D1505990

To Renew Books
PHONE (925) 258-2233

Handbook of
Counseling
BOYS
and
Adolescent
MALES

A Practitioner's Guide

EDITORS

ARTHUR M. HORNE
MARK S. KISELICA

Sage Publications, Inc.
International Educational and Professional Publisher
Thousand Oaks ▪ London ▪ New Delhi

For information:

Sage Publications, Inc.
2455 Teller Road
Thousand Oaks, California 91320
E-mail: order@sagepub.com

Sage Publications Ltd.
6 Bonhill Street
London EC2A 4PU
United Kingdom

Sage Publications India Pvt. Ltd.
M-32 Market
Greater Kailash I
New Delhi 110 048 India

Printed in the United States of America

Library of Congress Cataloging-in-Publication Data

Main entry under title:

Handbook of counseling boys and adolescent males :
  A practitioner's guide / Arthur M. Horne, Mark S. Kiselica, eds.
      p. cm.
  Includes bibliographical references and index.
  ISBN 0-7619-0840-4 (cloth: acid-free paper)
  ISBN 0-7619-0841-2 (pbk: acid-free paper)
  1. Teenage boys—Counseling of Handbooks, manuals, etc.
  2. Young men—Counseling of Handbooks, manuals, etc.
  3. Youth—Counseling of Handbooks, manuals, etc.
  I. Horne, Arthur M., 1942- II. Kiselica, Mark S.
HV1421 .H36 1999
362.7'0835'1—dc21   99-6436

99 00 01 02 03 04 05 7 6 5 4 3 2 1

Acquiring Editor:	Kassie Gavrilis
Editorial Assistant:	Heidi Van Middlesworth
Production Editors:	Astrid Virding and Sanford Robinson
Editorial Assistant:	Karen Wiley
Typesetter/Designer:	Marion Warren
Cover Designer:	Ravi Balasuriya

Contents

EDITORS' AND CONTRIBUTORS' INSTITUTIONAL AFFILIATIONS AND ADDRESSES

EDITORS

Arthur M. Horne, Ph.D.
Department of Counseling and
    Human Development Services
College of Education
402 Aderhold Hall
University of Georgia
Athens, GA 30602-7142

Mark S. Kiselica, Ph.D.
Department of Counselor Education
332 Forcina Hall
College of New Jersey
P.O. Box 7718
Ewing, NJ 08628-0718

CONTRIBUTORS

Jose Arcaya, Ph.D.
Psychology Department
John Jay College of Justice
445 West 59th Street
New York, NY 10019

Jill S. Barber, Ph.D.
Counseling and Testing Center
University of Georgia
Clark-Howell Hall
Athens, GA 30602-333

Christi L. Bartolomucci, M.Ed.
Department of Counseling and
      Human Development Services
College of Education
402 Aderhold Hall
University of Georgia
Athens, GA 30602-7142

Bill Blanks, M.S.W.
Phoenix Associates, Inc.
2200 Lake Avenue
Suite 260
Fort Wayne, IN 46805

Steve D. Brown, Ph.D.
Counseling and Testing Center
University of Georgia
136 Clark-Howell Hall
Athens, GA 30602-3333

Neil Cabe, M.Div., M.A.
Rainbow Counseling Center
147 East Aurora Road
Northfield, OH 44067

Chris Caldwell, M.S.
Ph.D. candidate
Department of Counseling and
      Human Development Services
College of Education
402 Aderhold Hall
University of Georgia
Athens, GA 30602-7142

Georgia B. Calhoun, Ph.D.
Department of Counseling and
    Human Development Services
College of Education
402 Aderhold Hall
University of Georgia
Athens, GA 30602-7142

Allison Cunningham, M.A.
Princeton Regional Schools
102 Scenic Drive
West Trenton, NJ 08628

Steven Danish, Ph.D.
Department of Psychology
Virginia Commonwealth University
Box 842018
Richmond, VA 23284

James Dean, Ph.D.
Private Practice
527 Sixth Avenue
Brooklyn, NY 11215-4908

Brian A. Glaser, Ph.D.
Department of Counseling and
    Human Development Services
College of Education
402 Aderhold Hall
University of Georgia
Athens, GA 30602-7142

Roger Herring, Ed.D., N.C.C.
Department of Educational Leadership
Counselor Education Programs
University of Arkansas at Little Rock
2801 South University
Little Rock, AR 72204-1099

Ken Hodge, Ph.D.
Physical Education Department
University of Otago
46 Union Street
Dunedin, New Zealand

David Jolliff, Ph.D.
Phoenix Associates, Inc.
2200 Lake Avenue
Suite 260
Fort Wayne, IN 46805

Donald B. Keat II, Ph.D.
Department of Counselor Education, Counseling
    Psychology, and Rehabilitation Services
327 Cedar Building
Pennsylvania State University
University Park, PA 16802

Courtland Lee, Ph.D.
Counselor Education Program
School of Education
University of Virginia
169 Ruffner Hall
Charlottesville, VA 22903

Shawn Leonard, B.S.
Pennington School
112 West Delaware Avenue
Pennington, NJ 08534

Michael Mobley, Ph. D.
Department of Education and Counseling Psychology
16B Hill Hall
University of Missouri, Columbia
Columbia, MO 65211

John Newbauer, Ed.D.
Phoenix Associates, Inc.
2200 Lake Avenue, Suite 260
Fort Wayne, IN 46805

Dawn A. Newman, M.A.
Department of Counseling and Human Development Services
College of Education
402 Aderhold Hall
University of Georgia
Athens, GA 30602-7142

Richard C. Page, Ph.D.
Department of Counseling and Human Development Services
College of Education
402 Aderhold Hall
University of Georgia
Athens, GA 30602-7142

K. Lynn Powell, M.A.
Department of Counselor Education
332 Forcina Hall
College of New Jersey
P.O. Box 7718
Ewing, NJ 08628-0718

Wendy Sabin, M.A.
Conover Road School
Colts Neck Township Schools
10-L Dennison Drive
East Windsor, NJ 08520

Warren Spielberg, Ph.D.
New School for Social Research
95 Pierreport Street
Brooklyn Heights, NY 11201

David Sue, Ph.D.
Center for Cross-Cultural Research
Western Washington University
Bellingham, WA 98225

Dougald M. Sutherland, B.A. (Hons.)
Department of Psychology
University of Otago
P.O. Box 56
Dunedin, New Zealand

Gail Tripp, Ph.D.
Department of Psychology
University of Otago
P.O. Box 56
Dunedin, New Zealand

Cynthia B. Webster, Ph.D.
Mental Health Division
Student Health Center
University of Georgia
Athens, GA 30602-7142

Acknowledgments

Appreciation is expressed for all those who have contributed so richly to the making of this book. First, to the hundreds of children and adolescents, mostly boys and teenage males, who have been part of our research and treatment programs both now and in the past, thank you for all you have taught me. Thanks also to the men and women who have participated in training workshops and the participants in men's groups I have been in, or led, or supervised for our graduate students. A sincere appreciation is expressed for your openness and sharing and for your contributions in helping me expand my awareness and knowledge.

Thanks and appreciation are expressed as well to my fellow faculty members and students for the great support they have provided over the years. My greatest stimulation comes from these people, for they help me think, challenge my beliefs, and make me aware of that which I have missed in my own scholarship and experiences. In particular, I thank the men's issues research team and support group: John Dagley, John Edwards, Richard Hayes, Karen Kampmayer, Jim Manley, Eric Roth, Robert Socherman, Shirley Taffle, Cindy Webster, Kevin Kulic, Ryan Scott, Curt Morrison, and Dawn Newman. Thanks to Dave Jolliff, Steve Brown, and Holly Forester-Miller for the workshops we've done together.

My appreciation for Mark, my coeditor, is immense. We moved from acquaintances to colleagues to close friends in the process of completing this book. From the beginning, Mark's joy and enthusiasm for this project have been a source of encouragement and inspiration. There have been ups and downs in the project, and each level strengthened the appreciation I have for Mark. Thanks for working with me on this exciting and rewarding project.

Thanks to my colleague and friend of three decades, Dave Jolliff. Dave has been the friend and mentor all people deserve but few experience. I have been most fortunate.

Love and appreciation are expressed for my family. My entire adult life, I've known it just can't be better than what I have experienced. Thanks for being part of the whole process. Special thanks to Gayle for the support and understanding, good humor, and fun times.

Thanks to Kassie Gavrilis and Jim Nageotte of Sage Publications for their excitement over this project and their professional expertise that brought it to fruition.

ARTHUR M. HORNE

This book is a sincere expression of the love I have for our nation's sons—a love that is an extension of the caring and tenderness I have received from my beautiful family. Sandi, you are a wonderful wife. Andrew and Christian, I am so proud and blessed to be your father. To my dear mom and dad, Winnie and Otto Kiselica, thank you for teaching me what it means to be a good parent. To my sisters, Mary and Patty, and my brothers, John and Matt, know that I appreciate you every day.

I have a very special regard for my coeditor, Andy Horne, for his faith in me and this project. Andy and I met nearly 10 years ago as copresenters on a conference panel focused on counseling men. Since that day, Andy has mentored me and affirmed my belief that society must direct more compassionate attention to the concerns of troubled boys. This book is the culmination of that concern, and it would not have been possible without Andy's devotion to it. Andy, you are a good buddy, a great coworker, and a model professional.

I am so very grateful to the fine people who contributed their ideas in this book. I am honored by their belief that this project is a worthy outlet for their valuable perspectives on helping boys. Also, I thank them for sticking with Andy and me over the course of the past 3 years as we shepherded this project to its completion.

I am proud to be associated with the many wonderful men and women of the Society for the Psychological Study of Men and Masculinity, Division 51 of the American Psychological Association. I thank all of you for your warmth, your influence on my thinking about clinical work with men and boys, and your trust in me as president of our organization.

I have the privilege of working with the finest people imaginable at the College of New Jersey. I appreciate my colleagues in the Department of Counselor Education, Marion Cavallaro, Bill Fassbender, MaryLou Ramsey, and Roland Worthington, who have been my friends and encouragers since I joined their ranks 5 years ago. I thank Suzanne Pasch, our Dean of Education, for always valuing my work as a scholar, educator, practitioner, and social advocate. Thank you Gloria Valeri, Debra Caroselli, Lynn Powell, Jennifer Schick, Jamie Sandes, and Kim Nash for the countless times you cheerfully assisted with many of the tedious chores associated with preparing this edited book for publication.

Last but not least, Kassie Gavrilis and Jim Nageotte of Sage Publications stood behind Andy and me as we undertook the monumental task of pulling this project together and making it a reality. Kassie and Jim, you are not only fine editors but also good friends.

MARK S. KISELICA

Preface: For the Sake of Our Nation's Sons

MARK S. KISELICA

ARTHUR M. HORNE

I've felt depressed and different from everybody else for as long as I can remember. I was always kinda shy and thought there was something wrong with me. I especially think people think I'm dumb or backward because I don't speak so well. But my dad was such a tough guy, and both him and my mom always told me not to worry about things whenever I tried to tell them about my feelings. They both wanted me to be a great wrestling star—like my dad was—and they believe that any guy who gives up or even looks down is a "wus." So, I decided a long time ago to hide my feelings and not let anyone see how scared I was inside. . . . [pause] A few times, I thought about goin' to see a counselor, but everybody would just laugh at me if the word got out about it, so I never went to see nobody. . . . [pause] I managed to get by, even though I felt like crap most of the time, at least until 2 weeks ago. That was when my girlfriend broke up with me. . . . [pause] I just couldn't take it anymore after that . . . [pause] so I got out a knife and wrote a suicide note to my mom and dad and my girlfriend and then I made these here cuts on my wrist. . . . [long pause] That's how I ended up here in the hospital.

> —Jessie, a 15-year-old wrestler admitted to a psychiatric hospital after a suicide attempt

I don't let nobody f*** with me and I don't let nobody get close to me! If you f*** with me, you're gonna pay and you're gonna pay big time! I don't give a s*** what anybody thinks about me either! My f***in' parents, my f***in' teachers, the f***in' cops, and all them f***in' shrinks I've seen in my life— they can all go to f***in' hell for all I care! None of 'em has ever tried to understand *me*! When the f*** is somebody gonna try to understand *me?*

> —David, 11 years old, incarcerated and convicted of aggravated assault

I was just a kid when I was abused for the first time. . . . [pause] I think I was 8 or 9 when it happened. . . . [pause] This guy from my neighborhood took me for a walk to a shed in the back of his house, where he made me do stuff to him and then he did stuff to me. I was scared and wanted to run away but he had locked the door and he was so big and I was scared of him. I knew what he wanted me to do was wrong, but I . . . I . . . I just couldn't say no to him. . . . [pause] And then he told me not to tell anyone—"it will be our secret" he said—and I was so scared and ashamed so I didn't tell anyone. He did it to me again and again. A couple of times, he even brought a friend with him and they made me do stuff with the both of them. . . . [pause] This went on for years, until he started goin' after my little brother. That's when I told him he'd better stop it or I'd *kill* him . . . and then he finally left me alone.

—Qawi, 19 years old

These statements all came from boys we met in our work as counselors. The voices of these and so many other troubled boys echoed in our minds when we started this book. As we recalled these boys and their difficult life circumstances, we wondered about the thousands of other boys in this country whose problems are legion. Consider the following sobering and staggering statistics:

▶ In 1995, 3,062 boys who were 18 years old or younger were murdered, and more than 393,000 boys were the victims of child abuse or neglect (U.S. Bureau of the Census, 1997).

▶ In 1995, 4,302 males between the ages of 15 and 24 years committed suicide. Another 234 boys between the ages of 5 and 14 years killed themselves that same year (U.S. Bureau of the Census, 1997).

▶ At least 3% and as many as 20% of all boys have been the victims of sexual abuse (Associated Press, 1998; Holmes & Slap, 1998).

▶ Among 8th-grade boys, 21.5% have been in a fight, 21.5% have been robbed, 44.6% have been threatened, and 22.5% have been attacked at school (Chadwick & Heaton, 1996).

▶ Among 10th-grade boys, 42% have been in a fight, 11% have been robbed, 33.1% have been threatened, and 11.4% have been attacked at school (Chadwick & Heaton, 1996).

▶ In 1992, 128,906 young men who were 19 years of age or younger fathered a child (National Center for Health Statistics, 1995), and the vast majority of their children were conceived and born out of wedlock (Children's Defense Fund, 1998).

▶ Of all boys between the ages of 3 and 17 years, 22.9% experience either a delay in growth or development, a learning disability, or an emotional problem that lasts 3 months or more or requires psychological help (Schmittroth, 1994).

▶ In 1996, 13.1% of all boys between 18 and 19 years of age were high school dropouts (National Center for Education Statistics, 1997).

▶ In 1994, 86.5% of all delinquency offenses were committed by boys (U.S. Bureau of the Census, 1997).

▶ In 1995, 77,464 boys under the age of 18 years were arrested for running away from home (Maguire & Pastore, 1997).

These statistics indicate that too many of our nation's sons are in trouble and troubled in a society that tends to disregard their problems or give them mixed messages about receiving help. We and the other contributors to this volume have worked for years to understand the struggles of boys and to develop effective means for helping them. This book is our attempt to raise awareness about the problems of boys and to share what we have learned about the developmental challenges of boys and adolescent males, their various cultural backgrounds, their special needs and concerns, and the process of counseling them.

Our young male clients have taught us that growing up to become a mature and responsible man is a confusing developmental challenge for many boys raised in contemporary American society. Throughout their formative years, boys and adolescent males receive contradictory messages about the meaning of masculinity. On one hand, they are exposed to the long-standing, traditional image that "real men" are strong and silent providers and warriors who avoid anything that hints of femininity, such as the expression of vulnerability and tender emotions (Levant, 1992). In its extreme form, this traditional portrait of a man is one of a fearless, take-charge, hyperaggressive individual who handles problems by fighting first and asking questions later. On the other hand, at the same time that they are bombarded with these macho images about men, many boys observe the significant adult men in their lives being asked by their wives and other women to take on roles and show care in ways that violate the traditional male role and require skills they tend to lack, "such as nurturing children, revealing weakness, and expressing their most intimate feelings" (Levant, 1992, p. 381). The effect of these contradictory depictions of masculinity on a large number of our male youths is "an unnerving sense of uncertainty about what it means to be a man" (Levant, 1992, p. 382).

This uncertainty is compounded when ethnic and gay conceptions of masculinity clash with those of the mainstream culture. For example, an African American boy may wrestle with the dilemma of adopting an African versus the dominant White model of masculinity (Lee, 1996). Similarly, a gay youth may be conflicted about feeling forced to accept a mainstream heterosexual definition of what it means to be a man while privately experiencing a homosexual orientation to manhood (Gluth & Kiselica, 1994). One of the major developmental tasks our sons must complete, then, is to sort through these many, conflicting messages about maleness and somehow create a personal, coherent, and healthy male identity.

Achieving this task is easier said than done. Because more and more boys are being raised in father-absent homes, the current generation of boys is less likely than prior generations to receive from their fathers ongoing, daily guidance about what it means to be a man (Blankenhorn, 1995). Those boys who are fortunate enough to enjoy the presence of their fathers in the home are more likely than prior generations of boys to encounter an adult male who is confused or in disagreement with his wife about the proper role of men in the family and society. Men who experience these sorts of dilemmas, known as gender role conflict, also tend to suffer from a variety of inter-personal and health-related difficulties (see O'Neil, Good & Holmes, 1996). We contend that a boy reared in a family system that produces male gender role strain may internalize inconsistent and disturbing messages about maleness. Thus, as a result of increased father absence and the transgenerational effects of gender role strain, a growing number of boys may be unsure of how they want to define themselves as men and how they should relate to women, as well as to other young men.

Amid these sources of confusion, a substantial number of our nation's boys are in turmoil in a culture that tends to disregard their hardships or responds to their difficul-ties in questionable ways. Boys remain highly overrepresented among children referred for counseling to remediate the highly disruptive problems associated with learning disabilities, hyperactivity, oppositional behavior, and conduct disorders (Beymer, 1995; Horne & Sayger, 1990). Overshadowed by the very visible nature of these problems are a host of other difficulties experienced by hundreds of thousands of boys that tend to go unnoticed. For example, recent research has revealed that although an alarmingly high number of boys (nearly a half million annually) are the victims of sexual abuse (National Center on Child Abuse and Neglect, 1996), their traumas are underreported to authorities and tend to be misdiagnosed and undertreated by child psychotherapists (Associated Press, 1998; Bolton, Morris, & MacEachron, 1989; Holmes & Offen, 1996). Other investigations have demonstrated that boys struggling with the challenges of adolescent parenthood (Kiselica, 1995; Kiselica & Sturmer, 1993) and shyness and anxiety (Kiselica, 1988) are largely ignored by mental health professionals. Many boys who do seek or are referred for professional assistance are hypocritically deemed poor candidates for counseling (Beymer, 1995) or are confronted with hostile adult attitudes about them (Kiselica, 1995), both of which have the effect of alienating boys from "helping professionals." In other instances, well-meaning, nonjudgmental practitioners make a valiant but ineffective and frustrated attempt to intervene with disturbed boys because they do not understand how to adapt their traditional counseling approaches to the relational styles and the unique emotional baggage of boys (Kiselica, 1995). Thus, the relationship between young men in need of counseling assistance and the counseling professionals charged with helping them is frequently like that of two distressed ships passing in the night, each unable to recognize and connect with the other, in spite of their physical proximity and a dire need for substantive contact.

The purpose of this book is to address these issues by providing practitioners with a comprehensive handbook on understanding and responding to the developmental, cultural, and special concerns of boys and adolescent males. Specifically, the purpose of this volume is to answer the following questions:

- ▶ What are the developmental challenges of boys and adolescent males?
- ▶ How can male youth achieve a mature and healthy sense of masculinity?
- ▶ What are the culturally salient issues of young men from different ethnic backgrounds?

▶ What are the most effective methods for establishing rapport and intervening with special populations of boys, including boys who present the stereotypic problems of males, such as aggression and hyperactivity, as well as other male youth, such as depressed boys and teenage fathers, whose concerns were historically ignored by society?

▶ How can we help boys who are victims, as well as those who are victimizers?

This scholarly and practical guide is intended to provide practitioners with the most comprehensive array of information on helping boys and adolescent males that has ever been assembled in one volume. Consisting of 19 chapters, this book is divided into three parts. Part I provides the reader with an understanding of how the psychological, career, and athletic development of boys, both adaptive and maladaptive, is shaped by a complex interaction of biological, social, cultural, and economic forces. Part II covers cultural considerations pertaining to counseling with African American, Asian American, Hispanic American, Native American, and White, non-Hispanic boys, respectively. Part III spans 10 chapters on special populations of boys, including gay boys, teen fathers, sexually abused boys, boy sexual offenders, developmentally disabled boys, shy and anxious boys, depressed boys, bullies, male youth gang members, and boy substance abusers. Parts II and III follow a handbook format that teaches the reader about the specific adjustment issues of different cultural and clinical populations as well as the most effective and practical methods for establishing rapport and intervening with these populations. Each chapter in Parts II and III also concludes with a summary of the major considerations for counseling with the particular population that was discussed in the chapter. We hope that this format enhances the efforts of counselors, psychologists, social workers, psychiatrists, nurses, ministers, and educators to engage and help a wide array of boys and adolescent males in counseling. In addition, we believe that this book can be used as a textbook by professionals teaching courses on counseling boys or children or in courses pertaining to gender issues in counseling.

Each of the contributors to this handbook is a recognized authority on counseling particular populations of boys. Our collaboration on this book represents the latest in a series of cooperative ventures, including a string of symposia (Andronico, 1998; Jolliff, 1994, 1995; Kiselica, 1996b, 1997) that were presented at national conventions of the American Psychological Association and the American Counseling Association. As a result of our ongoing efforts to raise awareness about the special needs of boys, an ever widening network of scholars and therapists dedicated to helping boys and adolescent males developed. The present edited text brings together many of these professionals with the intention of providing the most useful and up-to-date information on assisting male youth.

We hope that our book prompts mental health professionals to reevaluate how we look at boys and the therapeutic processes and strategies we use in our attempts to help them. First and foremost, a reconceptualization of how to help boys must rest on the compassionate realization that a substantial number of young men are in psychic pain. This anguish is associated with a wide range of adjustment difficulties that occur within a cultural context in which the passage to manhood is often confusing and unclear. We must recognize that these difficulties are not limited to the stereotypic problems of boys, such as disruptiveness and aggression. Although these types of problems certainly warrant our attention, they should not obscure other problems, such as shyness and anxiety, gender identity issues, cultural values conflicts, adolescent fatherhood, and incest, that many boys face on their own while they suffer in silence. We trust that our book will help bring these latter problems out of the shadows and illuminate strategies for supporting boys whose needs historically have been neglected. We must also confront the fact that the hardships of boys are sometimes exacerbated, rather than ameliorated, by our traditional approaches to counseling and psychotherapy—a state of affairs that challenges us to think more complexly about boys and to develop new methods for helping them. Ultimately, we must meet boys where they are and then guide them to an understanding of what it means to be a happy, competent man and how to become one. First, however, we must build a bridge between us and our nation's sons so that we can join them along the developmental road to manhood. We hope that this book serves as a blueprint for constructing that bridge, as well as a road map for guiding us on our journey.

PART

I

DEVELOPMENTAL CONSIDERATIONS

1

Growing Up Male

The Development of Mature Masculinity

DAVID JOLLIFF
ARTHUR M. HORNE

For several generations our sons have tried to become men not only without connecting to the teachings and energies of older men but also in the face of cultural denigration of the masculine. . . . We need to re-learn what masculinity really is. . . . The quest is now to discover how to renew manhood.
—C. T. B. Harris (1994, p. 21)

At a recent presentation to a university honors program for students and faculty, we raised our concerns about the developmental problems that boys and adolescent males are having today and the impact those problems have on the development of mature masculinity. We included in the presentation statistics about the extent of emotional pain and turmoil that today's young men are experiencing, as well as research data we had been collecting on boys who have been institutionalized in correctional facilities and juvenile centers. Some members of the audience responded with incredulous anger that we could be so concerned about the developmental problems of boys and young men, whom many in the audience referred to as the "privileged class in America." These respondents took the position that young males have such privilege that there should be little concern for the pain they experience. One member of the audience indicated that "the Rockefellers have problems too, but I don't have a lot of sympathy for them because they have such opportunities that they should be able to overcome their distress. Besides, men cause their own grief and should be able to take better care of themselves."

The attitude that men's needs do not need to be addressed because men are both the privileged group and the cause of the problems of society is prevalent in much of American culture today. Our experience has taught us, however, that there is great pain and confusion among males. If we value a mature masculinity in which men behave in responsible and caring ways, then we need to provide boys with the guidance and nurturing they need to achieve that goal. Promoting mature masculinity requires greater attention to the developmental concerns of boys and adolescent males than has been received in recent decades. Society needs a greater focus on teaching young males what mature masculinity is, with that teaching coming in part from men who have achieved it.

For mature masculinity to develop, boys and adolescents need nurturance and guidance *by both males and females*; one without the other is insufficient. Recent years have shown a strong trend toward the development of social institutions and situations in which boys have much more interaction with women than with men, institutions such as day care centers, preschool and early school years, and single-parent households. In a large-scale research project now underway, we are examining children at risk for academic, emotional, and behavioral problems. More than half of the 950 children are boys, but 48 out of 49 of their teachers, as well as 7 out of 8 of their administrators, are female. The after-school program serving the children is staffed by women, and almost half of the children reside in fatherless homes in which the only adult is the mother or grandmother. Although there are many explanations for such a situation, we must heed the call of Harris (1994) for connecting young men to the teachings and energies of mature men. This has not been happening. We believe that development of mature masculinity requires a continued strong presence of women in the developmental processes of young men, but it also is imperative that men reenter the picture and once again become involved in the rearing of all our children.

The following data illustrate the tragic consequences of fatherlessness in America today. Fatherless children are at a dramatically greater risk of drug and alcohol abuse, mental illness, suicide, poor educational performance, teen pregnancy, and criminality. Fatherless children are twice as likely to drop out of school (U.S. Department of Health and Human Services, 1993). Broken homes are the source of the majority of adolescents in psychiatric hospitals (Elshtain, 1993), and children who exhibited violent misbehavior in school were 11 times as likely as others to not live with their fathers (Sheline, Skipper, & Broadhead, 1994).

Hawley (1993) describes the "developmental trajectory" of boys and adolescent males in America and reports that, as has been clear for some time, males are experiencing considerable problems at all stages of growth. Noteworthy attention has been focused on developmental problems of girls in recent years, and the implied assumption was that if girls were experiencing difficulties in educational and emotional development as a result of social influences, then boys would be benefiting—at least comparatively—by not experiencing developmental problems. This simply is not the case. The actual situation is that too many of our children, both boys and girls, are in trouble or are at risk for developing emotional and behavioral problems. When we begin to examine developmental concerns of boys and adolescent males, we realize that, in fact, there are considerable areas of doubt and issue. For example, as described by Beymer (1995), boys and adolescent males constitute the largest numbers of young people who do the following:

- Drop out of school
- Commit suicide
- Are victims of violence
- Are incarcerated
- Are assigned to special classes in school (behavior disorder, learning disabilities, attention-deficit hyperactivity)
- Are referred in school for disciplinary actions
- Receive lower grades throughout their schooling
- Fail to progress at the end of a school year (grade failure)
- Have accidental deaths related to automobiles and motorcycles

So, although some males excel in school and personal life experiences, a significant number do not.

Ackerman (1993) has described men wounded in their developmental processes as "silent sons." He describes the silent son as having a number of identifiable traits, including an inability to maintain relationships, an inability to control anger, a tendency toward workaholism or other addictions, a fear of intimacy, a tendency toward violent behavior, and a likelihood of inadequate self-esteem. The silent son tends to keep feelings to himself, has a strong fear of criticism, is obsessively driven to succeed, and wants his life to be better but does not know how to change it. He also may have some very good traits such as being good under pressure, adventuresome, independent, hard-working, and a good problem solver. He may, in fact, be functioning very well but be in pain all the while.

Many silent sons are suffering from codependency, a condition that results from prolonged experience in an environment that disallows the open expression of feeling and direct discussion of personal concerns. Codependent men feel stuck and feel like they have lost many opportunities. They overidentify with being masculine. They believe they must not show emotion and that they must always be in control. Ackerman (1993) lists the following traits of the overly dependent man:

- Depends on a woman to act out his emotional side
- Controls situations to extremes
- Is a workaholic
- Is good at rescuing and protecting but not interacting
- If a father, may be living through his son
- Exhibits stress disorders
- Has relationships filled with anger

- ▶ Uses other males for ego strength
- ▶ Has a problem with addiction
- ▶ Lacks emotional expression
- ▶ Has one dimension of self-worth—his occupation
- ▶ Has a fear of intimacy
- ▶ Lacks spirituality
- ▶ Is externally validated only by what he does
- ▶ Exhibits extreme rigidity
- ▶ Overly asserts his masculinity

Ackerman further suggests that these codependent, silent sons hold highly stereo-typical images of being male, including being very competitive, courageous, distant, and silent. They tend to avoid showing pain, they may follow a "macho" credo, and they are very likely to be angry. Ackerman has classified these "silent sons" into seven types, all of which develop during the males' childhood and adolescence: the triangulator, the detacher, the achiever, the hypermature, the passive son, the conflict avoider, and the other-directed one.

The triangulator. The triangulator has never learned to deal with issues directly. He blames his problems on external causes. He has difficulty accepting responsibility for his behavior. He is angry at the world. He thinks of himself as very independent; in truth, he has difficulty being close to anyone. Because he believes that there are external causes for his behavior, he sees nothing wrong with his anger.

The detacher. The detacher is inclined toward ending or escaping an uncomfortable situation at the first sign of trouble, even before he finds out whether or not the problem can be worked out. He has not learned conflict resolution skills. He thinks that his physical detachment constitutes emotional detachment. He fears exposing his pain and his vul-nerability. At the first sign of trouble in a relationship, the detacher starts thinking that it is time to leave. His motto is "Safety at all times." The result is that he feels lonely.

The achiever. The achiever has an empty feeling inside that tells him he is never good enough and that his worth is dependent on accomplishments that others can see, because it was only through his achievements that he received recognition from his family or others. He is likely to be a workaholic. He is driven by external forces. He seldom has an internal sense of self-worth. He is likely to be a perfectionist, so he spends most of his life being disappointed. He says he values his family, but he does not value his time with them. In relationships, his need to perform and be in charge is often perceived as dominating. At the same time, he is dependent on his partner for emotional nurturance. He is the classic intellectualizer.

The hypermature. The hypermature son is overly serious, never lets his defenses down, is emotionally on guard, and attempts to maintain control over his life at all times.

He is likely to be far too self-critical, to have difficulty having fun, and to live under a high level of stress. He had too many responsibilities as a child and did not have sufficient time for a normal childhood. In relationships, he is often intense, analytical, and pressured by a sense of responsibility for the success of the relationship. He wants closeness, laughter, and warmth but does not know how to get them.

The passive son. The passive son sits on the sidelines watching the game of life go on, but he secretly wishes he were playing. He seldom takes a stand when it comes to his own interests and issues. He feels relatively unimportant, and he believes he has little to offer. In relationships, he puts his needs second, often tolerating a tremendous amount of inappropriate behavior from a partner. He believes he has few options, and he is in fact at high risk of being abandoned for a more interesting partner.

The conflict avoider. On the surface, conflict avoiders appear to be extremely competent at helping others with their problems; however, they are rarely able to handle their own. They help others with their issues to avoid facing their own. In relationships, they have tremendous difficulty receiving from others, and they are extremely uncomfortable with others' emotional support or help. They can give closeness, but they cannot receive it.

The other-directed one. The other-directed son has learned to display the exact opposite of how he feels. He makes jokes to cope with pain. He is afraid that if he stops laughing, he will cry. He strives to do what others think he should do to avoid rejection or being put down. He tends to see himself as he thinks others see him. He is easily influenced by others and fears they will abandon him. In relationships, he becomes a people pleaser and neglects taking care of himself. He is difficult to know. His partner may enjoy his charm and sense of humor for a while, but enjoyment disappears as the absence of openness and closeness becomes intolerable.

In addition to these seven "silent sons," all of whom are hiding from themselves and from others, Ackerman talks about an eighth type of wounded son who is not silent—the *healthy survivor.* The healthy survivor represents the small percentage of people who emerge from a seriously dysfunctional family relatively unscathed. He is his own man, he knows what he wants, and he is sensitive to the needs and feelings of others. He is a very resilient man, flexible in the face of stress, positive in attitude, and willing to receive assistance when needed. He does not deny his unhealthy family history; rather, he knows what he has learned from his experiences, and he builds on that. If he is in pain, he deals with it. He admits when he is vulnerable, he is not afraid to show his emotions, and he is not controlled by them. He likes who he is, and he is comfortable with life. The healthy survivor would not trade places with anyone today. He values what it took to get him where he is, and he values himself. He has achieved mature masculinity regardless of the childhood and family experiences he encountered. This is the goal we have for all boys and adolescent males, and the chapters of this book address differing ways of helping accomplish this goal.

TASKS AND ISSUES
FOR MALE DEVELOPMENT

A number of the chapters in this book describe developmental issues for boys and adolescent males. Our experience in working with children in schools and in institutions such as youth detention centers and state rehabilitation centers, as well as our work with adult men in therapy, has led us to attend to a number of issues related to growing up male. The issues actually emerged by our working backward through conducting counseling and therapy groups as well as workshops for adolescents and males for many years. From these groups, both those with a therapeutic focus and those with a training or educational focus, we began to recognize a consistent set of issues that men deal with that began when they were young boys and continue through their current life experiences. We work with men who ponder the question of how they came to be the persons they are. The answer is that they are who they are today as a result of the developmental life cycle they experienced growing up. That is where we need to begin, with the developmental cycle of boys and adolescent males. To do that, we have identified and examined themes that arise in our work with men; all of them revolve around grief.

We also have conducted numerous training groups for working with men in therapy. Based on extensive experiences in working with men (in therapy as well as through conducting training groups) covering two decades, we can assert that many men today report feeling alienated and lonely. They describe themselves as robots. They have few friends, they are estranged from their wives and children, they trust no one, and they are disengaged from their own feelings and sensations. They are numb, angry, and frustrated. Under these conditions, they find themselves in a deep well of grief, experiencing a sense of loss that is often difficult to identify or express but that affects their inner life and their outer world of relationships and activities.

Boys are taught from an early age to stifle tears and other emotional displays. The message is quite clear—push it down, stuff it inside, don't show that feeling or you will be seen as weak and as a failure. The stifled feelings do not disappear; they just become masked, and though masked, they remain below the surface, ready to emerge, often in the form of anger. We find that in many situations, men's anger is just the cap on a deep vessel of grief. The double bind for the male is that the culture's fear of male violence has resulted in his being shamed for his anger, leading to a further suppression of feelings. This suppression in turn leads to a fear of not being able to control feelings such as anger, or to grief over not being able to express the feelings with a caring and intimate person in a way that is safe.

The message to men and boys is clear: "Deny your grief and suppress your anger or you won't be a real man." Another expression, "Don't get mad, get even," reflects the same theme: Suppress feelings, and continue on your way. In William Shakespeare's play, Hamlet was told not to grieve the wicked murder of his father. His mother, who married within 1 month of her husband's death, admonished him to "cast thy knighted armor off [stop grieving] . . . and not seek for thy noble father in the dust." When young males accept this admonishment, they attempt to develop a way of being male that will prove to be acceptable to their peers and family. The price, though, is high: Young men pay the price of denying their feelings by expending enormous time and energy to force emotions into exile. Many men then stop attempting to understand and reconcile the grief and anger they experience, and instead live lives of sorrow, knowing that all is not right in their world but not having permission either from significant others in their lives or from their own personal worldview to be any other way. Medical knowledge is beginning to demonstrate how a lifetime of denial of strong emotional feelings may culminate in both emotional and physical death.

When boys grow up hearing parents and peers telling them messages about how to be a boy/man, including repressing their pain or sorrow, "negative" feelings become restricted, repressed, and denied. This repression of feelings results in access to the more "positive" feelings of tenderness and joy being restricted as well. To free up the ability to be in touch with one's feelings, to become acquainted with the full range of emotional experience, boys and young men must find the way to encounter their experiences—to become attuned to their emotions. The process is difficult, for there are extensive influences in the family and among peers for this not to happen.

The emotional "shutting down" that begins with boys is refined during adolescence, then becomes a "way of being" for adult males, a learned process. The emotions that make a man's life rich and full, and that make his relationships genuine and intimate, are encountered only by a period of turning in to oneself, and of developing a sensitivity to, and acceptance of, one's affective experiences. This is often a frightening prospect for a man and those close to him, but it is essential if his life is to be lived fully and maturely.

Recovery from grief is possible, but it is also difficult. Keen (1991) has said,

> When men who have spent their formative years in extroverted action first turn inward toward the unknown territory of the soul, they soon reach the desert—the vast nothingness. Before rebirth comes the painful awareness that we have long been dead. Before feeling comes the dreadful knowledge that we have been anesthetized and are numb. (p. 134)

The process of shutting off emotions begins early, with the teaching of boys to not cry or express pain, to be outgoing and gregarious, and to be "one of the guys." When, as adults, they realize the extent to which they have mastered the hypermasculine role of closing down feelings, they also realize that they cannot change or overcome the experience by being in a crowd. A true sense of loneliness overcomes the man, just at a time when support and encouragement would mean so much. To overcome this early socialized learning, men must learn to experience the sadness and fear of lost opportunity, for that is what years of emotional denial have been.

Our experience with men's groups and with men in individual therapy is that they are not aware of their grief. As they realize what they have been denied and what they have lost, they also become frightened and scared as the grief forces its way into awareness. Keen (1991, p. 134) states, "They must mourn before they can be born." Men have years of lost opportunity, and as they become aware of the passage of life, the knowledge that they have pursued the dream they were given instead of their own can lead to demoralization, to grief, and to despair.

What is the loss that men begin to grieve as they grow older? They grieve their lost innocence and the brevity of their childhood resulting from early admonitions to put away boyish ways. The responsible man will have begun his career and his family in early adulthood, working and caring for others willingly but with no knowledge of the cost. If the grief experienced by so many men is to be prevented, it is crucial that we learn better ways of teaching our boys and adolescents to address grief. At the same time, we have to help them become aware of more choices available so that they might possibly avoid being in an adult level of intense grief years down the road.

RELATING TO THE MASCULINE AND THE FEMININE

Both feminine and masculine nurturing are essential to the full development of the well-rounded young man. In today's world, an overarching loss comes from the experience of the absent father. Many boys lose their fathers through the tragedies of the Three Ds: divorce, desertion, or death. Even if the father was physically present, he may have been emotionally inhibited or too tired to form a close bond with his children, as may be the case with the workaholic father whose commitment is more to his job than to his family or child. Add to this the large number of mother-headed single-parent families, and it can be seen that too many of our sons are without the masculine nurturing necessary for healthy development. The same is true of our educational settings, in which boys are more and more taught and nurtured by women.

Young boys' early experience with both the feminine and the masculine energy of the grown-ups around him will be very influential in how he relates to both sexes as well as to himself in later life. A loving mother, historically the one who spends the most time in the nurturing role with the child, can have a very positive effect on her son's future relationships with women and the feminine side of his own personality if she is supportive, confident, accepting, and honoring of his boyness. A loving father can have a very positive effect on the son's identity development, self-image, success in later life, and honoring of his own maleness.

Inadequate or abusive relationships with these early nurturers can have an equally powerful effect on the developing boy. The narcissistic or codependent mother can overwhelm a boy with her attentions and her neediness. He becomes her metaphoric lover and, unwittingly, her victim. He has to be the little man in her life, the one for her to lean on, confide in, and flirt with. The neglectful or abusive father leaves a legacy of pain and anger in the boy that can manifest itself in any number of undesirable ways, including drug and alcohol use, arrests and court appearances, poor school participation, disrespect for women, and poor parenting skills when his own children are born.

Other female and male figures also play important roles in a boy's growing up. A boy's successful relationships with the females in his life influence the development of the softer side of his being as he grows. The relationships he has with his mother, sisters, aunts, and other women affect his way of being with women and influence how he will behave as a man. From birth on, women treat boys differently than men do, and the messages boys receive influence the extent to which boys and young men become nurturing. Those who encourage and nurture the caring side of boys will likely bolster the young man's proclivities to be gentle and nurturing.

A boy's successful learning of how to be with males in his life influences his ability to establish lasting, noncompetitive friendships. In friendships, boys learn that friendly competition is always present. Within their families, they also learn the role of men and how men relate to one another. They see the models in their lives—brothers, fathers, uncles, and neighbors—and how they interact with one another and with the women in their lives. They see the strong, silent men; the responsible men who persevere; and the irresponsible men who are shunned or held in disregard for failing to live up to the standard as a provider and protector. From these observations, young boys learn that life represents sacrifice, independence, and responsibility.

FRIENDSHIPS

One of the more poignant issues men deal with is a lack of friendships. A number of people have commented on the friendship of the two authors of this chapter; it is a deep and warm friendship that has evolved over the course of a third of a century. Men remark about how neat it would be to have a friend who is close, trusted, and concerned. When we have asked about their friendships, some indicate they had close friends when they were children, but that with time, a vacuum developed, an emptiness of friendship based on the male orientation they experienced. A theme of competitiveness and isolation evolved as they grew older, and rather than have a trusting friendship built on cooperation and collegial time, the boys were taught to compete, to develop a competitive edge, to work to be "the best" or at least one of the top players, regardless of the event. With this competitiveness came a lack of trust, a fear that others would seek control or domination, and a feeling that although people may be team members, there always is an issue of who is the best member of the team. Will the other team members become rejecting when one member fails to live up to expectations? The lack of trust leads to an isolation, a sense that the only one to be trusted is oneself.

TRADITIONAL MODELS OF COGNITIVE AND EMOTIONAL DEVELOPMENT

In the process of developing mature masculinity, a boy has to master number of tasks. He has to

- ▶ understand and develop friendships;
- ▶ learn his place in the family by observing the other men and observing the role models available;

> ▶ learn to interact with the women in their world and understand the messages the women send about how to be a man;

> ▶ monitor and regulate their expression of emotions; and

> ▶ establish a personal set of values to direct his life, seeking to balance the child's individuation and his place and role in the family.

These tasks have been described in different ways by developmental theorists, focusing on cognitive, affective, sexual, moral, and career aspects of growing up.

In the 1970s and 1980s, as feminist writers began to describe the need for new and different models of developmental theory to explain the experience of girls, adolescent females, and women, an explanation was offered for why the existing theories were inadequate. The explanation was that the existing developmental theories were developed primarily by White men, most of whom were now dead and who had studied mostly male issues. The extant literature described developmental and cognitive models that seemed inconsistent with the experiences many women had in their own development. Thus began very creative and insightful attempts to develop an alternative model, one focused on female development, and with an awareness of and focus on the sociopolitical influence of gender and sexism in human development.

The following sections briefly describe the more historically important theorists. After these reviews, we discuss a proposed alternative model of development for males.

FREUD

The first developmental theorist to have an impact on psychology was Sigmund Freud, with his theory of psychosexual stages of development. Freud indicated that children progress through stages in their personality development. In this model, emotional problems serve as indicators of a failure to successfully navigate the psychosexual stages to maturity. Within the theory, emphases are placed on psychosexual development (the life history), instincts (genetic impulses), libido (life energy), and unconscious motivation. In describing the psychosexual stages of development, Freud identified the first year of life as the oral stage, ages 1-3 as the anal stage, ages 3-6 as the phallic stage, ages 6-12 as the latency stage, and ages 12-18 as the genital stage. For boys, the psychoanalytic model had particular meaning because it was hypothesized that male children coveted their mothers and perceived their fathers as dangerous competitors who would debase, harm, or even kill the young male contender. Thus, Freud asserted that young males experienced a necessary trauma as they negotiated the need to establish a rapprochement with the father. This resulted in a love-hate relationship that had the boy both fearing the father for the threat that he was and regarding the father with jealousy, yet loving him for his strength, protectiveness, and power.

ADLER

Alfred Adler was a colleague of Freud, often referred to as a student but in fact a contemporary rather than a pupil. Adler disputed the psychosexual stages of development and instead proposed a model of development that focused on an urge for social interaction rather than sexual gratification. A key element of development, according to Adler, was a striving for significance and superiority, with superiority referring to obtaining a better position in life, not being superior to others. From an Adlerian developmental approach, though, young boys and men who are unable to develop social connectedness within their families become highly competitive as well as feeling insecure and lacking in value. Although the Adlerian model does not offer a theory of stage development as Freud's did, it does offer insights into developmental problems of young men.

ERIKSON

Erik Erikson, a student of Freud but influenced by the social interest theory of Adler, developed a theory from Freudian psychoanalytic psychology that built on Freud's original concept of psychosexual development. He stressed the psychosocial aspects of development and indicated that psychosexual and psychosocial growth take place simultaneously, and that at each stage of development people face the task of establishing equilibrium between themselves and their worlds. The initial stages of Erikson's psychosocial theory correspond to Freud's stages of psychosexual development. Year 1 (Freud's oral stage) involves trust versus mistrust. Erikson referred to years 1-3 (Freud's anal stage) as early childhood and identified the psychosocial stage as autonomy versus shame and doubt. Years 3-6 (Freud's phallic stage) were Erikson's stage of initiative versus guilt. Ages 6-12 (Freud's latency stage) were Erikson's industry versus inferiority. Ages 12-18 (Freud's genital stage) are the identity versus role confusion in Erikson's model.

The implications of Erikson's stages of development for boys and adolescent males are powerful. In Erikson's first stage, infant boys who are unable to develop trust, and whose physical and emotional needs are not met, fail to develop trusting interpersonal relationships. In the second of Erikson's stages, a failure to develop autonomy occurs when the young boy begins exploring and experimenting but is either overprotected (not allowed to explore and experience the consequences of trying new things) or is underprotected and experiences so much pain that doubt and shame develop.

Boys in the third stage of development desire to develop a sense of competence. Those boys who find themselves in competition with others, including parents, fail to achieve this sense of competence, and those who are restricted in their opportunity to make decisions and take action begin to feel guilty for wanting the initiative. They begin to allow others to make decisions for them.

The fourth stage of development finds boys reaching out, attempting to expand their experiencing of the world and to try on new roles and behaviors. Boys who are encouraged and supported at this stage of development develop a sense of industry, whereas those who are thwarted in their efforts develop a sense of inadequacy.

During adolescence, Erikson's model calls for young men to work toward identity versus confusion over roles. This is a period of time when adolescent males are attempting to break their ties of dependency to parents and family, try on new roles and behaviors, and establish an independent identity. Being thwarted in this experience results in a confusion about one's role and personal identity. The topics of interpersonal trust, autonomy, and competence in male role taking are central to the adult male experiences.

The developmental stages presented here address the psychosexual and psychosocial components of development. An implication of the models with stages is that males evolve from one level of development to the next, in part as a function of biological stages, in part in response to social interactions. Although Freud and Erikson proposed that people may become "stuck" or "fixated" at a particular stage or may fail to develop in an independent, autonomous, and contributing manner, there are markers in the life development of a male that carry a strong influence. Below, we present an alternative model of male development that focuses less on biology and stages and more on the male modeling and psychocultural/sociocultural influence that men have on the developmental characteristics of boys and young males.

AN ALTERNATIVE MODEL
<u>OF MALE DEVELOPMENT</u>

Horne, Jolliff, and Roth (1996) have presented a developmental process that describes five male roles that are influential in the development of mature masculinity (i.e., strong character) in boys and adolescent males. The five roles are the Nurturer, the Role Model, the Initiator, the Mentor, and the Elder. All five may occur at any age of a child, thus providing different influences in a boy's development. Whereas traditional models of psychosocial development describe the tasks of development for the individual going through the stages, this model describes the adult males who are important at different stages of a boy's development.

NURTURERS

Fathers provide the earliest male influence on boys. For bonding to occur, an attachment process must begin with the primary relationship at birth and continue throughout infancy. Fathers do not replace a mother's nurturing but, rather, provide additional, but alternative, caring for and with the child. Pruett (1988) identifies father nurturing as a key part of the early developmental attachment that occurs, and Lamb (1986) found that fathers are influential in children's development of an internal locus of control, empathy, and cognitive competence. Winnicott (1965a), in describing the "holding environment" in which children develop a sense of safety and security, reports that fathers contribute to their child's development by facilitating individuation and by initiating the child into group relations.

Boys begin to develop an identification with fathers ("being like") and a dissimilarity with their mothers ("being different") as their gender identity develops. Nurturance from the father encourages and contributes to the development of internal resources that allow a boy to take risks and to have a sense of strength and power—the ability to face life's inevitable challenges. A failure to develop a strong sense of identity will deprive a boy of the resources he needs to develop a healthy respect for himself and others and lead him to fear intimacy.

Under ideal circumstances, the nurturing male is the father, but ideal circumstances do not exist all the time; therefore, other males are expected to step in to fill the nurturing role as need be. These can include extended family members, such as uncles, or others who can offer the unconditional love and support, the acceptance and affirmation, so necessary for children.

ROLE MODELS

Although fathers or father surrogates are important as nurturers and serve as teachers throughout the life of a child, an effectively nurtured boy also learns from other role models in his life. Role models serve as representatives of the world beyond the parents and instill aspirations and ideals.

Role models may be found in a variety of sources. They may be friends and neighbors, but they also may be taken from the larger culture and include film and television characters, book and magazine personalities, and even comics, popular songs, and advertisements. They may be day care workers, teachers, religious leaders, or the local gang member or neighborhood bully. From the models that the boy observes, he internalizes the standards presented and begins to define the standards that will influence his behavior. From negative role models, the boy may copy stereotypic models of masculinity and develop a rigid, exaggerated hypermasculinity. Positive role models, on the other hand, facilitate the development of resiliency and the ability to persevere, encourage trying new skills and acquiring new behaviors, and encourage willingness to engage in reaching out to extend knowledge.

Boys with positive role models grow to have flexible, adaptive identities and confidence in their abilities. A common complaint we hear is that boys just need more role models, but we believe there are *abundant* role models; what we need is more role models who demonstrate mature masculinity. These role models provide a way for the boy engaged in vicarious learning through observation to elect to model the behaviors and emotional response patterns of mature men, so that his life will also be one of respect, dignity, and awareness of the full range of emotional experiences available to him.

INITIATORS

The function of initiation is to provide external validations for the transition from child to adult, to "overlay and counteract a hesitant and resisting nature" (Gilmore, 1990, p. 98). Given the developmental characteristics children learn from their nurturers and role models, boys may be focused on their ability to engage in individual achievement and may experience excessive egocentricity and self-centeredness. Initiators counterbalance that tendency by teaching the importance of teamwork, loyalty, and commitment to the larger group. There is a focus on the healthy inclusion of others and on the importance of balance between competition and cooperation.

A function of the initiation process is to help the young male learn to identify priorities, plan and execute strategies, and defer gratification. During the experience, boys and adolescent males learn the skills of setting standards for their personal performance and assessing their accomplishments. Self-efficacy is developed and enhanced as boys establish competencies and experience success in their activities.

Few opportunities exist for formal initiation rites for a boy in America; however, if a boy does not feel accepted and initiated into manhood by respected leaders of the community, he may remain in perpetual adolescence, with no commitment to either himself or his community. Successful initiation results in a sense of being a contributing member of the greater community.

MENTORS

Mentoring continues the process of growing and maturing. It provides a special relationship that contributes to a young man becoming a productive and contributing member of his community and work setting. Mentors are men who have a strong influence on a young man's development. "The true mentor serves as an analog in adulthood of the 'good enough' parent for the child" (Levinson, Darrow, Klein, Levinson, & McKee, 1978, p. 99). The mentor offers the young man advice, sponsorship, and guidance.

Successful mentoring relationships require that the young man has developed the character and ability to learn from others, to engage as a protégé in an intimate relationship with a person who can serve as teacher. This requires the ability to listen to advice, work in collaboration with others, and manage anger and other strong emotions well (Vaillant, 1993).

Levinson and colleagues (1978) reported that mentoring was one of the single most important relationships young men could have. Failure to work with a mentor early in one's career has been related to a failure to thrive in the career, a sense of bitterness and failure, and poorer likelihood of success in one's field of work. It might be assumed that lack of mentoring into other roles (fathering, husbanding) may contribute to deficits in these roles as well.

ELDERS

The elders in a person's life are those who have successfully served in earlier roles but through experience and age have moved to a concern with the broader cultural context of the community and to assisting in the establishment and guidance of the next generation. Elders are persons who are reflective and other-centered, and who can discriminate the authentic from the superficial (Heath, 1991). Their relationships feature collaboration and cooperation, not competition. There is a focus on meaning-making, a shift from the outside to the inside, from the physical to the spiritual, from egocentricity to community-centeredness.

Access to elders provides boys and adolescent males with the stability to engage in the other stages of development they must experience. Having elders to maintain the community and spirit, young men are able to experiment and stretch. Without the stability of elders available to them, they develop fear of the new, lose the vision of the community, and fail to grow.

THE FIVE TEACHERS

All five teaching roles are important in the lives of young men. They can enter the lives of boys and adolescent males at any point and be influential. Even more important, they may be absent at any stage, and the lives of the boys will suffer as a result. If we want boys to grow into mature men with respect for themselves and others, we need to enhance the opportunities for teachers to be available.

THE WHOLE MALE

Steinberg (1993) has described a model of development for males that corresponds to the model we presented above. He suggests that the ultimate goal of male development is "wholeness." He defines wholeness as "becoming a male human being" (p. 26). The goal, according to Steinberg, is to become fully developed in all human traits without selection on the basis of traditional gender roles. Immature males tend to avoid values and behaviors that are considered "feminine" by the society. The "whole man" has synthesized those traits considered masculine and those considered feminine according to what is true for him as a fully functioning human being. He has denied neither his masculine self nor his feminine self. He has become fully himself in spite of any social imperatives to the contrary.

To achieve this level of wholeness, Steinberg (1993) asserts that a man must journey through a number of stages. He has described a five-stage sequence leading to wholeness: cognitive, conformist, conscientious, autonomous and integrated—that corresponds to the five teachers described by Horne, Jolliff, and Roth, discussed above.

COGNITIVE STAGE

By the age of 4 or 5, most children have gained the cognitive awareness that there are two sexes, and they are able to identify themselves as either boy or girl. This first stage of gender identity may be no more than the awareness that female is like Mommy and male is like Daddy, but these categories become distinct and are experienced as opposites. Such a categorization is consistent with the need at this stage to understand the world by grouping nearly all concepts into opposites such as up-down, hot-cold, and wet-dry.

The child identifies with the more similar parent. For a boy, the concept of self is, in part, defined by his personal statement "I am a boy." The attributes that a boy is likely to value—competence, power, strength, and achievement—are those embodied by the father and significant other males in his immediate life space. Society then teaches the boy how to act in concert with these values by encouraging and discouraging particular behaviors. The boy at this stage then begins to acquire those gender traits that society has defined as appropriate for him.

CONFORMIST STAGE

The conformist stage normally peaks in early adolescence, when traditional masculine-feminine gender role patterns are at their height. The gender identity question has passed by the simplistic cognitive identification of sex to a full knowledge of the role expectations for maleness and femaleness. Not only do boys and girls know that there are gender differences, but their desire to be seen as attractive to the other sex and acceptable to their own sex motivates them to play out these different roles as prescribed by society. Adolescence is a time when the tendency is to describe oneself in socially desirable terms and to experience shame for transgressing the norms of what is socially acceptable. It is apparent that forming a traditional gender identity is necessary before one can develop an integrated identity.

CONSCIENTIOUS STAGE

During late adolescence and early adulthood, most people begin a self-conscious self-evaluation comparing acquired values, particularly those socially prescribed gender role values, against their own internalized value system and own self-image. Young people begin to compare and balance their collective definitions of masculine and feminine with their own true natures. This stage is represented by the search for a way to reconcile the external pressures one feels with the internal truths that often seem quite compelling.

AUTONOMOUS STAGE

For those who reach this stage of development, a stronger sense of self develops, partly as a result of a growing awareness of the autonomy of self and of others and partly as a result of growing tolerance of deviance from collective norms. As tolerance grows for those who choose other solutions to life's challenges, the individual learns to value his or her own autonomy. Men no longer have to conform to rigid, traditional stereotypes of masculinity, and women can experiment more freely with nontraditional roles. All of this is in contrast to the condemnation characteristic of the conformist stage.

INTEGRATED STAGE

For the fortunate ones who reach this stage, a sense of integration develops, a sense of inner peace that results from the emerging resolution of cognitive dissonance. Integrators move beyond coping to reconciling. They are able to more easily reconcile personal wants and needs with life demands. They can move beyond mere tolerance to a full appreciation of individual differences. They can move beyond role differentiation to a sense of integrated wholeness. This means an integration of masculinity and femininity. For whole men, self-assertion, competition, and externalization can become tempered with considerations of mutuality and interdependence. The stage is now set for personal integration and self-actualization, for wholeness, for becoming a male human being.

Steinberg postulates that there are two broad symbolic dimensions into which the psyche divides reality. He combines the labels of active versus passive from Freud with instrumental versus expressive from Talcott Parsons; he calls them "instrumental/ active" and "expressive/passive" (Steinberg, 1993, pp. 22-23).

INSTRUMENTAL/ACTIVE DIMENSION

This dimension is related to the achievement of goals through manipulation of the objects in the world. Initiative, decisiveness, and assertive activity are characteristic of this dimension. Activities include remaining emotionally neutral, achievement oriented, and rational. When people are functioning in this dimension, they are gathering information, solving problems, giving suggestions and opinions, and remaining task oriented.

EXPRESSIVE/PASSIVE DIMENSION

This dimension is focused on interpersonal connectedness and group harmony through expression and management of feelings and emotions. Expressions of warmth, caring, and affection are characteristic of this dimension. Laughing, playing, and sharing the small details of one's life are common. In interpersonal relationships, people who are functioning in this dimension tend to seek harmony, give direct expression of emotions, effectively mediate conflict, and release tension.

In the current environment of high consciousness about gender issues, it is a common observation that men are more instrumental/active and women are more expressive/passive. The origin of these specializations by each sex is subject to controversy. Is it biology that determines one's inclination toward one of these dimensions, are the inclinations archetypal, or are they the result of the gender socialization process? Or could it be that the result is an outcome of multivariate predictors including all of these and more? What is known is that these dimensions are historically and culturally consistent across most societies (Gilmore, 1990).

Although the psychological attachment to these dimensions may differ by sex, the abilities of aggression, nurturance, passivity, autonomy, focus, and expressiveness, among others, can be said to be human traits common to both females and males. Differences in preference and experience may not necessarily mean differences in ability.

The social developments resulting from actions representing each dimension over the life span of the human race have contributed, perhaps equally, to the evolution of the species. The problem for men today is that they are encouraged by their sociocultural environment to identify with the instrumental/active dimension to the near exclusion of the expressive/passive. This cultural imperative blocks men's continuance toward a true goal of wholeness, toward fullness as a human being.

It seems apparent that a boy, in order to feel adequate as a man later, must develop competency in the traditional characteristics of the instrumental/active dimension, especially during the conformist stage. It is as if he must fully identify with his maleness before he can move toward integration. Failure to reach this level of individuation may result in fixation at the conformist stage, which can be a disaster for the grown man and sometimes for the society in which he resides. When a man does not develop competence in the traditional masculine gender role, he feels inadequate. The positive qualities of that role remain undeveloped. Until a man has successfully mastered the instrumental/ active dimension and made those characteristics part of his conscious personality, he will not have the security to proceed further in his masculine development. Once he has identified successfully with the masculine role, however, he must begin the process of separating his masculine identity from his collective identity by his innate, transformational need to grow into wholeness.

MALE INITIATION AS A DEVELOPMENTAL PROCESS

A core component of the two developmental models presented by Horne, Jolliff, and Roth and by Steinberg is having initiators and an initiation process. The prevalence of the process is so powerful that boys and adolescent young men seek out opportunities for demonstrating their manhood, often through sports or other physical activities. This is a universal phenomenon. In East Africa, young boys are required to participate in an extended initiation process before they are considered men. This rite involves enduring excruciating pain, accomplishing strenuous feats of strength and endurance, and experiencing public challenge to meet the requirements of true manhood. Failure to meet these standards results in his being excluded from full participation in the male life of the community.

Gilmore (1990) has described initiation rituals from an anthropological perspective to illustrate the universality of the initiation process. African tribes such as the Masai, the Samburu, and other cattle-herding tribes are representative. A core experience in the initiation process for these tribes is the public circumcision rite. A boy must submit to the ritual without so much as a flinch; blinking or turning his head results in being shamed as unworthy of manhood, and his entire lineage is labeled as weaklings.

Other rituals may include accepting certain food taboos and stealing cattle (which is seen as a skill that sustains the main source of tribal wealth). Successful rustling bestows manhood on the young initiate and makes him attractive to young girls, who see such exploits as manly.

Although some of these practices may seem bizarre and unnecessary to Westerners, all societies distinguish between "female" and "male." Each, in some way or another, socializes its young into appropriate sex roles. When does a girl become a woman, a boy a man? In many parts of the world, menses is viewed as a benchmark signifying the onset of maturity into womanhood. Without a similar biological marker for men, cultures all over the globe have seen manhood as a status that is not conferred by biology but must be earned, and it must be earned by performing challenging tasks and overcoming powerful hardships. Females in many cultures also are challenged with stringent sexual standards, but rarely is their identity as a woman dependent on such tests of entitlement (Gilmore, 1990).

The purpose of all these rituals is to prepare young men to take their proper places and proper roles as contributing members of the community. Initiation rites serve to demonstrate that the young man is strong, can withstand pain, and has achieved manhood. A factor that differentiates other cultural markers of manhood from those in Western culture, though, is that with the movement to manhood the young man is also now responsible for his family and his community. There is a sense of responsibility that goes with the initiation process. Often, Western "initiation rites" include bravery and pain but not the taking of community responsibility. This is an area that needs further development in Western culture.

THE MASCULINE WOUND FROM SOCIETY

In Western societies, brutal tactics of initiation have all but disappeared; in fact, any semblance of initiation or rite of passage seems to have been forsaken. The result is that today's modern young man lacks the benefits of ritualized initiation to teach him exactly who he is and exactly what his role is to be as a contributing member of society. Also lacking is the public process of conferring onto the graduate his public status as a man. In traditional cultures, the public ritual is a powerful affirmation. The initiate has little doubt of his status in the community.

In the United States today, young men receive little training in what it means to be men and virtually no indication of when they have arrived. Consequently, our young men are confused about their identity, uncertain of their roles, and usually unprepared for mature manhood. Young men are not totally clueless, however: Few escape the socialization process. They know that they are to constantly and forever prove themselves in the three "W" areas: war, work, and women. They also seem to understand that, as men, they will be expected to perform the socially necessary "P" activities: protect, provide, and procreate. How do our young men know that they are to perform in these ways? They just do. Who teaches them these ways of manhood? No one—and everyone—and that's the problem.

Western society suffers from a lack of ritual practice in general and a lack of male initiation practice in particular. The devastating result is that we have boys pretending to be men. We have boys with men's bodies and the manly need to prove themselves, yet no one to show them how. Too often, they operate under the pretense of manhood, performing controlling, often violent behaviors and mistaking them for masculine strength. Too often, they participate in simulated initiation rituals such as high-risk physical activities and illegal acts—gang initiations, for example—all of which express a hunger for an experience that can be understood only at an archetypal level of awareness. Unfortunately, these attempts prove to be of no value. They may contain the physical challenge and pain, but they lack the necessary ingredient of the initiating elder: Boys cannot initiate boys into manhood; only men can do that.

The goal of all initiation processes is transformation. To be initiated is to be transformed in some way. Through initiation, people are helped to make transitions from one stage to another (Steinberg, 1993). The purpose of male initiation is the transformation from immature masculinity to mature masculinity (Moore & Gillette, 1990).

The initiation process is not intended to remove the boy and replace him with a grown up man. The boy in each of us, when well placed in our lives, is a source of great pleasure. He is the playfulness in us, the active energy, the fun, the sense of adventure, the source of wonder and joy. This kind of boy can be found in the mature male. There is that other kind of boy, however, who remains infantile, narcissistic, and ultimately destructive to himself and sometimes to society. He is the uninitiated male. Many men are trapped in this boy psychology. Moore and Gillette (1990) has gone so far as to suggest that most men are fixated at an immature level of development.

In speaking of the modern man, Hawley (1993) explains it this way: "It is not that he has a bad nature or that he is nature-less; the problem, rather, is that part of his true nature has been suppressed by contemporary culture. A deep, primitive, inalienable virility lies ominously in the unconscious of every male" (p. 9). These deep primitive drives must be acknowledged, honored, and guided for the good of the man and for the good of society.

Our society provides a number of pseudo initiation experiences. Acquiring one's driver's license is sometimes seen as a sign of maturing. Other milestones sometimes seen as maturity markers include reaching draft age or drinking age, first sexual activity, attending the prom, or graduating from high school or college. Unfortunately, none of these contains the basic elements of initiation: elders to guide the process, specific trials that must be passed in sequence, experiences that are unique to males in the culture, separation from mother and the other women of the community, extensive immersion into the male subculture, and affirmation from a broad representation of the community (Gilmore, 1990). Our young men today must, at best, synthesize in their own minds the experiences of growing up and form an identity of their own with little guidance.

THE MASCULINE WOUND FROM THE FAMILY

Even with little guidance in the form of ritual, our young men will continue, as past generations have, the developmental process as best they can. It is inevitable that boys growing up in our culture will suffer an emotional wound, a wound that is unique to them, a "masculine wound." Families too often are contributors to the wound.

Cultural models of both motherhood and fatherhood have made it likely that boys, while growing through the ages of nurturant neediness, will come up short. They will suffer the loss of what Winnicott (1965a) calls the "holding environment." They are destined to experience a premature, psychic separation from caregiving. Here is the scenario.

Boys and girls must separate and individuate from the parents and develop their separate identities, including sexual identities. They learn that boys are like Dad and girls are like Mom. When Mom is the primary early nurturer, both turn to Dad for assistance in separating from Mom. Dad becomes particularly important as the "other nurturer." When Dad is unavailable either physically or psychically or when Mom blocks the separation process by holding on, boys, especially, experience conflicted feelings of wanting to separate and at the same time wanting to hold on. They are doomed to feel either lost (alone and frightened) or shamed (enmeshed like a mommy's boy). They are trapped in a continuing struggle between their need to reaffiliate with Mother and their need to be separate and autonomous. Pollack, (1992, 1995, 1998) has indicated that boys (and later, men) are left at risk for disruptions in their friendships and family relationships. Men search endlessly for connections, yet because of a fear of retraumatization they fight off closeness, a true approach-avoidance conflict.

It is very possible that a man who has suffered such a wound as a child would have some likely, and familiar, residual traits. These might include being overly concerned about maintaining his independence, manifesting symptoms of anger and aggression along with condescendence toward the caregiving role, a devaluation of the need for connectedness, and pervasive emotional stoicism. It is important to realize that these young men are not necessarily bad or pathological; they are grieving. Any new loss experience can open them up to this well of accumulated grief.

SUMMARY: A TIME FOR CHANGE

The wounded boy or adolescent male may find himself picking stereotypic role models from society in his search for the meaning of masculinity. He is relegated to a conscious process because he was not able to obtain it naturally through receiving masculine nurturing. He imitates. He role-plays. Gangs may become places of enmeshment ritualized through role playing and pseudo initiation experiences that result from a lack of connectedness in his life. There is likely to exist an uninitiated boy/man searching for his masculine identity in all the wrong places. He must find a way to heal, to empower the masculine part of the himself, so that he can take his place in mature relationships with women, other men, and children. The culture's task is to put this young man in touch with his deep masculine power and teach him appropriate stewardship of that power. This is the only path to mature masculinity. The following chapters of this book address ways to assist boys and young men in this process of attaining mature masculinity.

2

A Cultural Critique
of Current Practices of Male
Adolescent Identity Formation

WARREN SPIELBERG

In Genesis 37, it is reported that Joseph's brothers plot to kill him because, as the chosen heir to the legacy of Jacob, he will have dominion over them. Already favored by his father, he has been given a multicolored coat, which symbolically reflects his full and flamboyant identity. Joseph's brothers have additional, more powerful reasons to be angry. According to later biblical philosophical commentary, the character and name of Joseph has been associated with the term *Yisod*. Translated literally, Yisod itself means male principle, or phallus, and suggests that it was Joseph alone who was intended to be the generational conduit of male vitality and transcendence. In this light, the envy and violence of Joseph's brothers reflected more than just the envy of preferential treatment and multicolored apparel; it also indicated a deeper rage about the frustrations involved in being excluded from the achievement of a sanctioned enduring sense of manhood.

In many ways, the fate of a significant number of young men in our culture today reflects the zero sum game of Joseph and his brothers. Although many young men function relatively well and some are destined for lives of enormous accomplishment and recognition, facing challenges and dangers that would entice the Greek adventurer Ulysses, many young men today face lives of despair, frustration, anonymity, and underutilization. A great many young men today, particularly those from minority and poor backgrounds, have been increasingly left out of a global economy, one that provides few outlets for their energies and ambitions. In this chapter, I argue that the astronomical rates of male youth violence in our culture are strongly related to our inability to provide avenues of constructive and heroic identity formation for a great number of young men.

Although the linkage between failed identity formation in adolescence and violence is not well understood, the extent of the problem of youth violence is now well known. More than 2 million violent crimes were committed annually by the late 1990s. The homicide rate in the United States has increased by 100% over the last 30 years. U.S. rates of violent crimes represent anywhere from 10 to 40 times the rates of other developed countries around the world. Approximately 90%-95% of these crimes are committed by males under the age of 30 (Miedzian, 1992).

Recent theories of male youth violence have highlighted the importance of television violence (Miedzian, 1992), difficult life conditions (Staub, 1996), various forms of family dysfunction (Hinshaw & Anderson, 1996), traditional notions of masculinity, and the role of testosterone in effecting male aggression (Doyle, 1995). Although all these theories have important merit, they do not have the explanatory power required to help us understand the enormous dimension of current youth violence. Moreover, violence on television, difficult life conditions, high levels of testosterone, family dysfunction, and macho codes of male behavior all exist in a number of developed and lesser developed countries around the world, but those countries do not exhibit the levels of youth violence currently present in the United States.

I believe that an adequate understanding of the problem of youth violence first requires an overview of the ways we raise boys prior to and during adolescence in our culture. Such an understanding includes many dimensions. I have suggested (Spielberg, 1993) that current male psychological development is characterized by difficulties young boys and men have in maintaining object constancy and self-esteem throughout their lives. Specifically, male development is characterized by the intrusion of shame into the self-system. States of shame lead to violence and to problems in identity formation (Lynd, 1958). Second, Pollack (1995) has observed, citing the work of Chodorow (1978), the brevity of many (but not all) men's attachment periods to their mothers and that the need to separate traumatically from them in our culture creates in them a vulnerability to loss and separation, such that they are vulnerable to emotional loss and trauma, and to transitions. I would also emphasize that the absence of the father makes this problem even more acute because often boys are unable to turn to a nurturing figure after their separation from their mothers. Finally, the preponderance of violence of men is currently related to recent cultural changes in both the economic and social spheres (Greene, 1996; Wilson, 1987). These changes have resulted in an inability of the culture to integrate and absorb young men productively.

BOYS, SHAME, AND IDENTITY

A major dilemma for boys, and later men, is the variability of their self-esteem maintenance. In our culture, most boys (and later, men) must learn to grapple with the intrusion of shame on the self-system, with ensuing struggles around issues of narcissistic vulnerability. In our culture, the emotional development of men, from infancy to adolescence, is fraught with the intrusion of shame and humiliation in the development of the self-system. These painful experiences are directly the result of traditional notions of masculinity that stress independence and emotional toughness. In early childhood, boys are taught to feel ashamed of their needs for support and nurturance.

A second source of development of male shame occurs in the context of boys' relationships with their fathers during middle and later childhood. Research has documented the positive effects on self-esteem and social adaptation that good fathering yields at these stages (Biller, 1982); however, it is equally clear that most men do not experience good fathering. A study by Sternbach (cited in Osherson, 1986) suggests that only around 15%-20% of men experience such an intimate connection with their fathers. Research on father absence indicates that men without good fathering suffer from a host of maladies: from poor male identification to greater rates of psychiatric disturbance and delinquency. According to Osherson (1986), most men suffer not only from the deprivation of father absence but also from the self-blame and shame with which they seek to explain and understand their father's absence.

Although early and middle childhood set the stage for men's inability to successfully accept and integrate their dependent and creative needs, I contend that it is during the juvenile period that young men most powerfully consolidate a sense of crippling shame around being dependent, creative, and vulnerable, as per the strictures of the traditional male role model. As many men can attest, juvenile society is extremely brutal and primitive. Boys from Boise to Brooklyn know the cruelty and ostracism that can befall those who transgress the schoolyard code of masculinity. This code favors cunning and cruelty over compassion, despair over idealism, competition over cooperation, disparagement over truthful evaluation, physical prowess over intelligent consideration, hierarchy over democracy, and stoicism over the expression of positive emotions. Many boys are spared, however, by the advent of the "chumship" (Sullivan, 1953), during which individual friendship protects boys from the excesses of the cruelties of their culture.

According to Sullivan (1953), a number of unfortunate factors coalesce during the juvenile period to amplify the emerging male's abhorrence at being seen as needy, vulnerable, or compassionate. During this period, the young boy must first and foremost become oriented to reality. Young boys must renounce their use of fantasy, imagination, and idealism or face considerable ostracism. Although imagination once protected the young boy from loneliness and distress, as the boy enters juvenile society he can become rejected for reporting fantasy material and for being too kind and sweet.

Second, as the juvenile becomes a social animal, he must learn new social skills—namely, cooperation and competition. Cooperation is vital to healthy development, but competition is much more valued in our culture. Getting ahead, putting others down, beating them, and, in some cases, humiliating them become the outstanding goals in the integration of interpersonal relationships. During this period, the manifestation of the need for tenderness becomes perceived to be linked with an inability to be successfully ruthless. This period of development also is marked by the juvenile's turn to the use of disparagement to cope with feelings of insecurity brought on by competition. One is taught during this period to protect one's self-esteem through the uncovering of the unworthiness of others, so the predominant understanding becomes the notion that "I am not as bad as the other swine" (Sullivan, 1953, p. 242).

Boys' experience with shame in the course of their development is usually tragic in a number of respects. First, it leaves a legacy of unhappy men, afraid of intimacy and truncated in their ability to communicate their feelings and needs. Second, with regard to the development of identity, the shaming of childhood puts men at great disadvantage in a number of other ways. Strong feelings of shame based on a young man's felt inability to be "manly enough" interfere with the development of pride in defining and reaching positive goals. At each stage of development, the accompaniment of successful passage is pride; however, the absence of a clear, attainable vision of manhood and the positive goals of boyhood often prevent successful passage. A feeling of shame and confusion based on attacks regarding dependence and or competitive failure often take the place of pride, because many boys never really know when they should feel good. That such feelings of shame are linked with the advent of violence is also well documented in the literature (Scheff, 1988). Studies of conflict among juveniles indicate that violence is very often the result of unexpressed shame that leads to rage under conditions of provocation.

Third, as men enter adolescence, most have dissociated large elements of their unique talents and capabilities. In their quest to be "one of the boys," they have paid the highest price, that being the renunciation of talents and interests that in our current culture are not deemed manly or rugged enough. In this way, the talented musician of 7 years of age can become the tone-deaf mediocre basketball player at 12; the interested reader of age 6 can become the schoolyard illiterate at 10; and the sensitive and helpful child of 8 can become, by the time he is 13, the distant and cunning observer of his fellow humans.

The advent of shame in men impedes the development of their identities in another way. Most boys are taught that compassion, empathy, thoughtfulness, commitment, and idealism are qualities of character that are more compatible with women. Taken together, however, precisely these characteristics may allow young men to achieve a new life of meaning and productivity away from their families.

SEPARATION AND INDIVIDUATION
FOR MALE ADOLESCENTS

Based on the foregoing, as young men enter the chasm of adolescence, most arrive dissociated from their talents and sensitivities, shamed, full of rage, and vulnerable to narcissistic injury. They are sorely conflicted in their desires for attachment and face intense assaults to their self-esteem maintenance. With puberty, they must now also face new challenges to their inner sense of continuity and emotional stability. The separation processes inherent in adolescent development once again expose young adults to intense states of annihilation anxiety. These anxieties are largely due to the enormous complexity involved both in separating from one's parents and in constructing a new synthesized identity. According to such theorists as Erikson (1959), Winnicott (1965b), and Blos (1962), the successful navigation of adolescence involves the following: the unconscious symbolic murder of one's parents; the repudiation of childhood identifications; a reworking and loosening of oedipal ties; the creation of a sexual identity; the choice of new interests, values, and ideals; and the placing of oneself into a particular historical period of present-future, which allows one to plan and live. Mastering anxieties represents a herculean, often lifelong challenge, too easily underestimated by the adults who must deal with male adolescents. Given the deprivation and lack of support that is all too common in boys' development, these tasks are very difficult to accomplish. As infant studies have shown, separation and individuation occurs optimally under conditions of continued parental support and encouragement.

According to Fromm (1947), the feared loss of self in primitive anxiety during adolescence reflects a neurotic lack of differentiation and intolerance for the anxiety necessary to maintain separateness. Although this problem is keen for all adolescents, the struggle to grow may be more acute in particular ways for adolescent boys. It is my contention that adolescence for boys heralds a period of renewed psychic annihilation and death anxiety. Indeed, the fears of separation and differentiation brought on by adolescence may be more intense for boys as compared with girls because of the differing course of female development, which emphasizes relational convergence. In contrast, male development emphasizes autonomy and contempt for dependency, which may leave boys at greater risk for primitive separation anxieties. Although girls at this period have their own set of vulnerabilities, as portrayed by Brown and Gilligan (1992), it may be that they are less prone to regressions of annihilation anxiety and ensuing paranoia and violence.

The fear of separation that young men face is no academic matter but, rather, signals the possibilities of violence in our culture. According to McCarthy (1995), in his seminal study of adolescent character disturbance, the homicidal and violent adolescent is someone who is characterized by intense fears of annihilating anxiety, strong intensely conflicted ties to inner maternal objects, and paranoid attempts to repair self-esteem. He is an individual who uses aggression to address object loss and other prior emotional wounds. Through the medium of violence, homicidal adolescents attempt to address prior experiences of abuse, abandonment, and emotional rejection. Studies of homicidal adolescents shed light on the problems faced by even minimally violent young people.

OBJECTS OF DEVOTION

It has long been known that violence on the part of adolescents is mitigated by the quality of their attachments to others. The likelihood of violent behavior is lessened if an adolescent can form meaningful emotional attachments with others who do not condone violence. For children who have not been well nurtured, even gangs provide an area of emotional and physical safety and serve to maintain structured control over the expression of violence (Canada, 1995).

What is less well understood in our culture, however, is the degree to which violence among adolescents is also mitigated by commitments to a cause, an idea, and/or a group. Adolescents who have an alternate group of attachments other than the family, which give them the opportunity to be idealistic, effective, and productive with their lives, are less prone to violence. This is true for two reasons. First, the need for adolescents to separate from their parents in early adolescence necessitates their search for alternate hero figures or groups with which to associate and identify (Miller, 1984). In this connection, adolescents project their ideal selves onto alternate attachments such as individuals and groups and then reintegrate them into their own personalities in the effort to grow and separate. Without the opportunity to forge new attachments, to have new opportunities for human effectiveness, and to reintegrate new productive experiences of themselves, adolescents are at great risk for feelings of alienation, impotence, and frustration. These feelings can cause great tension among adolescents, which they often seek to remedy through acting out in the form of violence. Often, because of the lack of new group attachments and constructive avenues of expression, many young men turn to the use of promiscuous sex, violence, and drugs as a means of integrating their energies and bolstering their self-esteem (Miller, 1984).

Second, the need for hero worship and heroic striving on the part of the adolescent can be part of a larger need to overcome the anxiety of separateness brought on by greater individuation. According to Fromm (1947), there are essentially two ways to grapple with the existential need to overcome the aloneness and separateness brought on by individual growth and freedom. One is constructive, the other destructive. The human capacity for self awareness requires a structured and cohesive view of self, a frame of orientation that helps overcome the terror of separateness. This frame of orientation, this road map for living that gives direction and meaning to our lives, also provides individuals with an ultimate goal for living, or what theologian Paul Tillich refers to as an "object of devotion" (Tillich, 1940, as cited in Fromm, 1947). This object, whether it is the God of Nazareth or the god of money, power, and violence, integrates our existence, silences our anxieties, and allows us, through dedication to our goals, to transcend the prison of our egocentricity. Although the various merits of differing and often competing systems of devotion can be debated, it is nevertheless crucial that such systems be constructive in their orientation. As Fromm warned in *Escape From Freedom* (1941), the dual challenges of coping with the problems of separateness and individuality and of becoming a man in a sanctioned fashion can easily tempt adolescents toward lives of destructive systems of devotion. For those adolescents who lack opportunities for group attachment and effective action in the world, the challenges of separateness and becoming "masculine" can be satisfied by systems of thought and devotion that encourage symbiosis, cruelty, and violence. Through the ecstacy of violence and the identification with an authoritarian leader (in our society, often an older peer), poorly developed adolescents often are able to find the unity of self in action they so desperately seek. As in Nazi Germany and in other totalitarian regimes, the end result of such a solution can easily become mass violence and genocide. The direction of this choice, between constructive and destructive forms of identity formation, is a complex phenomenon, dependent on many factors. Temperament, the course of individual development, familial influences, and the kinds of socialization opportunities provided for adolescents all play a role in the outcome.

Objects of devotion and the structure of adherence to them also provide opportunities to relate to others productively, independently, and effectively. The need to be competent and effective is a basic motivation of individuals. Violence is often an expression of impotence and of the inability or lack of opportunity to achieve effectiveness and self-realization. According to Sullivan (1953), feelings of power and influence in interpersonal relationships are vital for self-esteem and maturity. People who lack opportunities for effective action may make neurotic and destructive attempts to gain significance.

Finally, objects of devotion and the structures they provide also offer individuals stimulation and excitement. One of the many factors that generate destructiveness and cruelty is boredom. If the environment is insufficiently stimulating, as in aspects of our current adolescent male culture, instances of anger, rage, and predatory violence can be used to excite. Boredom and apathy are always dangerous because they provide the impetus to find reasons to hate, destroy, and control (Fromm, 1973).

In many ways, objects of devotion and the systems of meaning that are created around them fit well with current notions of the importance of meanings in life in helping young people to control their action and affect and learning how to improve their sense of time and judgment (Baumeister, 1992). Systems of meaning—which by definition provide purpose, clear values, and opportunities to feel effective and in control—have been demonstrated to counteract the violence-producing potential of poverty, even in the face of prejudice and discrimination. As Staub (1996) reports, this explains why in San Francisco's Chinatown, one of the poorest areas of the city, the murder rate remained extremely low (Staub, 1996). Others, such as Lasch (1979), have recently commented that our culture lacks systems of meaning that provide a broad, unchanging value base that guides behavior and helps people find solace when facing the difficulties of life. The consequences have been an elevation of self-interest as the ultimate moral criterion for behavior, a dangerous position to say the least. Reliance on the self as a consistent value base for young people augurs more instances of violence and regression. The elevation of self-interest over relatedness and shared mutual interest in our culture already has contributed to the advent of violence, as well as to depression rates 10 times as high as those of a previous generation.

Unfortunately, our society does poorly in meeting the normal developmental needs of adolescents, and, in particular, their needs for connection, commitment, and expression of their physical, creative, imaginative, and spiritual needs. Regarding basic child rearing, the family is a chaotic crucible. More than 1 million divorces occur every year, involving more than 1.5 million children. Well more than 10 million children now live in single-parent families (Prothrow-Stith, 1991). In such situations, children are less likely to receive the kinds of nurturance and opportunities for self-expression they require. In addition, adolescents (particularly if they are male) in such situations have difficulty establishing an acceptable and firm sexual and familial identity. Even intact families present ambivalent messages about the use of violence or drugs to their children (Canada, 1995).

On the societal level, there has been an "environmental failure" (Winnicott, 1971) in providing male adolescents with strong limits and confrontations (thus allowing for the growth of maturity, time perspective, and empathy), as well as with opportunities to dream and play in their own quest for connection and meaning. Through the transitional phenomena of life meaning, in the form of a "dream" (Levinson, 1978), young people can place themselves into a historical present and future, thus helping to allay their anxieties about the dissolution of their inner continuity.

Our society offers fewer and fewer opportunities for adolescents to create their own dreams and find meaning within a larger social context. First, our society offers fewer ideological avenues to its young people and far fewer heroic figures with whom to identify. Recently, when I asked the 6 members of my adolescent group which adults they admired as heroes, they were unable to offer anyone either from their own lives or from the culture. This example, which I believe could be replicated on a wider scale, is particularly tragic because it highlights both the lack of connection with adults in our culture and the lack of an ideological center in their lives. Second, and related, our culture provides fewer pathways for heroic action. Gone also are the days in which large-scale sacrifice and/or commitments were readily called for. Whereas the first part of the 20th century saw young men involved in industrial apprenticeship, military service, religious devotion, trade unionism, various political and or ideological struggle, and even fully employed; the last 30 years have seen a dilution of both heroic ideals and the avenues with which to achieve them (Becker, 1973).

The failure of our culture to provide young men with avenues of commitment, transcendence, meaningful work, and a call to effective action makes it intensely more difficult for them to separate from their families, to feel positive about themselves, to sublimate their aggressive urges into constructive action, and to master the anxieties brought on by individuation. It is my contention that only through the construction of a heroic identity based on the need to heal, protect, and contribute to the culture at large can young men find the transcendent and relational connection to the culture that they often unconsciously seek. The alternatives for young men are hero worship based on identification with the aggressor and/or a life based on the need to destroy and control.

Based on the foregoing, one might appropriately assume that the odds in favor of the development of psychologically healthy males capable of compassion and related-ness are nearly nonexistent. The dismal nature of the discussion, however, must be tempered by the knowledge of the myriad possibilities adolescents have to find alternate positive heroic figures and alternate groups for attachment in their lives.

A clinical example illustrates the process by which violent adolescents can be turned around to lead a life of productive action and, in so doing, heal themselves in the process. Sam is a 17-year-old young man with whom I have been working for the last 2 years. When I first met Sam, he was on the verge of being kicked out of high school, having attacked two students in a fight. Sam's violence was also escalating at home, where he had recently broken down a door and kicked his stepmother. During our initial interview, Sam factually related the death of his mother when he was 4 years old, his confusion surrounding his father's "wishy-washy behavior" toward him, and his con-fusion regarding his life in general. Dynamically, Sam presented himself as a young man with a tenuous connection to life, beleaguered by a rejecting internalized maternal figure and a supportive but weak father who tacitly encouraged his violence against others. In terms of his emerging identity, Sam saw himself as a "boat without oars" floating at sea. Not surprisingly, his heroic representation of himself was a compensatory one, that of "Hercules," a stereotypic male representation designed to help him overcome his own inner sense of weakness. Motherless and poorly related to his father (like Hercules) and similar to many violent youngsters, Sam was also a victim of violence. As a result, Sam saw himself as a wanderer/warrior in the fight for justice. His quest to confront others, however, often became a recipe for disaster. Socially, Sam had few friends and no outside activities and commitments, except for "hanging out" with other violence-prone youth outside school.

To help Sam feel more connected to others, he was placed in group therapy with other violent youngsters. The initial stages of therapy saw a young man at sea unable to connect to anyone or to any cause. A great deal of the early work centered around Sam's testing of the group leader, seeing whether his hostility and aggression would be contained. The refusal of the group leader to be drawn into "battle" with him forced Sam to confront his own behaviors. During this period, Sam also sought to learn more about the group leader and to earn his approval and admiration. As his first year of treatment ended, however, Sam began to see his desire to protect others in a different light. Through his identification with the group leader and his own growing interest in his own childhood, Sam began to get in touch with his desire to help children in ways in which he himself had not been helped. Eventually, it was suggested that Sam be enrolled in a group training program at the Young Adult Institute; he was trained to work on a volunteer basis with impaired preschoolers. This experience proved to be vital to his recovery in that it helped him to feel more effective in the world and gave him a sense of mission. Concomitantly, in therapy, Sam began to speak of his changing view of himself as a constructive individual rather than as feeling destructive. As his third year of treatment begins, Sam is free of violent episodes and has begun to develop new friendships with others that are mutually supportive. His identity is also more firmly planted toward becoming a healer, and he is currently making plans to attend college in the fall.

The foregoing highlights a number of important factors in my attempts to turn around violent youth. These include an active and ongoing commitment to containing acting out behavior, ongoing connections to positive adult figures (who serve as new models of identification), attachment to other productive groups of adolescents, working on a group project (the goal of which is to heal and help others), and, finally, a change to a transcendental notion of oneself from destructive to constructive.

On the larger societal level, the problem of youth violence is even more complex and difficult to solve. In the end, the job cannot be left to mental health professionals alone. The problem of youth violence stands at the crossroads of psychological, social, and political organization and spiritual credo. As such, it requires creative and eclectic solutions.

In terms of male development, it is now up to a new generation of parents to help rear young boys who are more attachment seeking and not ashamed of their needs for love and caretaking. In the area of families, we must strive to support families and children through legislation that provides appropriate resources for education, child welfare, and universal day care. In terms of adolescents, we must increase the opportunities we provide for meaningful contact with adults and with positive value systems, as well as with avenues for action and commitment. The need to create meaning in adolescence and adolescents' need for attachment to other peers and adults are inseparable.

In terms of policy, we must review current socialization practices for our adolescent population. National conscription with an option for a year or two of either military or public service is an interesting point of departure for discussion. Others include work/school scholarship programs, national school-based mentoring programs, youth employment programs, and a reconsideration of a national trend to increase the age at which young people are allowed to work on a part-time basis.

In the end, the most important tool in helping to curb youth violence may be the way adults approach their own lives. The challenge of living requires that we develop our own sources of hope and meaning that sustain and renew us in our quest to change and grow and that we find ways of passing these beliefs on to the next generation. Ultimately, it may be that such visions are the most powerful inoculation we have against a growing culture of destructiveness and despair.

3

Male Career Development
in the Formative Years

STEVE D. BROWN

Every man has memories of his boyhood dreams, of what he wanted to do when he grew up. As boys, some men wanted to be policemen, firemen, sports stars, or whatever caught their fancy at the time. During these same years, these men-to-be were observing their fathers and other significant men in their lives and developing ideas of what work was really like. Many of these boys accompanied their fathers to work and received glimpses of what it was like for their dads. During these early life experiences, they began forming preferences for some activities over others and developed opinions that influenced what they would choose to do in their future career life. Through the experiences of early socialization, many men were taught lessons about the importance of power, decision making, and setting limits. It is not difficult to perceive that these early experiences played a key role in how these boys began viewing their own career development and how they would later make occupational choices.

Some authors (Berger & Wright, 1978; O'Neil, 1981, 1982) suggest that men are taught that work is primary—more important than marriage, fatherhood, or any other role. Gaylin (1992) makes it clear that "nothing is more important to a man's pride, self-respect, status, and manhood than work" (p. 135). Everything else is secondary. Pleck (1981) indicates that for most men success in work is foremost in determining their sense of self-worth. Russo, Kelly, and Deacon (1991) consider that manhood and masculinity are determined primarily by career success. That being the case, many men turn to their work to fulfill their personal needs, including those more affective in nature. One has only to examine the common workplace to find men engaged in activities that meet needs across the spectrum of life, from social to emotional, from physical to relational. It is common for men to attempt to meet too many of their needs through their work, with the potential for creating a harmful imbalance that negatively affects other elements of their life, including their relationships with their spouses and children.

African American males generally were brought up with the same belief that work is central to life but often were confronted with a shortage of successful role models and with limited occupational alternatives from which to choose. Even though these men aspired to own the most expensive material possessions and experience the very best in life, many of them encountered social and educational obstacles that kept them from pursuing their boyhood dreams. The lack of successful role models left many young African American boys with work aspirations that were based on inaccurate media portrayals. When they looked for role models, all too often the image reflected was that work was unenjoyable. Even though work remained central in the development of African American males, the hope of becoming successful was often lost during their development.

Although some research has been conducted on early career development, Super (1990) indicates that career development in childhood has been inadequately researched. Those researchers who have been interested in child development have not reflected the same interest in the career development of children. Many questions concerning the interaction of identity and career development remain unanswered. The focus of this chapter is on males, and that bias will be evident as attempts are made to address questions concerning identity and career development. For example, what happens to boys as they develop to make work such an important element of life? How do genetics, environment, mentors, culture, and other factors influence a boy's development of identity? What can be done to help boys learn to find meaning in life roles other than work and to establish a better balance in their life roles? These are just a few of the questions concerning male development that need answers. The focus of this chapter is on finding some of these answers through exploring career issues in the development of boys and adolescent males.

RESEARCH ON CAREER
DEVELOPMENT IN MALES

In the early 1950s, researchers began examining the process of career development for young men and how it influenced occupational choice. Among these early researchers were Ginzberg, Ginsburg, Axelrad, and Herma (1951), who undertook a study of a group of boys and young men, ages 11 to 23, who were either attending a university-related school or attending a university. This group of young men were all from upper socio-economic backgrounds. Ginzberg and colleagues compared this first group to a second group of young men whose fathers were employed in unskilled and semiskilled occupations. A group of women who were college sophomores and seniors and who were also from upper socioeconomic backgrounds was used as another comparative group. The researchers concluded that the same general pattern of career development was followed by boys from lower-socioeconomic-level families as was followed by their wealthier counterparts. The primary difference between the two groups was the identification of a growing passivity among boys from lower socioeconomic homes as they matured. The pattern was one in which young boys from lower socioeconomic homes expressed considerable interest in future occupations, but as they grew older, this interest and goal-directed activity tended to decrease. In addition, Ginzberg and colleagues found that women in general appeared to have less focus on specific vocational goals than their male counterparts. Women tended to be more oriented toward marriage, a career, or a combination of both, and even those oriented toward a career were less focused on specific occupational goals than were the boys. It is important to note that the small size of each group used in this study limited its usefulness; the groups could not be considered representative of the general population. Even if the results of this study were representative of the normal population of that time, it would be interesting to see how the women's movement over the last two decades and the general change in societal norms would affect these findings.

With findings that supported the research of Ginzberg and colleagues, Burr, Hill, Nye, and Reiss (1979) found that children, not males exclusively, from working-class families tended to choose working-class occupations, whereas children with parents who were professionals tended to want to become professionals. Bell (1963) already had identified a potential exception to this pattern in that children whose parents had high ambitions for their children tended to aspire to occupations higher than those of their parents.

Boyle (1966) added the element of peer influence in his observations that children were more likely to have higher career goals than their parents if they associated with other children whose parents were from higher socioeconomic backgrounds. Boyle observed that peers served as models to be imitated. Of course, the primary models for children were their parents. Similar to Ginzberg and colleagues, Conger (1977) and Hoffman (1979) found that models tended to be sex specific, in that the occupation of the father had more influence on the career choice of sons and that daughters were more influenced by their mothers' occupation.

Swinton (1992) concluded that African American males were occupationally disadvantaged. Historically, education afforded some African Americans a means of achieving high ambitions; however, most of those who earned bachelor's or master's degrees were women (Brown, 1995). Even so, Swinton reported that African American women were more likely to be found in "bad" jobs. Many of the African American individuals who made it into college were the first in their families to do so and did not have parental models with college education. In reference to differences between men and women, the number of African Americans graduating with college degrees continues to be lower for men than for women.

In summary, researchers have found some clear differences between males and females, along with specific issues for African Americans, in career development. Socioeconomic level does not seem to alter a boy's career development process, although boys from lower socioeconomic groups tend to become more passive as they mature. Boys tend to be more focused on career goals than their female counterparts. Parents can have large influences on a boy's career aspirations, motivating him to aspire to goals

TABLE 3.1 Important Findings Regarding the Career Development of Boys

Socioeconomic level may not alter the career development process of boys.

Boys from lower socioeconomic levels tend to become more passive in their pursuit of a career goal as they mature.

Boys tend to be more focused on career goals than are girls.

Parents can raise the career aspirations of boys.

Peer groups can raise the career aspirations of boys.

Fathers have more influence on a boy's career choice than do mothers.

Among African Americans, fewer men than women graduate with college degrees.

that exceed his own parents' accomplishments. Peer groups can raise the career aspirations of boys. Boys are more influenced by their father's choice of occupation than their mother's, reflecting the importance of gender role modeling. African American males tend to pursue graduate school education, and occupations that require such, less frequently than do their female counterparts.

CONCEPTUALIZING MALE DEVELOPMENT

In their conceptualization of career development, Ginzberg and colleagues utilized the life stages concept of Buehler (1933), as did many early developmental career theorists. This chapter, however, focuses on stages as conceptualized by Donald E. Super as a framework to discuss early career development in males. Isaacson (1985) supports the idea that "no one has written as extensively or influenced thought about the process [of career development] as much as Donald Super" (p. 62). The stages of growth and exploration will receive foremost attention because these correspond to early career development, the time when boys move into being young adults.

As male career development is examined, the developmental stages of Erik Erikson will be integrated to compare and contrast the individual's personality development. Erikson's psychosocial theory provides considerable assistance in explaining how children are affected by social relationships and environments. As did Super, Erikson believed that children mature throughout their life span and that there is always the potential for individuals to work through their developmental issues. To maintain the focus on boys, Erikson's first five stages are examined as they relate to career development. The first five stages are trust versus mistrust, autonomy versus shame and doubt, initiative versus guilt, industry versus inferiority, and identity versus role confusion.

Steinberg (1993) also conceptualized five stages of identity development for men. These stages focus on a male's awareness of his masculinity and femininity and his ability to accept and integrate the same. The focus of Steinberg's work provides yet another way to conceptualize how males develop and what they need. The first four stages identified by Steinberg are examined as they relate to male career development. These stages end with adulthood and include the cognitive stage, the conformist stage, the conscientious stage, and the autonomous stage.

STAGES OF CAREER DEVELOPMENT
AND THE MALE EXPERIENCE

STAGE I: GROWTH

Super (1953) identified five stages of career development. He labeled the first stage "growth" and conceptualized that it extended from birth to the about the age of 14. He characterized the growth stage as a period when the primary emphasis is on physical and psychological development. During this developmental period, numerous attitudes, values, abilities, and skills, as well as interests, are formed that will have considerable influence on a boy's future choices, including those related to vocational direction. A boy's self-concept is largely formed during this period, and this affects vocational direction. Brown (1995) suggests that socioeconomic status may affect the vocational direction more for African American males than for others because of the effects that poverty and discrimination have on occupational choices. These impacts may be both direct and indirect. Super (1990) also argued that socioeconomic status affects the occupational and self-concepts of African Americans.

Models and the mentoring process play important roles in how a boy sees himself. Media, including television, may provide a variety of male role models, especially in the absence of a father or other significant male figure. Greenberg (1982) identifies characteristics such as strength, determination, and dominance as some of the messages conveyed by media to be characteristic of men. Doyle (1983) indicates that television portrays males as generally being aggressive and dominant. Jones (1991) finds that television commercials depict men in more dominant roles or as tough and rugged. In the absence of positive male role models, these characteristics can be exhibited in ways that are less than desirable, resulting in inappropriate aggression or other destructive behaviors.

That boys tend to be encouraged to behave more aggressively in their play than their female counterparts is supported by the work of Hyde and Linn (1986). The dominant and aggressive roles that males portray in the media have considerable impact on boys, sometimes leading them to pursue power and control in real situations. These dynamics may be influential in career success and achievement and may become measures of self-esteem and personal value for men.

Healthy role models are especially important to young boys and can provide examples that have particular impact on a boy's actual behavior. Leahy and Shirk (1984) found that as boys learn gender concepts there is an increasing agreement with adult stereotypes. Lindsey (1990) considers that once gender identity is developed a considerable amount of the individual's behavior is organized around it. Parents play a critical role in ensuring the availability of more positive role models. The games that boys play and the imaginary scenarios they act out often mirror the quality of the models to which they are subjected and that they value. A colleague, speaking about his son's resistance to engage in play, expressed that he simply could not understand why his son chose to read and study instead of playing games with other children in the neighborhood. It was easy to see from outside the system that all his son was doing was reflecting the workaholic modeling of his father. To change the intense focus of his son, the father had only to set aside more leisure time for relaxation, something that Solomon and Levy (1982) found was difficult for men. This example, like so many others, reflects the importance of modeling and makes it apparent that imitating these models is part of what a boy goes through in preparing for his working life.

Finding appropriate role models is important for all boys and a particularly salient issue for African American boys. Because of racism and other factors, African American boys have a more limited range of occupational role models to observe. Bowman (1995) indicates that African American children lack a variety of successful role models, even though African American parents tend to have the same aspirations for their children as do White parents. As a result, African American boys, as do boys from other cultural groups whose socioeconomic status is relatively low, tend to pursue occupations that either are limited in the potential for career development or provide extremely limited opportunities for success.

Growth, the first of Super's stages, is critical because it is associated with the early developmental years through preadolescence. The importance of the growth stage is that it serves as the foundation for later life. The toddler will follow his father around, modeling his father, picking up and attempting to use tools in mimicry of his father, all before he can utter a coherent sentence. This common image is consistent with the early stages of growth. As they grow older, boys may assume the soldier persona of G.I. Joe or the superhero characteristics of the Power Rangers, early attempts to try out how different occupational roles feel. The boys, of course, see themselves only as playing and having fun. It is during this stage that the boy's self-concept interacts with his physiological attributes in ways that determine his level of self-confidence for varying activities. The greater the success with activities and the rewards, the greater the affinity the boy tends to have for that activity. It is important to note that during this important phase, many boys are without a father to provide modeling. As Shapiro and Schrof (1995) indicate, 38% of boys spend at least a portion of their childhood without their biological father.

The activities that boys choose also tend to reflect gender preference. Simply talking to preadolescent boys makes obvious the general avoidance of the opposite sex and of activities that girls tend to engage in. David and Brannon (1976) refer to this rejection of femininity as "No sissy stuff." Subsequently, boys and girls have different toys, different activities, and different behaviors that are deemed acceptable. This, too, shapes the nature of things to come in a boy's occupational future.

Super (1990) emphasizes that career and occupational information plays an important role during the growth stage of development, stimulating curiosity and arousing interests that lead to the discovery of significant role models, feelings of internal control, acceptance of external controls, self-esteem, time perspective, and planfulness. Super perceives that information is instrumental in shaping attitudes and skills for career readiness. Etaugh and Liss (1992) found that the educational system has considerable influence on the development of gender-stereotyped work roles. Courses appropriate for women include language, home economics, and typing, whereas for boys the expectation is that they will take math and science courses. Education can either reinforce expectations learned earlier in life or provide alternatives for them. All too often, it reinforces societal expectations rather than providing boys with all their potential occupational and life alternatives.

What are we doing to prepare the male child to be ready for the working world? This question becomes even more interesting when one considers that we require people to have licenses to drive cars, to operate machinery, and to practice certain professions, but one does not have to receive any training before raising a child. How many parents have received the training to be effective, to develop the skills and awareness to help the child enter the working world? Table 3.2 identifies several strategies that parents can employ to begin the process of career education.

STAGE II: EXPLORATION

The exploratory stage as defined by Super follows the growth stage, beginning in adolescence and extending generally into the middle twenties. The key element defining entry into the exploratory stage is awareness that an occupation will be part of one's life experience. The teenager who dreams of being a rock star and attempts to dress like his favorite one or the young adult who dresses like the businessmen he knows are examples of behavior during the exploratory stage. The boy may have little understanding of what is actually involved in the occupation he dreams of attaining because he has little self-awareness and inadequate knowledge about the world of work. It is for this reason that the early period of the exploratory stage is called the fantasy phase.

During the fantasy phase, boys actively seek males who are attractive to them in terms of success and the respect that they receive from others. The career development of many boys receives little assistance during this critical period. Failure of parents and educational institutions to expose boys to occupational alternatives and an understanding of lifestyle development strands them in the fantasy phase. Although career interest tests may be administered during this stage, these may provide meaningless information or, even worse, information that may point to incompatible alternatives for the individual because the responses only reflect the misinformation and unrealistic expectations of the uneducated. Career tests are much more useful when the boy has a good awareness of his own personal characteristics, such as values and skills, and has a functional knowledge of the world of work. To administer interest inventories before a boy is adequately prepared tends to identify alternatives that are of no interest to him and may influence the boy to discount his utility in making a good occupational choice.

Self-awareness and career knowledge are instrumental in helping a boy move into the realistic phase of the exploratory stage. If the individual has high awareness of his

TABLE 3.2 Strategies for Career Development of Children

Spend considerable time with the child

Allow the child to follow adults around as they do tasks, provide appropriate tasks for the child that mimic the adult tasks, and demonstrate that tasks can be fun

Screen television programs to ensure that the programs your child watches have models that you respect, and discuss the occupational themes

Have significant others in the child's life describe to the child the parts of their job they enjoy

Show the child people who are working in a variety of jobs and talk about those people and their jobs

Model good career decision making

Talk to the child often about your job and what you enjoy about it

Encourage work-related play by purchasing certain tools and telling stories about what different people do in their work

Provide books appropriate for the child's reading level that have occupational elements

Provide opportunities for the child to see people at work in different settings and to shadow individuals who are on the job

Be aware of the impact of gender stereotypes on occupational choice and allow the child to experience tasks that are generally associated with the opposite gender

As an adult, learn the process of career decision making and keep yourself current on information related to the world of work

Discuss the different occupations of family members

Model and discuss the various roles in life, demonstrating how one's occupation fits into an entire lifestyle

Participate in play that relates to various occupations

Include the extended family in career development interventions

Discuss the potential barriers to career attainment associated with racism and other institutional factors

own personal values, preferred skills and abilities, interests, lifestyle preferences, and life goals, he can begin the task of comparing his own attributes to the various alternatives in the world of work. Deficits in his understanding of self and the occupational world may contribute to inappropriate choices for and subsequent dissatisfaction with work. Racial identity development also has consequences for career choice and work satisfaction for African American males. Understanding of self has different meanings for an African American male in the conformity and autonomy stages of development (Atkinson, Morten, & Sue, 1993) in a workforce dominated by White males. Because of the importance of work to males, the realistic phase is especially important in vocational development. During this stage, an emphasis on lifestyle development can do a great deal to help boys learn to focus on career development, which includes all of life's activities. Examining the balance in life from a "wellness" perspective can do much to help an individual understand how an occupation fits into life. Such a focus can enhance one's understanding of how career, social life, relationships, recreation, spirituality, physical activity, and learning all fit into establishing a healthy lifestyle. This focus also can help men, including minorities, develop strategies to compensate for and overcome barriers in their career and life planning that result from subtle or overt discrimination in the workforce. For example, consider a young man who applies for numerous positions, with no success, as part of a job search. It would not be unexpected for the young man to give up, following such a failure; however, if the young man invested his energy in social or volunteer activities or pursued a related internship in the field of interest, those endeavors might result in developing networks that eventually would lead to the desired occupation.

It is imperative that we question whether or not we are providing boys with the role models, education, and experiences that prepare them for a successful career. In a society where the average work week for men is increasing and the compensation for their services is decreasing, it is clear that the value of men's work is declining. For men to sustain a sense of value, they must pursue and be valued for roles other than that of worker. Evidence supports that some men are finding increased rewards from roles related to home as the amount of time they spend in housework and child care has increased. Juster (1985) found that men's time in these two activities had increased from 1.6 hours per day in 1965 to 2.0 hours per day in 1981. Although this increase is significant, it is important to acknowledge that this is only an average of 24 minutes a day, and the significance is due largely to the small amount of time that men invested in these roles to begin with. Furthermore, how significant a role is it if men are only spending an average of 2 hours a day in family-related activity?

We can also readily see that the number of men who are incarcerated in prisons is increasing. It is a remarkable statement about our society when we are willing to pay more money to keep one man behind bars than we are to pay a beginning teacher's wages. This travesty affects underrepresented populations to an even greater extent. What kind of reality is it that has 30% of African American males between the ages of 18 and 30 involved in some way with the criminal justice system, whether by being on probation or actually in confinement? This is a reality in at least two U.S. states and seems far from the kind of career path that we would encourage for our young men.

THE MALE'S PURSUIT OF IDENTITY

Erik Erikson's stages of development address the role that society and culture have on personality development. He emphasized that all of his stages have a special relationship to the basic elements of society. Erikson felt that as we become socialized as people, we are, in part, doing so by conforming to the expectations of society. This perception is largely reinforced by the work of Super, already discussed. The first five stages that Erikson conceptualized focus on a boy becoming a young adult and are appropriate to relate to Super's stages of growth, exploration, and establishment.

STAGE I: TRUST VERSUS MISTRUST

It would be difficult to prove that Erikson's earliest stage has a significant impact on one's career choice, but the primary issue of trust versus mistrust evolves into one's ability to trust one's self rather than trusting others to meet one's needs. This stage is dependent on the mother's ability to create a sense of trust in the child through sensitivity to the baby's individual needs that coincides with the culture's lifestyle. Erikson felt that it was not enough to guide the developing child through giving or denying permission; the parent must also be able to impart that there is meaning to what they are doing. According to Erikson, children develop characterological disorders from frustrations about rules that have little or no relevance to the society in which they live.

Work has been the primary role of men, and child rearing, at least in the societal frame, has been the primary role for women. Who, then, has had primary responsibility for establishing nonmeaningful rules for children that lead to developmental issues? As the number of individuals diagnosed with personality disorders rises in our society, what are we doing with the knowledge we have to improve the quality of child development through training primary caregivers? The sad reality is that we are doing too little. If the primary caregivers for children, still predominantly women in our society, have responsibility for the problems that many children have through their guidance, then the fathers or working mothers have responsibility through negligence. The future may have some interesting twists to this responsibility as the numbers of "house dads" and working mothers rise. In addition, with the advent of cloning, it may soon be a reality that two men (or two women) could have their own progeny without the assistance of any woman (or man). The bottom line is that we need to educate parents as to the responsibilities and necessary skills of effective parenting. If parents are unwilling to take these responsibilities, or disinterested in doing this well, we should at least consider removing their privilege of having children. In a society that licenses everything from driving a car to hunting to selling real estate, it is incredible and perhaps the most harmful example of negligence in our society that the only required criterion for parenting is that one be physically able to do so. The costs for our negligence increase with each generation of children raised with inadequate or negative role models and whose aspirations turn to living off society rather than contributing to its well-being.

STAGE II: AUTONOMY VERSUS SHAME AND DOUBT

As a boy grows, he is confronted with other challenges. Erikson's second stage, autonomy versus shame and doubt, is directly related to decision making. In this stage, there is an important balance that the child needs to learn, the balance between anarchic free will and positive restraint. Erikson felt that the child must be given enough autonomy to learn to make good choices and can learn to do so only if limits are placed on his behavior that protect him from making choices that result in shame or doubt. If autonomy is restricted too much, the child becomes obsessed with his own behaviors and attempts to micromanage his surroundings. The negative outcome of too much freedom is lowered self-esteem because of inconsistency in making good decisions.

There is a natural tendency for parents to attempt to make their children similar to themselves, and children reinforce this tendency by mimicking their parents. The greater the contact a parent has with the child, the greater the chance that the child will reflect behaviors and values that are similar to those of the parent. In a society in which both parents commonly work and day care has assumed the primary parenting role, it is no surprise that children are becoming less like their parents. Media and peer groups increase the exposure that children have to behaviors and values unlike those of their parents. This process provides considerable opportunity for children to be different from their parents and to receive rejection and criticism of their own ways, hence facilitating doubt and shame in the child. Subsequently, there is little surprise in findings that support day care as a positive alternative for child care. Consistency is an important element in child rearing, yet we continue to place more demands on parents that remove them from the parenting role. To facilitate the process whereby a child matures and secures compatible employment, respect for and guidance of the child's autonomous efforts are critical. This stage is very important in a child's acquisition of self-confidence in his or her ability to make good decisions.

STAGE III: INITIATIVE VERSUS GUILT

In Erikson's third stage, initiative VERSUS guilt, the boy begins making plans to achieve those things that he desires. Failure to limit initiative to what is actually possible to accomplish can result in feelings of guilt, self-doubt, and fear. Erikson (1963) suggests that this stage is different for the two sexes. Erikson stated that for a boy this stage is marked by pleasure in attack and conquest; for a girl it is the catching or snatching. Success for a boy lies in the identification of what he wants, pursuing it, and attaining it, and success is accompanied by a feeling of winning. The third stage is also where a child learns a sense of moral responsibility; where insight is gained into the institutions, functions, and roles that are integrated into the life experience; and where pleasure is associated with wielding and manipulating tools and meaningful toys. A child at this stage pursues the same activities as the parent who is seen as the model. Erikson believed that this is one of the most critical stages of development, where the child more readily learns to share obligation and performance than at any other stage. This is the stage where a child looks for opportunities that reflect identification with work, where a boy strongly identifies with his father's activities, and where role modeling is critical.

Initiative versus guilt is a stage that social and education experts contend is very critical for African American males. It is estimated that, by the time they reach the age of 30, 20% of African American males fall victim to drugs, alcohol, imprisonment, or death. If African American males are to survive into adulthood and prosper, they are identical to males from other cultural groups in their need to learn how to develop and maintain self-esteem, racial pride, respect for others, and the ability to make positive moral choices. These lessons can best be taught through a ready supply of positive role models in everyday working-class jobs instead of those with very limited potential for employment and success, such as sports or movie stardom.

STAGE IV: INDUSTRY VERSUS INFERIORITY

By the late elementary years, a boy is ready to begin real life. A life of virtually all play now sees real work activity. Recognition is achieved through productivity. During this stage, a boy recognizes that work is a part of life and that one needs to learn to survive. The child is subjected to systematic instruction concerning literacy and other work skills. The child begins moving away from the parents and developing an increasing sense of personal identity. This is a critical stage for a boy because it is the time when he may restrict his identity to that of the worker or provider as the only sense of identity and what will be the foundation of his feelings of success or failure. If a boy chooses to focus only on work, then the pleasures of other life roles are minimized; in addition, benefits to others in his life of fulfilling other life roles are lost.

STAGE V: IDENTITY VERSUS ROLE CONFUSION

With adolescence comes the stage of identity versus role confusion. This stage marks the end of childhood if the child has established a good awareness of skills and tools. Now the youth must connect those skills and roles he has learned with the occupational alternatives of the day. The sense of self that has been developed is now externalized and found meaningful, or not, to others. The youth has a growing sense of the role that a career will have in his life. Erikson indicates that this is the stage where childhood morality begins evolving into adult ethics. The boy needs rituals, creeds, programs, and/or ceremonies that confirm his identity. Parental and peer support that is consistent with the boy's personal perception of his identity are equally important because without such confirmation, role confusion and lowered self-esteem tend to result.

It is easy to see that if a boy has not developed a good sense of identity, one that is self-respected, then his choice of negative alternatives may be enhanced. One of the primary reasons why youth join gangs is to gain a sense of identity that is both consistent and reinforced as valuable by the other members of the gang. What a boy has not realized from his parenting role models, he obtains through other alternatives. At this stage, a boy can seek rewards and identity from numerous sources outside the home. As he does this, there may be increased conflict with parents as the boy reflects values through his choices that may go against the beliefs of his parents. If the parents have maintained a good relationship with their son and have provided appropriate guidance up to this point in the boy's development, the movement from the position of being responsible to others to the position of being responsible for himself will be easier for the boy.

As Erikson has demonstrated, the developing male has needs at each stage of development. These needs provide opportunities for growth, learning, and the evolution of individual identity. Failure to appropriately meet the developmental needs of a child may result in deficits in identity formation and subsequent difficulties in life. If deficits are present, the process of career decision making may be impeded as well. There

TABLE 3.3 Three Perspectives on the Stages of Male Development

Age	*Super's Stages*	*Erikson's Stages*	*Steinberg's Stages*
0-1		Trust vs. mistrust	Cognitive
1-3		Autonomy vs. shame and doubt	
3-6	Growth	Initiative vs. guilt	
7-11		Industry vs. inferiority	Conformist
Adolescence	Exploratory	Identity vs. role confusion	Conscientious

is simply no way to make a good choice of career without having a high level of personal awareness and knowledge about oneself.

Racial identity, the way one identifies with his or her own racial group, has a primary influence on identify formation. For example, colorism (Brown, 1995) plays an essential role in the pursuit of identity for African Americans. One's shade of blackness affects not only how an African American male views himself but also how he is viewed by other African Americans and the larger White community. It has been shown that light-skinned African Americans attain higher educational levels, socioeconomic status, and occupational status than those who are dark skinned. These findings, however, have had more significance for African American females than for males. Although it is difficult to determine the extent that racial identity development has on career choice, it seems apparent that it relates to career choice correlates such as self-efficacy.

DEVELOPMENT OF GENDER IDENTITY

Steinberg (1993) has identified five stages of identity development for males. The stages describe how the male identity evolves from one that is "collective" and requires considerable interaction with parents or surrogate parents, through stages where "personality identity" becomes better defined, to culmination in an "integrated identity." Four of these stages are related to the formation of the "collective identity" and the "personality identity"; these are relevant to the development of males from children into adolescents and eventually into young adults. Steinberg's stages are closely associated with the development of gender-specific identity.

When boys are very young and their survival is based on the quality of care they receive from their parents or other nurturers, Steinberg considers this to reflect collective identity. Steinberg's period of collective identity covers the same span as does Super's growth stage, 3 to 6 years of age. In the first or cognitive stage of the collective identity period, a boy may identify more with a similar parent and subsequently share an identity with that parent. As the boy matures, he enters the conformist stage, where he identifies himself with the traditional male stereotypes and associated male behaviors. During this stage, the boy models adult males and mimics their behavior. The conformist stage corresponds somewhat with the late parts of Erikson's stage of initiative versus guilt but predominantly with Erikson's stage of industry versus inferiority. As boys reach puberty and move into adolescence, they enter Steinberg's period of personality identity. This period is marked by the conscientious stage, wherein stereotypical definitions of male and female roles are compared and contrasted with the boy's own individual sense of self. Instead of outright rejection of opposite-sex characteristics, as in the conformist stage, the boy begins to accept that certain characteristics that have been stereotyped as being feminine are acceptable as self characteristics even though he is male. The process of individuation naturally begins during this stage as the boy sorts out his own identity from the models around him. As the boy becomes more accepting of his own individuality and accepts his unique characteristics that make him different from societal norms, he passes through what Steinberg refers to as the autonomous stage.

Steinberg's stages help us understand how boys become men and how they evolve stereotypical gender behaviors. The importance of fathering and providing time to model appropriate behaviors is evident within this framework. The fact that society is presenting increased competition for men's time, with increases in hours worked and other time demands, leads to the questions Who will be there to teach our sons to be men? How will our sons learn to develop other life roles so that they have a more balanced way of living and can increase men's contributions other than their working productivity? Some would say that androgyny is the wave of the future and that it is not important to preserve qualities associated with being male, especially if the society no longer values them. In response, others would voice the value of male identity and would support creating systems that assist boys in their evolution into men. As women have become more androgynous in their pursuit of traditional male employment, men have resisted their thrust. Similarly, many women remain biased that men are simply not equipped to fulfill the traditional female roles related to the home and raising children. Whatever the outcome of these different forces, it is essential that boys learn to have self-value, that they mature under conditions of respect and with the essential external care that will help them grow into functional, well-balanced, and productive individuals who make positive contributions to the world we share. It is quite clear that adults must do a better job of helping boys become men than they are presently doing.

FROM BOYS TO MEN?

Now that we have examined male development from three different developmental perspectives, what have we determined? First, work is to men as racing is to thoroughbreds: For most men, work is the predominant activity of life and the one from which they receive their greatest confirmations. Studies have provided insights into factors influencing the career development of men. The importance of the aspirations of parents and peer groups on career development has been established. The sad reality that boys need to have male models and the fact that fathers, in general, spend far too little time interacting with their sons has been noted. We have identified that considerable development for boys occurs at very young ages. The effects of the media on male development and their role in providing healthy models has been questioned.

We have examined the process of career development for boys and have identified that society as a whole is not doing a very good job of providing meaningful assistance. Self-awareness and decision-making skills are imperative if boys are to grow into men who are valued not only for their work but also for their contributions to other significant areas of life. The importance of helping boys define what is important to them as individuals, to clarify and operationalize their values, is critical in providing clues as to what other life roles can be fulfilling and in balancing the losses that work increasingly presents. Young boys need to learn that a career is important but so are relationships, spirituality, fathering, learning, recreation, and other valuable life endeavors.

Who will teach our boys to become good men? Who will teach our boys to find confirmation in areas other than work? We understand a considerable amount of what boys need to develop in healthy ways. Are we ready to pay the costs to provide the kind of education and developmental supports that will help boys evolve into healthy, fulfilled men, or will we continue to passively watch the erosion of the institutions and processes that have traditionally contributed to the value of men? This is the challenge: to implement what we know and to raise our children well, or to continue to devalue the traditional male roles without expanding other roles where men can be valued anew. Society provides all kinds of indicators that male youth are becoming lost and that they are searching for new ways to find meaning in their lives. We *will* have an impact on the future of our children, but the question remains as to what kind of impact that will be. Will our efforts be positive, or will we be looked on by future generations as a society more involved in other pursuits than in providing our young with the experiences and opportunities to guide them toward a meaningful future?

A POSITIVE CAREER-DEVELOPMENT
<u>MODEL FOR BOYS</u>

It would indeed be sad to leave the subject of career development for boys on such a negative note. The fact remains that although we have considerable knowledge concerning the process of career decision making and how to help individuals develop the self-awareness that is essential to the process, most boys are receiving little if any direct career guidance that would be useful in this process. What would a model career guidance program look like for young men?

The first component of a career guidance program for boys would be parents who are informed about the career decision-making process and the importance of self-awareness. The fact that many parents make strong attempts to make duplicates of themselves in their children is natural but can lead the children into life situations that are simply incompatible with their identity. Parents who are self-aware, who understand how to make decisions and can relate that process to their child, who make themselves available to their child, who are consistent, and who share their own experiences are ones who will serve their child best.

Prior to the Industrial Revolution, most children learned their future occupations by working with their parents from a very young age. Today, many children really do not understand what their parents do. This is at least partially the result of parents not taking their children to work with them. Modeling remains a powerful learning tool, and parents who expose their children to their own work as well as that of family friends and others are doing the primary task of educating young children about the world of work. Helping children process their own decision making, discussing values and goals, and assisting them in raising their own self-awareness and sense of responsibility all contribute to preparing the child to make a positive career choice.

As a boy gets older, late in elementary school and in high school it becomes increasingly important to expose him to occupational alternatives and to help him view himself in relation to these alternatives. With a good self-awareness, the process of comparing the self to alternatives is much easier. Providing reading materials, job observations, and shadowing opportunities increases a boy's awareness of alternatives as well as providing the opportunity to consider the personal match with various occupations. Table 3.4 and its illustration of the career decision-making process provides a model for what needs to occur at all stages of development. The trick is to provide age-relevant activities that raise self-awareness and knowledge of occupational alternatives.

As a boy enters junior high school, and throughout high school, deliberate instruction in decision making and career alternatives is critically needed. Such instruction requires access to professionally trained career counselors, teachers who have received education in the process of career decision making and how to implement career components into their classes, and up-to-date career information centers. A model program at one high school provided these resources and required that students receive instruction on choosing a career direction. During each year of the high school experience, each student was required to submit a written career plan. Subsequently, the student met with his or her counselor and discussed the plan. Over the 3-year span at this high school, students modified their plans based on their responses to coursework; their increasing self-awareness, which was facilitated by classroom activities provided by school counselors; and their general increase in knowledge related to careers, which was enhanced by instructional units on different careers and allocated time in the career information center.

By the end of the sophomore year, students had to choose whether to pursue college-track courses or preparation for vocational school. By the end of the junior year, students continued either their college track coursework or vocational preparation, but they could make adjustments based on their experiences and growth. By the end of the senior year, students who had taken college-track courses were required to identify a choice of major, and students who had pursued vocational training had to submit a plan for continued training or employment. This program provided a structure that helped students understand that the purpose of education was preparation for life and work. Because of the positive relationships that this particular school had with the community,

TABLE 3.4 A Basic Career Decision-Making Process

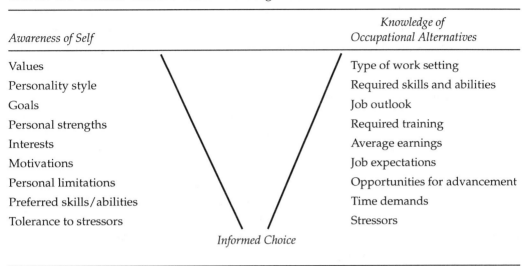

Awareness of Self	Knowledge of Occupational Alternatives
Values	Type of work setting
Personality style	Required skills and abilities
Goals	Job outlook
Personal strengths	Required training
Interests	Average earnings
Motivations	Job expectations
Personal limitations	Opportunities for advancement
Preferred skills/abilities	Time demands
Tolerance to stressors	Stressors

Informed Choice

many individuals in the vocational programs moved directly from school into employment. Many students who had followed a college track already had course credit from a local community college and were on their way to fulfilling the requirements for a major.

SHOP TALK WITH THE GUYS

Realizing that boys are not always very receptive to discussing their future plans, it is important to identify some strategies that may assist the parent, teacher, or counselor in discussing career issues. The most important variable in discussing career issues is making them relevant. Boys generally are focused on play, so discussing their choices as related to play activities can start them on the process of becoming aware as to what goes into making a decision. Helping boys sort out the difference between play and work at a young age can lead to increased motivation to pursue work. Just imagine what it would be like to get paid for your play. Well, why not? The primary difference between work and play generally is that people enjoy play but not work and get paid to work. The reality is that people can choose occupations that have many elements of personal enjoyment.

Availability and encouragement are key in promoting participation in activities related to self-awareness. For individuals to develop positive self-esteem, it is imperative that they learn about themselves, their uniqueness, and both their strengths and weaknesses. It is essential that such learning be promoted through family, school, church, and other environments. If relevant self-awareness activities are included in the basic societal institutions, they will become part of what is valued and a natural part of development. The fact that many institutions are engaged largely in the process of promoting structure and conformity, with little attention to helping boys develop a sense of personal responsibility, is all too apparent.

Perhaps the most important and most difficult area to discuss with boys is related to values. Values are the most stable aspect of an individual's affective identity and provide a framework that helps an individual make consistent choices that are focused on self-validation. The product of self-validation is happiness. The difficulty comes in that when individuals express values that do not validate others, especially significant others such as parents and teachers, they are often met with rejection and correction. Furthermore, too many activities that focus on values clarification fail to raise an individual's awareness to a level where the values can be operationalized. The basic question to a boy is simply this: "What's important to you?" Asking this question over and over at various times in life helps the boy focus on what is personally meaningful. Having the boy compare what life is like with one value versus another takes the process to a deeper level and provides a means of creating a hierarchy. The real test, of course, is applying the guiding principles provided through values to life decisions and maintaining a record of the results.

If a boy is asked if his parents are happy with their jobs, the answer too often is no. Regardless of the answer, it is often helpful to have boys talk with their parents and discuss the likes and dislikes of their jobs as well as what the parents may have done differently in their process of career development. The impact of a job on one's lifestyle is a critical piece of information and a frame that too many boys simply do not have. Reflecting on the different individual roles and on a holistic balance of life activities can help boys put their employment into a more complete and healthier life perspective.

A final element that helps boys understand the importance of making a positive career choice relates to how the process works in a free society. The following questions relate to this process.

- ▶ Where do you apply yourself more, in activities that you enjoy or those that you don't?
- ▶ Are you more productive in activities you like?
- ▶ What do you think happens in terms of quality and quantity of production if employees don't enjoy what they do?
- ▶ How easy is it to sell products that are of low quality and high cost?
- ▶ If a company can't sell its products, what happens to the availability of jobs?
- ▶ If the availability of jobs is low, what happens to your freedom to choose the job you want?
- ▶ Now, look back at where we started and consider how important it is to choose an occupation that you enjoy.

Such a discussion helps a boy understand the role that work plays in his life and in the greater society.

The most important factor in getting the attention of boys is providing models who are educated and who have found meaningful careers for themselves. The approaches and ideas already discussed can be quite helpful in orienting boys to making positive decisions, but availability and access to the essential resources also are necessary. To provide such is a small price for the outcome of young men entering the working world with more optimism and a better understanding of how work fits into their lives as a whole.

CONCLUSION

What would it be like if boys were educated to be self-aware and to make good decisions? It seems ironic that in a "free" society where decision making is imperative we place so little emphasis on teaching people how to make good decisions. This phenomenon is quite apparent in the reality that most individuals are not satisfied with their work (and other elements of society that depend on good decisions). It is clear that we know many ways to help boys make the major transitions into becoming productive and well-balanced men. The issues that remain concern discovering what is stopping us from providing such assistance and how can we overcome those obstacles. Whether we address these issues remains to be seen; boys and the men they become will provide the measure of our effectiveness in addressing them.

4

Promoting Life Skills for Adolescent Males Through Sport

KEN HODGE

STEVEN DANISH

Despite the popularity and success of youth sport programs today, debate continues regarding the potential benefits and costs of organized competitive sport for children. The key word in all these discussions is *potential*. The potential benefits of sport include physical development, such as skill learning and fitness; development of psychological characteristics, such as positive self-esteem and the ability to cope with stress; and development of social qualities, such as empathy for others and development of lifetime friendships (Weiss, 1995, p. 40).

The purpose of this chapter is to describe a specific model of intervention that uses life skills, especially as they relate to sport, as a means of promoting psychosocial development among boys and adolescent males. We begin with an examination of the role that sport plays in our society and its importance for the development of identity and personal competence among boys. As part of this examination, we consider both the benefits and the difficulties associated with sport. We then describe a conceptual framework for intervening with adolescent males and delineate a community-based psychoeducational intervention model that uses both sport and life skills. We also briefly discuss another example of a sport-related intervention that is consistent with the proposed psychoeducational model. Finally, we explore some of the future training, research, and implementation issues that must be resolved if we are to enhance the psychosocial development of adolescent males.

AUTHORS' NOTE: The authors gratefully acknowledge the insightful comments and suggestions from Alex McKenzie, who reviewed an earlier draft of this chapter.

The message that we hope to impart to the reader is that using sport to promote competence in youth has tremendous benefits and risks. The greatest risk is following the belief held by many that we can make a difference by just "throwing out a ball." On the contrary, we believe that teaching athletic skills without life skills sends the wrong message to adolescents. It reinforces the belief that their world can change if they become better athletes. For the overwhelming majority, this belief is not true. On the other hand, when both sets of skills are taught together, and when avenues to transfer skills from one domain to another are known, the effect can be very powerful.

THE RELEVANCE OF SPORT

There are several reasons why we have chosen to concentrate on sport. First, the impact of sport on our society is pervasive (Coakley, 1990). It is a major source of entertainment for both young and old—only family, television, and school involve children's time more than sport (Danish, Nellen, & Owens, 1996). If we expect to reach youth, we must reach them where they are and where they want to be (Danish, 1997). Second, sport is a significant factor in the development of adolescents' self-esteem, identity, and feelings of competence (Danish, Petitpas, & Hale, 1990; Fejgin, 1994; Fox, 1992; Kleiber & Kirshnit, 1991; Zaharopoulos & Hodge, 1991). This is especially true for boys. Third, sport skills and life skills are learned in the same way—through demonstration, modeling, and practice (Danish et al., 1993; Danish, Petitpas, & Hale, 1995).

Although sport provides many opportunities for psychosocial development, the potential benefits of participation are not necessarily transmitted through mere participation (Danish et al., Hodge, 1989, 1994a). There is nothing magical about a ball, other sporting equipment, or a sport venue for transmitting life skills. Both positive and negative skills and attitudes can be taught in the sport setting by coaches, teammates, and parents, and both can be learned by young athletes (Miracle & Rees, 1994). Indeed, as Weiss (1995) notes, if "the physical, psychological, and social benefits available though sport are to occur, they must be purposely planned, structured, and taught as well as positively reinforced. This does not always happen" (p. 40). Consequently, for benefits to accrue, sport has to be organized appropriately for the participants so that each player is able to reach her or his personal goals and derive satisfaction from doing so (Danish & Nellen, 1997; Hodge, 1994a, 1994b). Successful and satisfying goal accomplishment is regarded as a powerful mediator of psychosocial development.

Goal accomplishment is viewed as the foundation of healthy psychosocial development; thus, we need to examine the nature of the goals being accomplished to maximize the benefits of the experience and promote development. Sport, because of its inherently competitive nature, tends to reinforce an *ego-involved, other-referenced* goal orientation (Roberts, 1993); however, research suggests that a *task-involved, self-referenced* goal orientation is the most adaptive goal focus for psychosocial development (Duda, 1993; Roberts, 1993). If sport is to be a positive force for development, it must facilitate the attainment of both task and ego goals. Balancing goal orientations is often difficult to achieve because the focus in sport is predominantly on winning and other-referenced (social comparison) criteria for determining successful goal accomplishment. This is especially true for boys in sport. Indeed, it has been suggested that sport is *the* social context in which young boys use social comparison processes to determine their status with their peers and to determine their self-esteem (Veroff, 1969).

In summary, sport has considerable potential as both a venue for and a means of promoting psychosocial development for adolescent males. Because so many adolescent males are already engaged in sports and participating in athletic activities that have the potential for both positive and negative consequences regarding psychosocial development, we first need to understand the impact of sport on adolescent development.

DEVELOPMENTAL ISSUES FOR MALE ADOLESCENT ATHLETES

WHAT IS THE MOTIVATION FOR PARTICIPATING IN SPORT?

Participation motivation has been well researched over the past 25 years in sport psychology and related sport sciences such as the sociology of sport. There are many consistencies in why young athletes participate in sport (Athletic Footwear Association, 1990; Gould & Horn, 1984; Hodge & Zaharopoulos, 1992, 1993; Weinberg & Gould, 1995). Most research cites multiple reasons for involvement in sport. These diverse motives include having fun, seeking affiliation, demonstrating power, improving skills, pursuing excellence, exhibiting aggression, having something to do, experiencing thrills or excitement, being independent, receiving rewards, fulfilling parental expectations, and winning. The most common of the multiple motives for participating in sport are to improve skills (i.e., physical competency through a task orientation), to have fun, and to be with friends or make new friends (i.e., social competency through peer relations). Thus, for sport to be sought as an activity in which to participate, it must provide opportunities for competency building and enjoyment. We must also be aware of the potential conflict between an adolescent male's motives and those reinforced and rewarded in the sport environment (i.e., winning). This conflict is of particular concern when we take into account the considerable social status that success in sports has for adolescent boys.

HOW DOES SPORT MEET SOCIAL STATUS NEEDS?

Sport and school are perhaps the two most important social environments for children in the developmental period of 12-16 years of age (Battrick & Thomson, 1994; Coakley, 1990; Coleman, 1961; Weiss & Smith, 1995). Indeed, boys regard sport as being higher in social status than all other activities, including schoolwork, and some research indicates that among adolescent males, commitment to sport often exists at the expense of investment in schoolwork (Chase & Dummer, 1992; Fejgin, 1994; Miracle & Rees, 1994; Thirer & Wright, 1985). Although an overemphasis on sport over schoolwork is clearly counterproductive for adolescent males from a life skill and career perspective, the intrinsic motivation and enthusiasm they demonstrate for sport point to its importance.

Roberts (1993) contends that one of the reasons that sport is an important achievement context for boys is because being competent at physical skills is very important. It is a context where friendship patterns are established, acceptance from peers is attained, and social competence is developed. Because sport is so highly valued, it becomes a strong social asset, especially as one becomes more skilled. As Evans and Roberts (1987) state:

> Comparing themselves in games and sporting activities is a most important source of information to children about their relative competence and, by inference, their relative self-worth. . . . Given our society's strong achievement orientation, and the way in which sports and sport celebrities are idolized, we can begin to understand why physical competence is such a desired quality. . . . Merely being interested in and knowledgeable about sports can facilitate social acceptance. (p. 25)

In summarizing their research, they conclude that it appears reasonable to acknowledge the relationship among peer status, social competence, and sport competence. More will be said about this when we discuss the relationship between sport and self-esteem.

WHAT IS THE RELATIONSHIP BETWEEN SPORT AND SCHOOLWORK MOTIVATION?

Duda and Nicholls (1992) claim that the observed similarities and differences in the domains of school and sport suggest that more comparisons of these achievement contexts are warranted. They maintain that such comparisons can highlight the nature of the motivation to achieve in each context, and that given the prominence of both academic and athletic skills for adolescents, such comparisons may also have social relevance. The possibility of developing skills in one domain (e.g., sport) for use in another domain (e.g., schoolwork) also is relevant. This notion of "transferable skill" is at the heart of life skill interventions we will discuss in a later section of this chapter.

Research indicates that during adolescence, there is an increasing emphasis on ego-involved goals as a measure of success in both settings (Chaumeton & Duda, 1988; Eccles, Midgley, & Adler, 1984). This emphasis becomes a problem when adolescents begin to compete with one another in these settings. Those who do not compare well will perceive themselves as failures and, if the "discounting hypothesis" is accurate, may focus their energies in the areas where they compare favorably with their peers and ignore or "discount" those areas where the comparisons are unfavorable (Fox, 1992). Dropping out of sport has become commonplace and is a major concern if the psychosocial, physical, and health benefits of sport participation are to be realized (Weiss & Petlichkoff, 1989). Although beyond the scope of this chapter, dropping out of school or not "bonding" with school has become an even more serious problem than dropping out of sport (Hawkins, 1997).

Despite the increasing pressure to compete and compare, alternatives are still possible. A task goal orientation that focuses on task or skill improvement through carefully planned behavioral goal setting can allow adolescents of all academic and physical abilities to experience a sense of mastery and competence (Fox, 1992). Good coaching and teaching can redefine sport and academic excellence by encouraging the adoption and maintenance of task mastery as the primary goal in both sport and academics. Additionally, such a focus allows greater opportunity for all youth to experience positive feelings about themselves.

Dependent on whether one is task involved or ego involved, different achievement-related patterns are predicted. For example, task involvement, regardless of the level of perceived competence, relates to choosing moderately challenging tasks, the exertion of effort, intrinsic interest in the activity, sustained or improved performance, and persistence. These desirable behaviors are also possible for ego-involved people, as long as they have a high perception of their ability. Perceptions of competence, however, are believed to be particularly fragile in ego-involved individuals (Duda, 1993). When ego involvement is dominant and a person doubts her or his competence, maladaptive behavior such as lack of effort, cheating, or anxiety is likely to occur.

Given the central role that school and sport play in most adolescents' lives, a proneness for an ego orientation in these achievement situations can be expected. This is especially true if the adolescent is receiving similar socialization messages from the peer group, the media, and/or the family (especially parents). In one of the few studies that investigated these two achievement contexts concurrently, Duda and Nicholls (1992) found that there was considerable generality for goal orientations and beliefs about the cause of success across the domains of sport and schoolwork. The same dimensions of motivational beliefs as found in the classroom were also evident in sport (Duda & Nicholls, 1992). Parallel results were found for views about the larger purposes of sport with respect to issues such as developing the capacity for hard work, cooperation, and self-esteem (task orientation) versus social recognition, social status, and competitiveness (ego orientation) (Duda, 1993). The fact that these constellations of beliefs and goal orientations cut across the domains of schoolwork and sport indicates that interventions designed to encourage the transferability of skills from the sport domain to the academic domain may hold considerable promise as a means of preventing failure by at-risk children. Such development of transferable skills may also lead to a more general improvement in psychosocial well-being (Danish et al., 1996).

HOW DOES SPORT AFFECT
IDENTITY AND SELF-ESTEEM?

Perceived competence in sport has been demonstrated to be an important contributor to identity, self-esteem, and social status for many children (e.g., Fejgin, 1994; Thirer

& Wright, 1985). Nevertheless, to the extent that sport provides a structure that recognizes youth who surpass their peers in physical competence (an ego goal), it may harm the self-esteem for those low in physical competence. Those adolescents low in physical competence may not be able to readily discount sport competence because of dominant cultural imperatives that reinforce and reward success in sport as "social currency" for status (e.g., Coakley, 1990; Fejgin, 1994; Miracle & Rees, 1994). In contrast to those adolescents who may have lower self-esteem because of deficient physical competencies, those males who discount other competencies and rely exclusively on sport competence to define their identity are at risk of possible identity foreclosure (see Brewer, Van Raalte, & Linder, 1993; Coakley, 1992; Kleiber & Kirshnit, 1991; Murphy, Petitpas, & Brewer, 1996; Petitpas, 1978; Petitpas & Champagne, 1988).

When task-oriented goals are established in sport, or for that matter in any setting, the feedback from the activity can be positive for the development of self-esteem. Danish, Kleiber, and Hall (1987) note that sport can increase self-esteem when "competence is extended to meet expanding challenges and contributes significantly to one's self-concept and sense of well-being. Moreover, because greater challenges are sought as abilities expand, the process is inherently growth-producing" (p. 214); we note that it also is motivating.

Enhancing self-esteem through sport participation does not occur by default, despite the belief by many proponents of sport that some wonderful universal "self-esteem osmosis process" occurs as children grow up. Youth need supportive interactions with major socialization agencies such as the family, peers, school, coaches, and the media for such development to occur. When the natural socializing agencies either are not present or do not provide positive socializing experiences, sport-oriented intervention programs designed to enhance self-esteem and identity may be necessary. Some of these programs are described in a later section of this chapter.

DOES SPORT TEACH MORAL REASONING?

Whereas some programs exist that are designed to develop self-esteem through sport, many advocates of sport believe that involvement in itself is "character building." Sociologists and psychologists have been intrigued by the moral/prosocial dimension of sport and have contended that participation fosters fair play, sportsmanship, and character (Hodge, 1989; Lumpkin, Stoll, & Beller, 1994). Although some research supports this notion, most investigations have cast serious doubt on the role of sport in promoting moral development (see Shields & Bredemeier, 1995, for a review). In fact, it is proposed that "game reasoning" develops. This concept denotes the use of lower levels of moral reasoning in the sport environment as compared with everyday life environments. Particular elements of the sporting environment encourage and reinforce a sport/life dichotomy for several reasons: (a) The rule-bound, officiated nature of sport may encourage athletes to abdicate responsibility for their actions and adopt a "play to the ref, not the rules" mentality or a belief that it is not cheating unless you get caught; (b) the time-bounded and temporal nature of sport may encourage athletes to view sport as something separate from real life rather than part of everyday life; and/or (c) the emphasis in competitive sport on winning and sometimes winning at all costs may dictate an egocentric, selfish attitude. In other words, some athletes may come to believe that fair play and sportsmanship are luxuries that can be afforded only when the individual is winning.

This "game reasoning" level of moral reasoning is especially common for boys (Shields & Bredemeier, 1995). Hodge and Tod (1993) also contend that a high ego goal and an emphasis on winning at all costs will predispose an athlete to use lower levels of moral reasoning. Some research conducted supports this contention (e.g., Tod, 1996; Tod & Hodge, 1993).

The type of goal orientation one has also influences whether a moral/prosocial dimension within sport will be adopted. For example, Treasure and Roberts (1994) found that task orientation was related to the belief that sport facilitates personal development, such as teaching participants respect for authority, self-discipline, and cooperation with others as well as a commitment to lifetime health. In contrast, Treasure and Roberts (1994) also found that an ego orientation was related to negative social aspects of sport involvement such that "the higher the ego orientation, the greater the view that sport participation is a means to an end, namely acquiring status in school and providing an opportunity to feel important" (p. 24).

Moreover, when adolescents adopt a "game reasoning" perspective with an ego-oriented "win at all costs" attitude in sport and, as a result of their socialization experiences, either do not respect themselves or develop an inflated sense of their own importance, life can become an ongoing competition. More is said about this possibility in the next section.

HOW DOES SPORT PARTICIPATION AFFECT THE DEVELOPMENT OF AGGRESSIVE BEHAVIOR?

Many male athletes in contact sports learn very early in their sport careers that they will be evaluated on their ability to use violence in combination with physical skills (Coakley, 1990; Vaz, 1982). They are often reinforced and encouraged to be violent by their peers and teammates, coaches, and sometimes parents (Smith, 1983). For some, it becomes acceptable to use violence and physical intimidation as strategies to win games (Miracle & Rees, 1994).

More important, however, is whether learning to use violence in sport is carried over into nonsport situations (Coakley, 1990). To date, this question remains unanswered, although game reasoning research may provide a method to seek such an answer in the future. Coakley (1990) also suggests that, among males, learning to use violence as a tactic in competitive sport may not be as significant as whether they learn to define their masculinity as being willing to risk personal safety and intimidate others. If males do define their masculinity in this manner and believe it to be a natural or appropriate process, then the carryover of such violence to nonsport settings may become common, especially if these nonsport settings become arenas for proving themselves. The result may be that the nature of their interactions with others, both friend and foe, will almost parallel the win-lose sport environment (Danish, 1996), and aggressive and violent behavior may become a manifestation of inappropriate attempts at conflict resolution resulting from an overemphasis on social comparison and a win-lose perspective.

We believe that aggression can be reduced when a "win-win" environment in both sport and nonsport situations is fostered. To learn how to "win" while others also "win," adolescent males must learn to change the nature of how they compete (Lumpkin et al., 1994). A dominant ego-oriented approach to competition emphasizes social comparison with others, whereas a focus on a task-mastery orientation emphasizes a self-referenced comparison against personal standards (Duda, 1993; Roberts, 1993). Adolescents must learn to compete against their previous best performances and against their own potential (Danish & Nellen, 1997).

SUMMARY: DEVELOPMENTAL ISSUES

Although males generally experience a rewarding and supportive set of socialization experiences that predispose them toward sport (Greendorfer, 1992), they are also subject to greater expectations of success in sport, and their social status, identity, and self-esteem are often directly linked with their sporting success (Miracle & Rees, 1994). These expectations generate their own particular psychological climate for boys as they strive to achieve success in the explicitly competitive sport environment—an environment that is characterized by clear, unambiguous social comparison and public evaluation of their goal accomplishment efforts. Such social comparison and evaluation, coupled with a powerful cultural imperative that boys should participate and succeed at sport, make the athletic experience an exciting but precarious venue for psychosocial development.

DEVELOPING A FRAMEWORK
FOR PREVENTION AND INTERVENTION

We use two perspectives for developing our framework. The first is based on the writings of Perry and Jessor (1985), who identified four domains of health: physical, psychological, social, and personal. Within each of these domains, individuals can engage in either *health-compromising behaviors*, which threaten their well-being, or *health-enhancing behaviors*, which promote well-being. According to the authors, programs should be developed to teach and encourage health-enhancing behaviors and personality attributes as well as weaken health-compromising behaviors and personality attributes. Table 4.1 provides examples of such attributes.

By focusing on the creation of health-enhancing behaviors, personality attributes, and environments, Perry and Jessor (1985) sought to buffer youth against the impact of what many might consider "normative" risk-taking behaviors. In other words, instead of assuming that individuals can be taught to completely eliminate undesirable or unhealthy behaviors, they acknowledged that many risk-taking behaviors are norma-

TABLE 4.1 Behavioral and Personality Attributes

	Health Compromising	*Health Enhancing*
Behavioral attributes	Smoking	Regular exercise
	Fighting	Goal setting
Personality attributes	Hopelessness	Optimism
	Low self-esteem	High self-esteem

tive and suggested that it is necessary to optimize the chance that engaging in these behaviors would not place youth in any type of long-term danger (Meyer, 1994).

LIFE DEVELOPMENT INTERVENTION (LDI)

The second perspective used for the framework is a Life Development Intervention (LDI) and life skills orientation. LDI is based on a life span human development perspective emphasizing continuous growth and change (Danish & D'Augelli, 1980). Because change is sequential, it is necessary to consider any period of life within the context of what has happened in the past and what will happen in the future. As change occurs in one's life, it may result in problems or crises, but the results are not necessarily negative (Baltes, Reese, & Lipsett, 1980).

Because change disrupts our routines and relationships with others and may result in stress, most of us try to avoid change. We like continuity without having to confront life decisions and change. For this reason, change resulting from life situations has been called *critical life events*. We experience many critical life events throughout our life. For example, adolescent males are at an age where they are experiencing a number of stressful concurrent life changes and events. These changes include biological changes with the onset of puberty, a reference change from a child to an adolescent and then to a teenager, and physical relocation from elementary school to middle or junior high school (Crockett & Petersen, 1993). Until a child reaches early adolescence, family members usually are the strongest influence. With the onset of adolescence, significant social changes occur. Perhaps the most important is that peer groups become larger and become the most influential source for affecting behavior and values (Petersen & Hamburg, 1986).

Although critical life events are often considered as discrete, they are really processes that commence prior to the event and continue well after the event. Critical life events, then, have histories; from the time we anticipate them, through their occurrence, and until their aftermath has been determined and assessed. A number of characteristics of life events affect the impact they have on an individual. Three of these characteristics are the timing of the event, the duration of the event, and the contextual purity of the event (Danish, Smyer, & Nowak, 1980).

As noted earlier, and as can be seen in Figure 4.1, critical life events are not necessarily negative. One's reaction to a critical life event is dependent on the resources the individual has prior to the event, the level of preparation for the event, and the past history in dealing with similar events. Critical life events may lead to problems or increased dissatisfaction, or to little or no change in one's life, or these events may actually serve as a catalyst for increased opportunities and personal growth (Danish & D'Augelli, 1983).

In fact, critical life events are not all that dissimilar to one another. If past critical life events have been handled successfully, *and* the individual knows how this was accomplished, coping with the present event will be easier and increase one's feelings of confidence and likely success.

The specific goal of LDI is to enhance personal competence by teaching life skills. Personal competence is defined as the ability to do life planning, be self-reliant, and seek the resources of others (Danish, D'Augelli, & Ginsberg, 1984). Life skills are those skills, either behavioral or cognitive, that enable us to succeed in the environments in which we live. Some of the environments in which we live are families, schools, workplaces, neighborhoods, and communities. Most individuals must succeed in more than one environment. As one becomes older, the number of environments in which one must be successful increases. For example, a child need only succeed within the family; an adolescent must succeed within the family, at school, and in the neighborhood. Environments will vary from individual to individual; thus, the definition of what it means to succeed will differ across individuals, as well as across environments (Danish, 1995).

Individuals in the same environment are likely to be dissimilar from one another as a result of the life skills they have already mastered, their other resources, and their opportunities, real or perceived. For this reason, the needed life skills are likely to be different for individuals of different ages, ethnic and/or racial groups, or economic status. It is necessary to be sensitive to these differences, but it also is important to recognize that life skills enable individuals to transfer behaviors from setting to setting and across life situations as appropriate. An example of life skills that are transferable are those learned in sport that then have applicability at home and school.

The procedure used for implementing the programs is a psychoeducational approach (client dissatisfaction or ambition → goal setting → skill teaching → satisfaction or goal achievement). This approach can be distinguished from psychotherapy, which employs an illness or medical model (illness → diagnosis → prescription → therapy → cure) (Ivey, 1980).

COMMUNITY-BASED SPORT AND LIFE SKILLS PROGRAMS

In this section, we describe two programs and briefly mention a third. The two programs are GOAL (Going for the Goal) and SUPER (Sports United to Promote Education and Recreation). GOAL uses sport as a metaphor for life skills; in SUPER, the life skills are

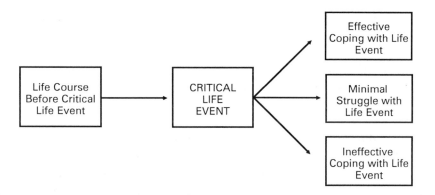

Figure 4.1. Coping With Life Events
SOURCE: Adapted from *Helping Skills II: Life Development Intervention* (p. 3), S. Danish and A. D'Augelli, © copyright 1983 by Human Sciences Press.

taught in sports clinics. As mentioned earlier, we have chosen sport as a vehicle for teaching life skills because adolescent males devote much of their time and energy to sport activities. Our objective in both these programs is to help teach adolescents the skills to succeed in the family, school, neighborhood, and community. These skills are similar to those described by the Task Force of Education on Young Adolescents (1989) as the five desired outcomes or characteristics for every young adolescent. These characteristics are

- to process information from multiple sources and communicate clearly;
- to be en route to a lifetime of meaningful work by learning how to learn and therefore being able to adapt to different educational and working environments;
- to be a good citizen by participating in community activities and feeling concern for, and connection to, the well-being of others;
- to be a caring and ethical individual by acting on one's convictions about right and wrong; and
- to be a healthy person.

GOAL (Going for the Goal)

GOAL is a 10-session, 10-hour program taught to youth at middle-school age. It is designed to teach adolescents a sense of personal control and confidence about their future so that they can make better decisions and ultimately become better citizens. To be successful in life, it is not enough to know what to avoid; one must also know how to succeed. For this reason, our focus is on teaching "what to say yes to" as opposed to "just say no." The GOAL program is the 1996 winner of the Lela Rowland Prevention Award given by the National Mental Health Association.

In the first workshop, *Dare to Dream*, the program and the leaders are introduced. The students discuss the importance of dreams and practice dreaming about their future. In the second workshop, *Setting Goals*, they learn that a goal is a dream they work hard to reach. They learn the value of goal setting and practice recognizing reachable goals. Sport examples are used as tangible evidence of the benefits of goal setting. The four characteristics of a reachable goal are that it is stated positively, is specific, is important to the goal setter, and is under the goal setter's control. In the third workshop, *Making Your Goal Reachable*, the students apply what they learned in the second workshop. They write a reachable goal to be attained within the next 2 months that meets the characteristics learned in the previous workshop. We have found that developing such goals is difficult for adolescents and adults alike; learning and applying this process is a key aspect of the program.

In the fourth workshop, *Making a Goal Ladder*, they learn how to make a plan to reach their goal by identifying all the steps needed to reach their goal and then placing them in order on the rungs of the ladder. Each rung of the ladder must include a step that has the four characteristics of a reachable goal. Students who miss either of these sessions or are unable to develop goals and concrete plans rarely benefit from the program. We consider these workshops the essence of the program.

In the fifth workshop, *Roadblocks to Reaching Goals*, the students learn how various roadblocks such as drug abuse, teen pregnancy, violence, dropping out of school, or lack of self-confidence can prevent them from reaching their goals in life. In the sixth workshop, *Overcoming Roadblocks*, they learn and practice a problem-solving strategy called STAR (Stop and chill out, Think of all your choices, Anticipate the consequences of each choice, and Respond with the best choice). In the seventh workshop, *Seeking Help From Others*, students learn the importance of seeking social support in achieving goals. As part of the activities, they identify a "dream team" of 10 individuals (family members, very close friends, good friends, and older friends and role models) who can help them reach their goals.

In the eighth workshop, *Rebounds and Rewards*, they learn how to rebound when a goal or a step on the goal ladder becomes too difficult to reach. They also develop a plan to reward themselves for their accomplishments. In the ninth workshop, *Identifying and Building on Your Strengths*, the students identify their personal strengths and learn how to further develop these strengths. They are also asked to identify an area in which they want to improve and a plan for how they can work toward improvement. In the tenth and final workshop, *Going for Your Goal*, the students play a game, "Know-It-All-Baseball," that provides an opportunity for them to integrate and apply the information covered in the nine other workshops (Danish, 1997).

The design of the GOAL program contains several unique aspects. First, skills are taught because they are concrete and are easily taught and learned, and when directed toward areas of everyday life, they are empowering. Facts or information presented to adolescents, such as the danger of using drugs, often is ignored and has not proven to be effective. Skills are taught differently than is knowledge. A Chinese proverb states "I listen—and forget. I see—and remember. I do—and understand." Just as learning to drive a car, dance, or play a sport cannot occur solely through listening to a tape or reading a book, skills for living cannot be taught in a passive manner. They are taught through instruction, demonstration, and supervised practice, and they require learning "how to." The mastery is very similar to learning to play sports or drive a car (Danish & Hale, 1981).

Second, GOAL uses sport as a metaphor for life skills because (a) life skills and physical (sport) skills are learned in a similar way, (b) the skills learned in sport are transferable to other life domains such as work and school, (c) sport is so pervasive in our society, and (d) sport is a major influence in the development of identity and competence among adolescents.

Third, the teachers of GOAL are high school student leaders chosen by their schools for their academic performance, leadership qualities, and extracurricular involvement. They receive special training on how to teach the program. Following the training, the student leaders teach the skills during middle/junior high school (often as part of the health curriculum) or in after-school programs. The ratio is approximately two to three high school student leaders to 15 middle/junior high school students. Successful high school students serve as concrete images of what early adolescents can become. Because these high school students have grown up in the same neighborhoods, attended the same schools, and confronted similar roadblocks, they serve as important role models and thus are in an ideal position to be effective teachers.

Fourth, there is a printed Leader Manual (Danish et al., 1992a) given to each high school student and a Student Activity Guide (Danish et al., 1992b) given to each junior high/middle school participant. A more complete description of the program and the research findings are described elsewhere (Danish, 1996, 1997; Danish & Nellen, 1997).

SUPER (Sports United to Promote Education and Recreation)

The objectives of the second program, SUPER, are for each participant to leave the program with the understanding that (a) there are effective and accessible student-athlete role models, (b) physical *and* mental skills are important for both sport and life, (c) it is important to set and attain goals in sport, (d) it is important to set and attain goals in life, and (e) roadblocks to goals can be overcome in both sport and life.

SUPER is a 30-hour, 10-session program that is currently being piloted. Sessions are taught like sports clinics, with participants involved in three sets of activities: learning the physical skills related to a specific sport, learning life skills related to sports in general, and playing the sport. Sometimes, the students learn several sports within a SUPER program; other times, the focus is on one sport. As with GOAL, there are manuals to facilitate dissemination.

The life skills taught include (a) learning how to learn; (b) communicating with others; (c) managing anger; (d) using positive self-talk; (e) giving and receiving feedback; (f) becoming part of a team; (g) increasing focus and concentration; (h) learning how to win, lose, and respect your opponent; (i) regulating arousal; and (j) becoming an effective decision maker and risk taker (Danish, 1998).

The SUPER leaders are college students, either athletes themselves or physical education majors so that they have some coaching and athletic skills teaching experience. They are often joined by high school leaders who have had experience teaching in the GOAL program. In preparation for teaching SUPER, the leaders learn many of the skills the GOAL leaders are taught, as well as how skills are learned, how to teach sport skills to athletes who are less able and experienced, and how to use sport observation strategies. Leaders are told that when they instruct, demonstrate, and conduct practices, they need to focus on *how* the students are participating as opposed to just *how well* they are performing and participating. Understanding "how" provides information on the life skills that the participants have in responding to direct instruction, coaching, or teaching and may be indicative of how they will respond to other forms of instruction, such as school and job training. Observing "how" participants react gives the leader the answers to such questions as these:

▶ Are the students attentive when given instructions or observing demonstration?

▶ Do they become frustrated with themselves when they cannot perform the activity to their expectations, and does this frustration impede or enhance later efforts?

▶ Are they first to initiate questions when they do not understand something being taught, or do they wait quietly for someone else to talk first?

▶ Are they first to initiate conversation with group members, or do they wait for someone else to talk to them first?

▶ How do they react when they have a good performance, and how do they react to a bad performance?

▶ How do they react when others have a good performance, or a bad performance?

▶ How do they react when someone gives them praise, or criticism?

▶ Do they give up when they can't do as well as they would like, or as well as others, or do they continue to practice in a determined manner to learn the skill?

▶ Do they compete or cooperate with the other student athletes?

The leaders observe the students' activities and help them explore what the activities mean to them. We expect that the leaders will spend at least several minutes with each individual to discuss the "hows" of their performance (separate from the "how wells") during each session of the sport clinics. Additional information about SUPER is presented elsewhere (Danish, 1996, 1997; Danish & Nellen, 1997; Danish et al., 1996).

In contrast to GOAL, which has been taught at many different sites, SUPER is still in a formative stage. We are just completing the methodology for teaching the life skills and integrating it into an ongoing recreation program. What we have learned is that the instruction must be fun and be something that the participants feel benefits their sports performance. We also recognize, as we discussed earlier, that boys use sport to determine their status with their peers and their self-esteem. As a result, SUPER activities must provide experiences where social comparisons (winning) as well as self-learning can take place.

Another community-based sport program has been developed by Don Hellison at the University of Illinois at Chicago. He has developed a program to use sport and exercise as a vehicle for teaching youth to take more responsibility for their well-being and to be more sensitive and responsible for the well-being of others. Through his book, *Teaching Responsibility Through Physical Activity* (Hellison, 1995), teachers and coaches are trained how to teach youth to be personally and socially responsible. He identifies five levels that encompass what it means for students to be responsible and for what they need to be responsible. These levels are the following: learning to respect the rights and feelings of others, understand the role of effort in improving their physical activity level and life situation, be self-directed in being responsible for their own well-being, be sensitive and responsible for the well-being of others, and apply what they have learned in different nonsport settings.

ISSUES IN TRAINING, IMPLEMENTATION, AND RESEARCH

If one is to conduct the programs described above, or develop similar programs, several knowledge and skill components are necessary. First, the intervention agent/person, hereafter referred to as the life skills educator (LSE), must have an understanding of adolescents: their physical, cognitive, affective, and social/interpersonal development and the changes taking place during this period. Second, LSEs must understand the settings in which they will be delivering the programs. If it is in schools, they must understand how schools operate and the "ins and outs" of the school environment; if it is in a sports environment, they must understand the game itself and the needs and motivations of the parents, coaches, and participants. They also must have the ability to work within these settings. Consequently, it is desirable for LSEs working with sport-based life skills programs to have a working knowledge of sport psychology principles and Psychological Skills Training (PST) programs specifically designed for sport (e.g., Danish & Hale, 1981; Hodge, 1994b; Orlick & McCaffrey, 1991; Smith & Smoll, 1996; Weiss, 1991).

Additionally, LSEs must understand the environment within which sports programs exist. On one hand, estimates by the Athletic Footwear Association (1990) suggest that there are 20 to 35 million 5- to 18-year-olds participating in nonschool sports and another 10 million 14- to 18-year-olds participating in school sports in the United States. On the other hand, sport is often seen as merely a big business, and its stars, who were once viewed as heroes, are often depicted in the media as contract-driven celebrities whose on-the-field conduct and off-the-field exploits overshadow their accomplishments. LSEs wishing to start a program like SUPER must contend with these contradictions. We have found that to begin our SUPER programs, we must emphasize the similarities between life skills and sport skills, especially how skills learned in sport can be transferred to other areas. Some of these skills are the ability to perform under pressure, solve problems, meet deadlines and challenges, set goals, communicate, handle both success and failure, work with a group and within a system, and receive feedback and benefit from it. The process of transferability is not a natural one, as de Coubertin, founder of the Olympic movement, noted:

> Sport plants in the body seeds of physio-psychological qualities such as coolness, confidence, decision etc. These qualities may remain localised around the exercise which brought them into being; this often happens—it even happens most often. How many daredevil cyclists there are who once they leave their machines are hesitant at every crossroads of existence, how many swimmers who are brave in the water but frightened by the waves of human existence, how many fencers who cannot apply to life's battles the quick eye and nice timing which they show on the boards! The educator's task is to make the seed bear fruit throughout the organism, to transpose it from a particular circumstance to a whole array of circumstances, from a special category of activities to all the individual's actions. (de Coubertin, 1918)

Third, because our sport-based life skills programs use an educational pyramid model of delivery (Seidman & Rappaport, 1974), LSEs must have the ability to be indirect service providers; that is, they must have skills in program development, training, supervision, and organizing and evaluating the implementation of these programs. Fourth, LSEs must have some training in counseling and listening skills.

Evaluation of life skills programs presents special problems. Few instruments enable a researcher to measure different outcomes and still have the properties necessary to compare experimental and control participants. Even fewer consider positive outcomes such as those identified in the Task Force on Education of Young Adolescents (1989) report. Although quantitative measures may permit such analyses, they are labor intensive, difficult to use, and expensive with large groups. For this reason, we have begun to use Goal Attainment Scaling (GAS) (Kiresuk, 1973; Kiresuk, Smith, & Cardillo, 1994) as a measurement strategy. GAS measures the specific level of success that a participant achieves in pursuing a stated goal. It is idiographic in that it allows participants to identify individual goals, but it is nomothetic in that it measures the level of success attained across participants on a 5-point scale from *much less than expected* to *much more than expected*.

The evaluations of GOAL have not, for the most part, focused on the specific life skills outlined in the report of the Task Force on Education of Young Adolescents (1989). Some of the findings were that participants

> learned the information the program teaches,
>
> were able to achieve the goals they set,
>
> found the process easier than they expected, and
>
> thought they had learned quite a bit about how to set goals.

They also had better school attendance (as compared to a control group). Male participants did not report the same increases in health-compromising behaviors—including getting drunk, smoking cigarettes, drinking beer, and drinking other liquor—as were found in the control group and also reported a decrease in violent and other problem behavior, as compared with a control group that reported an increase in these behaviors. Long-term longitudinal data are necessary concerning the effects of teaching life skills, as well as involvement in health-compromising behaviors. To date, outcome data have not been collected on the SUPER program.

CLOSING COMMENT

Enhancing the psychosocial development of boys and adolescent males requires new strategies. Traditional counseling approaches are either not likely to be effective or are too costly to promote development. We have proposed and described a community-based psychoeducational intervention that has the potential to reach large numbers of boys and adolescent males at a reasonably low cost. The programs described will not be sufficient for all boys. More intensive interventions may be required for males who have specific problems. Instead of starting with interventions that may stigmatize the "client" by treating him as "ill," however, psychoeducational approaches such as GOAL and SUPER provide positive alternatives. Such programs reach the adolescent males where they are and want to be—playing sports, watching television, and being with friends—and not where we as psychologists feel most comfortable. As we have tried to emphasize, for the benefits of sport to be realized, the activities must be purposely planned, structured, and taught as well as positively reinforced.

PART

II

CULTURAL CONSIDERATIONS

5

Counseling African American Male Youth

SHAWN LEONARD

COURTLAND LEE

MARK S. KISELICA

African American male youth face a significant number of social and educational hardships. In this chapter, we highlight these difficulties and document that young African American men are an at-risk population who warrant interventions tailored to their particular needs. We discuss several issues related to understanding and establishing rapport with African American male youth, and we describe several model service programs that have been designed to foster the positive development of this group. We conclude this chapter with suggestions for future training and research on psychotherapeutic work with African American male youth.

HARDSHIPS AND CHALLENGES

Both the popular and social science literatures indicate that over the past decade, Black men in the United States have been an at-risk population (Cordes, 1985; Dent, 1989; Gibbs, 1988; Johnson & Watson, 1990; Jones, 1986; McCall, 1994; Monroe, 1987; Parham & McDavis, 1987; Randolph, 1990; Salholz, 1990; Weathers, 1993; West, 1994; Wright, 1992). Populations that have been defined as "at risk" may not have available to them the same educational, social, and economic institutions that other groups may have (Herr, 1999); therefore, these populations suffer from restricted life chances and life possibilities.

AUTHORS' NOTE: Throughout this chapter, the terms "African American" and "Black" are used interchangeably.

One problem that certainly restricts the life chances and life possibilities of Black males is their shortened life span. In 1990, a report released by the National Urban League indicated that, because of disproportionate vulnerability to disease and homicide, Black males have a shorter life span than any other population group in America (Johnson & Watson, 1990). Another problem facing young Black males is an elevated victimization rate. The U.S. Department of Justice, Bureau of Justice Statistics (1986), reports that, among youths aged 14 to 17, the Black male victimization rate is almost eight times the White male victimization rate.

Along with a shorter life span, young Black males face a disproportionately high level of unemployment. The U.S. Bureau of Labor Statistics (U.S. Bureau of the Census, 1997) reports the unemployment rates of White and Black teenagers between the ages 16 and 19. During the years 1994, 1995, and 1996, White teenagers' unemployment rates were 15.1%, 14.5%, and 14.2%, respectively, while Black teenagers' unemployment rates were 35.2%, 35.7%, and 33.6%, respectively. These figures illustrate that the unemployment rate, in general, is about 2.4 times as high for Black teenagers as for their White counterparts.

Many authorities state that the most significant problem that young Black males encounter is an inadequate education (Green & Wright, 1991; Johnson & Watson, 1990; Narine, 1992; Reed, 1988; Wright, 1992). Information and statistics on the educational attainment of Black male youth come from a great many sources (Jones, 1986; Johnson & Watson, 1990; Narine, 1992; National Black Child Development Institute, 1990; Reed, 1988; U.S. House of Representatives, 1989). Each of these sources provides information and data that speak to the widespread struggles of Black males in the educational system. For example, compared with any other ethnic or gender group, Black males are more likely to be placed in general education and vocational high school curricular tracks than in academic tracks, and they complete high school at significantly lower rates. Black males are also three times as likely to be put into classes for the educable mentally retarded or learning disabled than to be placed in classes for the gifted and talented. More than any other ethnic or gender group, Black males drop out or are pushed out of school systems; they are also suspended from school more frequently and for longer periods of time. Given these statistics, it is not surprising that between 1976 and 1986, college enrollment rates of Black males ages 18-24 declined from 35% to 28%; this is true despite increases in overall minority enrollment.

In the light of these many hardships, it is imperative that counselors reach out to African American male youth in a manner that prepares them to meet the many developmental challenges they are likely to encounter. For counseling with this population to be successful, counselors must have an awareness of the African American culture.

AFRICAN AMERICAN CULTURE: ## IMPORTANT CONSIDERATIONS

The African American culture can be defined as "the attitudes, behaviors, and values which have developed in relatively homogenous Black communities where rudimentary

Afrocentric ways of life have been preserved to a great extent" (Lee, 1996, p. 25). Afrocentrism refers to perceiving the world in terms of African concepts, issues, and behaviors (Asante, 1987) and to understanding African relationships, social codes, and cultural customs from an African perspective (Asante, 1988). Important concepts related to Afrocentric life are highlighted here.

Despite cultural variations, African Americans tend to share many common characteristics (Franklin, Carter, & Grace, 1993). For example, Afrocentric life in the United States is greatly shaped by an African worldview emphasizing "the interrelationship of all things through the oneness of spirit, striving for harmony with nature, and stressing a group or collective perspective" (Landrum-Brown, 1990, p. 121). Consistent with this perspective, much of life in African American communities is defined by one's relationship with the extended family and the friendship networks existing in one's neighborhood (Boyd-Franklin, 1989).

[handwritten margin note: collective world-view]

The extended family has always been a vital source of support for African Americans (Franklin, 1993). Throughout the history of Black people in America, African American families have been characterized by strong kinship bonds between immediate and extended family members, including close friends who are viewed by the family as nonblood relatives (Daly, Jennings, Beckett, & Leashore, 1995; Franklin et al., 1993). Typically, African Americans turn to this family network for help during times of crisis as well as for assistance with meeting the responsibilities of daily living (Franklin, 1993). For example, in some situations, extended family members will share children or raise another family member's child. Such arrangements can exist for short or extended periods of time and demonstrate the great adaptability of roles within the family (Franklin et al., 1993; Hill, 1972, 1977).

[handwritten margin note: adaptability of roles within the extended family]

In addition to valuing flexible family roles, African American families, as a rule, value spiritualism, respect for elders, and sacrifice for others (Billingsley, 1968, 1992; Frazier, 1939; Hill, 1972; Martin & Martin, 1980; McAdoo, 1988; Stack, 1996; Staples, 1974). African Americans also value education and work, but many also fear that they face constricted work opportunities because of the high structural unemployment common to many Black communities and discriminatory work conditions (Smith, 1988).

IMPLICATIONS FOR COUNSELING

[handwritten margin note: reaching out to extended family, peers, & elders.]

Understanding the Afrocentric way of life provides direction for any counselor who hopes to reach out to African American youth. The counselor must know and respect the values, customs, language, and modes of expression of African American culture (Franklin, 1989; Lee, 1996). The counselor must also recognize that the identity of a young Black male is often rooted in an extended family. The counselor may need to reach out to that family, as well as to other important people in a young man's community, such as his peer group and respected male elders (Lee, 1996; Locke, 1995).

By remaining sensitive and responsive to the needs of these various people, the counselor is likely to communicate genuineness, earn trust, and transcend fears of the counselor's position as a member of the mental health system. Offering group-oriented counseling programs that are based in the community, are administered by African American men, and address the salient needs of African American boys is likely to have significant appeal to this population (Lee, 1996). A description of five pertinent programs follows. The first is designed to train adult African American men for volunteer work with African American boys. The remaining programs target young boys and teenagers, respectively.

ENSURING MALE ROLE MODELING
FOR BLACK MALE YOUTH

It is important that counselors initiate steps to acknowledge the importance of adult Black male influence on the development of Black male youth (Lee, 1996). In most Black communities, there is a wealth of positive Black male talent that can be employed to promote empowerment initiatives for young boys. These men can be found in a variety of settings, including churches, community agencies, fraternities and social/service organizations, Black businesses, and colleges and universities. Counselors should keep in mind certain criteria when selecting these men. The criteria include the following: (a) concern about the academic and social challenges facing Black male youth, (b) commitment to helping young Black males, (c) insight into being Black and male, (d) demonstrated success in their personal endeavors, (e) a sense of responsibility, and (f) a willingness to grow as Black men.

criteria

THE RESPECTED ELDERS TRAINING PROGRAM

Lee (1996) developed the Respected Elders Training Program, which has a goal of increasing the awareness and promoting the leadership skills of Black men who volunteer to conduct developmental group experiences with Black male youth in the school setting. Lee (1996) recommends that the initial training of the adult mentors be conducted in two sessions, preferably over a weekend so that participation is maximized. Lee also recommends that a follow-up session be held after the mentors have completed a structured experience helping African American male youth. The purpose of the follow-up session is to process the mentors' reactions to their mentoring experience. A Black male facilitates all three sessions. Ideally, 10-15 Black men should participate in the training. Highlights of each session follow. *training mentors*

The first session is referred to as "Reflections on Black Manhood" (Lee, 1996, p. 81) and is a modification of a program for Black men called "Reflections on the Native Son" created by Lee (1990). The purpose of this program is to provide the mentors with a group consciousness-raising experience about what it means to be a Black male in contemporary society. The facilitator conducts a video presentation containing images of Black men. Excerpts from a variety of video sources, such as the Public Broadcasting System television version of Lorraine Hansberry's (1988) play *A Raisin in the Sun* or the motion picture *Glory* (1990), can be used for this presentation. After viewing the video excerpts, the participants break into small groups and discuss their perceptions of the images of the Black men portrayed and how they relate to a number of important questions pertaining to life as a Black man. For example, the facilitator may ask the participants to discuss questions such as the following:

- ▶ How do you see yourself as a Black man?
- ▶ How do you feel about your father and the men in your family?
- ▶ Who are your male heroes and role models?
- ▶ How do you feel about the women in your family?
- ▶ As a Black man, what brings you a sense of purpose and satisfaction in your life?
- ▶ As a Black man, what makes you fearful and angry?

Afterward, the participants of the small group discussions come together to share their insights about Black manhood and what it means to be a "Respected Elder."

The purpose of the second session is to train the participants how to be male mentors for African American male youth. During the first part of this session, the facilitator provides an overview of an empowerment program that the mentors will conduct in their communities. Three examples of such youth empowerment programs are described later in this chapter. Next, the participants are taught the basics about group structure and processes, with an emphasis on their role as group leaders. Important interpersonal skills—such as nonverbal attending, encouragement, respect, genuineness, and empathy—are reviewed, and the concepts of commitment to the group and confidentiality are described.

After the second session is completed, the mentors are ready to begin their work helping African American male youth. Once the mentors have completed this service, they are invited back for a follow-up session that is designed to help them to analyze how the experience went, what it meant to them to be a "Respected Elder," and what changes they would like to make in their own lives or communities as a result of working with African American male youth. In addition, the participants discuss their readiness to work in an empowerment program again and recommend changes that might improve the effectiveness of the program.

CULTURE-SPECIFIC EMPOWERMENT PROGRAMS

Mentoring African American male youth can be a fulfilling and inspiring experience for adult Black men. In this section, we describe four empowerment programs in which Black men might serve in an effort to enhance the lives of African American male youth.

THE SIMBA WACHANGA PROGRAM

The notion of adult Black men serving as respected elders is applied in the Simba Wachanga program, which is described in Lindsay and Rodine (1989). *Simba Wachanga* (the Kiswahili name for young lions) is a rite-of-passage program developed by African Americans for African American male youth receiving services at the East End Neighborhood House in Cleveland, Ohio. The program is a culture-specific guidance system through which African American men serve as positive role models to young males. Other Simba programs have been developed throughout the United States in a widespread effort to maximize the human potential of African American male youth (Kunjufu, 1983, 1989). ← *the importance of instruction from elders*

Older men, who are known as the Council of Elders, teach the young men who participate in the Cleveland program their African identity. The coordinator of the program is selected from the Council of Elders. For approximately 2 to 4 hours per week, Elders engage the "young lions" in African rituals designed to steer African American male youth to manhood. Sex education and a wide range of training in life skills are also provided.

In the Cleveland Simba Wachanga program, a major emphasis is placed on teaching African American male youth the West African traditions of masculinity and fatherhood. According to Nsamenang (1987), West African men have a deep-rooted sense of community that is built on the strong and extended kinship system. Children and family members are deeply valued. Pregnancy is such a source of joy, and parents are the objects of such high regard that childlessness is considered the greatest of all personal tragedies. This feeling is so strong that a West African father would prefer to die in poverty and leave children than to die childless and rich. The father is the most esteemed member of the West African family, and he is responsible for serving as the governing authority for his wife and children. Once a man becomes a father, he is expected to play a major role in decision making regarding his children. Although he may rarely show tenderness and nurturance to infants, which in the West African tradition is the mother's role, he does take a more guiding role with his children from the time they are toddlers through the remainder of the life span. In particular, he will raise his children to be respectful and obedient and his sons to emulate his role as father (Nsamenang, 1987).

One of the important features of Simba Wachanga is that the Elders help the participants to address their concerns and make critical life decisions based on this Afrocentric tradition. For example, the Elders in the Cleveland program discuss with African American male youth the problems of adolescent pregnancy and parenthood in the African American community. The Elders instill in their protégés the belief that fatherhood represents the most important responsibility in a man's life. A man should not sire a child, they teach, until he is ready to commit to his child and the child's mother for life. The Elders talk with the African American male youth about Black men who have delayed fatherhood until they were fully capable of fulfilling their parental responsibilities, who have been outstanding fathers, and whose example they seek to emulate. By discussing these and other issues, such as acquiring an education, helping one's family, and refraining from participation in gangs and drug abuse—all of which are salient issues for the African American male youth residing in the East End of Cleveland—the Elders help the young lions to make a healthy and adaptive transition to manhood.

West African fatherhood

imparting a sense of responsibility

THE YOUNG LIONS PROGRAM

The image of the lion is utilized in another empowerment program, known as Young Lions, which was developed and described by Lee (1996). The goal of this program is to assist Black males in Grades 3 through 6 to develop motivation and skills for academic success, positive and responsible social behavior, and an understanding and appreciation of Black culture and history.

African American male youth participating in the program work with an adult male mentor for 1 hour twice a week to complete homework assignments, develop reading and mathematical skills, and address personal and social issues. The participants also meet twice a month in a large group session for social enrichment activities.

Throughout the program, the participants are taught to view their groups as a pride, which is a company of lions. This image is used to help the African American male youth to picture themselves as having the strength and courage of the lion to confront their current problems and to envision achieving a successful future.

In addition to the traditional African symbol of the lion, features of African culture and history are experienced and taught so as to foster the development of self-esteem. For example, the musical recording *Waaslu* by Olatunji (1970) is played, and the history of the great kings of Africa, such as Mansa Musa and King of Asante, is taught. The participants are asked to describe their impressions of Africa and of their heritage that result from these activities. In addition, they are encouraged to think about the qualities a young man must have and what he must do in school to become great like the majestic African leaders of old.

Considerable attention is also devoted to the struggles and accomplishments of famous African Americans. For example, the participants read and discuss the contemporary meaning of the poem "I, Too, Sing America," written by Langston Hughes (1970). The poem expresses a Black boy's strong declaration that he will prevail against segregation and will take his rightful place in American society. The participants also read and discuss biographical information about famous Black Americans, such as Frederick Douglass, W. E. B. DuBois, Martin Luther King, Jr., Jackie Robinson, and many other notable African Americans. In particular, the participants focus on what they can learn about pride from the examples of these fine role models.

Finally, several exercises are employed to help participants identify the skills and understand the training and education that are required for entry into a variety of occupations. Then, other methods are used to instill the value of remaining focused on achieving educational success. For example, participants listen to the "rap" recording "Keep Your Eye on the Prize," by Young MC (1991), and then discuss plans for winning the prize of academic success.

These and a variety of other educational and therapeutic activities described by Lee (1996) are employed in the Young Lions program to engender pride in African American male youth and to enhance the sense of brotherhood between them and their adult male mentors. The program concludes with a closing ceremony during which the mentors and the young lions explain what the group experience meant to them. The mentors present the young lions with certificates and a token, such as a candle, symbolizing completion of the program. The young lions are told to "keep the candle in a safe place and burn it on the day they graduate from high school in recognition of their educational success" (Lee, 1996, p. 51).

After the official program ends, the mentors conduct informal follow-up visits with the young lions to monitor their progress in school and in the community. In this way, the mentors help the youth to "keep their eyes on the prize" long after the program is over.

BLACK MANHOOD TRAINING: "BODY, MIND AND SOUL"

Black Manhood Training: "Body, Mind and Soul," which was also developed by Lee (1996), is designed to foster responsible behavior and positive Black male images among adolescent African American males. During initial meetings, adult mentors facilitate discussions about the challenges confronting Black males, what it means to be a Black male, and how the media depict Black men. In addition, the mentors invite the adolescents to view the program as an opportunity for strengthening one's body, mind, and soul, each of which then becomes a central focus of group activities.

In sessions related to caring for one's body, consultants are brought in to teach the participants how to remain physically fit. Black male health hazards are explored, such as AIDS and Black-on-Black crime, and participants are challenged to develop a wellness mentality.

During sessions devoted to developing the mind and appreciating the soul of the Black man, many of the same ideas and strategies utilized in Lee's (1996) Young Lions program are applied. For example, a variety of Black art forms and culture-specific curriculum materials are employed in both programs to promote an understanding about the African heritage and an awareness of the positive images of Black men that are illustrated by the lives of great African and African American male leaders. In Black Manhood Training, this information is used to motivate the participants to commit themselves to achievement and to recognize its importance for Black male survival. This information is also used to "promote the concept that a strong Black man has an indomitable spirit" (Lee, 1996, p. 66) and to explore what it means to be masculine and to be a responsible son, boyfriend, brother, husband, father, and uncle. The sessions focused on the mind and soul culminate with each member formulating personal definitions of a strong Black man as well as personal educational and career plans.

Two final events are held at the conclusion of the program: a test and an initiation ceremony. According to Lee (1996), each member must pass a "Test of Worthiness" (p. 71), which includes the following:

a. Test of the Body—for example, members might run a quarter of a mile in a specified amount of time to prove that their bodies are strong.
b. Test of the Mind—for example, members might complete a math test and get a certain percentage correct to prove that their minds are strong.

c. Test of the Soul—for example, members might participate in some responsible activity at school, at home, at church, or in the community to prove that their souls are strong.

Once these three tests are passed, a rite-of-passage ceremony is celebrated to mark the participants' entrance into manhood. The ceremony opens with welcome comments from the group's leader, a song, and the introduction of the Respected Elders, each of whom shares reflections on strong Black manhood. Guest speakers, such as a physician, a teacher, or a minister, then talk about the body, mind, and soul, respectively. After the male youth state what it means to be a strong Black man, they receive certificates, listen to closing remarks, and proceed out of the ceremony as men.

Although this ceremony represents the official conclusion of the program, the Respected Elders may engage the young Black men in follow-up activities, such as field trips to African and African American cultural institutions or participation in community service projects. These activities reinforce the values taught in Black Manhood Training and further assist the young men as they move toward successful manhood.

THE MAAT PROGRAM

Harvey and Rauch (1997) describe a 9-month rites-of-passage program for Black male adolescents that is based on the ancient Egyptian word *Ma'at*, which means an ethical way of life. This multifaceted empowerment service, known as the MAAT program, targets boys between the ages of 11 and 19 from Washington, D.C.

A major component of the MAAT program is the provision of educational/ enhancement services that are held for 2 to 3 hours per day. Modules on manhood development, sexuality, drugs, the creative arts, math, and science are offered. These modules are delivered within an Afrocentric rites-of-passage model, referred to as *Nguzo Saba*.

The Nguzo Saba consists of seven principles that permeate all the activities of the MAAT program. The first of these principles, *Umoja*, which means unity or interconnectedness, is expressed through group activities and special rituals that are conducted over the course of the 9-month program. For example, each meeting begins with the youths and their adult mentors forming a unity circle. "They hold hands, say a nondenominational prayer, and pour a libation in respect to the ancestors, requesting their presence at the sacred event. This ritual conveys to the youths that they and their meeting matter" (Harvey & Rauch, 1997, p. 34).

Kujichagulia, or self-determination, means defining oneself within an African culture. MAAT participants choose an African name as a way of affirming their African roots. It is believed that this act also symbolizes the rejection of the internalized racism that is often experienced by African American male youth.

Regarding the other five principles, the participants experience *Ujima*, or collective work and responsibility, by performing community services and learning skills in plumbing, painting, and electrical repair. *Ujama*, cooperative economics, occurs through entrepreneurial activities, such as designing, producing, and selling sweatshirts. *Nia*, or

(5) purpose   (6) creativity   (7) faith

purpose, is conveyed by emphasizing that African American male youth are "gifts of God" (Harvey & Rauch, 1997, p. 35) who are obliged to cultivate the earth. *Kuumba*, or creativity, is fostered during problem-solving exercises through which the participants learn to apply the wisdom of great African or African American historical figures to resolve contemporary dilemmas. *Imani*, or faith, is instilled by teaching about how African Americans have survived their historical struggles through their spirituality and their enduring belief that "tomorrow can be better, no matter how bleak things are today" (Harvey & Rauch, 1997, p. 35).

Living according to these principles promotes the "internalization of a positive sense of self, of other African Americans, and of African and African-American heritage" (Harvey & Rauch, 1997, p. 33). Once the youths demonstrate that they can live by these principles, they participate in a rites-of-passage ceremony during which they pledge to carry on the Nguzo Saba. This ceremony marks their successful transformation from boys to men.

SUGGESTIONS FOR FUTURE TRAINING AND RESEARCH

The culture-specific approaches to intervention described in this chapter accentuate healthy self-images of African American males. This emphasis represents a shift away from the application of traditional Eurocentric models with young Black men, which has tended to foster erroneous, ethnocentric interpretations of the Black experience in America and the misdiagnosis and maltreatment of African Americans in therapy (Anderson, Eaddy, & Williams, 1990; Daly et al., 1995; Franklin & Jackson, 1990). By comparison, a culture-specific approach has great potential to foster positive mental health among Black Americans, a claim that has merit on theoretical grounds (see Lee, 1989) and emerging empirical support from relevant outcomes research (e.g., D'Andrea & Daniels, 1992). We recommend, therefore, that educators of mental health professionals provide training on culture-specific approaches in their curriculums.

Although the clinical utility of a culture-specific approach such as Afrocentric counseling is promising, more research is needed to evaluate the long-term effectiveness of this approach with African American male youth. In addition, because many young Black males come from families and communities struggling with a host of psychosocial problems, more needs to be written about the integration of Afrocentric-group programs for boys with other therapeutic interventions, such as multisystems therapy (see Boyd-Franklin, 1989), which are known to be effective with multiproblem African American families. For discussions of related integrated interventions, the reader is referred to the work of Anderson Franklin and his colleagues (Franklin, 1989; Franklin et al., 1993), Lee (1996), and Kiselica (1995, 1999). We believe that such integration will help young African American males to develop positive self-images, cope with the hardships they face, and realize their potential to lead fulfilling and successful lives.

HIGHLIGHTS OF CHAPTER 5

▶ Relative to their White counterparts, African American male youth have a shorter life span, are more likely to be victims of crime, experience higher levels of unemployment, are more likely to drop out of school, and are less likely to attend and complete college. Thus, African American male youth are an at-risk population who warrant interventions tailored to their particular needs.

▶ For counseling with African American males to be successful, counselors must have an awareness of the African American culture.

▶ Despite cultural variations, African Americans tend to share many common characteristics and value a group/collectivist perspective, strong kinship bonds between immediate and extended family members, flexible family roles, respect for elders, sacrifice for others, spiritualism, and education.

▶ African American male youth fear that they face constricted work opportunities because of the high structural unemployment common to many Black communities and discriminatory work conditions.

▶ Offering group-oriented counseling programs that are based in the community, are administered by African American men, and address the salient needs of African American male youth is likely to have significant appeal to this population. Training adult male mentors in how to help African American male youth therefore is crucial.

▶ The Respected Elders training program is designed to increase the awareness and promote the leadership skills of Black men who volunteer to conduct developmental group experiences with Black male youth in the school setting. In this program, the men participate in a group consciousness-raising experience about what it means to be a Black male and are trained in how to serve in culture-specific empowerment programs as mentors for African American male youth.

▶ The Simba Wachanga program is a rite-of-passage empowerment program developed for African American male youth in Cleveland, Ohio. Older men, known as the Council of Elders, teach younger men about their African identity and help the youths to address their concerns and to make critical life decisions based on Afrocentric traditions.

▶ The goal of the Young Lions program is to assist Black males in Grades 3 through 6 to develop motivation and skills for academic success, positive and responsible social behavior, and an understanding and appreciation of Black culture and identity.

▶ Black Manhood Training: "Body, Mind and Soul" targets adolescent African American males and features sessions devoted to remaining physically fit, learning about African culture and great African and African American male leaders, and skills for achieving a positive Black identity and personal success in contemporary society.

▶ Based in Washington, D.C., the MAAT program targets African American male youth between the ages of 11 and 19. Modules on manhood development, sexuality, drugs, the creative arts, math, and science are offered within an Afrocentric rites-of-passage model emphasizing the African principles of Umoja (unity), Kujichagulia (self-determination), Ujima (collective work and responsibility), Ujama (cooperative economics), Nia (purpose), Kuumba (creativity), and Imani (faith).

6

Counseling Asian American
Boys and Adolescent Males

DAVID SUE

This chapter focuses on some of the issues involved in counseling Asian American boys and adolescent males. Before beginning the discussion, I would like to present some information regarding the Asian American population. First, the Asian American group is the fastest growing ethnic minority in the United States and is expected to reach a population of 20 million by the year 2020 (Ong & Hee, 1993). The continuing influx of immigrants and refugees has changed the characteristics of the different Asian groups in the United States. With the exception of the Japanese, Asian groups are composed primarily of foreign-born individuals. In 1990, approximately 64% of Asian Americans had been born in other countries, and it is estimated that even in 2020 about 55% will be foreign born (Hing, 1993). The continuing presence of immigrants and refugees ensures that traditional values of these populations will continue to have a strong influence in the life of many Asian families.

Second, the Asian American population is heterogeneous. It is composed of more than 25 distinct subgroups, each with its own set of values and its own language, religion(s), and customs. Adding to the diversity are within-group differences such as the degree of assimilation or acculturation; generational status; native-born, refugee, or immigrant status; and educational and socioeconomic levels.

Third, although Asian Americans are considered to be a model minority, progress has been uneven. Many Asian Americans are well educated, but others are undereducated. Only 31% of the Hmong have completed high school, and less than 6% of Cambodians and Laotians have a bachelor's degree (U.S. Bureau of the Census, 1995). Not all Asian groups do well. For example, in one area two thirds of Samoan middle-school students had grade point averages below 2.0, as compared with 21% of their White counterparts (Seattle Public Schools, 1986). Many Southeast Asian refugees show symptoms of post-traumatic stress disorder (PTSD) and depression. Stressors faced by many refugees include prior events, such as war trauma, and current resettlement problems (Clarke, Sack, & Goff, 1993). In one sample of refugees, 75% met the criteria for major depressive disorder and 14% had PTSD. Somatic complaints were common. Current problems involved difficulty with acculturation, getting jobs, and learning English, along with disrupted family ties (Chung, Bemak, & Okazaki, 1997). It is clear that Asian Americans must be considered to be a heterogeneous group.

Before discussing specific issues regarding the counseling of Asian American boys and adolescents, I offer two examples that illustrate difficulties inherent in cross-cultural encounters. First, a Chinese international student indicated in a counseling publication that he was discouraged from going into counseling because

> my advisor thought I was not qualified as a counselor because I always "held" something to myself. He did not understand that we seldom "confess" our "personal stuff" to someone else. . . . I tried to clarify these misunderstandings. (Chin, 1993, p. 2)

I was also contacted recently for a consultation regarding an Asian American student who was having difficulty in the counseling program. According to the program head, the student did not appear to have the skills necessary to be a successful counselor. He appeared to be problem oriented in working with clients and seemed to lack the ability to develop empathetic relationships during his counseling sessions. During the supervision sessions, the student would acknowledge deficiencies but did not seem to understand the feedback given about his performance.

In both these cases, cultural misunderstandings and difficulties may be involved. Part of the problem is that our training programs are still based on mainstream counseling approaches. This makes supervision and evaluation difficult when working with culturally different individuals. For example, because openness and emotional expressiveness are seen as positive qualities, we have difficulties dealing with cultural groups who believe that such behaviors indicate a lack of subtlety or immaturity. Should culturally based behaviors such as restraint of emotions and modesty be viewed as deficits in counseling encounters? How do we teach culturally different individuals "appropriate counseling skills"? How can the helping skills of other cultural groups be acknowledged? Also, what is the best format for conducting supervision sessions if the individual believes in respecting and not questioning authority figures? The "Guidelines for Providers of Psychological Services to Ethnic, Linguistic, and Culturally Diverse Populations" (American Psychological Association, 1993) provide some useful suggestions. Counselors and psychologists have to be aware of their own cultural background, values, and experiences and how these may have an impact when interviewing and evaluating an individual from a different culture. It is too easy to interpret differences as deficits. Until we can accept and acknowledge the fact that a wider range of skills needs to be developed in cross-cultural encounters, we will continue to mold trainees in a monocultural perspective.

Regarding the two Asian counselor trainees presented earlier, the supervisors should be aware of possible cultural issues and conflicts that could hamper cross-cultural communication. These should be discussed openly with the trainees. Also, instead of merely focusing on "deficits" in mainstream counseling skills, strengths of the individuals involving other cultural problem-solving skills should be identified. What can individuals from other cultural groups contribute in broadening our helping skills? Our counselor training programs have to be modified to incorporate cross-cultural principles. In working with Asian males, knowledge of some of the Asian values and of Asian family structure is important in understanding typical conflicts that occur in these families and in their interactions with society. This information is presented first before considerations of counseling issues with male Asian adolescents and children. It is important to remember that the following information refers to group characteristics and that within-group differences are quite large; individuals in a group might be quite different.

FAMILY STRUCTURE AND VALUES

The family structure of many Asian American families is hierarchical, with males and the older generation given higher status. The sons, especially the oldest, are obligated to take care of the parents and to carry on the family name. They have the responsibility of setting an example for the younger children and are expected to be good role models. It is said that when males are born, they are given a piece of jade to hold, whereas females receive a stone. A daughter generally is less valued because she will leave to take care of her husband's family. Sons are expected to continue the family line. Even when males marry, they are expected to demonstrate primary allegiance to their family of origin. In traditional Asian families, children are expected to be obedient. They are not allowed to argue or disobey parents. Communication flows downward. The decisions of the father are not to be questioned. Strong expressions of emotions are discouraged because they are disruptive to order.

Asian families display a collectivistic rather than an individualistic orientation. In other words, individual needs and desires are subordinated to the good of the family and the community. What an individual wants is less important than what is good for the family. Children are raised with the understanding that their behaviors, good or bad, reflect on the family name (Leong, Wagner, & Kim, 1995). They are taught to be sensitive to the reactions and evaluation of others. Achievements such as success in academic work are strongly reinforced. To ensure a family orientation, the obligation to the parents for their sacrifice in raising children is continually stressed, and guilt-inducing techniques are used to control children.

Asian parents tend to be more restrictive, more protective, and more emotionally unresponsive to their children than White parents. Shame is used as a means to train the children. Because of this, the emotion is strongly present in Asian children and adolescents (Ha, 1995). They are taught that the entire family will be evaluated according to the child's behavior. This may explain why Asian children between the ages of 11 and 13 report heightened levels of social-evaluative fears (Dong, Yang, & Ollendick, 1994). Asian families often display less affection than do White families. Care is shown by doing for the family rather than through giving compliments or physical contact. Fathers especially are less emotionally demonstrative and involved with their children than mainstream fathers (Lin & Fu, 1990). Chang-Rae Lee, a Korean novelist, talks about the Korean traditional lack of emotional display and describes the father in his book as "unencumbered by those needling questions of existence and self-consciousness." He states, "I wasn't sure he had the capacity to love" (Lee, 1995, p. 58). These cultural differences produce conflict in many Asian American youth who see different family patterns and values portrayed in the mass media and within the school system.

ADJUSTMENT ISSUES IN MALE ASIAN CHILDREN AND ADOLESCENTS

MALE IDENTITY CONFLICTS

> Some years ago, my five-year-old son came home from school, shortly after entering kindergarten in a predominantly White neighborhood, and asked me, "What am I? Am I a Korean or an American?" Trying to be a good mother, I told him he was a Korean American. . . . This did not comfort my son. . . . Instead he protested, "If I am a Korean, why can't I speak Korean like you do? And if I'm an American, how come I don't look like the American kids in my class?" He paused for a moment and then delivered the final blow: "Besides, they call me Chinese!" (Kim, 1980, p. 1)

Male children and adolescents straddle multiple cultures (mainstream, ethnic, and peer group). They have the burden of trying to integrate the sometimes conflicting values of these coexisting cultures. They need to be a different person at school from the one they are at home. Identity issues such as "Who am I?" and "Where do I belong?" are raised. Li-Young Lee, a Chinese American poet, describes his childhood in a small Pennsylvania town as "very alienating and brutal." He was the only Asian child in his school and always felt like an outsider (Ho, 1996). He knew he was different but had no one he could identify with and had mixed feelings toward his "distant" but "powerful" father.

Value conflicts also produce confusion in identity. In school, behaviors such as independence and autonomy are emphasized, whereas at home, issues of individual identity and self-differentiation are minimized. As acculturation develops, an identity crisis may occur. For example, a Vietnamese may be considered as "too Vietnamese" by American friends, "too old-fashioned" by Vietnamese peers, and "too American" by parents (Lee, 1988). Children may begin to feel that they are none of the above.

MALE ACCULTURATION ISSUES

Male children and adolescents acculturate more quickly than adults (Huang, 1994); however, because males are to carry on the family tradition, they appear to acculturate less quickly than females. This could produce problems in male-female peer interactions within their own ethnic group. Females may consider male Asians as being too old-fashioned and not possessing the qualities they find attractive. Because of problems with English proficiency, the parents have to depend primarily on their male children to act as interpreters and mediators with society. Instead of offering leadership, parents are often relegated to a state of dependence on their children. They worry that they are losing authority and respect, and they fear that their children are losing their traditional culture.

Disruptions in the family can be caused by role reversals (Rick & Forward, 1992). In one study of Asian and Caucasian adolescents, 74% of Caucasians identified adult role models, most of whom were parental figures. In contrast, only 52% of Asians identified any role models. Only 18 of 99 Asian adolescents identified parents as role models, and of these, only 3 selected their fathers (Lorenzo, Pakiz, Reinherz, & Frost, 1995). For a patriarchal culture, this finding may be indicative of the role reversals and acculturation problems between the children and their parents.

Although acculturation has a rapid onset, it may be a relatively slow process, with some values changing more quickly than others. Second-generation Chinese American high school students more resembled their Hong Kong peers on a "Measure on Autonomy Expectations" than they did their Caucasian peers (Feldman & Rosenthal, 1990). Both Asian groups valued autonomy less and conformity more than the comparison group and placed a high priority on filial piety and respect for and obedience to parents and other authorities.

Male children and adolescents may respond to the acculturation conflicts with one or more distinct reactions (Sue & Sue, 1990): conformity, marginality, traditionalism, and biculturalism. These are described below.

Conformity. This reaction shows a preference for majority cultural values and denial or rejection of one's own culture. Asian males who have learned from their parents that modesty, self-restraint, and formality in communication are signs of maturity are at a disadvantage in a culture that defines male characteristics as being dominant or forceful. Few male role models are present in the mass media; the values of Asians are not those associated with male heroes. Because of this, the physical features of the dominant culture may be seen as more acceptable than those of their own group. In one study, Asian American students rated opposite-sex Whites as more physically attractive than typical members of their own group (Liu, Campbell, & Condie, 1995).

Mura (1996) worries about the psychological development of his sons in a culture in which Asian males are generally portrayed as "villains or objects of ridicule." He was relieved when his first child was a girl because "I felt I could help her deal with the female Asian stereotypes better than helping my son deal with the ways the culture would emasculate him" (p. 8). At his first boy-girl party, a girl that he had a crush on rejected him because, she felt, "my features were not the stuff of all-American cinematic lovers" (p. 8).

A male child or adolescent may blame his own culture for his difficulties and his physical appearance, and reject its values. Lee (1994) identified a group of high school students, "New Wavers" who were easily identified because of their black clothes and spiked hair. Their primary goal was to party. They skipped classes and rejected all behaviors related to being a "nerd." They believed that they were "cool" and wanted to be "more American." In summary, for this group, attempts to deal with cultural issues are met with resistance.

Marginality. This reaction is characterized by a feeling of alienation from both cultures. Chang-Rae Lee reveals his sense of alienation from two cultures—those of the United States and Korea. He was raised in the United States from age 3 on and felt that he was straddling two cultures and at home in neither. The values he was exposed to at school were antithetical to the ones at home. This conflict or feeling of marginality was increased when he went back to Korea to assemble material for a new book. In Korea, he felt like a "complete alien" (Ho, 1996). A lack of identity with either culture can lead to a variety of psychological problems and possible gang membership or identification with other marginal groups.

Traditionalism. In this reaction, the values of the majority culture are seen as less important than the cultural values of the group. There may be little desire to interact with the dominant culture. In some cases, the majority culture is seen to be at fault for the plight of different ethnic cultures. In counseling, an ethnically similar counselor may be preferred.

Lee (1994) also identified a group of high school students who fit the traditional category. They spent much of their time studying even before school and during lunch, and they had career goals of entering engineering, computer science, or other science-related field. They indicated that their parent had admonished them to do well academically. Most of these students acknowledged discrimination but still felt they could succeed through hard work. They talked about getting good jobs so that they could support their parents.

Biculturalism. Most traditional values are accepted, but there is an openness to Western values. For many theorists, this would seem to be the best reaction to acculturation.

MALE ACADEMIC AND CAREER INTERESTS

In general, Asian American male students have done well academically. Performance is reinforced in the family and the peer group (Steinberg, Dornbusch, & Brown, 1992). The pressure to succeed academically is great, especially for males, because they are expected to carry on the family traditions and to financially assist the other members of the family. Two years after graduation from high school, 86% of Asian Americans versus 64% of Whites are in some kind of higher education (Sue & Okazaki, 1990). Asian American male students, however, show constriction in terms of career interests and opportunities. As compared to their Caucasian peers, they show higher interest in investigative (science, mathematics, architecture) (43% vs. 23.2% for Caucasian men) and conventional areas (office work, financial analysis) (10.5% vs. 0% for Caucasian men) (Park & Harrison, 1995). This pattern is reversed in the social area (counseling, school teaching), with only 17.4% of Asian men but 39.3% Caucasian men showing high interest. The lower interest in the social areas is thought to be due to factors such as difficulties with the English language, socialization that fosters self-consciousness, and low level of perceived control in the interpersonal sphere (Park & Harrison, 1995). Asian males may also believe that they are less likely to be accepted in fields in which social contacts occur frequently. Many Asians perceive the need for career counseling because their parents are unfamiliar with the educational and employment opportunities in the United States (Rick & Forward, 1992).

MALE ADJUSTMENT ISSUES

As compared with their Caucasian counterparts, male Asian adolescents score significantly higher in social isolation, depression and anxiety, and the internalization of conflicts. They appear to be less satisfied with their level of social support and report having few friends and after-school activities (Lorenzo et al., 1995). Conflicts concerning dating and marriage are also present (Lee, 1988). Many parents disapprove of their children dating non-Asian individuals. Because Asian parents tend to be restrictive, curfews and types of dating activities that are acceptable may be seen as more strict than those of the parents of peers. Male Asian undergraduates are significantly more conservative than non-Asian counterparts on all measures of interpersonal sexual behavior and sociosexual restrictiveness (Meston, Trapnell, & Gorzalka, 1996). Asian males are less likely to report light petting, heavy petting, and intercourse than are Caucasian peers.

STRATEGIES FOR ESTABLISHING RAPPORT

Rapport with male Asian children and adolescents can be established using many of the same skills used with other populations. Again, I wish to warn the reader that within-group differences exist among Asian Americans and that the following guidelines are merely suggestions. Some Asian Americans are very responsive to mainstream counseling approaches. Counselors must use their observational and clinical skills in working with specific individuals. They should show respect, a caring attitude, and willingness to assess the worldview of the client. Rapport is more likely to occur when cultural factors are brought up and discussed (with the exception of individuals at the conformity stage, who may be uncomfortable if this topic is presented). Demonstration that the counselor or therapist understands some of the areas of conflict, such as differences in expectations between the home and school, can increase credibility. A discussion of confidentiality with older children and adolescents and their parents is important, especially because any type of problem is seen to reflect on the entire family. Interpreting reluctance to share personal information as possibly an effect of cultural factors rather than as "resistance" is essential in establishing a good therapeutic environment.

For older male children and adolescents, it is important to determine their stage of ethnic identity. Male adolescents at the conformity stage would have different issues and reactions than those with a bicultural perspective. An attentive body posture with moderate levels of eye contact can be helpful. With some of the more traditionally oriented Asians, too much eye contact can produce discomfort.

Empathy can be established in several ways. It can be demonstrated cognitively by indicating an understanding of the individual and the problem. Rapport is more likely to be established if the counselor seems to know the issues involved (differences in expectations between the father and son, value conflicts, adjustment difficulties between the school and home environment). Another part of empathy is demonstration of an understanding of the emotional state of the client. I and others have found, at least in work with Asian college students, that cognitive empathy is effective and that some are responsive to emotional empathy. Many, however, were more responsive to emotional empathy that was problem focused ("that's a difficult situation to be in") rather than person focused ("you are having a difficult time"). Reflection of feelings should be used more sparingly because there is less labeling of feelings in Asian cultures and so may be considered intrusive. Somatic complaints are common and should be reacted to as "real" problems. Physical treatments such as relaxation or medications should be suggested. Issues dealing with cultural expectations for males, such as various responsibilities and expectations regarding dating and being the eldest son, should be discussed. For adolescents, developmental issues such as separation, autonomy, and personal identity should be considered in the context of family and cultural issues. Areas in which they can maintain interdependence with their family and cultural traditions, instead of being totally independent, can be reinforced.

INTERVENTIONS

As do adults, male Asian American adolescents underutilize mental health services. In one study, Asian Americans constituted 14.7% of the population but only 2.7% of the client population in the Los Angeles mental health system (Bui & Takeuchi, 1992). In general, problems are more likely to be overcontrolled (overconcern with the reactions of others, self-doubt, depression, feelings of isolation) or internal behaviors rather than undercontrolled or acting out behaviors. In designing an intervention program, the following areas should be considered (Huang, 1994; Sue & Sue, 1990).

First, for the male child or adolescent, generational status; acculturation level; means of dealing with culture conflicts, ethnic identity, and self-concept; perception of the father-son relationship; and feelings about other family members and language need to be assessed. What types of problems are being encountered? How does the child interpret them? How does the family deal with problems? What is the role of cultural differences or expectations in the difficulty?

Second, information should be obtained regarding migration history, acculturation level, salience of ethnicity, generational gaps, acculturation gaps, home-school gaps, role hierarchy, communication patterns, and affective expressiveness of the family members. How do the parents and other family members view the problem? What cultural variables are involved? In addition, if problems are occurring at school, information about the ethnic/racial composition of the student population and the way conflict is dealt with should be assessed.

TREATMENT STRATEGIES

In working with male children and adolescents either individually or in families, it might be important to use the following strategies:

Reframe: Because there is so much shame in acknowledging psychological or emotional problems, reframing a problem can be an effective strategy. Instead of talking about unhappiness or depression, the focus may be on helping the child meet academic goals.

Normalize: To reduce anxiety, the difficulties can be "normalized" by indicating that the problem is typical of those faced by other children, adolescents, or Asian families.

Follow hierarchical structure: In interviewing family members, start with the father, then the mother, and then children. Even if the father has difficulty expressing himself, his opinions need to be gathered first and be acted upon.

Act as the mediator: In traditional Asian families, have the communication go through you rather than directing family members to make responses to one another. For family members to express feelings toward a parent figure might produce discomfort and guilt (Fong, 1994). Reframe responses that may be considered too confrontational.

Culture conflict as the focus: To deflect problems in using the family as focus, discuss difficulties in terms of difference in cultural expectations and adjustments that have to be made in living in two cultures. The problem then becomes culture conflict rather than individual family members. Such an emphasis can promote problem solving and a joint effort in dealing with culture conflicts.

Structured exercises in groups: Asian males may feel uncomfortable in a group or classroom situation. They may feel self-conscious and intimidated. They may be amazed and astonished at the free expression of emotions. Many Asian clients perceive requests for self-disclosure, comments on group process, and requests for feedback as rude demands. Counselors who try to act as equals may be seen as insincere, inappropriate, or incompetent (Yu & Gregg, 1993). It may be helpful to establish some type of relationship by having all members indicate information about family members and their ages. A problem-solving focus can be taken initially.

Seek consultation: It is always important to consider cultural variables and their impact on behaviors. When in doubt, seek consultation.

The last of these strategies is illustrated in the following example (D'Andrea & Arrendondo, 1997). "A fifth grade Filipino student was referred to counseling by his teacher because he appeared to be having difficulty coping with the recent death of his mother. According to the teacher, this student had lost interest in his schoolwork and his classmates, was increasingly isolating himself from others, and recently began to talk to himself in class" (p. 63). The counselor talked to the boy and became alarmed when he mentioned talking to his deceased mother and even claimed she was kneeling on the floor beside him. The counselor, Kathy Shimabukuro, had to decide if the boy was having a break with reality. Because of her multicultural training background, Kathy decided to contact a Filipino Catholic priest to find out if there were cultural elements to the boy's reaction. She discovered that it was not unusual for Filipinos to "talk" to the spirit of a deceased family member to maintain a connection to the individual. It is similar to the practice of Westerners looking at photographs of the deceased person.

SUGGESTIONS FOR FUTURE TRAINING AND RESEARCH

Unfortunately, little research has been done on the effectiveness of training of mental health counselor for cross-cultural encounters. There is even less research and data on the developmental conflicts and adjustment of male Asian children and adolescents. Questions that require answers include the following:

- ▶ How do Asian boys and adolescents reconcile the values of interdependence from independence?
- ▶ Do they manage these conflicts by compartmentalization or by adjusting their response situationally—that is, showing a different set of behaviors when dealing with the family than with the broader society?
- ▶ What are "healthy" means of dealing with value conflicts?
- ▶ How do Asian boys and adolescents deal with issues of masculinity in a culture that extols behaviors very different from the ones that they have learned in their family?
- ▶ Because few male Asian role models exist, with whom do Asian males identify?
- ▶ Within their families, what are effective ways of moderating father-son conflicts produced by acculturation differences in a way that enhances their relationship?
- ▶ Very few male Asian adolescents consider their fathers as role models. How have both the fathers and sons been affected by this?
- ▶ Some cultural values change; what determines which are maintained, which are modified, and which are rejected?
- ▶ How do Asian boys and adolescents who don't fit the "success" profile deal with societal expectations?

▶ With continued acculturation, will there be significant increases in problems such as substance abuse, delinquency, and antisocial activities?

These and many other questions concerning the development of Asian boys and adolescents need to be researched.

The development of appropriate training procedures in working with Asian males must encompass three components (Sue & Sue, 1990). Adequate work has been done on only some of these.

The first is understanding of one's own values, assumptions, and biases during counseling. I believe this is one area where we are making progress in counselor training programs. This may be due to the introspective nature of Western societies. Trainees can identify their own set of values with a variety of training procedures and can assess their feelings, beliefs, and reactions to nontraditional families, nonegalitarian families, gender roles, sexual orientation, authoritarian parental patterns, and other client qualities. Understanding where these feelings and reactions to diverse populations come from is important. We need to assess the effectiveness of different exercises used to help counselors or trainees understand their own set of values.

Second is knowledge of other cultural groups and their values. Training in this component often involves a course in cross-cultural psychology. The values of other cultural groups are contrasted with those from the mainstream values in the United States. After counselor trainees take these courses, they can contrast ethnic group values with Western ones. Unfortunately, the training often involves the memorization of the values and characteristics associated with the different ethnic groups. After undergoing training, individuals often report that they feel less equipped to work with ethnic minorities because differences are stressed. In addition, stereotyping can occur because within-group differences are not given much consideration. The challenge is to have counselor trainees understand and assess cultural differences and attempt to develop "generic" means of dealing with them.

Third are the skills needed in cross-cultural encounters. This is another weak area in counselor training programs. The problem is that the vast majority of textbooks still come from a monocultural counseling perspective. Rapport, empathy, attending, and other micro skills in counseling are based on Western approaches. We generally inform students that people from different cultures may respond to a different set of micro skills and let it go at that. It is then no wonder when they feel inadequate when facing a client from a different culture. We cannot continue to teach "regular" counseling as a different entity from cross-cultural counseling. We need more attempts to identify the "generic" or "universal" aspects in counseling. Worldview exploration is one approach that seems appropriate to individuals from all cultures.

Little is known about the psychological development of Asian boys and adolescent males in the United States. Cultural values that emphasize modesty, respect for authority, and the inhibition of strong emotional expression clash with those attributes associated with masculinity in the majority culture. Because few Asian males appear to identify with their fathers, it is not clear how they adjust to these different perspectives concerning masculinity. The inability to accept fathers as role models because of acculturational differences and conflicts makes the development of "maleness" problematic. Identity issues are exacerbated because few Asian male role models are available in the mass media. The ways Asian boys and adolescents deal with these conflicts is unclear because they tend not to talk about these problems. Our primary sources of information have been fictional or autobiographical works of Asian authors. Asian boys and adolescents often indicate feelings of social isolation, depression, and anxiety. As more and more Asian boys enter and complete school, educators and counselors need to be aware of and be willing to discuss the issues involved in the development of male identity in this population.

HIGHLIGHTS OF CHAPTER 6

▶ The Asian American group is the fastest growing ethnic minority in the United States and is expected to reach 20 million by the year 2020. Most will be foreign born.

▶ The Asian American population comprises more than 25 distinct subgroups, each with its own set of values, language, religion, and customs. Each subgroup also has considerable within-group diversity in terms of degree of assimilation; native-born, refugee, or immigrant status; educational and socioeconomic levels; and psychosocial adjustment.

▶ Counselors working with Asian American boys must understand Asian values and family structure, which tends to be hierarchical, with males and the older generation given higher status. Children are expected to obey their parents, shame is used as a means to train children, and sons are obligated to care for their parents and to carry on the family name.

▶ Asian American families tend to have a collectivist orientation, practice restraint, value educational achievement, and be sensitive to the reactions and evaluations of others.

▶ Values conflicts between ethnic and mainstream culture produce identity confusion for many Asian American boys.

▶ Asian American boys commonly respond to cultural identity conflicts in the following distinct ways: conformity (preference for the majority culture, rejection of own culture), marginality (alienation from both majority and own culture), traditionalism (preference for own culture), and biculturalism (acceptance of both majority and own culture).

▶ Asian American males tend to have a strong achievement orientation, a preference for investigative (e.g., scientist, mathematician) and conventional (e.g., office clerk, financial analyst) careers, a low interest in social (e.g., teacher, counselor) careers, and a need for career counseling designed to teach them about the educational and career opportunities available in the United States.

▶ Asian American adolescent males tend to score significantly higher in social isolation, depression, and anxiety; to be more conservative and less experienced regarding sexual matters; and to be more restricted in terms of their social activities than their Caucasian counterparts.

▶ Counselors are more likely to establish rapport with Asian American boys by demonstrating an understanding of potential cultural conflicts and when both cognitive and emotional empathy are expressed. Emotional empathy tends to be more effective when it is focused on the problem ("that's a difficult situation to be in") than when it is focused on the individual ("you have a difficult time").

▶ Interventions with Asian American boys should be based on assessments of the client's level of acculturation, family history, and intergenerational conflicts.

▶ Effective treatment strategies include reframing and normalizing problems, following a hierarchical structure, acting as a mediator, and focusing on cultural conflicts during family sessions. Asian American boys also tend to respond well to structured group counseling experiences.

▶ Professionals who are unsure of how to interpret the behavior of an Asian American boy should consult experts who are familiar with the client's culture.

7

Hispanic American Boys and Adolescent Males

JOSE ARCAYA

The primary challenge facing every developing male is the extent to which he will be capable of meeting his responsibilities as an autonomous, responsible individual while simultaneously maintaining a sense of integrity or self-respect as he meets those obligations. This chapter is devoted to describing how so-called "Hispanic" boys learn to face that difficulty. This appellation is, in many respects, a fictional entity pasted together from the gamut of Spanish and Latin American cultures residing in this country. As noted elsewhere (Arcaya, 1996), it is an entirely arbitrary designation because first-generation immigrants and descendants of immigrants from Spanish-speaking countries, apart from speaking a common language, probably have more differences than similarities among them. For example, those from Argentina are quite distinct in physical and social makeup from Mexican natives, whereas Cubans typically have a greater entrepreneurial spirit than Puerto Ricans. For the sake of simplicity, however, this chapter presumes that broad, unifying characteristics exist within the Hispanic community, and that these characteristics serve to shape distinctively the personality of its young men.

Yet another caveat of a more academic nature needs to be mentioned. Despite the fact that many sociological and psychological theoretical perspectives (e.g., behavioral, cognitive, humanistic) could be invoked to understand the developmental needs and conflicts of this population of youth, the limited scope of this chapter does not permit an exhaustive review of that literature. Furthermore, any protracted academic discussion would likely divert the reader's attention from the practical matters related to this topic. Thus, to avoid this type of extended academic commentary, only the theoretical perspective deemed most relevant to this topic—Erik Erikson's (1963) psychosocial theory of development—is examined in detail.

I chose Erikson's model because he was one of the few thinkers to synthesize the third-person viewpoint of sociological understanding with the first-person perspective of psychoanalysis. His ideas are able to account for the reciprocal relationship between culture and biology in shaping personality. This fact makes Erikson's theory an appropriate model for describing the tension arising between mainstream social expectations and emotional growth needs of the culturally different child. Furthermore, because it is ultimately grounded in psychoanalytic treatment principles (e.g., transference, countertransference, ego defenses), Erikson's theory also implies practical ways of dealing with the kinds of cross-cultural problems confronting counselors of Hispanic boys. Because the ultimate aim of such therapy is to help Hispanic males acquire a responsible adulthood identity, professionals involved in such treatment need to understand how culture and individual psychology interplay to form character. In any case, counselors or therapists who would presume to treat young Hispanic males need to be aware of this cultural-individual matrix to avoid the twin evils of stereotypic thinking (e.g., "They are all the same") and excessive sentimentalizing (e.g., "These boys are the victims of societal discrimination") in counseling this population of males.

In the following pages, I discuss sociological-cultural realities of the Hispanic culture, describe Erikson's understanding of culture and personality, and present treatment strategies for dealing with the problems pertinent to Hispanic boys.

THE YOUNG HISPANIC MALE AND HIS CULTURE

As is the case with any ethnic influence on personality, the influence of Latin American or Spanish culture is diluted the longer that the individual remains in the United States. The culture no longer exists in its orthodox or pure form but as an Americanized (i.e., "melting pot") rendition of that way or mode of living. Our European-modeled society, which I will refer to as "mainstream" culture, prizes individuality, assertiveness, and self-efficacy. Additionally, because of its plethora of religious faiths and its Constitution's guarantee of separation of church and state, the United States is largely a secular country. These features are quite alien to people raised with the traditions of almost all Spanish-speaking countries insofar as the latter traditions tend to place family needs before individual aspirations, holding that communal needs supersede individual ambition (e.g., grown men often are expected to remain at home until married and afterward to be available to do their parents' bidding) and interdependency among family members is more important than personal independence. Adding to this somewhat conservative philosophy are the influence of Catholicism and the dictates of the Pope (which condemn free thinking) on these traditional Hispanic values.

As with all generalizations, these depictions are riddled with exceptions and are in the process of rapid transformation with the advent of global communication. These factors (i.e., family interdependence and acquiescence to religious authority) nevertheless have an abiding influence on the thinking of Hispanic males given that they are used as guides in daily decision making. Concession to authority and the importance of public image (e.g., "What will other people think?") means that one's personal reputation and that of one's family (even if justly criticized) must be defended against defamation. Character is determined to the extent that one fulfills the obligations of manhood. These ideals can be analyzed further in terms of how they influence Hispanic youth to form attachments (e.g., friendship patterns, family roles), develop personality configurations (e.g., modes of handling conflict, expressing desire), and choose their adult aims (e.g., job, place of residence).

To understand the first of these, the manner in which Hispanic youth form attachments, it is necessary to examine how the Hispanic family structure shapes male development. Unlike mainstream culture, it is a system premised on member dependence rather than individual emancipation. In this regard, Hispanic males are reminded continuously that their first loyalty is to their parents, siblings, and childhood friends, not to themselves or others outside the blood line. This dictate means that even though he tends to be much more indulged or fawned over than his mainstream counterpart (through the cult of *machismo*), the Hispanic male is also expected to live more in accord with a regime of family obligation than his contemporaries from European backgrounds. For example, even though schooling and economic progress might take the individual away from his childhood neighborhood to more sophisticated levels of society, these relatively recent bonds are not expected to take precedence, in either time or effort, over the needs of other family members. This observation is made to deny the well-known "fact" that there is disharmony between the rich and the less-well-off members of any cultural group. This type of conflict is particularly pronounced in the Spanish-speaking community.

Expected to assist the less-achieving family members (even when reasonable judgment might dictate otherwise), those who are more accomplished often find themselves enmeshed in trying to solve serious social-economic problems of others (e.g., bankrupt relatives, jailed cousins, unemployed brothers, physically abused sisters) that are not of the making of that more successful individual. Additionally, these same individuals are expected not to draw attention to their good fortune or attainments (in the self-conscious pursuit of "being the best" or "looking out for number one"). Instead, they are expected to display an attitude of humility rather than pridefulness ("Don't be arrogant"). Boastfulness and behavior designed to draw attention to the self are taken as signs of disrespect or impoliteness. For example, Hispanic males of the second generation or in the midst of the acculturation process would be viewed by their elders as excessively egotistical or even insolent if they were to pursue education in places remote from their homes or pursue technical careers beyond their parents' understanding. Given the fact that Hispanic youth are expected to follow tradition, an intergenerational strain can emerge easily between the traditional elderly (e.g., "Why don't you get a job just like mine?"; "Why are you moving so far away?") and the Americanized young man (e.g., desires to go away to college or leave his neighborhood, city, or state to find work). Thus, it can be said that Hispanic culture is founded on a kind of social conservatism that is at odds with the more innovative ideals of U.S. capitalism (i.e., "the newer, the better").

Regarding the second consideration, the manner in which Hispanic culture shapes personality, perhaps no example of how this influence operates is more important than the role of *personalismo* in the day-to-day thinking of Hispanic individuals. Referring to the propensity by Hispanics to use informality as the medium by which formal dealings are consummated, *personalismo* is a notion that allows the Hispanic to transcend specific formalities guiding society (e.g., business, legal), bringing to bear the power of family or personal reputation as leverage in daily transactions. For example, in many Latin American countries, it is the businessperson's family background that is decisive in expediting loans rather than the individual's objective credit history. Thus, because the family is believed to be of paramount value in affirming the self, the growing boy learns that he must promote a positive public image of the same and its members despite private knowledge to the contrary (e.g., "My uncle works as an officer in X bank"; "My cousin is friends with the chief of police") to promote his own place in society. Only "insiders" are expected to know the real workings of the individual's family, whereas the external community is expected to receive a highly controlled picture of its makeup. Most central to the family's configuration is its mother. Ascribed to her are the virtues of saintliness; any degradation of her reputation is seen as a degradation of the males who are expected to defend her honor.

Personalismo thus does not merely mean relating to others on a first-person basis but, instead, to making reference to one's entire kin system in an effort to give legitimacy or authority to one's social dealings (e.g., "He will defend his mother at any cost"; "Don't fool with his sister"; "His brothers will get you if you fight with him"). This form of cultural organization, as with all others, provides the developing boy with both advantages and problems. From a positive perspective, the developing male Hispanic (particularly if he comes from a large family) is never expected to act alone. Social isolation is comparatively rare because his sense of self—his *personalismo*—rests on the foundations of his family (particularly the reputation of his mother). From a more negative viewpoint, much of his fate is dictated by that same ancestry. His associates, his marriage partner, where he travels, and where he works are determined more by past tradition than by future considerations and conscious choices.

If the Hispanic male steps out of this circle of familiarity, he could encounter mockery, exclusion, or the accusation that he is "forgetting" where he comes from. In turn, his origins are defined not only by his biological family but also by his neighborhood or "barrio," which becomes a further extension of that youngster's nuclear family. The streets themselves thus become extensions of living rooms and the individual's living space (shared with the "siblings" of the streets), leading the Hispanic male to experience conflict between his kin family and the family of the streets.

Moreover, the creed of *personalismo* advocates that the Hispanic male should be an individual of his word, eschewing pretense (the opposite of *personalismo*) and embracing the values of physical toughness and bravery. As a corollary to this code of conduct, it is expected that he view women as essentially subservient but valued for their domestic abilities and physical allure. Furthermore, it is demanded that they receive his complete physical protection. Although the women's movement and the increase in general education undoubtedly have altered the rigidity of these old-fashioned sexual definitions, the fact remains that much less equality exists between the sexes within the Hispanic culture than in other groups. Hispanic males tend to categorize females into two broad types: the virtuous and the fallen. The budding youth is expected to fall in love with the former while getting his experience with the latter. Moreover, his ideal love object is supposed to be a kind of junior version of the youth's own mother: a girl who displays infinite patience and understanding, and is wholly attentive to his ongoing needs. On the other hand, the "fallen" woman is viewed as one to be pursued for pleasure; in many ways she holds interest more than his marital mate.

The counterpart to the Hispanic boy's idealized mother figure is the distant and often absent father. In this regard, the developing young man frequently finds himself striving to obtain the approval of someone who is more involved with affairs of the street or business than with his home obligations. Thus, compared to mainstream culture, the mother is more the source of day-to-day authority for her son than the father because of this retreat from the family situation (e.g., it is considered the mother's job to talk to his teachers, buy him clothes, pick him up from parties, etc.). As might be guessed, this dearth of a male presence in a boy's life can cause him to seek his masculinity ideal away from his biological family and in the streets.

At the same time, it should be noted that this absence typically is greater in the earlier years of development rather than later in childhood and adolescence, mostly because the older child is more capable of engaging in adult activities and is less likely to display the type of dependence to which many adult Hispanic males have trouble relating. Indeed, the fathers of Hispanic boys often show impatience with helplessness or vulnerability, urging their sons to "be a man" as quickly as possible.

This advice emerges from their hard-won knowledge that the world frequently is an unforgiving place, requiring that males fight for their rights or otherwise be taken for *pendejo*. This term, which is central to the thinking of many Hispanic males, refers to an individual who is weak, disrespected, taken advantage of, or otherwise domineered by others for their own whims. Such a label must be avoided at all costs given that it represents the exact opposite behavior expected of the ideal Hispanic man: self-reliant, tough, and unflinching in the face of external threats. The young male is socialized into the role of someone who is the ultimate authority of his household, views women with a mixture of idealism and disregard, and is highly protective of both his own reputation and that of his family.

Elements of the third component of this cultural matrix, the Hispanic male's adult ideals, dictate that a boy should grow to become resourceful and uncomplaining in his character, being an authority onto himself despite his clear dependence on or sensitivity toward the opinions of his family and neighbors. As such, he is supposed to be decisive in his actions and not betray the type of uncertainty that would categorize him as feminine, vulnerable, or a *pendejo*. The Hispanic male thus emerges from a conservative culture and is expected to accept a traditional occupation without question or conflict, leaving him with relatively little room for experimentation on his way to adopting a full-fledged adult identity. In this respect, he should act like a "man" in terms of marrying (or cohabitating) early, siring children, and taking on the requirements of a breadwinner as soon as he is capable of obtaining consistent employment. The type of "moratorium" suggested by Erikson (1963), wherein a youth takes "time off" from the path toward adulthood, is not tolerated in a Hispanic society. Probably because many Spanish speaking families live at the lower levels of economic existence, children are socialized to obtain, as soon as possible, remunerative or practical occupations with outcomes that are clearly apparent. The notion of "finding one's self" or experimenting with various roles before committing to a lifelong identity is relatively foreign to the Hispanic way of thinking.

Although the future often is presented in clearly narrow terms (e.g., in terms of specified kinds of work, acceptable marital partners), the growing male is also given a surprising amount of freedom to come and go as he pleases relative to his female counterpart. In keeping with the patriarchal value system of the Hispanic culture, the growing boy in that situation is expected to "sow his oats" during his late teenage years through his early twenties before assuming the more serious obligation of supporting his own family. Thus, it is not unusual for problematic drinking to begin in Hispanic youths' teenage years because alcohol usage and adult identity are viewed as being synonymous.

All of this is not to say that the Hispanic male is allowed to behave as he pleases, but instead that predefined rituals (e.g., drinking, carousing) in the company of older youths and men are tolerated behavior. At the same time, the growing youth is expected to remain closely bound to his parents and siblings, prepared to serve their needs even if this duty demands sacrificing his own desires or goals in the process. For example, it is not unusual for one of the brothers of a large family to defer his own education, job promotion, or advancement to rescue or otherwise attempt to rehabilitate one or more siblings who are chronically delinquent, unemployed, or otherwise maladjusted. It is expected that the most successful of the bunch will carry the less capable or fortunate on his back, as it were, even when it is quite clear that such individuals are past salvation. Fearing to be called disloyal, arrogant, or a traitor to his own people, the achieving Hispanic male is often dragged back to more humble origins or at least slowed in his progress by his obligations to the least successful of his clan. Many Hispanic males purposely lower their sights or otherwise achieve below their potential, realizing that unless they are willing to pull everyone up to their level they will be seen as objects of envy or competitiveness.

Depending on the country of origin and economic background of the male in question, greater or lesser degrees of ambitiousness are expected of maturing young men. The underlying ethos of Spanish culture, however, is that one's self-aggrandizing efforts always are secondary to one's loyalty to the family group. This expectation is often the basis of emotional conflict experience in the developing Hispanic male. On one hand, he is expected to make his way independently in the world ("Be a man"); on the other, he is required to remain a quasi-child in the face of the needs of his parents and siblings, ready to do their bidding whenever the need arises. Thus, the Hispanic male never feels completely emancipated from his family of origin or empowered as his own person because self-approval is often a function of parental affirmation.

This brief outline of Hispanic culture serves as preparation for a more extensive discussion of the psychology of the developing Hispanic boy. I will examine the ways in which such social factors interplay with his notion of masculinity. This discussion will be organized around Erikson's psychosocial theory of personality and his analysis of how social expectations, in combination with the individual's biological drives, forge human identity. This examination is followed by an enumeration of several types of psychological problems commonly displayed by young Hispanic boys.

ON THE WAY TO MASCULINITY: STAGES OF PSYCHOSEXUAL DEVELOPMENT

It is a truism to state that no life is led without pain or disappointment. Indeed, it was Erikson's (1963) insight that the basis of all psychological growth is a function of how individuals navigate through certain expected crises in their social existence. Drawing from Sigmund Freud's psychosexual theory of male development, Erikson postulated that the type of psychological conflicts described by Freud's psychosexual developmental theory (e.g., oral, anal, phallic, stages of sexuality) had their social equivalents in the type of interpersonal adversities arising at those same points in the individual's mental life. Thus, Erikson developed a theory of human development both paralleling and extending Freud's own, describing different kinds of social challenges confronting the child at specific growth points during his or her mental development.

Although Erikson posited eight stages of psychosocial growth (his so-called eight stages of man) bridging infancy into old age, of greatest concern in this section are those three periods of psychological growth spanning latency through early adulthood. Taken as a unit, they constitute the time frame when a young boy's sense of masculinity becomes established and where the typical developmental problems arise. Corresponding roughly to Freud's phallic, latent, and genital levels, these three stages (i.e., initiative versus guilt, industry versus inferiority, and identity formation and identity confusion) are now considered in detail.

The first, initiative versus guilt, refers to the developing child's need to thrust forward from his home environment or immediate circle of protectiveness, amplifying his horizons toward the larger, outer world. This stage is when he searches for affirmation of his capacities beyond his immediate family situation. In this stage, the child can be said to have a kind of exhibitionistic attitude, showing off his strengths and daring, and even defying parental rules as he forges the beginnings of his own identity. During this period of growth, occurring around the fifth year of life, the boy begins to idealize father figures, model himself around publicly acclaimed heroes (e.g., sports figures, television personalities), and accept the worth of those such nonfamily role models in an innocent or uncritical fashion. It is also here when the youngster begins to shape his identity through the approval or disapproval he receives from family members for his choice of such idols.

Erikson cautions that if the child is provided with no guidance at this stage or has little chance to "try out" the imaginative possibilities inherent in this gamut of champions, he can fall in danger of becoming conforming, disillusioned, or resigned, unable to find purpose in his actions. On the other hand, Erikson observes that it is possible for boys to become excessively interested in attention, hungry for approval, or seemingly grandiose in their self-aspirations as a result of receiving too much untempered praise. This is all to say that in this stage a boy assesses his first striving as a man, taking up what has been shown to him by his culture through imaginative play and mental fantasy.

Unfortunately, it is often the fact that Hispanic families do not provide their growing children with the same spectrum of possibilities offered to mainstream youths. Many Hispanic boys therefore suffer from stunted imaginations, for example, seeing themselves only in menial posts (leading to a devaluation of school) rather than having more professional or technical goals. Thus, in New York City, it is quite common for Puerto Rican youths to wish only to become building superintendents or porters rather than owners of those same buildings. In the Southwest, their Mexican American counterparts are prone to want to become car mechanics rather than airline pilots or auto dealers. Seeing an impoverished future, it is not unusual for such youths, lacking reasons to pursue goals with vigorous initiative, to turn to peer groups to bolster their fledgling identities. In this regard, the neighborhood or barrio is taken to be the context in which identity is described (e.g., gang member, neighborhood local) rather than the larger society.

This constraint on possibilities produces the recipe for despair and depression as the growing boy begins to learn that his initiative can carry him only so far, not just because of possible social prejudice but also because of the limiting horizons of who he is supposed to be. Erikson's stages are sequential and cumulative; thus, failure to properly master one stage leads to inevitable problems during the next. If the preschool boy's fantasy life is restricted (through lessened social and family expectations) during the initiative versus guilt stage, then it can be expected that he will be reduced in his academic, extracurricular, and general school activities. In other words, he will become diminished in his commitment to the learning enterprise, leading to the high dropout rate manifested by Hispanic schoolchildren.

The second of these three psychosocial stages, industry versus inferiority, occurs when the child is primarily concerned with achieving tangible results in his surroundings or otherwise taking a measure of his self-worth through the manner in which his work is assessed by others outside the family circle. Coinciding with his participation in the school system, where he must meet the objective expectations of adults who are detached from his family, this stage leads him to appraise his achievement not in terms of parental expectations but relative to other children of his own academic standing. Given appropriate psychological preparation (particularly in the light of how he confronted Erikson's earlier developmental crises), he is equipped to meet the challenges stemming from such an environment, deriving the pride of accomplishment through the objective evaluation of his capacities by a community of strangers.

It is for this reason that Erikson counterposes the sense of inferiority as a prime threat to the successful negotiation of this developmental stage. A sense of inadequacy can arise if children are expected to go beyond their intrinsic capabilities or if they are not supported in their efforts to move to new goals beyond the world of their household. Hispanic boys are particular vulnerable to the acquisition of such a negative self-image because they frequently are required to communicate in two languages without having a sound grammatical background in either language. Thus, the Hispanic male discovers that he speaks in a manner unacceptable to either mainstream society or his own Latin American background, causing him to be viewed as neither American nor truly Hispanic. Lacking an appropriate foundation of grammar, syntax, and vocabulary, many second-generation Hispanic boys mix both languages in a manner that is unacceptable to either the school system or society at large. Because of his limited access to an environment that can produce adequate linguistic competence, the Hispanic male frequently finds himself blocked in normal language attainment, producing a kind of linguistic "ghetto" (i.e., "Spanglish") that prevents him from integrating meaningfully into his social environment.

At the same time, "Spanglish" can serve as a unifying force among such children, providing a kind of in-group dialect that gives them a sort of marginal identity. This defensive maneuver, after repeated exposures to the electronic media (television, films, videotapes), serves as a reminder that his language is not the same as that of mainstream America: He speaks with an accent and at times uses unique syntax, whereas most movie, TV, and singing stars do not. This dawning realization that he speaks or communicates differently from the prevailing cultural ideal produces a larger and larger rift between what society tells him to achieve (i.e., "speak correctly") and what he is actually capable of performing.

Aggravating this source of inferiority is the essentially nonacademic tradition of many Latin cultures, which emphasize manual trades over intellectual accomplishment. Not reinforced at home for continuous school excellence, as boys of other social groups might be, the Hispanic male often learns that his place is not in the classroom but in the streets, among his friends. Neighborhood or peer-inspired vocational goals are of the manual type: repairing cars, fixing appliances, partaking in construction work, or helping adults with concrete technical work. Although such trades are not dishonorable in themselves, when they represent the only valid aspirations to which Hispanic boys can strive they block Hispanic children from identifying with the full breadth of American culture (i.e., "You're not good for anything other than working with your hands and backs"). Thus, the developing Hispanic boy faces the dilemma of trying to maintain his Spanish-speaking heritage while partaking meaningfully in mainstream U.S. culture. He is faced with the problem of blending in the norms of his family/community (e.g., "Don't sound or act too White") versus suppressing his native roots by assimilating the individualistic, competitive customs of American society and integrating productively. Most first- and second-generation immigrant youths face the ambivalence resulting from this dilemma. It is the age-old tension between foreign-born elders and their Americanized offspring, or the pull of the old versus the attraction of the new.

The final topic of concern in this section is Erikson's psychosocial stage of identity formation versus identity confusion. Corresponding roughly to the mid-teenage years to the early twenties, this phase of development concerns itself with the establishment of personal direction, autonomous decision making, and the creation of social identity. It is here that the young man involves himself fully with the opposite sex, although he may be far from making any long-term commitment. It is a period of experimentation with the real world, ending in a more or less focused way of life or values that will serve to guide the boy in later life. As such, it can be considered a time when idealism and romanticism figure prominently, providing a kind of ideology, justification, or philosophy that will guide later adult commitments.

In contrast to these rather positive outcomes emanating from the teenage years, the dangers of perpetual confusion, prolonged childhood, and deferred decision making are a constant set of obstacles to eventual maturity. The Hispanic male must resolve the same problem accosting all youths of his age: whether to identify with the values of society at large or to live in a state of perennial rebelliousness against his surroundings. It is not uncommon to see Hispanic men in their thirties, forties, and fifties still leading the lives of adolescents as they move from job to job, woman to woman, and residence to residence. This unsettled condition is also reinforced by the proximity of Latin American nations to U.S. borders, allowing a back-and-forth movement from one country to another (as evidenced by many people of Puerto Rican, Mexican, and Dominican background). Such fluid movement can act to prevent any real psychological commitment to either nationality.

The Hispanic male thus always has the option of retreating back into his own ethnic world or neighborhood and avoiding the kind of risk taking in a large world that would provide him with little basis for self-identity. Such is the case with so-called home boys, who are blocked by their own inhibitions and by social pressures from experimenting, sampling, or otherwise learning about the surrounding environment, instead staying within the confines of their own well-delineated neighborhood.

In this stage, the developing male is challenged with creating his own path in life, which threatens him with possible alienation from his surroundings or separateness from the familiar routines and world of his elders. Making this integration between old and new difficult is the pressure many Hispanic males feel to find a job quickly, contribute economically to their households, and assume the roles of adults without fully contemplating their own needs or wishes. In this respect, the effects of poverty (which is strongly present in many Spanish-speaking households) foreclose the possibilities for experimentation, risk taking, and genuine choice in personal direction. Those Hispanic males who are thwarted, abandoned, or excessively blocked in their aspirations are vulnerable to recruitment by gangs or antisocial peers who would provide their own images of competence and success to such confused adolescent males.

In the following final section of this chapter, I review some counseling approaches to dealing with the kinds of problems outlined in the foregoing pages, suggesting interventions that could be applied productively to the developing Hispanic male.

CLINICAL APPROACHES

Given the developmental emphasis characterizing this chapter, it is obvious that it would advocate a treatment approach focusing primarily on repairing or ameliorating those aspects of the psychological growth pattern that have been blocked, ignored, or diverted by negative family or social environments. Beyond the acquisition of "social skills" or altered "cognitive attitudes" (two of the most commonly advocated treatment goals advocated in this era of behaviorally oriented, short-term treatment), these youth, who are often divided in their allegiances to family, community, and school, tend to require help establishing their basic identities. They do not require a stopgap or Band-Aid approach. To accomplish the more ambitious task of character formation, Erikson's psychosocial theory, applied in conjunction with basic psychoanalytic principles of treatment, provides a productive method that can be adapted successfully within many counseling circumstances devoted to serving the needs of Hispanic boys and adolescents. Before presenting a case to illustrate this method, I review three basic psychoanalytic concepts—transference and countertransference, working through, and internalization— basic to all neo-Freudian approaches to therapy.

Transference was defined by Freud (1912/1958) as that tendency by all therapy clients to ascribe, irrationally, past aspects of their family relations to their current relations with their therapists. In the case of children, the border between transference and the real relationship is less clear than with adults; nevertheless, they also tend to distort their relationships with the therapist to conform to their particular developmental or parental histories. Often, the counselor is viewed in extreme terms as all "bad" or all "good." In turn, the kind of perception projected onto the counselor (assuming that he or she has done nothing objectively to deserve these exaggerated impressions) is dependent on the kind of emotional recognition that the boy has experienced in his earlier years. As might be expected, boys who have been abused or purposely mistreated are likely to view the counselor in negative terms. Normally, these boys behave in a jaded if not outright hostile manner in the face of positive solicitations. However, boys who have been frustrated in establishing bonds with their fathers or mothers (because of abandonment, neglect, or detachment) are more likely than the first group to view the therapist in positive or even idealized terms, even when little has occurred between the child and therapist to warrant such feelings.

Once a suitable relationship has been established, it is the job of the child therapist to help the child voice his fantasies about the therapist's background, personality, children, and interests. Expression of these feelings/ideas can take place through direct commentary or in the course of doing mutual activities (playing board games, puttering with cards, drawing pictures, working on the computer). The therapist's aim should be to help the boy internalize new ideals that provide him with greater hope, direction, and stability than his current state of mind. The more that the therapist can affirm the boy's cultural heritage, helping the child to appropriate Spanish customs (e.g., foods, holidays, music) and bond to his existing family, the more beneficial will be the effects of such treatment. As well, knowledge of the boy's psychosocial stage of development (e.g., initiative vs. guilt, industry vs. inferiority) is important in understanding his subjective world and the developmental challenges that characterize his situation.

Countertransference (Racker, 1953/1968) comes into play during all phases of counseling. It refers to the counselor's propensity to inject his or her own emotional needs and distortions into the therapeutic situation, overlooking the child's own situation in favor of the adult's unrecognized or unconscious drives. In particular, the boy's situation or behavior can be the cause of exaggerated anger, admiration, envy, or reactivity of every sort, well out of proportion to the objective facts characterizing the problem at hand (e.g., "Your teacher sounds as angry as the one I used to have when I was your age"). The counselor's unresolved issues (e.g., memories of discrimination, feelings of past victimization) can lead him or her to impose interpretations, make recommendations, or adopt treatment strategies that are self-serving rather than genuinely appropriate for the boy. Thus, impasses arising in the counseling situation require the therapist to examine critically (via individual therapy or supervision) his or her own emotional reactions to the child's situation and to ascertain the degree to which personal distortions and unrecognized biases are responsible for such problems rather than attributing them to external factors (e.g., failure of family cooperation, the child's intransigence). In short, the counselor must have a clear view of his or her emotional dynamics before presuming to deal with those of the child.

The notion of working through (Freud, 1914/1958) refers to the time necessary for any individual in counseling to make use of or otherwise incorporate insights derived from the treatment endeavor. With respect to the child therapy situation, it entails establishing a set of specific yet attainable goals (i.e., a contract) that can be reviewed during every treatment session to determine the boy's progress. Crucial to this endeavor is the family's or caretaker's conscientiousness in ensuring that the youngster attends treatment, monitoring compliance with the counseling aims (e.g., completing homework, curbing aggression), and establishing a home environment supportive of such change (e.g., quiet study area, timely praise for job well done).

As indicated previously, many Hispanic families can be quite wary of disclosing private matters with strangers. Thus, although they may strongly desire for their children's conduct to improve, they are prone to minimize the full extent of their domestic difficulties (e.g., father's drinking problem, ongoing financial pressures, past instances of sexual abuse) to outsiders. Unfortunately, this reticence serves to undermine the treatment process, because the child's challenges are minimized by such omitted information. To counteract this possibility, the counselor needs to assume an active role during the interview and initial phases of contact, asking about matters that may not have been volunteered but are crucial for understanding the child's living situation. Those may include the family's past and present immigration status, history of police or legal encounters by any immediate family members, nature of disciplinary practices employed in the household, financial status of the household, psychiatric history ("Do you or have you ever taken any medication for your nerves?"), or medical background (e.g., "Have you, your child, or other family members been interned in a hospital? Taken to an emergency room?").

Only after establishing an alliance with the family can treatment proceed effectively with the youngster. From the Eriksonian perspective, this means first determining—from both the boy's verbal material and collateral information—his psychosocial stage (it may not be congruent with the boy's chronological age) and then formulating statements that help the child feel understood as he struggles with the problems relevant to that stage (e.g., "Can I match the accomplishments of other boys in my grade?"; "Am I worthy of being accepted by other boys in my neighborhood?"). At the same time, awareness of the values intrinsic to the Hispanic culture can help the counselor to describe the youngster's specific psychological conflict in an empathic manner (e.g., "You don't want to be seen as a *pendejo* by your friends, yet you are afraid of shaming your family").

Finally, internalization (Erikson, 1956) refers to the process by which the child identifies with the counselor's values, perspective, and outlook. Presumably, this occurs following a process of idealization wherein the counselor becomes the boy's "hero" (or "heroine"). It arises from a supportive and trusting relationship in which the child begins fantasizing himself as having the kinds of attributes that he deems his counselor to possess. This situation can appear only if the counselor is perceived by the boy as genuine and possessing integrity. Honest communication, consistency, and awareness of the boy's ongoing struggles within the Hispanic subculture enable the counselor to acquire this kind of therapeutic credibility. Thus, the presence of these authentic qualities allows the youngster to appropriate or internalize (in a conscious as well as an unconscious manner) new values and attitudes from this valued adult figure. It is then that the child can begin to assume the role of a "man" that is congruent with his Hispanic background. The way in which the phenomena of transference, countertransference, working through, and internalization are manifested can be seen in the following case example.

Peter was brought to the therapist's attention because of school misconduct, poor grades, and a defiant attitude at home. The oldest of three children of a Puerto Rican mother who was a civil employee, he represented a significant source of anguish and strain to all adults with whom he dealt. Indeed, his mother was on the verge of remanding him to family court (the New York State equivalent of juvenile court) because of his obstreperous conduct. Having experienced only minimal contact with his biological father, he had never had any real adult male relationships in his life.

In keeping with this background information, Peter interacted initially with the therapist (a Hispanic male) in a rather reserved and somewhat sullen manner. Following the acquisition of a detailed social history from his mother and himself (from which it was learned that he suffered from lifelong reading problems), he admitted to a prevailing feeling of despair that he would never succeed in school. At age 13, his future adult image was that of someone who would be good only at "picking up trash."

Over the course of several months of regular weekly meetings (wherein the counselor reviewed Peter's homework and school progress, played video games, and learned of Peter's social situation with other boys), Peter began to be more forthcoming about his doubts and fears. From these conversations, it became clear that Peter derived whatever good feelings he had about himself by identifying with the fiercest boys in his neighborhood ("They aren't the goody-goodies; they have brothers and fathers who have been in jail"), even adopting a quite dramatic sullen and defiant street attitude whenever he became displeased during the counseling situation. During those moments, he might communicate to the therapist insulting phrases such as "You can't make me do anything. You're a sissy."

Such behavior, which was clearly transferential in nature (identifying the counselor with all adult men who had abandoned him), served to reject the counselor before he himself could be rejected. At the same time, it provoked the counselor to have self-doubts and questions about his own manly qualities. These thoughts were of an obviously countertransferential nature ("Maybe the kid sees something in me that is cowardly just like I felt myself at his age"). Although the therapist was tempted to reply to such communications with the same kind of toughness he had experienced in his own Hispanic upbringing, insights acquired from his supervisor and from personal therapy allowed him to gain perspective on the situation. Rather than matching strength with strength, the counselor broke through that particular power struggle (and potential treatment impasse) with the statement "I think that you want to make me fearful of you so that you can keep your distance from me." This kind of intervention, as well as many like it whenever Peter employed his "tough" act, helped to dissolve some of this youngster's resistance and anger.

The working through process consisted of encountering and reencountering Peter's anger, examining the ways in which it was and was not justified. Moreover, it involved revealing to Peter the way in which he wanted to sabotage the treatment process so that he would not be disappointed by another Hispanic father figure. In the course of a year, Peter's behavior improved both at school and at home. Although he continued to have flare-ups within the treatment situation, these decreased in intensity and duration. A sudden interest in reading (particularly the newspaper), even though he still struggled with his classroom work, evidenced that he had begun to identify with the counselor's personality. He seemed to have a more reflective ("white collar?") kind of existence than that which surrounded him. Unfortunately, at the start of the next academic year, Peter and his family moved to Puerto Rico. It is uncertain whether he was able to consolidate the gains he had made during the previous 11 months.

In conclusion, counselors working with Hispanic male youths must consider not only the individual aspects of their clients (i.e., idiosyncratic features of their personalities) but also the larger social context in which these boys live their lives. Even though the Latino or Hispanic culture has elements of sexism, paternalism, and authoritarianism, it is also informed by respect for authority, family loyalty, deference to the elderly, and emotional intimacy—aspects not normally encountered in the larger society. Therapists should not blankly approve of those constituents of Hispanic culture that are counterproductive to personal growth, but neither should they be condemnatory or dismissive of the same. Instead, counselors should first understand the total world of the developing Hispanic male, supporting those features that provide him with an authentic, productive identity while deepening his critical awareness of the unconscious forces shaping his character. Only in this way can Hispanic boys be helped to become their own men.

HIGHLIGHTS OF CHAPTER 7

▶ Although Hispanics probably have more differences than similarities among them, they share broad, unifying characteristics, such as speaking a common native language (Spanish) and placing family needs before individual aspirations and communal needs over personal ambition.

▶ Hispanic boys are raised to respect authority figures and to defend one's personal reputation and that of one's family. Their first loyalties are to their parents, siblings, extended kin, and childhood friends, not to themselves or others outside their family and community.

▶ The origins of Hispanic male identity are in a boy's immediate and extended family, as well as the neighborhood from which he comes. Thus his family and his community are an extension of who he is as a person and have a great influence on his choice of associates, marriage partner, where he travels, and where he works.

▶ The Hispanic culture advocates that males should be true to their word, humble, physically tough, brave, decisive, self-reliant, resourceful, and uncomplaining.

▶ Hispanic boys tend to have idealized images of their mothers, who handle the day-to-day matters of the home, and somewhat distant relations with their fathers, who are the providers for the family and the family's representative to the outside world.

▶ Predefined male rituals (e.g., drinking and carousing) in the company of older youths and men are tolerated as rites of passage to manhood. At the same time, Hispanic males are expected to sacrifice their own needs and desires (e.g., deferring an education) to assist family members in crisis. Furthermore, self-aggrandizing efforts always are secondary to one's loyalty to the family.

▶ Many second-generation Hispanic boys mix the English and Spanish languages in a manner that is acceptable to neither the school system nor the society at large and places them at risk for academic and acculturation difficulties.

▶ The limited life opportunities in many poor Hispanic communities lead to restricted academic initiative and premature career foreclosure among many Hispanic males.

▶ Because many Hispanic families live at the lower levels of economic existence and because many Latin cultures emphasize manual trades over intellectual accomplishment, large numbers of Hispanic boys are socialized to leave school, obtain practical occupations, marry or cohabitate, and sire children as soon as they are capable of doing so.

▶ Hispanic males are commonly conflicted as to whether to identity with the mainstream values of society or to remain loyal to the values of Hispanic culture.

► Because Hispanic families tend to be wary of disclosing private matters to strangers, counselors must take an active role to establish a working alliance with the family. This alliance permits the counselor to probe about domestic difficulties.

► Counselors who demonstrate honesty, consistency, and awareness of the boy's ongoing struggles within the Hispanic subculture can achieve therapeutic credibility with Hispanic boys.

► Counselors must carefully monitor personal distortions and unrecognized biases about Hispanics that might interfere with their ability to see a boy's problems objectively.

► Counseling with Hispanic boys is enhanced when the counselor affirms the boy's cultural heritage and helps the boy to appropriate Spanish customs and to bond with his family.

8

Helping Native American Indian and Alaska Native Male Youth

ROGER HERRING

Helping Native American Indian and Alaska Native male youth can be very challenging. Achievement of separation from the biological family and development of an independent identity are complicated by factors such as experiences of oppression and discrimination, low socioeconomic status (SES), limited access to publicly funded services, incongruity between traditional and mainstream cultures, and influences of culturation, as well as consequences of these factors (Herring, 1997a). This chapter accents the major content and process issues of this population and suggests selected appropriate strategies for helping interactions.

The term *Native* refers to Native American Indian and Alaska Native males when the context is applicable to both groups. The term *Native American Indian* depicts male youth indigenous to the lower 48 states; *Alaska Native* identifies male youth indigenous to Alaska. The term *youth* implies both children and adolescents.

DEMOGRAPHIC REALITIES

A central obstacle to understanding Native male youth is the myth of homogeneity (Thomason, 1995). This population reflects an incredible diversity in family patterns, customs, and languages. The Native population of nearly 2 million is steadily increasing, representing only 1% of the total U.S. population but 50% of the nation's diversity in terms of number of ethnic groups (Hodgkinson, 1990).

Census data, however, underreport Native population because many Natives do not participate in the census or do not want to be identified as Native. Census estimates also may be low because of Natives who choose to "pass," voluntarily concealing their ethnicity from people who do not accept their ethnicity; these Natives' physical appearance is such that they can "pass" for another ethnicity. A more realistic figure of Native population would be 2.5 to 2.8 million (Peregoy, 1993).

NATIVE AMERICAN INDIANS

The diversity of Native American Indians is illustrated in the 252 different languages (not dialects), 517 federally recognized tribes (196 in Alaska and 321 in the lower states), 365 state recognized tribes, 52 tribes without any recognition, and many bands too small to be recognized officially (Herring, 1994b, 1997a). More than 37% of this total population are 18 years of age or younger, and 41% are 20 years of age or younger. Birth rates reflect 95 males per 100 females. Of all Native American Indians, 22% live on tribal lands, reservations, or trust lands (U.S. Department of Commerce, 1992).

ALASKA NATIVES

More than 50% of Alaska Natives are Inuit (Eskimo), 36% are Native American Indian, and 12% are Aleut (U.S. Department of Commerce, 1992). The two main Inuit groups, Inupiat and Yupik, are distinguished by their language and geography. Native American Indian tribes include the Alaskan Athabascan in central Alaska and the Tlingit, Haida, and Tsimshian in the southeastern area (U.S. Department of Commerce, 1992). The Aleuts live mainly on the Aleutian Islands. A brief discussion of two Alaska Native groups provides insight into their culture.

Inuit (Eskimo). Historically, these peoples referred to themselves as simply *Inuit,* or "the people." The label *Eskimo,* meaning "raw flesh eaters," was bestowed on them by the Algonquians and adopted by the insensitive world (Herring, 1997b). The Inuits, never numbering more than 90,000, are remarkable in that they inhabit the harshest natural environment on earth, the desolate lands of the Arctic. Their existence historically was dependent on the meager resources of snow, stone, animal skin, and bone, yet they survived centuries of migrations. By the 1920s, traditional life was almost extinct as the "White man's culture" came to dominate.

The Aleuts. Stretching some 1,000 miles from Alaska's southwest coast is the Aleutian archipelago of nearly 100 treeless islands. For several thousand years, these islands have been home to the Aleuts. The Aleuts speak a language related to that of the Inuits, with whom they share other qualities.

In the 1740s, the traditional life of the Aleuts was shattered by the occupation of their islands by Russian sea otter traders. They were forced to accept the Russians' language, clothing and house designs, and names, which most of the Aleutian islanders retain today. Thousands died from brutalities or "White man" diseases during the century-long occupation. By the time the United States acquired the islands in 1867, the Aleut population had dropped from 15,000 to 2,500. Currently, more than 3,000 Aleutians remain, but only about half reside on the islands.

PARTICULAR ADJUSTMENT
OR CLINICAL ISSUES

Native male youth constitute an ethnocultural group with diverse values, problems, and resources. Helping professionals must be alert to particular adjustment or clinical issues for these youth. Experts agree that the most serious health problem facing Natives today is the psychological stress caused by pressure to assimilate into a society that conflicts with Native values (Herring, 1997a). Native male youth frequently experience depressed feelings and mental disorders associated with social stress, which are complicated by anxiety and the use of drugs (Nelson, McCoy, Stetter, & Vanderwagen, 1992). Major issues include experiences of oppression and discrimination, identity crises, stereotyping, culturation, value conflicts, suicide, sexuality, spirituality, and intergenerational conflicts.

EXPERIENCES OF DISCRIMINATION AND OPPRESSION

Native peoples have experienced hate crimes longer than any other group in the United States. Incidents of exploitation and victimization have been portrayed in many books and films. Unfortunately, such occurrences are not confined to the distant past. Natives continue to endure racist assaults, harassment, intimidation, and murder, yet crimes against Natives are the least reported both to law officials and in the news media (*The Hidden Victims*, 1994). The more militantly bigoted individuals and groups use direct confrontation, employing hate mail, harassment, vandalism, and violence to instill fear and instability in Native communities (Ryser, 1992).

Native male youth may present with experiences of discrimination. They have endured social problems including poverty, unemployed parents, inadequate health services, substandard housing, family dissolution, miseducation, and alcohol and drug abuse (Herring, 1997a). Many also have experienced separation from their families and being placed in non-Native homes (Herring, 1989).

IDENTITY CRISES

A major issue for Native American Indian male youth, especially nontraditional youth, concerns requirements for designation as "Indian." A generic label does not exist (Herring, 1994b, 1997a, 1997b). *American Indian* is the referent most frequently used (LaFromboise & Graff Low, 1989) and was first applied to the Arawak (a now-extinct tribe once indigenous to islands off the southeastern United States) by an Italian sailor who thought he had reached India. The term has since become institutionalized and accepted by many Native American Indians themselves (Trimble, Fleming, Beauvais, & Jumper-Thurman, 1996).

Native American Indians are the only ethnic group in this nation that has been legally defined. The Bureau of Indian Affairs (BIA) defines an *American Indian* as one who (a) is an enrolled member of a federally recognized tribe, (b) is at least one-fourth American Indian in blood quantum, and (c) can legally verify those facts. The U.S. Bureau of the Census definition is self-enumerative; that is, the bureau accepts the designation provided by census respondents themselves. The Department of Education recognizes someone as American Indian if he or she is a descendant of anyone who was once a member of a tribe. Thus, both recognize more individuals than does the BIA.

Issues of Native identity are compounded because more than 60% of Native male youth are genetically mixed. Many youth of mixed marriages are not seen as "ethnically pure" by some Natives and non-Natives and hence are not viewed as characteristically traditional Native (Trimble et al., 1996). In reality, differences in blood quantum are based in "legalistic genetics" and rooted in a non-Native paradigm (Wax, Wax, & Dumont, 1989). Moreover, ethnic identity is "not only a blood quantum or lineage relationship, but more specifically, a relationship of sociocultural affiliation, embedded in reciprocal recognition" (Peregoy, 1993, p. 166). Such ambiguity affects not only Native self-perceptions but also non-Native perceptions of Natives.

Native male youth experience not only the identity crises of adolescence (e.g., personal, career, and sexual) but also those of an ethnic identity. In addition, Native youth are often pressured to ignore traditional ways and assimilate into mainstream culture. For example, a Native male student's family may emphasize traditional values, whereas at school, teachers consciously or unconsciously reinforce the values of mainstream society. This conflict can result in feelings of low self-worth, frustration, alienation, and hopelessness (LaFromboise, 1988).

From an early age, traditional Native children acquire skills specific to their sex, and they receive most of the training they will need as adults during their first 10 years of life (Garrett & Garrett, 1994). In the traditional pattern, small males hone their hunting ability by observing their fathers, uncles, and older brothers, and by tracking small game themselves. They often present their first kills to old men, asking in return for prayers that will make them brave. Generally, males eschew dolls and prefer toys such as slingshots, stilts, darts, and tops that develop the quickness and coordination needed for hunting and warfare.

Native male children typically have tremendous freedom. A Sioux father, for example, might craft miniature bows, arrows, and quivers for his son and instruct him in their use. Sioux male youth play games emphasizing endurance, strength, and the ability to withstand pain. As soon as the child can straddle a small horse's back, he is given a pony or colt of his own to ride and look after.

Early morning swims in frigid waters are a common toughening stratagem used by many tribes. In the coldest part of the winter, Apache male children are ordered to jump into the river and then told to warm themselves by shouting (Boyer, 1979). Another procedure used by the Apache is to throw a male child naked into the snow and make him run. Once his circulation is high, he is asked to hold chunks of snow in his hands until they melt.

Childhood for traditional Native male youth typically ends after youngsters reach 10 years of age. With puberty comes another round of ceremony and increased responsibility. The Native male child has been prepared for his adult role. Few tribes celebrate the end of this happy time as the male youth begins to face the multiple crises of contemporary Native life.

STEREOTYPES AND AMBIGUOUS TERMINOLOGY

Helping professionals must avoid stereotypes by recognizing individual uniqueness. Some Native male youth have very traditional values, whereas others blend traditions with mainstream culture. A male student who does not reflect the physical stereotype of how a Native should look may easily be misidentified. He may appear Anglicized externally while remaining traditional internally.

Helping professionals must reject the stereotype of Native male students as being passive, withdrawn, and unexpressive (Herring, 1997a, 1997b). Although these qualities may describe the behavior of some, they are not typical of all Native male students, particularly nontraditional Native males. In settings where verbal interaction, assertiveness, and competitiveness are valued, however, traditional Native male students may be at a disadvantage.

Ambiguous terminology is a cogent area of stereotyping. The use of multiple labels of designation confounds Native male youths' difficulties with their ethnic identity. As suggested previously, the optimal designation is tribal affiliation. In addition, the extreme diversity of Native peoples merits individual recognition. Just as Native American Indians are stereotyped as the Plains Sioux, Alaska Natives are stereotyped as Eskimos (Inuits). Because insensitive aspects are embedded in both designations, tribal names are the most appropriate identifying labels.

DIVERSE CULTURATION

Native diversity is expressed in a full range of culturation (LaFromboise, Trimble, & Mohatt, 1990). The helping professional must initially determine the youth's degree of culturation to interact appropriately. For example, Herring (1997a, 1997b) divided Native families into four main groups. The *traditional* family attempts to adhere to culturally defined styles of living. Family members generally speak and think in their Native language and practice traditional ways. They prefer isolation from non-Natives and mainstream society. The *transitional* family retains only rudimentary elements of traditional life, preferring to live within the mainstream culture. The members generally speak both their Native language and English. This family does not fully accept the cultural heritage of its tribal group or fully identify with the mainstream culture. The *bicultural* family is generally accepted by dominant society. Family members simultaneously know, accept, and practice both value systems. The *assimilated* family is accepted by the dominant society, and family members embrace only mainstream values.

VALUE CONFLICTS

Although Native tribes are not identical, some unifying cultural values contrast with those of mainstream society. The following examples are not exhaustive, but they illustrate how traditional values differ from mainstream values. Neither are they intended to apply to all Natives because of individual diversity. Although counselors should avoid stereotyping any group and recognize that substantial within-group differences exist, some generalizations can be made about traditional Native male youth and mainstream male youth. Traditional Native male youth conflict with mainstream values in the relationship of humans to nature. Whereas middle-class European Americans emphasize control over nature, Native cultures believe in harmony with nature. Time orientation represents another area of conflict. Native cultures are oriented to the present, whereas mainstream society maintains a future orientation. Other conflicts include Native emphasis on cooperation, a being-in-becoming mode of activity, and a view of the nature of humankind as generally good. Mainstream society values competition, doing, and a view of the nature of humankind as both good and bad. The helping professional must understand that cultural clashes are inevitable for traditional Native male youth.

INCIDENCE OF SUICIDE

The second leading cause of death for Natives is suicide. Natives have the highest rate of completed suicide of any ethnic group, with age as a major risk factor. For Natives ages 10-24, the rates are nearly three times as high as rates for the total population, and suicide occurs predominantly among male members, with an age-adjusted completion rate of 24 per 100,000 (May, 1989). Suicide attempts by Native male adolescents are less frequent but more lethal than those of female adolescents (Howard-Pitney, LaFromboise, Basil, September, & Johnson, 1992). Suicide rates differ tribally, with lower rates among the tribes of the Southwest. Alcohol abuse contributes to suicidal behavior, with 80% of Native American Indian suicide attempters also having alcohol abuse problems (LaFromboise et al., 1990).

Suicidal behavior and ideation are resisted in most tribes (LaFromboise & Howard-Pitney, 1994). For example, the Tohono O'odham (Papago) consider these behaviors as evil or a sign of possession by bad spirits (Kahn, Lejero, Antone, Francisco, & Manuel, 1988). The Navajo believe that to ponder death is to invite it; therefore, a Navajo male youth willing to respond to questions about suicidal ideation is in actuality seeking help. Referrals for help from youth who later complete suicide are few because of the implied taint on the family (Kahn et al., 1988; LaFromboise & Howard-Pitney, 1994).

ISSUES OF SEXUALITY

Traditional Native children learn by observing and participating; thus they are reared with minimal direct sexual education by parents and elders. They may even be encouraged to experiment with sex-related activities with their brothers, sisters, and cousins. Partly because of the extended family and partly because of the male's traditional role as a hunter whose work took him outside the home, open displays of affection between males and females are rare even after marriage. Some men follow traditions of treating women as inferior, reluctance to have close interpersonal contacts, and same-sex nonkin social gatherings (Ho, 1992).

Masturbation among Native male children is strongly disapproved of but in most instances not censured. Traditional Apache male children's sexual explorations with girls are treated with tolerance and amusement, although the children engaging in them are told they are being bad. Later, they will be expected to conquer girls sexually; during their teens and later, they will sometimes be challenged to prove their manhood by sexual servicing of old women (Boyer, 1979).

Traditional Natives do not associate nudity and sexual intercourse with sin as many non-Natives do. In fact, many aspects of sexuality and reproduction have spiritual meaning that is reflected in puberty rites. For example, Apache children do much of their exploration in the outhouse/bathroom, to which they go with other children of both sexes. Their excited giggles are ignored by adults (Roscoe, 1994).

Homosexuality has been widely accepted by traditional Native tribes. For example, more than half of 225 interviewed tribes accepted male homosexuality, and 17% accepted female homosexuality (Roscoe, 1994). Many tribes (e.g., Zuni, Navajo, and Crow) also recognize a "third gender," known as *berdache*. Male berdaches have been documented in 150 Native societies; half of these groups also had female berdaches. Children with berdache tendencies receive special encouragement, and adult berdaches whose interests and abilities extend beyond customary gender-role behaviors usually demonstrate exceptional productivity and talent that the whole community respects (Roscoe, 1994). Sexual patterns may involve heterosexual, bisexual, or homosexual relationships, including same-sex marriages (Roscoe, 1994).

Although 81% of all adult male Natives with AIDS engage in same-sex eroticism, the social rejection that typifies "coming out" in other cultures may not be an issue for gay Natives. In certain tribes, concepts of gender are not dichotomized. The berdache may function as a "sexual outlet" for members who are without access to sex, such as men whose wives are pregnant and women without partners (Tafoya, 1989). Men who have sex with a berdache are not considered gay by either themselves or their tribes.

One disturbing aspect of Native sexuality issues is the sexual abuse of children. Child sexual abuse is compounded both by a reluctance within the community to openly discuss sexual abuse problems and by jurisdictional issues that can lead to difficulty in the arrest and prosecution of child molesters (Trottier, 1989). For example, in one small Alaskan village, one third of the children were described as neglected, abused, or homeless (Piasecki, Manson, & Biernoff, 1989).

Factors contributing to child abuse in Native homes include the cultural breakdowns that ended many traditional ways of life, the disappearance of many spiritual ceremonies, the removal of male leadership from the community by the federal government, and the weakened power of tribes to enforce Native methods of discipline (Trottier, 1989). Additional factors include marital disruption, parental alcoholism, chronic physical illness, inadequate caregiver-child bonding, severe educational deficits, and intergenerational conflicts (Piasecki et al., 1989).

Traditional Native male youth may manifest difficulties with their sexual identity. Media portrayals of violence and promiscuity as the norm conflict with Native values of being respectful and private about sex (Trottier, 1989). Today's Native males display a high degree of unconscious confusion of sexual identity.

SPIRITUALITY AND FAMILY LIFE

Traditional Natives regard spirituality as an integral part of tribal life. The Native male child is introduced early to spirituality as the tribe transmits a loving respect for nature, independence, and self-discipline (Ho, 1992). Because basic parental disciplinary roles are shared among several generations, biological parents have the opportunity to engage in fun activities with their children. Native male children experience intense, warm maternal care that generates a strong sense of security in them.

Traditional Native spirituality blends with the belief of being in harmony with nature. Thomason (1995) describes the Native perspective on mental health as a need for balance in all domains of the individual's life—social and community, spiritual, and right living. This whole cannot be divided into its parts. For example, the integration of the Four Directions (i.e., North, South, East, and West) with spiritual wholeness is simplistic yet profound. Many tribes interpret these directions as pathways to harmony and balance.

INTERGENERATIONAL CONFLICT

Two factors are prime in occurrence of intergenerational conflict: (a) degree of Native culturation and (b) influences of mainstream peers in acculturated settings (e.g., schools). As Native children mature, their mainstream culturation is in sharp contrast to the highly visible characteristics of their parents, creating even more generational separation, resulting in an enormous loss of family traditions and connections (Coleman, 1991). For example, the historical group identity of the Apache male, still retained by the older two or three generations, is that of the hunter, warrior, and horseman. In present reservation life, however, this identity is counterproductive to Apache male youth (Boyer, 1979). The desire to be accepted by non-Natives frequently leads to behaviors that contradict parental and tribal mores.

STRATEGIES FOR RAPPORT ESTABLISHMENT

The goal of most helping paradigms is to create a dialogue of growth with individuals. Embedded in this goal is the recognition of cultural and environmental influences. To accomplish this task, the helper must develop an open-mindedness toward Native individuals' worldview (LaFromboise et al., 1990).

AVOID PRECONCEPTIONS

The helping professional must avoid preconceptions about the presenting problems of Native male youth, many of whom will not have a clear understanding of counseling or how it can help. School counselors have more opportunities to orient Native male students to counseling than do private or agency professionals. School counselors can learn about students' needs and orient them to counseling precepts concurrently by having informal conversations in social situations or a drop-in policy. Native male students can socialize with other students, have access to career information, and talk with the counselor informally (Thomason, 1995).

OBTAINING INFORMATION

The helping professional may benefit by rethinking the nature of counseling (Thomason, 1995). For example, if the goal of counseling is to help Native male youth meet their needs, then intense talk about personal problems is not needed. In addition, Native male youth's residence (reservation or urban), level of culturation, specific tribal customs, and language spoken in the home deserve to be elicited immediately (Garrett & Garrett, 1994; Heinrich, Corbine, & Thomas, 1990, Herring, 1997a, 1997b). The most appropriate approach to acquiring information is a gentle, noninvasive one with few direct questions (Thomason, 1995).

GAINING TRUST AND RESPECT

To gain trust and respect, the helping professional must be attentive and responsive, give direction to the process, and display respect for values. Helping professionals can become involved in activities oriented to learning about tribal culture and its influences on the lives of their clients. Such behavior demonstrates an interest in the client and enhances the establishment of rapport. Showing respect also can increase the possibility of gaining a consultation. "Linking" services of traditional healers with traditional counseling can be very effective because it displays respect for traditions while offering a more comprehensive service to traditional Native male youth (Garrett & Garrett, 1994).

Another way of demonstrating respect for Native culture is to encourage the participation of the extended family in the therapeutic process. Traditional Native male youth are socialized in the presence of groups. Giving youth a choice about how to proceed with the process and encouraging the participation of family members reflects components of the traditional healing way (Garrett & Garrett, 1994).

Negative societal influences experienced by many of these youth may produce a high degree of alienation by adolescence. The psychological helplessness and increasing sense of hopelessness these circumstances create may serve to further alienate the youth. Helping professionals will understand this potential attitude and be prepared for its manifestation in the helping session.

CULTURALLY AFFIRMATIVE ENVIRONMENT

A final suggestion for establishing rapport is to ensure a culturally affirmative environment. Despite pressure from the dominant culture to conform, many Native male adolescents have learned to survive by becoming functionally bicultural. This cultural fluency has implications in the light of suggestions from some practitioners that counselors "go Native" when counseling (Eldridge, 1993).

A good initial session is vital to a successful counseling relationship with Native male youth. These youth will evaluate the total presentation of the helping professional (e.g., manner of greeting, nonverbal behaviors, appearance, and ethnicity). The helping professional must demonstrate knowledge of Native culture within the first few minutes of the session if respect and trust are to be gained.

If a non-Native helper attempts to use Native practices (e.g., burning herbs or wearing Native jewelry and clothing), traditional Native male youth may be offended. They may view these pseudo-Native practices with distrust or disdain (Eldridge, 1993). Similar recommendations that helpers dress informally and that women helpers use subtle makeup may also lead to negative perceptions. For example, one study that included counselor dress as a variable in client perceptions of empathy, warmth, and genuineness indicated that bicultural Native students may perceive such "dressing down" negatively (LaFromboise et al., 1990). These youths' ability to survive biculturally alerts them to mainstream values of professional dress.

Arguments have been made for the superiority of Native counselors to non-Native counselors in working with Native students (e.g., Herring, 1997a; LaFromboise, 1988). Trustworthiness, however, has been identified as a more significant variable in school counselor effectiveness than ethnicity. Native underuse of mental health services is often associated with the tension surrounding power differentials in counseling relationships and perceived conflicting goals between counselors and clients (LaFromboise et al., 1990).

Additional guidelines to aid helping professionals to provide a culturally affirmative environment include the following (Herring, 1994b, 1997a):

1. *Address openly the issue of ethnic relationships rather than pretending that no differences exist.* The client will perceive the helper as sensitive and aware of the tensions, as well as being open to discussing them without defensiveness.
2. *Evaluate the degree of culturation of the client.* The helper can use cues from dress, family and tribal involvement, friendship patterns, body language, and degree of eye contact.
3. *Schedule appointments to allow for flexibility in ending the session.* Traditional Natives prefer open-ended sessions to ensure closure to the presenting problem without time constraints.
4. *Be open to allowing other family members to participate in the counseling session.* Perhaps sessions can be held in the home environment, or, when working on a reservation, in the helper's car. Consultations with healers and elders should be accepted if they are requested.
5. *Allow time for trust to develop before focusing immediately on deeper feelings.* The helper should allow time to "warm up," talking about common interests or other neutral topics, before focusing on counseling issues. The first session should be extended.
6. *Use helping strategies that elicit practical solutions to problems.* The helper can take an active role in "joining" with the client to work together to solve a

problem. Nondirective approaches, however, may allow self-exploration and self-generated goals. A blend of techniques using myth and metaphor may be considered as an alternative to straight talk-therapy.

7. *Maintain eye contact as appropriate.* Even if the client avoids eye contact (as a culturally appropriate behavior), the helper may maintain eye contact (without staring).

8. *Respect the uses of silence.* Silence may signal the onset of a disclosure or the processing of deep thought. Nonproductive silence, or "waiting out the client," is not recommended.

9. *Demonstrate honor and respect for the client's culture(s).* Helping professionals need to be very aware of when their own values are having an impact. A strong emotional response (either positive or negative) to the client or session content indicates that this probably is the case.

10. *Maintain the highest level of confidentiality.* Native communities are extremely close. If confidentiality is betrayed, this will become known and destroy the helper's credibility.

PREVENTIVE AND REMEDIAL COUNSELING STRATEGIES

Below, I present several intervention approaches as prototypes in the further development, delivery, and evaluation of culturally sensitive approaches aimed at helping Native male youth overcome multiple and frequently conflicting concerns.

PROACTIVE PERSPECTIVE

The realities of Native male youth have been reiterated throughout this chapter. Effective counseling with this population is predicated on a proactive developmental perspective (Herring, 1997a, 1997b, 1997c). Helping professionals must be aware of the attitudes and customs particular to their own ethnic and cultural heritage and be knowledgeable about alternatives in a Native male youth's background, both self-disclosed and revealed from other sources. In this regard, the helping professional's goal is to uncover, respect, and learn to understand differences in culture, community, and experience (Herring, 1994b, 1997a, 1997b).

MAINSTREAM THEORETICAL OR SYNERGETIC PRECEPTS

Western counseling theories create numerous complications when they are applied to Native male youth. The techniques are founded on models heavily influenced by experiences of European American male theorists who acquired their training in institutions that mirror classic European traditions: The emergence and growth of counseling theory has been culturally encapsulated.

Helping professionals must develop strategies to modify the effects of political and socioeconomic forces on Native male youth. They also may need to become systemic change agents, intervening in environments that impede the development of Native male youth. For examples, school counselors can encourage curricular revision to include the impact of environment on Native male youths' behavior. They can also encourage tribes to assume an active role in providing adequate services.

The most appropriate theoretical approach to take in counseling with Native male youth is debatable; few outcome studies have been conducted with this population (Thomason, 1995). LaFromboise and colleagues (1990) have discovered strengths and weaknesses with person-centered, social learning, and behavioral models of counseling. Those researchers suggest the use of network therapy to be consistent with traditional Native community-oriented guidance systems. Network therapy represents the use of an integrated synergetic approach (Herring, 1997a, 1997b).

The first step is to meet the Native male youth as an individual and build rapport, patiently and without intrusive questioning. The client should be allowed to control the pace and, to some degree, the content of the conversation. A practical problem-solving approach to the presenting concern usually is more helpful than strictly psychodynamic, person-centered, behavior or a cognitive approach.

Traditional Native healing practices are gradually being incorporated into current approaches to mental health treatment. In particular, two such practices have demonstrated therapeutic effectiveness: (a) the four "circles"—concentric circles of relationship between client and Creator, spouse, and extended family as a culturally based structural concept of self-understanding; and (b) the "talking circle"—a forum for expressing thoughts and feelings in an environment of total acceptance without time constraints, using sacred objects, the pipe, and prayer.

Traditional healing systems utilized cultural metaphors to construct the illness reality and then symbolically manipulate it to effect healing. The use of metaphors allows helpers to tap into a world of symbolic language that is familiar to Native male youth. Helpers, however, must identify what these metaphors are within the Native male youth's reality. Familiarity with traditional healing practices can provide access to those metaphors.

One example of the use of metaphors is seen in the vision quest, which can be creatively incorporated into individual treatment strategies or integrated with ongoing treatment programs (Heinrich et al., 1990). Numerous education programs have used wilderness experiences in helping troubled adolescents to reduce rage, depression, and tension, and to develop a more positive self-concept. These experiences are similar to the vision quest without its cultural spiritualism. If the professional is concerned with helping a counselee find his purpose, the vision quest is an important, relevant metaphor (Heinrich et al., 1990).

Another example is the use of the sweatlodge as a metaphor in group work (Garrett & Osborne, 1995). Regardless of their versatility, helping professionals must remember the following limitations in therapeutic metaphors (Bowman, 1995):

1. Build metaphors from facts rather than from personal interpretations.
2. Accept that metaphors may be difficult to create spontaneously during the session.
3. Recognize the possibility of attacks by some organized religious groups and individuals for using New Age approaches (e.g., imagery, guided fantasy, and other relaxation techniques).
4. Do not impose metaphors into the natural flow of group processes.

In their pursuit of understanding Native cultures, persons outside these cultures must not be deluded by commercial efforts in shamanism (the belief that individuals, acting as mediums, may be able to summon good and evil spirits), vision quests, or sweatlodge bathing. Such commercial ventures aim to train instant medicine healers who can be injurious to non-Native participants as well as to Natives themselves (Dufrene & Coleman, 1992).

WITHIN-GROUP VARIANCES

Many Native male youth exist as both Natives and as non-Natives, trying to retain their traditional values but seeking as well to live in the dominant culture. This dualistic life increases the developmental stress on these youth. Within-group variances negate the treating of these youth homogeneously. Effective helping requires professionals to recognize a minimum of three within-group variances: cultural commitment, use of humor, and view of seeking counseling.

Cultural commitment. The historical idea of cultural assimilation as a solution to the so-called Indian problem remains untenable (Herring, 1989). "In general, Native peoples do not wish to be assimilated into the dominant culture. Over 62% of the Native population do not live on 'Indian land' " (U.S. Bureau of the Census, 1993). This physical separation from reservation culture has resulted in a varied degree of commitment to tribal customs and values. Natives are a people of many peoples whose diversity is played out in a variety of customs, languages, and family types (Garrett & Garrett, 1994). This diversity exists not only between members of different tribes but also among members within a single tribe.

The helping professional needs to be cautious of making assumptions about the cultural orientation of Native male youth. The continuum of culturation found in Native youth was presented earlier. Like members of other ethnicities, Native male youth wish to be recognized as individual people, as human beings, not as a category (Ho, 1992).

Use of humor. Contrary to the stereotype of Natives as solemn, stoic figures poised against a backdrop of tepees, horses, and headdresses or as fur-wrapped Eskimos in front of an igloo, the fact is that they love to laugh. Native peoples find humor important in cooperation, in reaffirming bonds of kinship, in relieving stress, and in creating an atmosphere of connectedness (Garrett & Garrett, 1994).

From the use of the clown motif in rituals to the use of practical jokes, humor is a prominent feature of Native culture (Herring, 1994a). Native humor is unique in its pragmatic observation of the obvious and the use of exaggeration. Natives understand the importance of not taking oneself too seriously, and humor prevents people from being too submerged in themselves and their problems. Caution is advised in using humor very discreetly (e.g., Herring & Meggert, 1993).

View of seeking counseling. Native value systems encourage a family or individual in difficulty to be reluctant to seek help. Many tribes believe that mental illness is a justifiable outcome of human weakness or the result of avoiding the discipline necessary to maintain cultural values (Herring, 1999). Research indicates that traditional Natives seldom look to non-Native counseling as a means of improving their way of life (LaFromboise, 1988). They recognize the need for professionals only when community networks are unavailable or undesirable.

Culturally sensitive professionals will recognize that traditional Native male youth have had little if any contact with mental health professionals. Tribe members may distrust non-Native personnel because of experiences of discrimination. Native families might exhibit variety in their attempts to assist members, and diverse family types may have different help-seeking patterns (Ho, 1992).

The varied family types do not imply a total erosion of cultural values. Many Native core values are retained, regardless of family type (e.g., Lewis & Ho, 1989). The traditional Native family is an extended network that includes several households, as well as grandparents, aunts, uncles, or nonkin persons. A nonkin person becomes a family member by being a namesake of a child and consequently assumes the responsibilities of child rearing and role modeling.

When a family needs help, the extended family network is the first source to be contacted. Second, a spiritual leader may be consulted to resolve problems. Third, if the problem is unresolved, then the family will contact tribal elders. Last, when all these fail, the family may seek help from mainstream options. Consequently, the counselor must recognize that the Native family seeking help from a professional may have experienced a series of frustrated attempts to resolve the problem. Also, the family may feel awkward during initial contacts with a professional, particularly if he or she is a non-Native. Remaining sensitive to these issues is a key to successful family work.

CONTENT AND PROCESS CONCERNS

Successful helping often hinges on understanding traditional belief systems and on being able to incorporate them into helping strategies. Helpers may need to become familiar with content and process concerns when working with Native male youth as well (Herring, 1990). *Content* concerns include worldview differences and the special needs and unique problems of Native male youth, whereas *process* concerns include varied levels of culturation and differences in SES.

CONDUCTING THE
SYNERGETIC HELPING SESSION

Synergetic helping involves selecting the most appropriate technique for the Native male youth in the present situation, with regard for environmental and historical influences (Herring, 1996, 1997c; Herring & Walker, 1993). No single paradigm can be applied to these male youth. Helping professionals must rely on content knowledge and a repertoire of appropriate process skills.

Although meager data support the following thesis, traditional healers in Native communities most likely exemplify empathy, genuineness, availability, respect, warmth, congruence, and concreteness (Trimble et al., 1996). Effective helping begins when a helper carefully attends to these basic characteristics. The helping professional integrates these interpersonal skills as the session continues, along with recognizing the following influences.

USE OF ORAL TRADITION

In helping activities, oral tradition can be integrated easily with the Native respect for elders. Community and tribal leaders can be effective resources in sharing customs and the "old way" through oral histories. Oral histories and legends can also be an important adjunct to school guidance activities.

For example, almost every tribe has tales of the trickster—a coyote, a spider, a raven, a mink, a hare, a blue jay, or an undefined being. The trickster is a slippery character, an ambiguous shape-shifter loaded with natural energy. As a fool but yet a feared character, the trickster reflects the ambivalent relationships that Natives have with one another (Boyer, 1979; Deloria, 1994). Not only does the trickster defy the flesh-and-blood limits of animal identity, but he also refuses to mirror mainstream society's worldview. Stupid and wise, reviled and respected, dangerous and clownish, the trickster reveals that the world is confusing and contradicting (Deloria, 1994).

Natives traditionally used such mythical and spiritual symbols in their efforts to instill values in their children. By telling stories and recounting legends, adults continually reiterated tribal values and instructed the children in appropriate behavior. Helping professionals could consider incorporating such oral traditions in their interventions. For example, the incongruencies between Native and mainstream values and ideologies can be illustrated with the trickster symbol.

USE OF MEDIA RESOURCES

Helping professionals also can use media resources in their interventions. Authentic and bias-free resources are available that depict Native art, crafts, music, and historical traditions. These materials can be obtained by contacting BIA offices, tribal organizations, and federal and state offices of Indian education. Media resources can improve non-Native perspectives as well as expand Native male youths' views about other tribes. Both Native and non-Native male youth can also benefit by vicariously experiencing "the Indian way." The helper, however, must be alert to avoid generalizing a particular presentation to all Native groups (Herring, 1994b).

PRACTICALITY

Native male youth are influenced by several cultures, and to classify them rigidly establishes yet another prejudicial system and contributes to a variation of oppression (Peregoy, 1993). Research indicates that Native male youth desire a counselor who understands the practical aspects of tribal culture and conveys sound advice. Peregoy (1993) concluded that although ethnically and culturally similar helpers are not necessary, these youth prefer helpers who possess an awareness of Native historical and current relationships with non-Natives, some specific tribal knowledge, an understanding of Native family patterns, and cultural sensitivity.

Many traditional Native male youth may view helping professionals as elders, expecting them to be more verbal than most European American youth do. Peregoy (1993) suggested that helping professionals briefly discuss the helping process, emphasize the importance of confidentiality, and describe a typical session. This action may enhance trust and indicate the expected roles.

Most Native male youth will experience discomfort with the demand for self-disclosure or with intrusive questioning (Herring, 1994b). The helper may make the youth more comfortable by initially modeling self-disclosure and then ask for reciprocity. A Native male youth who seeks assistance from an indigenous healer looks to the healer to identify the cause of the problem and work the cures (Peregoy, 1993). A helping professional must demonstrate patience, exemplified by not offering advice or interpretation without being invited to do so. At the same time, options must be described and solutions suggested, albeit with the realization that the youth himself may know or discover what is best to be done (Garrett & Garrett, 1994).

COMMUNICATION STYLE

The helping process, by its very nature, tends to be primarily verbal. Some Native male youth may feel uncomfortable if pressured to self-disclose personal concerns. The goal is not necessarily to get Native male youth to talk but to allow them the freedom to talk or not talk, as they wish. Such leeway increases the potential for trust and rapport.

GROUP WORK

Group work may be the most valuable approach to take with Native male students (Dufrene & Coleman, 1992). Two relevant topics are values clarification and cultural conflict resolution (Thomason, 1995). Note the following guidelines:

1. Ask group members to introduce themselves by describing their family background.

2. In dyads, ask group members to describe themselves in terms of what they like to do for fun.
3. Discuss how group members are different from non-Native students.
4. Use values clarification to stimulate discussion about different values.
5. Discuss the strengths of traditional culture and the conformity to non-Native ways.

Group work with Native male youth has been effective in teaching new behaviors and skills, especially with social cognitive strategies (LaFromboise, 1988). Social cognitive strategies reduce the emphasis on individual disclosure and introduce collective responsibility, responding to the collective approach characteristic of many tribes (LaFromboise & Graff Low, 1989).

Helping professionals need to recognize the influences that mainstream culture may have on the Native male's self-deprecating and irrational belief system (LaFromboise & Graff Low, 1989). Beliefs that are irrational by standards of the dominant culture may be perfectly legitimate given the historical experiences between Native and non-Natives (Herring, 1997a). For example, mistrust of the educational system may be rooted in mistrust based in assimilationist policy.

Dufrene and Coleman (1992) emphasize that helping professionals can best serve Native youth by using traditional Native spiritual dimensions in group work. These authors recommend that group sessions should begin and end with a prayer that would be acceptable to represented tribes. A prayer acknowledges that higher powers play a role in physical and mental happiness.

GUIDED IMAGERY

Another culturally appropriate technique is the use of guided imagery (Peregoy, 1993). For example, a Native male adolescent comes to a counselor's office with concerns related to self-concept. Guided imagery can direct the youth to visualize himself as he perceives himself to be and then have him visualize how he would like to be ideally. Once this is done, steps are developed, with the assistance of the counselor, to work toward the goal of improved self-image.

NONCLINICAL SETTINGS

School counselors have a greater opportunity to interact and facilitate growth with this population. They need to adhere to the same helping suggestions as other professionals do. Their helping processes generally emphasize developmental and educational concerns rather than mental health per se. Two major needs in educational settings are communication and bilingual needs.

Communication with parents. A primary need in schools is communication with Native parents. Little Bear (1988) identifies several reasons for this need. First, most teachers/counselors are non-Native and reflect monocultural training. Even if they are

Native, teachers may be urban and have little or no knowledge about reservation life. In addition, Native teachers/counselors from reservations may have accepted the values of mainstream society as being superior to those of Natives. The lack of curriculum materials that are tribally specific is another reason for parental collaboration in the learning process. Finally, Native male students are often judged in relation to historical circumstances not of their making, and these judgments have to be eradicated.

Little Bear (1988) recommends that educational personnel should avoid displaying a "savior" complex. They need to be aware of tribal/linguistic differences and not rely on preconceived stereotypes. Students should be introduced, at an early age, to alternatives to alcohol and drug use. These students should not be deliberately shamed because many tribes use shame as a discipline measure.

Parents also have a responsibility in the development of their children. They are the first educators of their children and must instill in them the need for education. Two aspects of a self-concept that become important when dealing with children not born in the dominant culture are a sense of belonging and a feeling of worth. Both need to be established prior to school enrollment.

Bilingual language needs. A second major need in schools is accommodating the bilingual needs of Native male youth. Subtractive educational programs seek to replace Native language with English, resulting in the failure of many Native students (also called pushouts). Additive educational programs teach English along with the Native language, creating the conditions for school success.

In addition, parents need to communicate in the language in which they are most fluent. The child benefits if each parent uses his or her own language. The child who learns little or none of the Native language and only "Indian English" at home is very much disadvantaged.

An illustration of how ideas and suggestions mentioned in this chapter can be integrated into helping interventions is presented in the following vignette:

C. H., a 10-year-old Cherokee boy, resided at a BIA boarding school during the week and spent weekends with his family. C. H.'s 5-year-old sister had fallen into a ditch over the summer and had suffered irreversible spinal damage. During the third month of school, C. H.'s teachers and dormitory monitors reported that he was extremely quiet and cried frequently.

The school counselor made a referral to a local Native mental health clinic. Both C. H. and his mother were seen. C. H. spoke of frequent dreams of dead kin since his sister's injury and admitted to hearing the voices of a dead sister asking him to join her. He admitted to loss of appetite, difficulty in sleeping, and fears of spirits who were after him. The mother, school counselor, and one dormitory aide were educated about the expression of bereavement and depression in childhood, and all were encouraged to aid C. H. in talking about his feelings. The therapist, aware of the taboo against talking about the dead, encouraged C. H. to draw pictures as a channel for ventilating his feelings. A traditional medicine man ceremony was held by the family, and C. H. was given antidepressant medication as he began ego-supportive therapy. His symptoms gradually remitted over a period of 6 months.

<u>CONCLUSION</u>

Effective counseling with Native male youth is predicated on adopting a proactive developmental perspective (Herring, 1991, 1997a, 1999). This view would include acquiring a thorough knowledge of past and current Native culture and history. It would also entail having an expanded understanding of these youth.

Helping professionals need to adopt strategies to modify the effects of political and socioeconomic forces on Native male youth. They also need to become systemic change agents, intervening in environments that impede development. In schools, for example, counselors can demonstrate the impact of cultural environment on Native male youths' behavior.

Helping professionals must integrate new information in their therapeutic interactions and continually seek to expand their knowledge base (e.g., through workshops) to enhance helping efforts with both traditional and nontraditional Native male youth. If helping professionals are to be prepared to face the challenges of Native male youth, their training programs will need to address those issues. In many situations, however, the trainers themselves are not willing or qualified to train students for multicultural counseling, especially with specific ethnic groups. Training programs must become introspective and challenge educators to ensure their credibility in this endeavor.

HIGHLIGHTS OF CHAPTER 8

▶ The Native population of nearly 2 million people consists of a wide variety of Native American Indians and Alaska Natives who are incredibly diverse in terms of their family patterns, customs, and languages.

▶ Native American male youth continue to suffer from the effects of centuries of oppression of and discrimination against Native peoples.

▶ Of all Native male youth, 60% have mixed ancestry Native and non-Native bloodlines. Consequently, most male youth with Native ancestry have multiple ethnic identities.

▶ Helping professionals must reject the stereotype of Native male students as being passive, withdrawn, and unexpressive.

▶ Native families can be categorized according to their degree of culturation. Traditional families adhere to tribal customs and prefer isolation from non-Natives. Transitional families neither fully accept the heritage of their tribal group nor identify with mainstream culture. Bicultural families practice traditions of both tribal and non-Native societies. The assimilated family is accepted by the dominant society and accepts only mainstream values.

▶ Native values—such as harmony with nature, a future orientation, cooperation, a being-in-becoming mode of activity, and a view of human nature as good—conflict with the mainstream values of emphasizing the present, competition, doing, and a view of human nature as both good and bad.

▶ Among Natives, suicide is the second leading cause of death. It occurs predominantly among males and usually is linked to alcohol abuse.

▶ Sexual norms of Natives differ greatly from those of non-Natives. Traditional Native children are encouraged to experiment sexually. Traditional Natives do not associate nudity and sexual intercourse with sin, as do many non-Natives. Homosexuality has been widely accepted by many Native tribes.

▶ Child sexual abuse is a serious issue among Native peoples and is believed to be linked to the weakened power of the tribal society, marital disruption, alcoholism, chronic physical illness, educational deficits, and intergenerational conflicts.

▶ Culturation of Native male youth to the mainstream contributes to intergenerational conflicts in Native families.

▶ Counselors can establish trust, respect, and rapport with Native male youth by avoiding preconceptions about Native youth; obtaining information about the client's cultural preferences, including the extended family in the helping process; and providing a culturally affirmative environment.

▶ Using indigenous healing practices (such as wilderness-based or vision quest experiences) and humor tends to enhance the effectiveness of problem-solving approaches with Native male youth.

▶ In a synergetic approach to counseling, the helper selects the most appropriate technique for the Native male youth in the present situation. Common techniques include the use of oral traditions, legends, and biased-free media resources concerning Native people and customs; dispensing practical advice on tribally related matters; providing the client the freedom to talk or not talk; group work; and guided imagery.

▶ In school settings, it is imperative that counselors collaborate with Native parents in the child's learning process and respond to the bilingual needs of Native male children.

9

Counseling Non-Hispanic
White Boys

K. LYNN POWELL
MARK S. KISELICA
ALLISON CUNNINGHAM
WENDY SABIN

One of the most perplexing conundrums about discussions of culture and counseling pertains to how one should talk about and treat Caucasian boys of non-Hispanic, European ancestry who reside in the United States. For starters, there is no simple way to either categorize or label this population. Although many demographers refer to this population as "Whites," such a labeling clearly is inadequate for discussions of culture because large numbers of Hispanics consider themselves to be "White" but culturally different from other Whites who are non-Hispanic and because there is great cultural variability among the tens of millions of Whites who are non-Hispanic. With regard to the latter, Axelson (1999) has observed that the cultural heritage of the early, White settlers of the United States from Great Britain merged with that of other early Northern European settlers from Sweden, Norway, Denmark, Finland, Holland, and Germany to create an American, Anglo-Saxon culture that has dominated the mainstream values and traditions of this country. Axelson notes, however, that many millions of other White peoples—such as Czechs, Greeks, Hungarians, Irish Catholics, Italians, Poles, Portuguese, Russians, Slovaks, and Jews from several European nations—who immigrated to the United States during the 1800s and throughout the 20th century were different in terms of their religious and cultural life from the ancestors of the early settlers. Consequently, these latter immigrants did not assimilate as readily into the American Anglo-Saxon culture and so have remained somewhat distinct in terms of their respective cultural heritages.

Axelson argues, therefore, that any consideration of culture and counseling that pertains to non-Hispanic White Americans should reflect these variations in cultural heritage.

Unfortunately, most of the counseling literature ignores the cultural diversity of non-Hispanic Whites as a factor to consider during the counseling process. This practice is problematic because it fosters the simplistic assumption that all White clients should be counseled the same way. The legion of Whites residing in our multicultural nation, however, hail from a vast array of cultures that color the many different ways in which White, non-Hispanic Americans perceive the world. For example, the respective world-views of a third-generation Irish American boy and a Jewish American boy raised in an Orthodox Jewish community are likely to be different from each other and have unique influences on how each boy approaches life and interprets experience.

To illustrate these differences, consider the subject of intercultural dating as an issue in counseling with both these boys. The Irish American boy is most likely to be comfortable and successful with this practice because intercultural dating and marriage are permissible practices among third-generation Irish Americans (see Fallows, 1979). In comparison, the Orthodox Jewish American boy probably would be hesitant to date any girl who is not Jewish because of strong Jewish cultural prohibitions against courting gentiles (see Rosen & Weltman, 1996). A well-intentioned counselor who supports the idea of intercultural dating but is not attuned to the cultural diversity among Whites may encourage both boys to forge ahead with initiating dates with culturally different girls. This naive stance could set up the Jewish boy for conflicts with his parents. Clearly, a much more complex and culturally sensitive handling of the issue of intercultural dating is required.

This example demonstrates the problems that can occur when counselors fail to consider the cultural backgrounds of non-Hispanic Whites in counseling. This example also underscores the importance of training mental health professionals how to adjust the counseling process with non-Hispanic White boys as a function of their particular cultural backgrounds.

The purpose of this chapter is to raise awareness about multicultural counseling with non-Hispanic Whites by discussing salient cultural issues to consider when counseling boys with the following cultural backgrounds: WASP (White Anglo-Saxon Protestant), Irish Catholic, Italian, and Jewish. We decided to discuss these particular cultural groups for four reasons. First, the unique features of the WASP, Irish Catholic, Italian, and Jewish heritages illustrate the cultural diversity that exists among non-Hispanic Whites. Second, each of the authors of this chapter can link his or her own ancestry to one or more of these ethnic groups. Thus, we wrote this chapter from the perspectives of individuals who were raised in, and are the products of, these groups of White Americans. Third, because we have extensive experience working with one or more of these groups, we were able to share our clinical observations about counseling with each group. Although we focused our discussion on these four populations of non-Hispanic White Americans, we recognize that there are numerous other European-ancestry groups of Whites residing in the United States whose cultures are not covered in this chapter because of space limitations. We hope that the examples of diversity provided in this chapter prompt counselors to learn about other ancestry groups of White non-Hispanics who are not covered here. Furthermore, because our discussions regarding the WASP, Irish Catholic, Italian, and Jewish cultures are terse and emphasize the role of men and conceptions of masculinity for each culture, we encourage counselors to learn more about each of these groups as well.

As a starting point for understanding the uniqueness of the cultural groups discussed in this chapter, we highlight key aspects of the WASP culture with which the Irish Catholic American, Italian American, Jewish American, and other ethnic American cultures are often erroneously lumped. Although there are some similarities among these different cultures, unique, deeply embedded features continue to distinguish one culture from the others. Comparing the WASP culture with that of the other three cultural groups illuminates these distinctions.

WHITE ANGLO-SAXON PROTESTANT BOYS

According to Axelson (1999), the WASP culture dominating much of U.S. society today can be traced to Europeans who established colonies in North America in the late 1600s and early 1700s. The majority of these people were English and carried with them the traditions of the Anglo-Saxon culture that had defined life in England. Brookhiser (1991) noted that most of these early English colonists were White and affiliated with several Protestant religions—hence the acronym WASP, for White Anglo-Saxon Protestants. Their lives were regulated by a value system that also shaped the experience of other European settlers, such as the Welsh, Scots, Protestant Irish, Swedes, Norwegians, Danes, Finns, Germans, and Dutch, who came to North America in large numbers during the 1800s (Axelson, 1999). The WASP value system has persisted and continues to exert a great influence on life in America today. A description of this value system, based on related discussions by Axelson (1999), Kiselica (1995), and Ponterotto and Casas (1991), is presented here.

In WASP culture, the individual is seen as the primary unit of the family or group, and independence and autonomy are highly valued. Competing and succeeding against others also are highly valued. Individual achievement and success are considered vital to one's self-esteem. Adherence to time schedules is important. Time is construed as linear ("don't lose or waste time because it never returns"). Accepted standards for nonverbal and verbal behavior include the following: maintaining eye contact while speaking, a firm handshake, and direct verbal expressiveness. The ideal family unit is the nuclear family, consisting of two parents, one male and one female, and their children. Dedication to one's family is a must and, for a man, is expressed by being a good provider. Written arrangements in the form of contracts are respected. Linear, analytic thinking, rather than intuitive and symbolic thinking, tends to dominate. WASPs are strongly influenced by Christian attitudes regarding sexuality and childbearing. Traditional, rigid moral codes prohibit out-of-wedlock childbearing and the open discussion of sexual matters. During times of crisis, individuals are expected to "pull themselves up by their bootstraps." Family problems represent highly personal issues that should be resolved within the immediate family.

IMPLICATIONS FOR COUNSELING

In spite of the fact that WASPs utilize formal counseling services more frequently than do racial/ethnic-minority individuals (see Atkinson, 1985; Cheung, 1991), WASPs prefer to work things out among themselves and to consider themselves lacking in self-sufficiency when they are unable to do so. Going to a professional to receive help is considered a sign of weakness, of being unable to help oneself. Consequently, WASPs tend to view counseling as a shameful experience. This is especially true for WASP boys who have a traditional masculine identity in which the expression of feelings and seeking assistance with emotional concerns is viewed with disfavor. Consequently, WASP boys typically do not initiate counseling on their own; they are more likely to be brought to a counselor by their parents seeking guidance for how to manage some crisis pertaining to their son. Once counseling is initiated, the parents tend to view the son's difficulties as "his problems," which need to be fixed, rather than as symptoms of a dysfunctional family system. Because problems are also highly personal matters that can be a source of shame if they are revealed to others, the parents may be reluctant to avoid involving extended family members in counseling (Kiselica, 1995).

Counselors can take several measures during the early stages of counseling to reduce the WASP experience of shame evoked by participation in counseling. At the onset of counseling, the counselor should assure the client of the confidential nature of the client-counselor relationship and define counseling as a psychoeducational process that involves the teaching of skills to enhance development rather than as a remedial process for "sick" people. It is also recommended that the counselor utilize written contracts specifying agreements between the counselor, the client, and the parents. It is advisable for the counselor to use specific questioning and formal procedures that are used to explore and understand problems. Being available promptly for scheduled appointment times and having defined time limits for sessions (e.g., a 50-minute session, once a week) are compatible with the WASP conception of time management. WASPs are also likely to appreciate a counselor who greets his or her clients with a firm handshake and maintains eye contact while speaking, patterns of relating that are consistent with a WASP communication style (Kiselica, 1995).

IRISH CATHOLIC AMERICAN BOYS

The vast majority of the nearly 40 million Americans who trace their ancestry to Ireland are Catholics (U.S. Bureau of the Census, 1997) whose descendants suffered through centuries of oppression at the hands of the British in Ireland. Between 1847 and 1920, nearly 4 million Irish Catholics migrated to the United States to escape famine as well as religious persecution and political domination by the British, only to encounter new economic and social hardships in Protestant English America (Axelson, 1999). The Irish Catholics were viewed by the well-entrenched WASP establishment with hostility and as inferior undesirables who should remain isolated from the mainstream (Galway, 1997). Because most of them were unskilled, uneducated peasants with little representation among the elite power brokers of the economic institutions of the United States, Irish Catholic immigrants struggled to survive as they either experienced difficulty finding employment or faced work options that were low paying and characterized by dangerous working conditions (McCaffrey, 1976).

Despite these initial prejudices and troubles, Irish Catholic Americans persevered, adapted to their difficult circumstances, and eventually flourished in the United States. This transition to a better life was aided by the fact that the Irish spoke English and were fair-skinned Whites; these characteristics gave them an edge over non-English-speaking, darker-skinned immigrants and gradually enabled them to make inroads into WASP society. Their accommodation to American life also was facilitated by the stability and strong local fellowship provided by the Irish Catholic church in their communities (McCaffrey, 1976). In addition, as McGoldrick (1996) notes, "Catholic schools run primarily by Irish nuns and priests transmitted Irish cultural values to generations of Irish American children" (p. 547). Thus, Irish Catholics adapted to American ways while preserving their Irish Catholic heritage. A synopsis of this heritage, culled from Greeley (1981), McCaffrey (1976), and McGoldrick (1996), follows.

IRISH CATHOLIC CULTURE

The Irish Catholic worldview was greatly influenced by the Irish Roman Catholic church. Traditional Irish Catholics follow the strict rules of the church and its priests without question. Traditional Irish Catholics experience tremendous guilt whenever they perceive themselves to have committed any sin against the church. Related to their fears concerning judgment about sin, they tend to be very anxious concerning what others think about them. There is a strong belief that one should suffer for one's sins and that such suffering should be borne alone. Similarly, problems are considered highly private matters between oneself and God; consequently, Irish Catholics tend to be reluctant to seek outside help—even among extended family members—when troubles occur. Sexual relations are also very private matters concerning a husband and wife, and they should occur for purposes of procreation. Rigid religious doctrines forbid premarital and extramarital sex, and they indirectly discourage tenderness, affection, and intimacy. Divorce is not permitted by the Catholic church because marriage is viewed as a sacred bond between a husband and wife. Abortion also is forbidden.

Although Catholic doctrines promoting marriage and prohibiting abortion have contributed to a relatively high birth rate among Irish Catholics, it should be noted that Irish Catholics also tend to have large families because "the Irish . . . simply like babies" (Greeley, 1981, p. 124). Irish Catholic parents take great pride in their children and typically consider a large family to be a blessing from God.

The Irish Catholic experience of oppression suffered under British rule has greatly influenced the Irish Catholic worldview and way of life. Irish Catholics tend to have a strong identity with oppressed peoples because of their centuries of struggles against British domination. In addition, Irish Catholics have long-standing traditions of hospitality to one's neighbors, humor, the "gift of gab," verbal obfuscation and ridicule, and the spirit of rebellion, all of which were means the Irish Catholics employed to survive British oppression.

The fact that Irish Catholic men were the direct targets of British oppression who were systematically deprived of any sense of power had particular effects on Irish Catholic family relations. Many Irish Catholic men often turned to their local pubs for companionship with other men and to alcohol to deaden their sense of powerlessness in a British-dominated nation. This practice contributed to high rates of alcoholism among Irish Catholics and to the familiar images of the Irish Catholic father as a distant family member and the mother as the ruler of the house. Mothers typically feared for the well-being of their sons and became quite protective of them, which led to the development of very strong mother-son bonds in Irish Catholic families.

Whether dealing with a son or a daughter, the Irish Catholic mother saw her primary responsibility as that of an unquestioned transmitter of the values and rules of the Catholic church to her children. Accordingly, Irish Catholic children are raised to be devout Catholics, to behave in an obedient and polite manner, and to never embarrass the family.

Although Irish Catholics enjoy periodic, jovial reunions with extended family members—particularly on holidays, and even at wakes and funerals, where feelings of grief are mitigated by a family celebration—"extended family relationships among Irish-Catholics are often not close" (McGoldrick, 1996, p. 558). Because respect for boundaries supersedes concern for relatives, Irish Catholics are unlikely to turn to the extended family for support during times of crisis, particularly if the crisis is one that could be viewed as an embarrassment for the family.

IMPLICATIONS FOR COUNSELING

Irish Catholic Americans are similar to WASPs in their tendency to experience shame in seeking counseling, to prefer individual counseling and family counseling limited to immediate family members, and to be comforted by reassurances that the client-counselor relationship is confidential. Unlike WASPs, Irish Catholics are likely to view counseling as being analogous to going to a priest for confession, a process in which they confess, if not spill out, their "sins" to the counselor (McGoldrick, 1996). Accordingly, we have observed that, although it is painful for Irish Catholic Americans boys to admit they need professional assistance, once they start counseling they describe their difficulties at length, as they would in a confessional, but with the indirect and superficially cheerful manner that the Irish maintain when they are troubled. The counselor's role during this self-disclosure is to be a very attentive listener and, like a priest commanding acts of penance during confession, to be ready to dispense some sort of advice or assignment to the boy afterward.

According to McGoldrick (1996), because Irish Catholics respond to the directives of therapists with the same sort of respect that is afforded to priests, they tend to be very diligent about completing therapeutic homework assignments. Furthermore, Irish Catholics prefer behavioral and solution-focused therapies because the particular kinds of homework assignments employed in these approaches are objectively focused on making changes in behavior. By comparison, Irish Catholics tend to be uncomfortable with gestalt therapy and psychodrama, which involve highly expressive and tactile forms of expression, and psychoanalytic models that overemphasize the dark or "sinful" side of humans (McGoldrick, 1996). Finally, the therapeutic process is greatly facilitated when the counselor mixes his or her reflections, interpretation, and assignments with timely humor and assurances that the client-counselor relationship is confidential.

Although humor is a useful tool for establishing and maintaining rapport with Irish Catholic American boys, it is sometimes necessary to explore with the client the negative effects that traditional Irish Catholic methods of communication might have on interpersonal relationships. According to Greeley (1981), Irish Americans tend to have difficulty expressing affection and anger, and they tend to avoid quarreling by relying on humor and "blarney" as indirect means of airing difficult emotions. These forms of communication are ill-suited for acknowledging and affirming the emotional states of loved ones. Furthermore, a boy who habitually expresses himself in this manner obscures his true inner world to others.

Because some Irish American boys are quite accustomed to these communication styles, they and their family members may not recognize how these styles impede the achievement of a more complete intimacy. It behooves the counselor to point this out to the boy in individual therapy and to his parents and siblings during family therapy. Not surprisingly, conveying this message is most effective when humor is involved in its initial delivery but follow-up relies on more direct, open discussions of the subject. For example, one of our Irish Catholic American clients once discussed in therapy his difficulties with his girlfriend, who was frustrated with the boy's inability to directly state his feelings for her. He reported that she became particularly upset whenever he ruined a potentially intimate moment by following up some romantic expression toward her with a joke. The counselor responded to this story by poking the boy in his shoulder, smiling, and saying "If you keep that up, fella, you're gonna laugh your girlfriend right out of your life." After a few humorous exchanges between the counselor and the client about this issue, the counselor became much more serious, confrontive, and emphatic about the matter and said

> Now, let's get serious about this for a moment. If you don't change your ways, you're gonna lose that lovely girl you've been dating and you won't even understand why. Is that what you really want? (A pause, while the client shakes his head no.) So, what do you say we get down to business here and discuss why you talk to her in this way and what you might like to do to about it?

The counselor and client then addressed the boy's Irish roots, the prototypical way people had related to one another in his family for generations, the historical reasons for these practices, and the pros and cons of his continued practice of this particular tradition. Addressing the boy in this manner—by first using humor, then direct serious discussion—the counselor maintained rapport with the client while modeling for him a different way of relating.

If the counselor hopes to address issues an Irish Catholic American boy has with his family, the best initial ally to recruit for this process is his mother, because Irish mothers traditionally are the masters of domestic matters in their families and enjoy very close relationships with their sons. This closeness can be a source of strength to utilize in counseling, as well as a potential source of concern. On the plus side, the deep feelings an Irish mother has for her son make her readily available to help him during times of crisis, and she is likely to be a pillar of strength throughout the counseling process. Many Irish mothers, however, have difficulty accepting a son's autonomy, and they may be uneasy when the son expresses serious plans to move away from home or romantic interests in a young lady. With regard to the latter, it can be fruitful to share an historical examination of mother-son bonds in Irish Catholic culture. When sons are made aware of this history, they become more understanding of maternal behavior that others might misconstrue as emotional enmeshment; when mothers are made aware of this history, they become more receptive to accepting the greater autonomy of sons that is practiced in mainstream American culture, especially if the mother's ambivalent feelings about the matter are empathically affirmed by the son and an understanding husband.

Although traditional Irish Catholic American fathers tend to view domestic issues as the domain of the mother (Fallows, 1979), our clinical experience indicates that fathers become alarmed when their sons are in trouble or are struggling with a significant emotional issue. Unlike Irish Catholic American mothers, who are better able to provide emotional support to their sons, fathers tend to feel awkward in knowing how to respond to their sons' affective needs. The father nevertheless should be encouraged by the counselor to take instrumental measures that can boost the son's emotional state. For example, Irish Catholic American fathers have a long-standing tradition of behaving as "bachelor husbands" (Fallows, 1979, p. 101), establishing a routine of engaging in recreational activities with groups of male friends while the mother attends to domestic matters. During outings together, it is common for these groups of husbands to discharge their own anxieties by joking with one another in a superficial way about their personal concerns. We have found it helpful to encourage Irish Catholic American fathers to think of ways that they could include their sons in these activities. One of our 14-year-old clients who was feeling depressed and anxious told us that he felt himself "to grow stronger" after his father began taking him to golf outings and poker games with the father's buddies, even though he and his dad did not talk much about the boy's concerns. Simply put, being around his father and seeing himself accepted as "being a man" gave this lad new confidence in himself. The boy's mother also reported that she felt great relief from this same intervention because it shifted some of the responsibility for the son's worries to the father, relieving some of the parental pressures she was experiencing. She also witnessed how much it helped her son. The father benefited from this intervention as well; he, too, was relieved to see his son improve, and he felt closer to his son by including him in some of the men's activities.

With some father-son interventions, it is necessary to caution the father to be careful not to model inappropriate consumption of alcohol, especially when the son has been referred for counseling to address alcohol abuse. Such boys have a particularly hard time recognizing that they have a problem in the light of the many Irish cultural messages that "tying one on" is OK. The male Irish tradition of patronizing a local pub and forming friendships while drinking has continued in the United States. Throughout the northeastern United States, there are countless bars with Irish names and Hibernian clubs where men of Irish ancestry get together to unwind with the assistance of alcohol. St. Patrick's Day, once viewed as a day to maintain Irish cultural heritage and pride, has become, for many Irish Americans as well as many non-Irish Americans, an excuse for having a big drinking binge. Alcohol typically is served at Irish wakes and on every major holiday. All these traditions can contribute to alcohol abuse in Irish American families. Although it is beyond the scope of this chapter to review all the addiction-treatment approaches that could be used with Irish American boys who develop alcohol abuse problems, it is important to recommend that substance abuse interventions involve awareness-raising strategies with Irish Catholic Americans concerning the influence of these traditions on drinking habits.

ITALIAN AMERICAN BOYS

Most of the nearly 15 million Americans with Italian ancestry (U.S. Bureau of the Census, 1997) are the descendants of the 4.5 million Italians who immigrated to the United States between 1880 and 1910 (Axelson, 1999). Like many of the Irish who immigrated to the United States, the majority of these Italian immigrants were illiterate, unskilled people who were very devoted to the Catholic religion. Compared to Irish Catholic immigrants, however, Italian immigrants placed a much stronger emphasis on the immediate and extended family, generally did not speak English well, were a darker skinned people, and practiced a less ascetic form of Catholicism (Axelson, 1999). Thus, Italian immigrants not only were very different from generations of WASPs who had lived in this country for more than a century but also were also noticeably distinct from fellow relative newcomers to the United States, such as the Irish Catholics. These differences contributed to the unique historical experiences of Italians in America and helped to shape the Italian American culture. Understanding this culture further illustrates the cultural diversity that exists among non-Hispanic White Americans.

THE ITALIAN AMERICAN CULTURE

Nothing is more important to traditional Italian Americans than the family. Because engaging in warm relations with both immediate and extended family members is central to the identity of Italian Americans, relatives have tended to live in close physical proximity to one another and visit one another regularly to share both the hardships and the joys of life (Axelson, 1999; Giordano & McGoldrick, 1996b). Perhaps this is best illustrated by the great celebrations enjoyed by Italian Americans over a Sunday dinner. At these get-togethers, which are held on a weekly basis by many of the Italian American families whom we have counseled, relatives gather for hours over multicourse meals to enjoy one another's company and to discuss family matters. In this manner, strong family bonds are established and maintained within and across generations. Thus, as Giordano and McGoldrick (1996a) note, for Italian Americans eating is "a symbol of nurturing and family connectedness" (p. 438).

The great emphasis placed on family solidarity places pressure on Italian American children to remain close to their families, both geographically and emotionally (Giordano & McGoldrick, 1996b). Because this cultural imperative is at odds with mainstream cultural values accentuating individual autonomy and separateness, Italian American boys often are confused about how close they should remain to their families. As Axelson (1999) explains,

> The mainstream culture emphasizes individuality and material achievement, often at the cost of breaking away from family, old friends, and the culture of parents and grandparents. For young Americans of ethnic Italian background, intergenerational cultural conflict follows from opposing messages: "move ahead" and "be successful" versus "don't change" and "remain close to us." (p. 104)

The strong ties that exist within Italian American families are, to a large degree, a survival mechanism that was developed centuries ago in Italy. According to Axelson (1999), throughout history Italians suffered oppression from invading foreign nations, as well as from their own governments. Consequently, Italians learned to rely on members of their extended family and fellow village residents and to distrust outsiders. Italian immigrants continued this tradition when they encountered prejudice in the United States. For example, they tended to settle in neighborhoods, known as "Little Italies," which had a very high concentration of Italians, who formed tight-knit bonds within and between families (see Giordano & McGoldrick, 1996b). These communities were viewed by Italian Americans as safe havens from the disparaging and exploitive behavior of outsiders.

One deeply entrenched prejudice about Italian Americans pertains to the widespread belief that they have ties to the underworld. Axelson (1999) observes that the stereotypic image of Italian Americans as members of the "mob" is highly insulting and unfair when one considers that only about 6,000 Italian Americans are involved in organized crime. Giordano and McGoldrick (1996b) argue that this stereotype has influenced many people to view Italian Americans as "inferior, dangerous, uneducated, violent and criminal" (p. 569). In our clinical experience, young Italian American boys exhibiting early signs of disruptive behavior are sometimes viewed in the same way and written off by judgmental adults as destined for an antisocial career.

The view of Italian Americans as criminals is contradicted by their close ties to the Catholic church and the manner in which Catholic traditions shape their behavior. The church and the parish community—not organized crime—are central institutions of the

Italian American way of life. Baptisms, first communions, confirmations, and mar-riages—all of which are sacraments of the Catholic church—are important landmarks in the lives of Italian American children and causes for great family and neighborhood celebrations. Italian Americans value religious rituals "for their pageantry, spectacle, and value in fostering family celebrations and rites of passage" (Giordano & McGoldrick, 1996b, p. 569), and there is a strong representation of Italian Americans in Catholic elementary and high schools. Although the vast majority of Italian Americans are Catholics, they tend to practice a different form of religiosity from that of other, more austere Catholics, such as the Irish Catholics:

> For most Italians, God is viewed a [*sic*] more as a benign friend of the family and the Church as a source of ritual and drama, in striking contrast to the Irish dire warnings about the Day of Judgment and emphasis of the Church's authority. However, because the Church represents tradition, family, and community, Italians still tend to support it. (Giordano & McGoldrick, 1996b, p. 569)

Although large numbers of Italian Americans have attended Catholic schools as an expression of their support for the Catholic church, historically Italian Americans were less likely than other Catholic school students to enter college. This relative lack of academic ambition was related to family pressure on children to leave school and find a job to assist in the economic support of the family (Axelson, 1999). Over the past two decades, however, attitudes about education have changed, and the pursuit of higher education among Italian Americans is on a par with that of other White ethnic groups, such as Irish Catholics. This change has been prompted by the belief among many Italian Americans that higher education is a key to success and economic security (Axelson, 1999). Italian American children nevertheless appear to prefer to live at home while completing college, a trend considered by some to be an expression of the value of staying close to family (Giordano & McGoldrick, 1996b). In some working-class areas of this country, Italian American children continue to have very high dropout rates (see Giordano & McGoldrick, 1996b).

Another changing tradition within the Italian American culture pertains to the role of the father and conceptions of masculinity. According to Italian custom, the father is viewed as the undisputed, authoritarian head of the household (Giordano & McGoldrick, 1996b). Although the traditional Italian American father may be rigid in his ways and expect his family to cater to his needs, he is also an affectionate and caring figure who provides for his family (Greeley, 1981) and acts as their sage (Giordano & McGoldrick, 1996b). Traditional Italian American fathers expect their wives to be faithful partners, good cooks, and the emotional providers for the family. They also raise their sons to be tough figures who can deal effectively with the outside world. According to Giordano and McGoldrick (1996b), "Sons are given much greater latitude [than daugh-ters] prior to marriage. Indeed, a bit of acting out is expected, even subtly encouraged, as a measure of manliness" (p. 573).

Although many Italian American boys and young men now question these traditional view of fathers and masculinity, others have great difficulty accepting the more androgynous gender roles of men and the more liberated role of women in mainstream America. Consequently, as Giordano and McGoldrick (1996b) assert, conflicts about gender role issues are common for young Italian American men.

IMPLICATIONS FOR COUNSELING

Several strategies are recommended for establishing a strong rapport with Italian American clients. First, a family systems approach to counseling utilizing both immediate and extended family members fits well with the strong family orientation of Italian Americans. During initial contacts with the family, the counselor should present him- or herself as a very warm person who greets the family with a high degree of hospitality. With many Italian families, this can be accomplished by the counselor sharing some kind of food and drink with the family while revealing some details about the counselor's life, such as where the counselor was raised, how many siblings the counselor has, and whether or not the counselor is married and the parent of any children. These gestures communicate a very personable style that tends to be appreciated by Italian American families and helps them to lower their guard about being in counseling.

The acceptance of food by the counselor from the family is sometimes a critical incident for gaining acceptance with Italian American families. For example, during a counseling session conducted by one of the authors of this chapter, an Italian American mother brought a large (and delicious!) square of sharp provolone cheese for the counselor. The counselor immediately made a genuine fuss over this gesture by expressing his gratitude, finding a knife and plate, cutting the cheese into cubes, and sharing it with his clients while they ate, laughed, and talked about the minor events that had occurred in their lives over the past week. This impromptu snack opened the door to discussing fights the boy had had in school and psychoeducational approaches the family might use to help him handle provocations with his peers more effectively. By comparison, responding lightly to the offering of the cheese and not eating some of it during the session would have insulted the mother and could have undermined making therapeutic progress with the family.

This example not only illustrates the importance of food and a personal approach but also highlights the need to take one's time with Italian American families. Italian Americans are less likely than WASP and Irish American clients to be in a rush, instead preferring an evolution of events within an atmosphere of warm sharing. With this in mind, it is recommended that counselors working with Italian American boys and their families forsake the traditional "therapist's hour" and reserve longer blocks of time for counseling, which can be utilized to weave relationship-building rituals into the therapeutic process.

Additional initiatives may be necessary when working with traditional Italian American fathers whose sons are having difficulties. These traditional fathers tend to view going for counseling as a sign of weakness, and they tend to be highly insulted if their authority is ignored. In the light of these considerations, we have found it helpful for male and female clinicians to work as cotherapists with Italian American families and that it is sometimes necessary for the male therapist to initiate special "man to man" meetings with traditional Italian American fathers before the first family session is conducted. These meetings are often successful when they are held in a pizzeria or restaurant where the two men can share some food while they discuss the father's concerns. During these discussions, it is imperative that the counselor listen with great respect to the father's perspective, while enlisting the father's help in therapy by stating how much the counselor "needs the father's strength and guidance" for the counselor to assist the family. These efforts are likely to win the father's commitment as an ally in counseling.

These strategies will foster trust within actual counseling sessions. Counselors can take other steps to establish a positive reputation in the community, which will facilitate the referral of Italian American clients for counseling. For example, in New Jersey many Italian American boys live in communities known as "Little Italies." Networking in these communities will increase the visibility and acceptance of the counselor as a person to whom families can turn when they are in trouble. This networking includes the following: dining in the many wonderful little Italian restaurants for which these communities are famous; getting to know the owners and patrons of these establishments; volunteering to assist organizations sponsoring Italian American festivals, such as "The Festival of Lights," which is celebrated annually in Trenton, or "Saint Rocco's Festival," which is held each summer in Elizabeth, New Jersey; attending Catholic church services in Italian neighborhoods and offering pro bono workshops for the parish community; establishing close ties with Roman Catholic priests, to whom Italian American parents often turn when their children are in crisis; and developing relationships with leaders of the trade unions, which represent many Italian American workers.

In addition to employing these strategies, counselors should be prepared to address certain issues commonly presented by Italian American boys in counseling. For example, Axelson (1999) and Giordano and McGoldrick (1996b) observe that many Italian American children experience conflicts with their parents about leaving home, including issues about living away from home during college or moving to any locale that is a great distance from home, which in our experience means more than an hour away from one's parents. We have found this dilemma to be very common among bright first-and second-generation Italian American boys who want to apply to excellent institutions of higher education that are located outside their home state. Many of these boys feel the pressure of their parents to stay at home and commute to a local school, yet they are strongly encouraged by their teachers and guidance counselors to apply to other schools that are often more highly rated academically but located farther away. Giordano and McGoldrick (1996b) recommend that counselors urge Italian American children facing this sort of dilemma to give their parents strong messages about the importance of family, in spite of the more limited contact that results from living far from home. For example, Giordano and McGoldrick advise counselors to encourage their clients to be very emotionally expressive with their parents when visiting home. Adding to this suggestion, we recommend frequent use of the telephone, for traditional Italian parents thrive on daily conversations with their children. These tactics tend to reduce the family's feelings of abandonment over time.

A second issue related to educational matters pertains to conflicts between parents and sons—especially fathers and sons—about career aspirations. Even though large numbers of Italian Americans are college educated and employed in white-collar professions, many of the Italian American boys we have encountered have fathers who are employed in the construction trades and other blue-collar jobs. Some of these fathers pressure their sons to work in the same kind of positions and discourage their sons from thinking about college. Boys who oppose such pressures are often rejected by their fathers and taunted with expressions such as "So the old man isn't good enough for you?" or "You're too good to do your old man's work!" Boys placed in these situations need emotional support from counselors who can help them understand the cultural roots of these reactions by their fathers. In addition, it is recommended that a male counselor use the "man to man" meeting strategy that was mentioned earlier. During this meeting, the counselor should take his time to empathize with the father's position and affirm that he is a good father because of the work he does. Over time, however, the counselor should probe the father's feelings about the less desirable aspects of the work he does. For example, one of our father clients was a carpenter who had been injured repeatedly on the job and had some nagging, long-term infirmities as a result. Tapping the father's anguish about these experiences helped the father to acknowledge his fears about his son having "to live a life of pain." Combining this effort with counseling designed to coach the boy on how to affirm his father helped to reduce the father's opposition toward his son's interest in college.

A final common issue pertaining to counseling with Italian American boys pertains to conflicts with girlfriends about gender role expectations. Italian American boys raised by a traditional father may have gender role expectations that clash with those of some of the girls they date. Boys from traditional homes often expect their girlfriends to accept traditional roles of women in heterosexual relationships, an expectation that can lead to arguments and short-lived relationships with girls espousing different gender role conceptions. With these boys, psychoeducational counseling designed to teach about nontraditional models of gender role behavior can open their eyes to taking a different approach to relating to the girls they date from nontraditional families. It should be pointed out that some boys ascribe very strongly to their traditional gender role upbringing. With these boys, the psychoeducational counseling has the effect of clarifying their desire to seek girls who accept traditional gender roles. Counselors working with these boys are urged to respect their client's values and not force their own preferences about gender role behavior on the client. At the same time, the counselor has an obligation to help such boys to recognize the potential implications of their gender role expectations on their heterosexual relationships.

JEWISH AMERICAN BOYS

Although the nearly 6 million Jews residing in the United States represent a small percentage of White Americans, Jewish Americans are considered a very distinct, visible, and powerful cultural group in this nation. Understanding the unique features of Jewish culture, especially Jewish expectations regarding the roles of boys and men in the family, is essential for practitioners who hope to help Jewish American boys in counseling. A discussion of the Jewish culture also demonstrates additional evidence of the cultural heterogeneity among non-Hispanic Whites in the United States.

The following overview about the Jewish culture was gleaned from information discussed by Rosen and Weltman (1996). Although this overview highlights salient issues of Jewish American boys, the reader should bear in mind that there are cultural differences among the descendants of Jews who came to the United States between 1880 and the 1940s (see Axelson, 1999) and more recent Jewish immigrants who came from Israel (see Fogelman, 1996) and the many nations that once constituted the former Soviet Union (see Feigin, 1996). In addition, the reader is asked to recognize that although we have accentuated traditional Jewish values and customs in our discussion, the degree to which these are embraced by Jewish American boys will vary according to the particular form of Judaism (e.g., Orthodox, Conservative, Reform) that is honored by a boy and his family and according to the family's level of acculturation to mainstream values and customs. Additionally, there is an ever growing number of so-called "secular Jews," who, despite a strong cultural affiliation to Judaism, do not subscribe to traditional religious practices and customs. Thus, counselors working with Jewish American boys are advised to use the ideas contained in this chapter as a lens for viewing their Jewish American clients and to adjust that lens according to the unique cultural background of each client.

JEWISH AMERICAN CULTURE

Dedication to one's family is a core value of Jewish Americans that is deeply rooted in the religious traditions of Judaism. As in the Italian experience, it is a survival mechanism inculcated by centuries of persecution and oppression. Jewish boys are taught at an early age that they are expected to show devotion to their parents, and family life remains important to Jewish men throughout their lives. Boys are expected to acquire a good education and be high achievers so that they can secure jobs that will provide them with the financial stability required for marriage and raising a family. A Jewish boy who achieves these expectations is a source of pride and status for the family, whereas a boy who fails to fulfill such hopes is often seen by the family as a failure and a source of embarrassment.

Traditionally, a Jewish man starting a family is expected to do so within the confines of marriage to a Jewish woman. A Jewish man who weds a Jewish wife in a ceremony conducted by a rabbi and goes on to raise children in the Jewish faith is considered a successful man who has demonstrated his devotion to the Jewish community. The dating of gentiles (non-Jews) and premarital sex are taboo in traditional Jewish families. Many Jews consider intermarriage—the marriage of a Jew and gentile—to be a violation of Jewish religious law and a betrayal of one's dedication to preserving the Jewish religion. Thus, although the intermarriage rate has increased significantly in recent years, an interfaith marriage might provoke intense conflicts with both the immediate and extended family and, in extreme cases, ostracism from the family.

The obligation of continuing the Jewish religion is closely linked with Jewish religious beliefs and the Jewish experience of persecution and discrimination. The Jews believe that they are God's "chosen people" who have a duty to raise their children in the teachings of the Torah and the Talmud. Preserving the Jewish religion and its traditions is also critical because Jews throughout the world have been the victims of subjugation and persecution. Memories of the atrocities of the Holocaust are still fresh in the minds of Jewish Americans, and they serve as horrifying reminders that the Jewish people are vulnerable to attack at any time. Maintaining the Jewish way of life in tightly knit Jewish families and communities traditionally has provided Jewish Americans with a safe haven from other people and institutions hostile to Jews. Thus, a Jewish father understands that his responsibilities include carrying on the many customs that are central to the Jewish way, including many of the following: naming his children after beloved relatives; teaching his children Jewish law; celebrating Jewish holidays (such as Passover and Hanukkah); honoring the rituals of bris (circumcision of a Jewish baby boy), Bar and Bat Mitzvah (ceremonies establishing boys and girls, respectively, as adult worshipers), sitting shiva (mourning the death of a loved one), and reciting Kaddish (saying a memorial prayer for a deceased family member); and loving one's wife and respecting her honored position in the family.

IMPLICATIONS FOR COUNSELING

Many aspects of Jewish culture are assets that can be utilized positively during counseling. Because the Jewish tradition emphasizes intellectual exchange, introspection, and the discussion of problems, most Jewish clients adapt easily and respond enthusiastically to counseling, insight-oriented psychotherapy, and bibliotherapy. Jewish families also respond well to family therapy because the family is viewed as an important feature of Jewish identity. Although some Jewish parents may contribute to the problems experienced by their children, they tend to seek help when their children are troubled and commonly commit themselves to counseling once they are engaged in the therapeutic process.

Orthodox Jewish parents of a troubled son tend to seek the assistance of a professional who is also Jewish and trusted by the local Jewish community. This practice occurs because some Jews believe that only a fellow Jew can relate to the difficulties experienced by Jewish families and because of the understandable historic Jewish mistrust of institutions that are dominated by non-Jews. Some Jewish parents who reside in areas populated with very few Jews will turn to a gentile counselor for help for their distressed child when no competent Jewish professional is available. Jewish parents whose son is committed to a psychiatric hospital or referred for special school counseling services sometimes have no choice in the selection of a therapist and may have to work reluctantly with a non-Jewish professional who is assigned to manage their son's case.

In those instances when the counselor is a gentile working with Jewish clients, it is recommended that the counselor explore with the family any concerns they might have about working with a non-Jew. Raising this subject may communicate the counselor's sensitivity regarding the family's Jewish heritage, mitigate any fears that the family has about the counselor, and obviate referring the family to a Jewish colleague. If the family continues to prefer the services of a Jewish professional, a referral to a Jewish clinician should be arranged if it is administratively possible to do so.

Jewish boys referred for counseling tend to struggle with several issues related to their cultural experience. Because Jewish boys are raised to be very devoted to their families, they tend to be highly sensitive to, and affected by, family problems. Worries about their families and the pressure to succeed academically can contribute to the emergence of somatic symptoms that have no organic origins (see Rosen & Weltman, 1996). During periods of extreme family distress, such as when parents have intense marital conflicts, some Jewish boys try to become superachievers in an attempt to maintain status for the family. Taking on this role can exacerbate somatic complaints and prompt maladaptive levels of arousal manifested as test anxiety. Thus, an eclectic approach to counseling is recommended, including individual stress- and anxiety-management strategies with the boy and family therapy exploring the potential contribution of family and cultural issues to the boy's symptoms.

The pressure to succeed academically can take a particularly high toll on Jewish boys with low intellectual potential or with learning disabilities. The pressure to succeed academically sometimes may also cause capable Jewish boys with high potential to underachieve or to drop out of school. According to Rosen and Weltman (1996), boys who are unable to fulfill high academic expectations may be a source of shame for the family. Typically, this shame is experienced by family members unconsciously and may be communicated to the boy implicitly. In response to these messages, the boy may doubt himself and question his prospects for finding a suitable mate later in life. These perceptions can hurt his sense of self-esteem and undermine well-intentioned remedial programs designed to foster his academic progress. A boy struggling with these issues is best served through family therapy designed to address the family's feelings about the boy's academic difficulties. Typically, after family members become aware of the harmful, unconscious messages communicated to the son, they rally to their son's side, become more accepting of his limitations, and help him to find his niche in the world.

In addition to the difficulties associated with high academic expectations, Jewish boys who are the ancestors of Jewish immigrants to this country sometimes contend with family conflicts over traditional versus nontraditional values. For example, second- and third-generation Jewish American boys may question prohibitions against dating gentile girls, or they may revolt against traditional Jewish religious practices. According to Rosen and Weltman (1996), boys embracing new value systems are often rejected and emotionally cut off by members of both the immediate and the extended family. Although family therapy can help some boys and their families to negotiate satisfactory compromises about values conflicts, in other families the boy's value system may be so at odds with that of his parents that a bitter impasse may occur. When this happens, both the boy and his parents require supportive counseling to help them adjust to the chasm that has developed between them. By remaining sympathetic to both parties, the counselor may serve as a bridge between the son and his parents in the future—even many years into the future—such as when a grandchild is born and both parties want to share in the joy of welcoming a new member into the family.

Finally, Jewish boys residing in communities dominated by gentiles often feel socially isolated and become the targets of anti-Semitism. They may seek support and guidance in counseling for how to deal with prejudice directed at them. In our clinical experience, it has been helpful to link these boys up with adult Jewish men in the community who have been successful in coping with anti-Semitism and are willing to teach a Jewish boy methods for survival in anti-Semitic environments. For example, we once recruited a local Jewish businessman to assist us in our work with a Jewish boy who recently had moved to a largely gentile community with his mother after his parents divorced. The adult male introduced the boy's family to a local synagogue and per-suaded the boy to read about his Jewish heritage. In addition, he had periodic heart-to-heart talks with the boy about overcoming prejudice by continually striving for excellence. In addition, he discussed with the client the possibility that there are many kind gentiles who could be friends and allies to the boy if they were made aware of his situation. These discussions were followed up by introductions of the client to gentile boys and men, especially teachers and coaches, who demonstrated unconditional accep-tance of the client and provided him with a sense of belonging in the community by inviting him to visit their homes and share their companionship. Knowing that he could rely on these people for support mitigated the sting of anti-Semitic treatment the boy sometimes encountered among unenlightened gentiles.

The experience of prejudice may be so common in the lives of some Jewish boys that they become hypersensitive to gentiles and misinterpret certain behaviors by others as being hostile when they are not. This hypersensitivity must be addressed or it can contribute to a self-fulfilling alienation from others. For example, one of our teenage Jewish clients reported feeling slighted when he went to work out in a weight room filled with gentile boys, none of whom greeted him warmly when he first began lifting weights in their presence. Although the boy interpreted this behavior as a sign of anti-Semitism, the counselor shared a different perception of the peers' behavior. The counselor explained to the client the norms of this particular weight room, where all boys, regardless of cultural background, were accepted only after they had become familiar in the facility and demonstrated diligence and competence at pumping iron. Indeed, after about 4 weeks of following his own power-lifting regimen, the client was made to feel like "one of the guys." This experience prompted the client to begin reinterpreting the behavior of other gentile boys in such a way that he was better able to distinguish real anti-Semites from imagined ones, a process that helped the client to develop a wider circle of friends his own age.

CONCLUSIONS AND IMPLICATIONS
FOR TRAINING AND RESEARCH

In this chapter, we have attempted to illustrate the great diversity that exists among non-Hispanic Whites by discussing salient cultural features of, and related implications for counseling with, WASP, Irish Catholic American, Italian American, and Jewish American boys. We hope that the information reviewed in this chapter prompts more mental health practitioners and the educators who train them to think more complexly about their cultural assumptions about non-Hispanic White Americans. Furthermore, we urge mental health educators and supervisors to broaden their multicultural training curricula to include coverage of White European ethnic groups their trainees are likely to work with in counseling. Such an expanded view of multicultural counseling will enhance the clinical effectiveness of practitioners working with non-Hispanic White boys.

We acknowledge that our recommendations are based on our own clinical experiences and those of others who have written about the four groups discussed in this chapter. Clearly, empirical research evaluating the clinical utility of our recommendations is required to further clarify which strategies are most effective with the populations covered in this chapter as well as many other populations we did not discuss. We hope that future research of this kind is conducted and yields more knowledge about culturally sensitive counseling with non-Hispanic White Americans.

HIGHLIGHTS OF CHAPTER 9

▶ Non-Hispanic White boys represent a wide variety of ethnic cultural groups, each of which is somewhat distinct in terms of its cultural heritage. To illustrate the cultural diversity among non-Hispanic Whites, salient cultural issues of the following four groups were discussed: White Anglo-Saxon Protestants (WASPs), Irish Catholics, Italian Americans, and Jewish Americans.

▶ The WASP value system was shaped by the early White, English colonists and other early European settlers of the United States, including the Welsh, Scots, Protestant Irish, Swedes, Norwegians, Danes, Finns, Germans, and the Dutch.

▶ The WASP culture emphasizes individuality, autonomy, competition, efficient use of time and a linear time perspective, Protestant moral codes, and privacy about personal matters.

▶ WASP boys tend to prefer to solve problems on their own. When they are referred for counseling, they initially prefer individual counseling or family counseling in which immediate, rather than extended, family members participate.

▶ WASPs prefer counselors who maintain confidentiality, take a psychoeducational approach to counseling, and have scheduled appointment times and set time limits for counseling sessions.

▶ The majority of the 40 million Americans who trace their ancestry to Ireland are Catholics whose descendants suffered through centuries of oppression at the hands of the British.

► Irish Catholics tend to adhere to the doctrines of the Catholic church, favor marriage and having children within the confines of a marital relationship, refrain from strong expression of emotion, and are reluctant to seek help for personal problems. They also are prone to experiencing guilt and shame regarding their shortcomings.

► Irish Catholic men tend to enjoy being "bachelor husbands" (the practice of engaging in recreational activities with other male friends), and Irish Catholic women tend to be the authorities regarding domestic matters and to be highly protective of, and close to, their sons.

► Although reluctant to seek counseling, Irish Catholic boys tend to respond well to behavioral and solution-focused approaches that are objectively focused on making changes in behavior rather than psychodrama or gestalt approaches, which emphasize high emotional expression, or psychoanalytic approaches, which overemphasize the pathological characteristics of humans.

► Although humor is an effective tactic for establishing rapport with Irish Catholic boys, some Irish Catholic clients may need to be challenged to learn nonhumorous, direct styles of emotional expression and tenderness to enhance their interpersonal relationships.

► In family counseling, Irish Catholic mothers are likely to be good therapeutic allies in counseling with their sons, although overly close mother-son ties in some families may need to be addressed to promote the son's autonomy.

► Irish Catholic fathers can bolster the emotional state of a troubled son by including him in group-oriented activities involving the father, the son, and other adult men.

► Because the consumption of alcohol is a tradition in many Irish institutions, Irish American boys who demonstrate early alcohol abuse can benefit from awareness-raising strategies regarding the influence of this tradition on their drinking habits.

► Fifteen million Americans have an Italian ancestry. Italian Americans tend to value the centrality of the family, including the immediate and extended family, the celebration of mealtime, and the traditions of the Catholic church.

► Historically, Italian Americans were less likely than other White ethnic groups to attend college. Although the pursuit of higher education by Italian Americans is now on a par with that of other White ethnic groups, Italian American children prefer to live at or near home during and after their college years.

▶ Although Italian American males historically have practiced traditional male gender roles, many young Italian American boys and young men are conflicted about continuing this tradition versus adopting androgynous gender roles.

▶ A family systems approach to counseling, utilizing both immediate and extended family members, is recommended with Italian American boys.

▶ Expressing warmth and hospitality, accepting and sharing food during counseling sessions, and having flexible time limits during counseling sessions tend to enhance the therapeutic process with Italian American clients.

▶ When counseling traditional Italian American families, it is recommended that counselors respect the authority of the father, which might entail meeting alone with the father to enlist his strength and guidance regarding his family.

▶ Networking in Italian American restaurants and festivals and developing close relationships with Catholic priests and trade union leaders are effective strategies for earning respect and trust in Italian American communities.

▶ Because of strong cultural expectations that a boy remain close to home and do what his father does, Italian American boys and their families may need special counseling addressing a son's desire to move far away from home or to choose a career path that is vastly different from that of his father.

▶ Italian American boys raised in traditional families may need assistance clarifying conflicts pertaining to traditional male gender role expectations and their implications for dating nontraditional females.

▶ Among the 6 million Jews who reside in the United States, there is considerable cultural diversity. Differences can be seen according to when Jewish individuals or their ancestors entered the United States, their country of origin, and the particular form of Judaism (Orthodox, Conservative, Reform) embraced.

▶ Traditionally, Jewish American parents expect their sons to achieve in school, pursue a respectable career, and start a family within the confines of marriage.

▶ Dating and intermarriage between Jews and gentiles (non-Jews) is considered by traditional Jews to be a violation of Jewish religious law and a betrayal of one's dedication to preserving the Jewish religion.

▶ Traditional Jewish boys and men are influenced by the doctrines and customs of Judaism, which include studying and respecting the Torah and the Talmud; teaching one's children Jewish law; honoring the rituals of bris, Bar Mitzvah and Bat Mitzvah, and sitting shiva; and loving one's wife and respecting her honored position in the family.

▶ Because the Jewish culture emphasizes the family and introspection, intellectual exchange, and the discussion of issues, many Jews respond well to family therapy, insight-oriented psychotherapy, and bibliotherapy.

▶ Orthodox Jewish families tend to prefer counselors who are also Jewish. Gentile counselors working with Orthodox Jewish families are advised to express their respect for, and sensitivity regarding, the family's Jewish heritage.

▶ The strong pressure to succeed academically is often related to many of the symptoms and problems for which Jewish boys are referred for counseling. These issues are best treated through family therapy in which the academic expectations held by the family are addressed systemically.

▶ Disagreement between parents and sons regarding traditional values (e.g., dating only Jewish girls) versus nontraditional values (e.g., dating gentile girls) can result in intense conflicts in Jewish American families and require family systems counseling.

▶ Many Jewish American boys require supportive counseling and the guidance and wisdom of adult male mentors to help them cope with anti-Semitism.

PART

III

SPECIAL POPULATIONS

CHAPTER

10

Counseling
Gay Adolescents

JILL S. BARBER

MICHAEL MOBLEY

This chapter provides an overview of the challenges and concerns of gay adolescents, who often find that simply by being themselves, they become alienated from family, friends, faith, and culture. The chapter also provides an overview of the tasks associated with identity development in this population, as well as recommendations and resources for concerned helping professionals. Savin-Williams (1995) points out that "a prevailing cultural assumption is that homosexuality is the province of adulthood; what these adults were as children and adolescents is a mystery" (p. 165). In the light of the recent finding by the U.S. Department of Health and Human Services (Gibson, 1989) that gay youth are 2 to 3 times as likely to attempt suicide as are other young people, the time is at hand for helping professionals of good conscience to begin to explore counseling strategies for this population.

COMING OUT

Perhaps one of the primary challenges faced by gay adolescents is the task of coming out to self and others. Research indicates that coming out may begin in childhood, adolescence, or any stage of adulthood (Cass, 1979; Troiden, 1989). From an early age, usually before adolescence, many gay youth report that they "feel different" from peers and family (Hunter & Schaecher, 1987). The ways in which that differentness is interpreted by self and others may determine the difficulty of the coming out process for the child or adolescent who lives through it. Additionally, Troiden (1989) notes that the age of coming out has dropped noticeably and that increasingly, lesbians and gays are becoming aware of their sexual orientation during adolescence. Newman and Muzzonigro (1993) found that in a multiethnic sample of gay male adolescents, the average age of realizing they were gay was around 12 years.

Unfortunately, the gay adolescent must often make the adjustment to his belonging in a stigmatized group without the support of family and faith experienced by some members of stigmatized ethnic minorities. This task may be even more difficult if the gay adolescent is also a member of an ethnic minority; he may feel forced to choose between identifying himself with his ethnicity and identifying himself with his sexual orientation. Newman and Muzzonigro (1993) point out that in both the African American and Hispanic communities, homosexuality is considered deviant and is viewed as "an aberration of Caucasian society" (p. 216). In his sample of African American gay adolescents, Edwards (1996b) reported that 89% of participants indicated that their parents would not be likely to accept their homosexuality. Furthermore, the gay community can be criticized for being oriented toward the needs of White middle-class individuals and for not being adequately responsive to the needs of people of color. With these considerations in mind, the gay adolescent of color faces the formidable task of integrating his racial, cultural, and ethnic background with his sexual orientation.

In summary, one of the primary challenges of a gay male is when, how, or if he should come out to his family. This gay rite of passage is particularly risky for adolescents who are dependent on parents for food, shelter, and educational opportunities. Remafedi (1987a) found that 48% of a sample of gay adolescents had run away from home; it is difficult to imagine that the running away was entirely the choice of the adolescent. Perhaps this fear surrounding coming out is best summarized in the words of Derek, a young gay man who was interviewed as a part of a research project:

> That was my biggest concern, that I was going to be kicked out . . . and there was good reason for fearing that . . . the look of disgust on my mother and father's faces. In their eyes I was being difficult. . . . At the time I needed my parents most . . . they were distant and unwilling to help. (quoted in Chandler, 1995, pp. 187, 190)

Derek was pushed out of his home, onto the street and into the workforce, before he was out of high school, which forced him to grow up fast. He added, "In some ways, I felt robbed of my childhood."

SPIRITUALITY

Unfortunately, the homophobic messages delivered in many religious traditions sometimes cause families to reject, abuse, or attempt to change the orientation of a gay child in the "name of God." Homosexuality has been perceived as a sinful choice, and as such condemned, leaving the gay adolescent to feel ashamed, alone, rejected, and abandoned by God. It seems likely that such a young person could be at increased risk for suicide or other self-destructive behavior. In some religious traditions, the expression of manhood required is to be a husband and father, leaving no place for a young gay man in the community of faith. Despite the homophobic teachings and the rigid expressions of manhood prescribed by traditional religions, however, many gay men have strong spiritual and religious convictions. Carl Jung (1959) made this observation concerning the spiritual life of his gay clients: "Often (gay people) are endowed with a wealth of religious feelings, which help [them] to bring the ecclesia spiritualis into reality, and give them a spiritual receptivity which makes them responsive to revelation" (p. 86). Certainly, in the age of AIDS, spiritual revelations are welcome to many. Perhaps one of the healing gifts of this era of disease is that the gay community, which once existed for the most part outside communities of faith, or invisibly within them, has been forced to answer some difficult spiritual questions and to be visible as never before. Recently, significant progress has been made in many denominations in welcoming and integrating lesbians and gays into the community of faith, offering opportunities for gay adolescents and their families to have spiritual support instead of condemnation or silence.

SCHOOL

Often, gay youths have school-related problems, including poor academic performance, truancy, failing a grade, and dropping out of school (Savin-Williams, 1995). These problems may result from enduring social isolation, verbal and physical abuse, family conflict, and the emotional turmoil of being different during a developmental time when belonging is essential. Sears (1991) reported that 97% of his sample recalled negative attitudes about homosexuality that were held by classmates, and more than half feared harassment, especially if they came out in high school. It is difficult to learn in the face of such fear. On the other hand, a gay adolescent who is a high achiever may have greater personal resources and experiences with success to support his self-esteem (Rotheram-Borus, Rosario, & Koopman, 1991). With this in mind, school, in some cases, has the potential to be the saving grace of a struggling gay adolescent.

School is the context for many of the social developmental activities of adolescence, such as playing team sports, developing leadership skills in clubs, and dating. Sears (1991) notes that for a gay student "high school is often a lonely place where, from every vantage point there are couples" (p. 326). A gay high school student is faced with the choice of watching from the sidelines as his peers pair off for the rituals of the prom and going steady or "passing" and going through the motions of the same activities himself. He may never be aware that his same-sex attraction could coexist with intimacy and love, and he is not likely to get that information at school.

SUICIDE

Perhaps the most basic challenge involves physical safety and protection from harm by self and others. One response to the pain of alienation experienced by many gay youth is to attempt suicide. Empirical studies indicate that suicide attempts are high among samples of gay male youths, ranging from 20% to 39% (Remafedi, 1987b; Remafedi, Farrow, & Deisher, 1991; Rotheram-Borus, Rosario, Van Rossem, Reid, & Gillis, 1995). One explanation for this alarming rate of self-harm is that gay youth often experience or expect physical and verbal abuse or rejection from those who would otherwise be expected to support them: family, friends, and community of faith. Furthermore, gay youth may internalize negative images of gay people that are readily available in a homophobic society. Without visible role models or accurate information about homosexuality, they may be unable to imagine that being gay could mean anything good. Finally, it is important to remember that adolescence, with its dramatic physical, emotional, and sexual changes, is difficult enough for adolescents who do not have to face the added pressure of being different in a way that carries the shame and stigma of homosexuality.

GAY-BASHING

Another challenge for the gay adolescent is the threat of harassment and violence from peers. A significant number of gay adolescents report that they have been physically assaulted, robbed, raped, or sexually abused (Martin & Hetrick, 1988; Peterson, 1989; Rotheram-Borus et al., 1991). Peterson (1989) found in a survey of the Los Angeles County school system that the abuse (with high prevalence) inflicted by classmates on gay male youths apparently is premeditated, rather than a chance occurrence, and that such incidents are escalating dramatically. These findings are consistent with the antigay violence that often occurs on college campuses (D'Augelli, 1992). The threat of violence may be a particularly difficult issue for a young gay man as he explores what it means to be male in a society that expects men to be physically powerful warriors.

SUBSTANCE USE AND ABUSE

One response to the emotional isolation, confusion, and self-hatred experienced by some gay adolescents is to numb the pain by using alcohol or drugs. Remafedi (1987b) found that 58% of the gay youth studied met *DSM-III-R* criteria for a substance abuse disorder. Rotheram-Borus, Luna, Marotta, and Kelly (1994) provide another explanation, suggesting that gay adolescents may be more likely to use alcohol or drugs to provide a socially acceptable explanation to themselves for engaging in same-gender sexual activity. In addition, gay bars historically have served as more than places to meet and drink; they have been community centers and part of the initiation process into the adult gay subculture. Unfortunately, the adult bar scene is permeated with substance use and is an inappropriate context for adolescent development. In response to the need for safe, substance-free meeting spaces for sexual minority youth, a number of youth organizations have emerged; however, such groups are located primarily in major cities.

HIV AND AIDS

The Centers for Disease Control (1998) estimates that at least one person under the age of 22 contracts HIV every hour of the day in the United States. Young people under 25 represent half of all new HIV infections in the United States. Gay adolescents may be at increased risk of becoming infected for several reasons, including a lack of appropriate information about prevention of infection. Additionally, Hetrick and Martin (1987) assert that stigmatized gay adolescents experience shame, guilt, depression, and self-hate; such an adolescent may engage in self-destructive sexual risk taking as a form of passive suicide. Savin-Williams (1995) points out that gay adolescents may never realize that sexual and emotional intimacy can be merged within same-sex relationships. The consequences for this disconnection can be damaging and even life-threatening as young men may have anonymous sex with older men or trade sex for drugs or money. In addition, part of the identity development process for a gay adolescent involves exploring his sexual orientation: "Many gay youths may engage in sexual activity as a means of such exploration, making sexual activity for gay youths normative, as a developmental marker of identity formation" (Rotheram-Borus et al., 1995, p. 84). With this awareness, it is critical that gay youth be as informed as possible about the prevention of HIV infection, so that they can explore their sexual orientation without risking their lives.

ADJUSTMENT

Most of the attention thus far has been on the problems, rather than the promise, of gay adolescents. There is no doubt that some of the struggles faced by gay adolescents are a consequence of the stigma they bear; however, those who survive may have developed a resiliency that enables them to cope effectively with other challenges in life. It is difficult to be different during a developmental period in which fitting in is so important. The experience of not fully fitting in may enhance a person's empathic understanding of others, his creativity, and his coping skills. We cannot forget that most gay adolescents cope with a world that, at best, does not affirm them and at worst offers them condemnation and abuse, yet they still manage to grow up to lead happy and productive lives. Recent findings in two studies of African American adolescent gay males (Edwards, 1996a, 1996b) suggest that, even with the existence of homophobia in society, the development of a positive and well-integrated self-perception and a good set of survival skills is possible in the lives of gay adolescents. Edwards suggests that for this to occur "the adolescent must develop an identity that is able to withstand the homophobic attitudes he will experience" (1996b, p. 353). He can be supported as he grows by having the opportunity to meet other gay youth and develop intimate relationships, by the presence of gay adult role models, by spiritual mentoring that affirms his sacred worth, by access to accurate information about what it means to be gay, and by having the opportunity to come out to himself and others.

IDENTITY DEVELOPMENT: SELF-EMERGENCE

The essence of the human soul contains a blueprint for the identity development process for every individual. As a male child grows into boyhood and young adulthood, internal codes (e.g., genetic and biological influences) and external codes (e.g., sociocultural and environmental influences) both strongly affect physical and psychosocial growth and development. During this process, a male child becomes aware of his likes and dislikes, his abilities and limitations, and his sexual desires and urges. A significant minority of male children develops a gay identity. The self-emergence process of personal identity reveals a unique cultural affiliation and identification with having a gay sexual orientation.

Given that the fabric and fiber of society are intricately heterosexist and homophobic in nature (Herek, 1996), the self-emergence process of developing a gay identity is constantly oppressed and suppressed. In many ways, it is not okay to be gay. Homosexuality is still considered by many to be a "sickness," "amoral," and simply "wrong." Thus, a male child/boy/young man who begins to gain an awareness and understanding of this aspect of his cultural identity will more than likely struggle to fully accept and integrate his gay identity because of a social environment that stigmatizes homosexuality (Cass, 1996; D'Augelli, 1996).

As counselors, it is our responsibility to nurture all precious souls. Our commitment is to provide a safe, nurturing, and supportive environment for all children. To be culturally competent counselors, we must understand the life experiences that foster and affect the growth and development of gay boys and young men. A later section of this chapter addresses multiple cultural identities associated with gay sexual orientation.

In the context of personal growth and awareness of one's identity, in general, Erikson (1968) has explicated an eight-stage developmental theory (only the first six stages of which are addressed here). It is crucial to understand how Erikson's theory may apply to the gay identity development process; a brief overview of Erikson's theory therefore is presented. One of the most cited gay identity development models, the Cass Sexual Orientation Identity (1979, 1996) also is discussed. In addition, the sociocultural and political significance of race in American society, including the gay community, commands that we also briefly offer a perspective on racial identity (i.e., Black identity, with implications for other minority groups). Finally, we present a conceptual framework for integrating the three identity models in an effort to foster a more holistic perspective on the gay identity development of males from boyhood to young adulthood. The chapter concludes with suggestions and recommendations for interventions.

ERIKSON'S PSYCHOSOCIAL DEVELOPMENT MODEL

Erikson's theory of human growth and development offers a developmental perspective on crucial tasks that an individual experiences and attempts to negotiate. A dichotomy of end states results as one matures in age and develops his personality and interpersonal style. Erikson's first six stages are as follow: trust versus mistrust, autonomy versus shame/doubt, initiative versus guilt, industry versus inferiority, identity versus role confusion, and intimacy versus isolation. Gladding (1998) notes that "the first five stages specifically focus on the formation of the person into a competent individual with adequate skills and identity" (p. 9). Furthermore, he asserts that the stages are sequential and that an individual needs to achieve a degree of success in each stage prior to advancing in pursuit of goals in the next stage.

What significance does Erikson's theory hold for gay male identity development? Erikson's psychosocial identity model offers a perspective on a gay male's general sense of self-concept. Self-concept may be defined as the self-understanding and self-image an individual develops; it includes personality characteristics and traits that relate to intrapersonal and interpersonal style. For instance, the optimal developmental outcome implied by this theory is for a young man to exhibit appropriate level of trust, autonomy, initiative, industry, identity salience, and intimacy in his relations with others.

At the end of the infancy stage and during the early childhood stage, some boys may have a sense of "being different" from others in their environments. Hanson and Hartmann (1996) note that "many gay men acknowledge that they felt different from a very early age as young as 2, 3, or 4 years old" (p. 262). Childhood recollections among these gay men also included an awareness of (a) having less defined masculine interests, (b) having more defined feminine interests, and in some cases (c) having a very strong attraction to men, including an erotic and excited interest in male bodies. During the task of developing trust and autonomy, a gay child/boy's conscious internal awareness of "feeling different" may hinder this process. How can he fully trust and establish a sense of individuality when he senses that this new level of self-understanding, an emerging self-concept of having interest in same-gender individuals, is unacceptable in his immediate environment of his family? Hanson and Hartmann (1996) believe that "some of these boys will keep their thoughts and feelings quite secret on the basis of guilt, shame, or fear of ridicule" (p. 263). It is important to recognize that for some gay males a sense of mistrust and shame/doubt related to his gay identity self-concept may have roots in early childhood, the first two stages of Erikson's model.

If the first four stages are negotiated successfully, a 12-year-old boy who begins to question his same-sex attractions may possess a strong self-concept that affords him strength during the exploration of his sexual identity process. If this same boy exhibited a general sense of mistrust, shame/doubt, guilt, and inferiority, however, he may experience enormous struggles and strains as internal concerns about his sexual identity surface. One has to wonder if this particular boy/adolescent may be prone to suicidal behaviors (D'Augelli, 1996; Hartstein, 1996). Thus, it is imperative that we assess a boy's or young man's personality style based on Erikson's theory. It is crucial for a gay boy/adolescent/young man to possess qualities and characteristics that help him mediate the negative and hostile attitudes toward gay males likely to surface in a heterosexist and homophobic society.

GAY IDENTITY DEVELOPMENT MODELS

In understanding the developmental process of gay identity, it is important to examine the social and cultural environmental influences of society. Several institutions, such as family, religion, education, government, military, and the world of work, provide strong messages about what is appropriate in terms of behavior, attitudes, beliefs, and values. Unfortunately, across these institutions, a strong heterosexist and homophobic bias exists. Heterosexism is defined as "the ideological system that denies, denigrates, and stigmatizes any nonheterosexual form of behavior, identity, relationship, or community" (Herek, 1996, p. 101). Furthermore, Herek (1995) notes that homophobia is often used "to describe hostility toward gay men, lesbians, and bisexuals" (p. 321) wherein heterosexual individuals may fear having contact with homosexuals.

As a boy grows and learns about himself and his role in society, he hears a loud and clear message encouraging, if not demanding, that he develop a heterosexual orientation. Many male role models both in the home and in public promote traditional gender role and sex role stereotypes for boys and young men. These messages are quite confusing for the child, boy, or young man who begins to sense that he is "different" from other males (Cass, 1996; Hanson & Hartmann, 1996). This initial level of conscious awareness signifies an internal self-discovery process about the nature of one's sexuality and sexual orientation. The male individual begins to recognize emotional, sexual, and physical attractions to other males. To further understand this process, we turn to Cass's gay identity development model.

CASS'S GAY IDENTITY MODEL

Cass (1979, 1996), using interpersonal congruency theory, has presented a six-stage model of gay identity development. In Cass's model, two forces, significant others' expectations and societal norms, are embedded within a gay male's interpersonal environment. These forces mediate the gay identity formation process. The interpersonal congruency theory as espoused by Cass (1979) posits that "stability and change in human behavior are dependent on the congruency or incongruency that exists within an individual's interpersonal environment" (p. 220).

Within this theory, the state of congruence represents an acceptable and comfortable way of being in the world. An individual experiences stability in his life during a state of congruency. Conversely, the state of incongruency represents an unacceptable and uncomfortable way of being in the world. An individual experiences instability in his life during a state of incongruency. The states of congruency and incongruency (Cass, 1979) are related to and indicative of how an individual experiences his gay identity. Cass contends that the state of incongruency serves as a catalyst to move an individual toward resolving experienced cognitive, affective, and/or behavioral dissonance related to his gay identity. Successful resolution of incongruency results in state progression and growth, whereas unsuccessful resolution leads to potential "identity foreclosure"; that is, the individual's gay identity development process may be postponed.

Cass (1996) later utilized a social constructionist psychology perspective to reframe her model. This perspective seems to supersede Cass's initial reliance on interpersonal congruency theory. Cass (1996) asserts that gay identity formation process is strongly influenced by the sociocultural environment in which the gay boy/adolescent/young man lives rather than being the result of inner psychological mechanisms that can be found in all human beings (p. 229). In general, Cass now encourages practitioners to recognize that an essentialist perspective, highlighting psychological inner developmental processes, must be weighed against a social constructionist perspective. An essentialist perspective holds that an individual's identity development and self-expression result from internal forces such as innate traits and cognitive and affective styles. The social constructivist perspective holds that an individual's identity development and self-expression result from his or her interactions with external forces such as family, peers, the church, schools, community, and political institutions. Stimulus from the sociocultural environment influences and contributes to an individual's identity development and self-expression.

In the essentialist perspective or naturalistic view, gay identity development unfolds based solely on inner psychological mechanisms. Such a perspective suggests that societal influences do not impede or support gay individual identity and self-expression. Various coming out stories and experiences of gay adolescents and youth would seem to discount this perspective on gay identity development. The social constructivist perspective as offered by Cass advances that the gay identity formation process mainly involves a "reciprocal interaction"; that is, the interaction between an individual gay male and his environment produces knowledge, behaviors, beliefs, and experiences about himself in relation to the development of a gay identity. Such a perspective seems highly plausible based on coming out stories and experiences of gay adolescents and youth.

Cass's model (1979, 1996) has six stages. An individual may move back and forth among stages. In Stage 1, identity confusion, the individual begins to question his sexual orientation. He experiences confusion because this new perception of himself as being gay is incongruent with the previous perception of himself as being heterosexual (especially given the ongoing and enduring heterosexist and homophobic messages promoted in society). In Stage 2, identity comparison, a boy or young man begins to explore externally and to compare himself with others to determine his sexual orientation. While in this stage, gay males tend to seek out gay reading material, identify with other gay males in their environment, and attempt to understand why they "feel different" from their peers. In Stage 3, identity tolerance, a gay male establishes increased contact with the gay community yet still presents himself as being heterosexual in nongay environments. This form of identity management has been referred to as "passing" or, in some cases, "being in the closet." As he becomes more comfortable with his sexual orientation, the gay male enters Stage 4, identity acceptance, and begins to embrace this aspect of his personal, cultural identity. Often, this is the stage when gay boys and young men begin to "come out" to significant others in their life, particularly family members and close heterosexual friends. They may already have "come out" to known and suspected gay and lesbian individuals in their social network. In Stage 5, identity pride, gay boys and young men begin to feel proud about their gay identity and begin to seek activities and environments that will nurture and support their sexual orientation identity. The emotional joy about being gay also sometimes coexists with intense anger toward heterosexuals who are not accepting of gay males. Finally, in Stage 6, identity synthesis, the gay boy or young man is willing to disclose the nature of his sexual orientation to anyone and simultaneously deal with the range of positive to negative reactions this may elicit from others. At this time, having a gay identity is perceived as being just one aspect of his entire personal, cultural identity. The awareness and observation of heterosexism and homophobia still makes him angry, but this feeling is not as intense as during the identity pride stage (Cass, 1979, p. 156).

This dynamic process experienced by gay boys/young men as they develop an awareness of their sexual orientation and develop a gay identity may be a turbulent period. An array of feelings may accompany movement back and forth among Cass's stages. Gay individuals in the earlier stages often experience emotional confusion, loneliness, frustration, isolation, and depression. It is important to understand that this range of affects and moods is the result of "feeling different" from mainstream society and of recognizing the potential dangers and costs that may occur after accepting and disclosing one's gay identity. In the stages of identity acceptance, identity pride, and identity synthesis, gay boys/young men feel assurance, contentment, connection with others, excitement, and joy and peace about their gayness. Finally, Cass (1996) encourages practitioners to view gay identity development as a process of interaction instead of as a set of discrete and stagnant stages. D'Augelli's (1994) human development life span perspective on gay identity development provides further understanding.

RACIAL IDENTITY AND GAY
IDENTITY DEVELOPMENT MODELS

The developed existing gay identity models generally reflect the experiences of White/European Americans, Canadians, and Australians (Levine & Evans, 1991). Too often, theorists have not incorporated the effects of race within their understanding of gay identity formation and development. In her revised model, Cass (1996) notes that her theory accommodates ethnic differences, yet she does not specifically provide information about the intersection of gay identity and racial identity.

Cornel West (1994) contends that race represents a strong influential role and force in the lives of Americans. Within the process of gay identity development, how does a non-White racial identification affect the acquisition of a positive, healthy gay identity? In Western society, the lives of members of "visible racial and ethnic groups," or VREG (Cook & Helms, 1988), are affected by stereotypes, prejudice, and racism (Helms, 1990). When VREG members ask the question "Might I be gay?" (Cass, 1996), their responses are mediated by the cultural norms, values, beliefs, and traditions ingrained in their community (Edwards, 1996a; Icard, 1986; Loiacano, 1989, 1993; Monteiro & Fuqua, 1994; Wall & Washington, 1991). The influences of parents, extended family, cultural peers, and the church (McGoldrick, Pearce, & Giordano, 1982) present unique cultural conflicts to negotiate within a social constructionist perspective (Cass, 1996) for gay boys/young men within VREG.

Tremble, Schneider, and Appathurai (1989) emphasize the salience of race as explicated by the voices of gay youth from a multicultural worldview. They report that a 20-year-old Pakistani-Canadian male stated "My parents are hurt. They see homosexuality as being against the Muslim faith. They think of it as a white people's thing. Being gay is something I picked up from my white friends" (p. 260). A gay Chinese adolescent from Hong Kong stated "I am a double minority. Caucasian gays don't like gay Chinese, and the Chinese don't like the gays. It would be easier to be white. It would be easier to be straight. It's hard to be both" (p. 263). Jones and Hill (1996) report that a 17-year-old African American gay youth stated "My parents say this gay stuff is a white thing. All of my homeboys from the neighborhood are always putting down gay people. And, when I come to programs for gay and lesbian youth, most of the adults are white. You white people are cool but I need to be with my own kind" (p. 557).

These voices of gay people from minority racial and ethnic groups offer a window about how they experience living in a socioracial society (Helms, 1996). Helms notes that race and how individuals respond to others based on skin color influence interpersonal and intrapersonal processes. Indeed, racism is alive and well in society, in general, and the largely White gay community is not immune. Research on gay boys/young men from VREG provides evidence of the prejudice and discrimination experienced in White gay communities (Greene, 1994; Icard, 1986; Loiacano, 1993). This current state of affairs makes it imperative that counselors carefully assess the interaction of gay and racial identity for males of VREG.

Helms's racial identity development model posits five "ego statuses": conformity, dissonance, immersion/emersion, internalization, and integrative awareness (cf. Helms, 1990, 1996). Each ego status reflects a composite of behavioral, attitudinal, and belief sets of a racial being and can be characterized as an "information-processing strategy," that is, how one encodes, analyzes, reacts to, and retrieves racial information. Ego status helps, for example, in understanding how a Black gay male may respond to individuals within the White gay community.

For example, a Black gay male with a conformity ego status tends to devalue his own racial group while idealizing Whites. Thus, for him, interaction in the White gay community is more comfortable and even preferable to being with Black gays or heterosexuals. The perspective changes when this Black gay male enters into the immersion/emersion ego status. He now idealizes his own racial group and devalues and denigrates Whites. At this time, he would tend to reject the larger White gay community. In the internalization ego status, this Black gay male critically and objectively assesses and responds to members of the White gay community on a case-by-case basis. If he perceives an effort to eliminate racism among White gay individuals, he may be likely to choose to remain committed to and involved with the group.

A CULTURAL IDENTITY
INTEGRATION MODEL FOR GAY MALES

Each gay boy/adolescent/young man possesses multiple levels of cultural identities, such as those of sexual orientation, gender, race, ethnicity, socioeconomic status, and religion/spiritual orientation. These indices form a unique "cultural identity matrix" for each gay male. In this section, we share a process model for dynamically and at times simultaneously assessing aspects of a gay male's cultural identity matrix.

This model suggests that two focuses be adopted. The first focus, a microscopic view, attends to the cultural identity anchor (i.e., sexual orientation) most important to the gay male's present functioning or concern. In this process, the gay male sets the agenda and guides the counselor's decisions about appropriate interventions. In selecting these interventions, however, the counselor needs to critically assess the particular identity "status" (i.e., sexual orientation) that dominates the gay male's current worldview.

For example, if a 17-year-old African American male presents with intense distress about his first awareness of having "sexual thoughts and attractions to other males," this would suggest Cass's status of identity confusion. Thus, an appropriate intervention might be recommendation for individual counseling. In counseling, initial dialogue needs to center on "sexual thoughts and attractions," not an assumed "gay identity." Again, this young man is in the very early process of self-exploration; thus, the counselor needs to avoid labeling or pigeonholing.

The suggestion to attend group counseling or a gay support group meeting may be quite inappropriate given his identity confusion status. Within the identity confusion status, this African American adolescent may feel extremely self-conscious and intensely fearful about others (i.e., group members) being aware of his sexual identity concerns. Moreover, membership within many counseling or gay support groups does not include visible racial/ethnic individuals. Thus, this young African American adolescent may feel more uncomfortable in a predominantly White group. In addition, if the counselor assesses that this young man expresses a general distrust of others, a cultural mistrust of Whites, feelings of shame or doubt, and difficulty initiating tasks, such a profile would further warrant individual focused intervention, perhaps with a non-White counselor.

If this same male stated "I am terrified that my parents, especially my father, will think I am a "White sissy" with no commitment to black folks! And, my girlfriend being a strong Christian woman would definitely tell me that I'm going to hell for being a sinner," then a second type of focus must be adopted: The counselor needs a macroscopic view. Using this perspective, the counselor verbally acknowledges the young man's "voiced" facets of his cultural identity matrix (i.e., sexual orientation, gender, race, familial, religious/spiritual). The delicate challenge here is to avoid contributing to the client's feeling of being overwhelmed when considering that a gay identity affects so many aspects of his life. It is important to assist the client in prioritizing the most immediate levels of his cultural identity presently being affected. The process of rank ordering and assigning degree of attending immediacy (perhaps using a 1-10 scale) will assist the client to regain a sense of control and/or state of congruency as he manages this interpersonal conflict. In a macroscopic view, as the client makes sufficient levels of progress in one facet of his cultural identity matrix (e.g., sexual orientation), the counselor needs to skillfully initiate dialogue about the impact on other facets. Thus, the counselor alternates between the macroscopic and microscopic views. This process model for cultural identity integration with gay males affords a holistic perspective and approach of intervention. It seeks to affirm and value the individual gay male's entire essence of being.

INTERVENTIONS FOR SUPPORTING GAY MALES

In offering support to gay males, it is crucial for counselors to establish rapport. The most immediate and credible rapport results when the counselor possesses awareness of, sensitivity to, and knowledge about what it means for a male to "think he might be gay" and/or "identify as being gay." A counselor's language, tone of voice, and nonverbal signals need to convey clearly a sense of comfort, safety, warmth, and genuine caring in assisting a gay male client.

During individual counseling, it may be helpful to explore gay identity development processes with the client. Providing a sociocultural context about gay male experiences will increase the client's level of self-understanding and "normalize" this potentially gay male's experience. The counselor needs to assess for internalized homophobia and assist in determining what societal influences lead to such beliefs. The client may benefit from a host of techniques of interventions, such as cognitive restructuring of negative self-talk/self-image about being gay; assertiveness training in confronting heterosexism/homophobia; and social skills training via role plays for building friendships, establishing romantic relationships, coming out, and/or establishing support networks as a newly self-identified gay male. More important, an exploration of the gay male's cultural identity matrix will also help him to acknowledge and integrate all aspects of his cultural identity in relation to his sexual orientation identity.

One of the most important interventions counselors can make is to help a gay client find age-appropriate ways to express his desires. Too often, gay youth and young men come out in gay adult environments. These environments do not provide age-appropriate experiences and/or role models for males who are in the early process of gay identity development. A counselor might recommend developmentally appropriate support systems such as social, support, or therapy groups; youth organizations; one-to-one peer mentoring; or contact with volunteer gay adult role models. Role models represent public and private visibility of being gay. Acknowledging a visibility continuum, it is important to identify both "open" (public) and "closed" (private) gay role models because one or both may help a gay client determine how he might navigate the expression of his gay identity. Why use "closed" (private) gay role models? With the awareness that the world is not a safe place, it is important for gay males to make decisions and develop skills in managing their identity. Career, family, religious, or political concerns, or concerns for a partner's safety, may prompt even those gay males having strong self-esteem and a healthy sense of identity to maintain a public image of heterosexuality in certain environments.

It is also crucial to consider other cultural facets of identity in suggesting role models. Racial, ethnic, religious/spiritual, and class issues may need to be considered in finding a potential role model. The counselor's responsibility is to ask the client what type of role model he might need.

RESEARCH

Research in the area of gay youth and adolescents is critical (Chandler, 1995; Herdt, 1989; Herdt & Boxer, 1993; Owens, 1998; Savin-Williams, 1998). Unfortunately, given the political and religious pressures associated with gay issues, large-scale investigations examining gay identity development and processes are nearly nonexistent. Unique challenges and barriers are present in studying how males, as they mature from boys, to adolescents, to young men, discover and experience themselves as gay individuals. One of the unique barriers is a presumption of heterosexual sexual identity directed toward developing males across the life span. Within the sociocultural "reciprocal interaction" process, significant others such as parents, siblings, and teachers respond to males as if they were heterosexual, often forcing males to portray a particular gender/sex role set regardless of internal stimuli that may contradict such notions. This condition highlights the heterosexist assumption that engulfs developing males across various sociocultural contexts and domains (e.g., clothing, play, sports, dating, hobbies).

It is essential that researchers find ways to study developing males outside a heterosexist framework. Child and adolescent researchers need to develop assessment measures that afford a reflection of nondominant sexual identity processes, sexual behavior variances, or sex role identification processes. In advancing understanding of the complexity of sexuality among males, researchers must adopt an inclusive perspective and conduct carefully crafted analyses that examine multiple expressions of sexual identity.

A second barrier relates to the sociopolitical and religious pressures against schools adopting any supportive, enriching posture toward gay boys/youth. Many gay and lesbian teachers remain in the proverbial closet in legitimate fear for their jobs. As long as they can be fired simply for being lesbian or gay, it is difficult to imagine a supportive climate in the schools for gay youth. It is essential, therefore, that nondiscrimination policies be put in place for school personnel so that gay youth have the opportunity to see healthy, productive role models. All too often, school boards, principals, teachers, and parent activists strongly object to any such policy and to any curriculum, extracurricular organizations, or health-oriented outreach efforts that acknowledge or support developing youth who might be gay. Research is needed to determine the most effective ways to overcome this particular barrier. Both quantitative and qualitative investigations surveying those who express homonegative attitudes would help to shed light on the resistant attitudes, behaviors, and affective responses of individuals in our society who deny appropriate sexual identity information and/or support services to gay and lesbian people.

Finally, another challenge for researchers is to cast a wider research net. Currently, most research data on gay youth reflect males who may be disconnected from their families, involved in mental health treatment, or actively engaged in political oriented gay community organizations. Sampling bias needs to be managed. A much more concerted effort needs to be directed toward including more diverse and varied participants across the life span. For instance, in standardized testing across grades K-12 that examines academic, social, and psychological functioning among males in schools, if a simple option of self-identifying one's sexual orientation existed, invaluable research data would be generated over time. Again, it is clearly recognized that implementing such a practice would incite war among political and religious bodies. The battles need to occur, however, if the souls of gay youth are to be saved.

An equally critical intervention domain involves counselors taking steps to effect systemic changes. Counselors need to advocate strongly for inclusive policies, procedures, and practices that affirm gay identity. For instance, it is vital to challenge institutions such as schools, churches, governmental agencies, workplaces, and unaware families. Gay males need to find safe havens in various settings. It is important for K-12 schools as well as universities and colleges to foster understanding and support of gay men and issues (Evans & Wall, 1991; Woog, 1995).

Counselors are in a pivotal role to forge bridges and alliances that foster the understanding and affirmation of lesbians and gay men and boys. To this end, some educators and counselors have chosen to identify themselves as allies with the lesbian/gay/bisexual community. Wall and Washington (1991) describe the process of becoming an ally, defining an ally as one who is joined with another for a common purpose. They note that although a member of an oppressed group can serve as an advocate for his or her own group the impact is often more powerful when the supporter is a member of the dominant group. Wall and Washington suggest that in joining to end lesbian/gay oppression, taking a position as an ally involves modeling advocacy and confronting inappropriate comments and behavior. In this context, heterosexual allies avoid making a point of being heterosexual, avoid joking about those who engage in nontraditional gender role behavior, and are equally physical with men and women. Additionally, advocacy involves making sure that issues facing gay and lesbian people are acknowledged and addressed. Such activities can include inviting speakers to address topics relevant to the lesbian/gay/bisexual community, advocating for nondiscrimination statements to include sexual orientation, and generally raising awareness of issues faced by lesbian and gay people.

Counselors are encouraged to seek and offer training experiences for other community members in increasing and fostering greater understanding about personal and political realities of gay life experiences (Buhrke, 1989; Buhrke & Douce, 1991). There is empirical support that educative interventions—including the use of discussion, small group problem solving, a gay/lesbian/bisexual discussion panel, and films—are effective in reducing homophobia among university undergraduates (Wells, 1991). Furthermore, Rudolph (1989) describes a promising 3-day multimodal intervention for mental health practitioners designed to instill needed attitudes and skills in counselors of lesbian and gay clients. The following resources are recommended (Evans & Wall, 1991) for use in programming around the issues of lesbian, gay, and bisexual awareness.

Alternatives: A Game of Understanding is available from P.O. Box 1050, Amherst, MA 01004-1050, telephone (413) 546-4523. *Opening Doors to Understanding and Acceptance: A Guide to Facilitating Workshops on Lesbian, Gay, and Bisexual Issues* can be obtained by contacting Kathy Obear, Human Advantage, 6 University Drive, Suite 125, Amherst, MA 01002, telephone (413) 584-0812. Finally, the Human Rights Foundation (1984) has published *Demystifying Homosexuality: A Teaching Guide About Lesbians and Gay Men.*

RESOURCES FOR SUPPORTING
<u>GAY MALE ADOLESCENTS</u>

Despite the multitude of challenges and barriers facing gay youth, we are quite pleased to note that resources are available in many geographic regions of the United States. These resources include support groups, mental health and medical services, gay schools, gay affirming religious/spiritual fellowships, professional career associations, family advocacy (e.g., Parents and Friends of Lesbians and Gays, or PFLAG), and local, state, and national gay organizations. The various national youth groups include the National Coalition of Advocates for Students, National Gay Youth Network, and National Network of Runaway and Youth Services. In addition, the Internet offers hundreds of resources and contacts for gay males. To this end, almost any search engine (e.g., Yahoo, Excite, Lycos) can be used to look up the term "gay youth"; numerous sources of support and connections are at hand. Space limitations prohibit a comprehensive list of all the organizations and resources available for gay youth; however, the resources listed below should provide a helpful start.

1. *How to Make the World a Better Place for Gays and Lesbians* (1995) by Una Fahy provides concrete, useful suggestions as well as a fairly comprehensive list of resources and contact information.
2. Parents and Friends of Lesbians and Gays (PFLAG) is a national organization with local chapters. PFLAG provides information and peer support for families and friends of lesbians and gays and also has excellent publications and conferences. It can be reached at www.pflag.org or (202) 638-4200.
3. The National Black Lesbian and Gay Leadership Forum is a national membership organization providing advocacy, public policy work, and education. It can be reached at (202) 483-6786.
4. The Hetrick Martin Institute is a social service agency established to enhance the well-being of sexual minority youth. It can be reached at http://cvisions.cat.nyu.edu or (212) 674-2400.

HIGHLIGHTS OF CHAPTER 10

▶ From an early age, usually before adolescence, many gay youth report that they "feel different" from peers and family. The ways in which that differentness is interpreted by self and others may determine the difficulty of the coming out process for the child or adolescent who lives through it.

▶ Newman and Muzzonigro (1993) found that in a multiethnic sample of gay male adolescents the average age at which respondents realized they were gay was 12 years. Developmentally, the challenge at this age is identity versus role confusion; thus, it is important to remember how difficult it can be for an adolescent who "feels" different during such a time when belonging is crucial.

▶ Often, gay youths have school-related problems including poor academic performance, failing a grade, truancy, and dropping out of school. Such problems may be a result of enduring social isolation, verbal and physical abuse, family conflict, spiritual conflict, and the emotional turmoil of not belonging.

▶ Empirical studies indicate that suicide attempts are high among samples of gay male youths, ranging from 20% to 39%. One explanation for this alarming rate of self-harm is that gay youth often experience or expect physical and verbal abuse or rejection from those who would otherwise be expected to support them: family, friends, and their community of faith.

▶ Gay youth may internalize negative images of gay people that are readily available in a homophobic society. Without visible role models or accurate information about homosexuality, they may be unable to imagine that being gay could mean anything good.

▶ Approximately 50,000 people are infected with the HIV virus annually, and 25% of these people are under the age of 21. Gay adolescents may be at increased risk of becoming infected. Stigmatized gay adolescents experience shame, guilt, depression, and self-hate; such an adolescent may engage in self-destructive sexual risk taking as a form of passive suicide.

▶ Research on gay boys and young men from minority racial and ethnic groups provides evidence of the prejudice and discrimination experienced by them within White gay communities.

▶ Cass (1996) asserts that the gay identity formation process is strongly influenced by the sociocultural environment in which the gay boy/adolescent/young man lives rather than being the result of inner psychological mechanisms that can be found in all human beings. She encourages practitioners to view the gay identity development as a process of interaction instead of as a set of discrete and stagnant stages.

▶ A counselor's language, tone of voice, and nonverbal signals should convey clearly a sense of comfort, safety, warmth, and genuine caring in assisting a gay male client. A counselor may recommend developmentally appropriate support systems such as social, support, and therapy groups; youth organizations; one-to-one peer mentoring; and contact with volunteer gay adult role models.

▶ Counselors are in a pivotal role to forge bridges that foster the understanding and affirmation of gay youth. To this end, some have chosen to identify themselves as allies of the lesbian/gay/bisexual community. This may involve making sure that one is aware of the resources available for gay youth in one's community, making sure that issues facing gay people are acknowledged and addressed in one's organization, inviting speakers to address topics relevant to the gay community, advocating for nondiscrimination statements to include sexual orientation, and generally being committed to raising awareness of issues faced by gay people.

CHAPTER

11

Counseling Teen Fathers

MARK S. KISELICA

Few social issues have captured the attention of our nation more than the problem of adolescent girls who bear children out of wedlock. The number and rate of premarital births to teen mothers has risen steadily over the past three decades, from 68,000 in 1960 (12% of all births to teenagers) to 361,000 (68% of all births to teenagers) in 1990 (Moore, Snyder, & Halla, 1992). This trend has heightened public concern because young, unmarried mothers and their children are at risk of dropping out of school and being poor and dependent on public welfare (Vera Institute of Justice, 1990). Concern for the well-being of adolescent mothers also has been generated by research findings indicating that the children born to young mothers are at risk for prenatal complications, premature birth, birth defects, mental retardation, and other health problems (Field, Widmayer, Stringer, & Ignatoff, 1980; Phipps-Yonas, 1980; Simkins, 1984).

In an effort to reduce the economic, social, and medical difficulties of young mothers and their children, multifaceted service programs for adolescent mothers proliferated during the 1980s and 1990s. Although these programs tended to be successful in addressing the many important needs of teen mothers, service providers generally neglected to consider the concerns of the male partners of teen mothers (Kiselica, 1995; Kiselica & Sturmer, 1993). According to several scholars (Allen-Meares, 1984; Robinson, 1988; Smith, 1989), this neglect is a manifestation of numerous misconceptions and stereotypes about young men who are involved in out-of-wedlock, adolescent pregnancies.

One of the dominant misconceptions about the teen pregnancy phenomenon in the United States is the public assumption that the vast majority of the partners of adolescent mothers are teenage boys. National statistics reviewed by Beymer (1995), however, indicate that approximately 70% of the male partners of married and unmarried teen mothers are over the age of 20. Nevertheless, as Robinson (1988) has documented, researchers and policymakers have tended to draw conclusions about teen fathers based on impressions and research that have been focused primarily on adult men who have sired children with teen mothers. Consequently, "teen fathers are the victims of massive misunderstanding" (Beymer, 1995, p. 26).

The purpose of this chapter is to clarify the role that teen fathers play in adolescent childbearing and to provide practitioners with suggestions for how to help adolescent fathers with their transition to parenthood. This chapter begins with an overview of the special concerns of males who beget children during their teenage years. Then, recommendations for establishing rapport with young fathers are provided. Next, strategies for crisis-oriented and long-term counseling are discussed. The chapter concludes with pertinent recommendations for training and future research.

TEEN FATHERS: WHO ARE THEY, AND WHAT ARE THEIR NEEDS?

Precise statistics on the number of teenage boys who become fathers and their demographic characteristics are difficult to generate because the identity of the fathers of children born to teen mothers are often not listed on birth registration forms (Sonenstein, 1986). The rough estimates that are available suggest that approximately 30% of the children born to teen mothers were sired by males who were teenagers (see Beymer, 1995). Although teen fathers are overrepresented among African Americans, the majority of adolescent fathers are White (see Kiselica, 1995). Cutting across racial and ethnic lines, teen fathers tend to be overrepresented among the poor (Vera Institute of Justice, 1990).

Recent research conducted by a handful of pioneering investigators has indicated that adolescent fathers tend to experience a host of adjustment difficulties associated with early paternity. These include the following: a wide range of troubling emotional reactions to the pregnancy, including depression, anger, and denial of responsibility for the pregnancy (Achatz & MacAllum, 1994; Elster & Panzarine, 1983b; Fry & Trifiletti, 1983; Vaz, Smolen, & Miller, 1983); conflicts regarding decisions pertaining to abortion and adoption (Robinson, 1988; Robinson & Barret, 1985); conflicts with the teen mother and her family and a related denial of access to the child (Achatz & MacAllum, 1994; Cervera, 1991; Elster & Hendricks, 1986; Kiselica, Stroud, Stroud, & Rotzien, 1992); concerns about their competency as a parent (Hendricks, 1988); declining contact with the child over time (Furstenberg, Brooks-Gunn, & Morgan, 1987; Hardy & Zabin, 1991); dropping out of school (Furstenberg, Brooks-Gunn, & Chase-Lansdale, 1989; Marsiglio, 1986); legal concerns (Achatz & MacAllum, 1994; Hendricks, 1988); relationship changes with peers (Achatz & MacAllum, 1994; Elster & Hendricks, 1986; Hendricks, 1988); and long-term career dissatisfaction, employment worries, and financial hardships (Achatz & MacAllum, 1994; Elster & Hendricks, 1986; Elster & Panzarine, 1983a; Furstenberg et al., 1987; Hendricks, 1988).

Recognizing that teen fathers need professional assistance to address these problems, several authorities have urged counselors to develop service programs that are tailored to the needs of adolescent fathers (Kiselica, 1995; Kiselica, Stroud, et al., 1992; Robinson, 1988). Kiselica (1995) recommends that teen father programs include the following service components: crisis pregnancy counseling, including abortion and adoption counseling; parenting skills training with an emphasis on the father's role in child development; legal advice; family and couples counseling; recreational services; educational and career counseling; and job training and placement services.

RAPPORT-BUILDING STRATEGIES

Adolescent fathers tend to be the victims of discrimination from adults who come into contact with them. According to Beymer (1995), teen fathers are "simultaneously rejected and ignored, disparaged and excluded, condemned and punished" (p. 26) for their role in the pregnancy. As a result, many teen fathers fear that they will be judged by counseling and social service professionals and, consequently, are unlikely to utilize even the best designed service programs. It is imperative, therefore, that helpers divest themselves of harmful stereotypes about this population and employ persistent outreach and rapport-building strategies with adolescent males facing early paternity (Kiselica, 1995; Robinson, 1988).

Accordingly, the process of effective counseling with teen fathers begins with a careful examination of the counselor's own attitudes and feelings about these youths. The counselor must guard against maintaining rigid stereotypes depicting the adolescent father as a manipulative young man who purposely gets a girl pregnant and then callously abandons the girl and her baby. A growing body of research indicates that although some teen fathers do fit this stereotypic image, most tend to support the adolescent mother before and after the pregnancy, and most also tend to support their children financially and emotionally during the early years of the children's lives (Achatz & MacAllum, 1994; Furstenberg, 1976; Panzarine & Elster, 1983; Rivara, Sweeney, & Henderson, 1986; Vaz et al., 1983). In the light of these research findings, counselors are challenged to reexamine how they view teen fathers. Moreover, even when the counselor encounters a young man who ignores his paternal responsibility, the counselor must move beyond knee-jerk judgments of the youth and entertain questions that will help the counselor to challenge the client to be an effective parent, such as the following:

- ► What are the circumstances that contributed to this young man's irresponsibility?
- ► How can I endeavor to mitigate those contributory circumstances?
- ► What role models can I enlist to help me to teach the young man what it means to be an effective father?
- ► What other forms of support does the client require to help him fulfill his crucial social role as a father?

Counselors who maintain positive perspectives about teen fathers are likely to be perceived by this population as trustworthy during initial contacts. To convince young fathers to enroll in service programs, however, counselors may need to employ a variety of outreach and rapport-building strategies. For example, it is recommended that the counselor establish a relationship with the family of the young father, through which the counselor communicates his or her willingness to assist the family with any of their concerns, not just those pertaining to the youth's paternity. Communicating this message over time can encourage the family to accept the counselor's initiatives and work as his ally in helping the young man to address his paternity issues (Kiselica, 1995). Hendricks has recommended that counselors be willing to arrange first meetings at the young father's residence, at a recreational center, or on some other familiar turf where the adolescent feels comfortable. This conveys to the teenager that the counselor is willing to enter the boy's world and comprehend its realities. I have found it particularly helpful to develop a relationship with the boy while taking turns shooting baskets, tossing a football back and forth, walking side by side down the street, or sharing a snack at a fast-food restaurant. Hendricks (1988) adds that it is a good idea to have flexible office hours and to create a male-friendly office environment by displaying sports magazines and offering the young man a soft drink and engaging him in nonthreatening, casual conversation during initial, brief encounters.

Throughout all their early contacts with teen fathers, counselors must carefully observe for, and adapt to, the relational style of the client. Counselors tend to be comfortable with intimate self-disclosure, but some teen fathers who have a traditional male relational style may recoil from counseling if the professional helper abruptly encourages the expression of private thoughts and feelings. I recommended, therefore, that the counselor utilize early, informal contacts with the youth to ascertain his relational style and adjust the approach to counseling accordingly. For example, with young fathers who demonstrate a traditional male relational style, it may be necessary to approach personal issues cautiously and to view the counseling session as a vehicle for providing the client with information pertaining to his concrete needs, such as how to obtain a job, legal advice, or facts about parenting and child development. Over time, the counselor should look for windows of opportunity during which the young man is less reticent regarding his emotional issues. Often, these opportunities emerge under the guise of a joke by the client or a passing comment that is shared by the client in the context of some other activity, such as tossing a football back and forth. The counselor must learn to judge how thoroughly the client is willing to focus on these issues at that moment and is likely to acquire important information by mirroring the client's manner of expression, such as the reciprocation of a humorous response or a related passing comment. Of course, with clients exhibiting a nontraditional male relational style, a more direct exploration of personal events usually is possible.

An understanding of, and sensitivity toward, the cultural background of the client is also a crucial factor in the development of a solid rapport with the client. As Kiselica and Pfaller (1993) observe, preliminary findings from multicultural research suggest that the experiences and counseling needs of teenage parents from different ethnic and racial backgrounds vary both between and within their cultures. For example, although most teenage fathers want help with practical concerns, such as finding employment (Hendricks, 1988), African American adolescent fathers also might need assistance with institutional barriers stemming from racism (Smith, 1988). Counselors who are uncomfortable with or incapable of addressing issues spurred by racism are likely to be rejected by those African American clients for whom racism is a salient issue (Kiselica, 1995). Ethnographic findings also suggest that the stigma associated with unwed parenthood might be more common in White than in Black families (Williams, 1991); therefore, counselors working with White families embroiled in the crisis of an unplanned, out-of-wedlock adolescent pregnancy are more likely to have to address the pregnancy-related shame and embarrassment of the client and his family during the counseling process (Kiselica, 1995). These are just a few of a multitude of culturally related concerns that can affect the counseling process with teen fathers. Because it is beyond the scope of this chapter to review each of these cultural issues, practitioners are urged to read *Multicultural Counseling With Teenage Fathers: A Practical Guide* (Kiselica, 1995) for a more thorough discussion of the topic. I also recommend that the reader incorporate the suggestions offered in this chapter with those contained in Part II of this book pertaining to different cultural populations of boys so as to develop multicultural counseling competency with adolescent fathers from different cultural backgrounds.

Regardless of the relational style or cultural background of the client, the most important message that the counselor can relay is that he or she is willing to serve as an advocate for the client over the long term. Such a commitment is likely to engender a foundation of trust that can sustain a therapeutic relationship through the prenatal and postnatal crises commonly experienced by young men involved in an unplanned pregnancy (Kiselica et al., 1992).

PHASES OF COUNSELING WITH TEEN FATHERS

Robinson (1988) suggests that the focus of counseling with teen fathers should vary according to the phase of pregnancy. Consistent with this recommendation, Kiselica (1995) describes at length the issues that emerge during the prenatal and postnatal phases of the pregnancy and concomitant counseling processes and interventions. An overview of these topics, gleaned from Kiselica (1995), follows. Also provided is a brief discussion of some case management issues that cut across the prenatal and postnatal phases of counseling.

COUNSELING DURING THE PRENATAL PHASE

Counselors working with an expectant teen father must be prepared to assist the client with three major dilemmas: How should the couple resolve the pregnancy? If the client is still enrolled in school during his partner's pregnancy, should he drop out of school? What does it mean to be a father?

Pregnancy Resolution Counseling

Teen fathers struggling to resolve a crisis pregnancy must contemplate a variety of options, each of which may pose an emotionally and morally laden conflict. Should he persuade his partner to have an abortion, or should he urge her to carry the baby to term? If the child is born, should the couple keep the baby, or should they give the infant up for adoption? If they keep the child, should they marry? If they marry, should they live on their own or with parents or relatives? If they don't marry, who should have custody of the baby? If the father is excluded from decisions regarding abortion and adoption, or if he chooses or is placed in a noncustodial role, what are his legal rights and obligations? What does unmarried, custodial fatherhood entail?

Obviously, these dilemmas are value laden as well, so it behooves the counselor to examine his or her attitudes and feelings about issues such as abortion and nonmarital paternity. According to Kiselica and Pfaller (1993), counselors have an ethical obligation to respect the values of their clients and to refrain from imposing their own values on teen parents as the couple attempts to make decisions about abortion and marriage. Instead, it is recommended that counselors adopt a decision-making paradigm in which they assist the client to clarify his or her own values pertaining to each of the possible options for resolving the pregnancy and to evaluate carefully the pros and cons of those options before a decision is made (Kiselica, 1995). Counselors who are unable to abide by these guidelines have an ethical responsibility to refer their clients to another professional (Kiselica & Pfaller, 1993).

While assisting the expectant father with these decisions, the counselor must remember that the pregnancy resolution process will be greatly affected, if not determined, by the expectant adolescent mother and her family. Furthermore, if the expectant father has informed his family of the pregnancy, they are also likely to exert influence on the decision-making process. Moreover, family members from both sides are likely to want to be involved in the process. I therefore recommend that the counselor explore with the client his willingness to involve all these parties in the decision.

With the client's permission, it is a productive strategy to extend oneself to the young mother, her family, and the father's family to enlist their support of the young couple during this emotionally draining time, solicit their input, and mediate any conflicts that emerge. With regard to the latter, it is common for the young couple's parents to express strong feelings of hurt, anger, and disappointment to the couple for the pregnancy. The counselor must empathize with these feelings while directing the families toward taking constructive action, such as that pertaining to making arrangements for an abortion, adoption, or who will have custody of the child. In addition, the counselor can gently help the families to reframe how they view the pregnancy; instead of seeing the pregnancy solely as an irresponsible act on the part of the couple and as a burden on the family, the family can be encouraged to entertain the love, hopes, and dreams that they have for the baby. Recruiting the support of extended family members and trusted members of the community, such as a local minister or close neighbor, can also to help the families feel less overwhelmed by the pregnancy and more positively directed toward the future.

Crisis Educational and Career Counseling

Throughout the pregnancy resolution process, important decisions regarding school and work must also be made. An unexpected pregnancy often prompts a teen father to drop out of school to find work to support his partner and child. According to Kiselica and Murphy (1994), the following measures may help the expectant father to avoid dropping out: referring the client to an in-school support program for expectant and parenting teens, placement in alternative schools that have cooperative work placements with local employers, and enlisting the assistance of the extended family in the form of financial support or child care provision for the child while the teen parents complete school.

Unfortunately, many teen fathers drop out of school in spite of taking such measures; others have dropped out of school prior to the conception. In both these cases, it is imperative that the counselor provide an orientation to the world of work, including training in job-seeking and job-keeping skills. Collaboration with job training and employment agencies is also necessary to help young fathers to develop employable skills and secure a job (Kiselica & Murphy, 1994).

Preparation for Fatherhood

It is common for expectant teen fathers to be worried about the impending responsibilities of parenthood (Achatz & MacAllum, 1994; Hendricks, 1988). Many ponder questions such as "Am I ready to be a father?" and "What is a father?" Expectant teen fathers whose partner will give birth to the baby therefore can benefit from assistance clarifying what it means to be a father.

Although an expectant young father can explore his parenting concerns through individual counseling and instruction, clinical experience indicates that a group psychoeducational approach to parenting skills training is more efficacious in preparing a teen father for parenthood. In a series of discussions on the subject, Kiselica and his colleagues (Kiselica, 1995, 1996a; Kiselica, Doms, & Rotzien, 1992; Kiselica, Rotzien, & Doms, 1994) have described how they utilize a group psychotherapeutic approach to fatherhood training in a three-module course that is tailored to the particular needs of young men facing paternity during their teenage years. In the first module of this course, the youths establish rapport with one another through a series of recreational activities, followed by more structured group sessions in which the participants clarify their attitudes about masculinity and their conceptions of fatherhood. A key component of this module is the development of a supportive group process through which the participants discuss the strengths and deficiencies of their own fathers. At the end of the first module, the participants identify their goals as parents and commit themselves to formal parenting skills training, which is conducted during the second module. Principles of child development and child-rearing skills are taught during this second module, with a particular emphasis on the important role of the father in child development. During the third and final module, the young fathers discuss issues of sexual responsibility and learn concepts of family/life management and family planning designed to engender realistic appraisals of family life and coping skills that the young men can use to help them avoid taking part in repeat unplanned pregnancies. Feedback from teen fathers who have completed the course suggest that the participants develop positive perspectives on fatherhood, effective parenting skills, responsible sexual attitudes and behaviors, and, most important, satisfying relationships with their children.

Responding to the couvade syndrome. Throughout the process of fatherhood training during the prenatal phase, teen fathers tend to express concern about the well-being of their pregnant partners. According to Kiselica and Scheckel (1995), a minority of expectant teen fathers who are intensely worried about the well-being of their partners during the pregnancy have been known to experience a cluster of somatic symptoms, referred to in the medical literature as the *couvade syndrome.* This stress-related reaction is believed to be the manifestation of physical aches and pains and anxieties about the birth and delivery of the baby (Bogren, 1986). The young man may feel acute anticipatory anxiety about his role during labor and childbirth. At the same time, he has empathy for his partner and typically attempts to be sensitive to the expectant mother's needs (Barnhill, Rubenstein, & Rocklin, 1979).

Kiselica and Scheckel (1995) describe several successful interventions they used during counseling with four adolescent boys affected by the couvade syndrome. All four clients were reported to recover from their symptoms after they were informed that these are common experiences of men during the prenatal period, received training about the childbirth process, and were taught specific strategies they could use to support their partners throughout the pregnancy and during labor and delivery. The authors recommended that the youth who is welcomed by the mother as a labor partner should be encouraged to join his partner in learning about the Lamaze method or some other form of birthing training. Kiselica and Scheckel also noted that expectant young fathers who have unstable, conflicted relationships with their partners may not be allowed by the partner and her family to be present at delivery. For these boys, the authors recommended that the clients receive some training about the birthing process to help allay their fears about the event and to assist them in understanding the experience of their partners during the delivery of the baby.

Supporting the adolescent mother. Because the couvade syndrome is a reaction closely tied to a young man's concern for his partner, the counselor should devote time to exploring how the client can support the expectant adolescent mother. Accordingly, in addition to receiving training about the supportive role of the father during the birthing process, it is recommended that expectant adolescent fathers be educated about the potential health risks associated with adolescent pregnancies. Expectant teenage mothers, especially those who lack prenatal medical care, are more likely than expectant adult mothers in their twenties to give birth to low-birth-weight babies (Children's Defense Fund, 1985). Low-birth-weight babies are at risk for a variety of medical complications (Baum, 1980). Most expectant teenage fathers are naive about such health risks and need to be encouraged to assist the adolescent mother in receiving adequate prenatal and postnatal medical care (Kiselica, 1995, 1996a; Kiselica et al., 1994).

During the prenatal phase, young fathers may require direct training in other behaviors for supporting the adolescent mother. For example, training in empathic listening skills and specific comforting behaviors can empower the client to be an important source of emotional support for his partner during the suspenseful months prior to the delivery and well into the postnatal period (Kiselica, 1995).

Counseling During the Postnatal Phase

Although counseling during the prenatal phase can help the client to weather the storms created by the crisis pregnancy, old issues may linger or reemerge, and new concerns and crises are likely to pop up as the young man matures. In particular, parenting difficulties, ongoing conflicts with (and hardships in) his and his partner's family, and long-term educational, career, and employment issues are likely to dominate the landscape of postnatal counseling.

Postnatal fatherhood issues. Some teen fathers may need to enter fatherhood training groups during the postnatal phase of counseling because they did not have access to such training during the prenatal phase. Although the content of such training is the same as that described earlier, the presence of young men who already are fathers can add several valuable dimensions to the group experience. These "veterans" can share with expectant fathers their views on how they handled prenatal crises and how they view their roles as fathers now that they have a child. In addition, during the parenting skills component of the course, it is a tremendous asset to the group when a current father brings his child to the class to demonstrate particular skills, such as comforting, feeding, changing, playing with—in other words, loving—his baby.

Although these latter experiences often contribute to the self-esteem and parental self-efficacy of the "veteran" father, his naiveté and insecurities as a parent are commonly apparent and warrant the counselor's ongoing attention. For example, parenting skills training rarely can prepare young men adequately for the shock and stress caused by the arrival of a colicky baby or for the strain that is created by the impinging responsibilities of parenthood, school, and/or work. A teenage boy facing these situations for the first time needs the support of the counselor, his family, and his peers in the group to help him to cope with the difficulties associated with raising a child as a teenager. He may also require refresher courses on parenting skills that have already been taught in an earlier module.

Another issue that may emerge during the postnatal phase pertains to young men who gradually neglect their parental duties. Although most fathers who are provided parenting skills training may be genuine in their desire to be an ongoing, positive presence in the life of their child, some do drift away from their responsibilities and require a balance of confrontation and encouragement to rekindle their devotion to their child. With regard to confronting the youth on this matter, the youth is more likely to accept constructive criticism about his behavior if it is posed by his peers in a group rather than by an adult counselor. It can also help to link the boy with an adult father from the community who is willing to serve as a father mentor. Often, the guidance and wisdom of an admired man can steer the young father on a course toward successful parenting.

Addressing ongoing family issues. Family issues that emerge during the postnatal phase can greatly affect the young father's transition and adjustment to fatherhood. One of the most detrimental crises is a decision on the part of his partner's family to deny him access to his child. Reasons for shutting him out can be varied: He and his partner may have had a fight marking the end of their relationship as a committed couple, he may have been unable or unwilling to provide adequate financial support, or the couple's parents may simply not like him or his family. Regardless of the reason for their decision, the counselor must quickly attempt to mediate some sort of agreement between the young father and his partner's family during this crisis. Empathizing with the concerns of both families is important during such work, as is an attempt to foster perspective taking among all parties about the other's position. Sometimes, a trusted minister, community leader, or mutual neighbor can help to resolve the crisis. When all else fails, however, the counselor may have to resort to referring the client to a lawyer who can advise him regarding his visitation rights as a father and the legal means to secure them. Throughout the entire process of gaining access to his child, the father will need the counselor's compassionate support.

Conflicts with his own kin are also common during the postnatal stage. His parents may continue to resent him for his "mistake" and express hostility toward him, his partner, and their child. Even when his parents and family are supportive of him during his early days as a father, disputes may erupt over how much the family can provide in terms of financial assistance and child care for the rearing of the baby. Boundary issues such as who sets the rules for the baby or who cares for the baby at what times can lead to other arguments that add to tension in the home. The reorganization of household space and time schedules to accommodate the baby may stress the family's ability to cope. Regular family counseling sessions can help the family to vent and manage their troublesome feelings, focus on the positive aspects of having a new member in the family, clarify the roles of family members, define what the family can or cannot do in terms of offering support to the young father, and identify what outside assistance the family may require.

Long-term educational, career, and employment issues. The counselor should bear in mind that educational and career decisions made during the prenatal phase of counseling typically represent a compromise between the teenage father's preferred plans and the rapidly emerging responsibilities of parenthood (Kiselica & Murphy, 1994). Many adolescent fathers periodically will need to be reminded of their aspirations and offered guidance in developing realistic educational and career plans that will enable them to realize their ambitions. This is particularly true in those cases in which the young father forsakes school or career plans because he is overwhelmed by the experience of early parenthood. This is also an important issue with those fathers who have left school for work and have been lulled into a false sense of security by their initial salaries earned while working in so-called unskilled positions. Many of these latter youths are naive about the world of work and the salaries they will need to earn in the future to ensure their economic self-sufficiency; consequently, they deem further schooling or training to be unnecessary. Such considerations underscore the importance of engaging these adolescents in long-term educational and career counseling (Kiselica, Stroud, et al., 1992).

Teen fathers are overrepresented among the poor, and large numbers of young fathers reside in economically depressed neighborhoods besieged by structural unemployment. Counselors working with adolescent fathers in such neighborhoods will have to become knowledgeable about local, state, and federal job training and placement programs that target at-risk youth from socioeconomically depressed areas to help these youths to develop the skills that will prepare them for the highly technical, service-oriented positions dominating the fastest growing occupations in our nation. In addition, these counselors must be catalysts for creative, holistic programs that enhance the life options of economically disadvantaged adolescents, such as The Children's Aid Society's Adolescent Sexuality and Pregnancy Prevention Program, which is a long-term, community-based, multidimensional program for adolescents in the Harlem section of New York. This program has been implemented at three community center sites, and it operates every afternoon and evening during the week and at two of the three sites on weekends. The components of the program include family life and sex education, academic assessment and help with homework, a job club, career awareness, mental health services, and self-esteem enhancement through the performing arts. In addition, all program participants—both adolescents and their parents—are guaranteed admission as fully matriculated freshmen at Hunter College of the City University of New York upon completion of high school or its equivalent and the recommendation of the program director. Financial aid for college expenses also is available. The features of college admission and financial aid for college provide young men with superordinate incentives that may help to offset the lure of teenage fatherhood. An evaluation of the program conducted after 3 years of operation indicated that 59% of the nearly 400 program participants were males. Participants were found to have generated significantly lower pregnancy rates than community adolescents who were not in the program (Carrera, 1992).

CASE MANAGEMENT CONSIDERATIONS

As indicated by the information shared in this chapter, adolescent fathers have a variety of service needs. Realistically, few professionals will be capable of responding competently to all of these needs themselves; therefore, it is likely that most counselors who have teen fathers as clients will provide some direct services to their clients and refer their clients to other professionals for other services (Kiselica & Pfaller, 1993).

In the light of this reality, the primary counselor is likely to serve as a case manager for the client. Regarding this role, several writers (e.g., Brindis, Barth, & Loomis, 1987; Robinson, 1988) have recommended that counselors serve as brokers of services for adolescent fathers. In this capacity, the counselor should work as an active advocate in securing such services as family life education, parenting and financial management training, and family counseling. As a broker, the counselor maintains an ongoing relationship with the teenage father, guiding him through the process of identifying and obtaining needed services. By offering the teenage parent key emotional support throughout this process, the counselor can help the youth to successfully negotiate the counseling services system (Kiselica & Pfaller, 1993).

IMPLICATIONS FOR TRAINING

If mental health practitioners aspire to make a substantive difference in the lives of teen fathers, then they will need to achieve the following: obtain training in multicultural counseling; develop a knowledge base and skills for working with teenage fathers; acquire supervised experience directly counseling young fathers; and learn how to deliver effective services in spite of the restraints of emerging managed care systems.

TRAINING IN MULTICULTURAL COUNSELING

Kiselica (1995) argues that because teenage fatherhood is a phenomenon that cuts across socioeconomic, racial, ethnic, and geographic lines, it is imperative that youth service professionals obtain extensive training in multicultural counseling: "This training will help practitioners to understand the diverse cultural contexts in which teenage pregnancy and parenthood occurs and to develop skills to make culturally appropriate interventions" (p. 346).

DEVELOPING THE KNOWLEDGE BASE AND SKILLS FOR COUNSELING TEENAGE PARENTS

Training would-be helpers to counsel adolescent fathers should include coverage of the subjects of both teenage fathers *and* teenage mothers, since an adequate understanding of adolescent pregnancy and parenthood must include a recognition that there are two partners involved in an unplanned conception, how the pregnancy is resolved, and, if the child is carried to term and delivered successfully, how he or she is parented. With this knowledge base, counselors will be able to serve the entire new family system that results from the pregnancy, thereby enhancing the development of the young father, mother, and baby. (Kiselica, 1995, p. 346)

Although preparing practitioners to work with both teen mothers and teen fathers is recommended, it is crucial that trainees learn effective counseling process and intervention skills specifically designed for teen fathers because the needs of this population historically have been neglected by educational, medical, and mental health professionals (Kiselica & Sturmer, 1993). Traditional models of training, which emphasize the teaching of basic counselor listening and responding skills, must be supplemented by the instruction of counseling process skills that are geared toward the relational style of males. For an in-depth review of these skills, the reader is referred to several excellent resources on the subject (e.g., Andronico, 1996; Kiselica, 1995; Levant & Pollack, 1995; Scher, Stevens, Good, & Eichenfield, 1987). In addition, the reader may consider joining Division 51 of the American Psychological Association, the Society for the Psychological Study of Men and Masculinity (SPSMM), because this organization publishes a newsletter and sponsors symposia highlighting current perspectives regarding the helping process with boys, adolescent males, and men.

Whether the training is focused on teen fathers, mothers, or both, pertinent instruction can be offered in graduate/professional schools and through continuing education programs in counseling, psychology, social work, nursing, medicine, divinity, home economics, vocational education, and other related fields. Educators can prepare their trainees to be competent service providers by infusing the topic of teenage parenthood into relevant courses and by teaching necessary helping skills (Kiselica, 1995).

Courses on adolescent counseling and development are an obvious choice for such infusion because they should address the current significant issues of adolescents (Carlson & Lewis, 1988). Similarly, sections of courses on multicultural counseling could be focused on cultural variations of adolescent childbearing and fatherhood. In classes on primary prevention and consultation, trainees can be taught skills for helping to prevent unplanned pregnancies among adolescents (Kiselica, 1995). Because many schools are beginning to offer school-based services for teenage parents, it is recommended that courses pertinent to school counseling include a review of the subject of teenage parenthood (Kiselica & Pfaller, 1993). Trainees will need to learn outreach strategies designed to identify teen parents and recruit them for services. Because so much of the work with teenage parents requires assisting them with critical decisions, helpers can benefit from training in decision-making counseling (Kiselica & Pfaller, 1993). Outreach and decision-making strategies could be taught in courses on the techniques of counseling (Kiselica, 1995). Courses on family and career counseling are appropriate venues for teaching counselors skills for addressing the family and educational/career conflicts that often are associated with the crisis of an unplanned adolescent pregnancy (Kiselica, 1995). Trainees will need to be taught referral and consultation skills as well as how to work collaboratively with other helping professionals (Kiselica & Pfaller, 1993). Finally, because research is critical for the advancement of knowledge about teenage fathers, training in a wide range of the methods of research, including experimental, qualitative, ethnographic, and single-study research procedures, is recommended (Kiselica, 1995).

As an alternative to covering discrete aspects of the subject of adolescent pregnancy and parenthood in a variety of courses, specialized courses and workshops on the topic can be offered. Another option is to provide in-depth coverage of the subject in a section of a course on adolescent counseling (Kiselica, 1995).

Dryfoos (1994) recommends that training include cross-disciplinary instruction involving schools of education, psychology, public health, nursing, and social work. This approach will prepare competent youth service workers adept at offering the type of comprehensive services deemed necessary for helping teenage parents.

BOX 11.1
Organizations Providing Information
Useful in Counseling Teen Fathers

Organizations providing information about
adolescent pregnancy and parenthood

Child Welfare League of America, Inc.
440 First Street, NW, Third Floor
Washington, DC 20001-2085
(202) 638-2952
http://www.cwla.org/

Children's Defense Fund
25 E Street NW
Washington, DC 20001
(202) 628-8787
http://www.childrensdefense.org/

National Organization on Adolescent Pregnancy,
  Parenting and Prevention, Inc.
1319 F Street, NW, Suite 400
Washington, DC 20004
(202) 783-5770
http://www.noappp.org/

Organization dedicated to understanding
and helping young boys and men

Society for the Psychological Study of Men and Masculinity
Division 51, Administrative Office
American Psychological Association
750 First Street, NE
Washington, DC 20002
(202) 336-5500
http://web.indstate.edu/spsmm/
(The SPSMM is Division 51 of the American Psychological Association.)

An emerging and ongoing educational challenge for any professional helping teen fathers is to keep abreast of government programs and policies that have an impact on the life circumstances of adolescents. As Herr (1999) cogently notes, counselors tend to be ignorant of the fact that "services are likely to be classified, articulated, and provided, directly or indirectly, through funds and policies implemented by federal, state, or local governmental units" (p. 4). Fortunately, several organizations and publications provide concise updates on pertinent government programs and regulations. For example,

BOX 11.1
Continued

Professional organizations monitoring government programs and policies that affect adolescents

American Counseling Association
5999 Stevenson Avenue
Alexandria, VA 22304-3300
(800) 347-6647
http://www.counseling.org/

American Psychological Association
750 First Street, NE
Washington, DC 20002
(202) 336-5500
http://www.apa.org/about/

American School Counselor Association
801 North Fairfax Street, Suite 310
Alexandria, VA 22314
(800) 306-4722
http://www.schoolcounselor.org/

Counseling Today, the official newsletter of the American Counseling Association; *The ASCA Counselor*, the official newsletter of the American School Counseling Association; and *NOAPP NETWORK*, the official newsletter of the National Organization on Adolescent Pregnancy, Parenting and Prevention, all publish news regarding the latest developments from Capitol Hill that may be of interest to helping professionals who serve youth. In addition, both the Children's Defense Fund and the Child Welfare League of America regularly publish books and pamphlets summarizing and analyzing the status and impact of public policy on children and families.

ACQUIRING SUPERVISED COUNSELING EXPERIENCES WITH TEEN FATHERS

Kiselica and Pfaller (1993) recommend that academicians and practitioners work collaboratively to develop internship experiences that provide trainees with the opportunity to counsel teenage parents. As an extension of this suggestion, Kiselica (1995) argues that

creative, dedicated planning and interprofessional collaboration may be required to expand the service mission of some internship sites which are focused on serving only teenage mothers. Some of the professionals employed in teenage mother programs may be interested in extending services to teenage fathers but lack the resources to do so. The addition of interns might allow these programs to include young fathers, since many interns work for free or are paid lower wages than full-time employees. Program coordinators might contract with educators to have interns placed at the site every semester so that a young fathers program can be offered on a continuing basis. (p. 349)

DEALING WITH MANAGED CARE

Effective work with teen fathers is rarely quick and easy. In this era of growing power of managed care companies, mental health professionals are constantly under pressure to practice short-term counseling under reduced rates of reimbursement from third-party providers. Consequently, counselors employed in both private practices and agencies dependent on third-party payments may be hesitant to accept teen fathers as clients, or they may find it difficult to provide teen fathers with the quality of care that is necessary to address clients' needs.

Counselors need to be trained in strategies designed to tackle these problems. Completing continuing education workshops on working with the managed care system is essential. In addition, counselors must receive training in program and organizational development skills so that they will be prepared to establish special state and local teen pregnancy task forces, which can help practitioners to bypass some of the obstacles created by the managed care system. One of the purposes of these specialized community networks is to identify the range of services that exist in the community and to develop a communitywide referral system. Through the utilization of such a system, professionals can avoid duplication of services and work collaboratively to overcome the confines of managed care that they tend to encounter when they work alone. Clearly, the benefits of having received training in referral and consultation skills, which was suggested earlier, will contribute to these efforts. For example, a private practitioner who is limited by managed care rules to conducting only 15 sessions with his client per year may provide the family counseling that his client requires; meanwhile, however, the counselor may contact a local agency through a teen parents organization to provide the youth with parenting skills training, and job training and job placement may be arranged under the purview of a government-sponsored employment service. Training counselors to work in this manner will help them to understand how they can cope with the frustrations and constraints associated with managed care.

One other issue that is rarely addressed in training programs is the role of volunteerism, both as a social responsibility and as a growing necessity in the light of the current managed care environment and the shrinking sources of governmental and private support for social service programs. One of the implications of the current economic climate is that practitioners are increasingly being asked to do more with less. Although the formation of teen pregnancy service networks can help to assuage the damaging effects of this state of affairs, it must be emphasized that these networks tend to depend largely on the generous work of many people who volunteer their time to make organizations successful. Educators have a responsibility to encourage trainees to consider how they might volunteer their time to address the difficulties that have been created by the managed care system. For example, trainees may wish to lend their support to volunteer organizations serving teen fathers by working in a part-time, pro bono capacity. Alternatively, the trainees might plan for how they can work on the behalf of activist groups that lobby the government to legislate parity of insurance coverage for mental health services or expanded coverage for the varied forms of counseling a teen father might require.

SUGGESTIONS FOR FUTURE RESEARCH

To date, extensive discussions and critiques of the research literature on teen fathers have been published by Robinson (1988), Kiselica and Pfaller (1993), and Kiselica (1995). A synopsis of their collective recommendations is provided here.

First, although several influential case studies (e.g., Kiselica, 1995; Kiselica & Scheckel, 1995) and demonstration projects (e.g., Achatz & MacAllum, 1984; Brown, 1990; Huey, 1987; Klinman & Sander, 1985) have generated results supporting the clinical efficacy of many of the process and intervention strategies described in this chapter, none was based on a design utilizing a completely randomized, pretest-posttest, control-group design. Consequently, more experimental research evaluating the efficacy of interventions with teen fathers is required. Second, although several writers have charged that practitioners harbor negative biases toward adolescent fathers (e.g., Allen-Meares, 1984; Robinson, 1988; Smith, 1989), empirical research on the subject is lacking. Future research therefore should be devoted to development of a reliable and valid measure of attitudes regarding teen parents, which should then be used to assess the attitudes of practitioners about this population. Third, although there is a burgeoning body of basic research on teen fathers, much of it is dated and confounded by a host of methodological problems (see Kiselica, 1995; Robinson, 1988); hence, we need more investigations into the characteristics of teen fathers, their responses to pregnancy, and their experiences as fathers.

CONCLUSION

We are in an era of a growing social awareness about the importance of the father in child development and the healthy development of the family. Concurrently, we are bombarded by the media with stories about teen mothers and their hardships. In the many high-profile discussions about teenage pregnancy and fatherhood, however, the topic of teen fathers continues to be neglected. It is high time that our nation recognize the difficulties that these young men face and the invaluable role they can play in the lives of their children and partners and in society. All professionals who are dedicated to enhancing the lives of our nation's youth must strive to see that the experiences of teen fathers are brought to the forefront of our national consciousness.

HIGHLIGHTS OF CHAPTER 11

▶ Approximately 30% of the children born to adolescent mothers are sired by males who are teenagers. Although teen fathers are overrepresented among African Americans, the majority of teen fathers are White. Cutting across racial and ethnic lines, teen fathers are overrepresented among the impoverished.

▶ Teen fathers tend to experience the following adjustment difficulties: an emotional crisis associated with an unplanned pregnancy, conflicts with their partners about how to resolve the pregnancy, concerns about their competency as a parent, friction with the adolescent mother and her family, declining contact with their child, dropping out of school, legal concerns, relationship changes with peers, and long-term career dissatisfaction, employment worries, and financial hardships.

▶ Although most teen fathers want help with the transition to parenthood, they tend to be neglected and misunderstood by service providers.

▶ Unlike the stereotypic depictions of teen fathers as manipulative young men who sexually exploit young girls and abandon them and their babies, most teen fathers tend to support their partners during the pregnancy and after the birth of the child.

▶ Effective rapport-building strategies with teen fathers include being nonjudgmental, creating a male-friendly counseling environment, understanding the cultural background of the client and its influence on paternity decisions, and working as a client advocate.

▶ During the prenatal period, counselors must help teen fathers with the pregnancy resolution process, short-term educational and career decisions, the impending responsibilities of fatherhood, manifestations of the couvade syndrome (sympathetic pregnancy symptoms), and the duties of supporting the adolescent mother.

▶ During the postnatal phase, counselors must help both noncustodial and custodial teen fathers with the responsibilities of raising a child, issues with his own family and with the family of the adolescent mother, and long-term educational, career, and employment issues.

▶ Because teen fathers have a variety of service needs, the counselor must work as a broker of services who helps the client to utilize the social service system.

► Professional training programs should include education about the needs of teen fathers and strategies for helping this population.

► Future empirical research should evaluate the efficacy of teen father service programs, measure attitudes of practitioners about teen fathers, and document the characteristics and experiences of adolescent fathers.

12

Abused Boys and Adolescents

Out of the Shadows

NEIL CABE

PREVALENCE OF THE
<u>ABUSE OF BOYS</u>

In 1955, S. K. Weinberg completed a study reporting that there were only one or two cases of child abuse per million children in the United States of America (Weinberg, 1955). In 1994, the National Center on Child Abuse and Neglect (NCCAN) counted 2.9 million reported cases of child maltreatment in 48 states, and 1,011,628 of those cases were substantiated. Male children accounted for 46% of those cases (NCCAN, 1996), or more than 465,000 boys. Although these higher numbers certainly reflect an increased aware- ness and reporting of child abuse in the United States, the number of reported cases and an ever increasing population suggest a frightening increase in incidence.

Finkelhor (1984) calls the abuse of boys an epidemic and estimates through various studies that between 3% and 31% of all young males have been abused. Hunter (1990) states, "If the rate of (sexual) abuse is constant from year to year, then at least 46,000 to 92,000 boys under the age of thirteen are sexually abused each year in the United States alone" (p. 26).

Unfortunately, the underidentification of male sexual abuse survivors is also epidemic. Hunter states that, despite mandatory reporting laws, two thirds of the child abuse cases suspected by professional helpers are never reported. This figure includes 87% of the cases of suspected abuse known to teachers (Hunter, 1990). Clinicians may be at fault as well. One study reported that clinicians are less likely to suspect male sexual victimization in patients presenting for therapy (Holmes & Offen, 1996).

Underreporting of male sexual abuse may occur for a number of reasons. Homophobia, a fear of being or being known as homosexual, and perhaps a fear of homosexuals themselves prevent many boys from admitting to inappropriate sexual contacts. Second, male socialization values such as being strong, self-reliant, and able to take care of himself keep many boys from admitting to sexual assault. Among the young male clients I have seen, the appearance of weakness or femininity is repugnant. This may be magnified if the perpetrator of the sexual assault is female. In fact, perhaps the most difficult young male clients to treat that I have encountered are those who were sexually abused by women, especially those abused by their mothers. Third, the clarity and dependability of memory is often questioned in sexual abuse cases. A child may be told that his memories are simply fantasies or wishful thinking. Finally, the sexual abuse of boys is an uncomfortable topic for therapist and client alike and is avoided, often to the relief of both.

The effects of the abuse itself, however, are devastating in the life of the young client. For example, it is an unfortunate fact, as reported in a study outlined in *Child Abuse and Neglect: The International Journal* (Levy, Markovic, Chaudry, Ahart, & Torres, 1995), that there is a reabuse rate of 16.8% within 5 years of a reported and investigated case of childhood sexual abuse, with the greatest risk arising within the 2 years following an initial discharge diagnosis of maltreatment.

Finkelhor summarizes a number of studies that seem to indicate which children are at high risk for sexual abuse. Boys and girls are at almost equal risk of maltreatment (46.7% and 52.3%, respectively), 4- to 6-year-old children are at about the same risk for maltreatment as teenagers, and 17% of victims in the NCCAN study were between 7 and 9 years of age. It is also important to note that fully 90% of all perpetrators are parents or other relatives of the child (NCCAN, 1996).

According to Finkelhor's summary, preadolescents (peaking at ages 10-12) are at greatest risk for sexual abuse. These victims may have lived at some point without a natural father in the home, the mother may be disabled or ill, and, according to Finkelhor, the child probably will have a poor relationship with his parent, causing the boy to seek an attachment figure outside the home. Stepfather families are at greater risk than biological father families, and parental conflict is common (Finkelhor, 1986). Children who present for therapy from homes representing these risk characteristics should perhaps always be questioned about sexual abuse.

Boys are being sexually abused at an alarming rate in the United States. What are the adjustment difficulties for boys and adolescents who have suffered a sexual assault?

ADJUSTMENT DIFFICULTIES FOR ABUSED BOYS

In 18 years of counseling, much of my work has focused on male survivors of childhood abuse. In that time, three major concerns for these young men have surfaced. First, are there indicators of sexual abuse before the boy discloses the abuse? This is especially important in light of the fact that boys are so reluctant to discuss the issue. Second, what are the difficulties these young men and boys are experiencing? The third issue lies in treatment, which is addressed below.

Put most simply, childhood sexual abuse affects every area of a boy's life. Physically, emotionally, psychologically, and spiritually, he is at odds with his world. In fact, even if a child develops few symptoms while still young, symptoms may occur later in his life. In cases I have seen, latency aged and younger children may require additional intervention when they reach puberty. At that point, I believe human sexuality takes on new meaning, and the move from family of origin toward procreational family puts the earlier sexual contact in an entirely new light. If I can identify the survivor client and address the issue with him, many of the effects of the abuse may be mediated, and the child may experience few if any symptoms later in his life.

My observation of and experience with abused boys has made it clear to me that the adjustment difficulties of sexually abused boys and adolescents may best be understood as arising in five separate clusters: relational, territorial, habitual, reactional, and physiological.

RELATIONAL CLUSTER

In light of the fact that the perpetrator of sexual abuse is often someone known to the child, and with whom he has some kind of relationship (see below), it is perhaps no small wonder that relationship issues become particularly difficult for the child. A *relational cluster* of symptoms develops, reflecting difficulty in forming both therapeutic and social relationships. In effect, the child learns to cope by developing a set of defense mechanisms that, on one hand, protect him from the reality of the abusive events but, on the other hand, inhibit healthy socialization. The two primary expressions of this defense in clients I have known are dissociation and rage; each prevents intimate contact with others. The client may become jealous, feel unable to love or care for others, have very few friends, and "zone out" or numb himself emotionally and even physically. Physical numbing may lead to self-mutilation in an attempt to rejoin reality or to master the lack of control crystallized by the abusive event. In some sense, survivor clients seem almost attracted to abuse, developing a victim stance in the world at large and reinforcing a perceived inability to trust anyone, especially adults.

TERRITORIAL CLUSTER

The lack of meaningful relationships further serves to reinforce a *territorial cluster* of symptoms, reflecting difficulty in personal space and the need for security. The child may become very aggressive or, conversely, withdraw from social contact. Hypervigilance and agoraphobia are common, as is the exaggerated startle response commonly seen in post-traumatic stress disorder clients. He may require space around himself constantly, often sitting with his back to the wall and establishing physical boundaries around himself. For some boys, perfectionism becomes a protection against a perceived vulnerability. Often, these boys are very afraid of being used, they develop a fear of smothering, and fight/flight behaviors become regular. It is something of a reversal that stressful situations often lead abused boys to sexual behaviors, many times recreating the abusive event itself in sexual contact with others. This reenactment is yet another attempt to master the powerlessness and helplessness of the abusive event. Although most sexual contacts for abused boys, especially adolescents, are age appropriate, sexual contacts may lead to perpetration, often with children near the same age at which the client was himself first sexually violated. It is very important for the clinician to realize that, although a majority of child molesters are sexual abuse survivors, *most* survivors of sexual abuse *never abuse anyone* (Finkelhor, 1986).

HABITUAL CLUSTER

In addition to the relational and territorial difficulties of survivor clients, a *habitual cluster*, reflecting a need for regularity and the security of repetition, often develops. Repetition tends to organize and regularize the chaotic thinking of abused boys, and this may lead to damaging habits. Drug and alcohol problems are regularly seen in boys who have been abused. In a sense, I believe these boys are self-medicating the psychic pain that the omnipresent memory of sexual assault generates. Other habits might include food, as a way of self-nurturing; sex, in an effort to forge some sort of relationship or engage in reenactment; masturbation, which unfortunately may reinforce the effects of the abuse itself; and compulsive behaviors, including self-mutilation, in an effort to force order into the chaos of his thinking. Some of my clients have become hyperreligious, fully accepting the dogma and doctrine of some religions. In this way, they can have an authority (the church) tell them what to do and establish a set of boundaries for them, however damaging those boundaries might be. Some of my clients have been retraumatized in the context of the church, both sexually and psychologically. Largely, the boys are unable to say "No!" to anyone, and especially so to authorities including teachers, coaches, religious leaders, and even some therapists.

REACTIONAL CLUSTER

Each of the three clusters so far mentioned has essentially involved external expressions of the need for the reestablishment of control and power in the boy's life following a sexual assault. Internal adjustments also are made. In large part, my feeling is that the boy's locus of control following a sexual assault shifts, depending on the developmental level of the child, from internal to external. That is, having been out of control and powerless in the assault, he loses any sense of an internal locus of control. Many of the behavioral concerns outlined above are an attempt on the part of the child to reestablish an internal locus of control, including aggression and fighting, sexuality, perfectionism, compulsiveness, and boundary construction.

The *reactional cluster*, a set of symptoms and behaviors illustrating how a child reacts to the abuse both internally and externally, evidences the loss of that internal locus of control.

Sleep disturbance is often reported by boys and adolescents who have been molested. Part of that sleep disturbance is frequently the result of nightmares that can be horrible for the child. Most often reported to me are nightmares of falling, being chased, shooting at others who will not die in the dream, tigers, fire, and demons of various shapes, sizes, and ferocities. Trouble falling asleep and terminal insomnia are common. Suicidal and homicidal thoughts are pervasive for many of these boys, and a sense of hopelessness permeates their daily lives. They feel helpless and broken; are beset by inappropriate guilt, as if the abuse was their own fault; feel stigmatized and shamed, as if others can "tell" somehow what was done to them; and have dramatically low self-esteem. Deep and recurrent depression and clinical anxiety are regular problems for boys who have been molested.

PHYSIOLOGICAL CLUSTER

Finally, there seems to be a *physiological cluster* of physical symptoms for young male survivors of sexual assault. Most frequent are enuresis, even into mid-adolescence, and encopresis, most often in younger clients. Some may experience colitis-like symptoms, and some may experience genital discomfort. Sexual dysfunction is not uncommon in those who are sexually active, including masturbatory difficulties. Some boys will suffer chronic illness, and I have encountered a few who develop eating disorders. Anorexia and bulimia are, in my opinion, also efforts at developing an internal locus of control: The child may feel that "he (or she) controlled my body during the sexual assault, now I can control it completely, even to the point of disappearing if I choose to do so."

Early in the treatment process, even before the client has disclosed any abusive events, if I can see symptoms in several of the clusters, I will suspect and question for sexual abuse. My experience is that most clients are enormously relieved to finally find someone who is not afraid to discuss what was done to them, who can be trusted, who is nonjudgmental, who believes them, and who can help them regain some control of their lives.

When a boy presents in therapy for treatment of sexual abuse, he already will be suffering from many of the symptoms outlined above. It is a daunting undertaking for the therapist, and based especially on the territorial and relational clusters of behaviors, rapport and the therapeutic relationship become of paramount importance. What are some strategies for building such rapport?

STRATEGIES FOR BUILDING
<u>RAPPORT WITH SEXUALLY ABUSED BOYS</u>

There is, in my opinion, no more important issue in the treatment of sexually abused boys than the therapist him- or herself and the nature of the therapeutic relationship. I believe, and my practice has reinforced this belief, that almost all mental health problems are the direct result of a breakdown in a relationship: with self, with others, or with an existential other (on some level, God, however he or she is perceived in the mind of the child). The therapeutic task at its basis lies in the reestablishment of relationships, first in therapy and then, by extension, socially. The relationship established with the therapist may extend to social relationships. From the reconnections and grounding established in therapy, connection elsewhere becomes possible.

For the sexually abused boy, boundaries have been horribly violated. A trusted other has violated the most personal space a child can inhabit: himself. Then, he comes to therapy, and we as clinicians expect him summarily to describe this violation—to a total stranger. In my workshops, I often ask participants to turn to their neighbor and tell them about their last sexual experience. This request is always greeted with laughter—it is ridiculous and we know it. Boys often have told a number of people about their sexual assaults before we ever meet them, and many have not been believed or have been told they are imagining the experience. Worse, they are sometimes told it was their fault. We nevertheless confidently expect them to tell us about it, yet again. How, then, can we as clinicians build rapport with these damaged young men, who are already suffering the kinds of disruptions in thought process and behavior mentioned above?

Moustakas (1992) says, "The word therapy has no verb in English, for which I am grateful; it cannot do anything to anybody, hence . . . [it] represents a process going on, observed perhaps, assisted perhaps, but not applied. Therapy comes from the Greek noun *servant*. The verb is *'to wait'*" (p. 1). Our obligation, as Moustakas states, is to serve and to wait. It may be that the key to rapport with the young male client who has been sexually assaulted is simply to *wait* until he is ready to talk, and to process in therapy the misery of his own condition. There must be no limit to our patience and no end to our willingness to serve by simply being there. Building rapport lies much more in *being* than in *doing*.

We can do some clear and practical things to help these young men. First, because boundaries were so horribly violated for them, it is our obligation to establish some. Limits and boundaries in the therapeutic relationship must be clear, consistent, rehearsed, rewarded, and consequenced. Sessions begin and end on time, we are extremely cautious about touch of any kind without the client's permission, and others are invited into the session only with the child's permission. This may include parents or foster parents. Further, I emphasize to parents that they know only a small portion of their child's inner life, and what he and I discuss in session will be given to them by him or by me only in extreme situations, which might include threats of suicide, self-injury, or impulses to hurt others. That is, the child must feel free to discuss with me the most intimate parts of his life without fear of unnecessary disclosure to others.

First, I am willing to wait. Second, I believe him, and I understand. The intensity of emotions felt by young male survivors of sexual assault is beyond the ken of many of us. Their rage is self-consuming, and their pain can be acute enough to literally double them over. One adult male client who had been gang-raped at the age of 9 told me I couldn't understand the energy it had taken all of his life simply to stay *alive*: not to function, not to get good grades and star on the football team in high school, not to get through college and find a job, just to simply stay alive.

As therapists for young male survivor clients, we must be aware of the enormity of their suffering, regardless of their age. The 6-year-old whose dreams are filled with tigers and burning demons is in pain equal to that of the adolescent whose days are filled with fistfights and hours lost to dissociation. In the end, each wants only a single person who can hear them and know the pain they feel. They often feel as if they have no voice, and it is our responsibility to give them one. They are eager to walk out of the pain; it is our obligation and privilege to accompany them.

Paramount in this effort is the requirement that the therapist be willing to endure the child's suffering with him. The word "rapport" has its roots in the French *raporter*: to bring back or to yield. It defines a relationship of mutual trust and emotional affinity (*American Heritage Dictionary*, 1970). If we are to develop such a relationship with our young male clients, we must feel their emotions with them, no matter now intense, and they must be able to trust us implicitly. Rapport is, at its most basic level, a willingness by the therapist to endure the suffering of the child with an accurate and child-focused empathy. If we recoil at his disclosures, no matter how horrific, he will not disclose. If we do not feel his pain, he will endure it alone. If we cannot be truly present with him, and allow him to be fully present with us and then allow ourselves to enter his pain, he will not heal. He cannot.

How can we facilitate that healing?

INTERVENTION STRATEGIES WITH ABUSED BOYS AND ADOLESCENTS

It is most important to remember that the child, regardless of his age, is involved in a healing *process*. That process itself is crucial, and regardless of the theoretical orientation from which we approach him, we must have one in mind. A number of models exist for the process itself, drawing primarily from developmental theory. Two such examples follow.

Moustakas (1992) describes a therapeutic process progressing through five stages: diffuse and pervasive anxiety, generalized anxiety and fear, focused hostility and fear, ambivalence, and preservation. Basic suffering for the child is described as a sense of the loss of self, and the child's only permitted expression of self-alienation comes in anxious behavior. In the therapeutic relationship, the child, through exploration of his feelings and attitudes, is able to realize a sense of personal worthiness, free from the damaging effects of his hostility and anxiety, allowing the recovery of himself as a unique individual. In that therapeutic relationship, the child is able to face himself, to become aware of his real feelings, to express these feelings in an accepting environment, and finally to allow the expression of positive feelings to emerge.

Maslow's hierarchy of needs describes the developmental process as one moving from physiological needs, to safety needs, to belonging, to esteem, and finally to self-actualization. In working with the abused boy, the same process should develop. Initial interventions with abused boys and adolescents necessitate the surety of physiological needs (housing, food, clothing), the regularity of safety needs (removal from the home when necessary, restraining orders if required, safety in the therapeutic setting, and legal intervention when required), and the development of a very real sense of belonging in the process. Belonging may include participation in team sports, clubs and groups at school, sessions with the non-offending parent to ensure that the child feels accepted and honored, and a simple acceptance by the therapist that the boy is normal and healthy and is valued as an individual. Following belonging, the therapist and the child work together to establish appropriate self-esteem in the child, noting his worth and value as a human being and providing the voice that has been taken from him. In this, the boy will learn to become what he is and not what he was made to be or made to do.

Maslow and Moustakas define theoretical directions for the treatment process as a whole; neither provides a model for therapeutic *practice*, and intervention may require an additional framework, especially because age is a factor in the intervention process. Although regression is not uncommon in abused children, there are significant differences in some treatment techniques for latency aged and younger boys, in contrast to adolescents. Although the issues as described above are fairly constant among all groups, the less verbal child will require more active intervention than an adolescent who may be more able to talk and think about his situation. Younger children tend to be much more metaphoric and deal more easily with play situations. What direction might the treating clinician take?

INTERVENTIONS WITH BOYS AND ADOLESCENTS

The Grounded Play Therapy (Cabe, 1997) approach to treatment may be applied to both adolescents and younger male survivor clients. Drawing on developmental theory and especially on the therapeutic continuum proposed by Lusebrink (1990), Grounded Play Therapy allows the boy to move at his own necessary pace from most resistive to least resistive media through a series of six stages. Media may be interpreted not only as tactile objects but also as therapeutic interventions. For example, the refusal to disclose abusive events either verbally or symbolically in play is resistive communication; discussion and play disclosure are fluid. Using drawing utensils as a further example, pencils are less fluid than paints. Following Montagu (1971), much of the process is tactile.

Stage 1 is homeostasis. Understanding the existing balance in a boy's life involves a thorough assessment, including psychosocial summary, testing for anxiety and depression, sexual history if necessary, family history, assessment of dissociative behaviors, appraisal for suicide risk with a noninjury contract if required, and possibly a genogram. In subsequent individual or family sessions, current functioning and behavior can be determined to assess for and establish the goals for each session.

Stage 2 is animation, a kinesthetic stage focused on consciousness and perception. Nondirective play, puzzles, safety concerns, systems interventions, communication exercises, and other kinesthetic activities apply during this stage. Commercial "silly putty" is an effective stress reliever for all ages, commercial clay and plasticine play clay are especially good for adolescents, and anger management exercises come into play.

Stage 3 is trust. Although the therapeutic relationship is a continual trust-building effort, art techniques with boys of all ages can be very effective in this stage, as can the use of drums and other rhythm exercises. This stage focuses on sensory and perceptual elements designed to help the boy build a sense of sanctuary and security not only in therapy but also in other areas of his life.

Stage 4 is vesting. Using affective and cognitive exercises, the boy develops a sense of residence within himself, reclaiming his own body and his own sense of himself. Full-body drawings, self-portraits, collages, mood drawings using only colors and shapes, and feeling checks and treatment of anhedonia are appropriate. In this stage, one useful technique is for the boy to review childhood photos from infancy to the present. This exercise is valuable to enhance self-esteem and help remove the sense of damage. The child will see that he looks "normal" and that he was a youngster who did not deserve what was done to him. Viewing pictures of himself as a small child also helps to remove the sense of personal responsibility so many young men carry, as if the abuse were somehow their own fault. They will see that a small child was incapable of defending himself against someone so much larger and more powerful.

Stage 5 is potency, with a focus on symbolic and creative tasks, emphasizing effective interaction with the environment and the necessary use and release of energy in self-affirming ways. Games such as the *Talking, Feeling, Doing Game* (Gardner, 1973) and *The Storytelling Card Game* (Gardner, 1988) can be very helpful for the boy. Unmailed letters to the non-offending parent and to the perpetrator can be difficult but healing for the boy at this point. Time lines, where the child marks high and low points in his young life on poster paper, help to point out existing problems. The time line can be a cathartic exercise, and abreaction, where suppressed emotions appropriate to the abusive events are openly expressed, may occur.

Finally, Stage 6 is preservation. The boy will generalize to the balance of his life appropriate behaviors that were learned and practiced in therapy. This stage may include school checks, parental conferences, legal follow-up as necessary, and rehearsals for court testimony. In the preservation stage, with permissions in place, I have occasionally asked older boys to help me with younger ones. The empathy and altruism inherent in this activity are very healing for many older boys.

The Grounded Play Therapy approach provides a model for each session during the therapeutic process. A child may actually move from most resistive media to least resistive in a single session while he still moves along the same continuum throughout the process. What are the issues that may be encountered as therapy progresses?

INTERVENTION ISSUES AND TECHNIQUES

Sgroi (1982) describes 10 treatment issues in dealing with sexual abuse. With qualification, these may be applied to boys and adolescent males.

1. A feeling of being "damaged goods"
2. Guilt
3. Fear
4. Depression
5. Low self-esteem and poor social skills
6. Repressed anger and hostility
7. Impaired ability to trust
8. Blurred role boundaries and role confusion
9. Pseudo-mature behavior with a failure to accomplish developmental tasks
10. Self-mastery and control

Perhaps all abused boys feel themselves to have been somehow permanently damaged and that they are somehow "damaged goods." In some cases, especially those involving force, physical injury may have occurred. In most of the cases I have seen, the boy will feel as if others can somehow tell what was done to him, and he feels as if others view him as damaged. A simple mirror in the therapy room may help to alleviate the second of those concerns, and a good physical examination can alleviate the first, assuming the physical damage is repaired. Self-portraits, photos of the child before and after the assault, full-body drawings for younger boys, and the positive, understanding, nonjudgmental regard of the therapist and significant others in the child's life will all help him heal his sense of damage.

Fear and guilt can be almost overwhelming for some boys following sexual abuse. First, they often feel as if they somehow caused the abuse—as if the perpetrator bears no guilt, and the child carries it all. With older boys, I often have them notice children of the age they were at the time of the abuse, and note how defenseless the little one is. With younger children, it is most helpful to repeatedly point out that no one is supposed to touch them in private places except themselves. Playing the abusive event or events out with puppets, teddy bears, even dinosaurs and toy soldiers will help the child to see his own vulnerability and allow him to place responsibility and culpability appropriately.

In addition to inappropriate guilt, fears for survivors of sexual assault can become pervasive. Younger boys often are frightened of the dark, strangers or all adults, loud noises, touch from almost anyone, deep voices, and more. Their dreams may be filled with monsters and fire, and their sleep will be irregular because of it. Relaxation training techniques are helpful as are cognitive reconstructions appropriate to the child's age. One of the basic principles in Grounded Play Therapy involves providing the child with a symbol that allows him to externalize his fear or emotion, and over which he may gain control. For example, balloons with angry faces or other representations of fears for the child can be batted around and "popped," and drawings representing nightmares can be "karate chopped," shredded, and thrown in the garbage. For the older boys, lists can do the same thing, and many of them will allow the playful use of balloons.

Depression and anxiety are perhaps the norm for young male survivor clients. Especially with adolescents, suicidal ideation can be severe, and suicide attempts may be part of the history. My youngest suicide survivor was 8 years old. In my opinion, aggression and acting out by my young male clients is one expression of their depression. In an attempt to gain mastery over feelings too powerful for him to enclose, the child literally acts the feelings "out" of himself. During the early assessment sessions, I regularly use the Childhood Depression Inventory (Kovacs, 1992) and the Revised Childhood Manifest Anxiety Scale (Reynolds & Richmond, 1985) not only to assess presenting levels but also to mark progress as therapy continues. For older adolescents, the Beck Depression Inventory (Beck, 1993b) and the Beck Anxiety Inventory (Beck, 1993a) may prove adequate. Each of these instruments is time sensitive and may be readministered successfully if the child is able to be honest in his responses.

Adolescents may also be particularly prone to self-medicate for depression, anxiety, and confusion. I use the Substance Abuse Subtle Screening Inventory (Miller, 1994) to help determine if alcohol and drug abuse present additional problems for the child. Gestalt techniques such as the "empty chair," along with cognitive behavioral techniques appropriate to the age of the child such as cognitive restructuring and reframing, are especially useful in treating anxiety and depression.

Low self-esteem and poor social skills in young survivor clients go hand in hand. That is, having been overpowered and intimately violated, the boy who is a product of 20th-century American male socialization feels worthless, helpless, and hopeless. This is particularly true for male adolescents raised in our chauvinistic, paternalistic, and homophobic social system. For many, if not most, of the adolescent male survivors of sexual assault I have treated, the single most damaging name they can ever be called is "gay" or "queer." If the boy achieved erection during the assault (if by a male), and more so if he reached orgasm, he feels as if he must be homosexual, that he must have "wanted it" somehow, and that it must have been his fault. Furthermore, sexuality becomes a very powerful reinforcement. I find this to be especially true of boys who have been involved in abusive sexual relationships for a number of years, as opposed to cases of single assault or rape. In fact, of the hundreds of boys I have treated, only two ever acknowledged themselves as homosexual. One was 12 years old, and the other 15. Almost all the adolescent boys I have seen, however, carried these unrealistic fears.

One very simple, and very effective, technique to help alleviate this faulty cognition is to have a "tissue fight" with the child. A tissue thrown at the eyes will cause a blink in almost everyone. Note to him that the blinking response was unavoidable, then explain to him that if anyone touches his genitals gently and for long enough, his body will respond the way his body is designed. It is not a thing over which he is always able to exercise conscious control. For latency aged and older boys, appropriate sex education may be an important part of the therapeutic process. I regularly use *The What's Happening to My Body Book for Boys* (Madaras, 1984/1988) for this purpose. In addition, explaining that the sexual assault may be more about power than about sex can help him to overcome some of this difficulty.

Because he feels so damaged, helpless, hopeless, and sexually stigmatized, his self-esteem plummets, as do his social skills. Tae kwon do or karate instruction may be helpful in a number of areas for the boy, and I often recommend them. House-tree-person drawings, especially with the younger boys, can be helpful in ascertaining the levels of damage the child feels and can be readministered to assess for progress. The changes in the tree and person drawings over time can be dramatic. Group therapy, if a group for abused boys can be found or started, can be extremely important for normalizing symptoms, removing a sense of isolation, and developing social skills. Such groups, however, are difficult to find.

In the workshops that I present, the most consistent request for intervention strategies involves anger management. Second perhaps only to dissociative symptoms, anger and hostility are the most prevalent of treatment issues for abused boys and adolescents. Resulting behaviors are also extremely difficult for parents and other caregivers to tolerate. First, the sexually abused boy has every right to his anger, which is a validation issue for the therapist. Second, the boy needs to learn some sort of appropriate expression of this anger. Unfortunately, the most trusted and/or loved persons in his young life usually receive the brunt of his anger. In some sense, he is choosing the safest person in his life as the object for his anger. Behavior modification techniques including time-outs and restitution are avenues to explore, but primarily the boy must learn where, how, and toward whom he may best express this deep need.

Pounding pillows, with the pillow representing the source of his anger, yelling into pillows, beating sofa cushions, and punching heavy punching bags all may provide some release. Several years ago, I bought a "Boppo" bag, the inflated thing with sand in the bottom, for a child to help him relieve his anger. It survived less than 1 minute; the boy was 7 years old. Almost any large muscle activity will provide relief for the boy. Running up and down stairs, swimming, wrestling if a partner can be found, walks in the woods, dancing, pounding, and breaking things all seem to help. I know of one boy who found great relief when he threw an entire set of dishes (with his mother's permission), breaking them in time to Tchaikovsky's *1812 Overture*. Experimentation relevant to the boy's life experience is important. My experience has been that throwing a dozen eggs one at a time in an appropriate way makes the boy feel better when anger and hostility arise. Crushing the containers, in the absence of eggs, also seems to help.

A decade or more ago, while teaching a class, I had my only experience with an earthquake. My most lingering memory is that my only thought was that there was absolutely nowhere I could go at that particular moment that was safe. Nowhere. Outside was perhaps as dangerous as inside the building. This is perhaps some of what the young male survivor of sexual abuse feels: Nowhere in his life is safe, and there is no one that he can trust. As a result of having been violated by a trusted other, there is no one to trust, ever. In this respect, the relationship between the boy and his therapist is primary. He must be able to trust the therapist. The hope is that he will become able to generalize, little by little, to the world at large, armored by the affirmative affective and cognitive environment of the therapeutic relationship and the normalizing of other relationships in his young life. One of the keys to this trusting relationship, addressed below, lies in appropriate boundaries.

BOUNDARIES

Boundaries exist personally, interpersonally, and intergenerationally. In each of those three systems, boundaries may be closed and rigid, appropriate, or transparent. In a closed boundary system, no one gets out, and no one gets in. That is, a closed family never allows sleepovers, seldom has company, and rarely communicates. Members do not talk with one another, and seldom with others. Affection is seldom if ever openly expressed, and touch is at a minimum. This sort of boundary system encourages abuse, because no one ever talks outside the family boundaries. Alcoholic families often exist this way, with the family keeping secrets. For a child with such rigid boundaries, conversation and disclosure of personal issues to others are extremely difficult.

When boundaries are transparent, a child never really learns where he stops and others begin. In this sort of system, doors are never locked, the bathroom is never sacred, and you never know who will be sleeping on the couch in the morning. Transparent boundaries may also breed abuse, especially if the boundary between adult and child is blurred. Unfortunately, children in the United States are often treated like miniature adults, which on some level allows abuse to occur. In such a home, a mother may sleep with anyone she chooses, and fathers may do as they please with their sons.

In an appropriate boundary system, adults are treated like adults, and children are allowed to be themselves within limits that are clear, consistent, fair, rewarded, and consequenced. Discipline is appropriate, privacy is respected, communication occurs, and affection is shared in acceptable ways. The abused child most often comes from a closed or transparent boundary system.

It is important that the therapist to an abused boy establish and teach appropriate boundaries quickly and consistently. Blurred boundaries lead to role confusion. The therapist should ask the following questions:

- ▶ As a boy, was my client allowed to be a child?
- ▶ Was he forced into the role of father to his brothers and sisters?
- ▶ Was he his mother's confidant, husband surrogate, and lover?
- ▶ What are normal touching behaviors among children and between children and adults?
- ▶ What is normal sexuality for a boy of my client's age?

These are boundary questions that must be addressed. As appropriate boundaries are taught and practiced in the therapeutic process, they can generalize to the rest of the boy's life.

One outgrowth of blurred boundaries and role confusion lies in the child's developing self-concept. If boundaries are transparent enough that he has been placed in roles inappropriate for a boy, especially with an adult, he may feel himself to be more mature than he is. Any child trying to be a tiny adult, employing what are really pseudo-mature behaviors, will fail to accomplish developmental tasks appropriate to his age. Developmental assessment of the younger boy may be accomplished through observation or the use of such testing materials as the Developmental Profile II (Alpern, Boll, & Shearer, 1984). For older boys, the Personality Inventory for Children (Wirt, Lachar, Klinedinst, Seat, & Broen, 1982) or other instruments may be helpful. In practice, allowing the boy to begin at the developmental level with which he is most comfortable and working toward more suitable levels is most appropriate. As he develops, he will gain more control of himself and of his life.

This is perhaps a key issue in working with sexually abused boys and adolescents. Having been victimized and living in a society that disdains weakness, he loses his sense of self-mastery. Masculinity must be asserted in some fashion, and this can occur in a number of ways. He may become "macho" in an effort to compensate for his victimization and to avoid the label of "feminine." Some boys will identify with their abuser and attempt to gain self-mastery by abusing others. Some will so completely identify themselves as feminine that they may engage in homosexual behavior because they think they must; this is pseudo-homosexuality and not homosexual orientation. Having been overpowered, they feel as if their only relief lies in overpowering others. These negative compensatory behaviors must be addressed. As they are replaced and appropriate behaviors relearned, the child will grow to be who he is and, again, not what was done to him or what he was forced to do.

SUGGESTIONS FOR FURTHER RESEARCH

As noted above, the abuse of boys and adolescent males is epidemic, yet only a small percentage of known cases is ever addressed, and many professionals who are mandated to report the suspicion of child abuse do not do so. Why? Is it because adults are so deeply entrenched in a faulty male socialization in the United States that they still somehow refuse to believe the enormity of the crimes being perpetrated against our young men? Furthermore, as more and more women admit to having sexually abused young males, the need for identification and treatment for these boys becomes of paramount importance. My most difficult clients consistently have been men and boys who were molested by their mothers. These issues beg for further investigation.

In addition to the questions surrounding reporting and prosecution, there remain enormous questions in terms of treatment of young males. What works? What is being tried and not working? What techniques are there that clinicians may employ that will help them deal with the plethora of symptoms with which young male survivor clients present? Much of the literature remains anecdotal and focused on case history. Although this is informative, treatment issues still need continuing research and evaluation in the literature.

One of the significant sequelae of early childhood trauma lies in the area of attachment formation. Although this too is a treatment issue, what can the clinician do to alleviate the range of attachment behaviors young male survivor clients exhibit? Especially in the light of male socialization issues, what is the place for human touch in therapy with boys and male adolescents (see Hughes, 1997)? How therapeutic might it be? Montagu (1971), in an early but still timely volume, considers human touch necessary to the formation, awareness, and expression of human emotions. James (1994) suggests that touch is critical in the development of a sense of self, that there is a deep need for touching in all trauma survivors, and that it is the initiating activity in the attachment process. In my opinion, these areas have yet to be addressed clearly in dealing with young male survivor clients.

In a fascinating article, Perry (1997) states that a persistent fear response (developmental trauma) in a child's environment will lead to an excessively active and reactive stress-response apparatus. These stress responses lead to the overdevelopment of certain areas of the brain and may lead to a predisposition to act in aggressive, impulsive, and potentially violent ways. Boys who have been abused over a period of time and those who live in other toxic environments may be more prone to violence.

The ecosystemic needs of the abused boy have yet to be clearly explored. In a provocative article, van der Kolk (1989) discusses endogenous opiates and the subsequent behavior of a traumatized child to reproduce them in situations of stress. In sum, the psychosocial, neurodevelopmental, and neurobiological impact of child abuse is only beginning to be understood. This, I think, is fertile ground for research.

CONCLUSION

The subtitle for this chapter is "Out of the Shadows." In many ways, young male victims of sexual assault are still shadowed in the therapeutic and research community. Their needs are far from met, and their treatment is far from sure. Indeed, it has been only a little longer than a decade since Porter published *Treating the Young Male Victim of Sexual Assault: Issues and Intervention Strategies* (Porter, 1986), one of the earliest volumes on the subject. Much has been learned. Much remains to be learned.

As therapists become more sensitive to the reality of the sexual abuse of boys and male adolescents, and as they continue to learn more and better ways to treat them, perhaps these young men will be able to emerge from the shadows healthy, happy, secure, and able finally to live without stigma or fear.

HIGHLIGHTS OF CHAPTER 12

► Hundreds of thousands of boys are sexually abused in the United States annually.

► Sexually abused boys tend to experience a wide range of adjustment problems, including relationship difficulties, withdrawal from social contact, self-mutilation, nightmares, insomnia, guilt, deep and recurrent depression, clinical anxiety, enuresis, encopresis, sexual dysfunction, eating disorders, drug and alcohol abuse, hyperreligiosity, perfectionism, and compulsiveness. Many victims develop aggressive tendencies and become sexual abusers later in life.

► For sexually abused boys, boundaries have been horribly violated. Trusting others again and talking about the trauma tends to be very difficult. Consequently, counselors must be very patient, avoid forcing the client to self-disclose, and wait until the client is ready to talk about his ordeal.

► Creating clear boundaries (e.g., beginning and ending sessions on time, being cautious about touch of any kind without the client's permission) and assuring the client of confidentiality will help the victim to trust the therapist with his problem.

► Abused boys desperately want counselors to hear their stories and to feel their pain. Thus, counselors must be fully present with abused boys and affirm their clients' shattered experience.

► Counselors must address the victim's physiological needs (e.g., arranging for housing, clothing), safety needs (e.g., advocating for removal from the home when necessary), and need to belong and to have self-esteem (e.g., facilitating ties with, and acceptance by, peers and the non-offending parent or relatives).

► Grounded Play Therapy is an approach to treatment with sexually abused boys that allows the boy to move at his own pace from resistive to least resistive media.

► Sexually abused boys typically feel damaged physically and emotionally. Self-portraits, photos of the child before and after the abuse, and the nonjudgmental regard of the therapist can help the child to feel healed and once again intact.

► Because sexually abused boys often feel that they somehow caused the abuse, the counselor must repeatedly and gently point out how defenseless children are against adults and that the perpetrator bears sole responsibility for the abusive event(s).

► Providing the sexually abused boy with a symbol of his negative emotions allows him to externalize and control his fears of the dark, strangers, loud noises, and other things and people. For example, drawings representing nightmares can be shredded and thrown in the garbage.

► Cognitive restructuring and reframing are effective strategies for treating overwhelming suicidal impulses and debilitating anxiety in sexually abused boys.

► Some victims who experienced any degree of sexual arousal during assaults perpetrated by another male often erroneously conclude that they are homosexual. To counter such faulty cognitions, the client must be taught that sexual arousal is sometimes unavoidable when another person touches the boy's genitals and that such arousal is not, by itself, indicative of a homosexual orientation.

► Hitting heavy punching bags and participating in karate and group therapy are some of the many outlets through which sexually abused boys can channel their anger about the abuse in socially acceptable ways.

▶ Regaining trust in others is the most difficult, yet crucial, challenge that sexually abused boys face. The caring relationship of the counselor can be the foundation upon which the client begins to recover from his sense of degradation and risks trusting the world again.

▶ Because sexually abused boys tend to come from families where there are highly dysfunctional boundaries, they must be taught rules about appropriate touching, normal sexuality, and the roles and responsibilities of children and parents.

▶ Some victims are forced to behave like pseudo adults by their perpetrators and dysfunctional families. These victims must be shown how to act in age-appropriate ways again.

▶ Sexually abused boys who adopt macho or abusive styles to compensate for their own victimization need help replacing these behaviors with more socialized ways of relating.

13

Treating Adolescent Sex Offenders

DAVID JOLLIFF

JOHN NEWBAUER

BILL BLANKS

Adolescents who commit sexual offenses against younger children represent one of the largest growing groups of juvenile offenders in today's society, a society that has not held youths accountable for their sexual offending acts in the past (National Task Force on Juvenile Sexual Offending, 1988). In the past, boys who offended sexually were dismissed as simply experimenting or as suffering an adjustment reaction. In many cases, it was considered by the court to be simply a matter of "boys will be boys," reflecting a gender stereotyping of sexual behavior. Implicit in this explanation is an assumption of a gender role definition that includes aggressive sexual behavior. Although it may be argued that this is not an attitude that pervades our culture, it is an attitude that has been, and is, held by many in our culture and is often portrayed in the media. Even when it is brought to the attention of the legal system, the response of the courts often have been inadequate (Ryan, 1986). It generally was hoped that these youth would find some normal outlet for their sexual behavior when they grew up, and then everything would be fine.

The combined results of these attitudes was a major underreporting of juvenile sexual behaviors (Knopp, 1982). In the 1980s, however, a number of researchers reported that adult sexual offenders often began their sexual offending behavior in their adolescent years (Abel, Mittelman, & Becker, 1985; Becker & Abel, 1985; Groth, Long, & McFadin, 1982). These findings seemed to stimulate the growth of programs and interest in intervention. In 1988, the National Task Force on Juvenile Sexual Offending published its preliminary report, which contained many recommendations for the development of treatment programs and evaluation of the effectiveness of these programs.

The juvenile sex offender typically is a youth whose potential for offending has gone unrecognized until the time he commits a sexual offense. This is probably because sexual offenses are committed by a rather diverse group of individuals. Awad, Saunders, and Levene (1984) found a large subgroup of adolescent sexual offenders to be lower in truancy, alcohol abuse, and temper tantrums than other adolescents. There is another group of adolescent offenders who are more aggressive and who seem to come from families where there is more abuse and chaos, and with generally discouraging conditions.

SEX OFFENDER TYPOLOGIES

O'Brien and Bera (1980) have theorized that there are different types of sexual offenders and have developed a very useful typology of adolescent sex offenders that includes low-risk as well as high-risk categories. The seven types identified by O'Brien and Bera include the following: naive experimenters, undersocialized child exploiters, pseudo-socialized child exploiters, group-influenced offenders, sexual aggressives, sexual compulsives, and disturbed impulsives.

Naive experimenters. These offenders tend to be younger adolescents. They have no previous history of acting-out problems. They usually have adequate social skills, though they lack sexual knowledge and experience. Their sexual acts are isolated, exploratory, situational, and nonviolent, usually with young children.

Undersocialized child exploiters. These offenders have more extensive patterns of sexual behavior, effected through manipulation, enticement, and entrapment. They are likely to be social isolates with poor social skills. They may have no history of acting-out behavior. They often feel inadequate, insecure, and worthless. Families are often disengaged.

Pseudo-socialized child exploiters. These generally are older adolescents. They feel confident and secure in most settings, and they exhibit good social skills. They have little or no history of acting out. Scores on personality inventories resemble those of the general population. They are often victims themselves, having survived sexual, physical, or emotional abuse as children. The sexual abuse behavior reflects a possible chronic pattern. These offenders rationalize their behavior by claiming that the act was mutual, intimate, and noncoercive. They likely feel little guilt or remorse.

Group-influenced offenders. These offenders have attempted to impress their peers, gain peer approval, or prove themselves worthy of peer acceptance. Typical offenses include gang rape, dare exposing, or bathroom surprise molestations. There is usually no previous history of sexually abusive behaviors. Personality and family characteristics test out normal. They are able to experience remorse.

Sexual aggressives. These offenders use force or violence in the commission of sexual assaults against peers, adults, or older children. They tend to be socially and sexually active with their peer group. They usually have a history of antisocial, acting-out behaviors from early childhood. They are likely to be regular users of drugs or alcohol. They have difficulty managing aggressive impulses. They are overly sensitive to criticism, tense and anxious, and emotionally labile. They use denial and projection as their defenses. Their families tend to be characterized by chaos, abuse, and violence.

Sexual compulsives. These persons engage in repetitive, sexually arousing behaviors that become compulsive and addictive in nature. They usually engage in hands-off behaviors such as voyeurism, obscene phone calling, exhibitionism, and fetish burglary. They tend to be quiet and socially withdrawn. They may be studious, tending toward overachievement and perfectionism. Tension and anxiety are a constant state of being, and they may be hypersensitive to failure. They have difficulty expressing anger appropriately. Emotional constraint and anxiety result in tension-reducing, acting-out behaviors that involve sexual arousal. Behavior becomes patterned, cyclical, and repetitive because it is self-reinforcing. The family system is usually rigidly enmeshed, with closed external boundaries. Parents may adhere to rigid and fundamentalist religiosity.

Disturbed impulsives. These persons are impulsive and demonstrate acute distortions of reality. The offense may be a single, unpredictable, uncharacteristic act or a pattern of bizarre and/or ritualistic acts. The offenses reflect a malfunction of normal inhibitory mechanisms resulting from thought disorders often caused by psychosis, either endogenous or drug induced.

SEXUAL OFFENSE ETIOLOGY

A variety of explanations have been offered in the literature for the development of sexually abusive behavior patterns (National Task Force, 1988). Several authors have suggested that feelings of powerlessness and helplessness combined with a lack of controls, both external and internal, trigger a sexual assault cycle with identifiable precursors, progressions, and antecedents. The cycle is accompanied by specific cognitive distortions associated with each stage (Lane & Zamora, 1984; Ryan, Lane, Davis, & Isaac, 1987).

Others have suggested that sexual arousal patterns develop in response to victimization or as the result of learned behavior and socialization over time (Longo, 1982). Our experience has taught us that trauma, patterns of family interaction that are discouraging, exposure to sexually explicit material, and other situations that can lead to feelings of helplessness or exaggerated images of power can combine to produce sexually deviant behavior. These sexually deviant behaviors are seen as powerful, especially by those who have been victims of a more powerful perpetrator in the past during either physical or sexual abuse. In other cases, exaggerated images of male sexual behavior portrayed in pornography or through in vivo models provide images of male sexual roles and behavior that are accepted by the youth as normal or even ideal. These misperceptions and exaggerations contribute to sexually aggressive behaviors and a masculine ideal that combines aggression with sex and feelings of power.

The desire to move from a felt minus to a perceived plus, from a feeling of inferiority to a feeling of power, provides an explanation of the motivation for many adolescent offenders. This conceptualization is a derivative of Adler's (1956) masculine protest and overall conceptualization of motivation. It also includes the element of teleology or purpose for the behaviors that are future or goal oriented rather than based on past events, or that imply drives (Adler, 1956). This element of goal orientation, along with misperceptions and cognitive distortions, is used extensively in our approach to treatment of sexual offenders.

THE ADOLESCENT OFFENDER TREATMENT PROGRAM

We developed the Adolescent Offender Treatment Program (ASOP) described here to treat the less violent and less dangerous types of offenders. Most of the offenders in this program are undersocialized child exploiters, pseudo-socialized child exploiters, or group-influenced offenders. The more aggressive or disturbed offenders are not appropriate for our program for community safety reasons, and the naive experimenters usually do not require the extensive experience in treatment that our program offers.

The ASOP program is a cooperative effort between the juvenile court and a group mental health practice. The juvenile court assigns two officers, either female or male, who specialize in sexual offenders. These officers participate in at least one of our treatment groups on a weekly basis in the role of cofacilitator. Their participation provides continuity from intake at the court through completion of the program. The officers have information from the police and victim reports as well as from prior arrest records, along with other collateral information that often proves helpful. The adolescents in the program are on probation or suspended commitment to Indiana Boys' School and have rather intense levels of supervision. Supervision includes at least weekly scheduled meetings with the probation field officer as well as unscheduled surveillance contacts by the field officers. Drug and alcohol urine screens are administered randomly to the participants. Participants may also be electronically monitored during the early phases of the program. Such monitoring, sometimes called house arrest, ensures that the participant will be at home during all times when not officially excused for activities such as work or school attendance.

The probation officers who specialize in working with sexual offenders are in frequent contact with the field officers and electronic monitoring officers regarding the behavior of the young men in the program. In addition, the field officers and electronic monitoring officers may contact the treatment therapists themselves. They also are invited to attend case conferences when advancement through the program is discussed.

SEX OFFENDER CHARACTERISTICS

The ASOP program is based on the assumption that there are four important characteristics of young male sex offenders. First, there is something deviant about their sexual response that allows them to be aroused by one or more of the following stimuli: younger, age-inappropriate children, violent acts that have become sexualized, or inappropriate sexual expression in general. For example, one young adolescent who was previously sexually abused (forced masturbation of a male baby-sitter) developed a fantasy of having a young child masturbate him, which he eventually acted out after a rather long period of time, using this fantasy for his own masturbation.

Second, we assume that some sexual offending is the result of inappropriate conversion of nonsexual problems into sexual behavior. Inappropriate sexual behaviors provide a degree of emotional satisfaction because of both the pleasure experience and the reduction of anxiety and powerlessness that they produce. The sexual behaviors in these situations serve to meet nonsexual needs associated with events that are perceived as threatening to one's self-esteem. The lowered self-esteem is frequently related to past traumatic experiences. These past traumas in no way cause the offense or excuse the offender; however, power and control behaviors serve to allow the offender to avoid uncomfortable life experiences while allowing him to pretend that he has mastered the situation. This pattern tends to mask the mastery deficits that most sex offenders exhibit, especially in regard to intimacy. We have seen many cases in which an adolescent is angry at a stepparent and has later anally raped or forced oral sex upon the stepparent's younger biological child (the adolescent's stepsibling).

Our third assumption is that there is something deviant or unusual about the offenders' personality or psychological makeup that allows them to act out sexually in an inappropriate manner, contrary to the mores and teachings of the community and often of their families as well. Something allows them to ignore the social rules, excuse their own behavior, and develop elaborate defense and denial systems that minimize the amount of harm that has been done to the victim and minimizes the significance of their activity. They have numerous irrational or dysfunctional beliefs and cognitive distortions as well as biased perceptions of reality. In addition, they also seem to lack internal controls and are prone to ignore external controls or to minimize their significance. These cognitive distortions and dysfunctional perceptions lead to inappropriate behavior. They are part of a system of thinking that includes rationalization, minimization, externalization of blame, and denial. These distortions give the offender permission to perform inappropriate, intrusive sexual acts, contribute to disinhibition when behaving sexually, and allow the offender to avoid feeling any sense of responsibility for his acts.

The fourth assumption is that sex offenders would not offend if they did not have an available victim. If a sex offender does not have access to vulnerable children or victims, he cannot commit the offense. Many programs that have good intentions fail to deal with this issue directly. In addition to the general conditions of probation, the ASOP program itself has rules for participants that restrict them from being with younger children or in places frequented by younger children. Activities like baby-sitting and helping in the care of younger children are strictly prohibited until successful completion of the program. We also emphasize with each perpetrator the lifelong need to protect himself from any potential accusation of molestation; the best safeguard is not to be alone with young children any time. Even a false accusation could land a known perpetrator in jail.

GOALS

Our goals for rehabilitation of offenders include the following:

1. Development of total responsibility for the sexual offense
2. Restructuring of cognitions so that the thinking distortions that triggered the sexual abuse are no longer problematic
3. Development of empathy for the feelings of the victim
4. The ability to experience remorse
5. Establishment of honesty as a mode in all communications
6. Institution of a program of amends including apology and restitution
7. Development of a protection plan to prevent any recurrence of the offense
8. Development of age-appropriate sexual/emotional response patterns
9. Healing of abuse issues in the perpetrator's own life and self-forgiveness

TREATMENT PROCESS

Information on which treatment modalities work best with adolescents for specific clinical dysfunctions is debated in the literature. Individual outcome studies, however, suggest that appropriate approaches for antisocial behavior include a combination of family therapy, individual therapy, and group therapy (Feldman, Caplinger, & Wodarski, 1983; Kolvin et al., 1981). The ASOP program includes all three modalities.

This program is an intensive outpatient program. In the beginning, participants meet twice a week for group therapy and once a week for individual or family therapy. That schedule thins out to a group meeting once a week as the participant progresses through the program. In addition, parents are expected to participate in a parent support group for at least the first 3 months. Multifamily group therapy is also provided. Aftercare is available following completion of the program.

Parent involvement. Parents are a very important part of this treatment program, so a contract is signed by them in which they agree to participate in parent support and family therapy groups, provide careful supervision to minimize any possibility of additional offenses, keep the program administrator informed of any changes in family circumstances that affect treatment, give assurance that their son will attend all sessions as required in a timely fashion, and, as parents, follow all confidentiality rules. Parents' involvement in the program is vital in minimizing the chances of overtly or covertly supporting the offender's denial. For this reason, they are invited to sit in on the group therapy session when their son describes the details of the abuse, details that include the grooming and setup of the victim, the planning, the rehearsal, and the act itself.

Participant/staff relationships. Throughout the program, emphasis is placed on the development of a caring relationship between the participants and the staff, and special attention is placed on helping the participants identify and express their inner experiences and emotional states. These are the two key conditions identified in most studies of successful therapeutic programs. Bremer's (1992) research on long-term effectiveness of treatment supports the validity of this finding. The participants said that the way they were treated was as important to the recovery as the content of the program (Bremer, 1992). This finding supports the importance of maintaining a positive therapeutic relationship between the treatment staff and the participants.

Prior victimization. In this program, we provide the participant with treatment for both the offending behavior and any victimization that has occurred in the participant's life. The majority of our participants are survivors of some form of childhood abuse, either sexual, physical, or emotional. Because these early traumas may have been precursors to the offending behavior, it is imperative that the participant's wounds be healed as a part of preventing any reoffense. It must be noted, however, that there is a sequence to the treatment program. The participant as offender must be treated before the participant as victim. This sequential pattern minimizes any chance that the participant will try to use his own victimization as an excuse for his offending behavior.

Personal responsibility. Another key issue is the maintenance of consistent limits for the purpose of teaching participants personal responsibility. Behavioral guidelines and expectations for performance of assignments as well as enforcement of consequences reflect the clinical staff's serious attitude toward the program and the issues it addresses. No breach of program rules is taken lightly, and lack of cooperation is confronted immediately. Boundaries are clearly established for behavior and then enforced consistently. Trust is something to be earned by both staff and participants in the program. Following through on what is promised is an important aspect of developing this trust and developing a sense of external controls that can be used as a model for the development of internal controls as well.

Program structure. The ASOP program is a highly structured, four-phase, sequential program. It is individualized so that the participant may move through at his own pace. It is expected that full completion of the program will take a minimum of 1 year; 2 years is average. Commitment of time to the program is greatest in the first phase. As offenders progress through the phases, they spend less and less time in the program, but more and more work and responsibility on the part of the participant is required. Each phase lasts about 3 months, longer in individual cases as needed. The aftercare component is central to preventing a reoffense. Graduates from the program may return at any time for support or if they feel they may be in danger of reoffending.

Psychosexual information. Treatment begins with a complete assessment. The assessment includes a review of the police report, an interview with the parents and with the program participant, and a well-formulated psychological evaluation. Additionally, the offender type is established using the O'Brien and Bera (1980) typology. All the following information is necessary for determining the participant's fit in the program and for determining the level of collateral support available.

1. The participant's version of the offense
2. How it was disclosed
3. Comparison of the participant's version with collateral information
4. A sexual history
5. The victim's statement
6. A mental status assessment
7. A social history (family, medical, educational, drug/alcohol use, mental health, victim history, and any previous legal history)

Psychological evaluation. The projective personality assessment typically includes the Rorschach Inkblot Method utilizing Exner's comprehensive system (Exner, 1991, 1993). Occasionally, the Thematic Apperception Test, the Children's Apperceptive Storytelling Test, or Robert's Apperception Test is used as well. The Rorschach or another standardized projective test seems to be particularly appropriate in those cases in which there is a great deal of defensiveness that seems to affect the adolescents' performance on the personality inventories, which are more obvious in terms of self-presentation to others.

Personality inventories include the Minnesota Multiphasic Personality Inventory for Adolescents (MMPI-A; Butcher et al., 1992) and the Millon Adolescent Clinical Inventory (MACI; Millon, 1992). We have found the MACI to be the most useful of the instruments. It is considerably shorter than the MMPI-A, which is a factor in adolescent testing, especially in situations such as these, when assessment is sometimes done with limited investment from the adolescent.

Intellectual screening is done with the Kaufman Brief Intelligence Test (KBIT) (Kaufman & Kaufman, 1990). The KBIT yields a score based on matrices and vocabulary that correlates strongly with longer tests such as the Wechsler Scales yet takes only approximately 30 minutes to administer and much less time to score.

Protection plan. Because the highest priority is placed on protecting the victim from any further chance of being reoffended, an immediate protection plan is implemented that separates the offender from the victim. The plan involves the participation of parents, probation officers, and the clinical staff. Typically, families need specific guidelines for their role in implementing the protection plan. There may be resistance to removing the offender from the home—for example, in cases of intrafamilial abuse. Relatives or friends may provide care for either the victim or the offender in lieu of keeping both in the same home.

PHASES

There are four phases to the ASOP program, plus an aftercare option. The first phase follows the offenders' assessment. In this phase, the commitment of time to the program is the greatest. As offenders progress through the phases, less and less time is spent in the program, but more and more work and responsibility on the part of the participant are required. Each phase lasts about 3 months, longer in individual cases if needed. That decision is made based on whether or not the adolescent has completed the objectives for that particular phase and on his participation in the program and cooperation with the clinical staff, probation or parole officers, and parents. The aftercare component is central to preventing a reoffense. Graduates from the program may return at any time for support or if they feel they may be in danger of reoffending.

Phase 1 Objectives

1. The participant will faithfully attend two therapy groups and one individual therapy session per week.
2. The participant will convincingly take full responsibility for the sexual abuse. This requires admission of a premeditated plan to commit the offense and recognition that the victim is blameless.
3. The participant will share specific details of the abuse in individual and group therapy sessions, with parents present in the group session. This objective includes a complete write-up of the details. All discrepancies between the participant's version of the abuse and the police report are resolved.
4. The participant will develop empathy for the victim and the victim's family, explaining how the victim and family must have felt and the impact of the abuse and trauma on them.
5. The participant will identify the distorted thinking through which the abuse was justified and be able to name the thinking errors, such as rationalization or denial.
6. The participant will acknowledge ongoing sexual fantasies toward children or other inappropriate subjects. He must demonstrate an awareness of the difference between inappropriate and appropriate sexual fantasies and thoughts and report any fantasies of reoffense since the previous therapy session.
7. The participant will understand the risk of reoffense and acknowledge the need for monitoring and intervention. He must adhere to an initial protection plan (stay away, look away, get away), including abiding by all the rules of the program and probation.
8. The participant will demonstrate an understanding of the reasons he offended. This means demonstrating a thorough understanding of the cycle of abuse and the lifelong danger of reoffending.
9. The participant will demonstrate a clear understanding of the misuse of power and control in the sexual abuse incident and be able to name his power tactics.

10. If the participant has been a victim of abuse, he will identify his own abuse issues as relevant.
11. The participant will work to improve school, social, and family interactions as necessary. The clinical staff will receive periodic reports from family member sand probation officials.

Phase 2 Objectives

1. The participant will faithfully attend one group and one individual session per week.
2. The participant will write an acceptable apology letter and, where appropriate, apologize in a therapy session with the victim.
3. The participant will perform such restitution as may be possible.
4. The participant will continue to actively participate in group therapy, remaining open to his own issues while supporting and challenging others.
5. The participant will display a willingness to examine deeper therapeutic issues in individual and group counseling, such as current sexual fantasies, relationship problems, mutuality of choice, expression of feelings, and a clear definition of sexual misconduct.
6. The participant will complete an intermediate protection plan that illustrates situations and places to avoid, the types of children that might elicit thoughts of reoffense, actions to take when recurring thoughts of molestation occur, and other necessary elements.
7. The participant will work to complete structured learning activities dealing with assertiveness, communication, thinking errors, social skills, and personal care.
8. The participant will show continuous improvement in school functioning, social behaviors, and family interactions.

Phase 3 Objectives

1. The participant will faithfully attend one group per week and individual counseling every other week.
2. The participant will share the details of his own victim history, if applicable, in a group session and focus on his victim issues in individual therapy.
3. The participant will share the details of his offense from the victim's point of view, showing a convincing awareness of the impact his offense had on the victim.
4. The participant will begin working toward self-forgiveness while recognizing the wrongness of his offense and the potential to reoffend.
5. The participant will continue to show improvement in school functioning, social behavior, and family interactions based on reports from probation officials and family members.

Phase 4 Objectives

1. The participant will consistently attend group therapy once a week and individual therapy once a month.
2. The participant will write an extensive autobiography and share it in group and individual therapy.
3. The participant will write a realistic and effective protection plan against the possibility of reoffense and share it in group and individual therapy.
4. The participant will demonstrate the ability to act as a facilitator of others' progress in the group therapy sessions by offering effective feedback, support, and confrontation.
5. The participant will demonstrate continued progress in school functioning, social behavior, and family interactions.

TREATMENT INTERVENTIONS

The structured exercises and worksheets described here are representative of those used in the ASOP program. Those not attributed to other authors were developed by the treatment staff based on the work of several authors in the field (Bays, Freeman-Longo, & Hildebran, 1990; Freeman-Longo & Bays, 1988; Way & Balthazor, 1990; Yokley, 1990). We are deeply indebted to them for their early work, upon which we built our program.

PHASE 1

In the ASOP program, participants are expected to break resistance and denial and to take full ownership and responsibility for their offense. To facilitate that process, they are asked to write a detailed description of their offending behavior using the "ASOP Details Outline" and the exercise called "Taking 100% Responsibility for the Abuse." Samples of both exercises are given below.

ASOP Details Outline

1. Give first names of all victims. Also give the ages of the victims when you molested them, your age when you molested, and the relationship of the victims to you.
2. Give the exact details of the sexual contact. What did you do to the victim? What did you have the victim do to you? When did the abuse take place? Where? How did you get the victim to do what you wanted?
3. What ways did you manipulate or force your victim to do what you wanted? How did you threaten or tell them not to tell?
4. What was difficult in your life at the time you molested? How did you feel about those difficulties?

5. How did you convince yourself it was okay to molest your victims?
6. How long before molesting did you begin planning it? What was your plan? Who else were you planning to molest?
7. Give five examples of the ways your thinking was distorted during the abuse.
8. What would stop you from molesting again?
9. Describe your most recent sexual thought for a child and what you did after you had the thought.

Taking 100% Responsibility for the Abuse

1. I was older and should have known better.
2. A [insert your age at the time of the molestation] is much better able to make decisions than a [insert the age of the victim at the time of the molestation].
3. Even if he or she started it, I should have said "no" and told someone.
4. The law says I am 100% responsible for molesting a child.
5. It's odd for a person my age to be playing with a child that age in the first place.
6. I made the choice to molest him or her. Children that age are accustomed to having other people make their decisions. I took advantage of that.
7. My excuse was that I was just curious. The law says that can be true only if the age difference is less than 3 years.
8. Even if he or she said, "I want to suck your dick," it was my responsibility to say "no" because I am older.
9. Even if he or she was talking dirty, I should not have taken that to mean it was okay to do sexual things.
10. Because I am older and bigger, I was the authority or even a hero in the situation, and I took advantage of that.
11. Even if something like this happened to me before, I don't have the right to do it to someone else.
12. I have a hard time admitting that I do anything wrong.
13. If the victim were as wrong as I say he or she was, that person would be in as much trouble as I am right now.
14. The other boys in the group accept that they are 100% responsible for molesting their victims.
15. The counselors are trained in sexual abuse counseling, and they say I am 100% responsible for what happened no matter how the victim behaved.

PHASE 2

Making amends for the offense is strongly emphasized. Amends by the ASOP definition contain the following two elements—an apology and restitution where possible. The apology process begins with the writing of an apology letter using the "Apology Letter Guide" below.

Apology Letter Guide

1. Give an apology: "I am sorry. . . ."
2. Tell what you did: "I was wrong when. . . ."
3. Explain that you take full responsibility for what you did.
4. Describe to the victim how he or she was in no way at fault.
5. Explain how you set up the abuse.
6. Explain why you are glad you got caught.
7. Describe how the abuse might negatively affect the victim, now and in the future.
8. Explain how you plan to avoid sexual offending in the future.
9. Remind the victim of his or her right to tell someone if you or anyone should ever try to sexually abuse them again.

This letter is written to the victim, read aloud in both the individual and group sessions, rewritten incorporating the acquired feedback, then read again and again until satisfactory. The question of whether to conduct a face-to-face apology, send the letter, or neither is not an easy one. A face-to-face meeting is held or a letter sent only when the best interests of the victim can be served by such an experience. Restitution of any kind must meet the same standard.

PHASE 3

A large majority of our participants were, or are, themselves victims of abuse—sexual, physical, or emotional. Their history of abuse seems to be highly related to their decision to offend. We believe that the victim experience of the adolescent, as well as his perpetration, must be a part of the overall treatment plan to facilitate full recovery and to minimize the chance of reoffending. The order of treatment is vitally important here. The perpetration must be treated first, and only when that work is nearing completion should the victim recovery begin. Model victim/survivor treatment programs are available elsewhere in the literature (Bolton, Morris, & MacEachron, 1989; Grubman-Black, 1990; King, 1995). The "victim history" format is used to assist the participant in exploring the details of his own victimization.

My Own Victim History

1. How old were you when you were abused? How old was the offender? Was the offender male or female? How many times were you abused? By how many offenders?
2. What kinds of abusive acts did the offender do to you? What did he or she have you do to them?
3. Was there the use of force in the abuse? If so, describe. Do you blame yourself?
4. How did the perpetrator manipulate or coerce you?
5. How did you feel about yourself after the abuse?

6. Did you think the abuse was partly your fault? If so, why?
7. If the abuse was sexual, did it cause you to think you were gay? Explain.
8. What effects did your abuse have on you later?
9. If you were to write an "anger letter" to your offender, what would you say?
10. What is the most important thing you would like to say to someone who has been molested?

PHASE 4

Nearly all the participants in the program live or have lived in a significantly dysfunctional family atmosphere. Each participant is assisted in understanding the contextual clues that distorted his views of violence, sex, or both. He is required to write an autobiography using the "Autobiography Outline." As it is being written, it is read aloud in individual and group therapy sessions, and revisions are made continuously until the document meets an acceptable level of honesty and forthrightness. This exercise is valuable in helping the participant understand the origins of his offense and, more often than not, the fact of his own childhood victimization.

Autobiography Outline

I. General information
   A. Age, date of birth
   B. Names and ages of brothers and sisters
   C. Parents' and/or stepparents' names and ages
II. Family history
   A. Parental divorces, stepparents, stepsiblings
   B. Serious illnesses in family members or self
   C. History of drug and alcohol abuse in the family
   D. History of trouble with the law in the family
   E. Grandparents: Any abuse issues or addictions of any kind
   F. Death of close family members
   G. Number of times and places family moved
   H. Number of schools you have attended
   I. Any relatives who have lived with you
   J. Describe your relationship to each family member
III. Childhood (from birth to age 12)
   A. Describe whether or not your childhood was happy
   B. Describe how you felt going to school for the first time
   C. Describe when you started making good friends. Who?
   D. Describe the one thing you liked best about childhood
   E. Did you feel like you fit in? Describe.
   F. Describe first experimental (not abusive) sexual experiences
   G. Describe any traumatic experiences in your life
IV. Childhood (from age 13 to present)

    A. Describe relationship with parents and siblings

    B. Describe your socialization process

        1. Relationship with friends

        2. Memberships in clubs, sports, etc. (church or school)

        3. Special opposite-sex relationships

        4. Previous experience with the legal system

        5. Your drug and alcohol use, past and present

    C. Describe your present sexual practices

  V. Sexual abuse history

    A. You as the offender

    B. You as the victim

    C. Other practices (peeping, pornography, obscene phone calls)

  VI. Personality characteristics

    A. Describe the kind of person you are

    B. Describe your personal values

    C. What "feeling word" best describes your personality?

    D. Which of your parents are you most like? In what way?

    E. What part do emotions play in your life?

  VII. Your future

    A. What will you be doing 10 years from now?

    B. What are your life goals?

An important part of Phase 4 is self-forgiveness. The goal here is to move beyond shame and self-loathing toward an adequate sense of self-worth and a positive self-image. One caveat: This task must be accomplished without diminishing the seriousness of the offensive behavior. It is successfully accomplished when the participant has a full acknowledgment of his own inappropriate behavior, has made amends, and is ready to go forward toward a healthy way of living based on learning and growth.

Forgiveness Cycle

1. How did you try to deny the sexual abuse when you first committed it?
2. How did you use anger or blame to cover up your feelings abut committing the sexual abuse?
3. Rate yourself on a scale from 1 to 10 in terms of how much you agree with this statement: I am ready to say that the sexual abuse I committed was a serious negative behavior. I am responsible for it. I am ready to put it aside and move forward.
4. Explain the rating you gave yourself. What is the next thing you would like to work out to give yourself a higher score?
5. What are the three ways you have grown and changed for the better since you entered treatment?

A final step in the full treatment process is the development of a protection plan to minimize the likelihood of reoffense. It is vital that this step be accomplished with sincerity and commitment before discharge from the program is completed.

My Protection Plan

1. What kinds of children am I at risk with?
2. What kinds of places or situations do I need to avoid?
3. What kinds of things that children do could "kick in" my distorted thinking?
4. When are the times I am most likely to push people away?
5. When I get an automatic thought of molesting a child, I will. . . .
6. I will avoid being around young children in the following ways.
7. When I find myself pushing people away, I will. . . .
8. If a child comes up to me and begins to become affectionate, I will. . . .
9. When I have a lot of thoughts about molesting or find myself planning to molest, I will talk to. . . .

Process Themes

The following descriptions are provided to give a flavor of the therapy process and the nature of the therapeutic themes often found in these cases. To be sure, not all these generalizations are true of every case, but they represent common threads that run through work with these adolescents.

One of the most common themes is the propensity for participants to deny the significance of their acts and even to deny the very acts that already have been substantiated by police investigation. It can be debated whether the denial is a conscious decision to lie or whether the distortions become so assimilated into the offenders' thinking that they no longer know for sure what they did. The truth probably lies on both sides. We do find participants who choose to lie or to be selective in their truth telling in hopes of minimizing the consequences by admitting to as little as possible. It seems quite clear that the opposite is also true. We also have seen participants who have repressed the experience, in part or in whole, or have repeated their distorted defense ("He or she wanted it or liked it, or asked for it or deserved it.") in their own minds so often that they have come to believe it to be the truth.

Those who have developed these survival tools will usually use them in a variety of situations, even those for which there is no real negative consequence. It becomes a mode of operation that is trusted because it has worked in the past. The treatment staff has often found that liars will also lie about what is happening in therapy, even to family members. The parent who then is upset and speaks to the therapist is often surprised to discover the actual truth. He or she will have a puzzled look when stating "But he said. . . ."

The most effective tool for challenging the withholding and distorting of facts is group confrontation. These young men have grown accustomed to lying to adults, but the pressure exerted by a group of peers is much more potent. To be sure, they will usually try to lie, but a group of other offenders, most of whom have tried the same game, eventually can wear down the resister. It is interesting that the participant who was the best at withholding the truth initially is often the best at catching others in their lies.

An example of effective group pressure may be helpful. A participant who had admitted to inappropriately touching a 9-year-old girl held fast to his claim that he never intended to penetrate her vagina with his finger. "It just slipped in," he insisted. The group facilitator gave an assignment to the entire group to find out the diameter of an average 9-year-old girl's vagina and that of an average boy's finger. Participants asked nurses, went to the library, and otherwise sought the information. The consensus at the next group meeting was that the vaginal diameter of a 9-year-old is about the same as that of a pencil. The individual participant held onto his story and was supported by one of the other participants. Then an interesting thing happened. The lone supporter suddenly yelled, "Stop. I now know he's lying. I just put my finger inside the opening of this pop can, which is much larger than a pencil, and my finger got stuck. He's lying!" The game was up, and the lie was admitted.

Because the young men we work with are among the less violent offenders, their offenses often resulted from their ability to groom the victim. They can become experts at grooming others to get what they want. Not only have they groomed their victims, but they also usually have groomed their parents and family members into believing their lies, and they have every hope of grooming the treatment staff as well.

A case example illustrates this grooming process. Terry groomed his victim by being exceptionally nice and kind to him. His victim was a 4-year-old boy named Billy who was pretty easy to please. Terry first made sure that Billy's parents trusted him to baby-sit for Billy. Terry was always very polite to Billy's mom and dad and offered to do extra things around the house for them, such as washing dishes, when he baby-sat. He also was very nice to Billy, letting him stay up late and giving him candy. He made sure Billy knew not to tell his parents about these favors and told him that they would both be in trouble if he did. Eventually, he began to play bedtime games with Billy in which he would get Billy undressed, and then they would dance on their way to the shower. Terry would wash Billy and make a game of that too. Eventually, Terry would take his own clothes off and take a bath with Billy, which then led to other sexual behaviors that eventually included sodomy. In the meantime, Billy's parents thought Terry was an exemplary baby-sitter, and in many ways he was. There were some problems with his baby-sitting, however, that got disclosed eventually when Billy complained that his bottom hurt.

In treatment, Terry was an exemplary group member who always did his home-work and never missed a session, although he complained that there was a misunder-standing about his abuse of Billy. Billy's parents were also convinced there was some misunderstanding until the day Billy had to explain the details of his sexual abuse to the group and to his parents. Through working with the other adolescents in the group, Terry had become aware that much of his behavior toward Billy had been purposive and directly related to his desire to build trust so that he could carry out his intention. During the early phases of his grooming, there had been very little sexual activity between Terry and Billy, although Terry admitted masturbating to images of sodomizing Billy from early in this relationship.

A major task during Phases 1 and 2 is to break the denial and grooming behaviors and to reorient the participant's cognitions toward facing the truth at all times. No distortion goes unchallenged, and consequences are meted out as needed. The presence of the probation officer in the group sessions is of immeasurable help with this task. He or she very often has information about the day-to-day life of the young person, including progress at school and behavior toward family members, plus access to the police report and court records. With the group confrontations, the perceptiveness of the therapist, and the information that can be provided by the probation officer, very few participants are able to maintain their distortions over the long term.

The most pervasive psychosocial characteristic that has been observed among the participants is a longing, a deep hunger, for a genuine connection with others, both family and nonfamily. They tend to be social isolates, and within their families they usually find very little acceptance and intimacy. As mentioned above, they may also be victims themselves, which would obviously mitigate against feelings of being loved unconditionally. They typically feel powerless in spite of the fact that their offense was one of overpowering another individual. Communication within their families tends to be indirect and often hostile. The typical family system could be described as disengaged or chaotic.

Work with these clients can be frustrating and maddening for therapists. The treatment seldom if ever begins with a willing client. All the participants are court ordered, and most are attending this program as a diversion from imprisonment in the Indiana Boys' School. Participants can be intransigent in their denial and clever in their manipulations. Often, they are caught in a life space not of their own making, one that must be tolerated and survived while they try to learn the skills of effective living. These skills typically are not being modeled by others in their day-to-day lives.

Work with these participants is also highly rewarding. As the transformation takes place from a frightened, distrustful, angry young man to one who is more honest, trusting, sensitive, and aware, memories of the frustration and discouragement felt by the therapy staff melt away. The joy of watching a young man grow from a frightened, immature little boy to a confident, mature young adult is one not describable in words.

CONCLUSION

There is no doubt that sex offenses against young children by adolescent offenders are a significant social problem. We now know that many of these adolescent "bad boys" will grow up to be adult offenders unless intervention is swift and successful. Models of treatment are emerging that offer great promise of success. This chapter has outlined in detail one such program. Ongoing development of treatment models is essential, as is the further development of evaluation methodology and models of training therapists who work in this area.

In this chapter, we have offered specific assessment and treatment guidelines. Careful selection of participants, an action-oriented program individualized for each person, a combination of treatment modalities, and a team effort are vital components of such a program. The most important outcome measure is the prevention of reoffending. Those of us who work with these young males are taking on the task of assisting them in directing their lives toward productive citizenship and helping to keep the children of the community safe. No effort is too great.

HIGHLIGHTS OF CHAPTER 13

▶ In the past, boys who offended sexually were dismissed as simply experimenting or as suffering an adjustment reaction. In many cases, it was considered by the courts to be simply a matter of "boys will be boys." This attitude also has been held by many in our culture and portrayed in the media. The combined results of these attitudes have been a major underreporting of juvenile sexual behaviors.

▶ This chapter describes a successful Adolescent Sexual Offender Treatment Program (ASOP). Topics include diagnosis and classification, treatment goals and objectives, selection procedures for treatment, a proven treatment process, and a case example for illustrative purposes.

▶ The ASOP program is a cooperative effort between the juvenile court and a private group mental health practice. Two probation officers who specialize in working with sexual offenders are assigned to the program and work closely with the treatment counselors.

▶ Most of the offenders in this program are undersocialized or pseudo-socialized exploiters or group-influenced offenders. More aggressive or disturbed offenders are not appropriate for this program.

▶ The program is based on four important assumptions. First, there is something deviant about the offender's sexual response that allows him to be aroused by age-inappropriate children or by violent acts that become sexualized. Second, the offending sexual behaviors serve to meet nonsexual needs that are often associated with past traumatic experiences. Third, something in the offender's personality structures allows him to ignore social rules, minimize empathy for the victim, and have numerous cognitive distortions about reality. Fourth, if a sex offender does not have access to vulnerable children or victims, he cannot commit the offense, so protections are set in place during treatment to prevent the possibility of reoffending.

▶ The program has several components: psychological assessment, selection procedures, individualized outcome goal and objectives, individual therapy, group therapy, homework assignments, treatment for their own past abuse history, parent involvement, victim protection, and aftercare.

▶ The treatment program is structured around a four-phase model. Each phase has specific behavioral criteria that must be met before the participant is allowed to move to the next phase. Discharge from the program occurs when the participant has successfully completed all four phases. The average length of treatment is 2 years, although some participants have taken up to twice as long.

14

Helping Mentally Retarded Boys and Their Families

JAMES DEAN

MARK S. KISELICA

Imagine an infant boy who is slow to crawl, walk, or talk. Imagine him as a preschooler having difficulty engaging other children in age-appropriate forms of play. Imagine him being teased by his peers and left out of their activities because he is "different." Imagine him being unable to evaluate accurately the safety of situations or the trustworthiness of strangers. Imagine him seeing most other children his age head off each week day to one school while he attends another. Imagine his frustration as he struggles to learn and perform the simplest of tasks. Imagine him growing older and finding himself not welcomed on youth league baseball, basketball, or soccer teams. Imagine him watching from the sidelines as other boys compete in sports. Imagine him sensing that he cannot match their physical skills and wondering if he will ever be able to do what other boys can do. Imagine him wanting to be like them and wanting to be liked by them. Imagine him as he enters adolescence, feeling socially isolated and limited in his opportunities to date girls whom he finds attractive. Imagine him feeling confused about his emerging sexual feelings and uncertain as to whether or not and when and how he should touch himself privately. Imagine him being taught that his sexual desires are wrong. Imagine him envying other boys as they hop in their cars and drive off on their own or with their buddies at great speeds to places and events to which he is denied access. Imagine him wondering what it means to go away to college and to live somewhere far away from where his parents reside. Imagine him as a young man facing difficulties in ordering food in a restaurant, riding buses, finding and keeping a job, and opening and maintaining a bank account. Imagine his loneliness in a world that tells him he should not marry or have children of his own. Imaging his fears as he wonders what will happen to him after his parents are too old or sick to care for him, or what his life will be like after his parents die.

You have just pictured what life is often like for many mentally retarded boys in an "ableist" culture, a society in which the value of people is determined by their physical and mental abilities to fit into the mainstream without requiring any special assistance; in which the ideal image of a man is that of an intellectually sharp individual who is also physically attractive, athletically competitive, and vocationally successful; and in which many people carry erroneous assumptions about the mentally retarded and fail to understand their special needs.

The purposes of this chapter are to raise awareness about the difficulties of mentally retarded boys and to suggest strategies for helping them. We begin by defining mental retardation and highlighting its causes, discussing common myths and stereotypes about the mentally retarded, and describing recent legislation designed to assist the disabled and protect their rights. Next, we outline some of the adjustment difficulties of mentally retarded boys and their families. Then, we discuss counseling with this population. We conclude with some comments about helping other populations of developmentally disabled boys.

DEFINITION AND DESCRIPTION
OF MENTAL RETARDATION

Mental retardation is a type of developmental disability that affects between 1% and 2.5% of the general population, or as many as 7 million people in the United States (Batshaw & Shapiro, 1997). "A developmental disability is any physical or mental condition that can impair or limit a child's skills or causes a child to develop language, thinking, personal, social, and movement skills more slowly than other children" (Pueschel, Bernier, & Weidenman, 1988, p. 3). "Being mentally retarded is technically defined as having scored below 70 on traditional intelligence tests and having difficulty adapting to the demands of everyday life" (Nielsen, 1996, p. 90).

According to Langone (1996), the American Association on Mental Retardation recommends examining 10 domains of adaptive functioning in assessing for mental retardation: communication, self-care, home living, social skills, community use, self-direction, health and safety, functional academics, leisure, and work. Deficits in adaptive functioning are determined by evaluating the individual's functioning in each of the 10 domains and comparing them against that of same-age peers who come from a similar cultural background.

Although no mentally retarded individuals ever develop the critical thinking and abstract reasoning skills associated with formal operational thinking, there is great variation in the skills that they are capable of learning. People who score between 50 and 70 on intelligence tests usually can be taught to read and write, and they usually can learn vocational skills in special education classes that enable them to become financially self-supporting. Individuals scoring between 35 and 55 on intelligence tests can be trained to take care of their own hygiene and can perform tasks that are useful in a sheltered environment, but they must live under adult supervision their entire lives. Those whose intelligence test scores fall between 20 and 40 can learn some very simple occupational tasks, but their serious speech and motor impairments prevent them from performing many of their daily hygiene tasks and from supporting themselves financially. Consequently, they must be under the constant supervision of adults. The mental and physical impairments of people with intelligence test scores below 20 are so severe that they cannot benefit from special educational training, and they require constant custodial care throughout their lives (Nielsen, 1996). The interventions described in this chapter target mentally retarded boys whose intelligence scores are 35 or higher and would be considered under most classifications systems as moderately to mildly retarded (see Patton & Jones, 1990). For a discussion of interventions designed for mentally retarded boys who are more seriously impaired, the reader is referred to Cleland (1979) and Sailor et al. (1986).

Batshaw and Shapiro (1997) report that "mental retardation occurs more frequently in boys than in girls. The ratio of males to females is 2:1 in mental retardation requiring intermittent supports and 1.5:1 in mental retardation requiring extensive supports" (p. 348). This is thought to be the consequence of links between the X chromosome and certain types of mental retardation, such as fragile X syndrome, which has rapidly become the most frequently diagnosed inherited cause of mental retardation (Batshaw, 1997).

CAUSES OF MENTAL RETARDATION

Nielsen (1996) concisely summarizes the causes of mental retardation:

> Mental retardation can be caused by both genetic and environmental factors. . . . Down's syndrome, for example, is a genetic abnormality that often causes mental retardation and is associated with certain physical characteristics such as slanted eyes, a short neck, and a very rounded face. . . . Other mentally retarded children, however, have no family history of retardation and have no evidence of brain damage or a genetic abnormality. In these cases, a severely impoverished environment at home might cause the retardation, especially in families in which the child was malnourished as an infant and toddler. (p. 91)

COMMON MYTHS AND STEREOTYPES ABOUT THE MENTALLY RETARDED

Throughout much of history, mentally retarded individuals have been viewed with pity, scorn, and contempt and contained on the periphery of society. Prior to the 16th century, people believed that the mentally retarded were possessed by evil spirits or the devil.

Consequently, they were typically hanged, imprisoned, tortured, or driven away from their communities (Tyor & Bell, 1984). Between the 16th and 19th centuries, special institutions for the mentally retarded and mentally ill were constructed, but the patients of these institutions were viewed as morally defective and were treated more like beasts than like human beings (Coleman, 1976). During the latter part of the 19th century, the medical community began to recognize that mental retardation represented some form of "defective mental development" (Diefendorf, 1918, p. 536). People throughout society, however, still referred to the mentally retarded as "imbeciles" and "idiots" whose deficits represented flaws in their characters. Furthermore, mentally retarded men were considered sexual perverts who posed a danger to society (see Diefendorf, 1918).

Recent advances in understanding about the causes of mental retardation have challenged these stereotypes about the mentally retarded and prompted more humane treatment of this population. Old myths about the mentally retarded nevertheless persist and influence how the mentally retarded are viewed by many people in contemporary society. In our clinical experiences working with the mentally retarded, we have encountered some people who still believe that the mentally retarded are possessed by the devil or that mental retardation is a contagious illness that can infect those who have close contact with people afflicted with this form of disability. We have also witnessed biased thinking about the intellectually disabled during heated debates at town meetings regarding plans to open supervised, community-based living services for the mentally retarded. Some of the opponents to such services were parents who expressed their fears that mentally retarded residents would harm their children. Mentally retarded men in particular were singled out as potential child molesters.

Daniels, Cornelius, Makas, and Chipouras (1979) discuss the following additional, and in some cases contradictory, stereotypes about disabled populations such as the mentally retarded: Disabled people are asexual; disabled people are oversexed and have uncontrollable urges; if a disabled person has a sexual problem, it is always the result of the disability; and if a nondisabled person has a sexual relationship with a disabled individual, it is always because he or she cannot attract anyone else.

In spite of the persistent fears of and biases regarding the mentally retarded, there is a growing recognition that very few mentally retarded individuals are in any way dangerous to other people and that many more of these individuals can be helped to lead productive and relatively normal lives (Nielsen, 1996). This recognition is evident in recent legislation regarding the disabled.

RECENT LEGISLATION REGARDING THE DISABLED

Over the past three decades, the U.S. Congress has passed several laws the reflect increasing concern in the United States for the needs of the disabled. Public Law 94-142, the Education for All Handicapped Children Act, passed in 1975, requires that education of handicapped children take place in the least restrictive, yet appropriate environment. This law also mandates that a written individualized educational plan be developed for every handicapped child. PL 94-142 also provides for special services as a part of public education for impaired children, such as the mentally retarded (Lay-Dopyera & Dopyera, 1987).

Since the passage of this landmark bill, Congress has passed numerous laws assisting the disabled, such as the Individuals With Disabilities Education Act (IDEA) of 1986, which is designed to provide an appropriate and free education to youth with disabilities from infancy through age 21 as well as special services for the disabled and their families (see Baker, 1996; Hanson, 1996a). In addition, the Americans With Disabilities Act of 1990 protects people with disabilities from being discriminated against on the basis of their disability. These legislative initiatives demonstrate that policymakers have shifted from shunning the mentally retarded to protecting their rights as citizens and promoting their well-being.

ADJUSTMENT DIFFICULTIES OF
<u>MENTALLY RETARDED BOYS AND THEIR FAMILIES</u>

Although great strides have been made in the understanding and treatment of the mentally retarded, mentally retarded boys continue to experience a host of adjustment difficulties and socially constructed barriers to leading a fulfilling life. They are likely to be teased or ignored by nondisabled peers, have low self-esteem, be shy and socially isolated, lack assertiveness skills, and feel lonely (Hallum, 1995). Because of parental restrictions against dating and rejection by female nondisabled peers, many mentally challenged boys rarely date, and some never do (Bernstein, 1985). When it comes to sexual matters, they tend to be confused about the physical changes brought on by puberty (Bernstein, 1985), less knowledgeable than the nondisabled about sexual reproduction (Hall & Morris, 1976), and less sexually experienced than nondisabled persons (Daniels et al., 1979), while being at risk for sexual exploitation and abuse (Polloway & Patton, 1990; Thompson, 1990). Few mentally retarded men ever marry (Hall & Sawyer, 1978), and many have difficulty finding employment environments that are tailored to their needs (Wehman & Parent, 1996; Wolfe, Kregel & Wehman, 1996).

Being the parent of a son facing so many potential difficulties is no easy task. Data from a variety of sources indicate that the parents of mentally retarded children tend to experience a variety of worries and hardships associated with raising an exceptional child. Most parents experience a mixture of intense sorrow and shock upon learning that their child is mentally retarded (Raech, 1966), followed by a long, emotionally draining process of revising the expectations they had for the child. For example, "Dreams for a child's college education, marriage, parenting, carrying on a family business, and so on often must be discarded or drastically revised" (Browder, Jones, & Patton, 1990, pp. 436-438). Olshansky (1962, cited in Smith, 1983) observes that many parents experience chronic sorrow for the remainder of their lives as they attempt to help their disabled child to find happiness and security in the world. Parents often report that many events will trigger grief, such as "seeing a neighbor's child learn to drive and realizing that their own child will probably never drive or own a car" (Browder et al., 1990, p. 438), and they tend to worry constantly about their child's future and what will happen to their child after the parents become old or ill or after they die (Hornby, 1995). Many parents experience an ever present fear that their child will be ridiculed, exploited, or abused by someone outside the family (Langseth, 1997). Some parents become so frustrated in trying to manage their children that they worry about their own potential to abuse their child (see Lutzker & Steed, 1998).

Fathers appear to have a harder time accepting mental retardation in sons than do mothers (Hornby, 1995), even though mothers tend to take on most of the domestic and child care duties related to raising the child (see Browder et al., 1990). Farber (1972) hypothesizes that men experience a loss of self-esteem when their sons are identified as mentally retarded. They also report feeling angry that when educators, physicians, and other professionals discuss their son's condition, needs, and treatment they are left out of the information loop (see Browder et al., 1990).

In addition to coping with these emotional reactions, parents must manage other physical and financial demands that are common in families with a disabled child. Completing simple tasks, such as feeding, bathing, and dressing a mentally retarded son, usually takes much more effort and time than is required for assisting a nondisabled child. The child care needs of a mentally retarded boy residing at home often prompt the parents, especially the mother, to readjust career expectations. At the same time, "the added expense of a child with special needs may increase a father's perception of needing to maintain and improve the family's financial situation" (Browder et al., 1990, p. 446).

The emotional and physical demands placed on a family can place a tremendous strain on a marriage. Although most couples gradually adjust to life with a disabled child, others have great difficulty making this adjustment (Pueschel et al., 1988). Attending to the needs of a mentally retarded boy can diminish the time a couple can spend alone as well as the frequency of spontaneous couple activities (Hallum, 1995). When the couple becomes obsessed with their parental responsibilities (Browder et al., 1990) and thus unable to establish a balance of addressing both their own and their child's needs (Langseth, 1997), their marriage is likely to suffer, especially if the couple had problems before the child's disability was discovered (Pueschel et al., 1988).

Siblings usually experience complex feelings about and burdens associated with having a mentally retarded brother. They may have ambivalent feelings, including empathy, envy, frustration, guilt, and anger, about having a brother who requires so much attention, especially attention from their parents. They also may attempt to compensate for their brother's disability by excelling, or they may become protective of their brother and act as surrogate parents (Browder et al., 1990).

Several writers (Browder et al., 1990; Hallum, 1995; Hornby, 1995; Langseth, 1997; Pueschel et al., 1988) have noted that most families establish a strong bond with the mentally retarded son and with one another in spite of—if not because of—the many stresses they face. For example, Pueschel and colleagues (1988) describe the great affection and caring that occurs in many families between the mentally retarded child, his parents, and his siblings. Hornby (1995) reports that some fathers believe that having a child with Down's syndrome brought them closer to their wives, thereby improving their marital relationship. It appears that the key to achieving these sort of satisfying outcomes is for the family to find a way to address each family member's needs (Langseth, 1997). This latter consideration should be a primary goal of counseling with mentally retarded boys and their families.

COUNSELING CONSIDERATIONS

According to Hanson (1996b), there has been a shift in the orientation of professionals and parents regarding the methods and process of intervention with developmentally disabled people. Historically, parents played a more passive role and left the selection and delivery of intervention methods to professionals. As practitioners began to realize that the development of mentally retarded children is greatly influenced by the family and the social ecosystem of the home, they began to conduct many of their assessments and interventions in the home and to involve parents in the clinical processes of setting treatment goals and conducting therapeutic activities with their children (Lutzker & Steed, 1998). Consequently, counseling with mentally retarded boys who reside at home with their families is "family centered or family focused" (Hanson, 1996b, p. 457).

In our work with mentally retarded boys, we have found it especially important to engage fathers in the therapeutic process of helping their sons. We have observed that mentally retarded boys truly crave and relish the guidance, affection, and attention of men, especially their fathers, as the boys attempt to find their way in life. Although all boys need men to teach them how to become men, mentally retarded boys need extra attention from caring men because of their cognitive limitations and because they are frequently rejected by their nondisabled male peers. We have found that mentally retarded boys acquire a high degree of self-confidence and self-esteem when their fathers and other adult men, such as uncles and friends of the family, show them affection, address their questions about life, teach them life skills, play and joke with them, and affirm their efforts to become independent. Thus, we make special efforts to reach out to the father as we provide supportive counseling, early assessment and interventions, and case management services and work with parents to teach their son life skills.

SUPPORTIVE COUNSELING

Supportive counseling is suggested to help families to resolve their feelings and attitudes about having a disabled family member. Counseling conducted when the family first learns about the boy's disability should be focused on validating the many feelings, such as shock, anger, depression, anxiety, shame, hatred, self-pity, and loneliness, that family members might have. It is crucial that the counselor affirm for the family that all these reactions are normal responses to a very stressful situation (Pueschel et al., 1988).

During family counseling sessions, many families need assistance clarifying role boundaries and communication issues associated with adjusting the family system to the demands placed on it by the addition of a child with special needs (Langseth, 1997). The counselor must help the parents to convey information about mental retardation to the disabled boy's siblings and to explain to the siblings what shifts in family functioning may be required to help the disabled child. The parents often need guidance about how to balance the respective needs of each family member, including their own marital needs, and how to prepare for the emotional ups and downs that come with raising a child with special needs (Pueschel et al., 1988). Although all these issues should be addressed in family counseling, it is also recommended that the family be referred to support groups for families with a mentally retarded child (Langseth, 1997) or multiple family group therapy (Szymanski & Kiernan, 1983) because the participants in such groups usually provide one another with great comfort and guidance in coping with the challenges of raising a disabled youngster. Local chapters of The Association for Retarded Citizens (The Arc) can be helpful in locating such support groups (Langseth, 1997).

EARLY ASSESSMENTS AND INTERVENTIONS

Part of the process of helping families to establish equilibrium in the home is to make sure that they arrange for early assessments and interventions focused on addressing their son's needs (Hanson, 1996b). Early assessments identify the son's capabilities and limitations. Once they are armed with this information about the son's abilities, families often replace unrealistic and frustration-producing expectations with realistic beliefs regarding what the son is capable of doing and when he might be capable of doing it (Pueschel et al., 1988). Early interventions help the disabled child to maximize his abilities and prevent the emergence of challenging secondary problems, such as aggression and self-injurious behavior (Hanson, 1996a, 1996c; Lutzker & Steed, 1998).

CASE MANAGEMENT SERVICES

Case managers must play a pivotal role in guiding the parents of a mentally retarded boy to the many professionals who can assess the child and provide early intervention services. The case manager should be knowledgeable about the special needs of mentally retarded boys and be able to coordinate services from a wide range of disciplines, including medicine, nursing, nutrition, social work, speech-language pathology and audiology, occupational therapy, physical therapy, and psychology (Hanson, 1996b). Moreover, the case manager should be able to devise an individualized service plan for the disabled child and his family (Hanson, 1996b). Once again, local chapters of The Arc as well as chapters of the American Association on Mental Retardation can be helpful in identifying the names of competent case managers for the mentally retarded.

Working With Parents as Teachers of Their Disabled Son

One of the central principles of early intervention is to convince the parents that their mentally retarded son is an active learner despite his disability and that the parents should become active participants in his development. Creating this mind-set empowers parents to see their child's potential and fosters their bonding with the child (Hanson, 1996a, 1996b). Accordingly, much of family counseling involves teaching parents child care skills and behavior modification principles so that they can be instructors and mediators of behavior change (Lutzker & Steed, 1998).

In their role as teachers, parents must work collaboratively with professionals to train their son in basic hygiene skills, appropriate forms of communication, and social skills (Langseth, 1997). Regarding these tasks, Langseth comments,

> Each parent needs to determine the most effective methods for teaching these skills. For some adolescents, verbal reminders or a pictorial or written checklist may be needed; for others, hands-on assistance may be needed initially; and for some, parents may need to do the task for a long time. (p. 290)

Hallum (1995) recommends encouraging parents to teach developmentally disabled boys how to assist with simple chores as a means to enhance self-esteem and self-confidence. These chores include setting the table, preparing a meal, cleaning the house, or shopping for food.

As is the case with any boy, a mentally retarded boy should be taught about male and female anatomy, sexual development, reproduction, and contraceptive use by the time he reaches adolescence (Langseth, 1997). (For a thorough discussion of sexual education with the mentally retarded, see Monat-Haller, 1992.) His parents should discuss their values about these issues with him and answer his questions regarding his dating, sexual desires, marriage, and having children. Some boys may need special guidance about appropriate times and places for masturbation (Langseth, 1997).

Because mentally retarded boys tend to be very agreeable, trusting, and willing to please, they are at risk for sexual abuse. Consequently, extra attention should be devoted to teaching about "good touch and bad touch." For example, parents and counselors can employ the Circles Game, which was developed by Walker-Hirsch and Champagne (1991), to help mentally retarded boys to develop boundaries between themselves and others regarding interpersonal and sexual closeness. The game consists of drawing different colored circles, each representing different degrees of interpersonal closeness. The boy may choose a purple circle to represent him. The blue circle may represent people the boy knows well and who can be trusted to hug him. To demonstrate the interpersonal closeness between him and these people, the circles may be placed near each other. A green circle may represent people who should not touch him and should be placed far away from the other circles. Then, the boy can be taught strategies for asserting himself if the green circle gets too close to him.

Educating mentally retarded boys about sexual matters is just one of several considerations related to the challenge of preparing them for independent living, which is a growing trend with the developmentally disabled. Langseth (1997) recommends that parents and professionals attempt to help the mentally retarded to achieve proficiency in the following areas, each of which is considered important for independent functioning: personal hygiene, household maintenance, social skills, money management, work ethics, transportation, home and community safety, medical care, and sound judgment. Langone (1996) suggests that all mentally retarded boys be taken to job sites and be exposed to and taught job skills as early as the elementary school years. Clees (1996) advocates for training in the utilization of recreational facilities and participation in leisure activities with both disabled and nondisabled people. Boys who are not proficient in several of these many areas of functioning may need to live with their parents or family members, or in state-supported, supervised living arrangements, when they become adults (Langseth, 1997). Whether the boy ends up living independently or under the supervision of adults, the collaborative training efforts of practitioners and parents can provide a mentally retarded boy with a supportive web that can help him to build on his strengths to achieve his highest potential (Hanson, 1996b).

CONCLUSION

In this chapter, we have tried to convey what it means to be a mentally retarded boy in our society and to suggest a variety of interventions designed to help mentally retarded boys to achieve fulfilling lives and a healthy sense of masculinity. We recognize that there are many other developmental disabilities, such as autism, cerebral palsy, seizure disorders, learning disabilities, and a wide range of sensory and communication disorders, that adversely affect thousands of boys and complicate their transition to manhood. We hope that his chapter will prompt counselors and psychotherapists to learn more about the special needs of these boys and to invest their time and energy in helping these youth in their quests to feel accepted, loved, happy, and productive in our ableist society.

HIGHLIGHTS OF CHAPTER 14

▶ Mental retardation is a type of developmental disability characterized by significant deficits in cognitive and adaptive functioning.

▶ Mental retardation is caused by both genetic and environmental factors, affects between 1% and 2.5% of the general population, and is more common among boys than girls.

▶ Although U.S. society has grown more enlightened about and accepting of developmentally disabled people, mentally retarded boys continue to be the victims of insensitive and inaccurate stereotypes.

▶ Mentally retarded boys and young men tend to be teased, socially isolated, confused and inexperienced regarding sexual matters, at risk for sexual and emotional exploitation, and unemployed or employed sporadically.

▶ Recent legislation, such as the Americans With Disabilities Act, protects the rights and promotes the well-being of the mentally retarded and other disabled citizens.

▶ Families of mentally retarded boys experience many difficulties associated with having a disabled family member. Parents tend to experience chronic sorrow and concerns about their son's future as well as the physical and financial demands of raising a disabled child. Siblings struggle with complex feelings about and burdens associated with having a mentally retarded brother.

▶ In spite of the hardships reported by families of the mentally retarded, most family members form a strong bond with the disabled boy and with one another, especially when the family finds a way to address the needs of each family member.

▶ Counseling with mentally retarded boys is family centered and focused on skills training and fostering strong family bonds, especially in the father-son relationship.

▶ Families require supportive counseling to help with the adjustments of the family system that are required to help the disabled child.

▶ Early assessments and interventions are crucial in facilitating the mentally retarded boy's development while preventing the emergence of secondary problems, such as aggression and self-injurious behavior.

▶ Case management counseling is necessary to help families to identify and utilize services that will address the many needs of their mentally retarded son.

▶ Parents require training in how to assist their mentally retarded son with learning life skills for independent living and assertiveness skills to prevent emotional and sexual exploitation.

15

Counseling Anxious Male Youth

DONALD B. KEAT II

The natural role of twentieth-century man is anxiety.
—Norman Mailer (1948, p. 237)

I have previously (Keat, 1990a, 1996) called anxiety one of the scarlet letters of emotion. The second scarlet letter was that of anger (Keat, 1980b). Anxiety, of course, is the focus of this chapter, and therefore the rest of my comments are directed toward the anxiety dimension. Management of anxiety has sometimes been called stress management. Learning how to handle anxiety appropriately is one of the most relevant areas that we can consider in the treatment of boys and adolescent males (both here condensed under the term *male youth.*)

ADJUSTMENT ISSUES FOR ANXIOUS MALES

The topic of anxiety has had at least a century of attention in the psychological literature. Freud began discussing anxiety more than 100 years ago. His introductory lectures on psychoanalysis included one on anxiety (lecture 25); that lecture took place in 1917. Therein, Freud stated "there is no question that the problem of anxiety is a nodal point at which the most various and important questions converge, a riddle whose solution would be bound to throw a flood of light on our whole mental existence" (Freud, 1966, p. 393).

One of my early mentors wrote a book on anxiety (May, 1950). This book was essentially the first multimodal book dealing with anxiety; May was concerned with how to interpret it biologically, psychologically, and culturally. Great interest remains concerning the meanings and dimensions of anxiety. This movement is evidenced by the writings of Kendall and colleagues (1992), Eisen and Kearney (1995), and Eisen, Kearney, and Schaeffer (1995). These books highlight how the importance of anxiety has increased over the years. There are more events impinging on a child's and adolescent's life today. Early day care, changing family structure, and moving and mobility are just some examples of the wide range of pressures that influence a youth's life today. Factors affecting anxiety are increasing, and anxiety continues to be an important dimension of everyday life.

Anxiety is common to us all. As Freud (1966) stated, "Every one of us has experienced that sensation, or, to speak more correctly, that affective state, at one time or other on our own account" (pp. 392-393). It is important to keep in mind that along with harms from anxiety there is an aspect of helpful anxiety that we use to mobilize our forces to deal with events in our lives. That is, anxiety can be helpful in the sense that it motivates people to prepare for a test or some other activity. There are times, however, when it can be more debilitating. This detracting aspect is the primary concern of this chapter.

DIAGNOSIS

Currently, there is only one *DSM-IV* (American Psychiatric Association [APA], 1994b) anxiety diagnosis specific to children and adolescence. This diagnosis is called separation anxiety disorder and has to do with younger children who are unwilling to separate from their major attachment figures of parents or from the home (APA, 1994b). The *DSM-IV* (APA, 1994b) lists extensive criteria for separation anxiety disorder, and Eisen and Kearney (1995) provide a detailed discussion. Eisen and Kearney note that there are other diagnoses applicable to children and adolescents, such as avoidant disorder, social phobia, social anxiety disorder, overanxious disorder, generalized anxiety disorder, panic disorder and agoraphobia, simple and specific phobias, obsessive-compulsive disorder, and post-traumatic stress disorder.

To this list of generally accepted diagnoses I would add two others I have observed in children and adolescents. The first is directly relevant for this book, in that it concerns only males. I call this the Male Anxiety Syndrome (MAS). This particular syndrome is reflected by the child or adolescent male covering his anxieties. The primary goal is to be "cool." Cartoonist Charles Schultz sometimes draws his Snoopy character as Joe Cool, a different persona or cover. The MAS covering has to do with keeping such concerns as health or physical and mental deficiencies covered up. In this syndrome, males keep these things to themselves and do not share them with others. Society demands that boys be immune to and mask their fears. These concerns are covered over (suppressed) and kept within the man's inner realm. The syndrome has even reached the realm of popular music, as in Oscar Brown's "But I Was Cool" (Brown, 1960). In this song, no matter what happened to him, the man remained cool until he was carried away, screaming, to be institutionalized. This song reflects several extreme situations that are not shared, and it is a caricature of what can happen when people keep things bottled up. When the blowup happens, everyone is surprised.

The second diagnosis I call the Watergate Anxiety Syndrome (WAS). The male with WAS covers up outer concerns so that he can appear as good as possible. Sometimes, he even fabricates so as to make situations look better than they are. An example is cheating on examinations and thereby misrepresenting skills. The WAS syndrome thus involves not only attempts to cover up outer concerns but also attempts to build up an image that is as good as possible to cover one's own inadequacies. The MAS indicates primarily that the person simply covers up and acts cool, but in the WAS, fabrications are stacked on the cover-up to attempt either to appear to remediate the deficiency (cheating on an examination) or to build up an image or story that makes the person look as good as possible.

Realization that anxiety is on the increase confronts us with the question of what to do about it. The assessment of anxiety usually is relatively easy. It is important to use a multidimensional assessment that involves semistructured interviews, self-report measures, parent-teacher rating scales, behavioral observations, and physiological recordings. These approaches are outlined well in other sources (e.g., Eisen & Kearney, 1995). The purpose of this chapter is to help anchor anxiety in a system in which a plan of action can be made. The assessment is comparatively easy; the treatment is more difficult. As I proceed, I will make this more concrete by presenting a comprehensive system to utilize in understanding the difficulty and then look at intervention strategies.

MULTIMODAL APPROACH: TREATMENT

I have utilized the multimodal approach for more than 25 years. Another important mentor, Arnie Lazarus (1972, 1973), originally proposed a comprehensive multimodal framework of the BASIC ID (behavior, affect, sensation, imagery, cognition, interpersonal relationships, drugs-diet). He has since contributed much to the literature in this area (Lazarus, 1976, 1985, 1989). I have utilized this same approach and applied it to the area of children (Keat, 1976a, 1976b, 1976c, 1979, 1985a, 1985c, 1990a, 1990b, 1996). In particular, I have published cases in my books (Keat, 1979, 1990b) as well as in the Lazarus (1976, 1985) case books. Additional cases have appeared in journal articles and books (Keat, 1972, 1974, 1980c). I proposed the multimodal approach as a systematic framework for assessing and planning effective intervention strategies to help children and adolescents. I outline in Table 15.1 the multimodal evolution, as it has moved from the Lazarus BASIC ID modes to the HELPING format, which describes the same seven modes. The acronym HELPING delineates the modes of health, emotions, learning, personal relationships, imagery-interests, need to know, and guidance of actions, behaviors, and consequences. This format provides the structure for the section that talks about intervention strategies. There structure is described in much more detail as it applies to first- and second-order analysis in cases as well as stress management procedures.

The next section of the chapter describes strategies for establishing rapport, which is necessary to effectively intervene with youth in counseling. The third section then

TABLE 15.1 Multimodal Evolution

Letter	HELPING Mode	BASIC ID Mode
H	Health	Drugs-diet (D)
E	Emotions-feelings	Affect (A)
L	Learning-school	Sensation-school (S)
P	People-personal relationships	Interpersonal relations (I)
I	Imagery-interests	Imagery (I)
N	Need to know-think	Cognition (C)
G	Guidance of ABCs (actions, behaviors, and consequences)	Behavior (B)

describes the multimodal approach as it applies both to cases and to the more general stress management paradigm as it is reflected in this approach. Specific procedures are introduced for each mode of intervention. The multimodal model is set up so that problems are delineated in diagnosis and then treatment interventions are planned based on assessment of the problem. This approach is similar to the format of a treatment planner written by Jongsma, Peterson, and McInnis (1996). In this manual, the first disorder listed is that of anxiety. For the diagnosis of anxiety, the short-term objectives are listed, and related therapeutic interventions are lined up on the page across from the objectives. These therapeutic interventions cover most of the modes and include both individual therapy and parent education as well as family counseling approaches. This strategy is similar to the multimodal approach, which delineates intervention strategies as related to the concerns expressed by the child or adolescent. The main difficulty for the counselor is to determine what to do to help male youth with their anxieties.

STRATEGIES FOR ESTABLISHING RAPPORT

Numerous relevant strategies exist for establishing rapport with child and adolescent clients. The two major ones discussed in this section are Epochè and the relationship itself. I first discuss and explain Epochè and then present procedures for establishing a relationship; finally, I present some procedures and intervention strategies.

EPOCHÈ

I initially presented the process of Epochè in my book on child multimodal therapy (Keat, 1990b). This component of the process of counseling was based on the writings of Moustakas (1988). *Epochè* is a Greek word meaning to stay away from, or abstain. In Epochè, we set aside prejudgments, biases, and preconceived ideas about things (Moustakas, 1988). Moustakas sees Epochè as a rare process, a preparation for life but also an experience in itself, the challenge of setting aside predilections, prejudices, and predispositions, and allowing things, events, and people to enter anew into one's consciousness, and to look and see and look again as if for the first time. Epochè is a way of looking and being, an unfettered stance, in which whatever or whoever appears in our consciousness is approached with an openness, a sense of just what is there and allowing what is there to linger. It includes emptying the mind, entering a pure place, being open and ready to embrace life in what it truly offers (Moustakas, 1988).

In his more recent writings, Moustakas (1995) not only establishes the importance of Epochè prior to the therapy session but also emphasizes that it needs to continue throughout contacts with the client:

> This process is needed during the actual interview as well when the therapist's thoughts or feelings interfere with listening and accepting the narrative being presented by the person in therapy. (p. 228)

Moustakas stresses the importance of this initial engagement in which

> the therapist develops a climate of safety and trust and supports the relaxation, freedom to communicate, and the dialogue between the therapist and person in therapy. The therapist enters into the world of the person in therapy and concentrates on his or her internal frame of reference. (p. 228)

In my personal practice, I attempt to get into the process of Epochè by suspending judgment and clearing myself so that I can really try to get ready to encounter what is going on in the child's word. What does this mean in practice? First, it means that I attempt to prepare myself for what the child is bringing into the session. I will outline the child's major concerns in life, such as getting along with siblings and parents, school functioning, and so forth. This outline is multimodal in nature and is written on a page where I have a map of where the child is and what his concerns are with regard to the major areas of functioning in his life. Then I ask myself what is keeping this concern in place and how I can help the child become "unstuckified" (Keat, 1990b, p. 7) from the problem. With this outline of thoughts and concerns, I get ready to enter into the child's world. Having this chart in mind, I always write myself a note to leave it "open" initially so that the child can bring in whatever is uppermost in his or her mind, unless there is some bridge from the last session that I can follow up on—something I said I would bring in or do. Usually, I try to remain open and do not enter into any component of my agenda until we are halfway through the session. Sometimes we do not even touch on the outline, but it is a guide for the journey in case it is needed.

This state of wonderment and searching is where I am in the 5 to 10 minutes prior to meeting with the child. I have prepared the multimodal outline of the major concerns of his or her life (more is presented about the multimodal framework later). From this, I have some ideas of what might be helpful for the child. With this outline in mind,

I spend the last few minutes in a trance state of self-hypnosis. The final minute before their appointment I arouse myself and heighten my awareness-alertness by getting out of my chair and moving around. I am focusing my attention back to the concerns but reminding myself to be open to receive them wherever they happen to be in their lives. (Keat, 1990b, p. 47)

With the Epochè state established prior to the session, we are ready to move into the stage of engagement, in which the relationship is of utmost concern.

ESTABLISHING THE RELATIONSHIP

After you have prepared yourself by the process of Epochè in getting yourself ready for the therapeutic encounter with the child, then the most important component of child counseling comes into existence: establishing the relationship. The relationship approaches I discuss find their basis in Rogers (1939, 1951), Allen (1942/1979), Axline (1947), Dorfman (1951), Moustakas (1959), Guerney (1964, 1977, 1983), and Guerney and Welsh (1993). Axline (1947), in particular, has delineated the basic principles advocated by the client- or person-centered framework. These were adapted by Keat (1974, p. 66) and presented in Keat (1990b, p. 47).

1. The deliberate establishment of a positive relationship (induced by providing the child with social approval, smiling behaviors, and other rewarding contingencies)
2. Acceptance of the child as he is
3. Permissiveness to allow the child freedom to express his feelings completely
4. Recognition and reflection of the child's feelings by the therapist so that the child gains insight into his behavior
5. Giving the child responsibility for his choices in problem-solving behavior
6. Allowing the child to lead the way, with the therapist following
7. Allowing the process to unfold gradually, without the therapist attempting to hurry things along
8. Setting certain limits that are necessary to anchor counseling in the world of reality and to make the child aware of his responsibility in the relationship

The crucial question that remains is that of how to establish a relationship with the child.

This question cannot be answered easily and varies with each particular child. The therapist must be one who cares for the child and attempts to find out what is reinforcing to the child. Once this is determined, then the therapist can proceed with establishing some kind of positive relationship with the child. This relationship is based upon both the therapist's and the child's personalities. The relationship could range from saying "hello's" to the child, building a model or engine over months of time, or being more deeply involved emotionally during contacts extending over a year or years. There are no quick, easy ways to advise a therapist how to establish this relation-ship. (Keat, 1990b, pp. 47-48)

Each counselor forms this relationship in his or her own way based on personal style. My style is generally quiet, gentle, and caring. Persons at the other extreme can be much more outgoing, with slap-them-on-the-back types of relationships. Of course, there are many degrees of active involvement in between these extremes.

I have previously stated that

the relationship approaches have been effective in about one-quarter of my cases. That is, in about one-quarter of one's cases, therapists can expect to find a relationship being the necessary and sufficient condition for therapeutic change. This situation is especially true in the case of emotionally deprived children who can grow through having a relationship with a significant other person. In the other three-quarters of the author's thousands of cases, however, the relationship was necessary but proved to be insufficient for improvement or promoting the desired behavior changes. (Keat, 1990a, p. 48)

Based on more recent experience, I would alter this statement to indicate that the relationship is necessary in almost all cases, but it is necessary and sufficient in 5%-15% of cases. In the other 85%-95% of cases, the therapist needs to go farther and implement additional procedures. The next section of this chapter concerns this topic—that is, looking at a broad range of procedures from the multimodal perspective that can be effective in helping to alleviate a child's anxiety state.

Before any of these techniques can be used effectively, it is necessary to have a constructive, therapeutic, collaborative relationship with a child in which you are functioning as a team. It is up to you as a multimodal counselor to orchestrate these experiences into meaningful lifelong learnings for the child (Keat, 1990b, p. 48).

In addition, there are three other important questions that I attempt to handle in every case that I encounter. The first important question is "How can I help this child?" That is, "In what way can I teach him or her something that will be useful in coping with whatever he or she is forced to deal with in life?" (Keat, 1990b, p. 48). I will relate this question to the helping approach described in the next section of this chapter.

The second important question is "How can I be different from significant others (adults such as parents and teachers) in the child's life?" The therapist needs to impress upon the child that he or she is someone different from the other persons in the child's life, because typically these other persons have not facilitated the child's growth. This formation of the relationship needs to be based on some premise other than the ones used by the other adults in the child's life (Keat, 1990b, pp. 48-49).

The third important question is "What can I leave with this child that will make him or her feel good or better throughout the day or week coming up?" It could be some statement such as "You are looking good today" or "You did a great job" on something that the child completed during the session. This positive reinforcement is usually in the form of a "warm fuzzy" that the child can use to help sustain him- or herself during the week. At other times, I try to give the child something of value to take away from the session. In addition to providing things a child can carry away in his or her head, there are sometimes situations in which I give a child a book to read or a tape to listen to as a means of carrying on our therapeutic work during the week between contacts (Keat, 1990b, pp. 48-49).

In summary, the process of getting ready for the client has been described as Epochè. Once you are ready, then you encounter the child or adolescent in the establishment of a relationship. This relationship is necessary for therapeutic encounters to be fruitful. It is, however, not sufficient in most situations. The counselor needs to be oriented for the therapeutic journey by utilizing a framework or way of viewing clients. The next section presents this framework for working with children and adolescents who are predominantly presenting anxious difficulties. The multimodal framework provides the integrative guide for bridging the components of counseling with children, from Epochè to the relationship to the actual implementations of intervention strategies, techniques, and procedures.

INTERVENTIONS

Interventions are the procedures or techniques we use in helping children and youth overcome their anxious difficulties. In utilizing this approach, we first need to determine the nature of the concerns. For the purposes of this chapter, anxiety is the presenting difficulty. To arrive at this assessment, we would typically utilize the referral form (Keat, 1990b) to help delineate the concerns that parents or teachers have regarding the child. After these problems are determined, then we could also utilize a procedure such as the "I'm afraid of" scale (Keat, 1990b, Appendix D), which helps to further delineate the anxieties or fears of the child. Once these are determined, the task of the counselor is to decide which techniques can be most useful in helping the child. From this viewpoint, pragmatic technical eclecticism (Keat, 1979, 1990b) is the approach from which I like to work.

In other writings, I have presented multimodal profiles for children and adolescents. In particular, the case of Anxious Ashley (Keat, 1996) presents a first-order multimodal profile for an 11-year-old male whose major presenting concerns have to do with anxiety. From this vantage point, the major interventions were focused around the one of the two major presenting concerns that I call the scarlet letters of emotions (i.e., anxiety and anger). For this chapter, the major focus is on the scarlet letter emotion of anxiety. Table 15.2 presents the multimodal profile for Anxious Ashley. This case is described in detail in a recent publication (Keat, 1996).

For the purposes of this chapter, I present a methodology in which the therapist takes the major affect or emotion of anxiety and does a second-order analysis of the concern (Keat, 1990b, chap. 10). Table 15.3 presents a second-order analysis for anxiety. In this approach, the therapist takes the major emotion of anxiety (from the first-order full-scale analysis) and then goes through the same seven helping modes to determine what the basic concerns are under this major presenting emotional concern of anxiety.

TABLE 15.2 Multimodal Profile: Anxious Ashley

Mode		Concerns	Intervention
Health	H1.	Overweight	You are what you eat
	H2.	Wellness	Audiotherapy
Emotions	E1.	Anxiety	Relaxation, hypnosis
	E2.	Anger	Madness management
	E3.	Enjoyment	Fun training
Learning	L1.	Visual: reading	Audiotherapy
	L2.	Auditory: math	Audiotherapy and videotherapy
Personal relations	P1.	Friends	Friendship training
	P2.	Girlfriend	Videotherapy
	P3.	Move	Bibliotherapy
	P4.	Adult Relationships	Winning Ways
	P5.	Parent's Skills	Counseling
Imagery	I1.	Self-image	I am lovable and capable (IALAC)
	I2.	Models	Hero imagery
Need to know	N1.	Perspectives	Cognitive restructuring
	N2.	Concerns	Problem solving
	N3.	Sex education	Bibliotherapy
	N4.	Outlook	Music Therapy
Guidance of ABCs	G1.	Behavioral goals	Reward Survey for Children (RSC)
	G2.	Appropriate behavior	Games-rules
	G3.	Stealing	Bibliotherapy

In the following pages, I take this second-order analysis and describe at least one procedure in each of the modes to delineate what types of approaches can be utilized to help alleviate the presenting concern of anxiety. These zones or modes are rank ordered in terms of importance. The rank order is determined by the presenting needs or press of the client (i.e., what is the greatest concern at this time?). The ordering is hypothetical in this illustration; each particular anxious male youth will have different concerns with different priorities.

EMOTIONS

The area of concern ranked highest was emotions, so that is where we begin. In the emotional zone, the first thing that I generally do with most children is train them in relaxation. An outline for relaxation training is presented in Table 15.4.

TABLE 15.3 Helping Anxiety: Stress Management

Rank	Mode	Procedures
7	H ealth	Directed muscular activity: exercise Nutrition education Adequate sleep
1	E motions	Relaxation training Madness management Fun experiences
2	L earning	Self-hypnosis Stress inoculation
6	P eople	Friendship training Shyness strategies Communication skills
4	I magery	Hero imagery Systematic desensitization Guided imagery and music
3	N otions	Corrective self-talk Lessening "musturbation" Cognitive restructuring
5	G uidance	Assertiveness training Coping Cat Time management

Relaxation Training

The five steps for relaxation training involve working with children to teach them breathing, then reviewing the muscle groups for relaxation procedures, developing pleasant scenes with them, figuring out self-sentences that help them to relax, and finally putting it all together. These relaxation procedures have been delineated both in sound (Keat, 1977) and in print (Keat and Guerney, 1980). These sources give detailed relaxation directions for children. Other authors also provide information on relaxation training for children, including Lupin (1977), Hertzfeld and Powell (1986), and Slap-Shelton and Shapiro (1992).

Teaching the child deep diaphragmatic breathing is the core to learning relaxation. After this breathing is learned, the various muscle groups can be tensed and relaxed (see Table 15.4). This tension-relaxation technique teaches the child to have control over tightness in particular parts of the body. Next, the child selects a relaxing scene/image or picture that is best for that particular child. This scene can be determined by discussing the relaxation images with the child and providing some suggestions, such as floating on a raft in a lake, watching a fire in a fireplace, or watching the waves roll in at the seashore. After choosing a relaxing scene or image, the child picks out a self-sentence that is relaxing for him, such as "Be calm and cool." Finally, the child can

TABLE 15.4 Five Steps of Teaching Children to Relax

1. Breathing: Key to relaxation
    a. Take deep breath; breath from way down in your stomach
    b. Hold for 5 seconds
    c. Let it out slowly, making a sound as you do: "Aaah" or "Sssss"

2. Muscles: Tension-relaxation
    a. Make the muscle hard
    b. Count to 3
    c. Take a deep breath
    d. Count to 5
    e. Let breath out slowly
    f. Shake loose
    [Do this for fists, arms, jaw, mouth, nose, neck, shoulders, back, stomach, and legs]

3. Pleasant scenes: Imagine the most pleasant, relaxing scene you can think of, then follow these steps
    a. Tighten a muscle
    b. Count to 3
    c. Take deep breath
    d. Let breath out at 5
    e. Imagine your pleasant scene

4. Self-sentences: Figure out a calm, relaxing sentence to tell yourself in place of a worry. Examples:
    a. "No worries."
    b. "I can do it."
    c. "Everything is cool."

5. Putting it all together: Combine all the steps for each muscle group. Example:
    a. Squeeze fist as hard as you can
    b. Count to 3
    c. Breathe in deeply
    d. Count to 5
    e. Let your breath out slowly and think of your pleasant scene and tell yourself "I'm calm and everything is cool."
    [Do this for other muscle groups as you relax your whole body]

put this all together by first tensing the muscle, and while tensing the muscle, breathing in deeply; then he releases both the muscle and the breath while closing his eyes and relaxing, turning on the pleasant scene, and saying the self-sentence subvocally. After a child practices these exercises for a while with you (as the counselor) or listening to instructional tapes at home, he can learn how to become a more relaxed person.

In working with youth, we need to involve parent(s) as much as possible. I also train the parents in relaxation and give them tapes so that they can learn it from an adult level and thus be models for their child. Such tapes as the one by Lazarus (1975) are helpful in training parents in the basics for relaxation. Some excellent books can help adults to learn about these procedures, such as those by Bourne (1995) and Davis, Eshelman, and McKay (1995). These sources describe ways in which parents can learn to cope with anxiety through relaxation training and provide a variety of other procedures that can then help them become better models for their children in learning to cope with the anxiety in their lives.

LEARNING

Learning was ranked as the number two mode for stress management (Table 15.3). In the area of learning, one of the major things I teach children after they have acquired the skills of relaxation is to move into my preferred procedure of self-hypnosis. I explain to them that I do this on a daily basis myself; I take a siesta for about 20 minutes. This time can allow the child to regenerate his or her batteries and go on for the second half of the day in a more positive fashion. The child can fit this in right after school, sometime between 3 and 4 o'clock, then carry out the rest of the day in a more positive and productive fashion.

The procedures for self-hypnosis are a little different from those for relaxation training. Self-hypnosis helps the person to move more and more deeply into a relaxed state. Elsewhere, I have presented exact directions for self-hypnosis (Keat, 1990b, Appendix A). In this source, I present a detailed self-hypnosis journey. This procedure is also presented on side 2 of a tape I prepared for children to use when they come home after school and are home alone (Keat, 1985b).

Both these sources invite children to go on a pleasant journey. As part of this journey, the first thing to do is settle down comfortably wherever they would like to be. This could be on the bed, in an easy chair, or lying on the floor or on the couch. The idea is that they get comfortable. The second component of the self-hypnosis training is to use the imagery that they are taking steps down a staircase; with each step, they become more and more relaxed. You can also use imagery such as going down an elevator or whatever other imagery the child feels comfortable with. When they are at the bottom, they become more and more deeply relaxed, and they sink into a state of euphoria. During this time, they are free to imagine whatever they want to because they are in control. They have their visualizations, which they can turn on to help them become more relaxed. One I like to use is watching the waves roll in at the seashore. Sometimes, I also utilize an ocean tape (Syntonic Research, 1979) that helps to enhance the effect of the imagery by providing auditory cues. I also describe these visualizations as their personal television screen or video playback, which they can put on anytime they want to during the day. When they have this pleasant scene on, they become more and more deeply relaxed. I also give them some positive affirmations regarding what they can do and accomplish in life.

I encourage them to think about this procedure and figure out when they can do it. They might be able to do it during the day, at the end of the day, or before they go to bed. If they play a sport, they could use it before the game/event to help them feel more energized. They are invited to enjoy these scenes as long as they like to feel calm and relaxed. When they are ready to come back up to wakefulness, they count backward from 10 to 1. At 1, they are awakened and feel fully refreshed and ready to go on to do whatever they want to. I often call this a pleasant journey because some people are concerned about the magical effects of hypnosis. A journey is more likely to be seen as useful in daily life.

NEED TO KNOW/NOTIONS

The third zone of intervention (Table 15.3) is that of need to know/notions. The need-to-know mode has to do with what children are saying to themselves about themselves. It is important that they tell themselves good things. They need to tell themselves something good, such as "I'm really competent in handling stress." They also need to lessen their mistaken ideas in this area. Finally, they need to learn to talk to themselves in a more positive way (Isaacs & Ritchey, 1989).

Corrective Self-Talk

The corrective self-talk process has several steps. First, irrational or mistaken ideas must be identified. For example, the child may have been told that he or she is not very smart. These thoughts should be written down on an index card, then crossed out with vigor. The child needs to lessen and eliminate this type of negative thinking.

The second step is to figure out more positive sentences. These positive self-sentences dispute the previously mentioned negative ones. These can be written down on the blank side of an index card. Examples include "I am really quite smart in certain things" and "I am doing okay in class and the teacher can't put me anywhere without my parent's permission." These types of sentences can help reassure the child regarding things that are going on in their lives.

The third step is work and practice. This means that children need to learn these new sentences and keep repeating them to themselves until they can replace the old ones and believe the new self-perceptions. If they practice disputing the irrational beliefs and work on repeating (subvocally) the positive self-sentences for several weeks, should be more able to cope in the future.

"Musturbation"

Another common type of cognitive restructuring approach with children is to help them lessen their "musturbation"—the shoulds, oughts, and musts that we lay on ourselves and others (Ellis & Harper, 1975). As in most work with children, this can be a joint effort with the counselor, parent, and child. With regard to parental musturbation, parents need to look for their musts and shoulds that they say to themselves (i.e., "I must be a perfect parent"). Once parents find these absolutes in their self-sentences, they should be able to lessen their distress by changing them. For example, a new self-sentence could be "I will do my best as a parent, but sometimes I will mess up." The following steps are useful in lessening musturbation:

1. Identify the musts, shoulds, and oughts that we lay on ourselves. For example, "I must do everything well."
2. Ask yourself, are these self-expectations realistic? If the answer is yes, then pursue these aspirations with renewed vigor. If the answer is no, then you are freed of some excess baggage and therefore will be able to enjoy other things more.
3. Lessen musts. With regard to children, some absolutes are unrealistic. That is, when we say that they must, should, or ought to do certain things, they really are not necessary. A child need not get all "A"s or be a good athlete to receive the parents' approval.

Once the parents get a handle on their own musturbation, then they are in better shape to help deal with their children. For example, in lessening their musturbation regarding their children, they first need to identify the categorical imperatives they are putting on themselves. For example, the parent could expect that the child should clean up his room daily. This expectation could be unrealistic and might be tempered to indicate that the room needs to be cleaned up weekly. Then the parent needs to ask whether the expectation is realistic. If the answer is yes, then a struggle to enforce it might ensue. If the answer is no, then the parent can reduce these conflicts (and stress) with the child.

It should also be remembered that there are different types of "shoulds." There are helping shoulds that need to be maintained for a society to run smoothly. Some examples are speed limits and showing consideration for others. There are also hurting shoulds; these are the ones that need to be lessened—such things as expecting your teenager to clean up his room or make his bed daily. Both parent and child would be better off and experience less conflict if these tasks were scheduled less frequently (less stress in both lives!). Also important regarding hurting shoulds is the rule of proximity: The closer someone is to you, the more you expect of them. Parents naturally expect more of their own child than they would of another person's child. Many people would be better off if we treated all people, including family members, like we would treat our good friends. Parents and children really should learn to lessen their expectations of themselves and others. As they work toward lowering unrealistic expectations regarding musts, shoulds, and oughts, then they can feel better about themselves in life and experience less anxiety.

IMAGERY

The fourth-ranked concern (Table 15.3) is imagery. Helping a child to develop a positive self-image is one of the core goals for counselors. This enhancement can come about in a variety of ways. Below, I discuss hero imagery, systematic desensitization, and guided imagery and music.

Hero Imagery

Sometimes, the copying of admired persons or heroes is an important aspect in the development of children. These heroes can come from the sports world, from school (teachers), or from other sources. Parents can be heroes for their own children. In all approaches related to imagery, it is important to think of how children view themselves. Children learn by modeling or copying heroes; they can picture their heroes doing what they do in a positive fashion.

In terms of training children to do this effectively, it is important for them to take a deep breath and relax whenever they are confronted with something that upsets them. This procedure combines aspects of the multimodal approach and points out the interrelatedness of each of the modes. That is, although we study these things separately, we need to put them together. When a child is upset, he or she needs to stop, relax, and think about how to handle the situation. This approach combines the emotional, learning, and the need-to-know ideas. By integrating a combination of approaches, youth can more effectively cope with their concerns.

Heroes can be helpful because they provide appropriate models. For example, at the kindergarten level, children could be afraid of attending school the first few days. Attempts to lessen children's fears may involve having them imagine they are someone like Big Bird (from *Sesame Street*) and they are going to walk into the school building and tell others how to do things appropriately. Once children can imagine that they are such a big person, they frequently can approach situations with less anxiety. Although some of this activity is done in imagination (make-believe), the test is if the child can then carry out imagined behaviors in real life. It is often necessary to get children who are receiving counseling to believe that they are heroes for the moment and then to introduce the situation in which the child, or the hero, acts competently. In a sense, this is similar to systematic desensitization (in which the child approaches things gradually, as explained in the next section), except in this approach they are imagining that the hero is coping with the feared situation. Once they can see their hero coping with the situation, they realize they can handle it on their own and the hero doesn't necessarily have to do it for them.

Another example with an older child would be to have Superman come to the rescue (Lazarus, 1977). For example, a 10-year-old who fears such things as traveling in the family car could imagine a series of scenes in which the child proudly shows the automobile to the favorite TV character (i.e., Superman). Then the child could imagine Superman being excited by being taken for a ride in the car. The child could be led through a series of scenes, building up (as in systematic desensitization) to an exciting chase in which the hero rides with the child in the car in pursuit of some international spies. After several scenes like this, the child's tension could be lessened, he probably would be able to go to family outings in the car (as Superman, himself) with less or no anxiety.

Such activities can be used when children are fearful when doing specific things (for example, riding in a car) or in certain situations (for example, speaking up in class). By imagining that he is someone "super," the child can overcome a lack of self-confidence do things he could not cope with as himself. Once children have successfully completed such anxiety-producing activities, their self-esteem will improve as they realize they can actually do these things themselves. With renewed self-confidence, they will then be able to carry on doing the new activity as well as some other tasks.

Systematic Desensitization

Systematic desensitization refers to gradually building up, in small steps, to something that is feared, such as speaking in front of a group. As discussed in the previous section, systematic desensitization is often used with children who are anxious about confronting things. Its efficacy, especially in combination with anxiety-reducing relaxation procedures, has been clearly documented. The relaxation exercises discussed earlier are a vital component of this approach. The second step in traditional systematic desensitization, following relaxation training, is the construction of anxiety hierarchies. These involve lists of graded steps for approaching the phenomenon that evokes anxiety. This process can be done in imagery, although in children it is generally best to practice desensitization in vivo. This real-life approach is described, for example, in treating a 9-year-old child's school phobia (Lazarus, Davison, & Polefka, 1965).

I have used similar procedures with children who have not attended school for more than a year (Keat, 1974). In this systematic approach, the hierarchy of experiences that gradually leads up to the child approaching school had 11 steps:

1. The child was visited at home to establish an anxiety-inhibiting relationship.
2. The child was taken out to eat so that he could associate leaving the house with a pleasant experience.
3. He came alone to the counselor's office, and the counselor took him home after the appointment.
4. He was taken to school and introduced to the school counselor so he would know a supportive person there to whom he could turn if he became too upset.
5. The child was to attend school on a half-day basis.
6. He was reinforced for coming to the office for his appointment.
7. He was introduced into a small activity counseling group with children.
8. A behavioral contract was established with him that divided the behavioral goals into small units.
9. He was taken to school on the first day of his contract.
10. His behaviors—from getting out of bed to eating breakfast to leaving the house and finally to attending school—were systematically rewarded.
11. His school attendance was maintained through constant support and reinforcements from the counselor (Green stamps) and his mother (money) (Keat, 1974, p. 69).

Each child would need to develop a personal reinforcement menu (e.g., the Reward Survey for Children [RSC]; Keat, 1979). The final phase of systematic desensitization is to counteract anxiety with relaxation exercises while the child works his way through a series of steps like that just described. Relaxation procedures and rewards are used to help the child complete the component parts of his contract. Both respondent (classical) and operant conditioning procedures were necessary in this particular case because the school phobia was composed of two factors: avoidance behavior that was motivated by fear of school and maintenance of it through various secondary reinforcers emanating from the mother. In this case, it was important both to deal with the fear of school and to remove him from the reinforcing home situation that helped to keep him there.

Guided Imagery and Music

Another component I like to use is that of music and imagery. The power of sound (Campbell, 1996) can help the child in learning to relax. For example, humming can be useful in trying to relax in particular situations. I also use ocean tapes (Syntonic Research, 1979) and sometimes background music (baroque largo movement) to help relax clients. A combination of music with pleasant imagery can be a very positive influence in a person's life. Children may need to learn when and where to utilize these things in their lives. The counselor can draw on his or her own musical interests and background experiences as well as those of the child being counseled. For example, with some anxious boys who experience trouble going to sleep at night, I utilize music as well as environmental sounds. The sound component also can be effective in inducing relaxed states during siesta times in the day. McFerrin (1989) adds in the need-to-know component as he encourages youth to change their perspective by learning to not worry.

GUIDANCE OF ACTIONS, BEHAVIORS, AND CONSEQUENCES

The fifth zone of intervention is that of guidance of actions, behaviors, and consequences. The behavioral mode examples are assertiveness training and the Coping Cat program.

Assertiveness Training

A shy or inhibited person may respond to interpersonal situations by withdrawing. It is theorized that each time assertive responses are enacted they will reciprocally inhibit the anxiety associated with a given situation and therefore inhibit the habit of anxiety responses (Wolpe & Lazarus, 1966). A child whose primary mode of behavior is withdrawn or passive, therefore, should be continually encouraged to perform stronger actions on his own behalf. That is, standing up for one's rights is important in acquiring "emotional freedom" (Lazarus, 1971).

The goal with such a withdrawn child therefore could be to encourage the expression of suppressed feelings. It is often necessary to lead children gently and systematically toward more assertive responses. This training can be accomplished in two ways. First, assertiveness can be practiced during the counseling session. For example, the child may want to do something in particular. The counselor will have given him a reinforcement survey schedule (Keat, 1979) or discerned the child's reward system from the interviews. The child may, for example, want to build a model during the counseling hour but be reticent in articulating his desires. He needs to be encouraged to voice his sentiments and stand up for his own rights. Specifically, he can be encouraged to express his wishes more quickly during the session. I counseled one child who would consume an entire session without stating his desires (Keat, 1972). I encouraged him frequently to speak up sooner; as a result, his ability to voice his preferences increased. For such improvements to carry over into the natural environment, as a second procedure the child can be assigned various tasks to carry out in his daily living. These include such psychological homework tasks as insisting on his rights in interactions with other people. This approach could mean such things as enlisting the aid of his father in constructing a model. The child should be prepared to behaviorally rehearse various reactions to different hypothetical responses from his father. Whatever the father's reaction, it is unlikely to be as bad as the child imagines. The parents, of course, must also be prepared for behavioral changes so that they will not sabotage the efforts of the counselor. The child's real-life behavior, of course, is much more difficult to assess than assertiveness during the counseling hour. Both behavioral rehearsal and psychological homework are necessary aspects of assertive training because progress must be generalized to the child's daily life.

Keat (1974) delineates several dialogues that occurred in counseling while encouraging the child to approach his father. These dialogues indicate how a child can learn to stand up for his own rights, thus allowing him to do things that he would like to do (Keat, 1974).

Coping Cat

Kendall (1990) developed an excellent program I have utilized with children. This approach is multidimensional in that it includes relaxation training in the emotional area, the learning of various acronyms to help lessen mistaken ideas and to learn to cope with anxiety-provoking situations, imagery, and aspects of various behavioral types of things. The Coping Cat approach thus utilizes at least five of the multimodal dimensions and therefore is a comprehensive program. Coping Cat materials include a workbook (Kendall, 1990) and a treatment manual (Kendall, Kane, Howard, & Siqueland, 1989). There is also a Coping Cat notebook for the child, which is his to utilize and take home.

The complete program is 16 sessions. It can be used in its entirety, or the counselor can pick up and use various components. For example, I used this program recently with a fourth grader who worried so much about performing in school that he wanted to be schooled at home. I utilized the relationship enhancement approaches discussed earlier, relaxation training, and consultation with the parents both before and after I met the child. I used the Show-That-I-Can (STIC) task orientation (Kendall, 1990) with the child as well as his notebook. We developed hierarchies of anxiety-provoking situations in school, utilized the self-talk approaches in some of the cartoons in the workbook, formalized the four-step plan for the child by using the FEAR acronym (i.e., Feeling frightened?, Expecting bad things to happen?, Attitudes and actions that will help?, and Results and rewards) (Kendall, 1990). The STIC and the FEAR acronyms were utilized periodically and reinforced so the child had a clear idea about what was involved in both of them as we explored ways to cope with his worries in school and at home. We also utilized some of the cartoon counseling approaches that are delineated in the work of Kendall. Some of these approaches were used during the counseling sessions, and some were carried out in school and at home. Through choosing useful dimensions of this multidimensional approach, I helped the child, over the course of 9 months, from not wanting to go to school at all to looking forward to going to school. He said that he felt good about the gains, had a good year, and was looking forward to summer camp. He hoped and expected that he would have a positive year in the upcoming school year as he moved into fifth grade.

PERSONAL RELATIONSHIPS

The sixth rank-ordered zone (Table 15.3) is that of personal relationships. Herein, the main considerations are friendship training and helping children to overcome shyness.

Friendship Training

One of the major things people present as social anxiety is getting along with peers. In counseling children to learn to get along with others, I recommend that they deal with three (nearly) rhyming words (Keat, 1980a). They should think about learning to *meet* friends, *greet* them, and then figure out ways that can be useful in *keep*ing them.

Meeting friends. Children need to put themselves in places where they can get together with other children. Then they need to get into activities that can be positive experiences for them.

Greeting friends. Once children are in a situation where they can meet other children, they need to learn ways and things to say to greet them more appropriately. Counselors can train them to do this by saying such things as "How are you doing?" or "What would you like to do today?" The counselor needs to help them figure out what to say before they meet others. Then they can practice this in their own imagination, or they can practice it during the course of a counseling session. In the counseling situation, you can initially take their role and show them what to say to the other child. Then you can switch roles; they can be themselves, and you can be the other child. This behavioral rehearsal can give them some reality practice in which they are encountering someone else and can give them ideas regarding what they can do and say when they meet other children. This practice can give them some confidence so that they can do what they need to do.

Keeping friends. Once children are put in the situation of meeting other children and having said something to get things going in their greeting, they are ready to go on keeping friends. One of the best things they can do is become aware of their areas of interest and develop game skills. One way you can move them to do this is by helping them learn to play various games that others like to play. These can be such sit-down games as cards or checkers, but children also might want to become involved in active games such as catch, jump rope, ball games, or soccer. They could move into video or computer games (Gardner, 1993), which are increasingly popular. Once they are involved in these games, children need to be aware of the ABCs of game playing (i.e., Actions of the games that will be more likely to be supportive of them in their interactions; Behaviors such as taking turns, sharing, and playing by the rules; and Communication in which they clearly state and talk about what they are interested in doing with the other child).

Another important part of keeping friends is to help children in counseling develop and enhance their areas of interest. Their interests can be crystallized from their reward survey schedule. You can then explore ways of enhancing what they are already doing. Their interests could be discussed, such as game playing, movies they have seen, television shows they like to watch, events and news they are aware of, and books they have read.

Counseling to learn ways of meeting, greeting, and keeping friends can help teach a child the do's and don'ts of being a friend. Some of the do's are to listen, show interest, be loyal, be open, be considerate, understand, share your feelings, give your friends the benefit of the doubt, talk over misunderstandings, and apologize (Kalb & Viscott, 1976). Helping children to get along better with others by putting them in positions where they can meet friends, teaching them ways to appropriately greet other children, and then helping them to develop a wide range of interests so they can be in a better position to keep their friends can aid them in their interpersonal relationships and thus nurture this very important part of life.

Shyness Strategies

Shy or socially withdrawn children can be a cause of concern. These children learn to behave shyly; they tend to avoid others and feel uneasy when they are called on to be with other people. Anxiety can be one of the inhibiting factors that leads children away from interacting with other children. Some approaches that have proven useful in counseling in helping children to overcome shyness are the following:

1. Help them to think about some of the situations they would like to approach. For example, you might want to talk with them about asking someone over to their house.
2. In the child's mind's eye or mental movie, they can imagine themselves or picture themselves in a situation of walking up to and meeting someone they know and that they are going to ask over. In the mental movie, have the child picture himself going up to this person.

3. Next, the counselor can help the child think about what he is going to say. The child could say some of the things he should have learned in friendship training, such as "Hello, how are you?" or "What are you going to be doing this weekend?" The counselor thus can help the child to find out what the other person is planning. As the counselor, you can practice this with the child so that he acquires the basic verbal and socialization skills that most adults take for granted.

4. The child can then try such communication on acquaintances and see how it works. As in gaining most skills, such as practicing a musical instrument or learning a sport, children need to think, work, and practice to learn to do these things better. If the strategies work well the first time, fine; if things do not go well, then more practice and encouragement may be necessary. By practicing how to behave more maturely, a child can overcome feelings of anxiety and uneasiness when around other children.

One of the stances of the counselor can be that of a caring coach. The caring coach is one who knows how to encourage players. This encouragement can be in the form of being a teacher of communication skills, a supporter, and a caregiver who is there to help the child learn whatever he needs to overcome difficulties.

Several important references deal partially with shyness (e.g., Schaeffer & Millman, 1981) or are concerned entirely with shyness (e.g., Zimbardo, 1977). Authors have written chapters on such difficulties as social anxiety disorders (e.g., Vasey, 1995). These sources delineate the previously discussed approaches of systematic desensitization, modeling, and cognitive procedures (i.e., corrective self-talk and musturbation). Cognitive behavioral group treatment as developed by Ginsburg, Silverman, and Kurtines (1995) is popular in counseling. Having children involved in group interactions provides situations in which they can practice developing their social skills.

HEALTH

The seventh mode in this rank ordering of stress management zones is that of health. The term *health* is a broad one that includes the biochemical balance of the child's body involving such things as exercise, eating, appropriate sleeping, and psychopharmacological interventions. The following technique involves physical outlets for dealing with anxiety.

Directed Muscular Activity: Exercise

One of the most important elements in counseling anxious children is helping them program their lives so that they have regular outlets for their physical feelings. This approach has been called directed muscular activity (DMA). DMA can be a good type of activity to use in conjunction with the relaxation procedures described earlier. Various exercises can have great attraction for children when they are told that "the Green Bay Packers and other professional athletes use them to increase their physical fitness for participation in athletics" (Keat, 1974, p. 68). This statement was made in relationship to the basic principle of isometric exercises, which are used to direct physical energy against an immovable object. These exercises include such activities as lifting up on a seat on which one is sitting, pushing against the wall, pushing one's hands against each other, and clenching the fist.

Although the use of DMA is utilized primarily in relationship to the other scarlet letter of emotions (anger), it can have a beneficial therapeutic effect in relationship to anxiety. A variety of directed muscular activities can be utilized. Keat and Guerney (1980, pp. 77-78) suggest the following:

1. Use of isometrics
2. Pillow pounding
3. Use of "Soccer Boppers" or punching bags
4. Throwing wet or dry sponges on the ground
5. Writing angry thoughts on paper, then crumpling the paper and throwing it away, or tearing it into small pieces and flushing it down the toilet
6. Getting on your back and doing exercises such as bike pedaling, or actually, if possible, riding a bike hard for a few minutes
7. Hitting balls very hard
8. Systematic exercises such as jogging, dancing, or swimming
9. Sports activities

Sports activities are highly rewarded ways and socially sanctioned ways of unleashing aggression and dispelling tension. All these socially sanctioned activities have the dual rewards of enhanced self-esteem and the experience of direct tension release. A child can be trained in counseling to program these activities into their lives as strategies for dealing with tension release on a physical level. Knowing that they have these outlets can lessen their anxiety and increase their feelings of ability to cope.

SUMMARY

In summary, this section has pointed out how the multimodal approach offers a comprehensive and holistic way of dealing with anxiety and stress difficulties. The modes are rank ordered in terms of sequence of implementation. Counselors should remember that intervention in one mode interacts with and affects reactions in other zones; the areas are interdependent. The particular procedures outlined in this section were relaxation training, self-hypnosis, lessening mistaken ideas such as musturbation, enhancing self-image and the utilization of guided imagery and music, systematic desensitization, assertiveness training, friendship training, shyness strategies, and directed muscular activity. By utilizing such a comprehensive approach in counseling, the counselor is more likely to be effective in helping a child or adolescent learn to cope with anxiety.

SUGGESTIONS FOR FUTURE
TRAINING AND RESEARCH

The multimodal approach offers a broad range of training based on a wide range of skills. Table 15.5 illustrates a wide range of training for the counseling psychology area. As delineated earlier, this model is an approach entailing specific effective intervention techniques from the basis of pragmatic technical eclecticism.

TRAINING

In considering the multimodal approach as a basis for training, it is important to note that persons are educated in the "pragmatic, technically eclectic" approach in which effective intervention strategies are gleaned from the literature of case studies and research. Within this framework, persons are trained in such broad areas as listed in Table 15.5.

Health

Wellness lifestyle education can influence all aspects of a person's life. By modeling such a wellness lifestyle, counselors can be more effective in their work with anxious male youth.

Emotions

The second area, emotions, illustrates the two major feelings discussed earlier as the scarlet letters of emotion (i.e., anxiety and anger). Stress management is a major training area for dealing with anxiety (Bernstein & Borkovec, 1973), and madness management is the major program for learning to deal with anger.

Learning

Counseling of learning skills involves teaching and supervision in one-to-one supervision and use of audio- and/or videotapes. As discussed in the next section, research can help to inform counselors on the most effective intervention strategies for anxious male youth.

Personal Relations

Group counseling is one of the major approaches used in counseling. Groups can focus on such things as stress management or conflict resolution skills. Training in conflict resolutions skills and mediation is the basis for helping persons learn to interact with others. In addition, community prevention programs can be important in this area. People who experience social anxiety can learn in group counseling or in community

TABLE 15.5 Counseling Psychology: Multimodal Training Areas

Mode	Training Areas
H ealth	Wellness lifestyle: education Health delivery systems
E motions	Stress management Madness (anger) management
L earning	Counseling skills Teaching and supervision Research
P ersonal relations	Group counseling Conflict resolution Community prevention programs Professionalization and socialization Mentors: professional practitioners
I magery	Professional image and identity Fire drills: inoculation
N eed to know	Cognitive restructuring Problem solving
G uidance of ABCs	Behavioral management Behavior contracts and rehearsal Practicums and internships

activities how to better get along with others, thus alleviating some of their anxious thoughts about such interactions.

Imagery

This zone includes the importance of the counselor presenting a professional image and identity. Meichenbaum (1985) mentions stress inoculation as important; for example, children might participate in fire drills as practice for a particular upsetting or anxiety-provoking situation.

Need to Know

The major approaches in this are cognitive restructuring of worries and problem solving. By learning to restructure thoughts dealing with tense moments, counselors and anxious male youth can learn to deal more effectively with such moments. A change in perspective also is involved in problem solving, the core of the multimodal approach. In the multimodal approach, the counselor and client identify a concern or problem and try to figure out effective intervention strategies to lessen or eliminate it.

Guidance of Actions, Behaviors, and Consequences

In this mode, the primary concerns are behavioral. Behavioral management is one of the main concerns in helping youth to learn to deal with their anxious feelings. Behavioral contracts and rehearsal are core interventions. Practicums and internships help counselors learn these skills.

RESEARCH[1]

As mentioned earlier, research can help inform training; that is, research into particular approaches can present the students with more effective ways of intervening with their clients (Thompson & Rudolph, 1996). Case studies provide the basis for much of what I view as relevant in work with clients. In practice, by gleaning what we can from client reports, we can learn what is effective in alleviating anxiety. My most recent case presented in the literature (Keat, 1996) indicates that the broad range of multimodal approaches can help to alleviate anxiety with a client who has anxiety as the primary presenting difficulty. This case illustrates the broad spectrum of approaches from the pragmatic, technically eclectic stance that can be effective in working with anxious clients (see Table 15.2).

One difficulty in finding the most effective modes of treatment has been the communication gap between clinicians and researchers (Kazdin, Siegel, & Bass, 1990). The Practice Research Network (PRN) in Pennsylvania is attempting to bridge this abyss. Researchers are contacting practitioners in an attempt to utilize a core battery of assessment procedures; they will follow up with regard to the treatment utilized and outcome of the approaches used.[2]

Another developing research area is investigations of the effects of technology. For example, I have been using taped relaxation and hypnosis instruction for clients to play on their home machines or on portable players. One line of research could compare utilizing learned relaxation responses with the use of audio- or videotapes during siestas or plane trips. Some anxious male youth like to have the support of a machine, such as a portable tape player, in stressful situations.

Computers have aided clients in acquiring coping skills. Various programs have been developed for small "palmtop" computers that clients can carry with them. One program allows clients to check in on their treatment progress (Newman, Kenardy, Herman, & Taylor, 1996, 1997). Another program has been developed by Michelle Newman (in press) for clients (ages 18-65) in the Generalized Anxiety Disorder (GAD) study at Pennsylvania State University. In this study, the clients are seen in six group sessions and then continue to use the computer on their own for 6 more weeks. The computer program cues people to use some behavioral techniques in which they have been trained. According to Newman (see Mahara, 1997, pp. 46, 48), when they feel anxious, they can turn on their computers, which will lead them through a number of questions about how they feel and what they are afraid of. Depending on whether they are experiencing uncomfortable physical sensations or negative thoughts, the computer will prompt them to use relaxation or cognitive restructuring techniques. Patients are motivated to use computers because the machines remind them what they are supposed to do and because they are portable (Newman, as told to Mahara, 1997, p. 48). Use of computers is helpful for research because every interaction with the computer is recorded. The program asks questions to assess users' anxiety before and after the intervention, thus providing information about choices people are making based on certain symptoms and how effective they are at that moment in the real world (Mahara, 1997, pp. 47-48). Newman thinks that it would be possible to gear these programs to be appropriate for anxious adolescents or children. The programs would need to employ simpler words for use with youth. Given the extensive utilization of computers by youth, such an extension seems worthwhile in research efforts.

Another approach would be to compare particular theoretical approaches and see which one helps most with clients. Beck, Sokol, Clark, Berchick, and Wright (1992) found that cognitive therapy was more effective than person-centered therapy for helping clients suffering from panic disorders. Their results indicated that 25% of the person-centered participants succeeded, whereas cognitive therapy was 71% effective in ending panic attacks. This type of research could be replicated using younger anxious clients instead of the older ones used in this study.

An additional research area is evaluation of the effectiveness of packages such as Kendall's (Kendall et al., 1989). Such approaches could compare the complete Coping Cat 16-session program with other approaches that utilize only parts of the program. Kendall has found support for using muscle relaxation, deep breathing, and cognitive imagery (systematic desensitization) in helping to reduce anxiety in children. In practice, I have found using components of the program to be effective in alleviating anxiety with children.

Another area that could be researched effectively is the utilization of small groups in working with anxious youths. Some studies with adults suggest that group cognitive behavioral treatments can be helpful with children. Some researchers are beginning to investigate the effectiveness of group treatments with anxiety-disordered children (Cadbury, Childs-Clark, & Sandhu, 1990), but there is need for more work in this area.

An additional area would be that of investigating parent training based on such programs as the relationship enhancement (RE) model (Guerney, 1977). Parents can serve as coping models for their children (Kendall et al., 1992) and demonstrate how to apply strategies appropriate for the management of anxiety. By training parents, we might help children to learn to cope more effectively with their anxiety. In working with families, I typically involve the parents in training similar to that which I use with the child; for example, I might provide relaxation training at the appropriate level for each person.

Family work also should be investigated. For example, Freeman, Carlson, and Sperry (1993) conducted a study of family counseling as applied to couples coping with economic stress. Their Adlerian emphasis on skill building, problem solving, goal setting, and rational thinking aided the couples in dealing with stresses that had broad-ranging effects on their marriages. Research investigating such approaches as compared to other orientations could help in delineating which would be most effective for interventions with families experiencing stressful situations.

Classroom interventions also should be considered a topic of research. Some school districts have implemented stress management for all the children at various grade levels in elementary school. In comparing groups of children exposed to this type of program to children in no program at all (currently, most schools), research should be able to support the efficacy of such training and thus support more preventive work with youth in the future.

Even broader programs could be implemented in communities. Stress management programs could be started at such places as youth centers and summer camps. Research could compare youth who participated in the programs to others who did not. Broader applications such as this could help to create a less stressful community or at least help its members cope better with stress.

One of the hallmarks of multimodal approaches is the counselor's armamentarium of procedures that can be effective in helping clients. With regard to anxiety, a whole range of procedures could be investigated. Books such as Gladding's (1992) suggest further areas of potentially effective tools for helping children deal with their anxiety. Counseling through the expressive arts that utilizes bibliotherapy, drama, music, puppetry, poetry, or play can be useful in helping children. Music can be an effective tool for helping children deal with their anxiety (Bowman, 1987). Combining poetry and popular music can also enhance the expressiveness of children (Mazza, 1986). Writing can be an effective way of helping a child learn to express and cope with anxious feelings (Brand, 1987). As discussed earlier, computers can be effective when employed in a whole range of coping skills for children (Johnson, 1987). By investigating a wide range of potential techniques to be used with children, the counselor can develop a variety of skills that can help in working more effectively with anxious children. Research investigating the utilization of certain modes could reveal whether, in particular situations, it is just as effective to work with just a few modes (Shapiro, 1994) as it would be to employ the comprehensive multimodal overview of concerns.

SUMMARY

The multimodal approach is a comprehensive one wherein the assessment of a concern leads to consideration of effective treatment interventions. In terms of anxiety treatment, counselors are called upon to learn specific skills of effective intervention techniques from a pragmatic, technically eclectic viewpoint. Tailoring approaches to fit individual clients' needs is of utmost importance. In this approach, counselors must trust their clinical intuition in learning from case explorations as well as from research in the area. The multimodal approach is the ultimate integrative approach in that it takes what is useful from the whole range of theories and applies techniques to the particular concern of the moment (i.e., anxiety). As such, it is informed by experience as well as research into various procedures. The pragmatic, technically eclectic approach of the multimodal counselor leads to more effective helping of clients.

Notes

1. This section was enriched by a consultation with Dr. Thomas Borkovec, codirector of Pennsylvania State University's Stress and Anxiety Disorders Institute, 544 Moore Building, University Park, PA 16802.

2. For further information regarding this effort, interested readers can contact the director of the PRN, Steven Raguseu, Psy.D., through the Pennsylvania Psychological Association (416 Forster Street, Harrisburg, PA 17102-1714).

HIGHLIGHTS OF CHAPTER 15

► In addition to generally accepted anxiety-related diagnoses, such as separation anxiety disorder, many male youth also demonstrate Male Anxiety Syndrome (the tendency to act cool and hide fears) and Watergate Anxiety Syndrome (fabricating an image to cover up personal inadequacies).

► Prior to each session with an anxious boy, it is recommended that the counselor engage in the process of Epochè: suspending judgment, clearing one's mind, and preparing for what the child will bring into the counseling session.

► Once the session with an anxious boy begins, the counselor should endeavor to establish rapport with the client by demonstrating a positive relationship, acceptance, permissiveness to allow the child freedom of expression, and reflection of the child's feeling. The counselor also should emphasize the child's responsibility in problem solving, allow the child to lead the way but let the process evolve, and place healthy boundary limits on the child/counselor relationship.

► During the first encounter with the client, the counselor should ask him- or herself the following questions: How can I help this child? How can I be different from significant others in the child's life? What can I leave with this child that will make him feel good or better throughout the day or week coming up?

► A multimodal approach to treating anxious male youth is delineated by the acronym HELPING, which denotes the modalities of health, emotions, learning, personal relationships, imagery-interests, need to know, and guidance of actions, behaviors, and consequences.

► With anxious boys, the emotions modality tends to be dominant. Relaxation training is an effective intervention because it helps clients to manage anxious emotions. Counselors are advised to teach parent(s) relaxation skills so that they can help to teach their children the same skills.

▶ In the learning modality, anxious boys are taught self-hypnosis, which is presented as taking a pleasant journey in which they learn to relax and travel mentally to a pleasant scene.

▶ Anxious children need to know what they are saying to themselves when they are anxious. Through training in corrective self-talk, they are taught how to identify irrational, anxiety-provoking ideas and to replace them with self-enhancing statements. "Musturbation," the process of telling oneself anxiety-provoking "must" statements (e.g., "I must be perfect"), is also addressed. Dysfunctional musts are distinguished from adaptive musts (e.g., "I must not hit others") and eliminated.

▶ Anxious boys tend to rank imagery in the middle among modalities. For this modality, hero imagery is used; children imagine that they are like a hero, such as Superman, facing anxiety-provoking situations bravely and successfully. Systematic and in vivo desensitization may also be employed.

▶ For guidance of actions, behaviors, and consequences, the boy is taught assertiveness skills and Kendall's (1990) Coping Cat approach, which utilizes cartoons, a workbook, and various child-oriented exercises.

▶ Friendship training (how to meet, greet, and keep friends) and shyness strategies (tactics for overcoming shyness) are effective in addressing problems in the personal relationships modality.

▶ Under the domain of the health modality, anxious boys respond well to directed muscular activity/exercise (e.g., pillow pounding, bicycle riding, and sporting activities to release pent-up emotions).

16

Counseling Depressed Boys

CHRIS CALDWELL

NATURE AND SCOPE
OF THE PROBLEM

Adolescent depression predicts future adjustment problems such as dropping out of school, becoming unemployed, abusing alcohol and drugs, and engaging in illegal activities (Kandel & Davies, 1986). Moreover, having an episode of depression during adolescence greatly increases the risk for future episodes in adulthood (Harrington, Fudge, Rutter, Pickles, & Hill, 1990). The lifetime prevalence of adolescent depression is estimated to be between 20% and 25%, with close to 3% of teenagers reporting symptoms justifying a diagnosis of a depressive episode at a given time (Lewinsohn, Hops, Roberts, Seeley, & Andrews, 1993). Although adolescent males, like their adult counterparts, report fewer incidents of depression than females (Weissman, Bruce, Leaf, Florio, & Holzer, 1991; Lewinsohn et al., 1993), they have particular risks associated with depression: Males typically are less prone to ask for or accept help for mental health problems, and, when engaged in counseling, tend to report less satisfaction and benefit from treatment (Good, Dell, & Mintz, 1989; Kessler, Brown, & Broman, 1981).

RISK FACTORS

Studies assessing causes of adolescent depression, like those concerning most mental health disorders, have focused predominantly on familial and environmental factors.

Compared with children of nondepressed parents, children of depressed parents have a significantly higher rate of psychiatric disorders, including depression. There is some support for a genetic hypothesis; however, it is more likely that circumstances of parental depression such as withdrawal of parents, restriction of child social activities, increased parental criticism or hostility focused on the child, and general ambivalence and avoidance on the part of a depressed parent toward the child have a greater impact. For similar reasons, studies have shown an increased potential for childhood depression when parents have other mental health disorders, such as alcoholism or drug addiction (Harrington, 1993).

In an extensive study of the psychosocial risk factors for adolescent depression, Lewinsohn, Roberts, Seeley, Rohde, Gotlib, and Hops (1994) described the most common determinants as (a) existence of any past mental health disorder or physical problems, (b) previous suicide ideation, (c) negativistic thinking style, (d) poor body image, (e) low self-esteem, (f) being excessively emotionally dependent, (g) being more self-consciousness, (h) having less effective coping skills, (i) having less social support, and (j) smoking more cigarettes. Surprisingly, in their study, death of a parent early in life was not associated with depression. Others have found evidence that exposure to early adverse experiences—such as any form of abuse; loss of a parent or loved one through either death or divorce; or failure to attain secure attachments with one or both parents—increases the likelihood of childhood depression (Harrington, 1993). Some studies have shown that extrafamilial factors, such as academic problems, may precipitate depression in adolescents, and there is strong evidence that problems of social support are associated with depression, but it is unclear whether academic functioning and inadequate social support precedes or antecedes depression in adolescents. The bottom line is that many studies have shown that depression in young people is associated with impairments in various types of interpersonal functioning (Becker, Heimberg, & Bellack, 1987). During adolescence, when developing academic and social skills is so critical and when having friendships is even more important, depression can be particularly devastating.

Most research on gender differences in depressive disorders focuses on the overrepresentation of women among those diagnosed as depressed. Some studies have shown that males are more likely than females to suffer from depression prior to puberty (Anderson, Williams, McGee, & Silva, 1987), but it appears that after puberty, females are more prone toward depressive disorders (Lewinsohn et al., 1993). One explanation of this is that females are more likely to engage in ruminating behaviors, thus increasing the severity of their symptoms, whereas males tend to distract themselves from depression by doing something they enjoy or thinking about other things and ignoring their problems. Being active and controlling one's moods are part of the masculine stereotype, but when taken to maladaptive extremes, the tendency to ignore or distract from moods may lead to other problems, such as aggressiveness, alcohol and drug abuse, and general acting out (Nolen-Hoeksema, 1990). It is evident that the passivity of mood disorders is less acceptable for boys (Schwarz & Schwarz, 1993) and therefore may be masked by other psychological problems, especially disruptive behavior disorders (Lewinsohn et al., 1993).

ASSESSMENT CONSIDERATIONS

Adolescence is a time of volatility of mood. As a result, depression is often not as straightforward and easy to recognize in teenagers as in adults (Schwarz & Schwarz, 1993). An accurate diagnosis based on skilled interviewing techniques and psychological testing is vital to provide direction for treatment (Oster & Montgomery, 1995). Accurately understanding adolescent development regarding mood, self-concept, and social functioning is also important for practitioners dealing with depressed teens.

When assessing for depression in adolescents, be prepared for difficult interviews (Schwarz & Schwarz, 1993). Adolescents in general (and males in particular) are reluctant to admit the need for help from adults because they are sensitive to embarrassment and do not want to appear childish (Meeks, 1988). Simultaneously, depression by its very nature causes problems with communication, focusing, and concentrating, such that depressed teens are likely to be slow to respond and easily confused, act sullen and display flat affect and speech, or be tense, fidgety, and restless (even more so than normal). They may have difficulty identifying and verbalizing their symptoms, so it is important to use short sentences and simplified explanations of the symptoms of depression (Schwarz & Schwarz, 1993). When possible, collateral information should be obtained from the adolescent's significant others, such as parents, teachers, counselors, and peers (Harrington, 1993).

Considering all the changes going on during adolescence, when one looks at the diagnostic criteria for a major depressive episode (American Psychiatric Association, 1994a), it is easy to see how assessing depression during adolescence can be very difficult.

Depressed mood or irritability is a fairly subjective experience. Teenagers typically lack the life experience to know what constitutes a normal mood or what ordinary sadness is. Mood and affect appear to be more environmentally influenced in adolescence than in adulthood, and younger teens report less persistence of dysphoric mood than adults (Emslie & Weinberg, 1994). Adolescence is a difficult time of gaining emotional independence (Schiamberg & Smith, 1982), and the fluctuation of hormones during puberty could easily contribute to periods of irritability and depressive symptoms.

Regarding diminished interest or pleasure in activities previously considered rewarding, adolescence is a time for sorting out identity issues (Schiamberg & Smith, 1982). One way teens do this is by trying some new activities and dropping out of others. Most choices of activities evolve around peer group identification, but these changes could mimic diminished pleasure or interest in activities once found pleasurable. Teens may feel an old pastime is childish and no longer desire association with what was once considered a key recreational outlet (Emslie & Weinberg, 1994).

The *DSM-IV* (American Psychiatric Association, 1994a) specifically warns against failure to make expected weight gains in children. Significant weight loss or weight gain is difficult to assess with any degree of clarity, however, because adolescents' bodies change so rapidly.

Many teens (and their parents) report major changes in sleep patterns during adolescence. Normal adolescents tend to sleep less during the week and sleep more during the weekends. Staying up late is fairly common for them; however, middle and terminal insomnia are fairly rare. Initial insomnia and trouble awakening are more typical of depressed teens (Emslie & Weinberg, 1994).

Regarding psychomotor agitation or retardation and fatigue, adolescents are typified by hyperactive or lethargic behavior. For some teens, the hormonal deluge leads to excess energy; for others, it leads to listlessness or maybe even significant periods of both. Once again, changes in sleep patterns and eating habits could account for energy fluctuations.

Feelings of worthlessness could be a result of the natural tension between the self and society during adolescence (Keniston, 1970). To look objectively at self-esteem during a time when the struggle with identity and self-doubt is at a peak can be a real challenge.

Regarding concentration problems, how many parents suspect their teens of having attention deficit/hyperactivity disorder (ADHD) during adolescence? In actuality, cognitive function increases quantitatively and qualitatively during adolescence (Schiamberg & Smith, 1982). Teenagers are inundated with new stimuli and choices that can be quite overwhelming.

Considering suicidal ideation, adolescents have more of a tendency to catastrophize what adults would likely consider a minor event, such as the failure of one's first romance (Emslie & Weinberg, 1994). Adolescence is a time when fantasies of death and dying are not uncommon. Teens may act as if they feel invincible, but in actuality, adolescence is a time when one begins to come to terms with mortality.

When considering the diagnostic criteria for depression, one must look at symptomatology as a function of age, gender, and developmental level, then weigh the effect of age-related phenomena on the development of depressive symptoms, and finally consider the impact of depressive symptoms on the personality of the child (Hodges & Siegel, 1985).

How are the depressive symptoms different from or more impairing than what would be considered normal for the male adolescent? First, one must differentiate depression from mourning or regular responses to loss or life stressors (Schwarz & Schwarz, 1993). Has the teen experienced any recent losses or traumas, such as loss of a loved one, a geographical move, a physical injury, or even loss of a favored recreational outlet? If so, a clinician must rule out bereavement or a phase-of-life problem (American Psychiatric Association, 1994a).

Next, it is important to assess functioning and skill level prior to the depressive episode (Schwarz & Schwarz, 1993). In this assessment, it is especially helpful to have information about past levels of functioning, such as previous grade reports, achievement scores, and medical information.

Finally, the degree or seriousness of the depressive symptoms, especially regarding the risk of suicide, must be assessed. For adolescents age 15 and older, suicide is the second leading cause of death, and males are overrepresented by a four to one margin (Oster & Montgomery, 1995). All threats of suicide ideation, therefore, should be taken seriously with this population. There is no evidence that questioning adolescents about their suicidal feelings is harmful to them. Moreover, depressed persons generally gain relief from talking openly about suicidal thoughts and plans, and it is important to obtain a full account of these to assess the strength of risk and head off any plans the child may have (Harrington, 1993).

Many assessment instruments and interviewing schedules can help in detecting and measuring depression in teenagers. It is advisable to make use of these, given the challenges of diagnosing adolescent depression. The Kiddie-SADS, Interview Schedule for Children, Child Assessment Schedule, Diagnostic Interview for Children and Adolescents, and Child and Adolescent Psychiatric Assessment are all structured interviews designed to assist clinicians in diagnosing depression and other mental health disorders (Harrington, 1993). It is especially important to assess for any secondary mental health problems because adolescents with a diagnosis in addition to depression tend to exhibit greater levels of behavior problems, somatic concerns, sleep problems, and suicide ideation (Carlson, 1981). Several self-report scales and checklists that are fairly brief also can assist with the assessment and treatment of adolescents by giving standardized measurements of depressive symptoms. The Children's Depression Inventory, Children's Depression Rating Scale (Western Psychological Services, 1995), and Reynolds Adolescent Depression Scale (Psychological Corporation, 1998) are some self-report measures of depression that are useful in assessment and treatment (Harrington, 1993). In addition, a widely used scale that provides measures of depression (as well as other problems of function) is Achenbach's (1991) Child Behavior Checklist. This assessment instrument has the added benefit of offering the therapist input from parents and teachers to gather collateral data on a child's behavior and symptom manifestation as well as information about any secondary problems a child may be experiencing (Achenbach & Edelbrock, 1983).

CLINICAL FEATURES: GENERAL AND MALE SPECIFIC

Lewinsohn, Gotlib, and Seeley (1995) discovered that the symptom reporting rate of adolescents varied somewhat from that of adults. In particular, prepubertal children were more likely to identify somatic complaints, psychomotor agitation, and mood-congruent hallucinations as their primary symptoms. Among adolescents, antisocial behavior, substance abuse, restlessness, irritability, and social withdrawal and malfunction were more predominant.

As previously mentioned, the rate of depression of boys is much lower than that of girls during most of adolescence; however, boys are diagnosed with conduct disorders at rates nearly double that of girls (Lewinsohn et al., 1993). Although girls report more internalized problems, such as dysphoric mood and poor self-esteem, males show elevations of externalized problems (Lewinsohn, Clarke, & Rohde, 1994) such as oppositionality, illegal acts, and especially substance abuse.

Boys are encouraged to compete more, to hide or mask their feelings, and to be more physically active and independent. These components may account for some of the role of gender socialization in diminishing depression rates for males. Parents are less likely to show warmth and affection to boys, however, and teachers tend to be more critical, reprimanding, and disapproving of boys. Boys also are more likely to be chastised for engaging in cross-sex activities. These are social components that could contribute to increased rates of psychological problems in males (Nolen-Hoeksema, 1990).

In studies of college-aged men, results of investigating the relationships between attitudes toward the male role, experiences of gender role conflict, and depression indicate that more traditional males have an increased likelihood of depression and are less likely to pursue counseling services. In particular, those who are more competitive and preoccupied with success, are more restricted emotionally, have more difficulty exhibiting affection, and exhibit other psychological problems are more likely to become depressed (Good & Mintz, 1990; Sharpe & Heppner, 1991). It is predicted that these gender role conflict factors surface in adolescent males as well.

AN INTEGRATIVE TREATMENT APPROACH

Numerous studies have demonstrated the positive effect of depression treatment for teenagers; however, to date, none show significant differences between the outcomes of the various types of treatment (Lewinsohn, Clarke, et al., 1994). Although data are lacking as to adolescent male preferences for treatment, it is probable that, like their adult counterparts, males tend to prefer programs that emphasize rational problem solving and independence over ones that focus on affective processing and relationship development (Kelly & Hall, 1992; Wilcox & Forrest, 1992). Males tend to need more assistance with recognizing and expressing their emotions as well as with improving their ability to relate (Moore, 1990), if they are to overcome depression. The remainder of this section integrates various models of adolescent depression treatments, with special attention given to considerations of the particular treatment needs of males.

Because males prefer action to rumination (Nolen-Hoeksema, 1990) and reason to affect (Johnson & Stone, 1989), the treatment approach prescribed here integrates skills training and cognitive remediations. Both of these are found in cognitive behavioral and social learning frameworks for treating depression. The key notion of social learning is that all behavior results from person-environment interactions, and depression in particular results from the lack of person-environment interactions with positive outcomes and/or a high rate of punishing interactions. There may be a lack of available positive reinforcers, a skills deficit in obtaining available reinforcers, or insensitivity to positive and heightened sensitivity to negative reinforcers (Lewinsohn & Arconad, 1981).

Cognitive behavioral techniques emphasize the role of maladaptive cognitions in the development of depression. They posit that a person's appraisal of a situation

TABLE 16.1 Principal Ingredients for Success in Working With Adolescents

1. *Trustworthiness.* Treat adolescents' feelings and vulnerabilities with sensitivity.
2. *Genuineness.* Adolescents are highly sensitive to disapproval and rejection. It is, therefore, important that those who work with youth have a genuine concern and appreciation for that age group.
3. *Empathy.* Display care toward youth and make every effort to relate to them on an individual level.
4. *Honesty.* Deal with youth truthfully and respectfully.
5. *Image.* Convey that you have the youths' best interests at heart.

SOURCE: Adapted from *Adolescent Life Experiences*, by G. R. Adams and T. Gullotta, © copyright 1983 by Brooks/Cole.

produces an emotional reaction that shapes behavioral inclinations. Behavior is then more likely to be maladaptive and lead to events that feed into initial cognitive appraisal, and the cycle repeats itself (Schrodt, 1992). It has been well documented that depressed children and adolescents demonstrate a distinct negative bias in their thinking and a negative, pessimistic outlook on life. They perceive that they have little influence over their environment and, as a result, see themselves as incapable of coping with distress (Schrodt, 1992).

Social learning treatment focuses on restoring an adequate schedule of reinforcement. The first goal of treatment is to redefine client problems in ways that give clients a sense of control. This involves pinpointing specific person-environment interactions and events that trigger depressive symptoms. The client and therapist can then focus on (a) changing those environmental conditions they can change, (b) developing skills to change detrimental patterns of interaction with the environment, and (c) increasing positive interactions with the environment (Lewinsohn & Arconad, 1981).

The objectives of cognitive behavioral treatment are to acquire awareness of one's own behavior, thoughts, and feelings, then learn alternatives to negative self-evaluations, overcome basic information processing errors, and learn how to reinforce oneself. Systematic increasing of pleasurable activities and learning how to reduce the symptoms of depression are also goals of cognitive behavioral treatment (Harrington, 1993).

EARLY PHASE OF TREATMENT

Children and adolescents, especially males, typically do not initiate requests for counseling. Parents, teachers, or social agencies often identify the problems associated with depression; youth tend to externalize the sources of these problems and contend that they do not need therapy. There may be additional issues of general mistrust of adults and, of course, hypersensitivity to being criticized or deemed "crazy" by others (Schrodt, 1992). This can make rapport building especially difficult with teens. A number of strategies can assist with developing a relationship of mutual trust and respect (see Table 16.1). First, warmth, empathy, patience, tolerance, and a nonjudgmental attitude

TABLE 16.2 Useful Factors in Evaluating Suicide Risk

1. *Direct verbal warning.* Take any statements seriously. Do not dismiss warnings as "hysterical gestures" or "attempts for attention."
2. *Developed plan.* The presence of any form of plan increases risk. The more specific, detailed, lethal, and doable the plan, the greater the risk.
3. *Past attempts.* Approximately 80% of completed suicides were preceded by a prior attempt. Clients with the greatest suicidal rate were those who had entered into treatment with a history of at least one attempt.
4. *Indirect statements and behavioral signs.* People may communicate suicidal intent through actions and words such as "talking about going away," giving away possessions, acquiring lethal instruments, and finding homes for pets.
5. *Depression.* The rate of suicide for individuals with clinical depression is 20 times greater than for the general population.
6. *Hopelessness.* Hopelessness is often an aspect of depression and appears to be more closely associated with suicide than any other characteristic of depression.
7. *Intoxication.* Approximately one-fourth of all suicides are associated with alcoholism as a contributing factor. A much higher percentage is associated with alcohol at the time of the suicide.
8. *Clinical syndromes.* Individuals suffering from depression or alcoholism are at much higher risk. The highest suicide rates exist within the clinical categories of primary mood disorders, psychoneuroses, organic brain syndrome and schizophrenia.
9. *Gender.* The suicide rate for men is three times that for women; however, the rate of suicide attempts for women is three times that for men.
10. *Age.* Risk increases over the adult life cycle, with the mid 50s to mid 60s the span of highest risk. Attempts by older people are more likely to be lethal. The ratio of attempts to completed suicides up to age 65 is seven to one, but two to one for those over 65.
11. *Race.* Caucasians have the highest suicide rate.
12. *Religion.* Suicide rates among Protestants tend to be higher than those among Jews and Catholics.
13. *Living alone.* The risk is lowest for those living with spouse and children, slightly higher with spouse only, higher still with partner or other, and highest living alone.
14. *Bereavement.* Select bereavement studies have found that 50% of those in their sample who had committed suicide had lost their mothers within the past three years (compared with a 20% rate among matched controls). There appears to be a link between childhood bereavement and suicide attempts in adult life, perhaps doubling the risk for depressives who lost a parent compared to those who had not.
15. *Unemployment.* Those out of work are at increased risk.
16. *Health status.* Physical illness and somatic complaints are associated with increased risk as are disturbances in sleeping and eating.
17. *Impulsivity.* Those with poor impulse control are at increased risk.
18. *Rigid thinking.* All or nothing thinking is characteristic.

TABLE 16.2 Continued

---

19. *Stressful events.* Negative events with unfortunate outcomes are associated with increased risk. For example, 52% of multiple-incident victims of sexual assault have attempted suicide.

20. *Release from hospitalization.* Risk is greatest during weekend leaves from the hospital and shortly after discharge.

SOURCE: Adapted from Pope, K. S., and Vasquez, M. J. T., *Responding to Suicide Risk* (1991), pp. 156-159, © 1991 by Jossey-Bass.

are vital for the development of a working alliance with teenagers (Schrodt, 1992). It is important to communicate to adolescents the nature and purpose of counseling in ways they can understand. It may be helpful to inform them of the prevalence of their disorder to assure them that they are not alone. Therapists should be forthright and honest about the limits of confidentiality, and they should be familiar with state guidelines about minors' rights in therapy. The child client's feedback and ideas about each aspect of treatment should be solicited so that he feels that his independence and capabilities are being respected. Any intervention that is planned should be discussed with the client beforehand (Brent & Lerner, 1994).

The immediate emphasis in counseling and psychotherapy with depressed adolescents is often suicide prevention (see Table 16.2). It may be necessary to involve the client's family in a cooperative effort involving educating them about the risks involved and how to take steps to prevent suicide attempts (Schwarz & Schwarz, 1993). If this is done with a respectful concern, therapeutic rapport can be salvaged and even enhanced. A contract shared among the client, therapist, parents, and other involved agencies needs to be established. An agreement as to what will happen if the youth has further incidents of suicide ideation, whom he will contact, and who will monitor the youth should be instituted (Boyer & Guthrie, 1985; Shafii & Shafii, 1992). Parents may need to be asked to eliminate from the home any objects the youth may use to hurt himself (Schwarz & Schwarz, 1993). Clients and parents may need information and help in obtaining additional services such as medical attention, psychiatric evaluation for medications, and crisis hot lines or nearby emergency mental health services. Given the risks involved, collegial consultation is warranted whenever dealing with suicidal teens (Pfeffer, 1988). Special caution should be taken with youth who are actively abusing alcohol or drugs, and this abuse should be dealt with in the agreement.

Once issues of suicide prevention and intervention have been resolved, a pretreatment measure of depressive symptoms should be taken, and a plan for treatment needs to be established. The treatment plan should specifically address any suicide prevention issues and should outline problems regarding the client's physical health, family or living environment, peer relations, education, and leisure activities (Raymer, 1992). It is important to couch client problems in terms that give the client a sense of control and a feeling of hope (Hoberman & Lewinsohn, 1985). A strategy for addressing each target behavior of the depression should then be outlined. Agreements should be made regarding clear expectations of the client to complete self-monitoring tasks and homework, abide by prescribed activity schedules, and attend sessions either individually or in group or family counseling (Becker et al., 1987; Matson, 1989). If deemed necessary, compliance with physician- or psychiatrist-prescribed medications should also be mentioned in the treatment plan.

Prior to the first session, clients and their parents should be given homework assignments. Clients should be given daily monitor sheets to fill out each day until the next meeting. Parents may be given recommended readings on childhood depression. Time should be spent reviewing the importance, purpose, and nature of out-of-office assignments.

One of the first tasks in the treatment of adolescent males experiencing depression should be getting them to accurately identify and appropriately express their feelings. This is especially difficult for males because typically they are not taught to recognize and express their emotions (Moore, 1990). In group, family, or individual counseling, time should be spent helping clients to get in touch with their current feelings and to describe feelings associated with identified daily monitor events. Daily monitor sheets should contain a rating scale of mood, a place to list activities engaged in each day, and a place to describe one or more events in the day that elicited feelings and the thoughts associated with them. These sheets then can be used to provide continual feedback regarding treatment interventions (Hoberman & Lewinsohn, 1985) as well as grist for the mill during sessions. Examples of activity schedules and daily monitoring and mood rating forms can be found in the appendix of Clarkin and Glazer's (1981) *Depression: Behavioral and Directive Intervention Strategies*; however, clinicians may want to devise their own, based on client needs and their own preferences.

Another early focus in treatment should be on changing aspects of the client's environment that contribute to depression. Environmental interventions may mean the change of physical or social settings if the client's environment is highly impoverished or aversive (Lewinsohn & Arconad, 1981). This may involve working closely with local child and family services in the event of abuse or neglect in the home. Work with the school may be necessary if misplacement or maltreatment at school is causing problems. There may be specific reasons for the child's depressive symptoms, and these must be assessed and dealt with before treatment will be effective.

If the environment is workable, then changing the consequences for the client's depression may be a focus of the treatment. Feedback and support from the client's significant others are important in evaluating and enhancing the effectiveness of treatment efforts. For example, the therapist can instruct parents on how to reward a child's progress by granting attention, praise, and physical displays of affection when their child uses adaptive behaviors, while ignoring or not reinforcing depressed behaviors (Lewinsohn & Arconad, 1981).

As early as possible in treatment, therapists should begin educating parents and other family members about childhood depression, through consultation or in family sessions. Bibliotherapy might be helpful for family members in understanding depression and how to help those who suffer. For example, Oster and Montgomery (1995) have written a user-friendly book titled *Helping Your Depressed Teenager*. It provides developmental information, straightforward advice on teen suicide, information on treatment and medications used for depression, and a list of organizations/support groups and selected readings for parents of depressed youth.

Another important aspect of early treatment is collaboration with community resources. After obtaining appropriate releases of information, the counselor should pursue referrals and consultation with a child's pediatrician, school counselor or nurse, and any other community organization with which the client and family are involved. Treatment efforts are maximized when they are coordinated with the social system of adolescents so that environmental problems can be addressed, hypotheses can be generated about information the client has about himself, and allies in treatment can be developed (Belsher & Wilkes, 1994).

MIDDLE PHASE OF TREATMENT

Once efforts have been made to enlist the support of the social system of the client and therapeutic rapport has been established, one can begin with the meat of cognitive behavioral and social learning therapies. The client should first be taught relaxation techniques to reduce symptoms of anxiety and tension, assist with lowering stress levels during difficult social interactions, and help the client exercise more control over the unwanted or distracting cognitions associated with depression (Hoberman & Lewinsohn, 1985). Below are three techniques that clinicians may teach. The first is deep breathing exercises. These are the simplest to learn and can reap the quickest benefit. Deep breathing requires little time and effort and can be used conveniently and frequently throughout the day. The next relaxation technique, deep muscle relaxation, is probably one of the best-documented successes of psychological interventions. Numerous resources and methods for teaching deep breathing and deep muscle relaxation are available (e.g., Barlow & Craske, 1989; Jacobson, 1987; Rapee & Barlow, 1991; Suinn, 1990), but I have found the wording and presentation of relaxation techniques in Wilson's (1987) *Don't Panic: Taking Control of Anxiety Attacks* particularly useful with adolescents. One resource specifically addresses relaxation training with youth (Carter & Cheesman, 1988). Finally, visual imagery techniques are particularly popular with adolescents.

Once the client has begun to learn techniques for how to alleviate distress, the next step is to engage the client in different types of social skills training. It is helpful to begin with basic skills regarding appearance and conversation. Personal hygiene should be evaluated honestly and goals set if it is inadequate. Begin work on other nonverbal assets of communication such as encouraging clients to smile, have an open posture, and use appropriate eye contact. A good tool for teaching and practicing communication skills is Carkuff's (1993) book *The Art of Helping*. It contains a step-by-step guide on how to attend to others in ways that communicate acceptance, openness, and concern. Clients can learn how to posture themselves directly facing the person to whom they are speaking, lean forward to communicate interest, and make appropriate eye contact. They can be taught simple reflective listening skills by learning how to respond to the content, feeling, and meaning of conversations. I have had particular success with making a game out of practicing communication skills by rating role-plays of conversations from 1 to 5 using an adapted version of Carkuff's (1993) levels of helping.

Other important social skills to teach depressed adolescents are how to improve their self-esteem and assert themselves more effectively. For assertion skills, I have had particular success using Alberti and Emmons's (1982) *Your Perfect Right: A Guide to Assertive Living*, though there are numerous assertiveness training resources available. Another useful tool for teaching assertiveness skills that also helps teens deal more effectively with social stressors is called *Fighting Invisible Tigers: A Student Guide to Life in the Jungle* (Hipp, 1985). Several books aid in working with youth on issues surrounding self-esteem. Frey and Carlock's (1984) *Enhancing Self Esteem* has several problems, exercises, and activities that are easily adapted for work with youth. Also, McKay and Fanning (1992) have a book on self-esteem that subscribes to cognitive-behavioral techniques for improving self-esteem. This book helps clients identify their negative internal messages and replace them with positive ones. It also encourages teens to be realistic about personal strengths and weaknesses and teaches them how to set reasonable expectations for themselves based on realistic self-assessments.

Finally, an important aspect of depression work with youth is to address cognitive errors and irrational beliefs. Ellis (1989) has set forth a fairly simple strategy that is effective in work with youth. By teaching teens the ABCs of rational emotive therapy, counselors can help clients identify events that *a*ctivate thoughts or feelings that lead to self-defeating behaviors, then recognize and challenge *b*eliefs or cognitions that lead to self-defeating behaviors or depressive *c*onsequences. Lewinsohn, Antonucciao, Steinmatz, and Teri (1984) have compiled a Coping With Depression Course that does an excellent job of explaining and applying rational emotive techniques with youth. Another cognitive approach effective with youth is Burns's (1989) adaptation of Beck's cognitive errors. In his *Feeling Good: The New Mood Therapy*, Burns provides an excellent description of 10 cognitive distortions and then offers several ways to "untwist one's thinking." Burns's work is written for the layperson and, as a result, is particularly useful for work with teens and their parents, either in session or as bibliotherapy homework.

LATER PHASE OF TREATMENT AND PREVENTING RELAPSE

Cognitive behavioral techniques are traditionally time limited and symptom focused. A client may not show adequate results or may attempt to terminate treatment prematurely for numerous reasons (Belsher & Wilkes, 1994). The first of these is inadequate social support. Many families have limited resources and may have difficulties making the changes necessary to address problems in the environment. In these cases, therapists should make special efforts to establish adequate support resources within or outside the family unit, such as through schools, social services, churches, or youth organizations. Sometimes, adolescents become overly dependent on the therapist. The task of the therapist then is similar, to see where else clients can get their needs met outside the therapeutic relationship (Belsher & Wilkes, 1994). Finally, there are times when the depression may be more severe or unresponsive to treatment efforts. In those cases, consultations and referrals to other providers, such as a child psychiatrist or a more intensive level of treatment, may be necessary (Schwarz & Schwarz, 1993).

Once the client has shown adequate progress and reduction of symptoms, the counselor or therapist should begin to lengthen the intervals between sessions to facilitate more client independence (Wilkes & Belsher, 1994). At this point, it would be good to begin getting posttreatment measures to see if the client is ready for termination. The therapist should begin discussing discharge planning and posttreatment referrals with the client. Relapse prevention should be a focus of treatment.

The good news is that preliminary research data show that adolescents with depression relapse at a lower rate than adults (Lewinsohn, Clarke, et al., 1994). It is still important, however, to ensure that clients have adequate social support to continue therapeutic gains and that they have information about how to detect relapse indicators. Using chemical dependency relapse prevention as an example, the objectives of relapse prevention are (a) early identification of warning signs and symptoms as well as situational variables associated with depression, (b) constantly developing social support and techniques learned in treatment to address those symptoms, and (c) knowing when, how, and whom to ask for help when one is unable to adequately alleviate depressive symptoms on one's own.

Highlights of Chapter 16

► Counselors need to become more cognizant of the impact of depression in boys because an episode of depression during adolescence greatly increases the risk for future episodes in adulthood, boys are less prone than girls to ask for help with depression, and they benefit less from counseling.

► In working with adolescents experiencing depression, the counselor characteristics of empathy, genuineness, honesty, trustworthiness, and working for the best interests of the adolescent are crucial.

► Adolescent statements about suicide should be taken seriously. When counselors hear such comments, they should examine whether the person has made a plan to carry out the suicide, including having access to the means to commit suicide. Completed suicides are, in most cases, preceded by a previous unsuccessful attempt.

► Depression in adolescence increases the likelihood of suicide to 20 times that of the general population, and a sense of hopelessness is closely associated with suicide in adolescents.

► Adolescents who have experienced the loss of a parent, alcohol and drug use, and/or poor impulse control are all at greater risk for suicide than other adolescents.

▶ Assessment of depression in male adolescents is difficult because they are reluctant to admit the need for help with depression, preferring to not be seen as childish or unable to handle their issues.

▶ One difficulty of assessing depression in adolescents is the wide range of changes that are occurring naturally and may mask the diagnostic characteristics of depression, such as weight gain/loss, sleeplessness or excessive sleep, self-esteem fluctuations, and changing interests in friends, sports, and other activities.

▶ An integrated approach to treatment is most effective. A focus on rational problem solving and developing independence is important, and social learning therapy and cognitive behavioral approaches both emphasize the role of maladaptive cognitions and the development of effective living skills.

▶ Because adolescents typically exhibit considerable mistrust of counselors, the early phases of treatment require efforts at establishing support, encouragement, and rapport.

▶ Daily monitoring sheets are very helpful for providing both the adolescent and the counselor with information about the extent and timing of depressive episodes, the reinforcers in life that ameliorate depression, and the effectiveness of an intervention plan in bringing about life changes.

▶ Social skills training is an important component of treating depressed adolescent boys and should be part of the counselor's repertoire of interventions.

17

Counseling Boys With Attention-Deficit/Hyperactivity Disorder

GAIL TRIPP

DOUGALD M. SUTHERLAND

Attention-deficit/hyperactivity disorder (ADHD) (see American Psychiatric Association [APA], 1994a) is one of the most common, and arguably most debilitating, disorders of childhood. The disorder is characterized by developmentally inappropriate levels of inattention, impulsivity, and overactivity that interfere with the child's behavioral, academic, and social functioning. Although it once was assumed that ADHD was a disorder of childhood only, there is now compelling evidence that children do not outgrow ADHD. As many as 80% of children with this disorder continue to experience symptoms in adolescence (Faigel, Sznajdeerman, Tishby, Turel, & Pinus, 1995; Hechtman, 1991), and for many, their adult life will be affected in some way by the disorder (Barkley, 1995).

BACKGROUND

Prevalence rates for ADHD vary as a function of the diagnostic criteria utilized and the population sampled. It is generally accepted that between 3% and 5% of school-age children meet criteria for this disorder, and up to 50% of child clinical referrals are for ADHD (APA, 1994a; Popper, 1988). The disorder is more frequently observed in boys than in girls, with sex ratios of approximately 3:1 reported among community samples (Szatmari, Offord, & Boyle, 1989). The discrepancy is larger still for clinic samples, reflecting the higher probability that boys with ADHD will be referred to a mental health professional. This referral bias is thought to be a consequence of the increased behavioral disturbance, particularly aggressive and antisocial behaviors, seen in boys with ADHD

(Barkley, 1990). Consistent with this, community studies have demonstrated that boys with ADHD are more aggressive than girls with this disorder (Befera & Barkley, 1985; Breen & Barkley, 1988).

Leaving aside referral bias, the higher prevalence of ADHD among boys has yet to be fully explained. An important consequence of this unequal sex distribution has been the almost exclusive focus by researchers on boys with this disorder. While acknowledging that most of the available literature on ADHD is derived from studies of boys with the disorder, we use the terms *children* and *adolescents* throughout this chapter.

ETIOLOGY

Over the past 30 years, numerous factors have been implicated in the etiology of ADHD, such as diet, lead poisoning, fluorescent lighting, retarded brain development, low hormonal levels, and "bad" parenting. The evidence that these factors actually cause ADHD is, at best, limited. Current opinion supports a biological contribution to ADHD. Although environmental factors such as poverty, family dysfunction, or poor parenting practices may exacerbate the disorder, there is little evidence that ADHD arises solely as a consequence of social and emotional factors (Barkley, 1990). Evidence is beginning to accumulate to support the theory that risk for development of ADHD is, at least in part, genetically determined. A number of studies have identified a higher incidence of ADHD in first-degree relatives of individuals with ADHD (Biederman et al., 1992; Goodman & Stevenson, 1989).

DIAGNOSIS

Historically, children exhibiting symptoms of inattention, impulsivity, and hyperactivity have been given a range of different diagnostic labels (e.g., minimal brain damage, minimal brain dysfunction, hyperkinetic impulse disorder, hyperkinesis, attention-deficit disorder), reflecting changing understanding of the disorder. The current *DSM-IV* (APA, 1994a) diagnostic criteria for ADHD require that the child exhibit a minimum of six symptoms of inattention and/or six symptoms of hyperactivity-impulsivity, with onset before the age of 7 years, and not better accounted for by other medical, psychological, or environmental conditions. Symptoms must be pervasive in nature, causing impairment in at least two settings. The disorder may be predominantly inattentive type, hyperactive-impulsive type, or combined type, depending on symptoms.

In Europe, the classification system (known as *ICD-10)* of the World Health Organization (WHO, 1990) is used, and children are diagnosed with hyperkinetic disorder if they exhibit developmentally inappropriate levels of inattention and hyperactivity in both the home and school setting, and these symptoms have been directly observed (WHO, 1990). Historically, the APA and the WHO diagnostic criteria for inattentiveness/hyperactivity have differed markedly, but under *DSM-IV* and *ICD-10,* the two classification systems are closer than they have been for some time (Tripp, Luk, Schaughency, & Singh, 1999).

COMORBIDITY

Attention-deficit/hyperactivity disorder is often comorbid with other disruptive behavior disorders. As many as 45% of children and 50% of adolescents with ADHD will also meet diagnostic criteria for conduct disorder. For the less serious oppositional defiant disorder, the comorbidity rates are around 40% for children and up to 65% for adolescents (Barkley, DuPaul, & McMurray, 1990; Barkley, Fischer, Edelbrock, & Smallish, 1990; Szatmari et al., 1989). The presence of comorbid conduct or oppositional behaviors complicates the assessment and treatment of ADHD. Although the occurrence of aggressive behavior can lead to inflated ratings of ADHD, we have worked with a small number of children whose severe conduct problems initially masked their symptoms of ADHD. Interventions with children who have coexisting conduct problems are necessarily more comprehensive and long term (Barkley, 1990).

Significant numbers of children with ADHD also have comorbid psychiatric disorders, the most common of these being mood disorders and anxiety (Biederman, Newcorn, & Sprich, 1991). ADHD is more prevalent among children who are mentally retarded and those with Tourette's disorder (Gillberg, Persson, Grufman, & Themner, 1986; Spencer, Biederman, Wilens, Steingard, & Geist, 1993).

ESTABLISHING RAPPORT

Establishing rapport is essential to the successful assessment and treatment of ADHD. Neither step can proceed effectively in the absence of a cooperative relationship between the therapist, the child, and those responsible for the child's care. Therapists working in this area must take the time to establish rapport with the child, his parents, and educators. Relationships with a child with ADHD and his carers are likely to be longer, more intense, and more difficult than those with other clients. Good rapport can help sustain these relationships.

PARENTS

The parents of children with, or thought to have, ADHD are often quite distressed on initial presentation. They often feel overwhelmed by their child's behavior, guilty that they are responsible for the child's difficulties, and sometimes angry at a perceived lack of support from professionals. More than at any other time, these parents need the opportunity to freely express their concerns and worries.

It is important that you, as a counselor, accept the parents' description of their child. This is how they perceive and experience their child. Listening carefully to parents' concerns also helps convey to them that you wish to fully understand their concerns and situation. Structured interviews and behavioral rating scales should be put aside until parents have had ample time to talk. Asking parents to engage in highly structured data collection at this time can give the impression that you are more concerned with data collection than with the parents' or child's difficulties.

Always check with parents why and how they have come to see you. There will be occasions when parents are not the instigators of a referral. These parents may be anxious about the involvement of a therapist and may feel they are being blamed for their child's behavior. In such cases, it is helpful if attention is focused on what can be done to help overcome the child's difficulties and parents' attendance is recast as a positive step toward assisting their child. If appropriate, make it clear to parents that they are not responsible for their son's ADHD but that the way they interact with their child may help or hinder their son's progress.

Prior to beginning both assessment and treatment phases, it is important to let parents know what is likely to happen, how long it will take, and who needs to be present. A cooperative relationship with parents is quickly eroded if they feel that they have not been fully informed of what is happening. It is important to give parents hope that they and their son can be helped; however, it is equally important not to promise more than you can hope to deliver. Attention-deficit/hyperactivity disorder is a pervasive and persistent disorder requiring concerted effort on the part of the parents and therapist. Failure to deliver on early promises will leave parents feeling let down and will reduce their motivation. Parents need to be given some indication at this time of their role in the assessment and treatment process.

On occasion, parents will express negative feelings about their child's teacher and/or school. These concerns need to be discussed openly. It is important to help parents understand that dealing successfully with ADHD requires the cooperation of all adults who have regular contact with the child. Therapists often can help parents find more effective ways of interacting with their child's teacher. When this is not possible, the therapist can act as a mediator for parents.

Make sure you give parents a chance to talk about their child's positive characteristics. Parents of children with ADHD seldom get to boast about their child. Focusing on a child's positive attributes reminds parents that their child is not all bad and can help to engage them in treatment. Finally, it is important to acknowledge that parenting a child with ADHD is both stressful and difficult.

TEACHERS

Therapists who do not routinely work in school systems often feel at a loss as to how to establish a working relationship with a teacher or school. Being open and honest about your role in the child's care is an excellent first step toward developing an effective working relationship. It also helps enormously if you take time to approach a teacher personally. Keep in mind that teachers may have 30 or more children requiring their attention. Your client is only one of perhaps many children a teacher is concerned about.

When asking teachers to assist with assessment or treatment, always give them plenty of warning about what you are likely to need from them. Explain why you want to collect certain information and the time it is likely to take. Keep requests to the minimum required and always remember to thank teachers for their help. Whenever possible, try to keep abreast of the local teaching situation, such as work loads, wage disputes, and class sizes. In this way, you can convey your concern for the teacher's situation, as well as that of the target child.

Allow time for the child's teacher to talk about his or her difficulties and successes with the child. It is important that you respect the teacher's views about the child's presenting problems. If you hold a different view from that of the teacher, do not impose your view but do acknowledge the difference. In the short term, agreeing with the teacher may assist in developing rapport, but longer-term problems will arise when the teacher determines your different viewpoint.

If different viewpoints or working styles threaten the working relationship, focus attention on the child's needs. Whatever differences exist, they usually can be put aside for the child's benefit. Remember that many teachers have limited knowledge of ADHD and may feel threatened by your involvement. This can be dealt with by acknowledging that the child's teacher has a unique knowledge of the child that is invaluable to you as a therapist. Also be aware that teachers may feel that their teaching style is being evaluated. Be clear from the outset of your involvement with a teacher that this is not the case. As with parents, it is important that you acknowledge the difficulties inherent in teaching a child with ADHD.

APPROACHING BOYS WITH ADHD

Boys with ADHD frequently find themselves in trouble with adults. As a consequence, they often assume that the therapist is another adult ready to complain about their behavior. In some cases, they will assume that you are an agent of their parents or the school. These perceptions must be dealt with soon after meeting the child so that rapport can be established.

It can be very helpful to find out what, if anything, the boy has been told about coming to see you. In some instances, boys will have been told nothing about you or what to expect. These boys may be fearful and unwilling to interact with you. Others will have been told that you are going to "sort them out." Depending on how parents have presented the therapeutic process, the boy may feel negatively toward you and refuse to cooperate. Explain in a developmentally appropriate manner what your role is and what they can expect to be asked to do when they are with you. For very young boys, this should be done in the presence of an adult with whom the boy is familiar. In the case of adolescent males, be sure to avoid saying or doing anything likely to be interpreted as condescending. Kamphaus and Frick (1996) provide model scripts for introducing the assessment process to children of different ages. Barker (1990) offers more general suggestions on developing rapport with children and adolescents.

In describing the assessment and treatment process, be sure to let the child know which other individuals are going to be involved and why you will be talking to them. As much as possible, you should involve the child in these processes. This will give him some sense of control and increase his motivation to assist you.

Watch out for fatigue when working with children with ADHD. The very nature of their difficulties makes the interview or testing situation more difficult for them than for other children. A distraction-free environment involving novel tasks and frequent reinforcement will maximize their performance. Frequent breaks should be scheduled, and these can often involve fun activities. Boys with ADHD will almost certainly have several failure experiences before being referred. It is important to realize they may be deliberately noncooperative to avoid further failure. Make sure you praise the child's efforts, and try to ensure that the assessment process is a cooperative endeavor.

ASSESSMENT

It is important to state from the outset that there are no medical or psychological tests for ADHD. Assessing a child with suspected ADHD involves the careful collection of information about the child's behavior from a variety of sources and settings. The assessment of a child with ADHD has two important functions: differential diagnosis and functional analysis of problem behaviors. Differential diagnosis is most useful for communicating about, and accessing the extensive literature on, the disorder, whereas a functional analysis is essential to development of an intervention plan.

In establishing whether a child has ADHD, it is necessary to determine whether the child's behavior differs markedly (in frequency and intensity) from that of other children of the same developmental age. The clinician must also establish that the child's behavior is the result of ADHD and not other factors such as mental retardation, hearing or visual difficulties, gross brain damage, severe language delay, childhood psychosis, autism, cerebral palsy, severe emotional disturbances, or other disorders with overlapping presenting problems (e.g., conduct disorder, oppositional defiant disorder, or learning disability).

In view of the significant role played by parents in the assessment and treatment of ADHD, it is essential that every effort be made to build rapport with the boy's caregivers. Rapport is enhanced by explaining to families what will happen during the assessment process, why certain information needs to be collected, and how long the assessment is likely to take. In addition, it is important to give parents the opportunity to talk about how their son's behavior affects them. Such discussion may also clarify for parents the role they play in maintaining their son's behavior. When the boy's parents are not living together, it is important to include the noncustodial parent as fully as circumstances permit.

Input from teachers is an essential component in the assessment of a child with suspected ADHD. Before contacting the child's school, it is important to gauge the parents' attitude toward the school and the child's teacher. In some instances, parents and teachers may disagree over the child's management. Knowing this in advance can be invaluable in making decisions regarding the best way to work with parents and teachers.

Teachers should be informed of the nature and purpose of the assessment process and the time involved. Be sure to arrange to talk with teachers and have them complete questionnaires and rating scales at times that suit them. It is important to establish how each school you work with prefers to handle requests for information. This often saves time and can make the difference between grudging agreement and active cooperation.

The assessment of a child thought to have ADHD is a time-consuming and often lengthy process. A thorough assessment should include interviews with parents, the boy, and his teacher; behavioral rating scales for completion by parents and teachers; child self-report measures; parent self-report measures; and observations of the boy alone, together with parents, and at school. Considerable time is saved if, prior to meeting with the boy's parents, permission can be obtained to access the results of any previous assessments of the boy (psychological, educational, and cognitive), to contact his physician to obtain information on his health and medication status, to send out child rating scales to parents and teachers, and to contact any social services involved with the boy or his family (Pelham, 1995).

INTERVIEWS

Interviews provide an opportunity to obtain a detailed account of the parents' perception of their child's difficulties, including the distress these problems cause other members of the family. They also offer some insight into the parents' current psychological functioning and relationships with each other, which may affect their ability to participate in any planned interventions. Higher rates of psychopathology have been observed in the parents of children with ADHD (Barkley, Anastopoulos, Guevremont, & Fletcher, 1992; Fischer, Barkley, Fletcher, & Smallish, 1993; Mash & Johnston, 1990). Given that development of ADHD is, in part, genetically determined, therapists may find themselves working with parents who also exhibit symptoms of the disorder. The presence of ADHD in the parents obviously will affect their ability to engage effectively in their child's treatment. To assist parents in providing specific information about their son's difficulties, the following strategies may be used: requesting recent examples of the behaviors the parents are concerned about, obtaining information on the specific situations in which the boy exhibits the behavior, and viewing the parents' responses to behavioral rating scales completed prior to the session.

There are no fixed rules regarding inclusion of the child in the parent interviews: Each case must be judged individually. If the parents are uncomfortable with their son being present, then they should be interviewed alone. Under these circumstances, inclusion of the child may result in the parents providing only partial information. If the boy is present during the parent interview, the therapist is able to directly observe parenting practices and interactions between the boy and his parents.

Parents also may be able to offer information about their son's school environment and his behavior in this setting. They should be asked for an account of the boy's schooling history (including preschool and/or day care) and questioned about any teacher concerns regarding behavioral difficulties or academic progress. The presence of any behavioral or emotional difficulties among the boy's siblings also should be assessed.

Depending on the boy's age, it may be helpful to interview him. Very young children often lack the verbal and cognitive skills to offer any information beyond that provided by the parents. Older children and adolescents, on the other hand, are able to provide useful information on their symptoms, family functioning, and school performance. The duration of any interviews with the boy will depend on his age, intellectual functioning, and language skills.

If the boy is interviewed, it is important to question him about his school progress, any difficulties he is having at home or school, and how he is getting along with peers, parents, and teachers. Be sure to finish up the interview with a discussion of topics that are positive for him. It is important that the therapeutic setting not represent a further failure experience for a boy with ADHD. Although children with ADHD typically underestimate their symptoms and difficulties, information on how a boy perceives his situation is useful in planning any intervention.

Regardless of whether the boy is formally interviewed, it is important that the clinician have the opportunity to interact with and observe him. This interaction provides important information about his level of cognitive functioning and should highlight any receptive or expressive language difficulties. Contrary to popular opinion, the boy's levels of activity and/or distractibility in the clinic setting do not predict functioning in children whose parent and teacher report hyperactivity (Tripp & Luk, 1997).

When practical, a face-to-face meeting with the boy's teacher should take place during the assessment process. If such a meeting is not possible, a telephone interview must be arranged. The teacher is able to provide important information on the boy's academic, behavioral, and social functioning in the school setting, relative to his peers. The presence of symptoms of ADHD can be assessed and information gathered on how the school and the teacher are currently managing the boy's behavior. In addition, a visit to the school permits observation of the playground and classroom environments, important elements of any school-based intervention.

Much has been made of the often low correlations between the reports of parents and teachers regarding children's behavior. This lack of agreement in part reflects the different settings in which these informants observe the child's behavior. Reliability can be enhanced by asking questions specific to the information required.

RATING SCALES

A number of behavior checklists and rating scales, which provide useful information on the extent of the boy's behavioral difficulties, are available for completion by both parents and teachers. These measures generally have good reliability and validity, together with extensive normative data for a wide range of ages. Some scales assess psychopathology generally, whereas others are specific to ADHD. Barkley (1990) provides an excellent summary (nature, reliability, and validity) of the rating scales available for use with children referred for an evaluation of ADHD. Although rating scales and checklists allow for normative comparisons and facilitate the collapsing of data across settings and times, they should never be used in place of interviews with parents and teachers. We have observed that some parents, typically those looking for a diagnosis of ADHD, use only the upper range of the response scales. Furthermore, there is evidence that teacher ratings of ADHD may be inflated in boys who display aggressive behavior (Abikoff, Courtney, Pelham, & Koplewicz, 1993; Hinshaw, 1987; Prinz, Conner, & Wilson, 1981).

In addition to information collected during the clinical interview, self-report questionnaires may also be used to assess the parents' psychological functioning. Care needs to be exercised in asking parents to complete these measures. By the time parents seek professional help for their son, many already have engaged in significant self-blame or been told by well-meaning friends that their parenting skills are at fault. It should be stated explicitly that in asking parents to complete self-report measures the counselor is not attempting to assign blame for the boy's behavior but that the information will be useful in planning how best to help them and their son. Areas that might be targeted include mood, psychopathology, marital adjustment, parent stress, and parenting style (Barkley, 1990).

BEHAVIORAL OBSERVATION

Various observational coding systems are available for coding school- and home-based interactions (see Barkley, 1990, and DuPaul & Stoner, 1994, for reviews). Home visits can provide an opportunity to observe the boy in the family context. Such visits can also provide important information on parents' expectations for their son and the degree of structure in the home environment. When home visits are not possible, clinic-based child and family interactions may still provide valuable information.

Classroom observations should be considered if time and resources permit. Although children may show some reactivity to the observation process, important information on a boy's classroom and playground behavior can be obtained. School observations are particularly valuable if the boy has specific school-based difficulties and intervention is planned for this setting.

LABORATORY MEASURES

A number of laboratory measures are available for use in the assessment of children with ADHD; however, the practical utility of these measures has been questioned on the grounds that they lack ecological validity (Barkley, 1991). The conditions under which these measures are completed have little in common with classroom or home settings.

EDUCATION OF FAMILIES AND TEACHERS

In working with parents and teachers, it is essential to check what they know about ADHD and to correct any misconceptions early. Accurate information on the diagnosis, etiology, treatment, and prognosis should be offered. Many research programs on ADHD have parent and teacher handouts that can be adapted to suit the therapist's own clients. Alternatively, organizations such as the Association for the Advancement of Behavior Therapy produce brief client handouts that can be purchased for a nominal fee. Be sure the information provided is correct and that parents and teachers have the opportunity to discuss the material. For families and teachers interested in obtaining more in-depth information about ADHD, Barkley (1995) provides an annotated bibliography.

Professionals who work, or intend to work, with children and adolescents presenting with ADHD must ensure that their own knowledge in this area is current. This includes being informed about relevant state and/or national public laws, legal entitlements, and specialist programs relevant to children with ADHD. Providing this information to caregivers is crucial to ensure that children, families, and teachers receive the maximum support and resources to which they are entitled.

TREATMENT

Clinically, the treatment of ADHD is moving toward the use of a multimodal approach, typically stimulant medication coupled with psychosocial treatments. Abikoff and Hechtman (1996) recently completed data collection for a two-site multimodal treatment outcome study comparing stimulant medication and psychosocial treatment with an attentional control group. The National Institutes of Mental Health (NIMH) are funding a six-site multimodal treatment study comparing medication, psychosocial treatment, combined therapy, and community-based intervention (Abikoff & Hechtman, 1996; Richters et al., 1995). Over the next few years, data from these studies will answer important questions about the longer-term effectiveness of these treatments. Below, we discuss three important components of any multimodal treatment: stimulant medication, parent management training, and school-based interventions. Treatment strategies focusing on the child are presented next, followed up by a brief discussion of treatments of limited efficacy.

MEDICATION

The prescription of psychostimulants, such as dextroamphetamine (Dexedrine), methylphenidate (Ritalin), and pemoline (Cylert), is the most common treatment for ADHD. It has been estimated that as many as 90% of American children with ADHD will receive stimulant medication during their primary school years (Pelham, 1995). These medications are generally safe and result in significant behavioral gains for many children (Greenhill, 1992). Other medications less commonly prescribed for this disorder include antidepressants (Biederman et al., 1991), clonidine (Steingard, Biederman, Spencer, Wilens, & Gonzalez, 1993), and neuroleptics (Gittelman-Klein, Klein, Katz, Saraf, & Pollack, 1976). The efficacy of these alternative medications is less well established (Brown, 1991; Greenhill, 1992). In the short term, the stimulants are reported to improve functioning across a range of domains including classroom disruption (Granger, Whalen, Henker, & Cantwell, 1996); on-task behavior (DuPaul & Rapport, 1993); academic productivity and accuracy (DuPaul & Rapport, 1993); compliance with adult requests (Barkley, 1989a); peer interactions (Wilens & Biederman, 1992); performance on laboratory measures of attention, impulsivity, and attention (Pelham, 1995); and aggressive behavior (Stewart, Myers, Burket, & Lyles, 1990). Response to medication varies, however, across behaviors and settings, and the stimulants do not actually normalize the behavior of children with ADHD (Greenhill, 1992; Pelham, 1995). Not all children diagnosed with ADHD respond to stimulant medication. The percentage showing a favorable response varies between 70% and more than 95% depending on the target group, (stimulant drugs appear less effective for preschoolers, adolescents, and adults compared with primary school–aged children), the trial medication, the criteria for determining a response, and the presence of comorbid difficulties (Barkley, 1990; Pliszka, 1989; Richters et al., 1995). Although these drugs generally are tolerated well, a range of side effects are reported, including insomnia; decreased appetite; headache; stomachache; increased irritability, moodiness, and tearfulness; evening rebound from medication; cognitive constriction; social withdrawal; motor movements and tics; and slowing of growth (Greenhill, 1992; Pelham, 1995). Many of these side effects can be overcome with a temporary reduction in drug dose; however, for some children the nature, or severity, of the side effects excludes stimulant medication as a treatment option.

The long-term benefit of stimulant medication in the treatment of ADHD has not been established. In general, the treatment outcome literature does not indicate that children receiving stimulant medication show lasting effects (Richters et al., 1995). It is possible that the lack of evidence for long-term benefits is an artifact of outcome studies that are too brief or include nonrandom samples, for example, children with more severe ADHD being assigned to the medication condition (Richters et al., 1995; Schachar & Tannock, 1993). In view of the proven short-term efficacy of the stimulants, therapists are encouraged to consider a medication trial when treating a boy diagnosed with ADHD. We encourage the reader to consult the following sources if considering a medication trial: Greenhill (1992) for a review of the pharmacological treatment of ADHD; Barkley (1990) for detailed information on setting up and evaluating a medication trial; and DuPaul and Stoner (1994) regarding the use of medications in educational settings.

Stimulants increasingly are being used in conjunction with other therapies (DuPaul, 1991; DuPaul & Barkley, 1993; Pelham, Vodde-Hamilton, Murphy, Greenstein, & Vallano, 1991). Pelham (1995) argues strongly for initiating any behavioral interventions prior to implementing a medication trial. Relative to the behavioral treatments, medication is an easier option for parents and teachers. If stimulants are introduced first, the often significant improvement in the child's behavior can reduce motivation to initiate and maintain the more time-intensive behavioral treatments.

PARENT MANAGEMENT TRAINING AND COUNSELING

Complaints of noncompliance and oppositional behavior are commonly heard from the parents of children with ADHD. In many cases, it is these difficulties rather than the core symptoms of ADHD that prompt referral. For such families, parent management training, alone or in conjunction with medication, may assist parents to deal more effectively with their son's difficult behavior. In some instances, it may be necessary to persuade parents that medication alone is not sufficient to address all their son's difficulties (Pelham, 1995).

Several excellent parent management programs for dealing with children's oppositional and defiant behavior are available (e.g., Forehand & Long, 1996; Forehand & McMahon, 1981; Horne & Sayger, 1990; Sanders & Dadds, 1993). These programs typically include an introduction to the principles of behavior management, specific skills training (e.g., attending, rewarding, ignoring, giving directions, and time out), skill rehearsal, and between-session homework assignments. Parents of boys with ADHD, however, face a number of difficulties in addition to noncompliance. Recognizing this, Barkley (1987, 1990) specifically adapted the Forehand and McMahon (1981) program for this client group. Changes to the program include the addition of an ADHD education component and parent counseling. Barkley (1990) draws attention to the influence that parents' perceptions of themselves and their child have on their ability and willingness to engage in treatment.

Typically, 8 to 12 sessions are required to complete parent management/parent counseling programs. The actual number of sessions spent with parents should reflect their individual needs and the speed with which they acquire the requisite parenting skills (Barkley, 1990). Whenever possible, the parents should be observed implementing the target parenting skills with their son. Parent management programs can be run individually or in a group format. If a group approach is used, session length needs to be increased. Each format has its strengths: An individual approach allows for greater tailoring of the program and increased individual practice, and the group format provides much-needed support for parents. Where possible, the format chosen should match the needs of the family.

The decision to include parent management training in the treatment of a boy with ADHD should be based on the information obtained during the assessment phase. If the boy's difficulties occur primarily in the school setting, parent management training may not be necessary. Barkley (1990), however, argues that parents who have received instruction in the principles of behavior management may be better able to cooperate with teachers. In the course of working with some families, serious marital or psychological problems, unrelated to the boy's behavioral difficulties, may become evident. It may be necessary to delay parent management training until these difficulties have been resolved.

Parent management training approaches like those identified above focus on parent skill acquisition, with limited child involvement. As such, they are better suited to families with younger children, typically between 3 and 11 years of age (Anastopoulos & Barkley, 1990; Forehand & McMahon, 1981). For older children and adolescents, the approach described by Robin (1990), which places greater emphasis on family sessions, is more appropriate.

SCHOOL-BASED INTERVENTION

The nature of ADHD, coupled with the demands of the school setting, almost invariably results in school-based intervention being required. At school, children with

ADHD frequently experience academic failure and peer rejection, and their behavior is often unacceptable to staff and fellow students.

In general, school-based treatment has focused on classroom behavior, although DuPaul and Stoner (1994) make a strong case for interventions that also address the child's academic difficulties. Intervention with academic failure will depend on the cause of the boy's problems. Academic failure can result from the symptoms of ADHD, the presence of learning disability, or both. Those responsible for assessing children in the school environment need to be on the lookout for deficits in academic skills as well as in academic performance. The latter may be addressed by medication and behavior modification procedures. Academic skills deficits are not addressed adequately by stimulant medication; they require behavioral intervention and careful programming of the learning environment. The reader is referred to the excellent book by DuPaul and Stoner (1994), *ADHD in the Schools*, which provides detailed information on both assessment and treatment of academic skills deficits.

Planning of a school-based intervention, while dictated by the needs of the child, must also take account of the school's and targeted teacher's attitudes toward, and resources for, dealing with ADHD. Teachers vary widely in their ability and motivation to implement a behavioral program, and this should be taken into account when planning teacher training and support. If the teacher of a boy with ADHD is unwilling to implement a behavioral program, the boy's parents may need to consider moving him to another class or school. Before taking such a step, the therapist should work with the teacher in an effort to overcome objections to a behavioral program (Barkley, 1990; Pelham, 1995). It is important that the therapist be sensitive to any negative interaction patterns that may have developed between the boy and his teacher. Teaching a child with ADHD can be very frustrating with few rewards.

The development and implementation of a school-based intervention is simplified if the therapist maintains regular contact with the teacher involved. If several teachers have regular contact with the boy, it can be helpful to have one teacher take a lead role, providing feedback to others involved. Close cooperation between home and school also facilitates the intervention. In some cases, relationships between teachers and parents may have become strained, and the therapist may play an important role in mediating between home and school (Pelham, 1995).

The well-established principles of behavior management apply equally well in the school setting as in the home. Children with ADHD, however, differ somewhat from their classmates in their response to these principles. First, evidence is accumulating that children with ADHD require more reinforcement (i.e., immediate, frequent, larger, and novel rewards) to maintain appropriate behavior (Barkley, 1989b; Douglas & Parry, 1994; Haenlein & Caul, 1987; Sonuga-Barke, Taylor, Sembi, & Smith, 1992; Wender, 1972, 1974). Second, positive reinforcement on its own probably will not be sufficient to manage the behavior of children with ADHD. The use of some mild negative consequences should be planned. Given the frequency with which these children experience failure, however, care should be taken to ensure that any reprimands are private and made in a brief, calm, and clear manner (Pelham, 1995; Pfiffner & Barkley, 1990; Pfiffner & O'Leary, 1993). In addition, children need to have appropriate behaviors demonstrated and need to be reinforced for engaging in them (Barkley, 1995). For more severe disruptive behaviors, time-out procedures are recommended (DuPaul & Stoner, 1994; Pfiffner & Barkley, 1990). These differences need to be conveyed to teachers and teacher aids, and care must be taken to ensure that both are familiar with the correct use of behavioral management techniques.

CHILD-FOCUSED TREATMENT

Although stimulant medication, parent management training, and school-based interventions are the key components of treatment for ADHD, many children with the disorder will require specific help with peer relationships, self-esteem, and aggressive behavior. Almost all children with ADHD experience some degree of peer rejection and/or negative evaluation, with many having clinically significant problems in this area (Greene et al., 1996). The children most at risk appear to be those with comorbid aggressive symptoms and/or learning disabilities (Erhardt & Hinshaw, 1994; Flicek, 1992).

Some ground is being made in child-focused treatment by Pelham and colleagues, with their intensive summer treatment program (Pelham & Hoza, 1996), and by Hinshaw (1996), who integrates self-evaluation strategies and anger management training with behavioral procedures. A key feature of these programs involves working with children in groups, allowing them to practice the skills they are being taught. An important outcome with these programs appears to be the maintenance or enhancement of the children's self-esteem.

TREATMENTS OF LIMITED EFFICACY

Dietary factors, in particular food additives and allergic responses to different foods, were previously thought by some to play a causative role in ADHD. Although these factors may be important for a small minority of children with this disorder, specialist diets (e.g., Feingold KP diet) and food allergy treatments largely have been discounted as effective treatments for this disorder (Rosen, Schissel, Taylor, & Krein, 1993). A number of other treatment approaches to ADHD have been proposed and subsequently discounted; these include biofeedback techniques, chiropractics, allergy treatments, motion sickness medication, perceptual/motor training, traditional psychoanalysis, and cognitive therapy (Barkley, 1995; Fonagy & Target, 1994; Lee, 1991; Pelham, 1995). Family therapy, cognitive behavioral therapy, and psychotherapy have demonstrated limited effectiveness in improving the behavior of children with ADHD but are of value in the treatment of adolescents (Faigel et al., 1995).

ADOLESCENTS WITH ADHD

The problems experienced by teenagers with ADHD are often heightened compared with those experienced by younger boys. The core symptoms of ADHD are combined with the normal problems of adolescence (e.g., increased parent-child conflict; adolescent's increasing desire for independence; coping with physical, hormonal and social changes brought about by puberty). It is not surprising that adolescent males with ADHD experience lower levels of self-esteem, more academic problems, increased difficulties in interacting with families and peers, and higher levels of substance abuse compared with their non-ADHD peers (Barkley et al., 1991; DuPaul & Stoner, 1994; Hechtman, 1991; Hoza, Pelham, Milich, Pillow, & McBride, 1993; Slomkowski, Klein, & Mannuzza, 1995).

The increased difficulties experienced by adolescents, their greater independence, and their better-developed cognitive skills require some modifications to the assessment and treatment guidelines given above. In assessing an adolescent referred for ADHD, it is essential to interview the parents and the young person and to obtain collateral information where possible. A history of the adolescent's difficulties should be obtained from the parents; however, the young person himself may provide more reliable information regarding current concerns and difficulties. Including an adolescent from the outset of assessment can assist in establishing good rapport and increase the chances of engagement in, and adherence to, any subsequent treatment program (DuPaul & Stoner, 1994).

Obtaining information about an adolescent's school behavior can be more difficult than is the case for younger boys. Adolescents often are required to shift between classrooms and will almost certainly take classes from several different teachers. Information about academic performance, peer relationships, and general behavior therefore must be obtained from multiple sources, and the therapist must take into account differences in personal interaction styles and discipline techniques across informants.

Behavior therapy with adolescents takes on a different form from that used with children. For home-based behavior management, Barkley and Robin (1995) suggest that parents establish clear rules about the adolescent's role in the house (e.g., a list of chores he is required to carry out) as well as more general rules covering areas such as curfews and dating. Parents should use positive and negative consequences to help shape behavior, but the specific rewards and punishments used must be altered so as to be applicable to an adolescent. In practical terms, rewards may include extra allowance or permission to go to a social event, while suitable punishments may include restricting telephone use or "grounding."

As the adolescent begins to take more responsibility for his life, behavior therapy should reflect this change in responsibility by focusing more on the teenager himself. DuPaul and Stoner (1994) recommend a program of cognitive and behavioral training in social skills, self-control, and study skills (e.g., training on how to take notes and study for tests) for adolescents with ADHD, although they warn that the efficacy of this program has not yet been confirmed. Robin (1990) advocates the use of family problem-solving techniques and communication training for families of adolescents with ADHD so as to address family structure problems and develop a strong parent-adolescent alliance in addressing problems brought about by ADHD. In some cases, particularly those in which there are comorbid conduct problems, parents may need help to reestablish appropriate boundaries for the adolescent (Robin, 1990).

Cognitive therapy can be useful for helping adolescents develop effective problem-solving techniques and recognize and challenge dysfunctional thoughts and assumptions (Faigel et al., 1995). Individual psychotherapy may also be necessary for adolescents with ADHD to help them address such problems as low levels of self-esteem and alcohol/substance abuse, which may accompany ADHD in this age group.

It is not always appropriate for a therapist who has worked with the family to see the adolescent individually. The young person may perceive the therapist to be an agent of the parents. It may be important for an adolescent male to work with a male therapist, especially if there is an absence of appropriate role models in his environment.

FUTURE RESEARCH

The main focus of research in the 21st century is likely to be the etiology of ADHD. Understanding the cause(s) of the disorder will advance the development of effective treatments and possible prevention. Future research should focus on finding the precise nature and location of any brain dysfunctions or abnormalities associated with ADHD, and understanding how these dysfunctions cause the behavioral symptoms of the disorder.

To date, a number of family factors, such as parental stress and parents' developmental expectations of the child (Sonuga-Barke & Goldfoot, 1995; Webster-Stratton, 1990), have been implicated in the behavioral, social, and academic outcome of children with ADHD. Unfortunately, research on these potentially important variables has taken place in a rather piecemeal fashion. Our own ongoing research in this area is attempting to identify the extent to which such family factors affect the child's short- and longer-term functioning.

Although psychostimulants are the drug of choice for treatment of ADHD (Ambrosini, Bianchi, Rabinovich, & Elia, 1993), other types of medication, including tricyclic antidepressants, also have proved effective in reducing the problematic behavior of children with ADHD (Wilens, Biederman, Geist, Steingard, & Spencer, 1993). Research should focus on evaluating the effectiveness of these drugs for children with comorbid disorders (e.g., mood or tic disorders) and the extent to which the available stimulants differentially affect children with different subtypes of ADHD (Richters et al., 1995). In addition, the long-term adult effects of childhood use of the stimulants are still largely unknown and need to be systematically monitored (Weiss & Trokenberg Hechtman, 1993).

Given that no single treatment modality seems to be maximally effective in the treatment of ADHD, future research should continue developing and assessing combined therapies. The recently instituted NIMH multisite multimodal treatment study of children with ADHD (Richters et al., 1995) provides an excellent example of this type of research, and results from this study will be awaited with keen interest.

TRAINING ISSUES

The assessment and treatment of ADHD is challenging even for therapists experienced in working with behavior-disordered children. Those inexperienced in working with children may feel overwhelmed. For therapists intending to work with boys and adolescent males with ADHD, we offer the following suggestions.

First, ensure that you have a thorough understanding of normal child development, particularly the range of behavioral difficulties typically experienced by boys and adolescent males. You must be able to distinguish between normal variations in behavior and ADHD. It also is important to familiarize yourself with the range of medical, developmental, and social factors that might also explain why a child is displaying ADHD-like behaviors.

Second, in developing your knowledge about ADHD, be guided by information from mainstream sources. ADHD has been the focus of significant media attention and populist writing, and not all the information offered by these sources is current or accurate. If possible, attend workshops on ADHD when they are offered by credible professional bodies.

Third, working with children with ADHD often requires a therapist to use his or her imagination in devising treatment plans that keep the child and family interested in therapy and motivated to change. This may involve working on the presentation of ideas and being sensitive to the family's strengths. It does not mean using unproved or fad therapies. Therapists are reminded to use well-proven behavioral principles in working with these boys and their families. If your training has not included specific instruction in the use of behavioral principles, you should consider obtaining training in this area.

Fourth, ADHD is one area of childhood psychopathology for which assessment and treatment methods are relatively well documented. Regardless of their theoretical orientation, we believe it is important that therapists take careful note of what is known about treating ADHD and incorporate it into their practice with boys and adolescent males with this disorder.

SM: AN EXAMPLE OF EFFECTIVE TREATMENT

SM is a 9-year-old boy who, together with his parents, presented for treatment. SM previously had been diagnosed with ADHD, combined type, and was prescribed methylphenidate. Although the medication controlled many of SM's symptoms, his parents were concerned about his difficulty following instructions, inability to establish a morning routine, forgetfulness (including taking his medication), difficulty interacting with his same-age peers, and small appetite. The latter had not resolved with a reduction in medication.

A team therapy approach was implemented, with one therapist focusing on the parents' concerns while a second (male) therapist worked one on one with SM. Initial sessions focused on listening to, and empathizing with, the concerns of SM's parents. This resulted in an observable reduction of parental stress. Significant time also was spent establishing rapport and building up trust and confidence with SM through listening and talking to him in a nonjudgmental manner and engaging him in a number of play activities.

Treatment then focused on improving SM's appetite and morning routines, the areas of most concern to his parents. SM's parents were taught basic behavioral skills, including attending to good behavior and ignoring undesirable behavior, setting up and maintaining a reward system for good behavior, and the appropriate use of punishment (i.e., withdrawal of privileges) for problem behavior. Using these behavior management techniques, SM and his parents worked toward goals in small steps until SM was eating appropriately sized meals and could independently get ready for school in the morning. SM's parents were also taught to give simple one- or two-step instructions to help his compliance. SM was kept informed of the strategies his parents were using and the goals they were working toward.

Individual treatment with SM focused on problem-solving approaches to dealing with provocation and teasing in the classroom, modeling of these strategies by the male therapist, and subsequent role-playing. A similar approach was used in helping SM develop strategies to aid memory. Addressing SM's socialization difficulties was more problematic. Many of his peers knew him prior to receiving any treatment for ADHD and maintained a negative view of him based on their earlier experience. The combined effects of medication, anger management strategies, and social skills training nevertheless reportedly improved his social status (teacher report).

Individual treatment sessions with SM were conducted in short, intensive blocks (lasting approximately 20 minutes), with breaks between blocks, and scheduling a fun activity (e.g., playing a game) at the end of each session. Sessions were structured in this manner to cope with SM's short attention span and concentration difficulties. There were marked differences in SM's behavior on and off medication. Without medication, sessions were disrupted by SM's constant high activity level and off-task behavior.

Throughout treatment, the therapists maintained regular contact with SM's teacher. Initially, this was done to establish the nature of SM's behavior in the school environment and to assess the teacher's concerns. As treatment with SM progressed, his teacher became involved in the management of his eating behavior and in helping SM to develop and maintain more appropriate anger management strategies and social skills.

For now, SM's parents are happy to manage their son's behavior without assistance, but they have been encouraged to refer themselves in the future should the need arise. We expect to see them again, possibly as SM approaches puberty.

HIGHLIGHTS OF CHAPTER 17

► Developmentally inappropriate levels of inattention, hyperactivity, and impulsivity that adversely affect behavior, academic performance, and social functioning characterize attention-deficit/hyperactivity disorder

(ADHD). Up to 50% of child clinical referrals are for ADHD. The disorder is more common in boys than in girls.

▶ A high proportion of boys with ADHD (as many as 80%) will continue to experience difficulties in adolescence; for many, their adult lives will be adversely affected.

▶ ADHD is often comorbid with conduct disorder or oppositional defiant disorder, which complicates assessment and treatment. Comorbid mood and anxiety disorders also are common.

▶ To date, there are no medical or psychological tests for ADHD. Information from interviews, behavioral rating scales/questionnaires, and behavioral observation are used in deciding if a boy has ADHD. Before making a diagnosis of ADHD, other possible causes for the boy's behavior problems must be excluded.

▶ Counselors involved in the assessment of ADHD must ensure that they are familiar with normal child development, particularly the range of behavioral difficulties typically experienced by boys and adolescent males.

▶ The participation of the boy, his parents, and his teacher(s) is essential to both assessment and treatment of ADHD. Adequate time must be set aside to develop a working relationship with all these individuals. This is facilitated by allowing parents and teachers to express their concerns freely and by making clear their role, and that of others, in the assessment and treatment process. The role of the counselor should be explained to the boy, along with what is expected from him.

▶ Intervention with boys and adolescents with ADHD is likely to be prolonged, involving several adults as well as the boy with ADHD. Counselors should plan interventions with this in mind. It is important that counselors be familiar with state or national laws and legal entitlements to ensure that caregivers, teachers, and boys receive the assistance and support to which they are entitled.

▶ A multimodal treatment approach incorporating stimulant medication, parent management training, and school-based interventions is currently favored. Component selection depends on the problems identified during assessment. Parent management training is most suited to families of younger children. School-based interventions should focus on classroom behavior and academic difficulties.

▶ Many boys with ADHD also require specific help with peer relationships, self-esteem, and aggressive behavior. The extent to which the counselor works individually with the boy is likely to increase with his age.

▶ The problems experienced by adolescents with ADHD are often heightened compared to those experienced by younger children. The core symptoms of ADHD are combined with the normal problems of adolescence. Assessment and treatment approaches should be modified to focus more on the teenager himself.

18

Bullies and Victims

A Theme of Boys and Adolescent Males

DAWN A. NEWMAN
ARTHUR M. HORNE
CYNTHIA B. WEBSTER

When I was a young boy, the bully called me names, stole my bicycle, forced me off the playground. I was victim to the ridicule he heaped on me. He made fun of other children, forced me to turn over my lunch money each day, threatened to give me a black eye if I told adult authority figures. At different times I was subject to a wide range of degradation and abuse—"de-pantsing," spit in my face, forced to eat playground dirt. . . . As I entered adolescence, I noticed that the bully could replicate himself. As part of male rites of passage, all boys were presented with a simple choice: suffer daily humiliation or join the ranks of the bully. We all had to answer the question, "Which side are you on?" I watched sweet childhood friends become hard and mean. I saw other sissy boys become neighborhood toughs. They formed gangs of bullies that tormented us. I witnessed the cycle of abuse which ensures the constant creation of new bullies and I vowed that this would never happen to me. Watching the powerlessness take on the trappings of power, I'd shake my head and withdraw into deeper isolation. . . . The world of children was a cruel place for me. (Rofes, 1994, pp. 37-38)

Bullying is a universal phenomenon and is no stranger to our society. Almost all boys and adolescent males have experienced or will experience bullying, either through being the direct recipient of the bully's attention or through observing classmates who were the victims of bullies (Horne, Glaser, & Sayger, 1994). Bullying behavior among students has long been a disruptive factor in the educational realm; in fact, bullying has risen to a threatening level, affecting the emotional and physical safety of students (Garrity, Jens, Porter, Sager, & Short-Camilli, 1994-1995). The U. S. Department of Justice and the National Association of School Psychologists (NASP) estimate that 160,000 children miss school each day because of fear (Lee, 1993). Bullying, a major cause of this fear, keeps children from perceiving school as a safe environment. Unfortunately, many of these children are reluctant to request aid from school staff for fear of reprisals and inadequate protection.

> If someone is pushing you around there is no one to tell . . . you have to take care of it yourself. . . . If you run and tell the teachers they think you are a punk. When they think you're a punk, you know you've got to watch your back. (13-year-old boy)

Isolated from assistance, children are left to their own devices to cope with feelings of fear and helplessness. Some refuse to attend school, experience physical ailments, drop out of school, associate with gangs for protection, or begin carrying weapons. Bullying research demonstrates why children may not feel safe from victimization, humiliation, and violence at school. A survey of 200 American students indicated that approximately 70% had directly experienced bullying at some point in their academic careers (Hoover, Oliver, & Hazler, 1992). Of the students surveyed, 14% believed that the exposure to bullying had a severe impact on their lives.

> Most of the bullying goes on at school between people who don't know each other. . . . When I'm at home, I just want to play with the people who know me. (12-year-old boy)

Bullying is a long-standing problem in our society; however, it was not until the 1970s that formal interest in this topic was sparked and researchers began a systematic examination of the problem (Ross, 1996). Since then, research has contributed a wealth of knowledge about bullies, their characteristics, and their families' characteristics (Horne, 1991; Norsworthy & Horne, 1994; Olweus, 1993, 1994). Researchers have also examined the characteristics of the victims of bullies (Olweus, 1978, 1993; Perry, Kusel, & Perry, 1988) and attempted to analyze the bully/victim dyad (Pierce & Cohen, 1995). Differing forms of bullying have been identified, including direct and indirect (Olweus, 1993), passive (Olweus, 1978), and that by proactive and reactive aggressors (Dodge & Coie, 1987).

In this chapter, we consider much of what is known about bullying, including variations of bullying, developmental and systemic factors influencing bullying, victims' characteristics and their role in the bullying relationship, and recommended interventions to reduce or prevent acts of bullying. Furthermore, within this context, we explore a notion of bullying that is socially prevalent—the "likable bully."

BULLIES

> I know a lot about bullies. I know they have a specific social function: they define the limits of acceptable conduct, appearance, and activities for children. They enforce rigid expectations. They are masters of the art of humiliation and technicians of the science of terrorism. They wreaked havoc on my entire childhood. To this day, their handprints, like a slap on the face, remain stark and defined on my soul. (Rofes, 1994, p. 37)

What is the definition of bullying? Olweus (1994) defines bullying in the following manner: "A student is being bullied or victimized when he or she is exposed, repeatedly and over time, to negative actions on the part of one or more other students. . . . It is a negative action when someone intentionally inflicts, or attempts to inflict, injury or discomfort on another" (p. 1173). As noted by Olweus (1994), in his definition bullying is characterized by three criteria: (a) It is aggressive behavior or intentional "harmdoing" (b) that is carried out repeatedly and over time (c) in an interpersonal relationship characterized by an imbalance of power.

Olweus (1994) distinguishes between two types of bullying: *direct bullying/ victimization*, such as open attacks on the victims, and *indirect bullying/victimization*, such as social isolation and intentional exclusion from the group. Each of these types of bullying can be devastating and destructive to the intended victim. The typical bullies are those that initiate aggression toward peers. Olweus (1978) refers to these as aggressive bullies. They are characterized as fearless, coercive, tough, and impulsive. Aggressive bullies have a strong inclination toward using violence, have a need to dominate others, and tend to express little empathy toward their victims (Olweus, 1994; Ross, 1996). These bullies tend to cognitively distort the meaning of their victims' behavior as well as overreact in ambiguous situations (Dodge & Coie, 1987). Aggressive bullies see the world with a paranoid's eye (Ross, 1996).

Passive bullies tend to be dependent, insecure, and anxious. They participate in bullying but typically do not initiate the aggression. Once the bullying is instigated, usually by an aggressive bully, the passive bullies actively participate (Ross, 1996). They may lack strong inhibitors against aggression, and when they observe the aggressive bully being rewarded, they often see bullying in a more positive light. Often lacking a defined social status among their peers, the passive bullies are eager to affiliate with the action-oriented bullies. Their alignment with the aggressive bully group has earned them the label of "camp followers" or "hangers-on" (Olweus, 1993, 1994; Ross, 1996).

Dodge and Coie (1987) further distinguish children's aggressive behavior into categories of proactive and reactive bullies. These authors describe proactive aggressors as internally motivated to use aggression for a desired goal, whereas reactive aggressors become hostile in reaction to perceived threats. Each of these subtypes of bullies carry out their bullying within a social system.

Society views the physically aggressive behavior of boys as representative of bullying. It appears that through socialization boys often inherit the label of "bully" when they have committed an offense toward another child. In contrast, girls' aversive behavior is often classified as "mean" (Ross, 1996). Interestingly, females usually bully other females, whereas males bully both sexes (Sharp & Smith, 1991). Boys tend to be exposed to a greater amount of bullying than girls, a trend that is marked primarily in junior high school (Olweus, 1994). Bullies are often the students who tease, kick, intimidate, threaten, and act aggressively toward adults (Olweus, 1993). The bully often shows little empathy toward the victim and demonstrates a need to dominate. Findings reveal that bullies are more likely to be absent and drop out of school (Bryne, 1994). Furthermore, several research studies note that males have a greater tendency to bully (Boulton & Underwood, 1992; Bryne, 1994; Siann, Callaghan, Glissov, Lockhart, & Rawson, 1994). In fact, worldwide research on bullying has consistently found that there is a higher incidence of bullying among boys as compared to girls (Ahmad & Smith, 1994).

> Bullies are the boys who think they can beat you at anything . . . basketball, grades . . . they think they can do anything better than you . . . they're so competitive. (13-year-old boy)

Past research has demonstrated that in the lower grades, the majority of bullying was committed by older boys. The boys who acted as the bullies were often found to be the oldest members of their peer group. It is interesting to note that the number of boys who bullied during a group's last year of elementary school decreased when the cohort entered middle school, and that boys who bully are often 1 to 2 years older than their victims. These boys engage in direct bullying four times as often as girls and are victimized twice as often (Olweus, 1993).

> When I was in the 7th grade, I could not stand this kid in 6th grade. I picked on him for like a year. Then one day, we just talked and we become cool. (14-year-old boy)

Sometimes, bullies are popular among their peers during their early school years. By junior high, though, this admiration often begins to show a marked decrease. It is not rare that these individuals become leaders of a group of willing accomplices who are subordinates rather than equals.

> For this group, the bully's word is law, which further reinforces the feeling of power and, in addition, eliminates the need for friendship with other children. Bullying allows children who are either bored with school or not doing well to be "good" at something, prove their courage and dominance to their peers. It allows them to feel superior. (Ross, 1996, p. 67)

> Most people bully to get attention . . . some just do it because that's the only thing they are good at. . . . "Hey man I can beat you up, but I can't read." (14-year-old boy)

ACCEPTANCE OF BULLYING

Bullying is not always regarded negatively and may even be seen as acceptable (Arora & Thompson, 1987; Oliver, Hoover, & Hazler, 1994). Olweus (1978) found that bullies were almost as popular as well-adjusted students and more popular than their victims. What causes some bullies to be likable while others are rejected and hated? What are the characteristics of the likable bully and of his social environment that allow for more accepting reactions and judgment?

> Likable bullies are the preppies. . . . The likable bullies are going to be more popular, unlike the rejected bully . . . they don't have many friends. . . . [What do you think makes the likable bullies more popular?] You know how girls are? They love boys like that. They like boys to be all big and bad. . . . They like a guy that can stand up for them and protect them. . . . The rejected bully only has a few friends. . . . They just don't care. They just bully for no reason, just to do it. . . . They fight and stuff. . . . The likable bullies don't fight. They pick on people. They pull pranks, poke fun at people. They make others laugh. . . . They'll do anything funny in front of a group of people. (13-year-old boy)

It seems difficult to imagine that the bully as defined, the perpetrator of threat and attack, could be perceived as likable. Although they may be popular with a small group of peers, bullies tend not to be generally popular (Cairnes, Cairnes, Neckerman, Gest, & Gariepy, 1988). Furthermore, aggression has been reported as the strongest factor for predicting peer rejection (Coie, Dodge, & Coppotelli, 1982).

All aggressive children, however, are not rejected. In their study of Australian children, Rigby and Slee (1991) found that students often admire the bully (the aggressor) and despise the victim. Their findings also uncovered a trend toward decreasing sympathy for the victims with increasing age. Olweus (1993) observed that passive bullies, at times, align with the active bully, in part because the active bullies are often as popular as other students and may even be well liked by the majority of students. It may be that students identify with the aggressor to vicariously experience rewards of power and control.

According to social learning theory (Bandura, 1986), aggression is likely to occur when rewards are probable. Batsche and Knoff (1994) indicate that bullies are rewarded by feelings of reduced anxiety and increased control. Furthermore, they are positively reinforced for their use of aggression by gaining a desired object or a goal, such as dominance status. Thus, social learning theory suggests that the rewards from the system somehow outweigh the costs for those who bully and that when a bully is liked rewards increase (Bandura, 1986). Hence, it is probable that the likable bully is further rewarded by acceptance and popularity among his peers. From this perspective, it appears that likable bullies also may be seen by peers as positive role models. They gain the rewards typically associated with bullying behavior without the peer rejection that often accompanies bullying and may play a role in the perpetuation of aggressive and bullying behaviors within a given system.

Furthermore, the act of bullying appears to be positively reinforced by those spectators who express interest and admiration for the manipulations of bullies. Thus, this modeling tends to promote bullying. For instance, onlookers who express interest may themselves turn to bullying, whereas teachers who bully their students serve as influential models.

> Teachers bully. . . . Sometimes we need it. For 2 years a teacher pushed me around, but I needed it. . . . She helped me get my act together. . . . She set me straight. I think she saw my potential. . . . Now she's my favorite teacher. (13-year-old boy)

An influential model that further promotes the "likability" of a bully appears in the homes of millions—the television. Often, in television programs, bullying is disregarded or is reinforced by approval. In fact, violent behavior frequently is depicted in the media as a means of obtaining what one desires (Eron & Huesmann, 1984, as cited in Clarke & Kiselica, 1997). For boys and adolescent males, repeated exposure to violent television programs and movies reinforces the message delivered by society that it is acceptable to be aggressive (Clarke & Kiselica, 1997). Continual exposure to bullying—in the classroom, on television, in the movies, and in songs—may serve to desensitize individuals against the unpleasant effects of being bullied (Ross, 1996).

> Dennis Rodman, he's a likable bully. He's a big talker and pushes a lot of people around and can be physical at times, but people really like him. They think what he does is okay. . . . He does it all for attention. . . . At times I would like him. (14-year-old boy)

Rehabilitation efforts of mental health workers dealing with the problems of bullies and aggression generally yield poor results (Kazdin, 1987). If we could identify differences between likable and rejected bullies and determine how these differences develop, we might begin to design more effective interventions directed at these bullying role models. Attention could be given to interventions that would alter the reward systems now in place.

VICTIMS

Every day, thousands of children in the United States fall prey to aggressive acts by peers. As children, we commonly hear the rhyme "Sticks and stones will break my bones, but names will never hurt me"; nevertheless, among aggressive acts, name calling appears to be the most prevalent and devastating to its recipients (Besag, 1989). The effects of victimization are far reaching and expand into adulthood, severely traumatizing 14% of both boys and girls (Hoover et al., 1992). This trauma has been linked to depression, helplessness, and, in severe cases, the tragedy of suicide.

Schoolboy Philip C. was driven to his death by playground bullying. He hanged himself after being constantly threatened, pushed around, and humiliated by three of his classmates. (Olweus, 1993, p. 8)

Sometimes you feel like dying because you can't face up to it. (15-year-old boy)

The term *bullying* clearly implies a victim as part of the process, as well as ongoing events that inflict threat on the victim(s). Bullying may include physical threat as well as psychological fear (Horne et al., 1994). Victims have described bullying as including such behaviors as teasing, ridiculing, vandalizing property, and being physically violent (Hoover et al., 1992). A large portion of the literature on victims has focused on the nature of the victim's relationships. Victims seem to demonstrate low levels of popularity and few friends (Hoover & Hazler, 1991; Slee & Rigby, 1993). Olweus (1993) discovered that victims are teased, intimidated, threatened, degraded, dominated, hit, and kicked.

There's one kid, he's just annoying. He's like a white Steve Urkel [a character from the television show *Family Matters*]. . . . He just bothers you . . . he pisses you off. . . . I just want to say "Shut up. . . . Get out of my face." If I were a teacher I'd like to kick him out the door before he set foot in my classroom and say "Boy, what are you thinking. . . . Get out!" (14-year-old boy)

Boys tend to attribute victimization to the victim (Mellor, 1990; Ross, 1996): "Bullying is brought upon the person by himself. . . . He might start acting smart and the group might keep on slugging him and hitting him" (14-year-old boy, cited in (Mellor, 1990, p. 5). This "just world" attributional process, blaming the victim for being the victim, is a predominant attitude (Ross, 1996; Shaver, 1975). When the victim is blamed for the harm wrought upon him or her, it is not uncommon for children to assume that the problems are also regulated by the victim. Thus, children often fail to offer help to those being victimized (Ross, 1996).

It's not always the victim's fault. . . . Sometimes it is, though. (13-year-old boy)

Victims of aggression appear to be subjected to different types of bullying behavior as a result of their sex. Analysis of the perceptions of 103 male and 97 female adolescent victims demonstrated that verbal bullying was experienced more often by girls and that physically aggressive bullying was experienced more often by boys (Hoover et al., 1992). Additionally, a study conducted in the United Kingdom indicated that violence and threats were more often made against boys and social and verbal bullying against girls (Sharp & Smith, 1991).

It is commonly assumed that individuals who are victimized have certain external characteristics that separate them from their peers, such as wearing glasses, being over/underweight, or having freckles. The characteristics that have been found to be related to the identity of a victim, however, are internal ones of cautiousness, sensitivity, quietness, anxiety, and insecurity. The male victims are likely to be smaller in stature and physically weaker than other boys (Olweus, 1983, 1994). It is not unusual for these individuals to possess low self-esteem and view themselves in a negative light, thus seeing themselves as failures, stupid, and unattractive (Olweus, 1994). Olweus (1993, 1994) identifies these victims as passive or submissive victims. Passive victims are the most frequently occurring type. They are abandoned at school and often do not share a solid friendship with a single child in their class. They try to avoid conflict by staying out of harm's way and often display emotional outbursts (e.g., crying) in response to the fear and frustration of being bullied. Their behaviors indicate to others that they are weak and therefore incapable of retaliation when attacked or insulted (Olweus, 1993, 1994).

> The abuse I suffered in the American public schools from kindergarten to my senior year of high school created deep psychic scars with which I have struggled throughout my lifetime. These same scars are shared by many others. We will never forget that we were tortured and publicly humiliated. (Rofes, 1994, pp. 37-38)

Interviews with parents of male, passive victims revealed that these boys exhibited characteristics of cautiousness and sensitivity at an early age. These attributes, when combined with physical weakness, are likely to contribute to their victimization, because these boys are unable to stand up for and assert themselves in the peer group. Furthermore, data indicated that these victimized boys demonstrated close, overprotective relationships with their parents, especially the mother. It is this tendency toward overprotection that has been considered both a cause and a consequence of the bullying (Olweus, 1993).

A second, less common category of victims are the provocative victims who, as the bullies would say, "ask" for abuse by being overly active. Provocative victims are distinguished from passive victims by the fact that they, like bullies, are also aggressive (Pellegrini, 1995). Their behaviors may provoke irritation and tension, resulting in negative reactions from others. It is in these cases that bullies take it upon themselves to "educate" the victim on the group's values and ways (Olweus, 1993, 1994).

Although the provocative victims are understudied, Pellegrini (1995) posits that they are particularly deserving of attention by researchers because they are the most rejected members of their peer group (Perry et al., 1988) and, consequently, are at an increased risk for negative developmental outcomes, such as peer rejection and suicide (Pellegrini, 1995). Pellegrini's (1995) proposed project, framed by dominance (Dunbar, 1988) and social cognitive theories (Bandura, 1986), places emphasis on the provocative victims. He postulates that the provocative victims associate with bullies as a means to increase their social status, (i.e., increase their dominance status). In return, these victims receive positive reinforcement from the bullies (i.e., attention). Additionally, they may learn aggressive strategies by modeling the bullies' actions. Pellegrini further proposes that the provocative victims may employ these tactics with their less dominant peers. Thus, the provocative victims may employ aggression as a method by which to establish dominance in a social situation (Pellegrini, 1995).

Who do these children turn to? Mottoes such as "Stand up for yourself," Don't be a crybaby," and "Don't be a tattletale" often prevent children from seeking help when they are victimized. Approximately half of primary school children and 35% of high school students who are bullied seek assistance from a family member. Self-reports indicate that in 65% of the bullying incidents teachers fail to intervene or do so only "once in a while." It is interesting that the proportion increases to 85% in high schools (Besag, 1989). When questioned, teachers report feeling powerless and unskilled to handle bullying situations; thus, in most cases, the child is left to defend himself or rely on his peers to intervene (Moran, Smith, & Thompson, 1993). Interviews with students, however, illustrated that 50% do not stand up to bullies to protect their peers because they feel ill-equipped to do so or feel it is none of their business (Boulton & Underwood, 1992). Thus, ignoring actions of bullies further substantiates the victim's devaluation of himself and his feelings of worthlessness (Horne et al., 1994).

MYTHS AND MISCONCEPTIONS ABOUT BULLYING

It is often thought that bullying and victimization are a corollary of large classes and schools—the larger the class, the more elevated the problems of bullying and victimization. Investigation into this premise, using Norwegian survey data, has illustrated no significant relationship between the percentage of bullying incidents and the size of class or school. The size of a class or school appears to be of inconsequential importance in predicting the frequency of bullying (Olweus, 1993, 1994).

A common conviction bears that bullying is a consequence of competition and striving for successful performance in school. More specifically, some believe that aggressive behavior of bullies results from school-related failures and frustrations. Results of a longitudinal Swedish study failed to support this premise: There was no significant evidence that aggressive behavior in boys was a result of poor academic success (Olweus, 1983, 1994).

Another extensively held belief is that victimization is caused by external deviations; that those who are fat, wear glasses, or speak with an unusual dialect are prone to becoming victims. Empirical results have revealed that the boys who were victims of bullying were found to be no more externally deviant than the control group. It can be surmised that the role that external deviations play in regard to the origin of bully/victim problems is quite small (Olweus, 1994).

Another frequent misperception is that bullying is likely to occur on the journey to and from school rather than at school. Bullying at school, however, tends to occur at twice the rate of bullying when traveling (Horne et al., 1994). Another misconception is that adults who know about the bullying take steps to prevent it. Olweus (1993) found that in the primary schools, only 35% of the time did a teacher become involved, whereas at the secondary level, the rate of involvement was only 15%. An additional misconception about bullying is that students will outgrow aggressive behavior as they age. This, however, does not appear to be the case. Patterson (1982, 1986) demonstrated that highly aggressive children tend to become even more aggressive as they age, unless there is some external intervention to reduce the level of aggression.

FAMILY CHARACTERISTICS OF BULLIES

Family characteristics and child-rearing conditions associated with bullying have been identified by multiple authors. Some attribute the bully's aggression to a compensatory behavior resulting from feeling inferior and inadequate (Besag, 1989). This, however, does not generally seem to be the case. Instead, it has been reported that the bully at school is often the victim at home, and this child has caretakers who use physical means of discipline; provide little supervision; are hostile, rejecting, and inconsistent in their parenting; lack effective problem-solving skills; and teach their children to strike back when provoked (Floyd, 1985, cited in Horne et al., 1994). Aggressive children tend to have family members who use ineffective discipline practices that include coercion, inconsistency, and harsh punishment (Patterson, 1986).

Additional characteristics found in the families of bullies have been identified by Olweus (1993). First, the parents are likely to display a lack of warmth or caring toward their children as well as a negative attitude toward parenting in general. Second, they often set inadequate limits on their children, provide insufficient supervision, and tolerate aggressive behaviors in their children. Third, the family has a propensity toward implementing corporal punishment, physical responses (e.g., hitting), and violent emotional outbursts. Olweus also identified a fourth characteristic—the temperament of the child. Children with poor impulse control and who anger easily are more likely to develop bullying behavior than children who have more stable emotional reactions.

> Raymond was incarcerated at the Youth Detention Center, where his good sense of humor and talkativeness made him popular with others at the institution, including fellow incarcerated youth and the officers. He bragged, "Everyone in my family loves to fight. That's why I'm in here. I love to fight." (Horne et al., 1994, p. 2)

Patterson (1986) indicated that the quality of early family interactions may be influenced by intraindividual factors. The characteristics of the aggressive child who bullies include temperament, genetic predisposition, and cognitive abilities (Horne, 1991; Norsworthy & Horne, 1994). Biological and genetic components contribute to some children behaving more actively than other children and to some children having temperament characteristics that provoke them to be more difficult as infants. Although not all active children become bullies, often children who are highly active at birth develop more aggressive behavioral patterns. This genetic predisposition, when fused with temperament issues, may result in children who are more difficult to parent than other children (Horne et al., 1994; Horne & Socherman, 1996). Additionally, aggressive children may perceive social cues quite differently from their peers and thus distort the intended meaning. For example, an aggressive child is likely to interpret an accidental shove by another as intended hostility and, in turn, is likely to react in an aggressive manner (Horne & Socherman, 1996). Hence, according to the researchers, temperament, genetic predisposition, and cognitive abilities appear to affect the manner in which children are responded to and how they respond to their environment.

> Bullying starts in the environment, neighborhoods, and families. . . . Some people grow up in homes where they learn to push others around so they think it's okay. (13-year-old boy)

The development of bullying behavior in boys and adolescent males may also be influenced by a number of environmental/systemic factors. These catalysts include parental pathology, antisocial behavior in the family, and inadequate family resources. In addition, marital conflict, single-parent households, and low-income may all contribute to the development of bullying behavior.

> I think we learn to be bullies. (12-year-old boy)

To keep a balance within the family structure in the home, children may learn to adopt the roles of "bully" and "victim" (Minuchin, 1988). Bullies and victims have been shown to have distinguishable home environments that are a causal factor in their school roles. Problems that occur within the home can prevent children from learning appropriate social skills required to be successful in other settings (Horne & Socherman, 1996). Bullies are likely to endure hostility in their homes and fail to learn skills related to negotiating, making group decisions without physical force, and learning to empathize (Hoover & Hazler, 1991; Horne et al., 1994). The primary caregiver often exhibits a lack of involvement with and aggressiveness toward the child, and usually utilizes inconsistent punishment and physical force. Parents of aggressive children who fight frequently or are involved in a conflictual divorce often fail to provide a warm and nurturing environment where the child can develop secure attachments. In addition, they may encourage the child to avoid being a "wimp" and to utilize violence and aggression to combat their issues with others (Loeber & Dishion, 1984).

Victims' families represent the opposite extreme from aggressive families. These families tend to be overinvolved and enmeshed. This enmeshment prohibits the child from discovering his own strengths, building confidence in his abilities, and becoming independent (Minuchin, 1974). The mothers of male victims tend to be overinvolved with the child's life, and often victims have a negative perception of their father (Olweus, 1993).

CULTURAL FACTORS

Bullying is an international phenomenon, occurring in most societies (Munthe & Roland, 1989). It has been recognized as a problem and studied in countries such as Scandinavia, the Netherlands, England, the United States, Canada, Australia, and Japan. Although bullying appears to exist across cultures, specific forms of bullying may differ from society to society. The characteristics of physical strength and aggression, however, apply universally to bullying behavior (Hoover et al., 1992).

The most extensive studies on bullies have been conducted in Scandinavian countries by Olweus. England and Japan have followed by engaging in research and intervention on bullying activities. The United States has directed less attention to this problem. Horne and colleagues (1994) attribute this minimal focus to the history of that country. America was settled by people who often did not fit in their country of origin. Many of the early settlers who came from Europe were adventurous and aggressive explorers or prisoners expelled from their home country because of their criminal history. Lawlessness was common early on, and aggressive behavior was often accepted as the norm. In fact, many of the American folk heroes could be described as people who abused the law and demonstrated aggressive and bullying behaviors (Horne et al., 1994).

Cultural context undoubtedly influences the identification of certain behaviors as bullying. In America, societal norms are highly influential in bullying. To some extent, Americans express admiration for the bully, for that person who demonstrates strength, individualism, aggression, and risk taking. Common themes in American schools often reinforce the toleration of bullying: "Don't tattle. Don't turn anyone in. Stand up for yourself. Mind your own business" (Horne et al., 1994, p. 6). With the "survival of the fittest" credo so prevalent in our culture, it is no wonder that some feel the weak deserve to be picked on. Acceptance of this aggressive behavior as part of social norms and the theme of "blaming the victim for being a victim" adversely affects many social systems, so much that it tends to reduce commitment to aiding those who experience the wrath of bullies (Horne et al., 1994).

In summary, there appear to be biological contributions to aggression and violence in many boys, beginning with highly active children whose temper lends itself to bullying. Furthermore, the home life of many boys models the behavior and provides support for maintaining an aggressive posture, and then the school system often ignores the bully/victim dyad with the expectation that children will work out their problems. Finally, the socialization of males in America often provides rewards and encouragement for bullying behavior, and at school the stronger children are often looked up to for their strength and size. Many cultural messages focus on boys developing a role of aggression, among them "Don't tread on me," "When the going gets tough, the tough get going," "I don't get mad, I get even," and "If you're looking for trouble, you're looking in the right direction."

<u>INTERVENTIONS</u>

Counselors, psychologists, educators, and other professionals are witness to the deep scars borne by boys and male adolescents who are victimized. Thus, the question is what can be done to prevent or reduce these acts of bullying as well as aid the victims. Sometimes, children have their own conceptions about what needs to be done:

I think the only way to handle it is to fight it out. . . . If they both want to fight, let them fight. You don't need to break it up because if you do when they get home they are going to bring out guns and stuff. (14-year-old boy)

Sometimes if you try to acknowledge the bully you'll find that they are a different person than you originally thought . . . once you get to know them they can become your friend. (13-year-old boy)

Numerous recommendations have been made for utilizing school-based programs for confronting the issue of bulling. Olweus's school-based intervention program was the first one focusing on bully/victim problems to be evaluated by systematic research. This intervention program was constructed to have an impact on the school environment, the classroom, and the individual participants. Olweus (1994) stressed the importance of working on all these levels. The core components, which are significant for implementation of the program, are cited by Olweus (1994, p. 1186) as follows:

    I. General prerequisites
       Awareness and involvement on the part of adults
   II. Measures at the school level
       Questionnaire survey
       School conference day
       Better supervision during recess
  III. Measures at the class level
       Class rules against bullying
       Class meetings
  IV. Measures at the individual level
       Serious talks with bullies and victims
       Serious talks with parents of involved students

Olweus's (1994) program was implemented in 42 Norwegian schools, and its effects were monitored in a sample population of 2,500 male and female students in the 4th through 7th grades. Analyses indicated marked reductions in levels of bully/victim problems 8 months and 20 months postintervention. This intervention program significantly affected existing victimization while concurrently reducing the number of new victims (Olweus, 1994).

Researchers have suggested that school counselors intervene via implementation of cooperative goal structuring, peer tutoring, and elevating public opposition toward bullying. Counselors may also initiate activities that teach democratic social behaviors and by placing bullies with older children and victims with younger children (Hoover & Hazler, 1991). Researchers have encouraged the use of peer solutions over adult solutions, because adult solutions have been shown to be less powerful change agents than solutions generated by the pupils (Sharp & Smith, 1991). Further recommendations to curtail bullying include the use of student-directed bully courts, improved supervision on the playground, and employment of assertiveness training for the victims (Whitney, Nabuzoka, & Smith, 1992).

Several scholars have recommended the use of family-based interventions. For bullies, family counseling, with a primary focus on cohesion and family structure, has been suggested (Oliver, Oaks, & Hoover, 1994). For victims, researchers have recommended a family counseling approach aimed at differentiating family members and discontinuing overprotective communications (Oliver et al., 1994). Additionally, researchers have investigated the effectiveness of social learning family therapy in maintaining the treatment changes in families of aggressive boys. The intervention resulted in significant increases in positive child behaviors at home and at school. After a 9- and 12-month follow-up analysis, results demonstrated that behavioral changes were maintained (Sayger, Horne, Walker, & Passmore, 1988).

SYSTEMIC SCHOOL INTERVENTIONS

"Bullying will continue to be tolerated in schools until there is a philosophical shift among school personnel about how they view and respond to coercive behavior" (Clarke & Kiselica, 1997, p. 320). The message sent by school counselors, staff, and administrators should be a "nontolerance policy"; that is, no bullying will be tolerated. Such policies prohibiting bullying need to be enforced on a consistent basis, as this will amplify the effectiveness of a schoolwide intervention (Clarke & Kiselica, 1997).

Interventions that involve the entire school can yield desirable effects; however, they take a great deal of time, energy, and commitment from those involved. Two programs designed to assist schools in prevention and reduction of bullying are "Action Against Bullying" and "Bully-Proofing Your School." The Action Against Bullying program was developed by the Scottish Council for Research in Education for use in school antibullying initiatives (Johnstone, Munn, & Edwards, 1992). The program was designed to help raise awareness about bullying and to suggest ways to combat it. As identified by the Scottish researchers, the single most important tactic to prevent bullying is for the school to have a clear policy to which staff, pupils, and parents are committed. Research shows that having a policy helps to combat bullying if everyone knows what the policy is, the policy is applied consistently, and everyone believes in the policy. Several areas should be attended to when developing a policy. First, if the school is interested in developing a practical policy to tackle bullying, an open, agreed definition of bullying is important—What counts as bullying? An example is that "any behavior which is the illegitimate use of power in order to hurt others is bullying behavior." Second, the aims of the policy need to be clear: preventing bullying, dealing with bullying if it occurs, building on a school discipline policy, and fitting in with social education policy. Third, it needs to be decided what the policy will consist of—for example, raising awareness through the curriculum, giving pupils opportunities to talk about bullying in general, supervision of key areas of the school, procedures for investigating incidents, and guidelines for listening to the victims, witnesses, and bullies. Fourth, the responsibilities of the teacher, pupils, parents, and staff need to be established. Finally, those involved need to be encouraged to commit to the policy.

The following outline, as presented in Johnstone and colleagues (1992, p. 11), will assist those who want to prevent bullying in their schools.

I. Start with a policy
   A. Discuss what counts as bullying in your school; set up a policy
   B. Emphasize prevention
   C. Relate the policy to overall social education and good discipline policies
   D. Act on your policy
II. Know your school—Where might the bullying occur? Consider:
   A. A survey
   B. Spot checks
   C. Getting pupils to write about the school, with danger areas marked
III. Support your pupils
   A. Reassess how you look after your pupils in general. Consider:
      1. Do all pupils know that the school cares about bullying?
      2. Do all pupils know they should speak out?
      3. Is there an available and accessible person clearly designated to help pupils?
      4. What are your procedures for integrating a pupil new to the school?
   B. Think ahead about supporting both victims and bullies. Consider:
      1. Can the victims be trained to be more assertive or more skilled socially? Who can do this, how, and when?
      2. Can the bullies learn to control their aggression or be empathic? Who can help them do this, how, and when?
      3. Can other pupils be drawn in to help victims and bullies?
IV. Use the curriculum. Do messages about acceptable behavior get transmitted in the classroom? Examine:
   A. Your social education program
   B. Positive ways of getting the message across through drama, role play, discussion, and games
V. Communication
   A. Keep publicizing your policy to pupils and to all staff
   B. Keep parents informed and let them know that the school wants to prevent bullying, not just deal with bullying incidents
   C. Build on what your school values

Teachers should be prepared for what to do in bullying situations. The Action Against Bullying model provides recommendations for teachers that explain how to handle bullying (Johnstone et al., 1992, pp. 8-9). They include the following:

- ▶ Remain calm and stay in charge
- ▶ Take the incident or report seriously
- ▶ Take action as soon as possible
- ▶ Reassure the victim; do not make him feel inadequate or foolish
- ▶ Offer concrete help and advice, and support the victim
- ▶ Make it clear to the bully that you disapprove
- ▶ Encourage the bully to see the victim's point of view
- ▶ Punish the bully if you have to, but be very careful how you do this
- ▶ Explain clearly the punishment and why it is being given

Johnstone and colleagues (1992) recommend that school personnel take time to acquaint themselves with students beyond those in their own classes. The more that educators are familiar with students, the better supervision they can provide and the greater the likelihood of identifying troublemakers (Horne et al., 1994).

Furthermore, the authors recommend the use of Bully Courts. A Bully Court consists of children who review and evaluate complaints brought against a bully. Children who have been brought up on charges of bullying are required to appear before a panel of peers, who question and hear testimony from the victim, the accused bully, and witnesses. If the bully is found guilty, the peer panel recommends an appropriate punishment. Often, a teacher is present during the course of the trial to assist in monitoring the hearing (Horne et al., 1994; Ross, 1996). The court demonstrates to the bullies that fellow pupils disapprove of their behavior and that bullying in the school will not be tolerated. Although this can be a very powerful intervention, caution must be exercised because some students admire bullies, and the court could have a negative impact.

The second school-based intervention, called Bully-Proofing Your School, is a comprehensive approach (Garrity et al., 1994-1995). Bully-Proofing Your School provides a blueprint for a school to easily implement a bully-proofing program. It is designed to meet one specific criterion: to make the school environment both physically and psychologically safe for children. The program is process oriented and includes all the necessary materials (e.g., outlines, strategies, handouts, and transparencies) for the adoption of a schoolwide program against bullying. This program comprises five main components: (a) staff training, (b) student instruction, (c) support of the victims, (d) intervention with the bullies, and (e) working with parents.

Bully-Proofing Your School is a preventive approach whose emphasis is on the positive rather than the punitive. Bullying behaviors are dealt with directly in a "matter-of-fact" fashion; that is, bullies are held accountable for their actions. The main goal of the program is to shift the balance of power and fear within the entire school. Understanding the theme of shifting the balance of power to the silent majority of students is critical to the success of the program. Because the silent majority view and experience acts of bullying but lack the confidence to take action, the development of skills and knowledge regarding bullying is essential (Garrity et al., 1994-1995).

The classroom curriculum is a key component of this systemic approach, which educates all participating students about bullying: what it is, what one can do if one is the victim of a bully, and what one can do if one sees another student being bullied. The classroom curriculum consists of eight weekly sessions in which the following topics are discussed: the concept of bullying, rules for bully-proofing the classroom, teaching strategies for the victims, practicing strategies for the victims, teaching strategies for the helpers, practicing strategies for the helpers, skill building, and review and reinforcement of all the skills presented in the classroom curriculum (Garrity et al., 1994-1995).

The Bully-Proofing Your School program is easy to implement and can be completed within a 2- to 3-month time frame. The reader is encouraged to refer to Garrity and colleagues' (1994-1995) manual for additional information.

Acknowledging that there is a problem of bullying within a school often is difficult. Admitting that there is a problem implies that the administrators have failed to address a problem. The administration may have ignored problems related to bullying for a variety of reasons: they may not know what to do; if they attempt to intervene, the aggression may escalate; and they may not view bullying as a problem (Horne & Socherman, 1996).

The first step is to acknowledge that the problem exists (Horne et al., 1994). This recognition frequently comes from the parents who refuse to accept their children being harassed. Parents may find it necessary to go beyond their child's school and extend their complaints to those at a higher level on the hierarchy, who may be more responsive (Horne & Socherman, 1996).

Once the problem is recognized, it may be helpful to work with representatives from the school community—students, teachers, administrators, and parents—to clearly define the nature of the problem. It also may be useful to generate a common definition of bullying as well as to cite examples of bullying (Horne & Socherman, 1996).

After the school community has established a definition and identified examples of bullying, the group needs to develop a plan of action to address the problem. The following are some recommended guidelines (Horne & Socherman, 1996):

- ▶ Tolerate absolutely no bullying behavior in the school environment.
- ▶ Establish an educational program to share in classrooms.
- ▶ Provide more effective monitoring of the school environments, including lunchrooms, hallways, and playgrounds.
- ▶ Institute a new "honor code" that reverses the traditional "not telling" code and replaces it with the expectation that reporting bullying is not only a good thing to do but also is expected as a means of increasing the safety and security in the entire school.
- ▶ Develop a set of consequences for bullies, one that is well publicized and known to all. Be consistent in applying the consequences; at the same time, recognize that bullies are often victims of abuse in their homes and communities, and provide interventions that will help them learn to manage the system better or find ways to assist them in getting out of the aversive situation.

► Establish a parenting component that provides an avenue for educators to work with parents of bullies. Involve them in the educational plan to reduce bullying behavior and help them understand the importance of reducing aggression and violence within the school community.

► Develop a plan to assist victims in learning more effective ways of managing themselves, including social skills training and assertiveness training.

► Work with parents of victims to help them learn ways to assist their children in their attempts to thwart the bullying episodes. Family support is extremely important in facilitating victims' movement from the victim role.

► Provide ongoing training and support for teachers and other educators to help them understand the importance of the program and methods for carrying it out. It is important to point out here that if a bullying program is implemented in the school, the rules apply to teachers as well as students. A major block to effective bullying programs involves teachers who bully students in the classroom and on the playground.

ADDITIONAL SKILLS AND SCHOOL-BASED INTERVENTIONS

To assist students in becoming aware that aggression is not and will not be acceptable, alternative ways of interacting can be learned. It is not sufficient to only provide punishment or consequences for bullying; we must also teach students effective alternatives to bullying. Some excellent programs currently being utilized teach alternative skills such as mediating and negotiating skills, refusal, empathy training, moral development processes, effective communication, problem solving, life-management skills, self-control, and rational decision making (Horne et al., 1994).

An additional tactic to aid in the reduction of bullying is the use of a "contact phone." This is an open line of communication available for students or others concerned about bullying to call; they can talk with a counselor, school psychologist, or other helping professional. The "contact phone" provides an opportunity for students to anonymously share their concerns and describe bullying situations they have encountered. It provides an opportunity for the student to talk with an adult about the problem as well as develop effective plans for handling the situation (Horne et al., 1994).

Another method to consider is cooperative learning. This intervention requires teachers to develop learning plans that require a group to work together to achieve solutions to an assigned task. It is preferable for the task group to be heterogeneous. This composition can teach bullies to work with less powerful students so that both can benefit. The success of each depends on the success of all; thus it is likely that the group will work more closely as a team (Horne et al., 1994).

INDIVIDUAL INTERVENTIONS

INITIATING CONTACT AND ESTABLISHING
RAPPORT WITH BULLIES

An important prerequisite to doing effective work with boys and adolescent males who are bullies is attitude. You have to like kids and have a belief that they are doing the best they can under the conditions they face, and that they have the potential to live differently if they are provided appropriate learning opportunities. If you do not have this orientation, then referral to others who may be more open to the bullies is highly recommended. If you as a teacher, counselor, therapist, or other helping person are so engaged in anger or fear that you cannot be open to providing a facilitative learning environment, you need to engage the services of someone else who may be more open to working with bullies. Fear and anger only block the development of a therapeutic experience. This is not to say that you cannot work with bullies, and you may have to if you are the only resource person available, but you must be aware that the attitude you bring to the relationship will determine whether the experience is therapeutic or merely a power struggle. You can change children's behavior by winning the power struggles with them in the short run, but such struggles seldom create permanent change.

Major components of helping bullies include teaching them self-control skills, providing them with social skills training, and helping them to take others' perspectives. The same is true for you, the change agent. We refer to this as "setting up for success" and believe that you have the opportunity of setting up for failure by engaging in a power struggle or of setting up for success by controlling your own feelings, using effective intervention skills, and understanding the worldview of the bully—why he thinks he behaves as he does. Ultimately, you do have the power—you can remove him from the environment by expelling him, locking him up, or taking other drastic actions—but that does not solve the problem.

One theme that counselors develop regarding bullies stems from their early experiences with bullies. Some avoid them because they see the bully as dangerous or fearful. Bullies pick up on this fear, just as a dog recognizes fear when a stranger approaches. Another mode is to not be intimidated by bullies because you are being bigger and stronger. One teacher, referring to his early experiences with bullies, said this: "Yea, though I walk through the Valley of the Shadow of Death, I shall fear no evil, for I am the meanest son-of-a-bitch in the Valley." He actively sought the opportunity for power clashes with bullies and modeled bullying behavior in the process. A third mode of being is to understand bullies, use social skills to establish rapport, and enlist the bullies' assistance in effecting change.

The third mode of interacting and engaging bullies involves having an "invitational" approach and owning the problem. The counselor might say something like the following:

Butch, we need to talk. I would like for you to talk with me about what's going on between you and Willy. You see, I've got a problem, and that problem is I am responsible for everyone in the school, and the way you have been intimidating Willy cannot continue. We have to find a way to fix this. I would like you to come to talk with me about this now.

This approach requires firmness, commitment, and willingness to listen. Bullies often feel they are being singled out and treated unfairly. You have to be able to communicate that fairness means allowing the bully to talk and share his perspective, but it also means that what happens has to be fair to all involved: the bully, the victim, and the others involved, including yourself. It often means explaining that "I like you, Butch, but this just can't keep happening. It is important for us to develop a plan so that you can be okay and keep being a leader with your friends but not hurt other people in the process. You have to learn to understand that what you do hurts Willy."

In the process of interacting with the bully, you should use a firm and controlled voice, have direct eye expression (an important demonstration of who is the alpha leader), and provide a way out of the dilemma. It is important to not lock the bully into a corner; everyone loses in that situation. Part of your discussion with him communicates that he is worth the time and energy you are putting forth, and that you are willing to work with him specifically because he is important and strong, but he is using his strength in the wrong way, and you believe he has the capacity to learn to use it more effectively.

PERSPECTIVE-TAKING SKILLS

A number of programs have been developed to help boys and adolescent males learn more effective methods for managing anger and bullying behavior. These include Goldstein's development of specific programs for children, including *Skillstreaming the Elementary School Child* (McGinnis & Goldstein, 1984), *Skillstreaming the Adolescent* (Goldstein, Sprafkin, Gershaw, & Klein, 1980), *Aggression Replacement Training* (Goldstein & Glick, 1987), and *The Prepare Curriculum* (Goldstein, 1988). Each of these programs provides leaders with instruction on how to teach children self-control skills, decision-making skills, and social interaction procedures. A very important component for each program is helping bullies and other children with behavior problems to take the perspective of other children. One finding from the literature on attachment and bonding is that children who have failed to develop an attachment relationship with a parent or other significant adult, and who are aggressive, fail to develop empathy with other children. They lack the ability to take the perspective of other children, to experience the world through others' eyes, and to appreciate the fear or pain experienced by others. Others' perspective taking thus is a very important component of treating bullies.

THERAPY WITH THE AGGRESSIVE BULLY

Ross (1996) recommends considering the aggressive bully's behavior within the context of Lazarus's (1966) theory. "Ambiguous actions by others, which most children would consider inconsequential, often are rapidly appraised by the bully as stressors that are threatening and controllable, a combination that within the bully's frame of reference merits direct action" (Ross, 1996, p. 45). In the case of the aggressive bully, the goal of therapy is to assist the bully in shifting from aggression-based appraisals to assertive ones. Thus, intervention should aim to alter both the speed and the content of his appraisals. Techniques such as punishment (e.g., deprivation of privileges and peer disapproval) combined with rewards for nonaggressive responses are recommended (Ross, 1996).

THERAPY WITH THE PASSIVE BULLY

The problem for many passive bullies is that their admiration for aggressive bullies and their need to be affiliated with them bias their appraisal of situations so that they, too, see danger that is often nonexistent (Ross, 1996). The passive bully needs changes that will facilitate peer acceptance of him, such as increased confidence and self-esteem, social and friendship skills, improved academic and athletic performance, and assertiveness. Before attention can be directed toward implementing these changes, the passive bully's desire to affiliate with the aggressive bully must be minimized. Live and symbolic modeling procedures can be utilized to illustrate that the aggressive bully is not a favorable model (Ross, 1996). To increase the success of this intervention, it is important to include the parents and encourage their cooperation.

GROUP INTERVENTIONS

Group interventions can aid in the reduction of bullying. Using a small group format, as opposed to working with an individual student, has several advantages (Garrity et al., 1994-1995). Groups are more efficient in terms of time, and the format provides an increased potential for learning, because several students are encouraged to share their experiences. When structuring a group, it is important to keep in mind that a heterogeneous group, one comprising both bullies and victims, will function more therapeutically than a group consisting solely of bullies. In a mixed group, the victims and bullies can learn to talk to each other. Furthermore, the heterogeneous group may provide the bully with a chance to experience the victim's abuse firsthand through talk therapy as well as role playing and other techniques. In contrast, a homogeneous group is not recommended because bullies may function to reinforce one another, thus perpetuating the behavior. Also, because bullies are good at blaming others and pointing out errors made by others, they are likely to confront one another within the group. This can be beneficial at times; however, it may also escalate into a negative group process and contribute to the maintenance of the bullying behaviors.

It is, however, acceptable to conduct a group for victims of bullies. These individuals can share their experiences, thus allowing them to realize that their experiences are by no means unique. It is preferable to keep the group "same gender" because boys may be embarrassed about describing their failure to cope with bullying episodes and their feelings of despair. The goal of the group is to have the victims become competent in coping with the type of bullying they are experiencing. Because boys generally engage in direct and physically aggressive bullying, it appears that a male group would be more conducive to achieving this goal. It is recommended that the group convene for at least 12 sessions, preferably 20, of approximately 1 hour each (Ross, 1996).

A major objective of the support group for victims is to provide reassurance that the victims are not alone and that others share the same experiences. This is one of Yalom's (1985) main therapeutic factors of group therapy—universality. The group experience provides the children with the opportunity to disclose personal experiences and feelings while other group members let the child know that they understand how awful the victimization experience is because they too share the same feeling (Ross, 1996).

In addition to the empathic support provided, the group also serves as an educational force assisting the victims to change their behavior to decrease the likelihood of being bullied. Skills and strategies that should be taught include protective strategies (e.g., how not to look like a victim), use of nonvictim body language (e.g., walking confidently), assertiveness skill, and social skills (Ross, 1996). Leaders should keep in mind that a variety of teaching methods will best serve the needs of group members. Role-play and symbolic modeling using videos and fictional accounts of bullying, combined with discussions, are recommended to facilitate the sessions (Ross, 1996).

USE OF BIBLIOTHERAPY TO INCREASE AWARENESS OF BULLYING

A technique becoming prevalent in the classroom is the use of bibliotherapy. Having access to books that narrate stories of differing forms of bullying, social exclusion, extortion, racism, prejudice, sexual harassment, and so on can assist in encouraging discussion of these topics as well as reports of bullying that children have experienced (Ross, 1996). Bibliotherapy, also known as bibliocounseling, can help children in several ways. Children unable to verbalize their thoughts and feelings may find them expressed in books. From selected stories, children can learn alternative solutions to problems and new ways of behaving. Furthermore, by reading about others who have experienced victimization similar to their own, children may not feel so alone or different (Berg-Cross & Berg-Cross, 1976).

In an article citing the benefits of bibliocounseling for children, Watson (1980) suggests that children may become psychologically and emotionally involved with characters they read about. Vicarious experiences through books can be similar to the child's own thoughts, feelings, attitudes, behavior, or environment. Directed reading can lead to expression of feelings or problem solving. Watson lists the goals of bibliotherapy as (a) teaching constructive and positive thinking, (b) encouraging free expression concerning problems, (c) helping people analyze their attitudes and behaviors, (d) looking at alternative solutions, (e) encouraging the client to find an adjustment to the problem not in conflict with society, and (f) allowing clients to see the similarity of their problems to those of others.

When employing bibliocounseling, counselors will want to discuss stories with the children who read them. Discussion focused around characters' behaviors, feelings, thoughts, and relationships, and about causes and effects, will be more effective than just asking the child to relate the story. Counselors can guide children to see the relationships and applications of the story to their own lives (Berg-Cross & Berg-Cross, 1976). It is assumed that once children have enough information about a problem, their attitudes and behaviors will change (Morgan, 1976).

USE OF ROLE-PLAY

Role-play can be used to aid children in acquiring an understanding of their behavior as well as increasing their capability to empathize with others. The role-play experience allows children to feel safe; it is a nonthreatening situation, one step removed from real-life interactions (Ross, 1996). In a typical session, the counselor provides a bully/ victim scenario and requests the bully to act as the victim while another student acts as the bully. By stepping into the role of the victim, the bully can experience the victimization first-hand. This increased awareness may serve to sensitize the bully to the harmful effects inflicted on the victim.

THE NO BLAME APPROACH TO BULLYING

The "No Blame Approach to Bullying" was developed by Maines and Robinson (1992). This counseling procedure is built on the assumption that "bullying is an interaction that demonstrates dominance and status at the expense of others; a change to more positive values on the part of the bullies is essential if the bullies are to abandon their antisocial behavior and coexist peacefully with the victim(s)" (Ross, 1996, p. 148). The critical components in executing this change in bullies consists of no blame or punishment of the perpetrators and no policing of the environment. Ross (1996, p. 149) provides an outline of the "No Blame" procedure:

1. Sit down with the victim and listen carefully to his story. Take notes and use prompts as necessary. Be sure to get the facts about the bullying incident so that when you talk to the bullies, you can consider the discrepancies in the two accounts.

2. Pay particular attention to the victim's account of the effects of the bullying on him. Note these in detail, and encourage him to provide details, either in writing or by drawing pictures.

3. Set up a meeting of those involved in the bullying. The optimum number is six or eight students. If there are only one or two perpetrators, try to include some students who saw the bullying and did not intervene.

4. Explain to the group that the victim has a problem., Tell his story clearly and in enough detail so that the group understands why he is upset.

5. Do not blame anyone. Merely state firmly that the members of the group are responsible and can do something about the problem. If some of the group were witnesses, suggest that they must have some ideas about what can be done even though they were not directly involved.

6. Arrange a meeting with each member of the group in about a week to find out how things are going. Convey a certainty that action will be taken by the group to help the victim.

7. Throughout this procedure, try to convey that those involved are basically good people and that they will be kind to the victim.

Research reveals 100% success with this method with primary school children and 97% success with secondary school students (Maines & Robinson, 1992; cited in Ross, 1996).

BEHAVIOR THERAPY: HINTS FOR SUCCESSFUL BEHAVIOR MANAGEMENT

Behavior modification techniques are based on empirically derived theory and have proved to be successful in the reduction and elimination of many childhood behavior problems (O'Dell, 1974), including childhood aggression. Employing behavioral strategies has several advantages, the first of which is that persons relatively unskilled in sophisticated therapy can be educated on the principles of behavior modification and can learn how to implement the treatment. This, in turn, allows for the practice of behavior therapy in more than one environment: Modification of the child's behavior is not limited to the confines of the counseling setting. Teachers, parents, and other adults can participate in the behavior modification. This implementation of behavioral strategies in the child's natural environment is an additional advantage of employing behavior therapy: It promotes setting generalization. Furthermore, the time required to train individuals to implement these behavior change strategies is minimal (O'Dell, 1974). The following are helpful strategies to assist in the management and modification of the bully's behavior:

I. Setting up for success
   A. Rearrange the environment
   B. Develop consistent routines
   C. Make commands and requests clear and polite
   D. Teach appropriate behavior
   E. Encourage treating others with respect
   F. Strengthen leader ties (parent/parent, teacher/principal, etc.)

II. Behavior change strategies: procedures for elimination
    A. Reinforcement of alternate behavior
        1. Use food, praise, or other reinforcer for the nonoccurrence of bullying behavior. Reinforce the child initially for a small period of time in which behavior does not occur and gradually lengthen the time period
        2. Successful when paired with time out or a punishment
    B. Removal of positive reinforcement
        1. Time out: Place child in time out contingent on bullying behavior
        2. Response cost: Loss of a reinforcer
    C. Punishment
        1. Overcorrection: Use restitutional overcorrection with bullying behavior. Have the child overcompensate for harm done (e.g., if a boy verbally abuses another child, have the boy make four positive comments about that other child)
        2. Reprimand
        3. Loss of privileges
        4. Logical consequences

IMPLICATIONS FOR TRAINING AND RESEARCH

TRAINING

A survey we completed recently indicated that the number one reason beginning teachers left the field of education was their frustration with children's behavior in the classroom and around the school. Of children's behavior problems, the number one difficulty was with aggression and acting out. As indicated at the beginning of this chapter, the individual and social costs of aggression in the school, family, and community are staggering, yet teachers and parents often are untrained and unskilled in how to work with acting-out children.

We believe that it is imperative for all schools to implement a training program for teachers and others in the school community to learn how to more effectively manage children's behavior. The training may be done by a school counselor, school psychologist, school social worker, administrator, or outside trainer; the important point is that we need to have this training widely available. Few graduate training programs, however, have addressed the problem; consequently there is little support for those most in need of help, and often, people in school systems seem to believe that it is someone else's responsibility to address the problem. Everyone should assume responsibility; as we have discussed, we believe that change occurs because of large-scale systemic interventions, and change therefore should involve all people engaged in the system. This instruction could occur through in-service training days for teachers but will most likely require an ongoing commitment covering several years.

Parents also need to have access to learning opportunities. Community agencies, churches, and neighborhood centers could provide the service, but this does not often happen. One of the reasons we focus so much on schools is that this is where children happen to be, and schools generally can get parents there too. Again, the difficulty is that so many fail to know whose problem bullying is and therefore wait for others to provide the training and services. In the meantime, the problem recurs and perpetuates itself. Training on managing bullying and other effective parenting skills should be a focus of the schools if community agencies are not providing the service. One program that effectively incorporates school and family involvement is FAST: Families and Schools Together (information is available from Lynn McDonald, Family Service Inc., 128 E. Olin Avenue, Madison, WI 53713).

RESEARCH

We know a great deal about bullying, but we still have much to learn. Research needs to investigate how changes occur and what maintains a change once it happens. A number of programs have been developed, as described in this chapter. Our own efforts are not always successful, however, and we may experience success in a short-term intervention but find that generalization and maintenance fail to occur. We do not yet know what all the variables are that influence the change process for bullies. Some children demonstrate considerable resilience to adverse conditions, but other children from what seem to be similar conditions become bullies. Why? We do not know the answers yet. Some teachers manage excellent behavior management skills with some children yet fail with others. Why? Some children who are small and appear to be likely victims of bullies fare very well; others are constantly picked on. Why?

Large-scale intervention evaluation programs need to examine what broad arrays of factors lead to success with some teachers, parents, and children but not with others. Such research requires a commitment that children are important and worthy of the time and energy the effort will take, that the victims deserve to feel safe and know they will be defended, and that everyone deserves the respect and dignity that go with living in a world secure from bullies.

CONCLUSION

The harsh reality of the bully/victim dyad is experienced by thousands of boys every day. Although it is unlikely that childhood bullying will be eliminated completely, there is reason to believe that with the cooperation of the schools, communities, teachers, educators, counselors, and students the problems can be reduced significantly. Schools can adopt collective remedies that will not only help the victims but also strengthen the relationship between parents, teachers, and pupils.

Bullying has been ignored too long. "Every [boy] should have the right to be spared oppression and intentional humiliation, in school and in society at large" (Olweus, 1993,

p. 48). This "democratic right" has been stripped away from many of today's youth. It is time to take the hallways back from the bullies. It is time for us to take responsibility as professionals and members of society to help create a safe learning environment where students are comfortable, feel confident, and are able to express themselves and their individuality.

We leave the reader with a memorable quotation from a 13-year-old boy's perspective related to bullying:

> It doesn't bother me if someone calls me a name . . . but if they start pushing you around you've got to stand up for yourself . . . no one else will protect you. . . . I've never been bullied to that point. I have been picked on though. If I get bullied, I don't have to fight, period. That's point blank. At home I fight a lot, but at school I don't do it because it is not in my best interest. I can't afford to get into trouble. I tell myself my future is important. . . . I want to go to college and stuff and if I have a bad record I will be judged by it in the future. I am always worried about what college I am going to get into and how I will be looked at. . . . That's important to me. . . . I always think, "What if I know someone who becomes famous?" I don't want to be known as the person who pushed them around.

HIGHLIGHTS OF CHAPTER 18

▶ Bullying occurs when a student intentionally and repeatedly harms another student, physically or psychologically, over time.

▶ Bullying is pervasive throughout the school system. Self-report surveys suggest that more than 70% of youth experience bullying during their academic careers. Approximately 14% of these youth believe their exposure to bullying has had a severe impact on their lives.

▶ There are two types of bullies: direct and indirect. Direct bullies commit aggressive attacks on their victims, such as hitting or kicking. Indirect bullies torment their victims by intentionally excluding or isolating them from their peers.

▶ Males have a greater propensity toward bullying than females. The bully is usually an older member of a peer group and tends to be viewed as powerful.

▶ Bullies do not typically outgrow their aggressive behavior. Most bullies, in fact, become more aggressive over time if they do not receive an external intervention focused on increasing their social skills and reducing their aggression.

► The bully is often the victim within his home environment. His parents tend to use physical means of discipline, provide little supervision, lack effective social skills, and be hostile and rejecting in their parenting style.

► Although the homes of bullies often lack warmth, the homes of victims tend to be the polar opposite. The victim's family tends to be enmeshed, which prevents the victim from establishing his independence and gaining confidence in his abilities.

► Family counseling is beneficial to bullies and victims. The bully and his family can benefit from therapy that focuses on problem solving and building family cohesion. Establishing boundaries and differentiating family members can prove beneficial for the victim and his family in therapy.

► Teaching students alternatives to bullying is essential. Numerous programs that teach skills such as mediation and negotiation, empathy building, effective communication, problem-solving abilities, life skills management, self-control, and decision making can provide the bully with personal resources to overcome the need to bully.

► Counselors, family members, and school personnel can use an invitational approach to assist bullies. This approach requires firmness, commitment, and a willingness to listen. Do not be intimidated by the bully; he can use this to his advantage. Instead, allow him to share his perspective in an attempt to understand his worldview and to enlist his assistance in producing a change in his behavior.

19

Counseling the Juvenile Offender

GEORGIA B. CALHOUN
BRIAN A. GLASER
CHRISTI L. BARTOLOMUCCI

Josh, a 15-year-old White male who is described by his teachers as a loner, is being held in a juvenile detention facility following his arrest at school. He is charged with possession of a firearm and attempted murder. Josh, who is normally very quiet, had recently found himself attracted to Carla, a gregarious and very popular young lady. Although she was initially polite to Josh and seemed interested in him, she had rejected an invitation from him to attend the upcoming homecoming dance. Several peers at school had learned of the invitation/rejection and began taunting Josh about Carla. The next day, Josh brought a loaded pistol to school, and when the taunting continued, he responded by pulling the gun out of his backpack and beginning to shoot. Fortunately, the bullets hit no one, and a teacher was able to tackle Josh and hold him until the police arrived.

Steven is referred to the juvenile court because of chronic, persistent truancy. The young man, despite warnings from the court about the consequences of missing school, continues to feign illness as a means of avoiding the middle school environment. The judge refers the child and his family to a local counselor who immediately recognizes school phobia.

Jason, an obese African American youth, is charged with simple battery following an altercation with a neighbor in which he used a ceramic planter to strike his victim on the head. The judge, a bit confused by the normally docile youth's behavior, refers him to a counselor for a consultation. The results indicate a youth who has been physically and emotionally terrorized by neighbors and peers because of issues related to his weight and effeminate mannerisms.

Bobby, a 16-year-old high school freshman, is arrested at school and taken to the local detention center following an altercation in which he threatened to kill the associate principal, Mrs. Dalton. School records reveal that, prior to this outburst, Bobby had perfect attendance with no disciplinary infractions. Bobby's mother indicates that the current misbehavior is not at all typical of her son and requests the services of a counselor to help sort things through. She reports that she has been a single mother to her only son for more than 14 years, until 3 weeks ago when she married a retired Air Force officer. The remarriage was followed by a move to a new home. The counselor finds that the incident at school was precipitated by Mrs. Dalton informing Bobby that he has not made the grades to ensure his promotion to the 10th grade.

Juvenile delinquency has many faces. From truancy to firearm possessions and from shoplifting to battery, a great deal of variability exists in those who either episodically or chronically find themselves involved in the juvenile court system. Those who work with these youth never cease to be amazed at the uniqueness of individuals, situations, and case presentations that so often fly in the face of the popular stereotypical perception of them as juvenile delinquents. This should not be construed as a celebration of, or as an apology for, these youth; rather, it is simply our observation of the complexity of circumstances and the multitude of pathways that have been involved in many a youth's entanglement with the juvenile justice system.

THE ISSUE OF DELINQUENCY

Adolescence is characterized as a period of exploration and experimentation with a variety of roles and behaviors as youth attempt to define their identity. These roles and behaviors may be benign and are necessary for the youth to become well adjusted adults. Dryfoos (1997), however, suggests that 50% of youth engage in at least two or more risky behaviors. This type of experimentation commonly indicates turmoil within the youth and their environment; for a large number of youth, it results in delinquency.

Clearly, juvenile delinquency is a widespread societal problem that threatens the well-being of families and communities throughout the country. Some statistics bear this out. The Office of Juvenile Justice and Delinquency Prevention (OJJDP, 1998) reported that U.S. law enforcement agencies in 1996 made an estimated 2.9 million arrests of persons under the age of 18. Delinquent behavior during childhood and early adolescence presents a major and costly problem for society. Recent statistics from the U.S. Department of Justice indicate that approximately 2 million children and adolescents in the United States were involved in the juvenile court system in 1996. Frequently, delinquency reports focus on the prevalence of male delinquency. Although the increasing presence of female juvenile offending cannot be ignored, 74% of all youth who adjudicate delinquent are male.

In general, the adolescent population is becoming more dangerous, posing a threat to themselves and the larger society. Of particular concern is the dramatic rise in violent offenses committed by adolescents (OJJDP, 1998). The rate of violent juvenile crime increased by 67% between 1986 and 1995. The rate of homicides committed by juveniles increased by 90% during this same time period (OJJDP, 1998). The age range of juvenile offenders is also increasing.

Juvenile offenses have serious consequences to society and to the youth themselves. Esbensen and Huizinga (1991) suggest that the probability of youths' victimization increases proportionately with their involvement with delinquency. Approximately 86% of youth who commit one felony will experience a personal assault (Esbensen & Huizinga, 1991). In addition, the costs include material ones such as government funding required for repair or replacement of material goods and needed rehabilitative services for the victims. Each year, taxpayers pay more than $1 billion to ensure the effectiveness of the juvenile justice system (Feldman, Caplinger, & Wodarski, 1983). It is estimated that between 6% and 16% of males under the age of 18 exhibit diagnosable disorders of conduct. Approximately two thirds of those will continue to display antisocial behavior into adulthood (American Psychiatric Association [APA], 1994a). The delinquent behavior of problem children and adolescents is a prevalent and relatively stable condition that frequently requires therapeutic attention (Horne, Glaser, & Calhoun, 1998).

COUNSELING INTERVENTION

If establishing rapport with an adolescent is difficult, then establishing rapport with a juvenile offender is a task of Herculean proportions. Frequently, these youth do not come to counseling of their own free will and volition but, rather, on an order from the court. Overcoming preconceived notions of the counseling process is difficult initially but can be aided by attention to a few important details. In getting started, remember the importance of a good first impression. First, although a three-piece suit accompanied by a serious countenance might be a useful presentation style for first meetings with many counseling clients, a more casual appearance will be perceived by the vast majority of juvenile offenders as less intimidating and more inviting. Second, it is important to diffuse the notion that counseling is for "crazy" people. It is not uncommon to hear the refrain "I'm not crazy, why do I need counseling?" This is a primary concern for many who seek counseling services, but it is especially true for adolescents. Third, issues related to confidentiality need to be addressed directly and early in the first meeting. A number of people have become involved in the lives of these youth as a result of their involvement with the court system. Ground rules regarding the limits of confidentiality must be established and agreed to by all parties involved. These parties must include, but are not limited to, the counselor, the youth, his parents, the probation officer, and school officials. Fourth, it is helpful in working with these youth to expand beyond many of the traditional intervention techniques that are useful with other populations. Overreliance on verbal therapy and the 50-minute hour is a common mistake made by many clinicians. It is important to remember that these adolescents are particularly skeptical of adult advice and opinions (Sommers-Flanagan & Sommers-Flanagan, 1997). Communicating one's effective listening and an understanding of the youth's feelings without validating destructive behavior are essential in effective work with this population. The following scenario illustrates an effective beginning to a counseling relationship.

Peter, a 16-year-old male, is mandated by the juvenile judge for counseling services. Peter meets with his counselor for an intake session and makes it abundantly clear that he will not talk to the counselor and that he is not "crazy." The counselor explains the counseling process to Peter and gives Peter the power of choice to participate.

> **Counselor:** Peter, this time is for you. If you choose not to engage in the session, that is fine with me; however, according to the judge, you do need to be here each week. I will leave it up to you to talk about the real issues in your life. Because we do have to be together each week, why don't we talk about some issues that aren't so close to home, maybe like music or what you like to do after school.
>
> **Peter:** I am not falling for your lines. I told you I am not talking to you.
>
> **Counselor:** Peter, I respect that decision; however, I am still trying to find a way that we can spend our time each week together so you can meet the obligation of your probation. Any suggestions? Remember, I am here each week for you. This is your time to speak and be heard.
>
> **Peter:** Yeah, well I got lots to say. I will entertain you, but I am not talking about my family or that teacher at school!
>
> **Counselor:** Well, it seems like there must be some things going on at school and at home. I am here if you decide you'd like to talk about it today or in the future. Just feel free to bring it up when you are ready.
>
> **Peter:** I'd rather just stick with music today.

The rest of the session is spent discussing Peter's favorite song and its meaning to him. Peter gets into talking about the music and begins to discuss his desire to start his own band. The counselor suggests that he write lyrics for his music, maybe based on his personal experiences. Peter considers this idea, still presenting as guarded, and tells the counselor he may look into this because it could be a way to make some money. Peter comes to his weekly sessions with his songs, which begin to expose more of Peter's true self. Although Peter is resistant to talk about issues outside his music, the music provides a means to discuss Peter's major concerns without him feeling threatened by the counseling process.

SOCIAL SKILLS DEVELOPMENT

Social skills are defined as "socially acceptable learned behaviors that enable a person to interact with others that elicit positive responses and assist in avoiding negative response" (Elliott & Busse, 1991, p. 64). Social skills are learned primarily through modeling (Bandura, 1969; Goldstein, Sprafkin, Gershaw, & Klein, 1980). The histories of many delinquents share commonalties such as inconsistent and severe discipline, parental conflict, family violence, and alcoholism. Exposing children to these dysfunctional models of social skills contributes to delinquency. In these stressed environments, the skills these youth need to respond appropriately to others and their environment are not acquired. These youth do not have the opportunity to observe constructive ways of coping with feelings, particularly angry feelings, and the result is observable aggression and disruptive behavior.

According to Peters and McMahon (1996), social skills deficits include (a) reading unreadiness, (b) inability to recognize intense feelings, (c) inability to resolve disagreements, and (d) inability to follow rules. Aggressive children have been found to show a cognitive deficit in the social domain, often jump to conclusions, do not have solutions for problems, and use aggression as the answer (Dodge, 1993b). This often leads to the youth feeling alienated and rejected by family, friends, and teachers as well as feeling alienated from the values and standards of society (Peters & McMahon, 1996). Instead of acquiring proper social skills through positive peer and family relationships, these youth begin to develop their own values, which are often quite different from societal norms (Hawkins & Weis, 1985).

Literature reviews regarding social skills training and delinquency often begin with the work of Sarason and Ganzer (1973), who demonstrated that group application of social skills training with juvenile delinquents could be effective in increasing locus of control and reducing recidivism. Numerous studies provided further empirical support for social skills training with delinquents (Goldstein & Glick, 1987; Hazel, Schumaker, Sherman, & Sheldon-Wilder, 1981). The program by Hazel and colleagues (1981) was prototypical. It focused on eight essential skills: giving positive feedback, giving negative feedback, accepting negative feedback, resisting peer pressure, problem solving, negotiating, following instructions, and beginning conversations. LeCroy's (1994) program included 11 essential social skills and corresponding sessions:

1. Creating Positive Interactions;
2. Getting to Know Others: Starting Conversations;
3. Making Requests: Getting More of What You Want;
4. Expressing Your Feelings Directly;

   5. Getting Out: How to Say "No";
   6. Asserting Your Rights: Tell It Like It Is;
   7. Identifying How Others Feel: The Art of Empathy;
   8. Dealing With Those in Authority;
   9. Responsible Decision Making: Think About It;
  10. Learning to Negotiate: Conflict Resolution; and
  11. When You're in Need: Asking for Help.

When working with juvenile offenders, it is important to be aware that they often lack the skills that allow them to interact positively and nonaggressively with others. Spence (1982) isolated three potential mechanisms whereby skills deficits may influence delinquency: (a) Difficulties in developing and maintaining peer relations result in offending as a means of obtaining approval and status (shoplifting is often a result of this), (b) difficulties with peers and teachers at school lead to truancy and hence increased opportunities to offend, and (c) mismanagement of encounters with the police increases the likelihood of arrest and conviction (don't run when a police officer approaches).

ANGER MANAGEMENT

Many juvenile offenders have problems controlling their temper. Their frequent and often inappropriate displays of anger often lead them into the juvenile justice system and often interfere with their attempts to extricate themselves from the system. The frustration, confusion, and anger a youth feels is often displayed as aggressive or hostile behavior. Authority figures often respond to these angry displays by utilizing punishment. Moreover, although punitive responses are often effective, they fail to instruct the youth in alternative, prosocial responses. When children are unable to cope appropriately with their angry feelings, they are more likely to act out in the forms of violence, crime, substance abuse, depression, suicide, and self-destruction (Omizo, Hershberger, & Omizo, 1988).

When working with such a youth, a counselor must first focus on helping the youth define his anger and develop an arsenal of appropriate responses. In many cases, if an adolescent were able to identify his feelings of anger and had a well-developed pool of appropriate responses from which to draw, the likelihood of a violent outburst would be diminished. Counselors can increase the likelihood of a positive outcome by helping the youth develop self-discipline, internal controls, and alternative means of expressing anger (Omizo et al., 1988).

Counselors frequently find it helpful to focus the youth's attention on his goals and the degree to which an inappropriate expression of anger serves to sabotage such goals. This intervention often helps most when these youth feel justified in retaliatory behavior. By pointing out that the youth is giving over his autonomy and personal power for the sake of revenge or machismo, the counselor can help him gain a new appreciation of the benefits of controlling his anger. For example, the counselor may point out that responding to taunts with a fistfight might provide instant gratification, but the long-term outcome might be loss of an important privilege (playing sports, increased probation time, suspension from school, not being detained). An important component of this perspective is the notion that the youth ultimately is giving control for what happens to him to someone else.

Feindler and Guttman (1994) describe an intervention, called the Chill-Out Program, designed to help adolescents control their anger. Adolescents are taught to recognize, moderate, regulate, and prevent anger and its accompanying aggressive component and to implement problem-solving actions in response to interpersonal provocation. Youth are educated about (a) interaction between cognitive, physiological, and behavioral components of their anger experience; (b) the adaptive and maladaptive functions of their anger; (c) the situational triggers that provoke their anger; (d) the concept of choice and self-responsibility in their responses to provocations; and (e) the importance of appropriate verbal expression of affect. In addition, Feindler and Guttman (1994) present a self-monitoring activity, the Hassle Log. This device provides the youth with an accurate picture of how he handled conflict situations during the week.

SELF-CONCEPT/SELF-ESTEEM

Counselors have long recognized the importance of self-concept and self-esteem in the successful development of individuals. The use of self-concept and self-esteem in the conceptualization of therapeutic cases has become so routine that it may have lost some of its clinical usefulness. First, there is the great danger of reification (e.g., "The adolescent is delinquent because he has low self-esteem." How do you know he has low self-esteem? Because he is delinquent!). Tautological thinking is a common clinical trap. It is further believed that the relationship between self-concept and delinquency is much more complex than generally believed, with other variables clouding the picture (socio-economic status, fragility of self-concept). In fact, the whole notion of self-concept is now being questioned in the literature. For example, Baumeister, Smart, and Boden (1996) have suggested that efforts to raise the self-esteem of juvenile offenders may have been misdirected. They pointed out that juvenile delinquents often have inflated self-esteem and that such narcissistic tendencies are related to violence. That is, when confronted with a criticism or slight, the youth may react with anger or rage.

Rose, Glaser, and Roth (1998) suggest that one of the problems in past research has been the use of global measures of self-concept. Delinquent youth tend to score within normal limits on global scales. When multidimensional scales are used, however, the youth report specific strengths (perhaps overestimations) of self-concept and some glaring deficits that are obscured when the subscales are compiled into a total or global score. For example, Rose and colleagues (1998) found that detained youth scored exceptionally high on scales measuring same-sex relations (75th percentile), opposite-sex relations (77th percentile), and physical appearance (68th percentile). On the other hand, deficits were noted on scales measuring emotional stability, parent relations, and verbal abilities. Emotional stability and perceived verbal abilities were both inversely related to antisocial traits as measured by the Minnesota Multiphasic Inventory (MMPI).

At present, we are not advocating the position that self-concept and/or self-esteem need to be discarded as useful therapeutic constructs. Henggeler (1989) proposes that the low self-esteem of delinquent adolescents is a realistic appraisal of their negative life experiences and concomitant failures rather than the cause of their difficulties; therefore, indiscriminate attempts to elevate self-esteem and/or self-concept may be counterproductive in that many of these youth are highly narcissistic. For the clinician who is concerned about focusing on self-concept or self-esteem, the important task is to carefully examine and determine where these adolescents may be overestimating some abilities while underestimating others.

CAREER COUNSELING

One of the basic functions of career counseling is to help the client plan for the future. Career-focused interventions, are, by definition, future oriented. Juvenile offenders, almost by definition, are not future oriented. Youth offenders often have poor judgment and behave impulsively, focusing on short-term versus long-term outcomes.

Counselors who work with this population have long recognized that the career aspirations of many juvenile offenders lack the level of maturity often found in their nonoffending peers. Extemporaneous discussions of career choices of those who are involved with the juvenile court system are often grandiose in nature, with dreams of basketball, football, or pop music stardom predominating. Juvenile offenders are often more narcissistic and thus tend to overestimate their skills and abilities. When the reality of unfulfilled fantasies finally begins to occur, an inevitable sense of deflation sets in. This counterbalance to the aforementioned grandiosity is often a sense of depression and hopelessness. For the counselor, paradoxically, this is good news. With dreams of million-dollar contracts beginning to fade in the light of detention, probation, and/or commitment, the counselor has the opportunity to help the youth pursue more realistic career plans.

The goal, then, is to help the youth take a more down-to-earth, practical approach to moving forward on a career path. The ideal is not to kill the dream but to teach the youth ways of building a bridge, one step at a time. Once the youth is able to obtain a realistic sense of hope in his future, he will be more apt to set goals for himself, which will then allow him to actively participate in the more task-oriented aspects of career development and planning (Robitschek, 1996). A primary goal of career guidance is to assist all persons to become competent, achieving individuals and to maximize their potential through the effective use or management of their own talents and their environment.

The next stage of career counseling involves examining external forces that may lead the youth to believe that his efforts will not be rewarded (Chartrand & Rose, 1996). It is important for the counselor to explore any realistic obstacles the youth may face, such as discrimination or limited job opportunities. When working with individuals whose "opportunities are limited or are perceived as limited, the need to understand client beliefs may be primary and interest exploration and goal setting secondary. For at-risk career clients, traditional interest exploration may be necessary, but not sufficient" (Chartrand & Rose, 1996, p. 343). In career counseling, it is important to emphasize the youth's feelings of control over his environment and his own destiny as well as taking responsibility for his relationships with both people and institutions.

Part of the goal-setting process of career counseling is a focus on identifying the youth's values and interests. Determining what interests the youth holds is an important starting point for considering possible careers. The values or beliefs the youth holds to be important influence the direction of his actions and choices, as well as allowing him to make good decisions regarding his future (Bingham, Edmondson, & Stryker, 1985).

Juvenile offenders typically inspire negative attributions about them, but these youth often display many positive characteristics. It is important for the counselor to identify those qualities and help the youth learn to utilize them in a prosocial fashion. These youth often have many talents but may not be using them the way society deems appropriate. For example, a very successful drug dealer is also a skilled businessman who is able to handle large sums of money and accounts. By reframing their skills into positive avenues, these youth learn that they have the potential to be successful without violating the law.

TIPS AND HELPFUL HINTS

Many of the youth seen in juvenile court have endured a great deal of pain and have created a lifestyle that meets what they perceive to be their most pressing needs. In circumstances that are often less than ideal, these youth draw on the resources that allow them to survive. Although these resources and decisions may be unlawful and differ greatly from basic societal norms, they often serve as a vehicle for the youth in coping with their environment. One of the roles a counselor can play is helping these youth examine the resources they use and expanding their repertoire of appropriate choices. Most delinquents have high energy, which often contributes to impulsive choices and decisions. By helping them use this energy in a positive direction, counselors can empower these youth to move in more prosocial directions.

In developing their styles of interacting with others, many delinquents have learned to be manipulative. Counselors who work with such youth will find themselves feeling tested both personally and professionally. In the majority of youth, this is a self-protective measure designed to shield them from the disappointment that they have experienced in relationships with other adults. As is true in all therapeutic relationships, they need time to trust you. They may try to tell you outlandish stories or attempt to push you away through their expressions of hostility or resistance. Remember, these youth often have well-developed defense mechanisms that require that you be found trustworthy before being allowed to enter their guarded palace.

Occasionally, juvenile offender counselors work with youth who have committed crimes of a serious and violent nature. It is crucial that those in such a position be able to separate the youth from his actions. The biblical entreaty to "love the sinner and hate the sin" is often helpful in trying to sort out the inevitable myriad feelings that occur in such work. These youth need counselors who will care about them unconditionally. Such genuine care and concern is crucial to building the type of relationship that will allow them to take an honest look at their issues and difficulties.

THE JUVENILE COUNSELING
AND ASSESSMENT PROGRAM

The Juvenile Counseling and Assessment Program (JCAP) was created as a means of addressing the issues of juvenile delinquency, contributing to the body of literature related to delinquency, and providing a training ground for graduate students who will assume professional positions working with these youth. The JCAP works to address the psychological, emotional, and educational needs of court-referred youth and their families through a collaborative partnership between the Athens Clarke-County Juvenile Court, the Department of Juvenile Justice, the Athens Regional Youth Detention Center, the Department of Counseling and Human Development Services in the College of Education, the University of Georgia, and the Athens-Clarke County community.

The JCAP is based on a three-tier model of service delivery, student training, and research. The program serves delinquent youth across a variety of settings, provides training to students in a master's program approved by the Council for Accreditation of Counseling and Related Educational Programs and an APA-approved counseling psychology doctoral program, and conducts research to advance the understanding of and development of effective treatment modalities for delinquency. This model allows emerging professionals to learn an effective, empirically based method to serve a therapeutically challenging population, while delivering quality services to offending youth in collaboration with a plethora of community agencies.

THE JCAP CLIENTELE

The JCAP team provides services to a diverse population of court-referred youth in northeastern Georgia. Each year, the JCAP provides approximately 250 juvenile offenders with therapeutic services. These youth represent males and females of diverse racial/ethnic and socioeconomic groups, ranging in age from 9 to 17 years. JCAP clients attend any one of the public, private, or alternative schools in the community or may be residing in the regional youth detention center. The degree of offenses committed by these youths also varies from status offenses (e.g., truancy) to felonies (e.g., aggravated child molestation).

The three facets of the overarching JCAP paradigm of service, research, and training provide a manner in which to conceptualize delinquency and to address needed interventions from a social learning theoretical foundation (Henggeler, 1989; Horne & Sayger, 1990; Patterson, 1986). Such research is based on the premise that delinquency is a direct or indirect product of the interactions of a youth with his environment; in working with delinquents, therefore, it is necessary to examine the complex reciprocal interactions between an individual's characteristics (e.g., temperament) and the characteristics of his family, peer group, school, and community to understand the issues encountered by each youth (Henggeler, Rodick, Hanson, Borduin, & Urey, 1986). Empirical evidence supports the socioecological ideology suggesting that offender behavior is multidetermined and that, therefore, interventions must involve the youth as well as his environment (Henggeler & Borduin, 1990; Patterson, 1986).

It is essential to address the multiple contexts that influence a juvenile offender's development. It is within these various contexts that youth learn behaviors, through their observations and interactions, and are able to process their experiences and consequently determine their behaviors (Dodge, 1993a). Dodge suggests that juvenile offenders' information processing becomes so closely tied to their behavior that they appear to be one and the same. For example, many juvenile offenders learn to perceive situations as more threatening than their nondelinquent peers and consequently may act aggressively. Exploring the interactions of the youth with his family, school, peers, and community provides insight into the youth's behaviors by examining his cognitive processes and emotions across the variety of contexts.

Naturally, youths' interactions and degree of involvement within each domain differ over the course of their development. The primary influence of the family on a child changes drastically as the child reaches adolescence. At this time, peers typically have a primary influence on the behavior of the youth (Hanson, Henggeler, Haefele, Rodick, 1984). The JCAP model therefore is not static but constantly accommodates the changing developmental stage and environment of the adolescent in considering interventions and prevention measures.

Examining the youth in the context of his environment can provide information concerning the youth's likelihood to engage in delinquent behavior. Protective or risk factors play an essential role in determining the resilience and vulnerability of each youth and his risk for delinquency (Jessor, VanDen Bos, Vanderryn, Costa, & Turbin, 1995). Environmental vulnerability, caused by such factors as violent neighborhoods and an inadequate degree of school support, increases the youth's likelihood for engaging in delinquency. Jessor and colleagues (1995) suggest that vulnerability and risk factors are separate entities and not on the same continuum as previously conceptualized. A youth is not bound for delinquency if he has a less enriched environment. Protective factors (e.g., religiosity, familial support) can create resiliency against delinquency. The JCAP model emphasizes the examination of protective and risk factors to aid the youth in becoming resilient by using assets to prevent further delinquency and achieve success.

JCAP THERAPEUTIC INTERVENTIONS
WITH JUVENILE OFFENDERS

The intervention and prevention services provided by the JCAP utilize several modalities including individual counseling, group counseling, psychological assessments, and family consultations to meet the holistic needs of each youth (Glaser, 1996; Kazdin, 1995). The JCAP attempts to provide this variety of services through addressing issues related to the youth's family, school, peers, and community as well as the individual issues of each youth. After examination of 400 juvenile programs, Lipsey and Wilson (1993) found that multimodal, skill-oriented programs focusing on behavioral change are most effective. The JCAP utilizes such an approach.

In examining the effectiveness of treatment modalities with juvenile offenders, individual therapy has been found to be the most effective in creating long-term changes throughout the individual's life (OJJDP, 1998). JCAP services therefore are provided primarily through individual therapy and complemented by additional services. In individual sessions, JCAP counselors-in-training collect information from the child (along with some initial information from the parent), through clinical interviews and assessments that identify areas of the youth's life in need of services. In collaboration with other community agencies, the JCAP is able to provide individual therapeutic attention to the youth while coordinating with other service providers to meet his additional needs. This method allows the JCAP to have an intense focus on the individual needs of the youth and provide him with needed interventions.

The interventions utilized by JCAP are individualized to meet the diverse needs of the juvenile offender. Particular interventions utilized within individual therapy, such as anger management and social skills training, are commonly needed in the majority of juvenile offenders to produce successful cognitive and behavioral changes. Ultimately, JCAP interventions aid the juvenile offenders in recognizing their strengths and responsibilities, ultimately reducing the likelihood that they will become further involved in the legal system.

DELIVERY OF SERVICE

The success of this multifaceted service paradigm requires cooperation and flexibility among the students and professionals involved. Numerous barriers to treatment, such as lack of transportation and fragmented services among agencies, can make providing necessary services to juvenile offenders challenging (Borduin, Mann, Cone, & Henggeler, 1995). With the aid of community agencies, such as the school system and juvenile court, the JCAP is able to combat these obstacles by delivering services to the youth in a flexible manner. JCAP counselors-in-training are able to meet with the youth at their school, at the juvenile court, or during their placement at the regional youth detention center. In addition, the collaboration helps to ensure that each system actively participates with the youth to provide comprehensive services across each agency.

JCAP has coordinated services with the juvenile court, local schools, and the regional youth detention center. When they encounter youth they believe to be in need of counseling, probation officers from the juvenile court refer them for mandatory JCAP services. Once the referral is received, the case is staffed and assigned to a JCAP counselor-in-training (CIT). The CIT will contact the probation officer and gather information about the youth's involvement with the juvenile court as well as related pertinent information. The CIT will then meet with the youth and his guardian at the juvenile court for an intake session that consists of a clinical interview and several psychological assessments. At this point, the youth is able to choose whether he would like to receive counseling at the juvenile court or at his school. Most youth choose to meet at their school for the sake of convenience. This provides an opportunity for the CIT to meet with the school counselor, guardian permitting, to acquire a greater understanding of the youth's school performance, grades, behavior, and attitude as well as to coordinate additional services (e.g., finding a mentor). Coordinating services through the school system has been successful in reducing the rates of clients missing their appointments; this, in turn, means that youth receive more consistent and effica-cious treatment.

A JCAP SUCCESS STORY

> Jimmy, a 14-year-old Hispanic male, was referred to JCAP services by his probation officer for assaulting a classmate after school. The probation officer suggested that Jimmy needs anger management and social skills. Jimmy, however, was having behavior problems only at school. Jimmy's counselor addressed these issues in therapy and recognized that much of his frustration was originating from feelings of lack of success in the classroom. Jimmy did not have much support with his schooling; his parents did not speak English and were unable to help him with his work. Other students were making ethnic remarks about him and his family as well as making fun of his classroom performance. Their taunting became too much for Jimmy, and he began acting aggressively.
>
> Jimmy's counselor utilized several community resources to help Jimmy acquire the skills he needed to feel positively about himself and his school interactions. The counselor contacted Jimmy's school counselor as well as his English teacher, with the permission of his parents, to gather a more complete idea of the problems Jimmy was experiencing. Through this meeting, it was identified that Jimmy needed individual academic attention. The counselor made Jimmy an appointment for bilingual tutoring provided by a local tutoring agency. This would provide Jimmy with the help he needed as well as allow his parents to be involved with Jimmy's education through the help of the tutor. In addition, Jimmy was referred to the school psychologist for testing to rule out the possibility of a learning disorder.
>
> Jimmy's counselor met with Jimmy on a weekly basis to address individ-ual and family issues. In addition, she referred Jimmy to an ongoing anger management group provided by the JCAP. The group environment provided Jimmy an arena to improve his social skills with peers as well as build a repertoire of tools to handle his anger and better cope with stressful situations.

Jimmy's teachers began to complete weekly evaluations of Jimmy's behavior for the counselor. His behavior improved dramatically over the school year, and Jimmy began to display more confidence in his abilities. He also discovered several strengths, such as his leadership and problem-solving abilities.

The JCAP has established a relationship with the counselors at the Athens Regional Youth Detention Center (ARYDC). This relationship permits the CIT to have clients referred by ARYDC counselors. In addition, it allows the CIT to continue services with court-referred youth who are detained while receiving JCAP services. The fluidity of the JCAP allows CITs to follow clients who are placed in the detention center as well as to continue services with local youth upon their release from detention. This continuity of service provides additional support for youth adjusting to the transition back into their family/community after being detained. This is a particularly vulnerable time for the youth; they may rejoin offending peers, dysfunctional homes, and a wary school system. This continuity allows the youth ample opportunity to prepare for their reinvolvement and is essential in aiding them in a successful transition into community living (Fagan, 1991).

SUMMARY

Treating juvenile offenders is challenging, and few programs have been effective in stemming the tide of recidivism among these youth. The JCAP program attempts to meet the needs of juvenile offenders, contribute to the body of knowledge related to delinquency, and aid in the understanding of the multidimensional influences on juvenile offenders. The JCAP's goal is to continue growing and to aid in the establishment of similar programs designed to meet the needs of these youth.

HIGHLIGHTS OF CHAPTER 19

▶ Juvenile delinquency is a widespread societal problem. An estimated 2.9 million juvenile arrests were made in 1996. There has been a dramatic rise in violent offenses, an increase of more than 67% during the past decade. Homicides by juveniles increased by 90% during this same period.

▶ Those classified as juvenile offenders exhibit great variability. Involvement in juvenile court can range from a single encounter to chronic adjudications. The type of crimes committed can range from minor status offenses to murder.

▶ Establishing rapport with the juvenile offender can be a Herculean task. Counselors must break from traditional therapy approaches and consider innovative ways to connect with these youth. Things to consider include the counselor's attire, ways of reframing the process, establishing clear boundaries, and utilizing approaches that do not rely exclusively on verbal interaction or the 50-minute hour.

▶ Important focus areas for interventions include social skills training, anger management, and career counseling. Many programs emphasize the importance of self-esteem and self-concept; however, recent research suggests that counselors need to be aware of the potential pitfalls of making these constructs the center of the therapeutic intervention.

▶ Juvenile offenders pose several specific challenges for counselors. In addition to the normal developmental issues of adolescence, the juvenile offender has, by definition, exhibited socially unacceptable and sometimes repugnant behaviors. The counselor must find ways of accepting the youth without accepting his behaviors.

▶ The Juvenile Counseling and Assessment Program (JCAP) was created to find effective means for dealing with the juvenile offender through an integrated approach involving research, service, and training. The JCAP's effectiveness stems in part from the counselors' willingness to "meet these youth where they are." This means that rather than attending scheduled sessions in a clinic, the youth are seen in the schools they attend, at the juvenile court, at the local department of juvenile justice, and, when necessary, at the regional youth detention center. This approach reduced typical barriers to treatment such as problems with transportation or youth forgetting their appointments. A decided advantage in utilizing this approach is the opportunity to observe the youth's environment. It also gives the counselor the opportunity to interact with professionals (teachers, principals, school counselors) who are actively involved in the youth's life.

▶ Counselors and counselors-in-training should take heart from an Office of Juvenile Justice and Delinquency Prevention report regarding serious and violent juvenile offenders. The report indicates that one of the most effective modalities for creating long-term change throughout the juvenile offender's life is individual counseling.

Counseling Substance-Abusing Young Males

RICHARD C. PAGE

Adolescence represents a time of change and personal development for young people. George (1990) has identified five tasks that adolescents must achieve to successfully make the transition to adulthood:

1. Accept the biological changes that the individual is experiencing
2. Learn to be comfortable with sexuality and one's sexual preferences
3. Choose a career identity
4. Learn to care for oneself and to be independent
5. Develop a sense of personal identity

Adolescence is a time of rebellion and experimentation for many male adolescents. In American society and in other societies around the world, male adolescents face tremendous pressures to achieve. More and more education or training is demanded of many adolescents for them to be able to compete in the world marketplace. Additionally, too many adolescents grow up in abusive families or in poverty. Gang membership has become an increasingly difficult problem to deal with in America and other countries. Many adolescents in America and other countries use illicit drugs, alcohol, or cigarettes as a way of coping with the pressures of modern life. For instance, Doweiko (1996) cites research showing that the average age at which boys first drink alcohol is 11.9 years and that about 19% of 8th graders have used inhalants at least once. Inhalants are cited as the first mood altering drug that many adolescents use. The reasons for adolescent drug abuse are complex and will be discussed later in this chapter. Patterns of adolescent drug abuse in the United States are summarized next.

Adolescents generally use either alcohol or other illicit drugs by the time they graduate from high school. Doweiko (1996) cites research showing that during most of the 1990s about 90% of high school seniors in the United States had drunk alcohol at least once and that about 28% of high school seniors consumed five or more drinks a week in 1992. Witters, Venturelli, and Hanson (1992) report that National Institute on Drug Abuse (NIDA) surveys show that about 90% of the high school students surveyed in 1989 had drunk alcohol at least once, about 62% had used cigarettes at least once, and about 44% had used marijuana at least once. However, only 19% of high school seniors had ever used stimulants, about 10% had ever used crack, and about 9% had ever used hallucinogens. Clearly, many adolescents in American society experiment with using alcohol, cigarettes, and illicit drugs by the time they become high school seniors. Many similar surveys do not include students who drop out of high school before they become seniors and who may have had drug abuse problems that caused them to drop out.

Adolescents who use or abuse drugs often need counseling or therapy. This chapter focuses on identifying and providing counseling to adolescent males who have a serious problem with alcohol or other illicit drugs. Although it is difficult to define precisely what addiction involves with adolescents because tolerance to drugs such as alcohol develops over a period of years, Farrow (1990) estimated that only 1% of all adolescent users are truly addicted, although as many as 15% of these users might meet the diagnostic criteria for alcohol or illicit drug abuse. Often, adolescent males who have drug abuse problems are referred for treatment by their families. Adolescent males who are abusing alcohol or other illicit drugs often are out of control and are causing havoc within their families. They may be gang members or may have run away from home. A multifaceted treatment approach generally is needed with these adolescents; it might include individual counseling, group counseling, family counseling, or placement in a residential treatment program. Too often, the treatment available for these adolescent males is limited or of ineffective types, and certain groups may be excluded from particular types of treatment. Before discussing the interventions that can be utilized with adolescent drug abusers, the adjustment issues and problems that are faced by adolescent drug abusers are summarized.

ADJUSTMENT ISSUES

It is necessary to distinguish between adolescents who are abusing drugs or who are addicted from adolescents who are using drugs without developing a dependence on them; this allows identification of adjustment issues of male adolescent drug abusers. The *DSM-IV* (American Psychiatric Association [APA], 1994a) specifies the features of both substance dependence and substance abuse. Some of these criteria also can be applied to adolescents to determine who has a substance abuse problem. For instance, the *DSM-IV* identifies tolerance, withdrawal, using more of the substance than intended, unsuccessful efforts to discontinue substance use, a lot of time spent in obtaining the substance, and having continuing physical or psychological problems associated with using the substance as part of the criteria that define either substance abuse or dependence. The *DSM-IV* additionally notes that substance abuse and dependence are associated with deterioration of important social, occupational, and recreational activities, although with adolescents it is necessary to include the deterioration of school performance and motivation to achieve in school. The *DSM-IV* indicates that the route of administration for using a substance, the speed of onset of a drug's effects, the duration of effects of a substance, the use of many substances, and the development of related mental disorders are associated with becoming dependent on a particular drug. Avis (1996) emphasizes that people addicted to drugs experience craving for the drug and demonstrate drug-seeking behavior.

Lewis, Dana, and Blevins (1994) and George (1990) mention several paper and pencil diagnostic instruments, such as the Adolescent Alcohol Involvement Scale, that can be used to determine which adolescents have serious drug abuse problems. Another instrument that can be used to diagnose teenage drug and alcohol abuse is the Personal Experience Inventory (Dahmus, 1992). Although all these methods of assessing whether an adolescent is dependent on a particular drug are helpful, in the final analysis it is the person providing counseling who has to determine, after a careful consideration of the individual dynamics, if counseling is recommended.

The attempt to determine the major factors associated with adolescent drug abuse has spawned much research. According to White (1989), this research has indicated that four primary sets of factors consistently have been associated with adolescent drug use and/or abuse: (a) social or cultural factors, (b) family interaction factors, (c) peer relationship factors, and (d) personal characteristics. The social or cultural environment that an adolescent is exposed to outside the home obviously influences the attitudes of the adolescent. For instance, if a male adolescent lives in a neighborhood where belonging to a gang is seen as important and cocaine use is part of the expected behavior of gang members, then this adolescent is at risk of developing a drug dependency problem.

White (1989) indicates that most adolescents are exposed to illicit drug use in their social and cultural environments in the United States and that many adolescents experiment with using drugs. Not all who experiment with using illicit drugs, including such drugs as cocaine, develop drug abuse or dependence problems. White (1989) says that family interaction factors, peer relationship factors, and personal characteristics are most often the problem areas associated with drug dependence among adolescents. Many adolescent drug abusers come from families in which one or both parents has an illicit drug and/or alcohol problem. One of the factors most highly predictive of adolescent male drug abuse is the peer group of these males. If male adolescents associate primarily with other adolescents who are abusing drugs and/or alcohol, the chances are high that these adolescents will abuse these substances as well. Most adolescent males who are abusing mind-altering substances do not adjust well to school, and many drop out of school. These factors represent some of the major adjustment issues that adolescent drug abusers face when they are young.

Below, I describe the major adjustment issues faced by adolescent drug abusers by presenting a profile of a hypothetical adolescent, Tom, who has a serious drug abuse problem. Although many differences exist among the types of adjustment problems faced by different adolescent drug abusers, I hope that the profile of Tom gives the reader some insight into the types of issues faced by many adolescent drug abusers. It is important to realize that adolescent drug abusers vary in characteristics such as race, socioeconomic status, education, type of drug used, specific family situations, intelligence, ability to succeed in school, and gang membership. It is also necessary to note that cocaine (a drug that Tom is described as abusing) is used in roughly the same amounts by members of different socioeconomic groups and different racial and cultural groups in American society. Most of the specific parts of Tom's profile are based on research that has been conducted on adolescent drug abuse (Amini, 1976; Beman, 1995; Brook, Gordon, Whiteman, & Choen, 1986; Doweiko, 1996; Holden, 1985; Lettieri, 1985; McDermott, 1984; Page & Powell, 1981; Segal, 1996; White, 1989; Witters et al., 1992) and on my experiences in working with adolescent drug abusers. The profile presented here is a constructed one, not drawn to represent the specific characteristics of any adolescent either I or anyone else has actually counseled.

PROFILE OF TOM

Tom is a 16-year-old African American adolescent who lives in a housing project in Atlanta, Georgia. Both his father and his mother live at home, but Tom's father uses a lot of cocaine and sells cocaine and other drugs to support his habit. Tom's paternal grandfather was an alcoholic who had been sent to prison for armed robbery. Tom has two brothers and a sister. Both of Tom's brothers use a variety of illicit drugs and alcohol, but Tom's sister does not use drugs. Tom is the youngest child in his family, and his sister is 2 years older. Neither of Tom's brothers lives at home. Sometimes, Tom's father hits him or his mother, and he once fought with his father to stop him from beating his mother. Tom's father has occasionally supplied him with cocaine. Tom is now using cocaine every week; he drinks a lot of alcohol and dabbles with using a variety of other illicit drugs. Tom's mother occasionally drinks, but she has never used any illicit drugs. Tom's mother and father often fight verbally, and Tom's mother wants to keep him at home to provide her with a sense of support in her otherwise dreary life. Tom's father is often gone from home for extended periods of time.

Tom's primary friends are other adolescents who use cocaine or other illicit drugs. Tom feels alienated from school. He does not participate in any extracurricular activities and often skips school to use drugs with his friends. Tom occasionally sells drugs to obtain the money for the increasing amount of cocaine he is using. Tom first used illicit drugs with his friends and not because his father supplied him with cocaine. Most of the time Tom spends with his friends revolves around drug-related activities such as using drugs or alcohol or trying to find ways to obtain them. Tom is thinking about dropping out of school, although his mother is encouraging him to remain in high school and graduate. Students at Tom's school who are motivated to graduate avoid Tom because they see him as being a "druggie."

Tom often boasts to his friends in the drug culture that he feels good about himself, but the school psychologist who once interviewed Tom perceives him as having low self-esteem, normal intelligence, and some of the signs of depression and as being anxious, rebellious, and impulsive. Tom does not view himself in any of these ways. He is beginning to use cocaine every day but denies he has a problem and thinks that he can still control the amount of cocaine he uses. Tom thinks he gets a real boost from this drug, and he loves the feelings associated with using cocaine. Tom feels more powerful as an individual when he is using cocaine, and he thinks he is able to cope with anything. When Tom is not using, he often feels depressed; the increasing conflict with his mother over his drug use does not help. Tom is beginning not to care if he is expelled from school, about his increasing number of school absences, or that he has no friends other than those who are abusing drugs.

The next section of this chapter suggests some ways that therapists counseling clients similar to Tom can establish rapport with them. I have purposely presented Tom as having serious problems so that more can be learned from this case example. I believe that unless an adolescent male with a serious drug or alcohol problem is minimally motivated to participate in counseling, it is difficult or impossible to counsel him successfully. Sometimes, adolescents who do not want counseling can be referred to residential drug treatment centers, but unless they become motivated to help themselves at some point during the treatment process, it is unlikely that they will discontinue using drugs after being discharged from treatment. For this reason, I assume that Tom has agreed to go to a therapist both to please his mother and because he has seen the effects that cocaine use has had on his friends in the drug culture.

STRATEGIES FOR ESTABLISHING RAPPORT

It is often difficult for therapists who work with illicit drug abusers to establish rapport with these clients. Most adolescent drug abusers are resistant to dealing with authority and have ignored the harmful effects of their drug abuse on themselves and others. Many adolescents who abuse drugs or alcohol glamorize the lifestyle associated with the drug culture and refuse to see how use of drugs or alcohol is beginning to control their lives. Often, male adolescents use drugs to get back at parents whom they see as restricting them or involving them in hurtful family dynamics. In Tom's case, he may both love and dislike his mother, who is threatened when he attempts to establish an identity that is separate from her and who wants him to stay at home to provide her with emotional support. He loves his mother because she cares about him, but he also dislikes the way she tries to control him, although he cannot admit this to himself.

Tom dislikes and at times even hates his father, although he cannot admit this to himself either. The first task of the therapist who works with Tom is not to confront these issues but, instead, to develop a therapeutic relationship with him so that he will continue to come to therapy. Another immediate task for the therapist is to help Tom to either stop using drugs altogether or develop coping strategies that reduce the harmful effects of the drugs and/or alcohol that he is using. For instance, if Tom is not willing to agree to stop using all illicit drugs, maybe he would agree as a first step to stop using cocaine and to use only a limited amount of marijuana and perhaps to go to school and change his lifestyle in other ways that enable him to cope better in society.

I first describe ways of establishing rapport with Tom or similar clients, an important first step in counseling. Following that, I describe counseling interventions.

The first counseling session that Tom attends is important because the therapist needs to establish rapport to keep him in counseling. The impressions that Tom or similar clients have of a counselor are related to the successful or unsuccessful completion of counseling. Unless Tom responds in a positive way to the counselor he is seeing, he probably will not come back to counseling, or if he does come back because he is forced to attend, he will not cooperate with what is occurring. Adolescents who have serious drug abuse problems need to perceive the counselor as a genuine person whose presence helps them to feel comfortable in the counseling relationship. Adolescent drug abusers need to believe that the therapist is concerned with their welfare if they are going to respond positively to therapy. This does not mean that the therapist should be naive, because male adolescent drug abusers will not respect this characteristic. It does imply that the therapist should be concerned with Tom's welfare and understand what Tom is experiencing. Because therapists subscribe to different theoretical orientations and have distinct personalities, it is difficult to describe the specific ways that empathy should be communicated by a particular therapist, but clients like Tom do need to perceive that the therapist empathizes with him regardless of how this is shown. Just because the therapist is able to empathize with Tom, however, does not mean that the therapist should unreservedly accept everything Tom says, especially when Tom tries to manipulate him/her or others.

Topics that often come up during initial counseling sessions with clients like Tom are reviewed next. The response of a counselor to these issues will affect how Tom or similar clients view the counseling process. Adolescent male drug abusers often attempt the following in counseling during the initial sessions: glamorizing the drug culture and previous drug use, discussing the drug use of the therapist, bringing up racial issues, bringing up gender differences, discussing negative opinions about authority figures, and trying to get the counselor to assume too much responsibility in counseling. These issues are often discussed partly because they are relatively safe issues for the client and partly because discussing issues that are threatening to the counselor is a way to test how the counselor deals with these issues. Different therapists often have their own ways of responding to these issues, but I hope it proves helpful to provide some opinions about how these topics can be handled in therapy.

When a client such as Tom begins counseling, he often wants to discuss a topic about which he knows as much or more than the therapist does. When adolescents have been involved in the drug culture or have used a certain drug, they have a lot of knowledge about life in the drug culture and the behavioral effects of the drugs they have used. It is important for them to see their peers and illicit drugs in the most positive light possible, even though they generally know (but will not admit) that their peers in the drug culture are unconcerned with their well-being. Others in the drug culture often have an investment in encouraging the people they associate with to keep using drugs; it is then easier for them to rationalize their own self-destructive behavior. For these reasons, it is a good bet that Tom will start glamorizing life in the drug culture or the use of certain drugs when he first enters counseling.

One way that a therapist can respond to these discussions is to initially avoid contradicting what is being said but not to agree either. When this occurs, the counseling sessions often reach a dead end because drug-related discussions that glamorize drugs or the drug culture are boring, are unrelated to the client's feelings, and are basically fabrications by the client. Life in the drug culture is not glamorous, and clients who maintain this kind of belief are fooling themselves or others. Usually, it does not take long for the client to become bored or restless when discussing drugs or the drug culture. Then the therapist can focus on what is boring in the session. If this is done successfully, the client gains the insight that if counseling is going to be successful he will have to reveal more about his personal thoughts and feelings. Sometimes, the counselor might want to say that he or she thinks these discussions are uninteresting. The timing of such a statement is important. It might be appropriate for the counselor to confront some adolescents about how drug-related discussions are boring; with others, it is more effective to let them come to these insights themselves by allowing them to get bored with their own talk. When this occurs in therapy, the client may blame the counselor for what is boring about therapy because he thinks the therapist is responsible for making counseling interesting.

Generally, it is unwise for the therapist to assume too much responsibility for making therapy interesting or for making male adolescent drug abusers stop using drugs. If the client starts to blame the therapist for the sessions' lack of direction after he has been glamorizing the use of drugs or alcohol, then the counselor can focus on the ways that using drugs has affected the client's life and on the role of the client in counseling. The therapist might say to Tom that only he can change his life. If progress is to be made in counseling, then it is up to Tom to make it, even though the therapist can provide a safe and supportive environment for him to begin to do this. The therapist might also tell Tom that if he or she does take responsibility for getting Tom to stop using drugs, then Tom will not respect this because he really knows that he must do this himself if quitting is going to work. Tom might get angry with the therapist if he is confronted in this way, but this is all right as long as Tom keeps coming to counseling. The counselor at this point might thank Tom for getting angry and examine with Tom what he or she did to make him angry. The therapist additionally might say that he or she thinks Tom is making progress in counseling because he is able to express his anger directly to the therapist. It is true that progress has been made: Focusing on anger can represent a significant theme in therapy for male adolescent drug abusers.

When a male adolescent drug abuser attempts to get a therapist to assume too much responsibility for his life, one way the therapist can respond is by placing responsibility back on the client. This means that therapists who counsel adolescent drug abusers should be aware of their own needs to assume responsibility for others. Male adolescent drug abusers often try to manipulate people in authority, and one way they can discredit counselors is to convince them to assume too much responsibility for changing the client and then resist that change. One way that counselors can relate to clients who are playing this kind of game is to avoid responding in the way the client wants them to respond. This might make the client angry, but, as stated above, such anger can lead to progress in therapy. If the therapist responds to the client's anger in a way that shows a lack of intimidation by the client, as well as showing that the therapist is interested in exploring the client's perceptions and feelings, then clients such as Tom will see that the counselor can deal with a client's anger in a facilitative manner. Tom might gain respect for the therapist by observing how he or she handles his anger or confrontational style. If the therapist does not respond to personal confrontations by resorting to a judgmental or authoritarian way of interacting, then Tom probably will gain trust in the counselor and the viability of the counseling process.

Another way that Tom might attempt to put the counselor on the spot is by asking if the therapist has ever used illicit drugs or had an alcohol problem. If Tom asked me this question and I thought he was asking this question to test me, I would probably avoid answering the question directly. Instead of answering this question with a yes or no, the therapist might ask Tom whether he thinks that the counselor has used illicit drugs or not. This avoids responding to the game that Tom is trying to play. If the counselor says he or she has used illicit drugs, then Tom may think he has discredited the counselor because he or she is a drug user just like him. On the other hand, if the therapist answers no to this question, then he can label the counselor by saying that he or she doesn't know anything about his experiences and life in the drug culture. By asking Tom to state whether he thinks the counselor has used drugs, the counselor can deal with Tom's transference issues by asking Tom how he would see the counselor if this question were answered in the affirmative, or if it were answered in the negative, and then point out to Tom that the counselor is still the same person no matter how this question is answered.

If I had Tom as a client, another topic that might come up at some point is that Tom is an African American and I am White. The ways racial issues are handled in counseling often depend to a large extent on the personality of the counselor. At the appropriate time, I might ask Tom directly how he feels about receiving counseling from a White male. If Tom can express the fact that he does not trust me or another counselor because of race, then I can explore with Tom the reasons for his mistrust. The therapist might ask Tom if he has noticed anything about the therapist's behavior that makes him think that the therapist is prejudiced. It is important for therapists who counsel male adolescent drug abusers to be aware of their own prejudices and to be aware of how their own values and behaviors affect their relationships with culturally different clients. Another idea that might be discussed with Tom is whether or not he wants to be referred to an African American counselor. This should be brought up only if there is an African American therapist available to see Tom. Culturally different clients can gain trust in a therapist by being encouraged to openly explore racial issues that come up in counseling. Prejudice and discrimination are facts of American life, and it is helpful for adolescent male drug abusers, some of whom have been victims of discrimination or prejudice, to explore how this has affected their lives.

If a woman were counseling Tom, it might be helpful to explore how he regards this and whether this affects his trust in the counseling process. Discussing what he thinks about the fact that his counselor is a woman might bring into the open any negative stereotypes Tom has of female counselors or women in general. It is important for a woman who counsels Tom to be aware of her own negative stereotypes of male adolescent drug abusers who may be racially different. If Tom can discuss openly how he feels about his relationships with women, this might become an important theme in counseling.

One further topic that Tom might want to discuss during the initial stages of counseling is how people in authority have mistreated him or misused authority. Tom might say that many people in authority are alcoholics, use cocaine, or have hurt others by misusing their power. Tom might say this as a way of rationalizing his own cocaine use. He might ask whether the therapist thinks marijuana or alcohol is more harmful to people. It is generally wise for counselors to avoid getting into debates with adolescent drug abusers about whether drug or alcohol use is good or bad for everyone. The therapist can instead ask Tom to examine how his own cocaine use is affecting his life and his relationships with others.

Tom might bring up how people in authority such as police officers or teachers have mistreated or hurt him. The therapist might ask Tom to clarify who has mistreated him and how his responses to these perceived injustices have affected his life. It is sometimes appropriate to ask clients such as Tom to examine how they feel about the counselor as an authority figure. These discussions can be productive because the negative perceptions that male adolescent drug abusers have toward authority often lead them to engage in self-defeating behavior. Counselors need to be comfortable in dealing with how rebellious adolescents perceive authority and to be aware of their own attitudes toward authority and how these attitudes affect counseling.

When the counselor notices that a continual theme in counseling is how the client perceives authority, then at the right time it might be helpful to explore how Tom perceives his family of origin. Tom's attitudes toward authority have developed in part from his experiences in his family of origin. Many adolescent drug abusers such as Tom have family problems that need to be addressed in counseling at some time.

The counselor's actions and attitudes in the initial sessions of counseling often affect whether or not rapport is established with an adolescent male drug abuser. If an adolescent fails to come back to counseling, the therapist should examine his or her own behavior to determine if anything more might have been done to establish rapport with the client. It is important for counselors to remember that it is not necessarily their fault when male adolescent drug abusers do not return to counseling. It is often difficult to get these adolescents to attend counseling, although they often do become willing clients. The next section explores different counseling interventions that can be utilized with adolescent drug abusers.

INTERVENTIONS

Many of the strategies discussed in the previous section related to approaches the counselor can use to gain the trust of a male adolescent drug abuser during the initial sessions of counseling. It is important to emphasize that different therapists, with different theoretical orientations and personalities, have different ways of approaching the issues discussed in the previous section. In this section, interventions are discussed that are often effective in helping adolescent drug abusers either to reduce the amount of drugs or alcohol they are using or to completely abstain from using drugs or alcohol. One dilemma of the therapist is to decide whether to see an adolescent who is abusing drugs or alcohol if this adolescent refuses to abstain from drug or alcohol use altogether. In some settings, it is appropriate to insist on complete abstinence for drug abuse counseling to occur (e.g., residential inpatient treatment centers), and in some settings, this is not appropriate.

Harm reduction models of drug abuse counseling have been debated for use in the United States (Cotton, 1996; O'Mara, 1995). This type of drug abuse counseling helps drug or alcohol abusers to manage the harmful effects of their use or abuse without insisting on complete abstinence. Harm reduction approaches to drug counseling often have practical use with male adolescent drug abusers. The ways that harm reduction models and abstinence models of drug abuse counseling can be used with adolescents are discussed below. Following this, individual, group, and family interventions are discussed, as well as the possible placement of an adolescent in a residential treatment center.

HARM REDUCTION APPROACHES

Many therapists who work in private practice or other settings are asked to work with males who are abusing drugs or alcohol but who are doing this primarily because they are rebellious adolescents. If an adolescent is engaging is risky behaviors by abusing drugs or alcohol but the therapist does not think this adolescent is at risk for becoming addicted, then the counselor might consider using harm reduction approaches. For instance, if an adolescent male refuses to quit drinking, it is often appropriate to ask him whether drinking is having any harmful effects on his life and to review with him how these harmful effects can be reduced. When this is done, an adolescent might decide not to drink and drive or to place more emphasis on doing well in school but continue drinking at selected times. Harm reduction models of drug abuse counseling allow many important issues to be discussed with adolescents, but it is important for the counselor using these approaches to determine that the adolescent is not at risk for becoming addicted to drugs or alcohol. Some of the risk factors associated with addiction were reviewed in the first section of this chapter. This model should be used for those adolescents unwilling to abstain from using all drugs and alcohol.

ALCOHOLICS ANONYMOUS

Adolescents who are using drugs such as cocaine or alcohol compulsively to escape personal problems or as a form of self-medication may be at risk for becoming dependent on (or addicted to) these drugs. When this is the case, the therapist might recommend to the parents that they send the adolescent to a residential drug treatment program. These kinds of programs are discussed later in this chapter. The therapist might also intervene by telling an adolescent like Tom that unless he stops using cocaine and other drugs, he is in danger of developing an addiction problem. The therapist can suggest to Tom that he should consider going to some Alcoholics Anonymous (AA) or Narcotics Anonymous meetings to receive support in dealing with his problem. The therapist should continue to see Tom whether or not he decides to go to AA meetings and should respect his decision not to go if he does not like the AA approach. AA can be used effectively as an adjunct to counseling with many adolescent drug abusers, but it is not effective with all adolescent drug abusers.

INDIVIDUAL COUNSELING

If the therapist has established a workable therapeutic relationship with Tom, then Tom might benefit from participating in individual counseling whether or not he attends AA meetings. In individual counseling, the therapist probably needs to be honest with Tom about the risks Tom is taking when he is using cocaine. Unless Tom can admit to himself that he has a serious problem with cocaine, he will not change his drug-taking behavior, and he may become dependent on cocaine. Tom probably also needs to admit that he cannot use any cocaine, because when he does he cannot control the amount he uses. Tom is probably fooling himself when he tells himself he can control his cocaine use; it is likely that in the past, his use has gotten out of his control.

One problem commonly encountered when counseling adolescents who are becoming dependent on drugs is that these adolescents generally have not had the life experiences to realize how their drug-taking behaviors can hurt them. Anything the counselor can do to help these adolescents to become aware of the harmful effects of their drug taking behavior can prompt them to decide to stop using drugs altogether before they become addicted. Because many adolescent drug abusers deny having a problem with drugs or alcohol, it is not easy for the counselor to help them to become aware that they cannot control their drug or alcohol use. If an adolescent with a drug dependence problem does stop using drugs or alcohol, then counseling can focus on relapse prevention. George (1990) lists relapse symptoms that the drug abuse counselor might want to deal with in counseling. AA can also provide group support for adolescents to help them avoid relapsing.

In addition to dealing with issues that relate specifically to avoiding the use of drugs and alcohol, many adolescent male drug abusers need individual counseling to deal with the same issues that nonabusing adolescents discuss in therapy. Many adolescent drug abusers have family problems that need to be addressed in therapy, including having family members who themselves are addicted to drugs or alcohol (Schroeder, 1989). It is often appropriate for the therapist to discuss with male adolescent drug abusers in individual therapy the problems they are experiencing in relating to family members (Page & Powell, 1981). Individual counseling can be an effective approach to use with adolescent males who are having school problems or relationship problems with their peers. Although individual counseling can be effective with adolescent drug abusers, group therapy approaches can be just as potent.

GROUP COUNSELING

Adolescents like Tom often listen more to their peers than they do to people they consider to be authority figures, such as counselors and teachers. Male adolescent drug abusers often know other people better than they know themselves; they need to know other people so that they can manipulate them to meet their needs to obtain drugs or alcohol. Adolescent drug abusers often lack self-awareness. They avoid awareness of negative feelings such as anger or guilt by taking drugs or alcohol, and they generally deny having any problems with drugs or alcohol to justify their use of these substances. For these reasons, group therapy, which uses the feedback of peers as a therapeutic modality, is often effective with adolescent drug abusers (Brinson, 1995; Smith, 1985). Adolescent drug abusers usually enjoy counseling groups more than they enjoy individual counseling because they enjoy giving and receiving feedback with their peers. Page and Berkow (1994) discuss the ways that unstructured therapy groups can be used effectively with adolescents and other people who have drug abuse problems. The goals of unstructured therapy groups include helping members to deal more effectively with personal problems and problems in interpersonal relationships. Male adolescent drug abusers often have one or both types of problems (Page & Berkow, 1994).

If Tom's counselor referred him to an effective therapy group, Tom eventually would receive feedback from the other members about how he is hurting himself and others by using cocaine. If he were participating in such a group, he would receive support from the other members for not using cocaine, and he would receive increasingly strong feedback from the members stressing the importance of his abstinence from cocaine use. Tom also would have the opportunity to discuss personal issues such as how he and his mother relate to one another and how he feels about his father. Page and Berkow (1994) show that unstructured therapy groups can help people with serious drug abuse problems develop improved self-esteem and more positive attitudes toward counseling. They also describe the kinds of therapeutic interactions that occur in unstructured therapy groups to promote these attitude changes among illicit drug abusers.

Structured therapy groups can be used effectively with male adolescent drug abusers to help them learn skills such as assertiveness in interpersonal relationships and ways to avoid relapse. Tom's therapist might consider referring Tom to participate in a therapy group that is being conducted in a private practice, a mental health setting, a school setting, a hospital setting, or some other setting. Unfortunately, this type of treatment is often unavailable for clients such as Tom.

FAMILY COUNSELING

Another intervention that Tom's therapist might consider is referring him to a family counselor. If Tom's therapist is seeing him in either individual or group therapy, it is probably better for someone else to conduct the family therapy sessions to avoid conflicts of interest. Because it is quite likely that Tom's father will refuse to attend these sessions because he is using cocaine, it might be necessary to do family therapy with just Tom, his mother, and any of his siblings who attend these sessions. As can be seen from the case study, Tom and his mother have a lot to discuss in family therapy. A problem associated with doing family therapy in this manner is that Tom's father might be threatened because he is not attending. The dilemma for the counselor is whether to meet with Tom and his mother if Tom's father does not come.

Many different kinds of family therapy have been advocated as being effective with adolescent substance abusers, including MRI Brief Family Therapy (Heath & Ayers, 1991), Contextual Family Therapy (Bernal & Flores-Ortiz, 1991), Solution Focused Brief Treatment (Berg & Gallagher, 1991), and Intergenerational Family Therapy (Chabot & Matteis, 1991).

COMPREHENSIVE RESIDENTIAL TREATMENT

If Tom does not stop using cocaine, or if his cocaine use increases, then it might be necessary to refer Tom to a residential drug treatment center for adolescents. One obvious advantage of referring Tom to a residential treatment center is that his use of cocaine can be monitored by the counselors working in the program. He can be given urine tests to make sure he stops using cocaine and other drugs.

Many residential treatment center programs in the United States primarily use group counseling to help adolescents with drug abuse problems rather than using individual counseling. Adolescents get feedback from their peers about how responsibly they are acting in the program, and they are expected to discuss their drug abuse and other personal and interpersonal relationship problems in group counseling. By living with other adolescents who are helping one another, Tom can learn how to form relationships that are drug free and based on mutual caring and support. Many of the current residential treatment centers in the United States use an AA Twelve Steps model of dealing with addictions and stress the importance of AA membership when residents leave the program. This might be a problem for Tom if he does not respond well to the AA approach.

Aftercare is an important component of residential drug treatment programs for adolescents, and the lack of aftercare services is associated with relapse. Fortunately, most residential treatment programs for adolescent drug abusers currently have counseling groups that adolescents can attend for a period of time once they graduate from the program. Many residential treatment programs for adolescent drug abusers are currently short term, keeping residents for 6 weeks or less. This is unfortunate because research consistently has shown that the longer the program (up to about 17 months), the greater the abstinence rate of the residents who graduate from the program (De Leon, 1986; O'Brien, Woody, & McLellan, 1986).

Many residential programs for adolescent drug abusers use techniques in which an adolescent is broken down through confrontation by the staff and residents and then is told by the group how to be a more socialized person. Other, more effective drug treatment programs use confrontation as a method of helping residents to become aware of themselves so that they can make better decisions (Page, 1983; Page, Smith, & Beamish, 1977). Research on the Synanon model of therapeutic communities of the 1960s showed clearly that programs that use confrontation to break clients down and then build them up again into what the group wants them to be do not have high success rates (Brecher, 1972). More supportive residential drug treatment programs are more successful with serious drug abusers such as heroin addicts; only 40% of the graduates of these residential treatment programs relapse (Simpson, 1986). It is important to keep in mind that the personalities of the counselors are an important component of a residential drug treatment program (Page, 1979). A review of the research shows that effective residential drug treatment programs typically include the following elements: Addicts have chosen to be in treatment, counselors are able to establish rapport with their clients, and the program is long enough for change to occur (Simpson, 1986). A therapist who considers referring a client like Tom to a residential treatment program should keep these elements in mind when making the referral.

HARSH REALITIES OF DRUG TREATMENT OPTIONS

It is unfortunate that the treatment options available to clients like Tom are often limited. Tom has some personal characteristics working against his rehabilitation. For instance, his father is abusing drugs and may not be supportive if he tries to rehabilitate himself. The possibilities of Tom being referred to a residential treatment program are not great because his family is disadvantaged and poor. Unless Tom can accept the AA model, it may be difficult for him to find help in the community from an organized group. If Tom drops out of school, he might be able to make more money selling drugs such as cocaine than he can through legitimate means of employment. It is important for counselors to be realistic when they are working with clients like Tom. It is also important for them to remember that Tom has a lot of responsibility for his own rehabilitation, and if he is motivated, he might be able to help himself. If Tom can learn to enjoy participating in counseling, he might become motivated to help himself from being in counseling.

SUGGESTIONS FOR FUTURE TRAINING AND RESEARCH

Tom and adolescents similar to him need to receive help in various ways if they are going to stop using drugs and become productive citizens as adults. Tom needs to get counseling to help him to stop using cocaine and other drugs so that he does not become an addict. He needs to receive an education that will enable him to support himself in a competitive society, so that he will not continue selling drugs and engaging in illegal means of making money. Tom's family situation needs to be improved so that he can receive appropriate support from his family if he decides to quit using drugs and alcohol. Tom's father needs to stop using and selling cocaine if he is ever going to be a responsible father. If Tom's father does not stop using cocaine, then Tom must decide not to follow the same path as his father if he is going to quit using drugs. Tom needs to relate to peers who do not encourage him to abuse drugs rather than adolescents who abuse drugs and encourage him to do the same. Tom needs to seek help from groups such as AA that encourage him to abstain from drug and alcohol use. The point here is that Tom and adolescents similar to him face many problems and obstacles in overcoming their drug abuse, and they may need help from various services.

If mental health and school professionals are going to provide effective help to male adolescent drug abusers, they need to be competent to work with this population. Standards are needed that describe counseling competencies in helping adolescents who have drug abuse problems. The National Board of Certified Counselors (NBCC), Certified Rehabilitation Counselors (CRC), National Association of Alcoholism and Drug Abuse Counselors (NAADAC), and International Certification Reciprocity Consortium (ICRC) are four national organizations that are cooperating in sponsoring a national certification for master's level drug abuse counselors. Standards have been developed for the course work, practicum, and work experiences that are needed to certify someone to become a Master Addiction Counselor, or MAC (Page & Bailey, 1995). Before someone can qualify as a MAC, he or she needs to have a master's degree in a helping profession and at least 3 years of counseling experience in the addictions field. Additionally, the NBCC requires course work in group counseling and family counseling. (For a further description of the MAC, refer to Page & Bailey, 1995.)

Training needs to be offered to professionals counseling male adolescents with drug abuse problems to help them to develop the requisite skills and knowledge to do effective work with this population. The section on interventions in this chapter describes some of the types of interventions that professionals counseling adolescent males can use. The certification standards developed for the MAC describe the knowledge and skills needed by drug abuse counselors. Much more training is needed by drug abuse counselors on the dynamics of drug and alcohol abuse and on applying individual, group, family, and residential treatment interventions with male adolescents with substance abuse problems. All helping professionals working with adolescent male substance abusers can benefit from such training, from those with doctorates to those with master's degrees or other degrees or certification.

Research is needed to assess the effects of different types of interventions for adolescent males with drug abuse problems. There is, unfortunately, little research available in the professional literature on this topic. Research is needed to help counselors learn about the types of individual counseling approaches that are most effective with adolescent males. For instance, do cognitive therapy approaches work better with adolescent males than more affectively oriented approaches? In this kind of research, it is necessary to control as much as possible for differences in the personalities of the therapists that might influence the experimental findings as much as or more than the type of intervention used. The same kind of research is needed to determine the types of family therapy interventions that are most effective with adolescent drug abusers. When research is done comparing different kinds of interventions, it is important for researchers to remember the limitations of this kind of research and to avoid overgeneralizing their results.

More research is needed to determine the kinds of group interventions that work with adolescent drug abusers. For instance, are unstructured group or structured group interventions more effective with adolescent drug abusers? What types of confrontation are most effective in counseling groups with adolescent drug abusers? Is it more effective to run counseling groups without allowing the members to receive individual therapy, or can individual and group therapy be done at the same time and complement each other? Does involuntary group or individual counseling work as well as voluntary counseling? Research on these kinds of questions is necessary to help professionals to develop more knowledge about counseling interventions that work with male adolescent drug abusers.

Research needs to be performed on the effectiveness of residential and hospital-based treatment centers with adolescent males. Many of these treatment centers are currently based in part on a Twelve Steps model of treatment (Le, Ingvarson, & Page, 1995). Research needs to be performed to determine whether this kind of treatment approach is effective with male adolescents. This research should investigate whether the AA approach is as effective with male adolescents who abuse alcohol as for those who abuse illicit drugs such as cocaine or heroin. Research is also needed that compares the effectiveness of short- and long-term residential treatment centers working specifically with adolescent drug abusers. Another area of research to explore is whether harm reduction models of drug and alcohol abuse work with male adolescents and whether this model is more effective with some male adolescents than with others.

More work is needed to determine what interventions work with male adolescent drug abusers, and training is necessary to help professionals providing counseling to these adolescents to develop the skills necessary to do this successfully. I have emphasized that if adolescents such as Tom are to be helped to overcome their drug abuse problems, then a large-scale social effort is needed on several fronts. Professionals providing counseling services can help in this effort, but the services that they provide are just one part of the equation. I hope that this chapter makes a contribution in describing counseling interventions that can be utilized with male adolescent drug abusers. This work is important because of its humanitarian value and because adolescent drug abusers often become adult addicts who cause untold pain to themselves and others.

HIGHLIGHTS OF CHAPTER 20

▶ The average age at which boys take their first drink is 11.0 years, and about 28% of high school seniors consume five or more drinks a week. Use of alcohol is the most serious drug problem for adolescent males.

▶ NIDA surveys show that about 44% of high school aged males had ever used marijuana, 19% of males had ever used stimulants, and 10% had ever used crack cocaine.

▶ The primary sets of factors consistently associated with adolescent drug abuse are cultural or social factors, family interaction factors, peer relationship factors, and the personal characteristics of the abuser. All these factors need to be dealt with in effective treatment programs.

▶ It is often difficult to diagnose adolescents who are at risk for addiction in later life. Early identification of male adolescents who are at risk for addiction is important so that they can receive help. Scales and other measuring instruments exist that can help in the identification of these adolescents, but counselors must evaluate the individual factors associated with addiction in each case.

▶ It is important that counselors, psychologists, and other professionals working with adolescents with drug abuse problems develop techniques for establishing rapport with these clients. It is important that the drug-abusing adolescent establish trust in the person helping him; otherwise, he will resist being helped.

▶ It is important that counselors, psychologists, and other treatment professionals choose interventions that meet the individual needs of the clients with whom they are working. For instance, some individuals may need to be referred to AA programs and others may not, and some clients may need to enter inpatient drug treatment programs but others may not.

▶ Individual counseling, family counseling, group therapy, and residential drug treatment programs can all be helpful in treating some male adolescent drug abusers. Clients should be referred to these types of programs based on their individual needs, not program needs.

▶ Many more treatment programs and treatment options are needed for male adolescent drug abusers. Too often, effective treatment options are not available within the communities of these clients.

▶ More research is needed to assess the effects of different kinds of treatment programs with various types of adolescent male drug abusers. The effectiveness of harm reduction programs, as well as that of other types of treatment programs, needs to be researched.

REFERENCES

Abel, G. C., Mittelman, M. S., & Becker, J. V. (1985). Sexual offenders: Results of assessment and recommendations for treatment. In H. H. Ben Aron, S. J. Hucker, & C. D. Webster (Eds.), *Clinical criminology* (pp. 191-205). Toronto: M & M Graphics.

Abikoff, H., Courtney, M., Pelham, W. G., & Koplewicz, H. S. (1993). Teachers' ratings of disruptive behaviors: The influence of halo effects. *Journal of Abnormal Child Psychology, 21*, 519-533.

Abikoff, H. B., & Hechtman, L. (1996). Multimodal therapy and stimulants in the treatment of children with ADHD. In E. D. Hibbs & P. S. Jensen (Eds.), *Psychosocial treatments for child and adolescent disorders: Empirically based strategies for clinical practice* (pp. 341-369). Washington, DC: American Psychological Association.

Achatz, M., & MacAllum, C. A. (1994). *Young unwed fathers: Report from the field.* Philadelphia: Public/Private Ventures.

Achenbach, T. M. (1991). *Child Behavior Checklist for ages 4-18.* Burlington, VT: University Associates in Psychiatry.

Achenbach, T. M., & Edelbrock, C. S. (1983). *Manual for the Child Behavior Checklist and the Revised Child Behavior Profile.* Burlington, VT: University Associates in Psychiatry.

Ackerman, R. J. (1993). *Silent sons: A book for and about men.* New York: Simon & Schuster.

Adams, G. R., & Gullotta, T. (1983). *Adolescent life experiences.* Monterey, CA: Brooks/Cole.

Adler, A. (1956). *The individual psychology of Alfred Adler* (H. Ansbacher & R. Ansbacher, Eds.). New York: Harper & Row.

Ahmad, Y., & Smith, P. K. (1994). Bullying in schools and the issue of sex differences. In J. Archer (Ed.), *Male violence* (pp. 70-83). London: Routledge.

Alberti, R. E., & Emmons, M. L. (1982). *Your perfect right: A guide to assertive living.* San Luis Obispo, CA: Impact.

Allen, F. H. (1979). *Psychotherapy with children.* Lincoln: University of Nebraska Press. (Original work published 1942)

Allen-Meares, P. (1984). Adolescent pregnancy and parenting: The forgotten adolescent father and his parents. *Journal of Social Work and Human Sexuality, 3*(1), 27-38.

Alpern, G. D., Boll, T. J., & Shearer, M. S. (1984). *Developmental Profile II.* Los Angeles: Western Psychological Services.

Ambrosini, P. J., Bianchi, M. D., Rabinovich, H., & Elia, J. (1993). Antidepressant treatments in children and adolescents: II. Anxiety, physical and behavioral disorders. *Journal of the American Academy of Child and Adolescent Psychiatry, 32*, 483-493.

American heritage dictionary of the English language. (1970). New York: American Heritage.

American Psychiatric Association. (1994a). *Diagnostic and statistical manual of mental disorders* (4th ed.). Washington, DC: Author.

American Psychiatric Association (1994b). *Diagnostic criteria from DSM-IV.* Washington, DC: Author.

American Psychological Association. (1993). Guidelines for providers of psychological services to ethnic, linguistic, and culturally diverse populations. *American Psychologist, 48*, 45-48.

Amini, F. (1976). Adolescent drug abuse: Etiologic and treatment considerations. *Adolescence, 11*, 281-299.

Anastopoulos, A., & Barkley, R. A. (1990). Counseling and training parents. In R. A. Barkley (Ed.), *Attention-deficit hyperactivity disorder: A handbook for diagnosis and treatment* (pp. 397-431). New York: Guilford.

Anderson, J. C., Williams, S., McGee, R., & Silva, P. A. (1987). DSM-III disorders in preadolescent children. *Archives of General Psychiatry, 44*, 69-76.

Anderson, L. P., Eaddy, C. L., & Williams, E. A. (1990). Psychosocial competence: Toward a theory of understanding positive mental health among Black Americans. In D. S. Ruiz & J. P. Comer (Eds.), *Handbook of mental health and mental disorders among Black Americans* (pp. 255-271). New York: Greenwood.

Andronico, M. P. (Ed.). (1996). *Men in groups: Realities and insights.* Washington, DC: American Psychological Association.

Andronico, M. P. (Chair). (1998, August). *Therapeutic groups for boys and men.* Symposium conducted at the annual convention of the American Psychological Association, San Francisco.

Arcaya, J. M. (1996). Latino males in group therapy. In M. Andronico (Ed.), *Men in groups: Insights, interventions, and psychoeducational work* (pp. 151-162). Washington, DC: American Psychological Association Press.

Arora, C. M. J., & Thompson, D. A. (1987). Defining bullying for a secondary school. *Educational and Child Psychology, 4*, 110-120.

Asante, M. K. (1987). *The Afrocentric idea.* Philadelphia: Temple University Press.

Asante, M. K. (1988). *Afrocentricity.* Trenton, NJ: Africa World Press.

Associated Press. (1998, December 2). Boys don't report sex abuse. *Bucks County Courier Times*, p. A1.

Athletic Footwear Association. (1990). *American youth and sports participation.* N. Palm Beach, FL: Author.

Atkinson, D. R. (1985). Research on cross-cultural counseling and psychotherapy: A review and update of reviews. In P. B. Pedersen (Ed.), *Handbook of cross-cultural counseling and therapy* (pp. 191-197). Westport, CT: Greenwood.

Atkinson, D. R., Morten, G., & Sue, D. W. (1993). *Counseling American minorities: A cross-cultural perspective* (4th ed.). Madison, WI: Brown & Benchmark.

Avis, H. (1996). *Drugs and life.* Dubuque, IA: Brown & Benchmark.

Awad, G. A., Saunders, E., & Levene, J. (1984). A clinical study of male adolescent sex offenders. *International Journal of Offender Therapy and Comparative Criminology, 28*, 105-116.

Axelson, J. A. (1999). *Counseling and development in a multicultural society* (3rd ed.). Pacific Grove, CA: Brooks/Cole.

Axline, V. (1947). *Play therapy.* Cambridge, MA: Houghton Mifflin.

Baker, S. B. (1996). *School counseling for the twenty-first century* (2nd ed.). Englewood Cliffs, NJ: Merrill.

Baltes, P., Reese, H., & Lipsett, L. P. (1980). Life-span developmental psychology. *Annual Review of Psychology, 31*, 65-110.

Bandura, A. (1969). *Principles of behavior modification.* New York: Holt, Rinehart & Winston.

Bandura, A. (1986). *Social foundations of thought and action: A social cognitive theory.* Englewood Cliffs, NJ: Prentice Hall.

Barker, P. (1990). *Clinical interviews with children and adolescents.* New York: W. W. Norton.

Barkley, R. A. (1987). *Defiant children: A clinician's manual for parent training.* New York: Guilford.

Barkley, R. A. (1989a). Hyperactive girls and boys: Stimulant drug effects on mother-child interactions. *Journal of Child Psychology and Psychiatry, 30*, 379-390.

Barkley, R. A. (1989b). The problem with stimulus control and rule governed behavior in attention deficit disorder with hyperactivity. In L. A. Bloomingdale & J. Swanson (Eds.), *Attention deficit disorders: Current concepts and emerging trends in attentional and behavioural disorders of childhood* (pp. 203-228). Toronto: Pergamon.

Barkley, R. A. (1990). *Attention deficit hyperactivity disorder: A handbook for diagnosis and treatment.* New York: Guilford.

Barkley, R. A. (1991). The ecological validity of laboratory and analogue assessment methods of ADHD symptoms. *Journal of Abnormal Child Psychology, 19*, 149-178.

Barkley, R. A. (Ed.). (1995). *Taking charge of ADHD.* New York: Guilford.

Barkley, R. A., Anastopoulos, A. D., Guevremont, D. C., & Fletcher, K. E. (1991). Adolescents with ADHD: Patterns of behavioral adjustment, academic functioning, and treatment utilization. *Journal of the American Academy of Child and Adolescent Psychiatry, 30*, 752-761.

Barkley, R. A., DuPaul, G. J., & McMurray, M. B. (1990). A comprehensive evaluation of attention deficit disorder with and without hyperactivity defined by research criteria. *Journal of Consulting and Clinical Psychology, 58*, 775-789.

Barkley, R. A., Fischer, M., Edelbrock, C. S., & Smallish, L. (1990). The adolescent outcome of hyperactive children diagnosed by research criteria: I. An 8 year prospective follow-up study. *Journal of the American Academy of Child and Adolescent Psychiatry, 29*, 546-557.

Barkley, R. A., & Robin, A. L. (1995). Getting through adolescence with an ADHD child. In R. A. Barkley (Ed.), *Taking charge of ADHD* (pp. 188-205). New York: Guilford.

Barlow, D. H., & Craske, M. G. (1989). *Mastery of your anxiety and panic.* Albany, NY: Graywind.

Barnhill, L., Rubenstein, G., & Rocklin, N. (1979). From generation to generation: Father-to-be in transition. *The Family Coordinator, 28,* 229-235.

Batsche, G. M., & Knoff, H. M. (1994). Bullies and their victims: Understanding a pervasive problem in the schools. *School Psychology Review, 23,* 165-174.

Batshaw, M. L. (1997). Fragile X syndrome. In M. L. Batshaw (Ed.), *Children with disabilities* (4th ed., pp. 377-388). Baltimore, MD: Paul H. Brooks.

Batshaw, M. L., & Shapiro, B. K. (1997). Mental retardation. In M. L. Batshaw (Ed.), *Children with disabilities* (4th ed., pp. 335-360). Baltimore, MD: Paul H. Brooks.

Battrick, S., & Thomson, R. (1994). *Sport and social status in New Zealand secondary schools.* Unpublished manuscript, University of Otago, Dunedin, New Zealand.

Baum, D. J. (1980). *Teenage pregnancy.* Toronto: Beaufort Books.

Baumeister, R. (1992). *Meanings of life.* Chicago: University of Chicago Press.

Baumeister, R., Smart, L., & Boden, J. (1996). Relation of threatened egotism to violence and aggression: The dark side of high self-esteem. *Psychological Review, 103,* 5-33.

Bays, L., Freeman-Longo, R., & Hildebran, D. (1990). *How can I stop? Breaking my deviant cycle.* Brandon, VT: Safer Society Press.

Beck, A. T. (1993a). *The Beck anxiety inventory.* Philadelphia: Center for Cognitive Therapy.

Beck, A. T. (1993b). *The Beck depression inventory.* Philadelphia: Center for Cognitive Therapy.

Beck, A. T., Sokol, L., Clark, D., Berchick, R., & Wright, F. (1992). A crossover study of focused cognitive therapy for panic disorder. *American Journal of Psychiatry, 149*(6), 778-783.

Becker, E. (1973). *The denial of death.* New York: Free Press.

Becker, J. V., & Abel, G. C. (1985). *Methodological and ethical issues in evaluating and treating adolescent sexual offenders* (DHHS Pub. No. ADM-85-1396). Rockville, MD: U.S. Department of Health and Human Services.

Becker, R. E., Heimberg, R. G., & Bellack, A. S. (1987). *Social skills training treatment for depression.* New York: Pergamon.

Befera, M. S., & Barkley, R. A. (1985). Hyperactive and normal girls and boys: Mother-child interaction, parent psychiatric status and child psychopathology. *Journal of Child Psychology and Psychiatry, 26,* 439-452.

Belsher, G., & Wilkes, T.C.R. (1994). Ten key principles of adolescent cognitive therapy. In T.C.R. Wilkes, G. Belsher, A. J. Rush, & E. Frank (Eds.), *Cognitive therapy for depressed adolescents* (pp. 22-44). New York: Guilford.

Bell, G. D. (1963). Processes in the formation of adolescents' aspirations. *Social Forces, 42,* 179-195.

Beman, D. S. (1995). Risk factors leading to adolescent substance abuse. *Adolescence, 30,* 201-208.

Berg, K. I., & Gallagher, D. (1991). Solution focused brief treatment with adolescent substance abusers. In T. C. Dodd & M. D. Selekman (Eds.), *Family therapy approaches with adolescent substance abusers* (pp. 93-112). Boston: Allyn & Bacon.

Berg-Cross, G., & Berg-Cross, L. (1976). Bibliotherapy for young children. *Journal of Clinical Child Psychology, 5,* 35-38.

Berger, M., & Wright, L. (1978). Divided allegiance: Men, work and family. *The Counseling Psychologist, 7,* 50-52.

Bernal, G., & Flores-Oritz, Y. (1991). Contextual family therapy with adolescent drug abusers. In T. C. Dodd & M. D. Selekman (Eds.), *Family therapy approaches with adolescent substance abusers* (pp. 70-91). Boston: Allyn & Bacon.

Bernstein, D. A., & Borkovec, T. D. (1973). *Progressive relaxation training.* Champaign, IL: Research Press.

Bernstein, N. R. (1985). Sexuality in mentally retarded adolescents. *Medical Aspects of Human Sexuality, 19,* 50-61.

Besag, V. (1989). *Bullies and victims in schools.* Milton Keynes, UK: Open University Press.

Beymer, L. (1995). *Meeting the guidance and counseling needs of boys.* Alexandria, VA: American Counseling Association.

Biederman, J., Faraone, S. V., Keenan, K., Benjamin, J., Krifcher, B., Moore, C., Sprich-Buckminster, S., Ugaglia, K., Jellinek, M. S., Steingard, R., Spencer, T., Norman, D., Kolodny, R., Kraus, I., Perrin, J., Keller, M. B., & Tsuang, M. T. (1992). Further evidence for family-genetic risk factors in attention deficit hyperactivity disorder. *Archives of General Psychiatry, 49,* 728-738.

Biederman, J., Newcorn, J., & Sprich, S. (1991). Comorbidity of attention deficit hyperactivity disorder with conduct, depressive, anxiety, and other disorders. *American Journal of Psychiatry, 148,* 564-577.

Biller, H. (1982). Fatherhood: Implications for child and adult treatment. In B. Wolman (Ed.), *Handbook of developmental psychology* (pp. 702-725). Englewood Cliffs, NJ: Prentice Hall.

Billingsley, A. (1968). *Black families in White America*. Englewood Cliffs, NJ: Prentice Hall.

Billingsley, A. (1992). *Climbing Jacob's ladder: The enduring legacy of African American families*. New York: Simon & Schuster.

Bingham, M., Edmondson, J., & Stryker, S. (1985). *Challenges: A young man's journal for self awareness and personal planning*. Santa Barbara, CA: Advocacy.

Blankenhorn, D. (1995). *Fatherless America: Confronting our most urgent social problem*. New York: Basic Books.

Blos, P. (1962). *On adolescence*. New York: Free Press.

Bogren, L. Y. (1986). The couvade syndrome. *International Journal of Family Psychiatry, 7*, 123-136.

Bolton, F. G., Morris, L. A., & MacEachron, A. E. (1989). *Males at risk: The other side of child sexual abuse*. Newbury Park, CA: Sage.

Borduin, C. M., Mann, B. J., Cone, L. T., & Henggeler, S. W. (1995). Multisystemic treatment of serious juvenile offenders: Long-term prevention of criminality and violence. *Journal of Consulting and Clinical Psychology, 63*(4), 569-578.

Boulton, M. J., & Underwood, K. (1992). Bully/victim problems among middle school children. *British Journal of Educational Psychology, 62*, 73-87.

Bourne, E. J. (1995). *The anxiety and phobia workbook*. Oakland, CA: New Harbinger.

Bowman, R. (1987). Approaches to counseling through music. *Elementary School Guidance & Counseling, 21*, 284-291.

Bowman, R. B. (1995). Using metaphors as tools for counseling children. *Elementary School Guidance & Counseling, 29*, 206-216.

Bowman, S. L. (1995). Career intervention strategies and assessment issues for African Americans. In F.T.L. Leong (Ed.), *Career development and vocational behavior of racial and ethnic minorities* (pp. 137-164). Mahwah, NJ: Lawrence Erlbaum.

Boyd-Franklin, N. (1989). *Black families in therapy: A multi-systems approach*. New York: Guilford.

Boyer, J. L., & Guthrie, L. (1985). Assessment and treatment of the suicidal patient. In E. E. Beckham & W. R. Leber (Eds.), *Handbook of depression: Treatment, assessment, and research* (pp. 606-633). Homewood, IL: Dorsey.

Boyer, L. B. (1979). *Childhood and folklore: A psychoanalytic study of Apache personality*. New York: Library of Psychological Anthropology.

Boyle, R. P. (1966). The effects of the high school on students' aspirations. *American Journal of Sociology, 71*, 628-639.

Brand, A. (1987). Writing as counseling. *Elementary School Guidance and Counseling, 21*, 266-275.

Brecher, E. M. (and the Editors of *Consumer Reports*). (1972). *Licit and illicit drugs*. Boston: Little, Brown.

Breen, M. J., & Barkley, R. A. (1988). Child psychopathology and parenting stress in girls and boys having attention deficit disorder with hyperactivity. *Journal of Pediatric Psychology, 13*, 265-280.

Bremer, J. (1992). Serious juvenile sex offenders: Treatment and long term follow-up. *Psychiatric Annals, 22*, 326-332.

Brent, D. A., & Lerner, M. S. (1994). Cognitive therapy with affectively ill, suicidal adolescents. In T.C.R. Wilkes, G. Belsher, A. J. Rush, & E. Frank (Eds.), *Cognitive therapy for depressed adolescents* (pp. 298-320). New York: Guilford.

Brewer, B., Van Raalte, J., & Linder, D. (1993). Athletic identity: Hercules' muscles or Achilles' heel? *International Journal of Sport Psychology, 24*, 237-254.

Brindis, C., Barth, R. P., & Loomis, A. B. (1987). Continuous counseling: Case management with teenage parents. *Social Casework: The Journal of Contemporary Social Work, 68*, 164-172.

Brinson, J. A. (1995). Group work for Black adolescent substance users: Some issues and recommendations. *Journal of Child and Adolescent Substance Abuse, 4*, 49-59.

Brook, J. S., Gordon, A. S., Whiteman, M., & Choen, D. (1986). Dynamics of childhood and adolescent personality traits and adolescent drug use. *Developmental Psychology, 22*, 403-414.

Brookhiser, R. (1991). *The way of the WASP*. New York: Free Press.

Browder, D. W., Jones, E. D., & Patton, J. R. (1990). Family issues. In J. R. Patton, J. S. Payne, & M. Beirne-Smith (Eds.), *Mental retardation* (3rd ed., pp. 429-459). Columbus, OH: Merrill.

Brown, C. S. (1991). Treatment of attention deficit hyperactivity disorder: A critical review. *DIPC: The Annals of Pharmacotherapy, 25*, 1207-1213.

Brown, L., & Gilligan, C. (1992). *Meeting at the crossroads: Women's psychology and girls' development*. Cambridge, MA: Harvard University Press.

Brown, M. T. (1995). The career development of African Americans: Theoretical and empirical issues. In F.T.L. Leong (Ed.), *Career development and vocational behavior of racial and ethnic minorities* (pp. 7-36). Mahwah, NJ: Lawrence Erlbaum.

Brown, O. (1960). *But I was cool: On sin & soul* (Record album, CL 1577). New York: Columbia Records.

Brown, S. (1990). *If the shoes fit: Final report and program implementation guide of the Maine Young Fathers Project.* Portland: Human Services Development Institute, University of Southern Maine.

Bryne, B. J. (1994). Bullies and victims in a school setting with reference to some Dublin schools. *Irish Journal of Psychology, 15,* 574-586.

Buehler, C. (1933). *Der menschliche Lebenslauf als psychologisches Problem* [The human life cycle as a psychological problem]. Leipzig: Hirzel.

Buhrke, R. A. (1989). Incorporating lesbian and gay issues into counselor training: A resource guide. *Journal of Counseling and Development, 68*(1), 77-80.

Buhrke, R. A., & Douce, L. A. (1991). Training issues for counseling psychologists in working with lesbian women and gay men. *The Counseling Psychologist, 19*(2), 216-234.

Bui, K.-V.T. & Takeuchi, D. T. (1992). Ethnic minority adolescents and the use of community mental health care services. *American Journal of Community Psychology, 20,* 403-418.

Burns, D. D. (1989). *Feeling good: The new mood therapy.* New York: Penguin.

Burr, W. R., Hill, R., Nye, F. I., & Reiss, I. L. (Eds.). (1979). *Contemporary theories about families.* New York: Free Press.

Butcher, J., Graham, J., Williams, C., Kaemmer, B., Hathaway, S., & McKinley, J. (1992). *Minnesota multiphasic personality inventory—adolescent.* Minneapolis: National Computer Systems.

Cabe, N. (1997). Conduct disorder: Grounded play therapy. In H. G. Kaduson, D. Cangelosi, & C. Schaefer (Eds.), *The playing cure* (pp. 229-253). Northvale, NJ: Jason Aronson.

Cadbury, S., Childs-Clark, A., & Sandhu, S. (1990). Group anxiety management: Effectiveness, perceived helpfulness, and follow-up. *British Journal of Clinical Psychology, 29,* 245-247.

Cairnes, R. B., Cairnes, B. D., Neckerman, H. J., Gest, S. D., & Gariepy, J. L. (1988). Social networks and aggressive behavior: Peer support or peer rejection? *Developmental Psychology, 24,* 815-823.

Campbell, D. (Author and speaker). (1996). *The power of music* (Cassette Recording No. 57290-3). New York: Simon & Schuster Audio Division.

Canada, G. (1995). *Fist stick knife gun.* Boston: Beacon.

Carkuff, R. R. (1993). *The art of helping* (5th ed.). Amherst, MA: Human Resource Development Press.

Carlson, G. (1981). The phenomenology of adolescent depression. *Adolescent Psychiatry, 9,* 411-421.

Carlson, J., & Lewis, J. (Eds.). (1988). *Counseling the adolescent: Individual, family, and school interventions* (pp. 21-40). Denver: Love Publishing.

Carrera, M. A. (1992). Involving adolescent males in pregnancy and STD prevention programs. *Adolescent Medicine: State of the Art Reviews, 3,* 1-13.

Carter, F., & Cheesman, P. (1988). *Anxiety in childhood and adolescence: Encouraging self-help through relaxation training.* New York: Croom Helm.

Cass, V. (1979). Homosexual identity formation: A theoretical model. *Journal of Homosexuality, 4,* 219-235.

Cass, V. (1996). Sexual orientation identity formation: A Western phenomenon. In R. Cabaj & T. Stein (Eds.), *Textbook of homosexuality and mental health* (pp. 227-252). Washington, DC: American Psychiatric Press.

Centers for Disease Control. (1998). *Young people at risk—epidemic shifts further toward young women and minorities* (CDC Update). Atlanta: Centers for Disease Control and Prevention and the National Center for HIV, STD, & TB Prevention.

Cervera, N. (1991). Unwed teenage pregnancy: Family relationships with the father of the baby. *Families in Society, 72,* 29-37.

Chabot, D. R., & Matteis, M. C. (1991). Adolescent substance abuse: A systemic intergenerational approach. In T. C. Dodd & M. D. Selekman (Eds.), *Family therapy approaches with adolescent substance abusers* (pp. 112-135). Boston: Allyn & Bacon.

Chadwick, B. A., & Heaton, T. B. (Eds.). (1996). *Statistical handbook on adolescents in America.* Phoenix, AZ: Oryx.

Chandler, K. (1995). *Passages of pride: Lesbian and gay youth come of age.* New York: Times Books.

Chartrand, J., & Rose, M. L. (1996). Career interventions for at-risk populations: Incorporating social cognitive influences. *Career Development Quarterly, 44*(4), 341-354.

Chase, M., & Dummer, G. (1992). The role of sports as a social status determinant for children. *Research Quarterly for Exercise and Sport, 63,* 418-424.

Chaumeton, N., & Duda, J. (1988). Is it how you play the game or whether you win or lose? The effect of competitive level and situation on coaching behaviors. *Journal of Sport Behavior, 11,* 157-174.

Cheung, F. K. (1991). The use of mental health services by ethnic minorities. In H. F. Myers, P. Wohlford, L. P. Guzman, & R. J. Echememdia (Eds.), *Ethnic minority perspective on clinical training and services in psychology* (pp. 23-31). Washington, DC: American Psychological Association.

Children's Defense Fund. (1985). *Black and White children in America: Key facts.* Washington, DC: Author.

Children's Defense Fund. (1998). *The state of America's children: A report from the Children's Defense Fund: Yearbook, 1998.* Boston: Beacon.

Chin, J. W. (1993). Multicultural education does not always include all cultures. *Guidepost, 35,* 2.

Chodorow, N. (1978). *The reproduction of mothering.* Berkeley: University of California Press.

Chung, R.C.-Y., Bemak, F., & Okazaki, S. (1997). Counseling Americans of Southeast Asian descent. In C. C. Lee (Ed.), *Multicultural issues in counseling* (2nd ed., pp. 207-231). Alexandria, VA: American Association for Counseling and Development.

Clarke, E. A., & Kiselica, M. S. (1997). A systemic counseling approach to the problem of bullying. *Elementary School Guidance & Counseling, 31,* 310-325.

Clarke, G., Sack, W. H., & Goff, B. (1993). Three forms of stress in Cambodian adolescent refugees. *Journal of Abnormal Child Psychology, 21,* 65-77.

Clarkin, J. F., & Glazer, H. I. (1981). *Depression: Behavioral and directive intervention strategies.* New York: Garland STPM.

Clees, T. J. (1996). Supported living and collaborative transition. In P. J. McLaughlin & P. Wehman (Eds.), *Mental retardation and developmental disabilities* (pp. 129-143). Austin, TX: Pro-Ed.

Cleland, C. C. (1979). *The profoundly mentally retarded.* Englewood Cliffs, NJ: Prentice Hall.

Coakley, J. J. (1990). *Sport in society: Issues and controversies* (4th ed.). St. Louis: Times Mirror/Mosby.

Coakley, J. (1992). Burnout among adolescent athletes: A personal failure or social problem. *Sociology of Sport Journal, 9,* 271-285.

Coie, J. D., Dodge, K. A., & Coppotelli, H. (1982). Dimensions and types of social status: A cross-age perspective. *Developmental Psychology, 18,* 557-570.

Coleman, J. (1961). *The adolescent society: The social life of the teenager and its impact on education.* New York: Free Press.

Coleman, J. C. (1976). *Abnormal psychology and modern life* (5th ed.). Glenview, IL: Scott, Foresman.

Coleman, S. B. (1991). Intergenerational patterns of traumatic loss: Death and despair in addict families. In F. Walsh & M. McGoldrick (Eds.), *Living beyond loss: Death in the family* (pp. 260-272). New York: W. W. Norton.

Conger, J. J. (1977). *Adolescence and youth: Psychological development in a changing world* (2nd ed.). New York: Harper & Row.

Cook, D. A., & Helms, J. E. (1988). Visible racial/ethnic group supervisees' satisfaction with cross-cultural supervision as predicted by relationship characteristics. *Journal of Counseling Psychology, 35,* 268-274.

Cordes, C. (1985, January). At risk in America: Black males face high odds in a hostile society. *APA Monitor,* pp. 9, 10, 11, 27.

Cotton, P. (1996). Harm reduction approach may be middle ground. In H. T. Wilson (Ed.), *Drugs, society, and behavior* (pp. 253-257). Guilford, CT: Brown & Benchmark.

Crockett, L., & Petersen, A. (1993). Adolescent development: Health risks and opportunities for health promotion. In S. Millstein, A. Petersen, & E. Nightingale (Eds.), *Promoting the health of adolescents* (pp. 13-37). New York: Oxford University Press.

Dahmus, S. (1992). Personal experience inventory. *Measurement and Evaluation in Counseling and Development, 25,* 91-94.

Daly, A., Jennings, J., Beckett, J. O., & Leashore, B. R. (1995). Effective coping strategies of African Americans. *Social Work, 40*(2), 240-248.

D'Andrea, M., & Arrendondo, P. (1997, November). Providing culturally-sensitive grief counseling services to Filipino clients. *Counseling Today,* p. 63.

D'Andrea, M., & Daniels, J. (1992). A career development program for inner-city youth. *Career Development Quarterly, 40,* 272-280.

Daniels, S. M., Cornelius, D., Makas, E., & Chipouras, S. (1979). Sexuality and disability: The need for services. In S. M. Daniels, D. Cornelius, E. Makas, & S. Chipouras (Eds.), *Who cares? A handbook on sex education and counseling services for disabled people* (pp. 1-19). Washington, DC: Sex and Disability Project.

Danish, S. J. (1995). Reflections on the status and future of psychology. *Community Psychologist, 28*(3), 16-18.

Danish, S. J. (1996). Interventions for enhancing adolescents' life skills. *The Humanistic Psychologist, 24*(3), 365-381.

Danish, S. (1997). Going for the goal: A life skills program for adolescents. In T. Gullotta & G. Albee (Eds.), *Primary prevention works* (pp. 291-312). Thousand Oaks, CA: Sage.

Danish, S. J. (1998). *The SUPER Program*. Richmond, VA: Life Skills Center, Virginia Commonwealth University.

Danish, S., & D'Augelli, A. (1980). Promoting competence and enhancing development through life development intervention. In L. A. Bond & J. C. Rosen (Eds.), *Primary prevention of psychopathology* (Vol. 4, pp. 105-129). Hanover, NH: University Press of New England.

Danish, S., & D'Augelli, A. (1983). *Helping skills II: Life development intervention*. New York: Human Sciences Press.

Danish, S., D'Augelli, A., & Ginsberg, M. (1984). Life development intervention: Promotion of mental health through the development of competence. In S. Brown & R. Lent (Eds.), *Handbook of counseling psychology* (pp. 520-544). New York: John Wiley.

Danish, S. J., & Hale, B. D. (1981). Toward an understanding of the practice of sport psychology. *Journal of Sport Psychology, 3*, 90-99.

Danish, S., Kleiber, D., & Hall, H. (1987). Developmental intervention and motivation enhancement in the context of sport. In M. Maehr & D. Kleiber (Eds.), *Advances in motivation and achievement: Enhancing motivation* (Vol. 5, pp. 211-238). Greenwich, CT: JAI.

Danish, S., Mash, J., Howard, C., & Curl, S., Meyer, A., Owens, S., & Kendall, K. (1992a). *Going for the goal: Leader manual*. Richmond: Department of Psychology, Virginia Commonwealth University.

Danish, S. J., Mash, J. M., Howard, C. W., Curl, S. J., Meyer, A. L., Owens, S., & Kendall, K. (1992b). *Going for the goal: Student activity book*. Richmond: Department of Psychology, Virginia Commonwealth University.

Danish, S. J., & Nellen, V. C. (1997). New roles for sport psychologists: Teaching life skills through sport to at-risk youth. *Quest, 49*(1), 100-113.

Danish, S., Nellen, V., & Owens, S. (1996). Teaching life skills through sport: Community-based programs for adolescents. In J. Van Raalte & B. Brewer (Eds.), *Exploring sport and exercise psychology* (pp. 205-225). Washington, DC: American Psychological Association.

Danish, S., Petitpas, A., & Hale, B. (1993). Life development intervention for athletes: Life skills through sports. *The Counseling Psychologist, 21*, 352-385.

Danish, S., Petitpas, A., & Hale, B. (1995). Psychological interventions: A life development model. In S. Murphy (Ed.), *Sport psychology interventions* (pp. 19-38). Champaign, IL: Human Kinetics.

Danish, S., Smyer, M. A., & Nowak, C. A. (1980). Developmental intervention: Enhancing life-event processes. In P. B. Baltes & O. G. Brim, Jr. (Eds.), *Life-span development and behavior* (Vol. 3, pp. 339-366). New York: Academic Press.

D'Augelli, A. R. (1992). Lesbian and gay male undergraduates' experiences of harassment and fear on campus. *Journal of Interpersonal Violence, 7*, 383-395.

D'Augelli, A. R. (1994). Lesbian and gay male development: Steps toward an analysis of lesbians' and gay men's lives. In B. Greene & G. M. Herek (Eds.), *Lesbian and gay psychology: Theory, research, and clinical applications* (pp. 118-132). Thousand Oaks, CA: Sage.

D'Augelli, A. R. (1996). Lesbian, gay, and bisexual development during adolescence and young adulthood. In R. Cabaj & T. Stein (Eds.), *Textbook of homosexuality and mental health* (pp. 267-288). Washington, DC: American Psychiatric Press.

David, D. S., & Brannon, R. (Eds.). (1976). *The forty-nine percent majority: The male sex role*. Reading, MA: Addison-Wesley.

Davis, M., Eshelman, E. R., & McKay, M. (1995). *The relaxation and stress reduction workbook*. Oakland, CA: New Harbinger.

de Coubertin, P. (1966). What we can now ask of sport (J. Dixon, Trans.). In *The Olympic idea: Discoveries and essays*. Kolm: Carl Diem Institut. (Original work presented 1918)

De Leon, G. (1986). Program-based evaluation research in therapeutic communities. In F. M. Tims & J. P. Ludford (Eds.), *Drug abuse treatment evaluation: Strategies, progress, and prospects* (pp. 69-88). Rockville, MD: National Institute on Drug Abuse.

Deloria, V., Jr. (1994). *God is red: A Native view of religion*. Golden, CO: Fulcrum Printing.

Dent, D. (1989, November). Readin', ritin' and rage: How schools are destroying Black boys. *Essence*, pp. 54-59, 114-116.

Diefendorf, A. R. (1918). *Clinical psychiatry: A textbook for students and physicians*. London: Macmillan.

Dodge, K. A. (1993a). The future of research on the treatment of conduct disorder. *Development & Psychopathology, 5*, 311-319.

Dodge, K. A. (1993b). Social-cognitive mechanisms in the development of conduct disorder and depression. *Annual Review of Psychology, 44*(26), 559-584.

Dodge, K. A., & Coie, J. D. (1987). Social-information-processing factors in reactive and proactive aggression in children's peer groups. *Journal of Personality and Social Psychology, 53,* 1146-1158.

Dong, Q., Yang, B., & Ollendick, T. H. (1994). Fears in Chinese children and adolescents and their relations to anxiety and depression. *Journal of Child Psychology and Psychiatry, 35,* 351-363.

Dorfman, E. (1951). Play therapy. In C. R. Rogers (Ed.), *Client centered therapy* (pp. 235-277). Boston: Houghton Mifflin.

Douglas, V. I., & Parry, P. A. (1994). Effects of reward and nonreward on frustration and attention in attention deficit disorder. *Journal of Abnormal Child Psychology, 22,* 281-302.

Doweiko, H. E. (1996). *Concepts of chemical dependency.* Pacific Grove, CA: Brooks/Cole.

Doyle, J. A. (1983). *The male experience.* Dubuque, IA: Wm. C. Brown.

Doyle, J. A. (1995). *The male experience* (3rd ed.). Dubuque, IA: Wm. C. Brown.

Dryfoos, J. G. (1994). *Full-service schools: A revolution in health and social services for children, youth, and families.* San Francisco: Jossey-Bass.

Dryfoos, J. G. (1997). The prevalence of problem behavior: Implications for programs. In R. P. Weissberg, T. P. Gullotta, R. L. Hampton, B. A. Ryan, & G. R. Adams (Eds.), *Healthy children 2010: Enhancing children's wellness* (pp. 17-46). Thousand Oaks, CA: Sage.

Duda, J. (1993). Goals: A social-cognitive approach to the study of achievement motivation in sport. In R. Singer, M. Murphey, & L. K. Tennant (Eds.), *Handbook of research on sport psychology* (pp. 421-436). New York: Macmillan.

Duda, J., & Nicholls, J. (1992). Dimensions of achievement motivation in schoolwork and sport. *Journal of Educational Psychology, 84,* 290-299.

Dufrene, P. M., & Coleman, V. D. (1992). Counseling Native Americans: Guidelines for group process. *Journal for Specialists in Group Work, 17,* 229-234.

Dunbar, R. (1988). *Primate social systems.* Ithaca, NY: Cornell University Press.

DuPaul, G. J. (1991). Attention deficit-hyperactivity disorder: Classroom intervention strategies. *School Psychology International, 12,* 85-94.

DuPaul, G. J., & Barkley, R. A. (1993). Behavioral contributions to pharmacotherapy: The utility of behavioral methodology in medication treatment of children with attention deficit hyperactivity disorder. *Behavior Therapy, 24,* 47-65.

DuPaul, G. J., & Rapport, M. D. (1993). Does methylphenidate normalize the classroom performance of children with attention deficit disorder? *Journal of the American Academy of Child and Adolescent Psychiatry, 32,* 190-198.

DuPaul, G. J., & Stoner, G. (1994). *ADHD in the schools: Assessment and intervention strategies.* New York: Guilford.

Eccles, J., Midgley, C., & Adler, T. (1984). Grade-related changes in the school environment: Effects on achievement motivation. In J. Nicholls (Ed.), *The development of achievement motivation* (pp. 283-332). Greenwich, CT: JAI.

Edwards, W. J. (1996a). Operating within the mainstream: Coping and adjustment among a sample of homosexual youths. *Deviant Behavior: An Interdisciplinary Journal, 17,* 229-251.

Edwards, W. J. (1996b). A sociological analysis of an in/visible minority group: Male adolescent homosexuals. *Youth & Society, 27*(3), 334-355.

Eisen, A. R., & Kearney, C. A. (1995). *Practitioner's guide to treating fear and anxiety in children and adolescents.* Northvale, NJ: Jason Aronson.

Eisen, A. R., Kearney, C. A., & Schaefer, C. E. (Eds.). (1995). *Clinical handbook of anxiety disorders in children and adolescents.* Northvale, NJ: Jason Aronson.

Eldridge, N. M. (1993). Culturally affirmative counseling with American Indians who are deaf. *Journal of Rehabilitative Counseling, 26,* 1-18.

Elliott, S. M., & Busse, R. T. (1991). Social skills assessment and intervention with children and adolescents: Guidelines for assessment and training procedures. *School Psychology International, 12*(1-2), 63-83.

Ellis, A. (1989). Rational-emotive therapy. In R. J. Corsini & D. Wedding (Eds.), *Current psychotherapies* (4th ed., pp. 197-240). Itasca, IL: F. E. Peacock.

Ellis, A., & Harper, R. A. (1975). *A new guide to rational living.* Englewood Cliffs, NJ: Prentice Hall.

Elshtain, J. B. (1993, July). Family matters: The plight of America's children. *The Christian Century,* pp. 14-21.

Elster, A. B., & Hendricks, L. (1986). Stresses and coping strategies of adolescent fathers. In A. B. Elster & M. E. Lamb (Eds.), *Adolescent fatherhood* (pp. 55-66). Hillsdale, NJ: Lawrence Erlbaum.

Elster, A. B., & Panzarine, S. (1983a). Adolescent fathers. In E. R. McAnarney (Ed.), *Premature adolescent pregnancy and parenthood* (pp. 231-252). New York: Grune & Stratton.

Elster, A. B., & Panzarine, S. (1983b). Teenage fathers: Stresses during gestation and early parenthood. *Clinical Pediatrics, 22,* 700-703.

Emslie, G. J., & Weinberg, W. A. (1994). Diagnosis and assessment of depression in adolescents. In T.C.R. Wilkes, G. Belsher, A. J. Rush, & E. Frank (Eds.), *Cognitive therapy for depressed adolescents* (pp. 45-68). New York: Guilford.

Erhardt, D., & Hinshaw, S. P. (1994). Initial sociometric impressions of attention-deficit hyperactivity disorder and comparison boys: Predictions from social behaviors and from nonbehavioral variables. *Journal of Consulting and Clinical Psychology, 62,* 833-842.

Erikson, E. (1956). The problem of ego identity. *Journal of the American Psychoanalytic Association, 4,* 56-121.

Erikson, E. (1959). The problem of ego identity. In *Psychological issues* (Vol. 1, pp. 101-171). New York: International Universities Press.

Erikson, E. (1963). *Childhood and society.* New York: Norton.

Erikson, E. H. (1968). *Identity: Youth and crisis.* New York: Norton.

Eron, L. D., & Huesman, L. R. (1984). The control of aggressive behavior by changes in attitudes, values, and the conditions of learning. In R. J. Blanchard & D. C. Blanchard (Eds.), *Advances in the study of aggression* (Vol. 1, pp. 139-171). Orlando, FL: Academic Press.

Esbensen, F., & Huizinga, D. (1991). Juvenile victimization and delinquency. *Youth & Society, 23*(2), 202-228.

Etaugh, C., & Liss, M. B. (1992). Home, school, and playroom: Training grounds for adult gender roles. *Sex Roles, 26,* 129-147.

Evans, J., & Roberts, G. (1987). Physical competence and the development of children's peer relations. *Quest, 39,* 23-35.

Evans, N. J., & Wall, V. A. (Eds.). (1991). *Beyond tolerance: Gays, lesbians, and bisexuals on campus.* Alexandria, VA: American College Personnel Association.

Exner, J. E. (1991). *The Rorschach: A comprehensive system: Vol. 3. Interpretation* (2nd ed.). New York: John Wiley.

Exner, J. E. (1993). *The Rorschach: A comprehensive system: Vol. 1. Basic foundations* (3rd ed.). New York: John Wiley.

Fagan, J. (1991). Community-based treatment for mentally disordered juvenile offenders. *Journal of Clinical Child Psychology, 20*(1), 42-50.

Fahy, U. (1995). *How to make the world a better place for gays and lesbians.* New York: Warner Books.

Faigel, H. C., Sznajdeerman, S., Tishby, O., Turel, M., & Pinus, U. (1995). Attention deficit disorder during adolescence: A review. *Journal of Adolescent Health, 16,* 174-184.

Faller, K. C. (1987). Women who sexually abuse children. *Violence and Victims, 2*(4), 263-276.

Faller, K. C. (1993). *Child sexual abuse: Intervention and treatment issues.* McLean, VA: U.S. Department of Health and Human Services Administration for Children and Families, National Center on Child Abuse and Neglect.

Fallows, M. R. (1979). *Irish Americans: Identity and assimilation.* Englewood Cliffs, NJ: Prentice Hall.

Farber, B. (1972). Effects of a severely retarded child on the family. In E. P. Trapp & P. Himelstein (Eds.), *Readings on the exceptional child* (pp. 225-245). New York: Appleton-Century-Crofts.

Farrow, J. A. (1990). Adolescent chemical dependency. *Medical Clinics of North America, 74,* 1265-1274.

Feigin, I. (1996). Soviet Jewish families. In M. McGoldrick, J. Giordano, & J. K. Pearce (Eds.), *Ethnicity and family therapy* (2nd ed., pp. 631-637). New York: Guilford.

Feindler, F. L., & Guttman, J. (1994). Cognitive-behavioral anger control training. In C. LeCroy (Ed.), *Handbook of child and adolescent treatment manuals* (pp. 170-199). New York: Lexington.

Fejgin, N. (1994). Participation in high school sports: A subversion of school mission or contribution to academic goals? *Sociology of Sport Journal, 11,* 211-230.

Feldman, R. A., Caplinger, T. E., & Wodarski, J. S. (1983). *The St. Louis conundrum: The effective treatment of antisocial youths.* Englewood Cliffs, NJ: Prentice Hall.

Feldman, S. S., & Rosenthal, D. A. (1990). The acculturation of autonomy expectations in Chinese high schoolers residing in two Western nations. *International Journal of Psychology, 25,* 259-281.

Field, T., Widmayer, S. M., Stringer, S., & Ignatoff, E. (1980). Teenage, lower-class Black mothers and their preterm infants: An intervention and developmental follow-up. *Child Development, 51,* 426-436.

Finkelhor, D. (1986). *A sourcebook on child sexual abuse.* Newbury Park, CA: Sage.

Fischer, M., Barkley, R. A., Fletcher, K. E., & Smallish, L. (1993). The adolescent outcome of hyperactive children: Predictors of psychiatric, academic, social, and emotional adjustment. *Journal of the Academy of Child and Adolescent Psychiatry, 32,* 324-332.

Flicek, M. (1992). Social status of boys with both academic problems and attention-deficit hyperactivity disorder. *Journal of Abnormal Child Psychology, 20,* 353-366.

Fogelman, E. (1996). Israeli families. In M. McGoldrick, J. Giordano, & J. K. Pearce (Eds.), *Ethnicity and family therapy* (2nd ed., pp. 638-645). New York: Guilford.

Fonagy, P., & Target, M. (1994). The efficacy of psychoanalysis for children with disruptive disorders. *Journal of the American Academy of Child and Adolescent Psychiatry, 33,* 45-55.

Fong, R. (1994). Family preservation: Making it work for Asians. *Child Welfare, 73,* 331-341.

Forehand, R. L., & Long, N. (1996). *Parenting the strong-willed child: The clinically proven five-week program for parents of two- to six-year-olds.* Chicago: Contemporary Books.

Forehand, R. L., & McMahon, B. (1981). *Helping the noncompliant child: A clinician's guide to parent training.* New York: Guilford.

Fox, K. (1992). The complexities of self-esteem promotion in physical education and sport. In T. Williams, L. Almond, & A. Sparkes (Eds.), *Sport and physical activity: Moving towards excellence* (pp. 383-389). London: E & F. N. Spon.

Franklin, A. J. (1989). Therapeutic interventions with urban Black adolescents. In R. L. Jones (Ed.), *Black adolescents* (pp. 309-337). Hampton, VA: Cobb & Henry.

Franklin, A. J. (1993, July/August). The invisibility syndrome. *The Family Therapy Networker,* pp. 33-39.

Franklin, A. J., Carter, R. T., & Grace, C. (1993). An integrative approach to psychotherapy with Black/African Americans. In G. Stricker & J. R. Gold (Eds.), *Comprehensive handbook of psychotherapy integration* (pp. 465-479). New York: Plenum.

Franklin, A. J., & Jackson, J. S. (1990). Factors contributing to positive mental health among Black Americans. In D. S. Ruiz & J. P. Comer (Eds.), *Handbook of mental health and mental disorders among Black Americans* (pp. 291-307). New York: Greenwood.

Frazier, E. F. (1939). *The Negro family in the United States.* Chicago: University of Chicago Press.

Freeman, C., Carlson, J., & Sperry, L. (1993). Adlerian marital therapy strategies with middle income couples facing financial stress. *American Journal of Family Therapy, 21,* 324-332.

Freeman-Longo, R., & Bays, L. (1988). *Who am I and why am I in treatment?* Brandon, VT: Safer Society Press.

Freud, S. (1958). *The dynamics of transference* (J. Strachey, Ed.). London: Hogarth. (Original work published 1912)

Freud, S. (1958). *Remembering, repeating, and working-through* (J. Strachey, Ed.). London: Hogarth. (Original work published 1914)

Freud, S. (1966). *The complete introductory lectures on psychoanalysis.* New York: Norton.

Frey, D., & Carlock, C. J. (1984). *Enhancing self esteem.* Muncie, IN: Accelerated Development.

Fromm, E. (1941). *Escape from freedom.* New York: Avon Press.

Fromm, E. (1947). *Man for himself.* New York: Holt, Rinehart & Winston.

Fromm, E. (1973). *Anatomy of human destructiveness.* New York: Holt, Rinehart & Winston.

Fry, P. S., & Trifiletti, R. J. (1983). Teenage fathers: An exploration of their developmental needs and anxieties and the implications for clinical-social intervention services. *Journal of Psychiatric Treatment and Evaluation, 5,* 219-227.

Furstenberg, F. F. (1976). *Unplanned parenthood: The social consequences of teenage childbearing.* New York: Free Press.

Furstenberg, F. F., Brooks-Gunn, J., & Chase-Lansdale, L. (1989). Teenaged pregnancy and childbearing. *American Psychologist, 44,* 313-320.

Furstenberg, F. F., Brooks-Gunn, J., & Morgan, S. P. (1987). *Adolescent mothers in later life.* New York: Cambridge University Press.

Galway, T. (1997). The new Irish: Keeping a culture alive. In M. Coffey (Ed.), *The Irish in America* (pp. 227-259). New York: Hyperion.

Gardner, J. E. (1993). Nintendo games. In C. E. Schaefer & D. M. Cangelosi (Eds.), *Play therapy techniques* (pp. 273-280). Northvale, NJ: Jason Aronson.

Gardner, R. (1973). *The talking, feeling, doing game.* Cresskill, NJ: Creative Therapeutics.

Gardner, R. (1988). *The storytelling card game.* Cresskill, NJ: Creative Therapeutics.

Garrett, J. T., & Garrett, M. W. (1994). The path of good medicine: Understanding and counseling Native Americans. *Journal of Multicultural Counseling and Development, 22,* 134-144.

Garrett, M. T., & Osborne, W. L. (1995). The Native American sweatlodge as metaphor for group work. *Journal for Specialists in Group Work, 20,* 33-39.

Garrity, C., Jens, K., Porter, W., Sager, N., & Short-Camilli, C. (1994-1995). *Bully-proofing your school: A comprehensive approach for elementary schools.* Longmont, CO: Sopris West.

Gaylin, W. (1992). *The male ego.* New York: Penguin.

George, R. L. (1990). *Counseling the chemically dependent: Theory and practice.* Englewood Cliffs, NJ: Prentice Hall.

Gibbs, J. T. (Ed.). (1988). *Young, Black, and male in America: An endangered species.* New York: Auburn House.

Gibson, P. (1989). Gay male and lesbian youth suicide. In M. Feinlaub (Ed.), *Report of the Secretary's Task Force on Youth Suicide: Vol. 3. Prevention and interventions in youth suicide* (pp. 3-111–3-143). Washington, DC: U.S. Department of Health and Human Services.

Gillberg, C., Persson, E., Grufman, M., & Themner, U. (1986). Psychiatric disorders in mildly and severely mentally retarded urban children and adolescents: Epidemiological aspects. *British Journal of Psychiatry, 149*, 68-74.

Gilmore, D. D. (1990). *Manhood in the making: Cultural concepts of masculinity.* New Haven, CT: Yale University Press.

Ginsburg, G. S., Silverman, W. K., & Kurtines, W. M. (1995). Cognitive-behavioral group therapy. In A. R. Eisen, C. A. Kearney, & C. E. Schaefer (Eds.), *Clinical handbook of anxiety disorders in children and adolescents* (pp. 521-549). Northvale, NJ: Jason Aronson.

Ginzberg, E., Ginsburg, S. W., Axelrad, S., & Herma, J. L. (1951). *Occupational choice: An approach to a general theory.* New York: Columbia University Press.

Giordano, J., & McGoldrick, M. (1996a). European families: An overview. In M. McGoldrick, J. Giordano, & J. K. Pearce (Eds.), *Ethnicity and family therapy* (2nd ed., pp. 427-441). New York: Guilford.

Giordano, J., & McGoldrick, M. (1996b). Italian families. In M. McGoldrick, J. Giordano, & J. K. Pearce (Eds.), *Ethnicity and family therapy* (2nd ed., pp. 567-582). New York: Guilford.

Gittelman-Klein, R., Klein, D. F., Katz, S., Saraf, K., & Pollack, E. (1976). Comparative effects of methylphenidate and thioridazine in hyperkinetic children: I. Clinical results. *Archives of General Psychiatry, 33*, 1217-1231.

Gladding, S. T. (1992). *Counseling as art: The creative arts in counseling.* Alexandria, VA: American Counseling Association.

Gladding, S. T. (1998). *Family therapy: History, theory, and practice.* Upper Saddle River, NJ: Prentice Hall.

Glaser, B. (1996). *Juvenile counseling and assessment program* (Brochure). Athens: University of Georgia Press.

Glory [Film]. (1990). Hollywood, CA: Tri-Star Pictures.

Gluth, D., & Kiselica, M. S. (1994). Coming out quickly: Brief counseling for gay and lesbian adjustment issues. *Journal of Mental Health Counseling, 16*, 163-173.

Goldstein, A. (1988). *The Prepare curriculum.* Champaign, IL: Research Press.

Goldstein, A., & Glick, B. (1987). *Aggression replacement training.* Champaign, IL: Research Press.

Goldstein, A. P., Sprafkin, R. P., Gershaw, N. J., & Klein, P. (1980). *Skillstreaming the adolescent: A structured learning approach to teaching prosocial skills.* Champaign, IL: Research Press.

Good, G. E., Dell, D. M., & Mintz, L. B. (1989). Male role and gender role conflict: Relations to help seeking in men. *Journal of Counseling and Development, 69*, 17-21.

Good, G. E., & Mintz, L. B. (1990). Gender role conflict and depression in college men: Evidence for compounded risk. *Journal of Counseling and Development, 69*, 17-21.

Goodman, R., & Stevenson, J. (1989). A twin study of hyperactivity: II. The etiologic role of genes, family relationships and perinatal adversity. *Journal of Child Psychology and Psychiatry, 30*, 691-709.

Gould, D., & Horn, T. (1984). Participation motivation in young athletes. In J. Silva & R. Weinberg (Eds.), *Psychological foundation of sport* (pp. 359-370). Champaign, IL: Human Kinetics.

Granger, D. A., Whalen, C. K., Henker, B., & Cantwell, C. (1996). ADHD boys' behavior during structured classroom social activities: Effects of social demands, teacher proximity, and methylphenidate. *Journal of Attention Disorders, 1*, 16-30.

Greeley, A. M. (1981). *The Irish Americans: The rise to money and power.* New York: Harper & Row.

Green, R. L., & Wright, D. L. (1991, March). *African American males: A demographic study and analysis.* Paper presented at the National Workshop of the W. K. Kellogg Foundation, Sacramento, CA.

Greenberg, B. (1982). Television and role socializations: An overview. In National Institute of Mental Health (Ed.), *Television and behavior: Ten years of scientific progress and implications for the eighties* (pp. 179-190). Washington, DC: Government Printing Office.

Greendorfer, S. (1992). Sport socialization. In T. Horn (Ed.), *Advances in sport psychology* (pp. 201-218). Champaign, IL: Human Kinetics.

Greene, B. (1994). Lesbian and gay sexual orientations: Implications for clinical training, practice, and research. In B. Greene & G. M. Herek (Eds.), *Lesbian and gay psychology: Theory, research, and clinical applications* (pp. 1-24). Thousand Oaks, CA: Sage.

Greene, M. (1996). Youth and violence: Trends, principles, and programmatic interventions. In B. Simon & R. Apfel (Eds.), *Minefields in the heart* (pp. 128-148). New Haven, CT: Yale University Press.

Greene, R. W., Biederman, J., Faraone, S. V., Ouellette, C. A., Penn, C., & Griffin, S. M. (1996). Toward a new psychometric definition of social disability in children with attention-deficit hyperactivity disorder. *Journal of the American Academy of Child and Adolescent Psychiatry, 35*, 571-578.

Greenhill, L. L. (1992). Pharmacological treatment of attention deficit hyperactivity disorder. *Psychiatric Clinics of North America, 15*, 1-27.

Groth, A. N., Long, R. E., & McFadin, J. B. (1982). Undetected recidivism among rapists and child molesters. *Crime and Delinquency, 28*, 450-458.

Grubman-Black, S. D. (1990). *Broken boys/mending men: Recovery from childhood sexual abuse.* Bradenton, FL: Human Services Institute, Inc. and TAB Books.

Guerney, B. (1964). Filial therapy description and rationale. *Journal of Consulting Psychology, 28*, 303-310.

Guerney, B. G., Jr. (1977). *Relationship enhancement.* San Francisco: Jossey-Bass.

Guerney, L. (1983). Introduction to filial therapy. In P. Keller & L. Ritt (Eds.), *Innovations in clinical practice: A source book* (Vol. 2, pp. 26-39). Sarasota, FL: Professional Research Exchange.

Guerney, L. F., & Welsh, A. D. (1993). Two by two: A filial therapy case study. In T. Kottman & C. Schaefer (Eds.), *Play therapy in action* (pp. 561-588). Northvale, NJ: Jason Aronson.

Ha, F. I. (1995). Shame in Asian and Western cultures. *American Behavioral Scientist, 38*, 1114-1131.

Haenlein, M., & Caul, W. F. (1987). Attention deficit disorder with hyperactivity: A specific hypothesis of reward dysfunction. *Journal of the American Academy of Child and Adolescent Psychiatry, 26*, 356-362.

Hall, J. E., & Morris, H. L. (1976). Sexual knowledge and attitudes of institutionalized and non-institutionalized retarded adolescents. *American Journal of Mental Deficiency, 80*, 382-387.

Hall, J. E., & Sawyer, H. W. (1978). Sexual policies for the mentally retarded. *Sexuality and Disability, 1*, 34-43.

Hallum, A. (1995). Disability and the transition to adulthood: Issues for the disabled child, the family, and the pediatrician. *Current Problems in Pediatrics, 25*, 12-50.

Hansberry, L. (1988). *A raisin in the sun* [Television production]. Los Angeles: NBLA Production.

Hanson, C., Henggeler, S., Haefele, W., & Rodick, J. (1984). Demographic, individual, and family relationship correlates of serious and repeated crime among adolescents and their siblings. *Journal of Consulting and Clinical Psychology, 52*, 528-538.

Hanson, G., & Hartmann, L. (1996). Latency development in prehomosexual boys. In R. Cabaj & T. Stein (Eds.), *Textbook of homosexuality and mental health* (pp. 253-266). Washington, DC: American Psychiatric Press.

Hanson, M. J. (1996a). Early interactions: The developmental context for infants whose development is atypical. In M. J. Hanson (Ed.), *Atypical infant development* (pp. 3-16). Austin, TX: Pro-Ed.

Hanson, M. J. (1996b). Early intervention: Models and practices. In M. J. Hanson (Ed.), *Atypical infant development* (pp. 451-476). Austin, TX: Pro-Ed.

Hanson, M. J. (1996c). Early interventions: Goals and outcomes. In M. J. Hanson (Ed.), *Atypical infant development* (pp. 477-513). Austin, TX: Pro-Ed.

Hardy, J. B., & Zabin, L. S. (1991). *Adolescent pregnancy in an urban environment: Issues, programs and evaluation.* Washington, DC: Urban Institute Press.

Harrington, R. (1993). *Depressive disorder in childhood and adolescence.* New York: John Wiley.

Harrington, R., Fudge, H., Rutter, M., Pickles, A., & Hill, J. (1990). Adult outcomes of childhood and adolescent depression. *Archives of General Psychiatry, 47*, 465-473.

Harris, C. T. B. (1994). *Emasculation of the unicorn: The loss and rebuilding of masculinity in America.* York Beach, ME: Nicolas-Hays.

Hartstein, N. B. (1996). Suicide risk in lesbian, gay, and bisexual youth. In R. Cabaj & T. Stein (Eds.), *Textbook of homosexuality and mental health* (pp. 819-838). Washington, DC: American Psychiatric Press.

Harvey, A. R., & Rauch, J. B. (1997). A comprehensive Afrocentric rites of passage program for Black male adolescents. *Health and Social Work, 22*, 30-37.

Hawkins, J. D. (1997). Academic performance and school success: Sources and consequences. In R. G. Weissberg, T. P. Gullotta, R. L. Hampton, B. A. Ryan, & G. R. Adams (Eds.), *Healthy children 2000: Enhancing children's wellness* (pp. 278-305). Thousand Oaks, CA: Sage.

Hawkins, J., & Weis, J. (1985). The social development model: An integrated approach to delinquency prevention. *Journal of Primary Prevention, 6*, 73-97.

Hawley, R. A. (1993). *Boys will be men: Masculinity in troubled times.* Middlebury, VT: Paul S. Eriksson.

Hazel, J., Schumaker, J., Sherman, J., & Sheldon-Wilder, J. (1981). The development and evaluation of a group skill training program for court-adjudicated youths. In D. Upper & S. Ross (Eds.), *Behavioral group therapy, 1981: An annual review* (pp. 117-137). Champaign, IL: Research Press.

Heath, A. W., & Ayers, T. C. (1991). MRI brief therapy with adolescent substance abusers. In T. C. Dodd & M. D. Selekman (Eds.), *Family therapy approaches with adolescent substance abusers* (pp. 49-69). Boston: Allyn & Bacon.

Heath, D. H. (1991). *Fulfilling lives: Paths to maturity and success.* San Francisco: Jossey-Bass.

Hechtman, L. (1991). Resilience and vulnerability in long term outcome of attention deficit hyperactive disorder. *Canadian Journal of Psychiatry, 36*, 415-421.

Heinrich, R. K., Corbine, J. L., & Thomas, K. R. (1990). Counseling Native Americans. *Journal of Counseling & Development, 69*, 126-133.

Hellison, D. (1995). *Teaching responsibility through physical activity.* Champaign, IL: Human Kinetics.

Helms, J. E. (Ed.). (1990). *Black and White racial identity: Theory, research, and practice.* New York: Greenwood.

Helms, J. E. (1996). Towards a methodology for measuring and assessing racial as distinguished from ethnic identity. In G. Sodowsky & J. Impara (Eds.), *Multicultural assessment in counseling and clinical psychology* (pp. 143-192). Lincoln, NE: Buros Institute of Mental Measurements.

Hendricks, L. E. (1988). Outreach with teenage fathers: A preliminary report on three ethnic groups. *Adolescence, 23*, 711-720.

Henggeler, S. W. (1989). *Delinquency in adolescence.* Newbury Park, CA: Sage.

Henggeler, S. W., & Borduin, C. (1990). *Family therapy and beyond: A multi-systemic approach to treating the behavior problems of children and adolescents.* Pacific Grove, CA: Brooks/Cole.

Henggeler, S. W., Rodick, J. D., Hanson, C. L., Borduin, C. M., & Urey, J. R. (1986). Multisystemic treatment of juvenile offenders: Effects on adolescent behavior and family interaction. *Developmental Psychology, 22*(1), 132-141.

Herdt, G. (1989). *Gay and lesbian youth.* New York: Haworth.

Herdt, G., & Boxer, A. (1993). *Children of Horizons: How gay and lesbian teens are leading a new way out of the closet.* Boston: Beacon.

Herek, G. M. (1995). Psychological heterosexism in the United States. In A. R. D'Augelli & C. J. Patterson (Eds.), *Lesbian, gay, and bisexual identities over the lifespan: Psychological perspectives* (pp. 321-346). New York: Oxford University Press.

Herek, G. M. (1996). Heterosexism and homophobia. In R. Cabaj & T. Stein (Eds.), *Textbook of homosexuality and mental health* (pp. 101-114). Washington, DC: American Psychiatric Press.

Herr, E. L. (1999). *Counseling in a dynamic society: Contexts and practices for the 21st century* (2nd ed.). Alexandria, VA: American Counseling Association.

Herring, R. D. (1989). The American Indian family: Dissolution by coercion. *Journal of Multicultural Counseling and Development, 17*, 4-13.

Herring, R. D. (1990). Understanding Native American values: Process and content concerns for counselors. *Counseling and Values, 34*, 134-137.

Herring, R. D. (1991). Counseling Native American youth. In C. C. Lee & B. L. Richardson (Eds.), *Multicultural issues in counseling: New approaches to diversity* (pp. 37-47). Alexandria, VA: American Association for Counseling and Development.

Herring, R. D. (1994a). The clown or contrary figure as a counseling intervention strategy with Native American Indian clients. *Journal of Multicultural Counseling and Development, 22*, 153-164.

Herring, R. D. (1994b). Native American Indian identity: A people of many peoples. In E. P. Salett & D. R. Koslow (Eds.), *Race, ethnicity, and self: Identity in multicultural perspective* (pp. 170-197). Washington, DC: National Multicultural Institute.

Herring, R. D. (1996). Synergetic counseling and Native American Indian students. *Journal of Counseling & Development, 74*, 542-547.

Herring, R. D. (1997a). *Counseling diverse ethnic youth: Synergetic strategies and interventions for school counselors.* Fort Worth, TX: Harcourt Brace.

Herring, R. D. (1997b). Counseling indigenous American Indian youth. In C. C. Lee (Ed.), *Multicultural issues in counseling: New approaches to diversity* (2nd ed., pp. 53-70). Alexandria, VA: American Counseling Association.

Herring, R. D. (1997c). *Multicultural counseling: A synergetic approach.* Alexandria, VA: American Counseling Association.

Herring, R. D. (1999). *Counseling Native American Indians and Alaska Natives.* Thousand Oaks, CA: Sage.

Herring, R. D., & Meggert, S. (1993). The use of humor as a counseling intervention with Native American Indian children. *Elementary School Guidance and Counseling, 29*, 67-76.

Herring, R. D., & Walker, S. S. (1993). Synergetic counseling: Toward a more holistic approach. *Texas Counseling Association Journal, 22*, 38-53.

Hertzfeld, G., & Powell, R. (1986). *Coping for kids: A complete stress-control program for students ages 8-18.* West Nyack, NY: Center for Applied Research in Education.

Hetrick, E. S., & Martin, A. D. (1987). Developmental issues and their resolution for gay and lesbian adolescents. *Journal of Homosexuality, 14*, 25-44.

The hidden victims: Hate crime against American Indians under-reported (Report No. 75). (1994, October). Montgomery, AL: Southern Poverty Law Center.

Hill, R. (1972). *The strengths of Black families.* New York: Emerson Hall.

Hill, R. (1977). *Informal adoption among Black families.* Washington, DC: National Urban League Research Department.

Hing, B. O. (1993). Making and remaking Asian Pacific America: Immigration policy. In *The state of Asian Pacific America* (pp. 127-140). Los Angeles: LEAP Asian Pacific Public Policy Institute and UCLA Asian American Studies Center.

Hinshaw, S. P. (1987). On the distinction between attentional deficits/hyperactivity and conduct problems/aggression in child psychopathology. *Psychological Bulletin, 101,* 443-463.

Hinshaw, S. P. (1996). Enhancing social competence: Integrating self-management strategies with behavioral procedures for children with ADHD. In E. D. Hibbs & P. S. Jensen (Eds.), *Psychosocial treatments for child and adolescent disorders: Empirically based strategies for clinical practice* (pp. 285-309). Washington, DC: American Psychological Association.

Hinshaw, S., & Anderson, C. (1996). Conduct and oppositional defiant disorders. In E. J. Mash & R. A. Barkley (Eds.), *Child psychopathology* (pp. 113-150). New York: Guilford.

Hipp, E. (1985). *Fighting invisible tigers: A student guide to life in the jungle.* Minneapolis: Free Spirit Press.

Ho, M. K. (1992). *Minority children and adolescents in therapy.* Newbury Park, CA: Sage.

Ho, V. (1996, April 3). Feelings of alienation never far from reality for Asians in America. *Seattle Post Intelligencer,* pp. E1-E2.

Hoberman, H. M., & Lewinsohn, P. M. (1985). The behavioral treatment of depression. In E. E. Beckham & W. R. Leber (Eds.), *Handbook of depression: Treatment, assessment, and research* (pp. 39-81). Homewood, IL: Dorsey.

Hodge, K. (1989). Character-building in sport: Fact or fiction? *New Zealand Journal of Sports Medicine, 17,* 23-25.

Hodge, K. P. (1994a). Mental toughness in sport: Lessons for life. *Journal of Physical Education New Zealand, 27,* 12-16.

Hodge, K. P. (1994b). *Sport motivation: Training your mind for peak performance.* Auckland, New Zealand: Reed.

Hodge, K., & Tod, D. (1993). Ethics of childhood sport. *Sports Medicine, 15,* 291-298.

Hodge, K., & Zaharopoulos, E. (1992). Participation motivation and dropouts in netball. *New Zealand Coach, 1,* 6-7.

Hodge, K., & Zaharopoulos, E. (1993). Dropouts in rugby. *New Zealand Coach, 2,* 7-8.

Hodges, K. K., & Siegel, L. J. (1985). Depression in children and adolescents. In E. E. Beckham & W. R. Leber (Eds.), *Handbook of depression: Treatment, assessment, and research* (pp. 517-555). Homewood, IL: Dorsey.

Hodgkinson, H. L. (1990). *The demographics of American Indians: One percent of the people; fifty percent of the diversity.* Washington, DC: Institute for Educational Leadership.

Hoffman, L. W. (1979). Maternal employment: 1979. *American Psychologist, 34,* 959-865.

Holden, C. (1985, January). Genes, personality and alcoholism. *Psychology Today,* pp. 38-44.

Holmes, G., & Offen, L. (1996). Clinicians' hypotheses regarding clients problems: Are they less likely to hypothesize sexual abuse in male compared to female clients? *Child Abuse and Neglect: The International Journal, 20,* 493-501.

Holmes, W. C., & Slap, G. B. (1998). Sexual abuse of boys: Definition, prevalence, correlates, sequelae, and management. *JAMA, 280,* 1855-1862.

Hoover, J., & Hazler, R. J. (1991). Bullies and victims. *Elementary School Guidance and Counseling, 25,* 212-219.

Hoover, J. H., Oliver, R., & Hazler, R. J. (1992). Bullying: Perceptions of adolescent victims in the midwestern USA. *School Psychology International, 13,* 5-16.

Hornby, G. (1995). Fathers' views of the effect on their families of children with Down syndrome. *Journal of Child and Family Studies, 4,* 103-117.

Horne, A. M. (1991). Social learning family therapy. In A. Horne & J. Passmore (Eds.), *Family counseling and therapy* (2nd ed., pp. 463-496). Itasca, IL: Peacock.

Horne, A. M., Glaser, B. A., & Calhoun, G. B. (1998). Conduct disorders. In R. T. Ammerman, C. G. Last, & M. Hersen (Eds.), *Handbook of prescriptive treatments for children and adolescents* (2nd ed., pp. 84-101). Boston: Allyn & Bacon.

Horne, A. M., Glaser, B., & Sayger, T. V. (1994). Bullies. *Counseling and Human Development, 27,* 1-12.

Horne, A., Jolliff, D., & Roth, E. (1996). Men mentoring men in groups. In M. Andronica (Ed.), *Men in groups: Insight, interventions, psychoeducational work* (pp. 97-112). Washington, DC: American Psychological Association.

Horne, A. M., & Sayger, T. V. (1990). *Treating conduct and oppositional defiant disorders in children.* New York: Pergamon.

Horne, A. M., & Socherman, R. (1996). Profile of a bully. Who would do such a thing? *Educational Horizons, 74*, 77-83.

Howard-Pitney, B., LaFromboise, T., Basil, M., September, B., & Johnson, M. (1992). Psychological and social indicators of suicide ideation and suicide attempts in Zuni adolescents. *Journal of Consulting and Clinical Psychiatry, 60*, 473-476.

Hoza, B., Pelham, W. E., Milich, R., Pillow, D., & McBride, K. (1993). The self-perceptions and attributions of attention deficit hyperactivity disordered and nonreferred boys. *Journal of Abnormal Child Psychology, 21*, 271-286.

Huang, L. N. (1994). An integrative approach to clinical assessment and intervention with Asian-American adolescents. *Journal of Clinical Child Psychology, 23*, 21-31.

Huey, W. C. (1987). Counseling teenage fathers: The "Maximizing a Life Experience" (MALE) group. *School Counselor, 35*, 40-47.

Hughes, D. A. (1997). *Facilitating developmental attachment: The road to emotional recovery and behavioral change in foster and adopted children.* Northvale, NJ: Jason Aronson.

Hughes, L. (1970). I, too, sing America. In L. Hughes & A. Bontemps (Eds.), *The poetry of the Negro: 1746-1970* (p. 182). Garden City, NY: Doubleday.

Human Rights Foundation. (1984). *Demystifying homosexuality: A teaching guide about lesbians and gay men.* New York: Irvington.

Hunter, J., & Schaecher, R. (1987). Stresses on lesbian and gay adolescents in schools. *Social Work in Education, 9*, 180-189.

Hunter, M. (1990). *Abused boys: The neglected victims of sexual abuse.* Lexington, MA: Lexington Books.

Hyde, J., & Linn, M. (1986). *The psychology of gender.* Baltimore, MD: Johns Hopkins University Press.

Icard, L. D. (1986). Black gay men and conflicting social identities: Sexual orientation versus racial identity. *Journal of Social Work & Human Sexuality, 4*, 83-93.

Icard, L. D. (1996). Assessing the psychosocial well-being of African American gays: A multidimensional perspective. In J. Longres (Ed.), *Men of color: A context for service to homosexually active men* (pp. 25-50). Binghamton, NY: Harrington Park Press.

Isaacs, S., & Ritchey, W. (1989). *I think I can, I know I can.* New York: St. Martin's.

Isaacson, L. E. (1985). *Basics of career counseling.* Boston: Allyn & Bacon.

Ivey, A. E. (1980). Counseling 2000: Time to take charge! *The Counseling Psychologist, 8*(4), 12-16.

Jacobson, E. (1987). Progressive relaxation therapy. *American Journal of Psychology, 100*, 522-537.

James, B. (1984). *Handbook for treatment of attachment-trauma problems in children.* New York: Free Press.

Jessor, R., VanDen Bos, J., Vanderryn, J., Costa, F. M., & Turbin, M. (1995). Protective factors in adolescent problem behavior: Moderator effects and developmental change. *Developmental Psychology, 31*, 923-933.

Johnson, J. M., & Watson, B. C. (Eds.). (1990). *Stony the road they trod: The African American male.* Washington, DC: National Urban League.

Johnson, M., & Stone, G. L. (1989). Logic and nurture: Gender differences in thinking about psychotherapy. *Professional Psychology: Research and Practice, 20*(2), 123-127.

Johnson, R. (1987). Using computer art in counseling children. *Elementary School Guidance and Counseling, 21*, 262-265.

Johnstone, M., Munn, P., & Edwards, L. (1992). *Action against bullying: Drawing from experience.* Edinburgh, Scotland: Scottish Council for Research Education.

Jolliff, D. S. (Chair). (1994, August). *Boys and adolescent males: Developmental and intervention processes.* Symposium conducted at the annual meeting of the American Psychological Association, Los Angeles.

Jolliff, D. S. (Chair). (1995, April). *Working with boys and adolescent males: Issues and intervention processes.* Symposium conducted at the annual meeting of the American Counseling Association, Denver.

Jones, B. E., & Hill, M. J. (1996). African American lesbians, gay men, and bisexuals. In R. Cabaj & T. Stein (Eds.), *Textbook of homosexuality and mental health* (pp. 549-562). Washington, DC: American Psychiatric Press.

Jones, K. M. (1986). Black male in jeopardy. *Crisis, 93*, 16-21, 44-45.

Jones, M. (1991). Gender stereotyping in advertisements. *Teaching of Psychology, 18*, 231-233.

Jongsma, A. E., Peterson, L. M., & McInnis, W. P. (1996). *The child and adolescent psychotherapy treatment planner.* New York: John Wiley.

Jung, C. G. (1959). *The collected works* (Vol. 9). New York: Pantheon.

Juster, F. T. (1985). A note on recent changes in time use. In F. T. Juster & F. Stafford (Eds.), *Time, goods, and well-being* (pp. 313-332). Ann Arbor: University of Michigan Institute for Social Research.

Kahn, M. W., Lejero, L., Antone, M., Francisco, D., & Manuel, J. (1988). An indigenous community mental health service on the Tohono O'odham (Papago) Indian reservation: Seventeen years later. *American Journal of Psychiatry, 140*(6), 689-694.

Kalb, J., & Viscott, D. (1976). *What every kid should know.* Boston: Houghton Mifflin.

Kamphaus, R. W., & Frick, P. J. (1996). *Clinical assessment of child and adolescent personality and behaviour.* Boston: Allyn & Bacon.

Kandel, D. B., & Davies, M. (1986). Adult sequela of adolescent depressive symptoms. *Archives of General Psychiatry, 43,* 255-262.

Kaufman, A. S., & Kaufman, N. L. (1990). *Kaufman Brief Intelligence Test manual.* Circle Pines, MN: American Guidance Service.

Kazdin, A. (1987). *Conduct disorders in childhood and adolescence.* Newbury Park, CA: Sage.

Kazdin, A. (1995). *Conduct disorders in childhood and adolescence* (2nd ed.). Thousand Oaks, CA: Sage.

Kazdin, A. E., Siegel, T. C., & Bass, D. (1990). Drawing on clinical practice to inform research on child and adolescent psychotherapy: Survey of practitioners. *Professional Psychology: Research and Practice, 21,* 189-198.

Keat, D. B. (1972). Broad-spectrum behavior therapy with children: A case study. *Behavior Therapy, 3,* 454-459.

Keat, D. B. (1974). *Fundamentals of child counseling.* Boston: Houghton Mifflin.

Keat, D. B. (1976a). Multimodal counseling with children: Treating the BASIC ID. *Pennsylvania Personnel and Guidance Association Journal, 4,* 21-25.

Keat, D. B. (1976b). Multimodal therapy with children: Two case histories. In A. A. Lazarus (Ed.), *Multimodal behavior therapy* (pp. 116-132). New York: Springer.

Keat, D. B. (1976c). Training as multimodal treatment. *Elementary School Guidance and Counseling, 11,* 7-13.

Keat, D. B. (1977). *Self-relaxation for children* (Cassette Recording No. C-600). Harrisburg, PA: Professional Associates.

Keat, D. B. (1979). *Multimodal therapy with children.* New York: Pergamon.

Keat, D. B. (1980a). *Friendship training for children* (Cassette Recording No. C-590). Harrisburg, PA: Professional Associates.

Keat, D. B. (1980b). *Madness management programs for children* (Cassette Recording No. C-580). Harrisburg, PA: Professional Associates.

Keat, D. B. (1980c). Multimodal therapy with children-adolescents: The case of LOU. *Journal of Counseling and Psychotherapy, 3,* 35-44.

Keat, D. B. (1985a). Child-adolescent multimodal therapy: Bud the boss. *Journal of Humanistic Education and Development, 23,* 183-192.

Keat, D. B. (1985b). *Latchkey children: HELPING yourself* (Cassette Recording No. C-570). Harrisburg, PA: Professional Associates.

Keat, D. B. (1985c). Multimodal therapy with children: Ernie the enuretic. In A. A. Lazarus (Ed.), *Casebook of multimodal therapy* (pp. 70-80). New York: Guilford.

Keat, D. B. (1990a). Change in child multimodal counseling. *Elementary School Guidance & Counseling, 24,* 248-262.

Keat, D. B. (1990b). *Child multimodal therapy.* Norwood, NJ: Ablex.

Keat, D. B. (1996). Multimodal therapy with adolescents. *Psychotherapy in Private Practice, 15*(2), 63-79.

Keat, D. B., & Guerney, L. B. (1980). *HELPING your child.* Alexandria, VA: American Association for Counseling & Development Press.

Keen, S. (1991). *Fire in the belly: On being a man.* New York: Bantam.

Kelly, K. R., & Hall, A. S. (1992). Toward a developmental model for counseling men. *Journal of Mental Health Counseling, 14,* 257-273.

Kendall, P. C. (1990). *Coping cat workbook.* (Available from the author, 238 Meeting House Lane, Merion, PA 19066)

Kendall, P. C., Chansky, T. E., Kane, M. T., Kim, R. S., Kortlander, E., Ronan, K. R., Sessa, F. M. & Siqueland, L. (1992). *Anxiety disorders in youth.* Boston: Allyn & Bacon.

Kendall, P. C., Kane, M. T., Howard, B. L., & Siqueland, L. (1989). *Cognitive-behavioral therapy for anxious children: Treatment manual.* (Available from the lead author, 238 Meeting House Lane, Merion, PA 19066)

Keniston, K. (1970). Youth: A new stage of life. *The American Scholar, 39,* 631-641.

Kessler, R. C., Brown, R. L., & Broman, C. L. (1981). Sex differences in psychiatric help-seeking: Evidence from four large- scale surveys. *Journal of Health and Social Behavior, 22,* 49-64.

Kim, B.L.C. (1980). *Korean American children at school and at home* (Technical report). Washington, DC: Administration for Children, Youth, and Families.

King, N. (1995). *Speaking our truth.* New York: Harper Perennial.

Kiresuk, T. J. (1973). Goal attainment scaling at a county mental health service. *Evaluation, 1,* 12-18.

Kiresuk, T., Smith, A., & Cardillo, J. (1994). *Goal attainment scaling: Applications, theory, and measurement.* Hillsdale, NJ: Lawrence Erlbaum.

Kiselica, M. S. (1988). *An anxiety management primary prevention program for adolescents.* Unpublished doctoral dissertation, The Pennsylvania State University, University Park.

Kiselica, M. S. (1995). *Multicultural counseling with teenage fathers: A practical guide.* Thousand Oaks, CA: Sage.

Kiselica, M. S. (1996a). Parenting skills training with teenage fathers: A group psychotherapeutic approach. In M. P. Andronico (Ed.), *Men in groups: Realities and insights* (pp. 283-300). Washington, DC: American Psychological Association.

Kiselica, M. S. (Chair). (1996b, August). *Reducing violence among inner-city male youth: Theoretical and clinical considerations.* Symposium conducted at the annual meeting of the American Psychological Association, Toronto.

Kiselica, M. S. (1997, August). Is emotional constriction in boys and men the product of a normative or an aberrant developmental pathway? In W. S. Pollack (Chair), *Rescuing Ophelia's brothers: What about boys?* Symposium conducted at the annual meeting of the American Psychological Association, Chicago.

Kiselica, M. S. (1999). Culturally sensitive interventions with African-American adolescent fathers. In L. Davis (Ed.), *African American males: A practical guide* (pp. 205-218). Thousand Oaks, CA: Sage.

Kiselica, M. S., Doms, J., & Rotzien, A. (1992, March). *Improving societal excellence through courses on fatherhood for adolescent boys.* Paper presented at the annual meeting of the American Association for Counseling and Development, Baltimore, MD.

Kiselica, M. S., & Murphy, D. K. (1994). Developmental career counseling with teenage parents. *Career Development Quarterly, 42,* 238-244.

Kiselica, M. S., & Pfaller, J. (1993). Helping teenage parents: The independent and collaborative roles of school counselors and counselor educators. *Journal of Counseling and Development, 72,* 42-48.

Kiselica, M. S., Rotzien, A., & Doms, J. (1994). Preparing teenage fathers for parenthood: A group psychoeducational approach. *Journal for Specialists in Group Work, 19,* 83-94.

Kiselica, M. S., & Scheckel, S. (1995). Teenage fathers and the couvade syndrome (sympathetic pregnancy): A brief primer for school counselors. *The School Counselor, 43,* 42-51.

Kiselica, M. S., Stroud, J. C., Stroud, J. E., & Rotzien, A. (1992). Counseling the forgotten client: The teen father. *Journal of Mental Health Counseling, 14,* 338-350.

Kiselica, M. S., & Sturmer, P. (1993). Is society giving teenage fathers a mixed message? *Youth and Society, 24,* 487-501.

Kleiber, D., & Kirshnit, C. E. (1991). Sport involvement and identity formation. In L. Diamant (Ed.), *Mind-body maturity: Psychological approaches to sports, exercise, and fitness* (pp. 193-211). New York: Hemisphere.

Klinman, D. G., & Sander, J. H. (1985). *The teen parent collaboration: Reaching and serving the teenage father.* New York: Bank Street College of Education.

Knopp, F. H. (1982). *Remedial intervention in adolescent sex offenders: Nine program descriptions.* Orwell, VT: Safer Society Press.

Kolvin, I., Garside, R. F., Nicol, A. R., MacMillan, A., Wolstenholme, F., & Leitch, I. M. (1981). *Help starts here: The maladjusted child in the ordinary school.* London: Tavistock.

Kovacs, M. (1992). *The childhood depression inventory.* North Tonawanda, NY: Multi-Health Systems.

Kunjufu, J. (1983). *Countering the conspiracy to destroy Black boys.* Chicago, IL: Afro-Am Publishing.

Kunjufu, J. (1989). *A talk with Jawanza: Critical issues in educating African American youth.* Chicago, IL: African American Images.

LaFromboise, T. D. (1988). American Indian mental health policy. *American Psychologist, 43,* 388-397.

LaFromboise, T. D., & Graff Low, K. (1989). American Indian children and adolescents. In J. T. Gibbs & L. N. Huang (Eds.), *Children of color: Psychological interventions with minority youth* (pp. 114-147). San Francisco: Jossey-Bass.

LaFromboise, T. D., & Howard-Pitney, B. (1994). The Zuni life skills development curriculum: A collaborative approach to curriculum development. *Journal of the National Center Monograph Series, 4*(4), 98-121.

LaFromboise, T. D., Trimble, J. E., & Mohatt, G. V. (1990). Counseling intervention and American Indian tradition: An integrative approach. *The Counseling Psychologist, 48,* 626-654.

Lamb, M. E. (1986). *The father's role: Applied perspectives.* New York: John Wiley.

Landrum-Brown, J. (1990). Black mental health and racial oppression. In D. S. Ruiz & J. P. Comer (Eds.), *Handbook of mental health and mental disorders among Black Americans* (pp. 113-132). New York: Greenwood.

Lane, S., & Zamora, P. (1984). A method for treating the adolescent sex offender. In R. Mathias (Ed.), *Violent juvenile offenders: An anthology* (pp. 347-363). Washington, DC: National Council on Crime and Delinquency.

Langone, J. (1996). Mild mental retardation. In P. J. McLaughlin & P. Wehman (Eds.), *Mental retardation and developmental disabilities* (pp. 98-106). Austin, TX: Pro-Ed.

Langseth, D. R. (1997). Role of the family. In S. M. Pueschel & M. Sustrova (Eds.), *Adolescents with Down syndrome* (pp. 287-300). Baltimore, MD: Paul H. Brooks.

Lasch, C. (1979). *The culture of narcissism.* New York: W. W. Norton.

Lay-Dopyera, M., & Dopyera, J. (1987). *Becoming a teacher of young children* (3rd ed.). New York: Random House.

Lazarus, R. S. (1966). *Psychological stress and the coping process.* New York: McGraw-Hill.

Lazarus, A. A. (1971). *Behavior therapy and beyond.* New York: McGraw-Hill.

Lazarus, A. A. (1972). *Multimodal behavior therapy* (Six cassette tapes). Fort Lee, NJ: Behavioral Sciences Tape Library.

Lazarus, A. A. (1973). Multimodal behavior therapy: Treating the BASIC ID. *Journal of Nervous and Mental Disease, 156,* 404-411.

Lazarus, A. A. (1975). *Learning to relax.* New York: Institute for Rational Living.

Lazarus, A. A. (Ed.). (1976). *Multimodal behavior therapy.* New York: Springer.

Lazarus, A. A. (1977). *In the mind's eye.* New York: Rawson.

Lazarus, A. A. (Ed.). (1985). *Casebook of multimodal therapy.* New York: Guilford.

Lazarus, A. A. (1989). *The practice of multimodal therapy.* Baltimore, MD: Johns Hopkins University Press.

Lazarus, A. A., Davison, G., & Polefka, D. A. (1965). Clinical and operant factors in the treatment of a school phobia. *Journal of Abnormal Psychology, 70,* 225-229.

Le, C., Ingvarson, E. P., & Page, R. C. (1995). Alcoholics Anonymous and the counseling profession: Philosophies in conflict. *Journal of Counseling and Development, 73,* 603-610.

Leahy, R. L., & Shirk, S. R. (1984). The development of classificatory skills and sex-trait stereotypes in children. *Sex Roles, 10,* 281-292.

LeCroy, C. (1994). Social skills training. In C. LeCroy (Ed.), *Handbook of child and adolescent treatment* (pp. 126-169). New York: Lexington.

Lee, C. C. (1990). Black male development: "Counseling the native son." In D. Moore & F. Leagren (Eds.), *Problem solving strategies and interventions for men in conflict* (pp. 125-137). Alexandria, VA: American Association for Counseling and Development.

Lee, C. C. (1996). *Saving the native son: Empowerment strategies for young Black males.* Greensboro, NC: ERIC Counseling and Student Services Clearinghouse.

Lee, C.-R. (1995). *Native speaker.* New York: Riverside Books.

Lee, E. (1988). Cultural factors in working with Southeast Asian refugee adolescents. *Journal of Adolescence, 11,* 167-179.

Lee, F. (1993, April 4). Disrespect rules. *New York Times Educational Supplement,* p. 16.

Lee, S. W. (1991). Biofeedback as a treatment for childhood hyperactivity: A critical review of the literature. *Psychological Reports, 68,* 163-192.

Lee, S. (1994). Behind the model-minority stereotype: Voices of high- and low-achieving Asian American students. *Anthropology and Education Quarterly, 25,* 413-429.

Leong, F. T. L., Wagner, N. S., & Kim, H. H. (1995). Group counseling expectations among Asian American students: The role of culture-specific factors. *Journal of Counseling Psychology, 42,* 217-222.

Lettieri, D. J. (1985). Drug abuse: A review of explanations and models of explanation. *Advances in Alcohol and Substance Abuse, 4,* 9-40.

Levant, R. F. (1992). Toward the reconstruction of masculinity. *Journal of Family Psychology, 5,* 379-402.

Levant, R. F., & Pollack, W. S. (Eds.). (1995). *A new psychology of men.* New York: Basic Books.

Levine, H., & Evans, N. J. (1991). The development of gay, lesbian, and bisexual identities. In N. J. Evans & V. A. Wall (Eds.), *Beyond tolerance: Gays, lesbians, and bisexuals on campus* (pp. 25-38). Alexandria, VA: American College Personnel Association.

Levinson, D. (1978). *The seasons of a man's life.* New York: Ballantine.

Levinson, D., Darrow, C., Klein, E., Levinson, M., & McKee, B. (1978). *The seasons of a man's life.* New York: Knopf.

Levy, H. B., Markovic, J., Chaudry, U., Ahart, S., & Torres, H. (1995). Reabuse rates in a sample of children followed for 5 years after discharge from a child abuse inpatient assessment program. *Child Abuse and Neglect: The International Journal, 19,* 1363-1377.

Lewinsohn, P. M., Antonucciao, D. O., Steinmatz, J., & Teri, L. (1984). *The coping with depression course: A psychoeducational intervention for unipolar depression.* Eugene, OR: Castalia.

Lewinsohn, P. M., & Arconad, M. (1981). Behavioral treatment of depression: A social learning approach. In J. F. Clarkin & H. I. Glazer (Eds.), *Depression: Behavioral and directive intervention strategies* (pp. 33-67). New York: Garland STPM.

Lewinsohn, P. M., Clarke, G. N., & Rohde, P. (1994). Psychological approaches to the treatment of depressed adolescents. In W. M. Reynolds & H. F. Johnston (Eds.), *Handbook of depression in children and adolescents* (pp. 309-344). New York: Plenum.

Lewinsohn, P. M., Gotlib, I. H., & Seeley, J. R. (1995). Adolescent psychopathology: IV. Specificity of psychosocial risk factors for depression and substance abuse in older adolescents. *Journal of the American Academy of Child Adolescent Psychiatry, 34,* 1221-1228.

Lewinsohn, P. M., Hops, H., Roberts, R. E., Seeley, J. R., & Andrews, J. A. (1993). Adolescent psychopathology: I. Prevalence and incidence of depression and other DSM-III-R disorders in high school students. *Journal of Abnormal Psychology, 102,* 133-144.

Lewinsohn, P. M., Roberts, R. E., Seeley, J. R., Rohde, P., Gotlib, I. H., & Hops, H. (1994). Adolescent psychopathology: II. Psychosocial risk factors for depression. *Journal of Abnormal Psychology, 103,* 302-315.

Lewis, J. A., Dana, R. Q., & Blevins, G. A. (1994). *Substance abuse counseling: An individualized approach.* Pacific Grove, CA: Brooks/Cole.

Lewis, R., & Ho, M. (1989). Social work with Native Americans. In D. Atkinson, G. Morten, & D. Sue (Eds.), *Counseling American minorities* (pp. 51-58). Dubuque, IA: William C. Brown.

Lin, C.-Y. C., & Fu, V. R. (1990). A comparison of child-rearing practices among Chinese, immigrant Chinese, and Caucasian-American parents. *Child Development, 61,* 429-433.

Lindsay, J. W., & Rodine, S. (1989). *Teenage pregnancy challenge. Book two: Programs for kids.* Buena Park, CA: Morning Glory.

Lindsey, L. L. (1990). *Gender roles: A sociological perspective.* Englewood Cliffs, NJ: Prentice Hall.

Lipsey, M. W., & Wilson, D. B. (1993). The efficacy of psychological, educational, and behavioral treatment: Confirmation from meta-analysis. *American Psychologist, 48,* 1181-1209.

Little Bear, D. (1988). Teachers and parents: Working together. In J. Reyhner (Ed.), *Teaching the Indian child: A bilingual/multicultural approach* (2nd ed., pp. 270-280). Billings, MT: Eastern Montana College.

Liu, J. H., Campbell, S. M., & Condie, H. (1995). Ethnocentrism in dating preferences for an American sample: The ingroup bias in social context. *European Journal of Social Psychology, 25,* 95-115.

Locke, D. C. (1995). Counseling interventions with African American youth. In C. C. Lee (Ed.), *Counseling for diversity* (pp. 21-40). Needham Heights, MA: Allyn & Bacon.

Loeber, R., & Dishion, T. J. (1984). Boys who fight at home and school: Family conditions influencing cross-setting consistency. *Journal of Consulting and Clinical Psychology, 52,* 759-768.

Loiacano, D. K. (1989). Gay identity issues among Black Americans: Racism, homophobia, and the need for validation. *Journal of Counseling and Development, 68,* 21-25.

Loiacano, D. K. (1993). Gay identity issues among Black Americans. In L. Garnets & D. Kimmel (Eds.), *Psychological perspectives on lesbian and gay male experiences* (pp. 364-375). New York: Columbia University Press.

Longo, R. E. (1982). Sexual learning and experience among adolescent sexual offenders. *International Journal of Offender Therapy and Comparative Criminology, 26,* 235-241.

Lorenzo, M. K., Pakiz, B., Reinherz, H. Z., & Frost, A. (1995). Emotional and behavioral problems of Asian American adolescents: A comparative study. *Child and Adolescent Social Work Journal, 12,* 197-212.

Lumpkin, A., Stoll, S., & Beller, J. (1994). *Sport ethics: Applications for fair play.* St. Louis, MO: Mosby.

Lupin, M. (1977). *Peace, harmony, awareness: A relaxation program for children.* Hingham, MA: Teaching Resources.

Lusebrink, V. B. (1992). *Imagery and visual expression in therapy.* New York: Plenum.

Lutzker, J. R., & Steed, S. E. (1998). Parent training for families of children with developmental disabilities. In J. M. Briesmeister & C. E. Schaefer (Eds.), *Handbook of parent training: Parents as co-therapists for children's behavior problems* (2nd ed., pp. 281-307). New York: John Wiley.

Lynd, H. M. (1958). *On shame and the search for identity.* New York: Harcourt Brace.

Madaras, L. (1988/1984). *The what's happening to my body book for boys.* New York: Newmarket Press.

Maguire, K., & Patore, A. L. (Eds.). (1997). *Sourcebook of criminal justice statistics: 1996.* Washington, DC: Government Printing Office.

Mahara, R. (1997, February). Don't worry, be happy: Researchers at Penn State worry about stress. *Town & Gown,* pp. 44-50.

Mailer, N. (1948). *The naked and the dead.* New York: Henry Holt.

Maines, B., & Robinson, G. (1992). *Stamp out the bullying: Never mind the awareness, what can we do?* Portishead, Bristol, UK: Lame Duck.

Marsiglio, W. (1986). Teenage fatherhood: High school completion and educational attainment. In A. B. Elster & M. E. Lamb (Eds.), *Adolescent fatherhood* (pp. 67-88). Hillsdale, NJ: Lawrence Erlbaum.

Martin, A. D., & Hetrick, E. S. (1988). The stigmatization of the gay and lesbian adolescent. *Journal of Homosexuality, 15*, 163-183.

Martin, E. P., & Martin, J. M. (1980). *The Black extended family*. Chicago: University of Chicago Press.

Mash, E. J., & Johnston, C. (1990). Determinants of parenting stress: Illustrations from families of hyperactive children and families of physically abused children. *Journal of Clinical Child Psychology, 19*, 313-328.

Matson, J. L. (1989). *Treating depression in children and adolescents*. New York: Pergamon.

May, P. (1989). Social, economic changes seen as crucial factors for alarming rise in suicide. *NIHB Health Reporter, 4*(13), 4-7.

May, R. (1950). *The meaning of anxiety*. New York: Pocket.

Mazza, N. (1986). Poetry and popular music in social work education: The liberal arts perspective. *Arts in Psychotherapy, 13*, 293-299.

McAdoo, H. (1988). *Black families*. Newbury Park, CA: Sage.

McCaffrey, L. J. (1976). *The Irish diaspora in America*. Washington, DC: Catholic University of America Press.

McCall, N. (1994). *Makes me wanna holler: A young Black man in America*. New York: Random House.

McCarthy, J. (1995). *Adolescence and character disturbance*. Lanham, MD: University Press of America.

McDermott, D. (1984). The relationship of parental drug use and parent's attitude concerning adolescent drug use. *Adolescence, 19*, 89-97.

McFerrin, B. (1989). *Don't worry, be happy*. New York: Delacorte.

McGinnis, E., & Goldstein, A. (1984). *Skillstreaming the elementary school child*. Champaign, IL: Research Press.

McGoldrick, M. (1996). Irish families. In M. McGoldrick, J. Giordano, & J. K. Pearce (Eds.), *Ethnicity and family therapy* (2nd ed., pp. 544-566). New York: Guilford.

McGoldrick, M., Pearce, J. K., & Giordano, J. (1982). *Ethnicity and family therapy*. New York: Guilford.

McKay, M., & Fanning, P. (1992). *Self esteem* (2nd ed.). Oakland, CA: New Harbinger.

Meeks, J. G. (1988). The many faces of adolescent depression. *The Early Adolescence Magazine, 3*(2), 34-42.

Meichenbaum, D. (1985). *Stress inoculation training*. New York: Pergamon.

Mellor, A. (1990). Bullying in Scottish secondary schools. *Spotlights, 23*, 1-8.

Meston, C. M., Trapnell, P. D., & Gorzalka, B. B. (1996). Ethnic and gender differences in sexuality: Variations in sexual behavior between Asian and non-Asian university students. *Archives of Sexual Behavior, 25*, 33-72.

Meyer, A. (1994). *The effectiveness of a peer-led positive youth development program for sixth graders*. Unpublished doctoral dissertation, Pennsylvania State University, State College, PA.

Miedzian, M. (1992). *Boys will be boys*. New York: Anchor.

Miller, D. (1984). *Attack on the self*. New York: Jason Aronson.

Miller, G. A. (1994) *The substance abuse subtle screening inventory*. New York: Harcourt Brace.

Millon, T. (1992). *Millon Adolescent Clinical Inventory*. Minneapolis, MN: National Computer Systems.

Minuchin, S. (1974). *Families and family therapy*. Cambridge, MA: Harvard University Press.

Minuchin, P. (1988). Relationships within the family: A systems perspective on development. In R. A. Hinde & J. Stevenson-Hinde (Eds.), *Relationships within families: Mutual influences* (pp. 7-26). Oxford, UK: Clarendon.

Miracle, A. W., & Rees, C. R. (1994). *Lesson of the locker room: The myth of school sports*. Amherst, NY: Prometheus.

Monat-Haller, R. K. (1992). *Understanding and expressing sexuality*. Baltimore, MD: Paul H. Brooks.

Monroe, S. (1987, March 21). Brothers. *Newsweek*, pp. 54-66.

Montagu, A. (1971). *Touching: The human significance of the skin*. New York: Columbia University Press.

Monteiro, K. P., & Fuqua, V. (1994). African American gay youth: One form of manhood. *The High School Journal, 77*(1-2), 20-36.

Moore, D. (1990). Helping men become more emotionally expressive: A ten week program. In D. Moore & F. Leafgren (Eds.), *Problem solving strategies and interventions for men in conflict* (pp. 183-200). Alexandria, VA: American Association for Counseling and Development.

Moore, K. A., Snyder, N., & Halla, C. (1992). *Facts at a glance*. Washington, DC: Child Trends.

Moore, R., & Gillette, D. (1990). *King, warrior, magician, lover: Rediscovering the archetypes of the mature masculine*. New York: Harper Collins.

Moran, S., Smith, P., & Thompson, D. (1993). Ethnic differences in experiences of bullying: Asian and White children. *British Journal of Educational Psychology, 63*, 431-440.

Morgan, S. (1976). Bibliotherapy: A broader concept. *Journal of Clinical Child Psychology, 5*, 39-42.

Moustakas, C. E. (1959). *Psychotherapy with children: The living relationship*. New York: Harper.

Moustakas, C. E. (1992). *Psychotherapy with children: The living relationship*. Greeley, CO: Carron.

Moustakas, C. E. (1988). *Phenomenology, science and psychotherapy.* Sydney, Nova Scotia, Canada: Family Life Institute, University College of Cape Breton Press.

Moustakas, C. E. (1995). *Being-in, being-for, being-with.* Northvale, NJ: Jason Aronson.

Munthe, E., & Roland, E. (1989). *Bullying: An international perspective.* London: David Fulton.

Mura, D. (1995, June 28-30). Of racism, sexism and fatherhood. *USA Weekend,* pp. 8-9.

Murphy, G., Petitpas, A., & Brewer, B. (1996). Identity foreclosure, athletic identity, and career maturity in intercollegiate athletes. *The Sport Psychologist, 10,* 239-246.

Narine, M. L. (1992). *Single-sex, single race public schools: A solution to the problems plaguing the Black community?* Washington, DC: U.S. Department of Education.

National Black Child Development Institute. (1990). *The status of African American children: Twentieth anniversary report 1970-1990.* Washington, DC: Author.

National Center for Education Statistics. (1997). *Digest of education statistics: 1997.* Washington, DC: U.S. Department of Education.

National Center for Health Statistics. (1995). *Vital statistics of the United States, 1992* (Vol. 1). Washington, DC: U.S. Public Health Service.

National Center on Child Abuse and Neglect, U.S. Department of Health and Human Services. (1996). *Child maltreatment 1994: Reports from the states to the National Center on Child Abuse and Neglect.* Washington, DC: Government Printing Office.

National Task Force on Juvenile Sexual Offending. (1988). The preliminary report on juvenile sexual offenders [Special issue]. *Juvenile and Family Court Journal, 39*(2).

Nelson, S. H., McCoy, G. F., Stetter, M., & Vanderwagen, W. C. (1992). An overview of mental health services for American Indians and Alaska Natives in the 1990s. *Hospital Community and Psychiatry, 43,* 257-261.

Newman, G., & Muzzonigro, P. (1993). The effects of traditional family values on the coming out process of gay male adolescents. *Adolescence, 28,* 212-226.

Newman, M. G. (in press). The clinical use of palm top computers in the treatment of generalized anxiety disorder. *Cognitive and Behavioral Practice.*

Newman, M. G., Kenardy, J., Herman, S., & Taylor, C. B. (1996). The use of hand-held computers as an adjunct to cognitive-behavior therapy. *Computers in Human Behavior, 12,* 135-143.

Newman, M. G., Kenardy, J., Herman, S., & Taylor, C. B. (1997). Comparison of palmtop-computer-assisted brief cognitive-behavioral treatment to cognitive-behavioral treatment for panic disorder. *Journal of Consulting & Clinical Psychology, 65*(1), 178-183.

Nielsen, L. (1996). *Adolescence: A contemporary view* (3rd ed.). Fort Worth, TX: Harcourt Brace.

Nolen-Hoeksema, S. (1990). *Sex differences in depression.* Stanford, CA: Stanford University Press.

Norsworthy, K., & Horne, A. (1994, July). *Social learning family therapy: An intervention and teaching model for families with aggressive children.* Paper presented at the International Conference on Family Psychology, Padua, Italy.

Nsamenang, A. B. (1987). A West African perspective. In M. E. Lamb (Ed.), *The father's role: Cross-cultural perspectives* (pp. 273-293). Hillsdale, NJ: Lawrence Erlbaum.

O'Brien, C. P., Woody. G. E., & McLellan, T. (1986). Psychotherapeutic approaches in the treatment of drug abuse. In F. M. Tims & J. P. Ludford (Eds.), *Drug abuse treatment evaluation: Strategies, progress, and prospects* (pp. 69-88). Rockville, MD: National Institute on Drug Abuse.

O'Brien, M., & Bera, W. (1980). Adolescent sexual offenders: A descriptive typology. *Preventing Sexual Abuse, 1*(3), 1-4.

O'Dell, S. (1974). Training parents in behavior modification: A review. *Psychological Bulletin, 81,* 418-433.

Office of Juvenile Justice and Delinquency Prevention. (May, 1998). *Serious and violent juvenile offenders* (Juvenile Justice Bulletin). Washington, DC: Government Printing Office.

Olatunji, B. (1970). Wasslu. [Track from the album *More drums of passion,* C29307]. New York: Columbia Records.

Oliver, R., Hoover, J. H., & Hazler, R. (1994). The perceived roles of bullying in small-town Midwestern schools. *Journal of Counseling and Development, 72,* 416-421.

Oliver, R., Oaks, I. N., & Hoover, J. H. (1994). Family issues and interventions in bully and victim relationships. *School Counselor, 4,* 199-202.

Olweus, D. (1978). *Aggression in the schools: Bullies and whipping boys.* Washington, DC: Hemisphere.

Olweus, D. (1983). Low school achievement and aggressive behavior in adolescent boys. In D. Magnusson & V. Allen (Eds.), *Human development. An interactional perspective* (pp. 353-365). New York: Academic Press.

Olweus, D. (1993). *Bullying at school: What we know and what we can do.* Cambridge, MA: Blackwell.

Olweus, D. (1994). Annotation: Bullying at school: Basic facts and effects of a school based intervention program. *Journal of Child Psychology and Psychiatry, 35,* 1171-1190.

O'Mara, R. O. (1995). Maintenance isn't cure, but it's limiting HIV, crime in Britain's drug picture. In E. Goode (Ed.), *Drugs, society, and behavior* (pp. 254-256). Guilford, CT: Brown & Benchmark.

Omizo, M. M., Hershberger, J. M., & Omizo, S. A. (1988). Teaching children to cope with anger. *Elementary School Guidance and Counseling, 22*, 241-245.

O'Neil, J. M. (1981). Patterns of gender role conflict and strain: Sexism and fear of femininity in men's lives. *Personnel and Guidance Journal, 60*, 203-210.

O'Neil, J. M. (1992). Gender and sex role conflict and strain in men's lives: Implications for psychiatrists, psychologists and other human service providers. In K. Solomon & N. B. Levy (Eds.), *Men in transition* (pp. 5-44). New York: Plenum.

O'Neil, J. M., Good, G. E., & Holmes, S. (1995). Fifteen years of theory and research on men's gender role conflict: New paradigms for empirical research. In R. F. Levant & W. S. Pollack (Eds.), *A new psychology of men* (pp. 164-206). New York: Basic Books.

Ong, P., & Hee, S. J. (1993). Twenty million in 2020. In *The state of Asian Pacific America* (pp. 11-24). Los Angeles: LEAP Asian Pacific Public Policy Institute and UCLA Asian American Studies Center.

Orlick, T., & McCaffrey, N. (1991). Mental training with children for sport and life. *The Sport Psychologist, 5*, 322-334.

Osherson, S. (1986). *Finding our fathers: How a man's life is shaped by his relationship with his father.* New York: Fawcett Columbine.

Oster, G. D., & Montgomery, S. S. (1995). *Helping your depressed teenager: A guide for parents and caregivers.* New York: John Wiley.

Owens, R. E. (1998). *Queer kids: The challenges and promise for lesbian, gay, and bisexual youth.* New York: Haworth.

Page, R. C. (1979). Staff and resident involvement in a therapeutic community: For better or worse? *Personnel and Guidance Journal, 57*, 361-364.

Page, R. C. (1983). Social change in a therapeutic community. *International Journal of the Addictions, 18*, 769-776.

Page, R. C., & Bailey, J. (1995). Addictions counseling certification: A comparison of approaches. *Journal of Counseling and Development, 74*, 167-172.

Page, R. C., & Berkow, D. N. (1994). *Creating contact, choosing relationship: Dynamics of unstructured group therapy.* San Francisco: Jossey-Bass.

Page, R. C., & Powell, G. (1981). Family counseling with illicit drug users. *Journal of Offender Counseling, 1*, 48-57.

Page, R. C., Smith, M., & Beamish, P. (1977). Establishing a drug rehabilitation center. *Personnel and Guidance Journal, 56*, 180-184.

Panzarine, S. A., & Elster, A. B. (1983). Coping in a group of expectant adolescent fathers: An exploratory study. *Journal of Adolescent Health Care, 4*, 117-120.

Parham, T., & McDavis, R. (1987). Black men, an endangered species: Who's really pulling the trigger? *Journal of Counseling and Development, 66*, 24-27.

Park, S. E., & Harrison, A. A. (1995). Career-related interests and values, perceived control, and acculturation of Asian-American and Caucasian-American college students. *Journal of Applied Social Psychology, 25*, 1184-1203.

Patterson, G. R. (1982). *Coercive family process.* Eugene, OR: Castalia.

Patterson, G. R. (1986). Performance models for antisocial boys. *American Psychologist, 41*, 432-444.

Patton, J. R., & Jones, E. D. (1990). Definition, classification and prevalence. In J. R. Patton, J. S. Payne, & M. Beirne-Smith (Eds.), *Mental retardation* (3rd ed., pp. 33-76). Columbus, OH: Merrill.

Pelham, W. E. (1995). *Attention deficit hyperactivity disorder: Diagnosis, nature, etiology, and treatment* (Booklet). Pittsburgh: Author.

Pelham, W. E., & Hoza, B. (1996). Intensive treatment: Summer treatment program for children with ADHD. In E. D. Hibbs & P. S. Jensen (Eds.), *Psychosocial treatments for child and adolescent disorders: Empirically based strategies for clinical practice* (pp. 311-340). Washington, DC: American Psychological Association.

Pelham, W. E., Vodde-Hamilton, M., Murphy, D. A., Greenstein, J., & Vallano, G. (1991). The effects of methylphenidate on ADHD adolescents in recreational, peer group, and classroom settings. *Journal of Clinical Child Psychology, 20*, 293-300.

Pellegrini, A. D. (1995). *Victims as aggressors.* Unpublished manuscript, University of Georgia.

Peregoy, J. J. (1993). Transcultural counseling with American Indians and Alaskan Natives. In J. McFadden (Ed.), *Transcultural counseling* (pp. 163-192). Alexandria, VA: American Counseling Association.

Perry, B. D. (1997). Incubated in terror: Neurodevelopmental factors in the "cycle of violence." In J. D. Osofsky (Ed.), *Children in a violent society* (pp. 124-149). New York: Guilford.

Perry, C., & Jessor, R. (1985). The concept of health promotion and the prevention of adolescent drug abuse. *Health Education Quarterly, 12*, 169-184.

Perry, D. G., Kusel, S. J., & Perry, L. C. (1988). Victims of peer aggression. *Developmental Psychology, 24,* 807-814.

Peters, R., & McMahon, R. (1996). *Preventing childhood disorders, substance abuse, and delinquency.* Thousand Oaks, CA: Sage.

Petersen, A., & Hamburg, B. (1986). Adolescence: A developmental approach to problems and psychopathology. *Behavior Therapy, 17,* 480-499.

Peterson, J. W. (1989, April 11). Gay runaways are in more danger than ever, and gay adults won't help. *The Advocate,* pp. 8-10.

Petitpas, A. (1978). Identity foreclosure: A unique challenge. *Personnel and Guidance Journal, 56,* 550-561.

Petitpas, A., & Champagne, D. (1988). Developmental programming for inter-collegiate athletes. *Journal of College Student Development, 29,* 454-460.

Pfeffer, C. R. (1988). Child and adolescent suicide risk. In C. J. Kestenbaum & D. T. Williams (Eds.), *Handbook of clinical assessment of children and adolescents* (pp. 673-688). New York: New York University Press.

Pfiffner, L. J., & Barkley, R. A. (1990). Educational placement and classroom management. In R. A. Barkley (Ed.), *Attention-deficit hyperactivity disorder: A handbook for diagnosis and treatment* (pp. 498-539). New York: Guilford.

Pfiffner, L. J., & O'Leary, S. G. (1993). School-based psychological treatments. In J. L. Matson (Ed.), *Handbook of hyperactivity in children* (pp. 234-255). Boston: Allyn & Bacon.

Phipps-Yonas, S. (1980). Teenage pregnancy and motherhood: A review of the literature. *American Journal of Orthopsychiatry, 50,* 403-431.

Piasecki, J. M., Manson, S. M., & Biernoff, M. P. (1989). Abuse and neglect of American Indian children: Findings from a survey of federal providers. *American Indian and Alaskan Native Mental Health Research, 22,* 43-62.

Pierce, K. A., & Cohen, R. C. (1995). Aggressors and their victims: Toward a contextual framework for understanding children's aggressor-victim relationships. *Developmental Review, 15,* 292-310.

Pleck, J. H. (1981). Men's power with women, other men, and society: A men's movement analysis. In R. A. Lesis (Ed.), *Men in difficult times: A book of original readings* (pp. 242-243). Englewood Cliffs, NJ: Prentice Hall.

Pliszka, S. R. (1989). Effect of anxiety on cognition, behavior, and stimulant response in ADHD. *Journal of the American Academy of Child and Adolescent Psychiatry, 28,* 882-887.

Pollack, W. S. (1992, August). *Boys will be boys: Developmental traumas of masculinity—Psychoanalytic perspectives.* Paper presented at the symposium "Toward a New Psychology of Men" at the centennial meeting of the American Psychological Association, Washington, DC.

Pollack, W. S. (1995). No man is an island: Toward a new psychoanalytic psychology of men. In R. F. Levant & W. S. Pollack (Eds.), *The new psychology of men* (pp. 33-67). New York: Basic Books.

Pollack, W. S. (1998). *Real boys: Rescuing our sons from the myths of boyhood.* New York: Random House.

Polloway, E. A., & Patton, J. R. (1990). Psychosocial factors in retardation. In J. R. Patton, J. S. Payne, & M. Beirne-Smith (Eds.), *Mental retardation* (3rd ed., pp. 161-193). Columbus, OH: Merrill.

Ponterotto, J. G., & Casas, J. M. (1991). *Handbook of racial/ethnic minority counseling research.* Springfield, IL: Charles C Thomas.

Pope, K. S., & Vasquez, M. J. T. (1991). *Ethics in psychotherapy and counseling: A practical guide for psychologists.* San Francisco: Jossey-Bass.

Popper, C. W. (1988). Disorders usually first evident in infancy, childhood, or adolescence. In J. A. Talbott, R. E. Hales, & S. C. Yudofsky (Eds.), *Textbook of psychiatry* (pp. 649-735). Washington, DC: American Psychiatric Press.

Porter, E. (1986). *Treating the young male victim of sexual assault: Issues and intervention strategies.* Syracuse, NY: Safer Society Press.

Prinz, R. J., Conner, P. A., & Wilson, C. C. (1981). Hyperactive and aggressive behaviors in childhood: Intertwined dimensions. *Journal of Abnormal Child Psychology, 9,* 191-202.

Prothrow-Stith, D. (1991). *Deadly consequences.* New York: Harper Perennial.

Pruett, K. D. (1988). *The nurturing father.* New York: Warner Books.

The Psychological Corporation, Harcourt Brace & Company. (1998). *1998 catalogue for psychological assessment and intervention products* [Catalogue]. San Antonio, TX: Author.

Pueschel, S. M., Bernier, J. C., & Weidenman, L. E. (1988). *The special child: A source book for parents of children with developmental disabilities.* Baltimore, MD: Paul H. Brooks.

Racker, H. (1968). *Transference and countertransference.* London: Hogarth. (Original work published 1953)

Raech, H. (1966). A parent discusses initial counseling. *Mental Retardation, 4,* 25-26.

Randolph, R. (1990, August). What can we do about the most explosive problem in Black America—the widening gap between women who are making it and men who aren't. *Ebony,* p. 52.

Rapee, R. M., & Barlow, D. H. (1991). *Chronic anxiety: Generalized anxiety disorder and mixed anxiety-depression.* New York: Guilford.

Raymer, K. A. (1992). Inpatient treatment of depression. In M. Shafii & S. L. Shafii (Eds.), *Clinical guide to depression in children and adolescents* (pp. 233-248). Washington, DC: American Psychiatric Press.

Reed, R. J. (1988). Education and achievement of young Black males. In J. T. Gibbs (Ed.), *Young, Black, and male in America: An endangered species* (pp. 37-96). New York: Auburn House.

Remafedi, G. (1987a). Adolescent homosexuality: Psychosocial and medical implications. *Pediatrics, 79,* 331-337.

Remafedi, G. (1987b). Male homosexuality: The adolescent's perspective. *Pediatrics, 70,* 326-330.

Remafedi, G., Farrow, J. A., & Deisher, R. W. (1991). Risk factors for attempted suicide in gay and bisexual youth. *Pediatrics, 87,* 869-875.

Reynolds, C. R., & Richmond, B. O. (1985). *Revised Childhood Manifest Anxiety Scale.* Los Angeles: Western Psychological Services.

Richters, J. E., Arnold, E., Jensen, P. S., Abikoff, H., Conners, C. K., Greenhill, L. L., Hechtman, L., Hinshaw, S. P., Pelham, W. E., & Swanson, J. M. (1995). NIMH collaborative multisite multimodal treatment study of children with ADHD: I. Background and rationale. *Journal of the American Academy of Child and Adolescent Psychiatry, 34,* 987-1000.

Rick, K., & Forward, J. (1992). Acculturation and perceived intergenerational differences among Hmong youth. *Journal of Cross-Cultural Psychology, 23,* 85-94.

Rigby, K., & Slee, P. (1991). Bullying among Australian school children: Reported behavior and attitudes toward victims. *Journal of Social Psychology, 131,* 615-627.

Rivara, F. P., Sweeney, P. J., & Henderson, B. F. (1986). Black teenage fathers: What happens when the child is born? *Pediatrics, 78,* 151-158.

Roberts, G. (1993). Motivation in sport: Understanding and enhancing the motivation and achievement of children. In R. Singer, M. Murphey, & L. K. Tennant (Eds.), *Handbook of research on sport psychology* (pp. 405-420). New York: Macmillan.

Robin, A. L. (1990). Training families with ADHD adolescents. In R. A. Barkley (Ed.), *Attention-deficit hyperactivity disorder: A handbook for diagnosis and treatment* (pp. 462-497). New York: Guilford.

Robinson, B. E. (1988). *Teenage fathers.* Lexington, MA: Lexington Books.

Robinson, B. E., & Barret, R. L. (1985, December). Teenage fathers. *Psychology Today,* pp. 66-70.

Robitschek, C. (1996). At-risk youth and hope: Incorporating a ropes course into a summer jobs program. *Career Development Quarterly, 45,* 163-169.

Rofes, E. E. (1994). Making our schools safe for sissies. *High School Journal, 77,* 37-40.

Rogers, C. R. (1939). *The clinical treatment of the problem child.* Boston: Houghton Mifflin.

Rogers, C. R. (1951). *Client-centered therapy.* Boston: Houghton Mifflin.

Roscoe, W. (1994). Beyond sexual dimorphism in culture and history. In G. Herdt (Ed.), *Third sex, third gender.* New York: Zone Books.

Rose, C., Glaser, B., & Roth, E. (1998). Elevation and deflation in self-concept level among juvenile delinquents: Implications for placement and intervention. *Journal of Offender Rehabilitation, 27,* 107-122.

Rosen, E. J., & Weltman, S. F. (1996). Jewish families: An overview. In M. McGoldrick, J. Giordano, & J. K. Pearce (Eds.), *Ethnicity and family therapy* (2nd ed., pp. 611-630). New York: Guilford.

Rosen, L. A., Schissel, D., Taylor, S., & Krein, L. (1993). Nutrition. In J. L. Matson (Ed.), *Handbook of hyperactivity in children* (pp. 282-304). Boston: Allyn & Bacon.

Ross, D. M. (1996). *Childhood bullying and teasing: What school personnel, other professionals, and parents can do.* Alexandria, VA: American Counseling Association.

Rotheram-Borus, M. J., Luna, G. C., Marotta, T., & Kelly, H. (1994). Going nowhere fast: Methamphetamine and HIV infection. In F. J. Battjes, A. Sloboda, & W. C. Grace (Eds.), *The context of HIV risk among drug users and their sexual partners* (NIH Pub. No. 94-3750, pp. 155-182). Washington, DC: Government Printing Office.

Rotheram-Borus, M. J., Rosario, M., & Koopman, C. (1991). Minority youths at high risk: Gay males and runaways. In S. Gore & M. E. Colten (Eds.), *Adolescents, stress, and coping* (pp. 181-200). Hawthorne, NY: Aldine de Gruyter.

Rotheram-Borus, M. J., Rosario, M., Van Rossem, R., Reid, H., & Gillis, R. (1995). Prevalence, course, and predictors of multiple problem behaviors among gay and bisexual male adolescents. *Developmental Psychology, 31,* 75-85.

Rudolph, J. (1989). Effects of a workshop on mental health practitioners' attitudes toward homosexuality and counseling effectiveness. *Journal of Counseling and Development, 68,* 81-85.

Russo, N. F., Kelly, R. M., & Deacon, M. (1991). Gender and success-related attributions: Beyond individualistic conceptions of achievement. *Sex Roles, 25,* 331-350.

Ryan, G. (1986). Annotated bibliography: Adolescent perpetrators of sexual molestation of children. *Child Abuse and Neglect: The International Journal, 10,* 125-131.

Ryan, G., Lane, S., Davis, J., & Isaac, C. (1987). Juvenile sexual offenders: Development and correction. *Child Abuse and Neglect: The International Journal, 11,* 385-395.

Ryser, R. (1992). *Anti-Indian movement on the tribal frontier.* Washington, DC: Center for World Indigenous Studies.

Sailor, W., Halvorsen, A., Anderson, J., Goetz, L., Gee, K., Doering, K., & Hunt, P. (1986). Community intensive instruction. In R. Horner, L. Meyer, & H. B. Fredericks (Eds.), *Education of learners with severe handicaps: Exemplary service strategies* (pp. 251-288). Baltimore, MD: Paul H. Brooks.

Salholz, E. (1990, December 4). Short lives, bloody deaths: Black murder rates soar. *Newsweek,* p. 116.

Sanders, R. R., & Dadds, M. R. (1993). *Behavioural family intervention.* Boston: Allyn & Bacon.

Sarason, I., & Ganzer, V. (1973). Modeling and group discussion in the rehabilitation of delinquents. *Journal of Counseling Psychology, 20,* 442-449.

Savin-Williams, R. (1995). Lesbian, gay male, and bisexual adolescents. In A. R. D'Augelli & C. J. Patterson (Eds.), *Lesbian, gay and bisexual identities over the lifespan: Psychological perspectives* (pp. 165-189). New York: Oxford University Press.

Savin-Williams, R. (1998). *"—And then I became gay—": Young men's stories.* New York: Routledge.

Sayger, T. V., Horne, A. M., Walker, J. M., & Passmore, J. L. (1988). Social learning family therapy with aggressive children: Treatment outcome and maintenance. *Journal of Family Psychology, 3,* 261-285.

Schachar, R., & Tannock, R. (1993). Childhood hyperactivity and psychostimulants: A review of extended treatment studies. *Journal of Child and Adolescent Psychopharmacology, 3,* 81-97.

Schaefer, C. E., & Millman, H. L. (1981). *How to help children with common problems.* New York: Van Nostrand Reinhold.

Scheff, T. (1988). *Shame and violence.* Berkeley: University of California Press.

Scher, M., Stevens, M., Good, G., & Eichenfield, G. A. (Eds.). (1987). *Handbook of counseling and psychotherapy with men.* Newbury Park, CA: Sage.

Schiamberg, L. B., & Smith, K. U. (1982). *Human development.* New York: Macmillan.

Schmittroth, L. (Ed.). (1994). *Statistical record of children.* Detroit: Gale Research.

Schrodt, G. R. (1992). Cognitive therapy of depression. In M. Shafii & S. L. Shafii (Eds.), *Clinical guide to depression in children and adolescents* (pp. 197-217). Washington, DC: American Psychiatric Press.

Schroeder, E. (1989). Practical approaches in treating adolescent chemical dependency: A guide to clinical assessment and intervention. *Journal of Chemical Dependency Treatment, 2,* 95-129.

Schwarz, A., & Schwarz, R. M. (1994). *Depression: Theories and treatments.* New York: Columbia University Press.

Sears, J. T. (1991). *Growing up gay in the South: Race, gender, and journeys of the spirit.* New York: Harrington Park.

Seattle Public Schools. (1986, February). *Disproportionality task force preliminary report.* Seattle: Author.

Segal, B. M. (1996). Substance use and abuse in adolescence: An overview. *Child Psychiatry and Human Development, 26,* 193-210.

Seidman, E., & Rappaport, J. (1974). The educational pyramid: A paradigm for training, research, and manpower utilization in community psychology. *American Journal of Community Psychology, 2,* 119-130.

Sgroi, S. M. (1982). *Handbook of clinical intervention in child sexual abuse.* Lexington, MA: Lexington Books.

Shafii, M., & Shafii, S. L. (Eds.). (1992). *Clinical guide to depression in children and adolescents.* Washington, DC: American Psychiatric Press.

Shapiro, J. P., & Schrof, J. M. (1995, February 27). Honor thy children. *Newsweek,* pp. 39-49.

Shapiro, L. E. (1994). *Short-term therapy with children.* King of Prussia, PA: Center For Applied Psychology.

Sharp, S., & Smith, P. K. (1991). Bullying in UK schools: The DES Sheffield bullying project. *Early Child Development and Care, 77,* 47-55.

Sharpe, M. J., & Heppner, P. P. (1991). Gender role, gender-role conflict, and psychological well-being in men. *Journal of Counseling Psychology, 38,* 323-330.

Shaver, K. J. (1975). *An introduction to attribution processes.* Cambridge, MA: Winthrop.

Sheline, J. L., Skipper, B. J., & Broadhead, E. W. (1994). Risk factors for violent behavior in elementary school boys: Have you hugged your child today? *American Journal of Public Health, 84,* 661-663.

Shields, D., & Bredemeier, B. (1995). *Character development and physical activity.* Champaign, IL: Human Kinetics.

Siann, G., Callaghan, M., Glissov, P., Lockhart, R., & Rawson, L. (1994). Who gets bullied? The effect of school, gender and ethnic group. *Educational Research, 36,* 123-134.

Simkins, L. (1984). Consequences of teenage pregnancy and motherhood. *Adolescence, 19,* 39-54.

Simpson, D. D. (1986). National treatment system evaluation based on the Drug Abuse Reporting Program (DARP) follow-up research. In F. M. Tims & J. P. Ludford (Eds.), *Drug abuse treatment evaluation: Strategies, progress, and prospects* (pp. 29-42). Rockville, MD: National Institute on Drug Abuse.

Slap-Shelton, L., & Shapiro, L. E. (1992). *Take a deep breath: The kids' play-away-stress book.* King of Prussia, PA: Center for Applied Psychology.

Slee, P., & Rigby, K. (1993). Australian school children's self appraisal of interpersonal relations: The bullying experience. *Child Psychiatry & Human Development, 23,* 273-282.

Slomkowski, C., Klein, R. G., & Mannuzza, S. (1995). Is self-esteem an important outcome in hyperactive children? *Journal of Abnormal Child Psychology, 23,* 303-315.

Smith, L. A. (1988). Black adolescent fathers: Issues for service provision. *Social Work, 33,* 269-271.

Smith, L. A. (1989). *Windows on opportunities: An exploration in program development for Black adolescent fathers.* Unpublished doctoral dissertation, City University of New York.

Smith, M. (1983). *Violence and sport.* Toronto: Butterworths.

Smith, R., & Smoll, R. (1996). Psychosocial interventions in youth sport. In J. Van Raalte & B. Brewer (Eds.), *Exploring sport and exercise psychology* (pp. 287-315). Washington, DC: American Psychological Association.

Smith, S. (1983). The link between sexual maturation and "adolescent grieving" in parents of the dependent disabled. *Sexuality and Disability, 6,* 150-154.

Smith, T. E. (1985). Groupwork with adolescent drug abusers. *Social Work With Groups, 8,* 55-64.

Solomon, K., & Levy, N. B. (Eds.). (1982). *Men in transition.* New York: Plenum.

Sommers-Flanagan, J., & Sommers-Flanagan, R. (1997). *Tough kids, cool counseling: User-friendly approaches with challenging youth.* Alexandria, VA: American Counseling Association.

Sonenstein, F. L. (1986). Risking paternity: Sex and contraception among adolescent males. In A. B. Elster & M. E. Lamb (Eds.), *Adolescent fatherhood* (pp. 31-54). Hillsdale, NJ: Lawrence Erlbaum.

Sonuga-Barke, E. J. S., & Goldfoot, M. T. (1995). The effect of child hyperactivity on mother's expectations for development. *Child: Care, Health and Development, 21,* 17-29.

Sonuga-Barke, E. J. S., Taylor, E., Sembi, S., & Smith, J. (1992). Hyperactivity and delay aversion: I. The effect of delay on choice. *Journal of Child Psychology and Psychiatry, 33,* 387-398.

Spence, S. H. (1981). Social skills training with adolescent male offenders: II. Short-term, long-term, and generalized effects. *Behavior Research and Therapy, 19,* 349-368.

Spencer, T., Biederman, J., Wilens, T., Steingard, R., & Geist, D. (1993). Nortriptyline treatment of children with attention-deficit hyperactivity disorder and tic disorder or Tourette's syndrome. *Journal of the American Academy of Child and Adolescent Psychiatry, 32,* 205-210.

Spielberg, W. (1993). Why men must be heroic. *Journal of Men's Studies, 2,* 173-188.

Stack, C. (1996). *Call to home: African Americans reclaim the rural South.* New York: Basic Books.

Staples, R. (1974). The Black family in evolutionary perspective. *The Black Scholar, 5,* 2-9.

Staub, E. (1996). Cultural-societal roots of violence: The examples of genocidal violence and of contemporary youth violence in the United States. *American Psychologist, 51*(2), 117-131.

Steinberg, L., Dornbusch, S. M., & Brown, B. B. (1992). Ethnic differences in adolescent achievement: An ecological perspective. *American Psychologist, 47,* 723-729.

Steinberg, W. (1993). *Masculinity: Identity conflict and transformation.* Boston: Shambhala.

Steingard, R., Biederman, J., Spencer, T., Wilens, T., & Gonzalez, A. (1993). Comparison of clonidine response in the treatment of attention-deficit hyperactivity disorder with and without comorbid tic disorders. *Journal of the American Academy of Child and Adolescent Psychiatry, 32,* 350-353.

Stewart, J. T., Myers, W. C., Burket, R. C., & Lyles, W. B. (1990). A review of the pharmacotherapy of aggression in children and adolescents. *Journal of the American Academy of Child and Adolescent Psychiatry, 29,* 269-277.

Sue, D. W., & Sue, D. (1990). *Counseling the culturally different* (2nd ed.). New York: John Wiley.

Sue, S., & Okazaki, S. (1990). Asian-American educational achievements. *American Psychologist, 45,* 913-920.

Suinn, R. M. (1990). *Anxiety management training: A behavior therapy.* New York: Plenum.

Sullivan, H. S. (1953). *The interpersonal theory of psychiatry.* New York: Norton.

Super, D. E. (1953). A theory of vocational development. *American Psychologist, 8,* 185-190.

Super, D. E. (1990). A life-span, life-space approach to career development. In D. Brown & L. Brooks (Eds.), *Career choice and development: Applying contemporary theories to practice* (pp. 197-261). San Francisco: Jossey-Bass.

Swinton, D. H. (1992). The economic status of African Americans: Limited ownership and persistent inequality. In B. J. Tidwell (Ed.), *The state of Black America 1992* (pp. 61-117). New York: National Urban League.

Syntonic Research. (1979). *Environments—Disc 9* (Record album, SD 66009: Side A—Pacific Ocean, Side B—Caribbean Lagoon). New York: Author.

Szatmari, P., Offord, D. R., & Boyle, M. H. (1989). Ontario child health study: Prevalence of attention deficit disorder with hyperactivity. *Journal of Child Psychology and Psychiatry, 30,* 219-230.

Szymanski, L. S., & Kiernan, W. E. (1983). Multiple family group therapy with developmentally disabled adolescents and young adults. *International Journal of Group Psychotherapy, 33,* 521-533.

Tafoya, T. (1989). Pulling the coyote's tale: Native American sexuality and AIDS. In V. M. Mays, G. W. Albee, & S. F. Schneider (Eds.), *Primary prevention of AIDS: Psychological approaches* (pp. 280-289). Newbury Park, CA: Sage.

Task Force on Education of Young Adolescents. (1989). *Turning points: Preparing American youth for the 21st century.* New York: Carnegie Corporation.

Thirer, J., & Wright, S. (1985). Sport and social status for adolescent males and females. *Sociology of Sport Journal, 2,* 164-171.

Thomason, T. C. (1995). Counseling Native American students. In C. C. Lee (Ed.), *Counseling for diversity: A guide for school counselors and related professionals* (pp. 109-126). Boston: Allyn & Bacon.

Thompson, C. E. (1990). Transition of the disabled adolescent to adulthood. *Pediatrician, 17,* 303-313.

Thompson, C. L., & Rudolph, L. R. (1996). *Counseling children.* Pacific Grove, CA: Brooks/Cole.

Tod, D. (1996). *The moral of the sport story: Motivationally derived morality?* Unpublished master's thesis, University of Otago, Dunedin, New Zealand.

Tod, D., & Hodge, K. (1993). Moral reasoning and achievement motivation in rugby: A case study. *Journal of Physical Education New Zealand, 26,* 14-18.

Treasure, D., & Roberts, G. (1994). Cognitive and affective concomitants of task and ego goal orientations during the middle school years. *Journal of Sport & Exercise Psychology, 16,* 15-28.

Tremble, B., Schneider, M., & Appathurai, C. (1989). Growing up gay or lesbian in a multicultural context. *Journal of Homosexuality, 17,* 253-267.

Trimble, J. E., Fleming, C. M., Beauvais, F., & Jumper-Thurman, P. (1996). Essential cultural and social strategies for counseling Native American Indians. In P. B. Pedersen, J. G. Draguns, W. J. Lonner, & J. E. Trimble (Eds.), *Counseling across cultures* (4th ed., pp. 177-209). Thousand Oaks, CA: Sage.

Tripp, G., & Luk, S. L. (1997). The identification of pervasive hyperactivity: Is clinic observation necessary? *Journal of Child Psychology and Psychiatry, 38,* 219-234.

Tripp, G., Luk, S. L., Schaughency, E. A., & Singh, R. K. (1999). DSM-IV & ICD-10: A comparison of the correlates of children identified with ADHD and hyperkinetic disorder. *Journal of the American Academy of Child and Adolescent Psychiatry, 38,* 156-164.

Troiden, R. R. (1989). The formation of homosexual identities. *Journal of Homosexuality, 17,* 43-73.

Trottier, I. (1989). Prevention of child sexual abuse requires increased awareness, education. *NIHB Health Reporter, 4*(13), 14-16.

Tyor, P. L., & Bell, L. V. (1984). *Caring for the retarded in American: A history.* Westport, CT: Greenwood.

U.S. Bureau of the Census. (1993, September). *We the . . . first Americans.* Washington, DC: Economics and Statistical Administration, U.S. Department of Commerce.

U.S. Bureau of the Census. (1995). *Population profile of the United States.* Washington, DC: Government Printing Office.

U.S. Bureau of the Census. (1997). *Statistical abstract of the United States: 1997.* Washington, DC: Author.

U.S. Department of Commerce. (1992). *Census bureau resources for the Congress—1990 summary.* Washington, DC: Government Printing Office.

U.S. Department of Health and Human Services, National Center for Health Statistics. (1993). *Survey on child health.* Washington, DC: Government Printing Office.

U.S. Department of Health and Human Services, National Center on Child Abuse and Neglect. (1996). *Child maltreatment 1994: Reports from the states to the National Center on Child and Neglect.* Washington, DC: Government Printing Office.

U.S. Department of Justice, Bureau of Justice Statistics. (1986). *Correctional population in the United States—1986.* Washington, DC: Author.

U.S. House of Representatives. (1989). *Barriers and opportunities for America's young Black men* [Hearing before the Select Committee on Children, Youth, and Families]. Washington, DC: Government Printing Office.

Vaillant, G. (1993). *The wisdom of the ego.* Cambridge, MA: Harvard University Press.

van der Kolk, B. A. (1989). The compulsion to repeat the trauma: Re-enactment, re-victimization, and masochism. In B. James (Ed.), *Handbook for treatment of attachment-trauma problems in children* (pp. 389-406). New York: Free Press.

Vasey, M. W. (1995). Social anxiety disorders. In A. R. Eisen, L. A. Kearney, & C. E. Schaefer (Eds.), *Clinical handbook of anxiety disorders in children and adolescents* (pp. 131-168). Northvale, NJ: Jason Aronson.

Vaz, E. (1982). *The professionalization of young hockey players.* Lincoln: University of Nebraska Press.

Vaz, R., Smolen, P., & Miller, C. (1983). Adolescent pregnancy: Involvement of the male partner. *Journal of Adolescent Health Care, 4,* 246-250.

Vera Institute of Justice. (1990). *The male role in teenage pregnancy and parenting: New directions of public policy.* New York: Author.

Veroff, J. (1969). Social comparison and the development of achievement motivation. In C. P. Smith (Ed.), *Achievement-related motives in children* (pp. 46-101). New York: Russell Sage.

Walker-Hirsch, L., & Champagne, M. P. (1991). Circles revisited: Ten years later. *Sexuality and Disability, 9,* 143-148.

Wall, V. A., & Washington, J. (1991). Understanding gay and lesbian students of color. In N. J. Evans & V. A. Wall (Eds.), *Beyond tolerance: Gays, lesbians, and bisexuals on campus* (pp. 67-78). Alexandria, VA: American College Personnel Association.

Watson, J. (1980). Bibliotherapy for abused children. *The School Counselor, 27,* 204-208.

Wax, M., Wax, R., & Dumont, R. V., Jr. (1989). *Formal education in an American Indian community* (Cooperative Research Project No. 1361, Study of Social Problems Monograph). Prospect Heights, IL: Waveland.

Way, I. F., & Balthazor, T. J. (1990). *A manual for structured group treatment with adolescent sex offenders.* Notre Dame, IN: Jalice.

Weathers, D. (1993, December). Stop the guns. *Essence,* pp. 70-71, 132-137.

Webster-Stratton, C. (1990). Stress: A potential disruptor of parent perceptions and family interactions. *Journal of Clinical Child Psychology, 19,* 302-312.

Wehman, P., & Parent, W. (1996). Supported employment. In P. J. McLaughlin & P. Wehman (Eds.), *Mental retardation and developmental disabilities* (pp. 118-127). Austin, TX: Pro-Ed.

Weinberg, R., & Gould, D. (1995). *Foundations of sport and exercise psychology.* Champaign, IL: Human Kinetics.

Weinberg, S. K. (1955). *Incest behavior.* New York: Citadel Press.

Weiss, G., & Trokenberg Hechtman, L. (1993). *Hyperactive children grown up* (2nd ed.). New York: Guilford.

Weiss, M. (1991). Psychological skill development in children and adolescents. *The Sport Psychologist, 5,* 335-354.

Weiss, M. (1995). Children in sport: An educational model. In S. Murphy (Ed.), *Sport psychology interventions* (pp. 39-69). Champaign, IL: Human Kinetics.

Weiss, M., & Petlichkoff, L. (1989). Children's motivation for participation in and withdrawal from sport: Identifying the missing links. *Pediatric Exercise Science, 1,* 195-211.

Weiss, M., & Smith, A. (1995, September). *Quality of friendships in youth sport: Measurement development and validation.* Paper presented at the annual meeting of the Association for the Advancement of Applied Sport Psychology, New Orleans.

Weissman, M. M., Bruce, M. L., Leaf, P. J., Florio, L. P., & Holzer, C. (1991). Affective disorders. In L. N. Robins & D. A. Regier (Eds.), *Psychiatric disorders in America: The epidemiologic catchment area study* (pp. 53-80). New York: Free Press.

Wells, J. W. (1991). What makes a difference? Various teaching strategies to reduce homophobia in university students. *Annals of Sex Research, 4,* 229-238.

Wender, P. H. (1972). The minimal brain dysfunction syndrome in children. *Journal of Nervous and Mental Diseases, 155,* 55-71.

Wender, P. H. (1974). Some speculations concerning a possible biochemical basis of minimal brain dysfunction. *Life Sciences, 14,* 1605-1621.

West, C. (1994). *Race matters.* New York: Vintage.

Western Psychological Services. (1995). *1995-96 catalog of tests, books, software, and equipment* [Catalog]. Los Angeles: Author.

White, J. L. (1989). *The troubled adolescent.* New York: Pergamon.

Whitney, I., Nabuzoka, D., & Smith, K. (1992). Bullying in schools: Mainstream and special needs. *Support for Learning, 7,* 3-7.

Wilcox, D. W., & Forrest, L. (1992). The problems of men and counseling: Gender bias or gender truth? *Journal of Mental Health Counseling, 14,* 291-304.

Wilens, T. E., & Biederman, J. (1992). The stimulants. *Psychiatric Clinics of North America, 15,* 191-222.

Wilens, T. E., Biederman, J., Geist, D. E., Steingard, R., & Spencer, T. (1993). Nortriptyline in the treatment of ADHD: A chart review of 58 cases. *Journal of the American Academy of Child and Adolescent Psychiatry, 32,* 343-349.

Williams, C. W. (1991). *Black teenage mothers: Pregnancy and child rearing from their perspective.* Lexington, MA: Lexington Books.

Wilson, R. W. (1987). *Don't panic: Taking control of anxiety attacks.* New York: Harper.

Wilson, W. J. (1987). *The truly disadvantaged: The inner city, the underclass, and public policy.* Chicago: University of Chicago Press.

Winnicott, D. W. (1965a). *The maturational process and the facilitating environment.* New York: International Universities Press.

Winnicott, D. W. (1965b). *Maturational processes and the healing environment.* London: Hogarth.

Winnicott, D. W. (1971). *Playing and reality.* London: Tavistock.

Wirt, R. D., Lachar, D., Klinedinst, J. E., Sear, P. D., & Broen, W. E. (1982). *Personality Inventory for Children.* Los Angles: Western Psychological Services.

Witters, W., Venturelli, P., & Hanson, G. (1992). *Drugs and society.* Boston: Jones & Bartlett.

Wolfe, P., Kregel, J., & Wehman, P. (1996). Service delivery. In P. J. McLaughlin & P. Wehman (Eds.), *Mental retardation and developmental disabilities* (pp. 187-198). Austin, TX: Pro-Ed.

Wolpe, J., & Lazarus, A. A. (1966). *Behavior therapy techniques.* New York: Pergamon.

Woog, D. (1995). *School's out: The impact of gay and lesbian issues on America's schools.* Boston: Alyson.

World Health Organization. (1990). *International classification of diseases* (10th ed.). Geneva: Author.

Wright, W. (1992). The endangered Black male child. *Educational Leadership, 49,* 14-16.

Yalom, I. D. (1985). *The theory and practice of group psychotherapy* (3rd ed.). New York: Basic Books.

Yokley, J. M. (1990). *The use of victim-offender communication in the treatment of sexual abuse: Three intervention models.* Orwell, VT: Safer Society Press.

Young MC. (1991). Keep your eye on the prize [Track from the album *Brainstorm,* C4-96337]. Los Angeles: Capitol Records.

Yu, A., & Gregg, C. H. (1993). Asians in groups: More than a matter of cultural awareness. *Journal of Specialists in Group Work, 18,* 86-93.

Zaharopoulos, E., & Hodge, K. (1991). Self-concept and sports participation. *New Zealand Journal of Psychology, 20,* 12-16.

Zimbardo, P. G. (1977). *Shyness.* New York: Jove.

AUTHOR INDEX

SUBJECT INDEX